KU-014-611

Mental Health and the Environment

EDITED BY

Hugh Freeman MSc MA BM BCh FRCPsych DPM

Senior Consultant Psychiatrist, Salford Health Authority; Lecturer, Department of Psychiatry, University of Manchester; Editor of the British Journal of Psychiatry

CHURCHILL LIVINGSTONE
LONDON EDINBURGH MELBOURNE AND NEW YORK 1984

CHURCHILL LIVINGSTONE
Medical Division of Longman Group Limited

Distributed in the United States of America by
Churchill Livingstone Inc., 1560 Broadway, New York,
N.Y. 10036, and by associated companies, branches and
representatives throughout the world.

© Longman Group Limited 1984
© Figs 17.1--17.8 Randolph Langenbach 1984

All rights reserved. No part of this publication may be
reproduced, stored in a retrieval system, or transmitted
in any form or by any means, electronic, mechanical,
photocopying, recording or otherwise, without the prior
permission of the publishers (Churchill Livingstone,
Robert Stevenson House, 1–3 Baxter's Place, Leith
Walk, Edinburgh EH1 3AF).

First published 1984

ISBN 0 443 02780 3

British Library Cataloguing in Publication Data
Mental health and the environment.
1. Social psychiatry   2. Man — Influence of environment
   I. Freeman, Hugh L.
   616.89'071   RC455

Library of Congress Cataloging in Publication Data
Mental health and the environment.
Includes index.
   1. Mental health. 2. Mental illness — Etiology.
3. Man — Influence of nature on. 4. Environmental
psychology. I. Freeman, Hugh Lionel. [DNLM: 1. Mental
Health. 2. Mental Disorders. 3. Social Environment.
WM 31 M5487]
RA790.5.M418 1984   155.9   84–9421

Produced by Longman Singapore Publishers (Pte) Ltd.
Printed in Singapore.

Acknowledgements

My thanks are due in the first instance to the contributors, who have provided most of the content of this book, and who have responded patiently to editorial interventions. Secondly, the advice and support of the publishers has been enormously helpful in the long and complex process of seeing a book like this through from conception to launching.

Like many other people, I owe a great deal to the inspiration provided by the late Dr J.L. Burn, Medical Officer of Health of the City of Salford, who helped to direct my thoughts and professional activities towards the relationship of environment and health. Dr Bill McQuillan did the same at a later stage. Over the course of some years, my concern with this subject has also been much influenced by discussions with a number of people who have themselves made significant contributions to the subject; amongst these, I am particularly grateful to Oscar Newman, George Brown, Graham Ashworth, Alice Coleman, Peter Willmott, and Tom Fryers.

I am grateful for the secretarial assistance provided particularly by Mrs Helen Aldcroft and Miss Helen Shearwood, while the staff of Prestwich Hospital Professional Library have uncomplainingly obtained innumerable references. The excellent photographs of Salford were taken by David Chadwick.

Some previously published work of my own is reproduced here by permission of the British Journal of Psychiatry (which I now edit) and of Faber & Faber Ltd in respect of a chapter in 'Imagination and Precision in the Social Sciences', edited by T. J. Nossiter, A. H. Hanson & S. Rokkan. For Professor Webb's paper, material has been quoted with permission from 'Mental Health in the Metropolis, 1978' edited by Leo Srole & A. K. Fischer (New York University Press) and from his own paper 'Mental health in rural and urban environments' in Ekistics, Vol 45, No 266. Material illustrating Dr Giggs' chapter is reproduced by permission of McGraw Hill, Ltd. and illustrations to Chapter 11 by permission of Presses Pocket, Paris.

The generosity of the Rockefeller Foundation allowed me to spend a period at the Villa Serbelloni, Como, Italy with enormous benefit to the progress of the book. Finally, in this as in all things, I owe more to my wife than can ever be acknowledged.

Salford
1984

Hugh Freeman

Contributors

Christopher Bagley PhD
Burns Professor of Child Welfare, University of Calgary, Alberta, Canada

Paul F Brain PhD
Reader, Department of Zoology, University College of Swansea, South Wales, UK

G. M. Carstairs MD FRCPE FRCPsych
(Formerly Professor of Psychiatry, University of Edinburgh and Vice-Chancellor, University of York), UK

Charles Clark BSc PhD
Senior Psychologist, HM Prison, Wormwood Scrubs, London, UK (formerly Research Worker, Institute of Psychiatry, London)

Kenneth Dean PhD
Lecturer in Geography, College of St Mark and St John, Plymouth, UK

Hugh L. Freeman MSc MA BM BCh FRCPsych DPM
Senior Consultant Psychiatrist, Salford Health Authority; Lecturer, Department of Psychiatry, University of Manchester, UK

John A Giggs PHD
Lecturer, Department of Geography, University of Nottingham, UK

D. R. Hannay MD PhD FFCM MRCGP DCH
Senior Lecturer, Department of General Practice, University of Glasgow, UK

P. M. Higgins FRCP FRCGP
Professor of General Practice, Guy's Hospital Medical School, London, UK

Howard James MRCP MRCPsych DPM
Consultant Psychiatrist, Moorhaven Hospital, Ivybridge, Devon UK

J. M. Kellett MA MRCPsych MRCP DPM
Senior Lecturer, St George's Hospital, Blackshaw Road, London, UK

Randolph Langenbach MArch
Assistant Professor, Department of Architecture, University of California, Berkeley, USA

A. C. P. Sims MD FRCPsych
Professor of Psychiatry, University of Leeds, St James University Hostpital, Leeds, UK

Christopher J Smith PhD
Associate Professor, Department of Geography, State University of New York at Albany, New York, USA

Alex Tarnopolsky MD MRCPsych
Consultant Psychotherapist, The Maudsley Hospital, London, UK

S. D. Webb PhD
Professor, Department of Sociology, University of Victoria, British Columbia, Canada

Keith Wedmore MA LLB
Barrister-at-Law (formerly Research Fellow, State University of San Fransisco) 5 Cornelia Avenue, Mill Valley, California, USA

Contents

SECTION C: **Case studies**

EPILOGUE

Introduction

The impulse which led to the production of this book derived from my personal experience — now over 20 years — of working as a clinical psychiatrist in an inner city area of the North of England, which has an overwhelmingly working class population. From the start, the influence of the local environment was unmistakable in such features as a dirty atmosphere, overcrowded slum housing, unpleasant industrial processes near people's homes, obtrusive transport routes, and dilapidated public buildings. Overall, Salford people were not noticeably subject to a greater or less degree of psychiatric disorder than others, but such unfavourable aspects of the environment often figured prominently in their case histories, and could be seen when they were visited at home. At the same time, this nineteenth century industrial settlement had its positive side — 'a closely knit community, based on long residence and inter-marriage, with its own institutions and customary ways by which everyday life of the district was determined. Social groups centred on the physical environment with its familiar streets, small shop and other informal meeting places' (Nicholson 1961). But during the 1960s and 1970s, the Salford townscape was totally transformed; most of the 'Coronation Streets' of terraced houses (by no means all of them slums) were demolished, smoke control cleaned up the atmosphere, much local industry moved away or closed down, the transport network was partly replaced by urban motorways, and a new city of tower blocks emerged where the old had disappeared, together with the 'megastructure' of an integrated shopping centre.

In all this, there was much to be thankful for; clean air meant the eventual end of Salford's appalling legacy of chronic bronchitis; a high-rise flat with central heating, bathroom and all-electric kitchen was healthier than a damp and crumbling terraced cottage; new health centres, schools, and leisure facilities gave the people better services. But from the beginning, the negative side of these environmental changes emerged strongly, and was often to be heard in the psychiatric consultation (see Chapter 7).

What disturbed me more than anything, though, was that no-one in authority apparently regarded it as their province to be concerned about the harmful effects of uprooting people, turning their living environment through 90 degrees, and setting it in surroundings from which virtually every familiar feature had been erased. Nor did those responsible for the creation of 30-storey blocks of flats seem to have given a moment's thought to how a woman was to live in one of them with several small children and little money. As a result, I began to look into the scientific study of mental health aspects of the environment and, in collaboration with Professor Graham Ashworth, a symposium was organised at the University of Salford in 1974, opened by HRH Prince Phillip; the proceedings may be seen as a forerunner of this volume (Freeman 1975).

In 1971, Rapoport had described the scientific study of relationships between the built environment and behaviour or states of mind as being in a 'pre-paradigmatic stage . . . one can find a study to support any position and can quote in favour of any decision'; Fischer (1975) referred to the 'absence of a social psychology which is able to account for the connection between structural factors and individual action', and Piha et al (1979) to 'the lack of a comprehensive psychiatric frame of reference which would in a meaningful and understandable way link together the pathogenesis of mental health disorders and the properties of the physical environment'. Mullin (1969) points out 'the lost opportunity to evaluate the experience of British new towns:

> because we have largely failed to develop methods of interdisciplinary study appropriate to such an environmental situation we have not been able to judge whether any successes we have achieved have been the result of conscious action or of entirely separate and perhaps fortuitous factors.

In fact, the huge volume of public investment that went into the building of these new communities was accompanied by the most puny efforts to study their human consequences. Progress in recent years has not been dramatic, but it does justify a book to assemble what is now known, and what reasonable hypotheses or views have been put forward about the relationship between environment and mental health.

THE PSYCHIATRIC VIEW

Psychiatrists today acknowledge that the disorders which concern them have in general a multifactorial origin, resulting from interaction between the organism's genotype and outside influences experienced from the time of conception. All such factors up to death could, strictly speaking, be described as environmental, and to consider them all would be to encompass the whole of psychiatry except for its genetic aspects. But such scientific imperialism is to be avoided, and the present volume is concerned with those characteristics of people's physical and social surroundings for which there are reasonable grounds to suggest that they are likely to be significant in relation to mental health and illness.

Though Cheyne (1733) considered 'the Humour of living in great, popular and consequently unhealthy Towns' to be one of the main causes

Fig. 1.1 Salford central redevelopment area. Multi-storey public housing of the 1960s (photograph by David Chadwick)

of 'Distempers, with atrocious and frightful symptoms, scarce known to our Ancestors, and never rising to such fatal heights, nor afflicting such Numbers in any other known Nation', interest in this subject as an entity is surprisingly recent. Both the clinical–phenomenological tradition and psychoanalysis, which are the twin foundations of present day psychiatry, have been overwhelmingly concerned with the individual and his immediate family. Adolph Meyer emphasised the importance of social stress, but his psychobiology — influenced by Darwinism and the concept of adaptation — failed to resonate with the clinical and social climate of that time (Brill 1980). More recently, social psychiatry has dealt with relevant human interactions — between individuals and between groups, both within the family and outside — but it is still a young discipline, working out its basic parameters of knowledge and theories of causation; it emphasises that the social and biological aspects of mental disorder are complementary, not mutually exclusive. Social psychiatry was defined by an Expert Committee of WHO in 1959 as the 'preventive and curative measures which are directed towards the fitting of an individual for a satisfactory and useful life in terms of its own environment' (quoted by Shepherd, 1983). A psychiatry of the environment should be one of its constituents, yet at this stage is still, as Freud said of the infant psychoanalysis, 'not so much a science as the hope of a science'; it lacks not only adequate scientific data, but even properly defined concepts.

As a sociologist, Elias (1969) criticised psychiatrists for vaguely conglomerating family, neighbourhood, community, and other social configurations into a single factor of 'environment' or 'social background', whereas for sociology, each of these represents a separate, highly structured element, with dynamics of its own. This is in much the same way as non-psychiatric physicians tend to dismiss the whole of a highly complex psychopathological state as 'functional overlay'. In Elias' view, psychiatric terminology and thinking imply a separation between a highly structured situation within the individual on the one hand and an apparently unstructured network of relationships and communications in the background; this is likely to make collaborative efforts with the social sciences extremely difficult. Much of what has passed for social psychiatry has certainly remained at a rather naive level, in terms of sociological thought, but Elias seems to have equated psychiatry too much with psychoanalytical theory. He also suggested that both psychiatry and sociology have the tendency to try and reduce each other's explanation of problems to its own, as being the more fundamental — in other words, a kind of conceptual 'one-upmanship'.

There is another, similar problem. Although some sociological work is based on the view that a person's social adjustment is considerably influenced by conditions of housing and neighbourhood, and by such stress as a recent move to an unfamiliar district, we do not really know how far the sociological concept of adjustment is equivalent to the medical concept of mental health (Hare 1966). In fact, there seems to be a need for much greater sophistication by both disciplines when dealing with the other. Human personality is not exclusively a product of physiological or biological factors, and to the extent that it is shaped by sociocultural influences, the environment seems likely to be one such major factor (Gold 1982). Yet there is a lack of empirical research to define this relationship, so that the social-psychological aspects of a process such as urbanisation, have often been treated as a relatively unimportant aspect of urban social systems. Since sociology has accepted socioeconomic variables as primary aetiological factors, and since they tend to have a strong relationship with environmental variables (especially at the aggregate level), measurements of environmental effects are likely to be unreliable. As a result, the physical environment has been a relatively neglected factor in most sociological studies, e.g. of delinquency (Gillis & Hogan 1982).

Probably most directly relevant to this book is urban sociology which evolved from the European classic tradition of Max Weber and Georg Simmel to the Chicago School of Park, Burgess, and Wirth, though the types of social organisation which the latter described may have been more characteristic of 20th century industrial society in general than of cities as such. On the other hand, Gans (1962) suggested that contrasts between

urban and suburban societies were explained more by the personal characteristics (e.g. social class) of the people who lived in each setting than by
the size, density, or heterogeneity of each type of community. Different
aspects of the individual–community relationship are examined in a number
of subsequent chapters here.

THE ENVIRONMENTAL PROFESSIONS

But if psychiatrists have not been as involved as they should have been with
the surroundings of patients' lives, what of those whose professional concern
is the surroundings themselves — architects, planners, engineers, politicians, administrators? In general, the story is a melancholy one of essential
lack of interest in the human consequences of structure, transport developments, or changes in the patterns of industry and commerce. Economic
considerations have been overwhelming, irrespective of the political
ideology on which any society operates. Environmental psychiatry may be
at a primitive stage, but so far as architecture is concerned the failure seems
to be equally great:

> no method exists of objectively describing and analysing configurations of built form in such
> a way that they can be easily related to 'human' factors; and . . . no real attempt to distin-
> guish and describe those 'human' factors which might be affected by spatial configurations
> (Hillier & Hudson 1984).

Nor has much research been carried out on the psychological impact
of different environments from the aesthetic point of view, though a study
by the Department of the Environment (1972) found that satisfaction with
a public housing estate was closely related to its appearance and to the way
it was looked after, rather than to density, building form, or to living on
or above the ground. Therefore, environmental psychiatry should have as
much to teach these professions as personnel concerned directly with mental
health; it might perhaps teach them many things which should really have
emerged within these environmental disciplines themselves. Though Walter
Gropius wrote that 'Architects should conceive of buildings not as monuments, but as receptacles for the flow of life', that message was little heeded,
least of all by the Modern Movement in architecture.

The man–environment science then, can be divided into two aspects: for
architects and planners, it is the systematic analysis of human behaviour
related to the settings they create; for human scientists, it is the environmental contexts of that behaviour (Craik 1973). These two aspects have been
seen as contrary, but environmental psychiatry should be equally concerned
with both.

DEFINITIONS

What are the terms, though, of this discussion? To try and define either
'mental health' or 'environment' is to enter a semantic Slough of Despond

from which little useful may emerge. Sells (1968) refers to the 'conflicting guidance offered by the literature in which the conceptualisation of mental health is represented in a most contradictory and confused manner', while measuring it is scarcely possible 'when the acknowledged experts disagree on what is to be measured'. Giggs (1980) states that 'comprehensive and permanent definitions are irrelevant for practitioners in (this) field'. Any piece of research uses definitions and classifications which are appropriate to its specific requirements and the particular population being studied. A classification of possible criteria of mental health was made by Kasl & Rosenfield (1980) into: (a) indices based on treatment data; (b) psychiatric signs and symptoms; (c) indicators of mood, well-being, satisfaction, etc.; (d) indices of functional effectiveness and role performance; and (e) indices derived from notions of 'positive mental health', e.g. adequacy of coping. All these have been used at different times as the basis for theoretical or empirical studies.

Better then for our present purpose to define mental health in common sense and pragmatic terms as the absence of identifiable psychiatric disorder, according to current norms. At this, hands will be thrown up in horror, particularly by non-psychiatrists, but as Jablensky (1982) points out, 'Attempts to operationalise and measure positive mental health . . . have produced either trivial results or lists of desirable traits and behaviours reflecting the characteristics of particular social groups or culture'. In these terms, mental health is both a value concept, determined by individuals, and a 'loosely demarcated area of activities and concerns', whereas psychiatric disorder is neither, though its minor forms must represent a continuum with normal experience. When Hare & Shaw (1965) asked: 'if by environmental changes we were able to reduce the number of persons in a population who admitted to symptoms of undue anxiety, depression, etc., in response to a questionary, should we have improved the mental health of the population?', the answer must surely have been yes.

Similarly, Sir Aubrey Lewis (1967) pointed out that

> Sociological attempts to state the denotative characteristics of mental illness . . . do not stand on their social legs, but are propped up by medical struts and stays, which have three criteria — the patient feels ill; he has disordered functions of some part; and he has symptoms which conform to a recognisable clinical pattern.

Lewis' conclusion was that 'though the social effects of disease, like the social causes, are extremely important, it is impossible to tell from them whether a condition is healthy or morbid'; that decision must be based on the assessment of its physiological and psychological components, which requires medical skills.

However, the problem of measuring morbidity remains, since most data have been of treatment or service contacts, rather than of distribution of illness, and these professional interventions must depend primarily on a community's level of economic and social development. If the activities of specialist psychiatric services can be recorded in relation to defined communities, as is done by British case registers (Wooff et al. 1983), it can reasonably be assumed that most cases of severe disorders will be included, at least in industrialised countries. But in the case of milder neurotic and personality disorders, not much more than 5 per cent of individuals receive specialist treatment for them in the UK, and the proportion in most other countries is probably less. Therefore, the alternative method of measurement is by investigating a random sample of the general population; here, the instruments of measurement become particularly important, and different approaches to this problem will be referred to in several of the following chapters.

While cross-cultural comparisons of morbidity have a great potential for determining the relative significance of environmental factors, there are two major problems involved. These are the need to establish comparable definitions of psychiatric symptoms across cultures, and the lack of suitable techniques for measuring the relevant sociocultural parameters (Carstairs & Kapur 1976). Epidemiological studies have used such diverse dependent variables as happiness, psychophysiological complaints, psychotic symptomatology, behaviour problems, and social functioning (Mechanic 1973). In spite of the methodological difficulties of such studies, social class, age and sex roles, residence, social mobility, ethnic and cultural differences, and community networks have all been found to be important in relation to psychosis, though the precise role of each of these factors in different conditions is not yet known.

However, definition becomes rather more complicated by the question of 'social pathology', which is generally understood as a significant deviation from prevailing norms of behaviour, expressed in such forms as delinquency and crime, disordered or broken family relationships, sexual deviation, and addictions. Choldin (1978) describes such behaviour as 'individual events, negatively valued by society in general, and aggregated into neighbourhood rates' for scientific or administrative purposes. Clearly, most of those who behave badly are not psychiatrically disordered (though the exact proportion who are is unknown), but the relative aetiological importance of individual disturbance and external social forces may as yet be unresolvable, while in the case of children and adolescents, disturbed behaviour is often the leading feature of psychiatric abnormality. Just as morality is 'in the nature of things', so appears to be the fact that communities with high rates of mental illness also tend to show high levels of behavioural deviance and of psychiatric sequelae to crime and social disturbance. The association of these problems has been particularly well synthesised by Rutter (1981), who points out that 'city living is associated with an increased susceptibility to a quite wide range of problems' — not only crime and delinquency, but depression, emotional disturbance, educational problems and family breakdown. For this reason, two contributors here deal primarily with behavioural social pathology — one with the social ecology of deviance in young people, and one (in collaboration with myself) with the possible relationship of urban size to crime. There should be evidence enough in both these chapters that their subject matter deserves to come under the rubric of mental health, though using measures of social deviance as indirect indices of psychiatric disorder is a risky procedure, which may lead to 'psychiatric reductionism' (Keller & Murray 1982).

On the other hand, mental retardation or handicap has been excluded from this book, on the mainly practical grounds that it is now a substantial discipline of its own, which could not be covered adequately without enlarging the scope of the work unmanageably. Nor does it cover the micro-environment of psychiatric hospitals, for instance, which comes more into the province of environmental psychology — another largely independent discipline. But early nineteenth century psychiatry, like the rest of medicine then, was based on the view that all parts of the body were interdependent, and that both health and disease resulted from the interaction of individuals with their environment. 'The physician, by manipulating environment and patient, could overcome the past associations that led to the disease and create an atmosphere in which the natural restorative elements could reassert themselves' (Grob 1983). The concept of 'moral treatment' was largely equivalent to the construction of a specific environment that would have a therapeutic effect. Like almost every other form of psychiatric intervention, before and since, this one had more success with acute disorders than with the chronic; it tended to fall into disrepute with the advance of scientific medicine, later in the century, until its rediscovery in the 1940s as the 'therapeutic community'.

'Therapeutic environments' are interpreted by Canter & Canter (1979) in two different ways — either as providing places in which treatment and care can occur, or as creating situations which will directly contribute to therapeutic processes, e.g. arranging chairs so that social discourse is encouraged. At the same time, physical surroundings can have related roles, as when they are both symbolic of their function and facilitate therapy, through people 'reading' from a physical setting the potential interactions which may take place in it. A location for therapy derives its major characteristic from being an identifiable place, but in the case of psychiatric disorder, this itself can be a source of conflict, because that same identity may also label and stigmatise the people dealt with in it. The fact that environments often fail to be therapeutic may be due to inadequate definition of their therapeutic goals; these are often expressed in such general terms ('improve hospital morale') that there is no way of showing whether progress has occurred towards them. Furthermore, staff involved respectively in the planning, designing, and operating of such an environment may have completely different views as to what those aims should be.

Canter & Canter (1979) emphasise that the design for a therapeutic environment can only be effective when related to a particular context; fashions come and go which focus on one environmental feature, such as large gardens or bright decor, but these are bound to be unsuccessful if used on their own. Providing contemporary furnishings for the mentally retarded or those handicapped by chronic mental illness may simply allow them to vegetate in more comfort than before, and new buildings may achieve nothing if the institution retains an archaic form of administration. Acute general hospitals, rather than being coherent communities with common goals for the provision of patient care, now seem to be industrial complexes, having a number of separate processes, each with its own set of skilled operations, and its own criteria for evaluating the success of its product. In the 1950s, Thomas McKeown cogently argued the case for hospitals to be flexible structures, which could be adapted to constantly changing needs. Instead, exactly the opposite has been produced in Britain and many other countries — the 'technological fix' solution of skyscraper buildings with huge energy consumption, extreme vulnerability to anything going wrong, and a disorientating and often frightening atmosphere for patients treated in them.

'Environment' also suffers from a surfeit of definitions, but is seen here primarily in structural and social terms. It therefore refers to people's surroundings as expressed in their homes, districts, regions, and sometimes countries. It also includes the social groupings outside their immediate family, beginning at the level of a residential community or ethnic or occupational group. However, since settlements of those doing the same job are increasingly unusual in western countries, the last of these categories will now tend to be restricted to military camps (Freeman 1958), oil industry housing, etc. Beyond this are other relevant levels of social organisation. Assuming that different kinds of social action will occur in different kinds of residential areas, American social ecologists (Rosen et al. 1978) have suggested that much of the important behaviour related to residence can be understood in terms, respectively of household, neighbourhood, local area, and (sometimes) municipality. Lawton (1977) points out that to consider 'environment' as a unitary independent variable does an injustice to the complexity of the concept; further precision is needed both to distinguish between its different aspects and to permit allocation of some processes to the environment, to the individual, or to their interface respectively.

It is not proposed to deal here with the immediate family environment, except in so far as it is involved in wider issues, nor at any length with such conceptual developments as social network theory (Henderson 1980), since this does not necessarily relate to specific forms of physical environment and would move the focus of discussion into another large scientific field (though Chapter 2 contains a summary of this work). Attempts to incorporate the whole of sociology are to be avoided as much as those involving the same with psychiatry.

Another exclusion is the toxicological aspect of environmental sciences; substances such as lead which are environmental pollutants can certainly have effects on psychological and emotional functioning, but the subject is a vast and controversial one, with its own literature, which could not usefully be sampled here. However, the fact that prolonged exposure to high levels of ambient air lead, such as occurs in areas of dense motor traffic, may possibly cause brain damage to young children should surely have had more influence on transport and fuel policies than it has done up to now. Brain (1972) has suggested that common pollutants such as lead and carbon monoxide fumes might add to the stress experienced in certain environments, through activation of the adrenals, while a study of psychiatric admissions in St Louis, during summer and autumn months, suggested that certain types of psychiatric patients (especially with alcoholism and organic brain syndrome) are unusually sensitive to the effects of atmospheric nitrogen dioxide. In addition, mean levels of carbon monoxide in the air seemed to be associated with increased emergency room visits by psychiatric patients (Strahilevitz et al. 1979).

A completely new aspect of the environmental sciences whose significance cannot yet be judged is that of electromagnetic fields. Until fairly recently, these were thought to have no detectable physiological or biological effects, but it now appears that the enzyme structures and RNA systems of cells may well be influenced by applied magnetic fields at a critical, fairly low level. In fact, the mean generation time of $E.\ coli$ cultures was found to be significantly reduced, when subjected to alternating magnetic fields (Aarholt et al. 1981). At the same time, pain relief has been obtained through electrically stimulated production of endogenous opiates, and it is quite possible for people to experience currents in excess of those involved in such mechanisms, in proximity to high-voltage power cables, through accumulation of positive ions. In that case, the continuous production of β-endorphin over extended periods induced by environmental electrical influences, might result in unpleasant symptoms when the subject withdraws from the field or the current is reduced, e.g. through frosty or foggy weather. If the ambient electrical fields or biochemical anomalies in the body were only sought when symptoms were reported, it is likely that nothing would be found, since the body would then be approaching its more normal biochemical state. But symptoms which have been reported at an incidence greater than normal amongst people living close to power cables (headaches, exhaustion, insomnia, loss of appetite, depression) do seem to have some similarity with those described in connection with chronic abuse of and withdrawal from morphine (Smith & Aarholt 1982). Perry (1981) recorded a surprising number of suicides from a small community in Shropshire which was exposed to power cables; in collaboration with American workers, he then recorded significantly higher magnetic field intensities at the former homes of 590 people who had committed suicide, compared with control addresses. These findings are at present disputed by the electrical power industry, but indicate the need for much more careful monitoring of physical and chemical influences in the environment.

Related to this aspect of the subject is the fact that under environmental conditions of high humidity and low temperature, certain species of

Fusarium (soil microfungi) can produce secondary metabolites which cause mycotoxicoses in both animals and man. Male rats which were affected perinatally by these mycotoxins showed intra-species aggressive behaviour, which persisted throughout their lives; at post-mortem, they were found to have abnormalities in the testes and pituitary. Since foodstuffs stored under damp and cold winter conditions are more likely to contain mycotoxins than those used soon after harvesting, it is possible that severe weather could have a permanent effect on the behaviour of those born at such times. The higher risks of developing schizophrenia which have been found in people born during winter months could be relevant to this possibility (Schoental, 1982).

LIMITS OF THE DISCUSSION

It should also be made clear at the outset of this work that its objective is not to construct some psychiatric blueprint for the future of society — of whatever political complexion. The view that psychiatry could play an important part in resolving or preventing social problems of all kinds has been prevalent in the United States since William Alanson White, and if societies could be changed so that frustration, conflict, and aggression were reduced, much psychiatric disorder could no doubt be prevented. However:

> the psychiatrist functions solely in the realm of behavioural dysfunction. He is not an expert in dealing with poverty, overpopulation, urban renewal, automation or war . . . he should be capable of (helping) the behavioural difficulties that might arise in people who suffer from deprivation, crowding, slums, unemployment or massive stress (but) lacks the power to implement social action outside the mental health field. (Grinker 1982)

In the same volume, Jablensky (1982) points out that attempts to apply psychiatric knowledge to the social field, e.g. in prevention of traffic accidents or advice to urban planners and industrial managers, have so far rarely produced more than trivial recommendations. Though 'there is nothing intrinsically wrong in the search for new and useful social roles', the present state of knowledge and pitifully small resources devoted to such applied research make psychiatry's contribution to social development so far very unimpressive.

One of the reasons for this relative failure is that efforts tend to be focussed at the wrong level, usually one that is far too ambitious. For instance, Rutter (1981) says that when preventive policies are considered, there is a tendency to assume that these must in some way deal with 'basic' causes, but that 'this model involves a most naive and simplistic notion of causation'. There are, as he points out, many practical ways in which society could reduce psychiatric and social pathology, on the basis of established knowledge and within the limits of its resources. Instead, the tendency is to wait for the millenium, mostly because of unproved assumptions that these pathologies are direct expressions of an abnormal structure of society. In the 1960s, it was widely believed that the millenium had in fact arrived, and a few psychiatrists were happy to be carried along as gurus on a band-waggon of mysticism, contempt for social usages, and ill-digested Marxist theory. Their views have not stood the test of time, and did nothing for the improvement either of psychiatric disorder or of the many other social problems on which they were only too ready to pronounce. In fact, progress can only come through scrupulous, painstaking research, based on clear concepts, and through action which is directly related to what has been scientifically demonstrated. Society does not need psychiatrists to tell it such truisms as that good housing is better than bad.

At the same time, it would be as well to bear in mind the warning of Melvin Webber (quoted by Briggs 1982), that:

> neither crime-in-the-streets, poverty, unemployment, broken families, race riots, drug addiction, mental illness, juvenile delinquency, nor any of the commonly noted 'social pathologies' marking the contemporary city can find its cause or cure there. We cannot hope to invent local treatments for conditions whose origins are not local in character, nor can we expect territorially defined governments to deal effectively with problems whose causes are unrelated to territory or geography.

But neither, as Briggs points out, can the nation state deal with them on its own, since there are now too many interdependencies of countries and continents. Economic depression spreads throughout industrialised nations, drugs are trafficked from Asia to Europe and America, people migrate from less to better developed societies with very different cultures. The search for pragmatic solutions to problems of mental health in different environments is not helped by constant changes in the scenario, but this does not mean that it is a fruitless one.

Before drawing conclusions about the relationship of any individual's mental health to current environmental conditions, though, it would be as well to be reminded of the anthropological and biological context of this discussion:

> Our evolved repertoire was not intended for this environment . . . We are certainly evolved to be gregarious, but not in nations of 600 million, or in cities of 15 million . . . we were formed slowly over several million years, and at least 99 per cent of our existence — when our uniqueness was probably being moulded on the African savanna — was the existence of a small-scale hunter. The agricultural sedentary world is a mere 10 000 years old; and the industrial world with its even more alarming transformations is only 200 years old. Only yesterday. We are an old animal coping with a startling new world of its own creation that has got out of hand. (Fox 1982)

With that background, the subject of mental health and environment in its scientific aspects needs to be approached with a due sense of humility.

It also has to be remembered that a generally pessimistic view of the effects of socio-cultural change goes back at least to the 18th century, and has focussed particularly on the processes of industrialisation and urbanisation. As a result, it has come to be assumed that those inevitably have harmful effects at individual, social and cultural levels, yet as Chapter 7 shows, there is little evidence that the mental health of rural populations is consistently better than that of people who live in urban settlements.

Certainly, cities do tend to house concentrations of multiply disadvantaged people, who may show poor mental health along with other unfavourable attributes, but it would be quite wrong to extrapolate this picture to whole city populations (Freeman, 1984). There may, however, be an optimum size beyond which the costs of cities start to outweigh their benefits, resulting in an escalation of levels of social pathology (see Chapter 11).

PSYCHOLOGICAL CONSERVATION

On the basis of the evidence presented in this book, there would seem to be an urgent need to pay attention to the psychological conservation of the environment — retaining familiar landmarks and forms of housing — in the same way that physical Conservation Areas have been established in Britain.

> The need to sustain the familiar attachments and understanding, which makes life meaningful, is as profound as other basic human needs . . . the townscape ought to reflect our need for continuity, and the more rapidly society changes, the less readily should we abandon anything familiar which can still be made to serve a purpose. (Marris 1974)

Thus the social matrix which forms the identity of place, and which is almost certainly related to the identity of person and group (Canter 1977), may be preserved or restored. By contemporary standards, the great cities of the nineteenth century were mostly quite small, and a few, such as Vienna, still are; they had comprehensible boundaries and remained in touch with the surrounding countryside. But the sheer size of today's urban settlements may involve what Cappon (1975) has called 'the destruction of whatever natural order of territoriality was established by historical and social usage'.

Ødegard (1972) points out that important sources of ecological danger have been neglected because the power of adaptation of the human species has been relied on uncritically.

> We psychiatrists should perhaps have had better opportunity than most of predicting this unfortunate development, because we have experienced the breakdown of the homeostatic mechanism so often. As prophets we have failed as badly as have the physicists and technologists.

But it can reasonably be maintained that mental health is unlikely to be promoted by incomprehensible urban sprawl, severed by dangerous, polluting motorways, and full of monotonous blocks, standing between empty, impersonal spaces. The pioneer environmentalist John Barr referred (1970) to 'the same cars on the same sort of asphalt strips, growling, fuming past . . . the mobile squalor that, more than any single thing today, is annihilating urban Britain'. Since he wrote, the process has gone on relentlessly in many parts of the world.

There are also the likely ill-effects of population dispersal, based on the fallacy (promoted by the motor lobby) that because movement is technically possible over long distances at a high speed, it is therefore, desirable or necessary. There can be little doubt that the time and energy wasted by many millions of people every day in travelling — whether in overcrowded mass transit or in crawling private cars — together with the stress that comes from this frustrating activity, must be factors harmful to all aspects of health. As a consequence, city centres are deserted at night and weekends, and suburbs empty during the weekdays, causing further undesirable social and psychological effects.

More recently, the construction of orbital motorways around the outer suburbs of cities has produced a new generation of suburb-to-suburb traffic, pulling industry, business, and even professional activity out of the central areas. Sold to the public as a solution to urban traffic congestion, these developments tend to create a 'suburban gluepot' of new traffic movements, while accelerating the decline of city centres and making suburb-to-centre public transport uneconomical through loss of passengers.

Instead, there is a need to restore to human settlements the benefits of urbanity — of a social matrix in which a worthwhile quality of life and work can grow. This objective is not mere whimsical folkiness, but would regain a milieu that can be a very efficient one for conducting business and other essential activities. In contrast, Papanek (1974) has estimated that in present-day Chicago, the chances against an individual human-to-human contact are more than 3 million to one. To obliterate a community's landmarks and replace familiar environments with the tasteless impersonality of most present-day buildings seems like a recipe for social disaster in the long run, but it remains the task of scientific enquiry to demonstrate these dangers in a way that can influence the political process.

In particular, one contribution which social psychiatry might make, in collaboration with other disciplines is to oppose the overwhelming preoccupation that planners, architects, and local governments have had for many years with reduction of high urban density. Following a review of the scientific evidence, Choldin (1978) points out that 'Reducing urban densities does not appear to be a worthwhile goal . . . It is more important to recognise that high density is a basic feature of the urban community and to discover ways in which to organise community life and to build satisfying environments'. It is even more important, in fact, to recognise — as Durkheim did originally — that high density is actually essential for the positive qualities of towns and cities, such as cultural life and specialised professional services; the low densities of suburbs make these facilities difficult to provide without imposing a degree of car travel which is both environmentally damaging and unjust to the more disadvantaged sections of society (see Chapter 7).

Furthermore, in the post-industrial society which the old manufacturing nations of Europe and North America are now entering, conventional views on the relative situations of commerce, industry, communications, and residential building need to be completely revised with respect to land use. Most British and American cities, for instance, have enormous amounts of unoccupied space in the buildings of their central areas, which are unlikely to have any commercial or industrial use in the foreseeable future. Converting these to residential occupation would be economical of resources and have immense social consequences for the better. The harmful effects of mass commuting and of the abandonment of city centres by those in the upper half of the socioeconomic scale form one of the principal themes of Chapter 11. Marris (1974) points out that 'There is a virtue in rehabilitating familiar forms which neither economic logic nor conventional criteria of taste can fully take into account, and we should at last recognise this, before we decide what to destroy'. Similary, Sampson (1982) suggests that the British, 'with their long tradition of close communities, privacy, leisure, houses and gardens, could be better equipped to manage the process of deindustrialisation than most Europeans, with their competitiveness, their cooped-up apartments'; he hopes that patterns of family and friendship might still partly compensate for social life at the work-place, and that people might occupy themselves by exchanging services within neighbourhood communities. The importance of family and other social networks will be referred to throughout this book, even though their precise relationship to psychiatric disorder remains to be established.

A report from Hartlepool (Gregory, 1984) — an industrial area with the highest rate of unemployment in mainland Britain — remarks on the absence there of any overt sign of protest, or even much evidence on the streets of people without jobs. This might be related to the fact that there was hardly any redevelopment, and that the established pattern of terraced streets, shops, and semi-detached council estates remained relatively undisturbed — 'the fabric of the town is these interlocking streets and interlocking lives'. Because they were not uprooted, extended families continue to flourish there, usually with at least one member receiving a full-time wage, and the benefits of this are shared around the rest. Others find whatever part-time work they can; if this is done by women, their children may be minded by unemployed husbands, helped out at times by mothers and mothers-in-law who live close by. Gregory adds that 'the home is now a bolthole for all the members of the family, who equally need a place where they are recognised as individuals . . . The stress laid by women upon the value or relationships inside the home is now being echoed by men, whose loss of work has meant the loss of its camaraderie'. This contrast, though, between the social integration of a north-east English town and the violence experienced in redeveloped inner city areas does not take enough account of the population movements and racial heterogeneity of the largest conurbations. But even there, it is very likely that massive redevelopment has made things far worse.

Another contribution to social policy of social psychiatry and sociology, as Carstairs (1969) has pointed out, is to show that the clustering of such forms of social pathology as alcoholism, parasuicide, and violent crime in the overcrowded, underprivileged areas of large cities cannot be explained simply on grounds of material circumstances; equally important seems to be the alienation from participation in the general life of society which is felt by many people living in such situations. In historical terms, this recalls the widespread demoralisation, following periods of social and economic disruption, which have at times resulted in millenial or revolutionary movements (Cohn 1957). Carstairs summarises such circumstances as: long-settled means of production and traditional occupations being rapidly superseded by new techniques, throwing many people out of work; different sectors of a population experiencing widely contrasting standards of living; weakening of traditional values, with protective functions no longer being fulfilled by customary authorities; and an all-pervading sense of uncertainty about the future. This fits the situation of our own times in many parts of the world too closely for comfort.

The result of these processes has been described in the case of Chicago by Saul Bellow (1982) as: 'huge rectangles, endless regions of the stunned city — many, many square miles of civil Paaschendael or Somme. Only at the centre of the city, visible from all points over fields of demolition, the tall glamour of the skyscrapers'. As for the human consequences of such environmental changes, they are likely to produce 'that black underclass . . . which is economically "redundant", a culture of despair and crime'. Thus, those who are multiply disadvantaged become ecologically trapped, unable to work because employment has moved to far suburbs or become strung along motorways, and there is no accessible public transport to take them there. Economic activity now tends to occur increasingly in inter-urban clusters, focussed on road and air travel, and linked more by telephone, telex, and computer than by the meeting of people; it is a capital-intensive, high technology environment, needing fairly small numbers of personnel, who will mostly have to be young, intelligent, and mentally and physically healthy to measure up to its demands. This dispersal and differentiation of human activities also makes the control of deviant behaviour more difficult, since people are constantly on the move (except for the poor and handicapped), and the unofficial monitoring that neighbours and workmates carry out in less complex societies is no longer possible.

In the case of Liverpool, for instance, the combination of massive de-industrialisation with ill-conceived redevelopment (clearing central areas and moving investment out to satellite towns) has produced a ' city on the dole'. Visitors are astonished at the areas of empty space near the city's heart, at the absence of a rush hour, at the ghostly feeling of activities and people no longer there, at the lines of waiting taxis which recall a Third World city. In some districts, hardly anyone is employed, except by the public sector; so far, transfer payments and social services have avoided severe destitution, but what of the mental health of such a population?

THE BOOK

The contents of this volume are divided into three sections. In the first, environmental aspects of mental health are seen primarily in terms of their scientific background and from the points of view of psychiatry, biology, geography, and sociology. An introductory chapter also considers a number of relevant theoretical issues, particularly Brown's hypothesis of the aetiology of depression, in relation to environmental factors. The second section deals with specific issues, on which reasonable amounts of evidence now exist; these are housing, urban–rural differences, aircraft noise, urban disasters, urban scale, and migration. Finally, there are a number of illustrative examples, which it is hoped will form a useful amalgam with the more general material earlier; these deal with a new community in London, depression and schizophrenia in an English city, inner city health, and the situation in developing countries. There is finally a contribution by an architect on continuity and the sense of place. Certain topics, such as the role of stress, and possible explanations for excess of psychiatric disorder in central city locations, appear in more than one chapter. Throughout, contributors will be referring to original research of their own, and in a number of cases, this is published here for the first time. Also, they have advanced and reconceptualised their earlier work, so that both in terms of data and of scientific consideration, it is hoped that the whole subject will have moved significantly forward. The last word, though, may be left with Adolph Meyer, from an address of 1907:

> Insanity is not merely a matter of fate, at least if we learn to consider social conditions as to some extent of our own making.

REFERENCES

Aarholt E, Flinn E A, Smith C W 1981 Effects of low-frequency magnetic fields on bacterial growth rate. Physics Medicine & Biology 26: 613–621

Barr J 1970 The assaults on our senses. Methuen, London

Bellow S 1982 The Dean's December. Harper & Row, New York

Brain P 1978 Stress as an urban pollutant. Journal of Environmental Planning and Pollution Control 1: 28–35

Briggs A (Lord) 1982 The environment of the City. Encounter 59: 25–35

Brill H 1980 Notes on the history of social psychiatry. Comprehensive Psychiatry 21: 492–499

Canter D 1977 The psychology of place. St. Martin's Press, New York

Canter D, Canter S 1979 Designing for therapeutic Environments. John Wiley, Chichester

Cappon D 1975 Designs for improvements in the quality of life in downtown cores. International Journal of Mental Health 4: 31–47

Carstairs G M 1969 Overcrowding and human aggression. In: Gurr G (ed) The history of violence in America. Praeger, New York

Carstairs G M, Kapur R L 1976 The great universe of Kota. Hogarth Press, London

Cheyne G 1733 The English Malady; or, a Treatise of Nervous Diseases of All Kinds, as Spleen, Vapours, Lowness of Spirits, Hypochondrical and Hysterical Distempers. London

Choldin H M 1978 Urban density and pathology. Annual Review of Sociology 4: 91–113

Cohn N R C 1957 The pursuit of the millenium. Secker & Warburg, London

Craik K H 1973 Environmental psychology. Annual Review of Psychology 24: 403–422

Department of the Environment 1972 The estate outside the dwelling. Design Bulletin 25. HMSO, London

Elias N 1969 Sociology and psychiatry. In: Foulkes S H, Prince G S (eds) Psychiatry in a Changing Society, Tavistock, London

Fischer C S 1975 The study of urban community and personality. Annual Review of Sociology 1: 67–89

Fox R 1982 Of inhuman native and unnatural rights. Encounter 58: 47–53

Freeman H L 1958 Common stresses in a military environment. Journal of the Royal Army Medical Corps 104: 31–35

Freeman H L 1984 Mental health in the inner city. Environment and Planning A 16: 115–121

Giggs J A 1980 Mental health and the environment. In: Howe G M, Loraine J (eds) Environmental Medicine. Heinemann, London

Gans 1962 Urbanism and Suburbanism as Ways of Life.

Gillis A R, Hogan J 1982 Density, delinquency and design. Criminology 19: 514–529

Gold H 1982 The sociology of urban life. Prentice Hall, Englewood Cliffs, N J

Gregory P 1984 You don't heave a brick through your uncle's window. The Guardian February 18th

Grinker R 1982 In Shepherd M (ed) Psychiatrists on psychiatry. Cambridge University Press, Cambridge

Grob G N 1983 Mental illness and American society, 1875–1940. Princeton University Press, Princeton

Hare E H 1966 Mental health in new towns. What next? Journal of Psychosomatic Research 10: 53–58

Henderson S 1980 A development in social psychiatry. Journal of Nervous and Mental Disease 168: 63–69

Hillier W R G, Hudson J 1984 Creating life: the relation between people and space in urban localities. Architecture and Behavior (in press)

Jablensky A 1982 In: Shepherd M (ed) Psychiatrists on psychiatry. Cambridge University Press, Cambridge

Kasl S V, Rosenfield S 1980 The residential environment and its impact on the mental health of the aged. In: Birren J E, Sloane R B (eds) Handbook on mental health and aging. Prentice Hall, Englewood Cliffs, N J

Keller P A, Murray J D 1982 Handbook of rural community mental health. Human Sciences Press, New York

Lawton M P 1977 The impact of the environment on aging and behavior. In: Birren J E, Schaie K W (eds) Handbook of the psychology of aging. Litton Educational, New York

Lewis, Sir Aubrey 1967 The state of psychiatry. Essays and addresses. Routledge & Kegan Paul, London

Marris P 1974 Loss and change. Routledge & Kegan Paul, London

Mechanic D 1973 The contributions of sociology to psychiatry. Psychological Medicine 3: 1–4

Meyer A 1952 Modern psychiatry: its possibilities and responsibilities. In: Collected papers, vol 4. Johns Hopkins Press, Baltimore

Mullin S 1969 I'm sorry, I'll build that again New Statesman 78: 818–819

Newman O 1980 Community of interest. Anchor, Doubleday, New York

Nicholson J H 1961 New Communities in Britain. National Council of Social Service, London

Ødegard O 1972 The future of psychiatry. British Journal of Psychiatry 121: 579–590

Papanek V 1974 Design for the real world. Paladin, London

Perry F S 1981 Environmental power-frequency magnetic fields and suicide. Health Physics 41: 267–277

Rapoport A 1971 Some observations regarding man-environment studies. Architectural Research & Teaching 2: No 1, November

Rosen B M, Goldsmith H F, Redick R W 1978 Demographic and social indicators from the US census of population and housing: uses in mental health planning in small areas. WHO, Geneva

Rutter M 1981 The city and the child. American Journal of Orthopsychiatry 51: 610–625

Sells S B 1968 The definition and measurement of mental health. Public Health Service Publication No. 1873, US Government Printing Office, Washington

Shepherd M 1983 The Psychosocial Matrix of Society. Tavistock, London

Smith C W, Aarholt E 1982 Possible effects of environmentally stimulated endogenous opiates. Health Physics 43: 929–930

Strahilevitz M, Strahilevitz A, Miller J E 1979 Air pollutants and the admission rate of psychiatric patients. American Journal of Psychiatry 136: 205–207

Wooff K, Freeman H L, Fryers T 1983 Psychiatric service use in Salford. British Journal of Psychiatry 142: 588–597

SCIENTIFIC BACKGROUND

The scientific background

To start on a note of caution, it is very unlikely that direct cause-and-effect relationships will be found between specific features of the environment and abnormal mental states or forms of psychological malfunctioning. The intervening processes must be extremely complex, and Kasl (1977) has pointed out that three factors must be included in this equation of person–environment fit; these are the objective social environment; the individual's perceptions of it, related to his personal characteristics; and finally the physiological, affective, and behavioural reactions which act as mediators. However, there are many difficulties in translating this metatheory into effective research designs; in defining what specific dimensions of the environment and of the person need to be examined in these studies, the distinction between physical and social environmental dimensions tends to be blurred (Kasl & Rosenfield 1980).

At any time, interactions are continuously occurring between social, cultural, and physical aspects of the environment on the one hand and different levels of the human nervous system on the other. If a neurotic illness or psychosomatic condition should occur later, this would only be after many variables had played their part in the intermediate processes. Furthermore, one feature of the environment will have widely varying effects on the different people who may be exposed to it, and these different effects result both from the variations between individuals' genetic constitutions and from the influence on them of their life experiences. The latter, mainly through setting up conditioned reflexes, cause particular bodily organs to respond to environmental stimuli in particular ways, and some of these responses will be maladaptive. Therefore, two individuals exposed to the same environmental stress might show respectively a psychiatric disorder or a physical disorder (Fig. 2.1). In other individuals, it is possible for the same environmental influences to have no ill-effect at all, or even a beneficial efect, as when the moderate anxiety of a situation improves performance. Furthermore, people react back to their milieu, so that the relationship is a transactional one (Stokols 1978).

Though certain social situations may be coincident with a high rate of a particular psychiatric disorder, this in itself allows us to say no more,

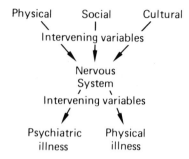

Fig. 2.1 Environmental effects on mental and physical health

scientifically, than that a connection between the two could exist, and the connection might be a very indirect one. Environmental input consists of a series of signals, which are received by the body's sense-organs and transmitted through psychological and physiological processes of enormous complexity, mainly in the central nervous and endocrine systems, which have a common governing centre in the hypothalamus. Eventually, some of the environmental signals will be experienced as emotion, but the biological significance of these emotions depends on factors such as the individual's culture and the way he has come to terms with his environment in the past. For instance, bodily reactions involving the adrenals may be less related to an objective degree of danger in the immediate environment than to the psychological significance of perceived events there; Frankenhaeuser (1975) showed that urinary excretion of adrenaline increases linearly with stress as perceived.

On the other hand, positive mood has been shown to enhance interpersonal attraction and affiliative and helping behaviour (Mehrabian & Russell, 1974). At the same time, higher levels of arousal tend to increase an individual's primary emotional reaction to a setting or situation, so that an environment primarily experienced as pleasant will appear more pleasant and vice versa. Thus, a crowded and noisy urban setting, generally experienced as unpleasant and highly arousing, would be the kind of environment likely to set up avoidance reactions in people within it — both to the environment and to others there. An empirical study of behaviour in a newly pedestrianised central area of an Australian city showed that helping strangers was more common there and friendly greetings more readily returned than before. However, when pedestrian density was high, rates of helping were not significantly higher than in the old environment, though one of the most important factors attracting people to new settings of this kind is usually thought to be the presence of other people (Amato, 1981).

Thus, where a climate of danger has been established — as in many American cities — otherwise trivial environmental stimuli such as a shadow will take on sinister significance. Trichopoulos et al (1983) conclude that 'because of pre-existing conditioned reflex pathways, symbolic danger can generate stress as effectively as real danger', though the extent to which this diminishes by adaptation seems to be uncertain.

Even at the macro level, the investigation of cause-and-effect relationships with environmental factors remains formidable; Gans (1968) interprets the relevance of the physical environment to behaviour as occurring through the social system and culture of the people involved or through its effects being taken up into their social system. There is thus 'a social system and a set of cultural norms which define and evaluate portions of the physical environment relevant to the lives of the people involved and which structure the way people will use (and react to) this environment in their daily lives'. So far as mental health is concerned Giggs (1979) points out that there are 'very few spatial analyses at the intra-urban scale which successfully demonstrate causal relationships, and this is particularly the case with psychiatric illness, where there is little unequivocal scientific evidence for specific aetiological factors for most forms of disorder'.

SOCIAL NETWORKS

Probably the greatest unresolved problem in studies of psychological effects of the environment is to fill in those considerable areas of *terra incognita* which represent the processes of interaction between individual personality or behaviour and the social structure of a community. Since community characteristics, at an ecological level, do not usually explain much of individual variation in behaviour, it is easy to conclude that communities are not significant forces on individuals (Fischer 1975), but more detailed analysis may reveal complex and even contradictory effects operating on different sub-populations, e.g. the young or the elderly. 'What is missing in the study of intra-community variation are compelling theories which connect settlement patterns, in terms of ecological variables, to community and personality'. In Fischer's view, the most promising conceptual tool for this purpose is analysis of social networks.

These networks are the people with whom an individual associates regularly, and who are significant to him in terms of qualities such as support and influence. Within the internal fabric of a community, networks are linked, but do not merge; they might provide a means of examining scientifically such concepts as alienation or anomie (see pp. 37,51), but up to now, their lack of objective criteria leaves it still largely a matter of opinion as to who does or does not constitute part of a network. Whilst deficiencies of social bonds are considered a regular *consequence* of psychiatric illness, it also appears that some of the increased prevalence of neurotic morbidity observed in the lowest socio-economic class can be partly explained by failures of social networks (Henderson 1980). However, which of these elements is primary, or whether a third — such as personality — leads to both is a question which remains unresolved. It has been suggested (Hammer, 1983) that one of the ways in which the social networks of schizophrenics become depleted is through a failure of cross-connectedness of the individuals involved; however, this seems more a descriptive restatement than an explanation of the situation.

There also may be confusion at times between the effects of deficiencies of social relationships and effects of life events of an 'exit' kind from a person's social field. Killilea (1982) suggests that whereas in times of personal crisis a small, dense network with strong ties may be most valuable, at times of psychosocial transition (and perhaps of psychiatric disorder), a low-density network with relatively weak ties is possibly more helpful; this is because high-density networks may put more normative pressure on their members to maintain existing roles, and so provide less support for those who are interested in effecting major role changes (Mitchell & Trickett 1980). Theoretically, mental health might be improved by identifying informal community care-givers, and developing consultative relationships with them; however, it is not known in what way this process of intervention might change the networks of which they are part, so that the results might not be what was hoped. What has often been described as 'environmental manipulation' in treating psychiatric disorder is, in fact, more the attempt to manipulate social networks (Greenblatt et al, 1982).

A linkage between social support and the course of psychiatric disorder is proposed by Goldstein and Caton (1983), who followed up for one year 119 schizophrenics with a history of multiple admissions, returning to a variety of living arrangements in poor areas of New York City. Little earlier research exists on the effects of either physical characteristics of the environment or the conditions within different living settings on discharged patients' level of functioning and length of stay within the community, but these latter have been found to be influenced by the social–emotional circumstances of the home, such as social support and interpersonal stress (Vaughan & Leff 1976). In this study, patients' living arrangements were separated into six categories (e.g. with parents, or alone in the patients' own flat) but these categories were found to have no significant differential effect on rate of rehospitalisation, level of clinical functioning, or degree of adjustment in the community. Similarly, no major social or clinical differences were found between those living with their families and those who had a solitary living environment; the latter experienced less interpersonal stress, but had poorer social supports. Although some patients changed their home during the course of the year, the new environments tended to be quite similar to the old ones. Outcome over the year was more strongly predicted by social support and interpersonal stress within the home than by the use of available treatment services, those patients who were in high stress/poor social support environments having the highest risk of rehospitalisation. Goldstein & Caton conclude that since interpersonal stress and social support are strong predictors of rehospitalisation, regardless of the patient's type of living arrangement, the most valuable community care resource might be natural support environments such as families, and improvement of these should perhaps have more priority for resources. These results are open to some selection bias, for instance through living arrangements not being randomly assigned, and it is possible that more effective treatment services than the ones available to these patients would have shown a stronger effect on outcome, but the New York study indicates an important direction for further research.

STRESS

In the search for a general explanation of the mediating processes between environment and individual reactions, the concept of stress has emerged as generally most valuable (see also Chapter 8). Research on this subject has been dominated by two models (Evans 1982); the physiological, derived from Selye, implies both a homeostatic concept of bodily function and negative effects from the processes of coping with stress, independently of the impact of the stressor itself. The psychological model, on the other hand, emphasises cognitive interpretation of environmental conditions, influenced by characteristics of the individual and of the context; it is not clear, though, which model is more crucial in determining human reactions. Biological approaches tend to overemphasise pathogenic outcomes of a physical kind, but psychological effects, e.g. on mood or interpersonal relationships, are also very important, both as outcome measures in themselves and through affecting the susceptibility of the host organism to disease.

The impact of environmental stressors on people is likely to depend on both the importance (salience) and controllability (congruence) of the setting in which the stressors occur (Stokols 1978). It can be wrongly concluded, however, that certain stresses have no negative effects because of successful efforts by the individual to maintain normal performance through adaptation, though these efforts themselves may well be harmful to him in the long run (Evans 1982). If various kinds of changes in environmental conditions can all be conceptualised as 'stressful', then they must share some common mechanism, or else the construct of stress fails to remain credible.

However, the processes that make certain environmental conditions stressful can also be seen in various terms: an arousal model proposes that they affect the reticular activating system, and that stress will result if arousal levels thereby move outside an optimum range; an overload model assumes that an excess of environmental stimuli has harmful effects (discussed later in this chapter); and a systems model sees stress as resulting from individual needs being thwarted by environmental conditions (Evans, 1982). Cassel (1974) points out that because of the habit of thinking in mono-aetiological terms, much work on the social and psychological antecedents to disease has tried to identify particular forms of stress that would have a specific causal relationship to clinical entities. Yet animal data show that a wide variety of pathological conditions may emerge following changes in the social milieu, and in humans also, variations in group relationships could be expected to enhance susceptibility to disease in general, rather than having a specific aetiological role; this seems to be confirmed by the fact that certain regions of the US, have a higher death rate than the national average from all causes. In different individuals, the specific manifestations of disease following stress would depend on their genetic predisposition, metabolic state, etc., as well as on any adverse physico-chemical or infective factors to which they might have been exposed. Unfortunately, research on stress up to now has nearly all been restricted to short time spans, and results are not available from studies over the lengths of time that are needed to provide answers to these unresolved questions.

Another way of connecting personality to the environment is via the family. Piha et al. (1979) suggest that since the family is the primary mediating unit between the individual and society, it should therefore be crucial in the psychiatric study of the relationship between environment and mental health. This might be examined by analysing firstly, the compatibility between the physical environment and family developmental tasks, and secondly, those qualities of the environment which have a current meaning for the family, and which enter into its transactions. The housing environment may represent a positive factor in the family's mental health if the properties of this environmental stage, and if the utilisation of these properties is connected with adequate interpersonal processes within the family. However, the family's mental representation of its environment can also be unrealistic, and involve shared myths. These provocative ideas would require a great deal of empirical research to establish their validity, though, and seem to include many subjective value judgements.

SPACE AND DENSITY

The theme of personal space is one that recurs throughout this volume, particularly in relation to topics such as crowding, density, and privacy, which are interrelated and often confused with each other; it is the main subject of Chapter 3. The whole concept of territory and of the need for personal space is of uncertain significance for humans, but can be seen in terms of the structuring of that part of static space for which a person feels possessiveness. Since some space has to be shared in most environments, elaborate social systems are contrived to allow this, but, 'the differences from animals are so great that it seems more profitable to concentrate on the ways in which (it) is culturally learned' (Lee 1976). Mercer (1975) regards the same concept as a primitive rule system; in situations where normal cultural constraints do not apply, people will tend to fall back on this, and use it to communicate intention in their interaction with others. An example (Lipman 1968) is the use of chairs in an old people's home, which is both an assertion of identity and a means of limiting social inter-action to a feasible level.

So far as an independent territorial instinct is concerned, Freedman (1975) argues against the existence of one even in animals, since lack of space *per se* does not seem to trigger aggressive or defensive responses, nor have other negative effects. Therefore, 'territoriality' represents little more than a description of behaviour, while any expression in humans would be likely to be merely symbolic, even more than in the case of animals. In other words, its functions are cognitive and social-organisational, rather than biological (Stokols 1978). However, territoriality is considered a useful concept by Altman (1975), as one of the behavioural mechanisms for boundary control which is an important fact of social behaviour. He divides human territories into three types, mainly according to the length of time they are occupied, and their importance to the lives of individuals; 'secondary territories', such as entrances and staircases in blocks of flats, are relevant to Newman's *defensible space* theory. A central construct in the regulation of self/other boundaries between people and the social and physi-cal environment is privacy, which Altman regards as a selective process, whereby people vary the permeability of these boundaries through a variety of behavioural mechanisms, including the verbal, non-verbal, cultural, and environmental. Various combinations of these are used to communicate intentions as to interaction or withdrawal, and to optimise a desired degree of access to the environment. Altman recognises that the related concept of stimulus overload is important, but considers that privacy is the key to an understanding of crowding.

Personal space

Whether or not this view is accepted, it would clearly be wrong to under-estimate the significance of spatial factors, for which Hall (1968) has constructed a body of theory (proxemics), consisting of 'the inter-related observations and theories of man's use of space'. He maintains that mental processes and behaviour take place within a cultural context, transmitted both through language and codes of spatial use; these codes vary from culture to culture, and may also be subject to individual differences. Prox-emic studies do not deal directly with mental health outcomes, though they may examine behavioural precursors of variations in people's mental health status (Kasl and Rosenfield 1980.)

Sommer (1969) described as 'personal space' or 'portable territory' the area surrounding the body into which intrusions by others are seen as threat-ening, thus resulting in anxiety and defensive behaviour, while Horowitz et al. (1964) labelled it the 'body-buffer zone', and emphasised that its extent is subjective, governed both by culture and by personal character-istics of the individual. It has been suggested that these phenomena might be explained in terms of cerebral arousal, so that introverts and schizo-phrenics would become overloaded at a lower level of sensory input, but this hypothesis does not seem to have been tested neurophysiologically. Tech-niques such as encounter groups specifically involve the temporary disrup-tion of Western society's normal rules for the use of personal space. Silberman (1979) described this space as the 'mental transition sphere', which controls and modulates the constant flow of stimuli and exchange of communication with the outside world, influencing the development of the ego. In the case of the schizophrenic, it has been suggested that 'The boundary between self and environment is infirm, and that between fantasy and perception can, at times, dissolve altogether. The fragility of his own ego is projected onto the external environment' (Tuan 1979); this interpre-tation seems to be confirmed by the sensitivity of schizophrenics to their social environment.

Human territorial behaviour in New York underground railways was investigated by Fried & De Fazio (1974), on the basis that in any social system, parameters of personal distance are maintained by physical en-vironments, law, and social custom, though expectations about these are mostly unconscious. They found passengers' behaviour greatly influenced by the prevailing density; at rush hours, seating which provided physical separation from others was unavailable and bodily contact between strangers occurred. Then, territorial defence becomes largely psychological, e.g. avoiding eye contacts, ignoring each other, and seeming to be unaware of intruders. Despite overcrowding, however, behaviour remains regularised and predictable, indicating adaptation of biological tendencies to a very unnatural environment. When there is choice, through low density of passengers, people tend to sit as far apart as possible, which minimises boundary conflicts and satisfies the need continually to avoid contact with strangers. Thus, the assured privacy of the personal car may be one reason for the declining use of public transport.

Crowding and density

Whereas *density* is a physical state, which can usually be represented by a mathematial ratio, *crowding* is predominantly a psychological experience; at the same time, though, density of areas is a complex matter in itself, including factors ranging from residential acreage per square mile to number of persons per room (Kirmeyer 1978). These different components may vary independently, so that a low density might result either from relatively little of an area being used for residential purposes, or from it being occupied entirely by detached, single-family dwellings; the larger an urban area, the more likely it is that its use will be very heterogeneous.

Crowding has been examined experimentally by Freedman (1975), who found that the sensation is certainly related to having little space, but distinct from it. When such factors as smell, heat, fear, or discomfort —

usually associated with crowding — were excluded, no negative effects were found in either physical, psychiatric, or social terms. Freedman's findings led to the *denstiy–intensity* theory, i.e. that crowding merely intensifies an individual's characteristic reaction to any situation, but this will not apply if the presence of others is irrelevant to a particular behaviour. Urban sociology has also been much influenced by the *density–pathology* hypothesis — that high density is responsible for numerous forms of social pathology, including an excess of psychiatric morbidity. In the study of these phenomena, a distinction has been made between high density and very large numbers; the latter situation may have generally negative effects at times, influencing people to withdraw socially and be more defensive, in a way which would not be caused by high density alone, though this point remains to be established conclusively.

Kirmeyer (1978) points out that theoretical links between density and medical or social pathologies have not been empirically established, though it is generally assumed that high density is a stressor with important long-term psychological consequences. For instance, the physical and psychological energy required to cope with excessive stimulation possibly results in frustration and physical weakness, leading to increased mobidity and mortality. Various ways have also been suggested in which high density might encourage delinquency (Galle et al. 1972). However, the information so far available on populations does not include reliable indicators of stress or of coping mechanisms, and gross rates of pathology are not closely related to the experience of stress in any dimension (Webb & Collette 1975). It is very difficult to establish causal relationships from correlations of any of these factors, particularly as density tends to co-vary with social and economic measures, and as the populations studied in different areas are not comparable; but one of the more consistent findings is a relationship between living alone and poor mental health, as both Galle et al. and Webb & Collette found.

Rapoport (1975) suggests that if crowding is equivalent to cognitive overload and the need to organise behaviour very tightly, there may be a difference between the effects of increased group size and effects due to reduction in the amount of space per person. Here again, the probable difference in effects between high density and large numbers emerges. Furthermore, cultural differences make it very difficult to set any absolute standards for crowding: though Chombart de Lauwe (1959) reported that rates of illness and disorganisation increased in France with less than 8–10 square meters per person in a dwelling, under half that space in Hong Kong was associated with low rates of mortality, morbidity, and criminality. This suggests that any effects of crowding on behaviour would depend on the mediating social structure; in Chinese culture, for instance, privacy is defined in terms of groups, not individuals, and although a particular number of people in a house might have negative effects if they were non-kin, they do not do so when are defined as kin (Anderson 1972). Another factor is technological and economic development; Carey (1972) suggested that as societies advance in this respect, the empirical relationship between density and crowding in urban areas will decline almost to zero; it was then 0.270 for Washington, DC. Within Western societies, though, such concepts as privacy and adequate personal space are likely to be strongly related to social class, expectations about them rising with higher status, though whether family relationships improve with more spacious dwellings, above a certain minimum level, has not yet been clearly established.

In some societies at least, an association between crowding and physical disease may derive from the particular kind of stress that arises from accompanying disordered social relationships (Cassel 1970, 1971); adverse effects of living at high density might be confined to periods following migration, and once settled, people may generally adapt to these conditions. Levy & Herzog (1974) concluded from a review of the literature that crowding is unlikely to be a serious problem in the absence of abject poverty, lack of sanitation, or poor nutrition; otherwise, it is more of an irritant and social strain, which may precipitate psychoneurosis or other mild forms of maladjustment, but is probably irrelevant in the main to physical disease and major mental disorder. This was confirmed in New York by Kahn & Perlin (1967), and in Toronto by Booth (1976). The latter investigated people in households, rather than in areal units such as census tracts, and included medical examinations of half the respondents; although household crowding was associated with greater prevalence of stress-related diseases among males, the detected effects of density and crowding were generally small. The finding that men who were experiencing crowding for the first time in their lives were most strongly affected suggested that successful human adaptation to compressed living conditions may be quite rapid, perhaps no more than one generation. However, this sample was limited to members of intact families, and it is likely that other kinds of people would show different results; in fact, Gove et al. (1979) state that because of problems relating both to the sample and to the measurement and analysis, it is difficult to draw any conclusions about crowding from this study.

Freedman et al. (1975) also studied data from New York City, concluding that density explained little or none of the variance in physical, mental, and social pathology, in addition to that explained by income and ethnicity; these findings were approximately the same for density per acre and per room, although the two measures are themselves only moderately correlated. They add that 'The burden of proof is firmly on those who would argue that density does have substantial effects' and that 'intuitions notwithstanding, humans do not have generally negative reactions to high density'. Dye (1975) compared eight indicators of social pathology for 243 American central cities with three measures of population density: population per square mile, persons per house, and room crowding. He concluded that for cities as a whole, these pathologies are more closely related to the age, race, ethnicity, and social class characteristics of the population than to its densities, though room crowding was significantly and independently associated with poverty, residential segregation, and income inequality. Most ecological studies of the density–pathology relationship, however, have suffered from the use of units of analysis which were too large; variation in environmental conditions and in the sociodemographic composition within the area may then be so great as to obscure any possible effect of spatial variables on the aetiology of medical or social pathologies (Choldin 1978). Similarity, Gove et al. (1979) state that though density at the level of the macro-environment is not important in terms of pathological effects, disruption of relationships in the home due to overcrowding is likely to have very serious consequences.

An exotic contribution to the subject has come from Abbott (1979), who examined 1897 census data from Moscow, finding that infant non-survival rates had an inverse association then with density. As there was also a negative association between social status and pathology, it was concluded that it was not density but low status which accounted for the pathology measured. Abbott points out that in the case of Chicago and other communities conforming generally to the Burgess zonal model (see Chapter 14 for explanation of this model) areal density and lower status are correlated, and it is then difficult to distinguish between the effects of either density or status on pathology. Another problem of macro-level research is that as urban areas increase in size, population distribution within them becomes more unequal, and overall density fails to be a constant measure of potential interaction across sub-areas. Furthermore, Roncek (1981) using data from Cleveland and San Diego, found that although increasing overall density correlated with lower crime rates, the various components of density (space per person, group size, interaction level) follow different trends.

The indicators of 'pathology' which have been generally used in this research are of three main kinds: crime, mortality and physical morbidity, and psychiatric disorder (Kirmeyer 1978); other rates, such as divorce and fertility have sometimes been included also. Clearly, these factors are not homogeneous, and methodological difficulties may arise when they are treated as being equivalent. In Aberdeen, however, Bain (1974) found a significant positive association between referral rates for all psychiatric disorders and both overcrowding and the number of shared households. In this connection, overcrowding of social roles may be more important than the number of persons per square unit of measurement; but even this distinction is very much dependent on the cultural features of any society, though density has a general tendency to be associated with increased complexity of role behaviour.

Surveying the literature on social behaviour, Korte (1976) found no convincing evidence that either population density or crowding in themselves produced measurable changes, while Kasl & Rosenfield (1989) suggest that many ecological studies of pathological conditions probably reflect no more than the impact of aggregated individual characteristics. If so, they would not have identified significant ecological or environmental variables, and 'impressive statistical associations would fail to illuminate anything about environmental factors in the aetiology of such pathologies'. In other words, it is more nearly the case that suffering people come to live densely than that density causes suffering (Fischer 1976). The ecological approach is discussed further, later in this Chapter.

There are two main sociological views on the subject of high population density, whose positions are historically opposed (Miller 1974). The Behaviourists, represented by Simmel and Wirth, argued that it leads to much psychological and physiological strain, inputs of low priority being deliberately reduced. On the other hand the Structuralists, such as Durkheim, saw it as allowing the refined division of labour and thus greater expression of each individual's aptitudes and needs; this is the notion of 'moral density'. In other words, there is a polarisation effect, in which the dense community — typically a city — contains both the best and worst of its particular society. However, this argument tends to ignore the size of the community, and probably has little relevance to the motorised megalopolises of today (see Chapter 11). Furthermore, most of Wirth's hypotheses about density are similar to his hypothesised effects of community size, so that the two characteristics should probably be treated together as a causal pair (Morris 1968), another example of possible density–size confusion.

It is hard, in fact, to separate density from other social, economic, and political factors, while a number of social-ecological aspects of the community either buffer or accentuate its effects on individuals' psychology, e.g. the visual and architectural qualities of the environment, conditions such as noise and light, and the number of interpersonal contacts per unit of space and time. Density effects also seem to be greater when there is incongruity between the environment and the behaviour occuring within it, a feature related to the concepts of 'behaviour setting' and 'manning' in environmental psychology (Barker 1968) (see also Chapter 11). 'Behaviour settings' refer to those recurring patterns of human activity that take place within specific boundaries of time and space, e.g. sports matches or concerts; 'manning' refers to the number of people required to maintain a setting at an optimal level. However, many theoretical aspects remain to be resolved before practical use can be made of this work.

Perceived density

A particularly individual view, but one deserving great interest, is that of Rapoport (1975), who regards density as a perceived experience, rather than merely a mathematical ratio. Thus, depending on the individual's previous experience, the social organisation of the setting, and the relationship between people and objects involved, places containing identical numbers per unit area can have quite different perceived densities. These are 'read', or decoded, according to cues — both physical and social — which indicate that the environment is dense or not dense, and which convey an expected level of interaction. For instance, when a population is homogeneous, it is easier to disregard other people, and the area is seen as having a relatively lower density, whereas people who are different cause uncertainty, a high rate of stimuli, and thus a 'reading' of high density. Judgement of density is made from the amount of information which needs to be processed; should this be evaluated as unwanted or uncontrollable, then a feeling of crowding or, at the other extreme, of isolation will be experienced. Just as sensory overload and sensory deprivation are extreme ends of a continuum, so there is a limited range of acceptable and perceived densities for any given group and context, with extremely low densities having undesirable effects as much as extremely high ones.

Rapoport sees crowding, then, as an incongruence between perceived density and norms or desired levels of interaction, which are culturally defined in terms of kinship, age, sex, rituals, etc.; lack of open space, traffic, industrial and commercial activities, and noise are other aspects of the environment which may be related to feelings of being crowded. Effective boundaries (physical or social) reduce perceived densities and, depending on whether or not non-members of the individuals' reference group are present, density will be decoded differently and behaviour altered accordingly. Perceived density is also reduced by fixed and recognised relationships in space, homogeneity of people, and by agreed rules, cues, symbols, and markers, all of which make behaviour more mutually predictable and reduce the need for constant communication. Thus, high density need not lead to stress if the group concerned is stable, homogeneous, and well organised. Rapoport is convincing in his view that the experience of density is highly dependent on perception, but whether it is then true to say that the objective nature of density is altered by perception of it is a matter perhaps for philosophers.

Rapoport's general position was supported by a study in Detroit (Rodgers 1981), where many factors other than objective density were found to affect an individual's perception of the crowdedness of his residential environment; for instance, it is generally recognised that high density housing tends to be for those of low income. Although residents' satisfaction with their environment was investigated, measures of satisfaction were considered to have no empirically verified place in conceptualisation of any social process, being useful primarily because of the meaning they give to objective indicators. However, material conditions which can be modified have only a small influence on people's evaluations of the environment, and improving them may not increase levels of satisfaction, due to the rising expectations which are provoked at the same time. Though much better understanding is needed of the psychological processes involved in evaluations of the environment, much of the dissatisfaction with the city expressed in this study by residents of central Detroit, compared with those in the suburbs, seemed to be explained by room crowding and neighbourhood density.

Conclusion on density

When social structural differences between urban neighbourhoods are held constant, population density appears to make a relatively trivial difference in the prediction of rates of social pathology in their populations (Choldin 1978). Earlier ecological studies, e.g. in Chicago, made the fundamental mistake of not appreciating that factors associated with density (particularly poverty, minority status, and prevalence of migrants) had not been separated from any effects of density itself; as Choldin points out, 'The sections of the cities with the most pathology were dense and crowded, but they were also very poor and full of migrants.' Efforts continued for many years to resolve this problem of co-linearity of factors, and eventually, overall urban density failed to emerge as a significant factor. However, when urban sub-communities are examined in detail, household crowding does seem to represent an important social indicator, though so far as social pathologies are concerned, it is probably those same associated characteristics of the local populations that are influential, rather than the crowding itself. Mediating factors such as anonymity were hypothesised by Roncek (1981) to exist between areal density and crime rates in two American cities, but their role has not yet been empirically demonstrated, as with other intervening processes between the environment and the individual.

Even though high density may not contribute importantly to medical or social pathologies, it may still have significant effects on the quality of life — for instance, the amount of socialising that takes place in the home, or degree of neighbourly contacts (Kirmeyer 1978). Since these medical and social pathologies are usually of complex origin and develop over long periods, it should not be surprising that measures of density for large urban populations do not figure as important causes of them. Schizophrenia is an important example of this weak relationship.

THE URBAN ENVIRONMENT

Interest in the urban dimension of psychiatric disorder may derive in the first place from the sheer aggregation of human beings, and so from the multiplicity of interactions between them. Urbanisation is mainly a feature of the modern era when, as Tuan (1979) points out, the built world effectively withstands the normal fluctuations of nature, but paradoxically:

> it is in the large city — the most visible symbol of human rationality and triumph over nature — that some of the old fear remains. The urban sprawl . . . is seen as a jungle, a chaos of buildings, streets and fast-moving vehicles that disorient and alarm newcomers. But the greatest single threat in the city is other people. Malevolence, no longer ascribed to nature, remains an attribute of human nature.

At any rate, that is how one geographer has seen the question, while as a sociologist, Simmel (1950) referred to 'the intensification of emotional life due to the swift and continuous shift of external and internal stimuli'. It was mainly this view which gave rise to discussions of the psychological climate of cities that have gone on since the beginning of the century, though very little of this work has scientific validity.

The Chicago School of Sociology saw the difference between urban and rural life as involving different qualities of interpersonal relationships, and concluded that the type to be found in cities was generally harmful to the functioning of human personality. This was explained in terms of a particular type of stress — social alienation — which involved the demoralisation of those who were no longer part of a meaningful group process. Since urbanism is usually associated with industrialisation and (in certain continents) with Westernisation, it is likely that the effects of these various factors may be confused, and that urban–rural comparisons should therefore be specific to time and place. Although there is increasing discontent about the urban–rural dichotomy in studies of communities, no substantial alternative to it has yet been developed (Fischer 1975). This question is discussed further in Chapter 8.

Stimulus overload

In a very influential article, deriving from Wirth's view that high urban densities required special forms of human interaction and social organisation, Milgram (1970) points out the need to link the demographic circumstances of urban life with the psychological experience of the individual. One such link is through the concept of information overload, which requires adaptations, such as reserving time and energy for only essential interpersonal contacts, or blocking off channels of communication, e.g. by keeping doors locked, or telephone numbers unlisted. In a situation of high density and large numbers, new norms of behaviour evolve, which are basically those of non-involvement but which also permit greater tolerance of the unusual than is likely in a small community. One relevant factor, particularly in areas with high crime rates, is an increased sense of physical and emotional vulnerability, and Cappon (1975) has pointed out that the American middle class is paying a high price to the urban poor in terms of continual over-vigilance of the nervous system. However, adaptation may allow the long-term city resident to ignore aspects of its life which seem striking to the newcomer, and overload could be thereby reduced to some extent (Chapter 11).

Lipowski (1975) has provided a particularly useful discussion of information overload, as a probable result of the man-made transformation of the physical environment and of the mass production of symbols and messages produced by information technology. This process acclerates both cultural change and shifts in value systems, which make great demands on human adaptive capacity; such excessive demands might well be concerned in the high mortality from diseases such as coronary thrombosis in developed societies. If, as seems likely, the ability of the human organism to process information is limited by its channel capacity, information overload would constitute a form of psychosocial stress, caused by excess of stimuli relative to a person's processing ability. This could result in distress and in increased liability to disease.

On the other hand, the coping strategies which a person may use to escape from this situation, such as excessive use of drugs or withdrawal by psychiatric breakdown, may well be harmful in themselves. Such a model clearly has relevance for schizophrenia, which now appears to involve a constant state of overarousal in the central nervous system, associated with a break from reality. Lipowski points out that all the hypotheses involved in this theory require validation by multidisciplinary research, which should be seen as an urgent challenge by the scientific community: there is little sign, though, that this is yet happening.

An allied concept is that of social overload. McCarthy & Saegert (1976) compared residents, who had similar accomodation and demographic characteristics, in high and low-rise buildings respectively of a public housing estate in New York. In these two situations, the subjects' daily experiences, social relationships, and orientation to the housing were significantly different; the high-rise tenants saw more people, and felt more crowded, felt less satisfaction, privacy, and safety, and had greater difficulty in social relationships with neighbours or people outside. The difference was more marked for tenants on higher floors, who had even more casual contacts. Whereas low-rise residents identified with their building, yet had outside social relationships, high-rise tenants saw it mainly as a conglomerate of alien spaces and threatening people. McCarthy & Saegert regard the unmanageable number of unrelated residents in high blocks as causing social overload, related to the feeling of being crowded, which does not seem to diminish significantly by adaptation. Though striking, these findings do not extrapolate to people of higher social status and seem to involve some of the common confusion between crowding and density; according to Freedman (1975), it is the large numbers rather than the density of people that is harmful in this situation. Newman (1975), however, makes a related point that the smaller the number of families sharing a defined environment, the stronger are their feelings of possession and concern for it.

Another relevant study was that of Bornstein & Bornstein (1976), who measured the average speed of walking over a constant distance of people in 15 cities and towns in Europe, Asia, and North America. A direct relationship was found between these speeds and the size of the communities' populations, but not with degree of crowding in the street or the presence of shop windows, suggesting an adaptive mechanism, in the form of social withdrawal from the 'overloading' stimulation of highly populated areas. It was concluded that the immediate social and physical environment affects cognitive and behavioural processes in a fairly predictable manner, even between varied cultures. Surprisingly enough, pedestrians on an urban pavement were found to maintain a greater distance from an attractive female than from an unattractive one (Dabbs & Stokes 1975); this may reflect the status attaching to beauty, which could result in people being wary of it. In a field study in Holland, Korte et al. (1975) found that the probability of helping a stranger was inversely related to the level of environmental stimulation, which included the density of both pedestrians and motor traffic.

Noise

Among those stimuli which may overload people's receptive capacity, noise must certainly be one of the most important, though a number of factors intervene between exposure to noise on the one hand and annoyance, or possibly illness in the individual on the other. Cohen & Weinstein (1982) suggest that factors determing individuals' responses to any particular noise include its physical properties (e.g. unpredictability), its meaning, and characteristics of the individual, e.g. his perception of control over the noise, or whether an important goal is being disrupted. The deleterious effect of noise on performance may be particularly related to its masking of auditory communication.

This question has been particularly prominent in recent years in connection with aircraft noise (discussed fully in Chapter 9), though Tuan (1979) points out that:

> Noise is not the egregious defect of modern cities. The commercial quarters of traditional cities were sometimes much more raucous . . . In Imperial Rome . . . on the streets there reigned an intense animation, a breathless jostle, an infernal din. The prosperous medieval town was full of the sound of bells and bustling people.

Nevertheless, there can be little doubt that present-day machinery and amplification have added a new dimension to the problem, not least in the fact that traffic on main routes continues through most of the night. Ashmore & McConahay (1975) state that those living in urban areas 'who are bombarded with the unpredictable and uncontrollable high-intensity noise of freeways, subways, jet airports, jackhammers, neighbours' stereos, and school playgrounds, suffer from a very effective 'one-two punch'. The noise we adapt to at work will make us irritable and unable to do complex cognitive tasks at home . . . and the noise which disrupts our sleep will make us irritable and unable to function on complex tasks at work'. Though most people can certainly adjust to even the severest conditions, Kasl & Rosenfield (1980) suggest that noise may affect well-being and mental health via curtailment of valued activities, including social contacts; less mobile groups such as the elderly (and especially the relative social isolates among them) may be less able to cope with these adverse effects of noise. From a survey of the literature, Monahan & Vaux (1980) conclude that 'Under certain circumstances, noise may decrease attraction and affiliative behaviour between people, increase aggressive behaviour, decrease the probability that people will come to one another's aid, and contribute to tension-related illness'.

Urban malaise

A different conclusion about urban life, though, is reached by Fischer (1973); secondary analysis of the published literature failed to support the view that malaise increases along with urban size, or that urban residence *per se* is independently related to malaise. In fact, so far as data exist worldwide, there is more evidence of this phenomenon in rural than in urban areas, though the difference is small when social class is controlled, since greater economic opportunities represent one of the most positive qualities of cities. In American cities, some evidence of malaise (particularly in central areas) may be an effect of migration, because those with the ability to do so may move away to smaller communities, which American and Dutch people — but not French — generally prefer. Such moves are likely to be influenced by idealised images of non-city life, and by possibly unreal hopes of maintaining urban opportunities in the small community, which represents something of high value in the American ideology. Nevertheless, when all covariates are controlled, there is said to be evidence of a small trend for the largest cities to show malaise in their populations, and for this to be greater in city centres than in more peripheral areas.

The data analysed by Fischer were mostly obtained in the 1960s, though, and a different picture would emerge today from western cities, as well as from many in the developing world, as a result of such processes as central decay, uncontrolled expansion, and endlessly growing traffic (see also Chapter 8). Ridley (1981) says of the inner city parts of Liverpool that they:

> are generally depressing beyond belief. Housing standards are bad and accomodation is overcrowded; there are few amenities; . . . 15 per cent of the land is actually vacant or derelict; apartment blocks . . . have been vandalised beyond repair . . . all adding to the atmosphere of decay. Other indicators of malaise are just as bad; poor health, low educational achievement, low incomes, high crime rates, many problem families and, of course, massive unemployment'.

As an anthropologist, Gutmann (1980) believes that the urban environment reduces the absorption of cultural ideas, and loses its power to bind narcissism to the collective good, such as occurs in smaller and less complex societies. Therefore, 'egocentricity tends increasingly to become the general coinage of social relations', the bases of association between people tend to change, and 'all unproductive, dependent cohorts are at risk'. The possible effect of such a process on the aged is discussed below, though Gutmann seems to view non-urban and non-industrialised societies through rather rosy spectacles.

The environment and children

But the urban environment is immensely complex, and relationships between its individual aspects and specific forms of psychosocial disturbance very difficult to identify. Rutter (1981) has concluded that it is not possible to say by which mechanisms inner city life has adverse effect on families, and through families on children, when these are compared with children in a more rural setting; the critical factors are not overall population density, urbanisation, or industrialisation in themselves, since different cities in Britain have different rates of pathology. The excess of both psychiatric disorder and crime affects children and parents equally, and both sexes; it includes not only personal illness and disturbance but marital discord, family breakdown, and educational problems. In children, it mainly applies to chronic disorders of early onset, associated with serious family difficulties, and less to psychiatric conditions beginning in adolescence. Though socially alienated and psychologically disturbed people tend to congregate in inner cities, there seems to be an additional factor producing disorders, which may be the stress of life in that setting. Not everyone there is poor, and most psychosocial problems in British children are not due to lack of money of low social status; nor is social isolation common in these areas. When families were scored on an Adversity Index, the likelihood of disorder for a child was the same in the city and the country, for families with the same scores, but high scores were much more common in London.

Adverse effects from the school (which only increased the risk for children of non-disadvantaged families), when included in the analysis, resulted in the whole inner city excess of childhood psychiatric disorder being accounted for by the combination of these school and family effects; it is unnecessary to invoke any broader ecological influences on children's behaviour (Rutter & Quinton 1977). In the area studied of South London, the rate of disorder was just as high in children born and bred there, whose parents had been born and bred there, as it was in families who had migrated in from other parts of the UK; also, a four-year study of outward migration showed that this was not such as to leave families with a high rate of psychiatric disorder behind (the 'social residue' explanation). However, school effects clearly cannot explain the relatively high city rates of adult psychiatric disorder and criminality. As far as women were concerned, the rate of psychiatric abnormality was only higher in London for those of the working class. Because psychiatric problems in the mother often impair parenting, they will tend to lead to childhood disorder, but Rutter states that what effects of social structure interact with family influences to produce the high rate of inner city pathology remains unknown.

Similarly, rates of child guidance and delinquency referrals in various districts of Croydon differed widely according to area of residence (Gath et al. 1977). The two rates, however, were associated with similar demographic and socio-economic indices, particularly social class, type of housing, and density of population. The highest rates of both clients were in the poorest and most dilapidated areas, but there was little overlap between the membership of the two groups; those attending child guidance clinics who were not recorded as 'conduct disorders' largely shared the same poor social circumstances. Environmental factors were thus important in all forms of maladjustment, but this kind of study cannot reveal the way in which they act, e.g. whether through family processes or independently. This work is also referred to in Chapter 6.

The environment and the elderly

At the opposite end of the life-cycle, the relationship of the mental health of the elderly to different environments assumes even greater importance in industrialised countries, as old people form a steadily growing proportion of their population. Old age is marked by high morbidity in both physical and psychiatric terms, and is associated with problems of social behaviour, e.g. isolation through bereavement. These problems are strongly influenced by both cultural and environmental factors, seen in the contrast between an old person living on her own in a high-rise flat in Britain, compared with one at the centre of a multi-generation family home in India.

When the extended family structure largely breaks down through loss of cultural support, social mobility, and the dispersive effects of massive redevelopment, the life of old people is likely to be governed to a significant extent by environmental circumstances. This will be further enhanced by the relatively recent phenomenon of large-scale migration of the elderly, seen particularly in places such as the 'Costa Geriatrica' of Sussex or retirement colonies in Florida. Kasl & Rosenberg (1980) state that for old people, neighbourhood characteristics such as proximity to shopping and transport are more important than their housing in influencing residential satisfaction, whereas for younger adults, the reverse is true.

Since old people tend to live in areas of older buildings, they are very likely to become caught up in processes of urban redevelopment, which will involve enforced moving. On common-sense grounds, they would seem more vulnerable than other age-groups to the adverse effects of such changes, but Kasl (1972) points out that little is known about these psychological and health consequences, which have not yet been systematically studied. Neither is it known which components of an environment are important to the elderly, though there is evidence for the following statements: psychological well-being is positively related to their amount of social interaction; geographical distance is a strong determinant of the amount of contact with kin; working-class elderly are particularly dependent on physical proximity for frequency of contact with friends; loss of friends creates some insecurity as well as loneliness, since friends are partly relied on for help in emergencies; the longer old people have lived in a former neighbourhood and the stronger were their social ties there, the more dissatisfied they are likely to be in a new district; better housing conditions in a new area cannot adequately compensate for loss of friendship ties and convenience of services in the old one. Lawton (1970) has tried to explain these aspects in terms of an hypothesis of 'environmental docility', i.e. that the behaviour of people of reduced competence (mentally ill, aged, economically deprived, etc.) is more determined by environmental influences than is that of people of higher competence; some empirical data exist to support this view, but mainly from institutions.

Massive growth of cities is usually associated with modernisation and rapid social change — in England at the time of the Industrial Revolution, and now in Asia, Africa, and South America. This environmental and cultural shift from remote agricultural societies involves the elderly in a loss of social prestige, and so is likely to impair mental health. Some of the lost social supports may be rebuilt through a matrilocal version of the extended family (Young & Willmott 1957), but this does not have the same value for older urban men as for women. Higher mortality of males in urban than in rural populations may indicate 'the peculiarly troubling effects that the urban environment seems to have on the mental health of men' (Gutmann 1980).

Gutmann goes on to suggest that the aged suffer in urban environments because they depend on 'the inner controls of younger, stronger individuals and on the external social controls that are maintained by a cultural consensus . . . The reduction in culture turns them into strangers, and it also brings about an increase in the numbers of those who would victimise them'. Other vulnerable and dependent groups in the population are likely to suffer in the same way, as affiliations are focussed so as to exclude them, e.g. in the contemporary 'youth culture'. A result is that fear of violence and crime, of kinds that would be unthinkable in most non-urban societies, has become a major aspect of the life of old people in cities. However, it is much affected by the degree of their integration into informal social networks; greater social support reduces their fear and perception of danger (Kasl & Rosenfield 1980). A study of elderly people in small towns of the American Midwest (Windley & Scheidt 1892) suggested that greater satisfaction with their housing improved morale and happiness, while lessening the likelihood of psychiatric complaints; also, lessening of social and physical barriers to their participation in the life of the community heightened psychological well-being. Those older people who were more involved in community affairs were healthier and psychologically happier, but to some extent this is a tautologous statement, and it becomes difficult here to separate the effects of personality and of environment respectively.

Some surprising results emerged from a comparative study of the elderly in New York and London (Gurland et al, 1983), which was part of the larger US–UK Cross-National Project. It had been assumed that a number of features of life in New York would be more stressful and depressing for the elderly than would be the case in London; these included higher crime rates, more expensive medical care, financial problems, housing inadequacies (with less owner-occupation), more population heterogeneity and language problems, and a higher rate of hospitalisation. However, the major determinants in the elderly were thought to be physical illness, disability, and dependence, which (perhaps not surprisingly) were of similar frequency in the two cities, as were isolation and transiency of domicile — but neither living alone nor having fewer social contacts were found to be associated with depression in either city. In spite of environmental differences between the two places, fear of crime and complaints of a deteriorating or changing neighbourhood were equally common in both, so that the discrepancy between the actual and perceived situation tended to even out the differential impact of the two environments. Though New Yorkers complained of housing deficiencies more than Londoners, the latter experienced such problems as inadequate heating, outside WCs, or poor kitchen equipment at least as much. Possibly the New York elderly had higher expectations in those matters, while the Londoners expected more in the way of public order and environmental civilities.

THE ENVIRONMENT AND DEPRESSION

Though schizophrenia has been the subject of many theories of social environmental determination, knowledge of its aetiology remains seriously incomplete and it is in fact depression for which a coherent causative model now exists, through the work of Brown and his colleagues (Brown 1979; Brown & Harris 1982). In their view, depression is essentially a social phenomenon, whose occurence is highly related to the presence of severe, long-term life events, mostly distinguished by the experience of actual or threatened major loss ('severe events'). Examples of these which are specially relevant to this book include moving to escape difficult neighbours, arrangements to obtain a new flat falling through, or receiving notice to quit one's home. Aetiology is considered multifactorial, in that certain people are vulnerable to depression (as they are to other illnesses) for genetic, constitutional, or other reasons and the onset of a psychiatric disorder can occur either because of these or because of current environmental factors, in varying degrees. Past losses are strongly associated with the type and severity of subsequent depression ('symptom formation factors').

A second group of aetiological factors (but not so important as severe events) are 'major difficulties'. These are defined as being severe, lasting at least 2 years, and not involving health, e.g. poor housing (which featured in 28% of the cases of chronic depression); the indices of poor housing were: overcrowding, extreme physical deprivation, problems with noise, and lack of security of tenure. Severe events and major difficulties together constitute the category of 'provoking agents'. Although both severe events and major difficulties have been found to be more common in working class women (the research having been done with females), this in itself could not explain the excess of psychiatric disorder in them, compared with the middle class.

The explanation was found in the third group of factors ('vulnerability factors'), which relate to the support received from social relationships and — when this is present — to low self-esteem. They both increase the chances of depression developing and, once its onset has occurred, reduce the changes of specialist help being received, so that female cases of depression seen by psychiatrists tend to show an excess of middle-class patients. Vulnerability factors are said to play a crucial aetiological role through limiting a woman's ability to develop an optimistic view about controlling her world; since three of the factors concern the present, the current environment is the most powerful influence on the risk of depression, but only when a major life event or difficulty is occurring. The three elements of this aetiological model (all psychosocial) are linked to background factors, such as social class, and its theoretical implications may vary with the social setting.

Thus, it is impossible for simple measures (e.g. those based on education or occupation) to reflect accurately what is happening in an individual's environment, since the underlying social processes linked to class are extremely complex. For instance, the risk of a burglary, or of an accident to a child is probably much greater for a working-class woman, who may also have to cope with such experiences as enforced rehousing, debt, unemployment, or police trouble, which are not on the whole met by middle-class women. It therefore becomes necessary to study the immediate environment in terms of aetiological processes, if traditional measures of social class fail to reveal significant correlations with rates of psychiatric disorder. In Brown's view, this work reveals 'not only something about the aetiology of affective disorders, but something of the quality of life in the societies in which we live'; he adds that 'all is not well with women in our cities'.

In this research, depression was defined as of 'caseness' level if its severity was such that, had the woman concerned appeared in a psychiatric outpatient department, she would have had been regarded as psychiatrically ill. Though clinical depression is common in the general population, its distribution is far from uniform; in inner cities, about 15 per cent of people will have an episode of 'caseness' level in any year, and about half of these episodes will have lasted for at least 12 months. However, social class differences are not found in those illnesses which are of less than 'caseness' severity. Some sub-populations will have much lower rates, but working-class women with children are particularly at risk; in some inner city areas, 15–25 per cent of them, at any time, will have definite affective disorders and twice that number will ·have significant depressive symtoms. Three-quarters of the social class difference in levels of 'caseness' depression was explained by differences in vulnerability factors.

Bebbington (1978) has criticised this body of work on the grounds that the mechanism of incubation is unknown by which life events can generate the onset of depression, that life events are not unitary in their social effects, and that their importance may be lost in over-simple analyses. It has also been suggested that low intimacy in the relationship with the partner (vulnerability factor) and marital difficulties (provoking agent) may be confounded, although they are treated as independent variables. Mueller (1980) proposes that because life events of an exit type involve significant disruptions in a person's social network, the stressfulness of an event may be closely tied to the degree of that disruption, which in turn affects the availability of social support; but since measures of stressful events and of social support are highly inter-related, it is difficult to establish whether social support has an independent effect or merely moderates the impact of the stress of life events. Finally, Werry & Carlielle (1983) suggest that 'one person's or one culture's stresses are not necessarily the same as another's'; they ask 'whether results of studies in London and other huge cities are typical of anywhere except themselves and whether or not some of the ominous findings would also be true of the millions of women who live in less crowded and less insecure circumstances'. Their own study of women in suburban areas of Auckland showed that depressive-type symptoms were very common, but were mostly regarded by the subjects as part of life, self-resolving, and requiring no treatment; while this might be partly due to favourable living conditions, a 'cultural stoicism factor' was also proposed.

However, Brown's aetiological concepts are now widely accepted; they are supported to some extent by the learned helplessness model, which suggests that depression is caused by uncontrollable situations which lead the individual to perceive that his responses are generally ineffective in obtaining reinforcement. One study comparing depressed and non-depressed students showed that performance deficits associated with unsolvability in depressed subjects can be eliminated by instructions to blame failure not on incompetence, but on the harshness of the environment (Klein et al. 1976).

Subsequently, Brown and his colleagues repeated their investigations in the Hebridean islands of North Uist and Lewis (Brown et al. 1977; Brown & Prudo 1981; Prudo et al. 1981); in the former, the rate of depression in women over a three-month period was half that found in London, while the social class differences in rates of 'caseness' depression were absent, as they were in Rutter's Isle of Wight study. It was considered that the same aetiological model still broadly applied, but severe life events, major difficulties, and vulnerability factors were all less common. The lowest rate of depression occurred in those women who remained closest to the traditional crofting and religious way of life; however, they were more subject to chronic anxiety and phobic states, which seemed to be mediated through intense attachment to their kin, e.g. following death of a parent. It is possible that this anxiety is caused by the society's strong normative framework, which can be a source of social criticism, and that it is encouraged by women's subservient domestic and marital role there. Such a community may simultaneously provide support, by giving a place and meaning in life and thus reducing vulnerability to depression, while promoting suscepti-bility to anxiety through the oppressive nature of the closeness.

Social change from such a society in the direction of urbanisation may bring about a very high rate of depression among working-class women, though even those of the middle class in cities experience a greater level of depression than women in more traditional communities. Thus a simple urban–rural dichotomy did not give an accurate picture of the differing rates of depression within the populations of Camberwell and the Hebrides respectively, since the immediate environment seems to be of critical aeti-ological significance. However, the current structure of the environment and historical development of the individual psyche meet in relation to a person's attachments, which are culturally influenced, and in this way the sociological and psychological perspectives are intimately linked. Leighton (1981) considers that hypotheses such as this by medical sociologists rep-resent a social-environmental determinism which has been derived mainly from the study of deviance and from the relationship theories of G. H. Mead.

Brown's model was also tested on a sample of 110 working class women in Oxford, all of whom had at least one child aged 14 or under living at home (Campbell et al. 1983). Lack of an intimate relationship with a male partner was found to act as a vulnerability factor, increasing the risk of depression in the face of a provoking agent, and there was also a trend for women with three or more children to have increased vulnerability. However, unemployment was not found to be a vulnerability factor here, and it is suggested that employment might be protective only for those women with unsatisfactory housing, a common problem in South London, but rare in the Oxford group. In a North American town which had been exposed to the stress of an accident at a nearby nuclear power plant, lack of a confiding relationship was again found to be a vulnerability factor, but the other two were not (Solomon & Bronet 1982). However, in this study, the temporal relationship between stress and depressive symptoms was not established.

A possible explanation for Brown's findings has been proposed by Mueller (1981), based on evidence that urban living seems to be associated with decline of social support from neighbours and of participation in the local community (Fischer 1976). This pattern is not homogeneous across urban populations, but might well be especially characteristic of the inner city, where there tends to be high turnover of residents and changing ethnic composition. Within such areas, the effects of reduced supportive ties would be greater in those not in regular contact with people outside the immediate locality, e.g. housewives (particularly with young children at home or not working) and the elderly. They might not find adequate supportive rela-tionships among neighbours, especially if neither had lived there for long, and so would have to rely increasingly on the immediate family. But if there was no suitable husband or partner, women would then be very vulnerable to depression, particularly at times of personal crisis. Mueller emphasises that it is not yet certain whether deficits in support from social relationships play an aetiological role, but greater urban prevalence of depression has been found not only in working class women, but also in people aged over 65 (Gurland 1976)

SOCIAL PROCESSES

It will be evident, both from Brown's work and from the earlier discussion, that mental health is related not so much to the environment in its physical, structural sense, but more to the social processes connected to that setting. In their turn, these processes are not only determined by the structure of any environment, but also by the culture, economy, and political ideology which govern it. The relationships of all these forces are enormously complicated, therefore, and are constantly changing over time, so that scientific study of them needs to be approached with great caution. Associations (of varying consistency) have been found in many communities between higher than average rates of psychiatric disorder and a variety of sociocultural and social-environmental factors, such as low social class, social isolation, stressful life events, and social disintegration. Though there is no agreement on the causes of these findings, it is possible to find common factors in absence of social support or disruption or individuals' social networks, but such situations may be specific to particular socio-demographic groups or psychiatric conditions (Mueller 1980). Nevertheless, social network factors might be the underlying mechanisms of these statistical relationships, and provide the basis for an integrating framework in which to assess the contribution of the social environment to psychiatric disorder.

Kasl & Harburg (1975) have analysed the literature of epidemiological surveys of mental health in terms of urban environments. Their rather pessimistic conclusions were: that this work generally does not concern itself greatly with the urban environment; that studies most directly concerned with potentially pathogenic aspects of the urban environment do not deal with mental health; that satisfaction-dissatisfaction with housing and neighbourhood have an unknown link to mental health, and do not compare in importance with family relationships, job satisfaction, or social adjustment; that 'social disorganisation' cannot easily be linked to living in the slums; that studies of non-enforced rehousing have not demonstrated any significant mental health benefits; and that parameters of the urban environment are likely to interact with psychosocial variables in ways that are bound to complicate the aetiological picture. From these, three even more parsimonious conclusions were drawn: that the interest of psychiatric epidemiology in the urban environment has been more apparent than real; that our knowledge of the influence of the various parameters in the urban environment on mental health is extremely limited; and that the available evidence does not encourage the idea that urban environmental variables by themselves account for much of the variance in mental health. Though this point of view may be somewhat overstated, it is difficult to disagree with its basic propositions, and the various scientific disciplines involved clearly need to improve both their conceptualisations and their standards of empirical evidence.

Social disintegration

Social psychiatry has been much concerned with the concept of 'integration', i.e. the extent to which a society has a coherent, identifiable, and stable structure, to which individuals and groups can be related, and feel themselves to be related. Where such a structure can be most strongly identified, it is likely to be connected to geographical patterns of settlement, i.e. different districts being occupied by clearly defined socio-economic religious, racial, or occupational groups — for instance, the Italian enclaves of American cities in the middle decades of this century, or hierarchical rural communities in Asia. It is generally assumed that social integration or cohesion is a factor promoting mental health, and vice versa, though this is almost certainly an over-simplification, and there are problems of definition with almost every one of the factors involved. For instance, it may be relatively unimportant for those affluent and mobile people in Western societies who see the world as their oyster (and have what Webber (1963) called 'community without propinquity'), but very significant for a population which, for economic and cultural reasons, is largely tied to its area of settlement (see Chapter 7).

Most explanations of geographical differences in social problems, such as delinquency or violence, have been based on the social disorganisation or disintegration model, i.e. fragmentation of the usual bonds between people (social network ties) that underpin the stability of any society; it is assumed to arise in heterogeneous and rapidly changing populations, where adequate socialisation fails to occur (Murray & Boal 1979). These authors draw a distinction between aetiological theories of social pathology which blame the immediate environment (stress, disorganisation, sub-culture) on the one hand, and those which blame the socio-economic structure of society and the way in which certain social groups are treated (drift, labelling, alienation) on the other, but the two categories are by no means clearly separated.

In their classic studies on the distribution of delinquency in Chicago, Shaw & McKay (1942) established strong correlations between high juvenile crime rates and manifestations of social disorganisation — changing population, sub-standard housing, poverty, foreign-born and Negro residents, tuberculosis, and also psychiatric disorders. All these factors were most pronounced in inner city areas and persisted over time, even when the composition of their populations changed greatly. However, later work (e.g.

Downes 1966) showed that delinquent sub-cultures, with their own learning processes and opportunities, might be present at the same time as social disorganisation, and that anomie could also be an important underlying factor.

Social disintegration was regarded by Leighton (1959) in the Stirling County study as occurring between the sub-systems of society, and as resulting from the rate of social change exceeding the rate of adaptation to it; such societies become vulnerable to cultural crises, e.g. those of the late 1960s in many Western countries. Then, the coping guidelines of culture that have been passed down from previous generations cease to work effectively, and people try new kinds of behaviour, but these often random reactions tend to conflict with each other, and may make things worse. The stability of cultures, their coherence, their capacity to function as wholes, and their meanings are undermined, so that for many people, it is change itself which becomes most important in determining their behaviour. When societies are in this process of disintegration, 'other people then appear unpredictable, and the institutions of society no longer dependable in a society where nearly all values are in flux', and this uncertainty may extend to the definition of mental illness (Leighton 1981). It thus becomes difficult to tell what constitutes allowable behaviour. Socio-cultural disintegration tends to be associated with demoralisation (consisting of distress associated with subjective incompetence), but this is less likely to occur in the presence of adequate social bonds, linking an individual to others by positive affect (de Figuerido, 1983).

In Leighton's view, social disintegration is causally related to psychopathology through: increase in the frequency of organic disease, some of which is associated with brain damage; failure of child-nurturing and child-rearing patterns; lack of shared values, standards and codes of behaviour, and of opportunity for the satisfaction of basic needs, e.g. sense of belonging to a worthwhile group. At the same time, the malfunctioning of their organisations decreases these societies' ability to meet the needs of the population for care. The psychological states generated by sociocultural disintegration were linked with psychiatric disorder through the concept of stress, but it was accepted that people may have neurotic personalities as a result of experiences in early life, and would than manifest disorder at a lower level of stress that others. The stressor and the individual's reaction to it — in terms of his internalised standards — together form a 'stressful situation' which the person has to resolve within himself (de Figuerido, 1983). However, Cassel (1974) suggests that the underlying mechanism may be people's lack of feedback that their actions are leading to desirable and/or anticipated consequences, particularly when these actions are designed to modify their relationships to important social groups. In addition to excess psychiatric disorder, social disintegration has been related to increased rates of tuberculosis, stroke deaths, and hypertension.

Social indices used by Leighton et al. (1963) to measure this phenomenon included poverty, cultural confusion, poor leadership, high crime rates, and fragmented communication networks. Higher prevalence rates of psychiatric morbidity (particularly affective and personality disorders) in the area of Maritime Canada where these studies were carried out were related to evidence of social disintegration, but the severe process was confined to a few small clusters of population. In disintegrated areas, the probability of being a psychiatric case was lower for females, whereas the reverse was true in the county as a whole. In terms of lifetime-prevalence, about two-thirds of the population were thought to have shown some evidence of psychiatric disorder, and about half these had some degree of impairment; however, rates of period-prevalence (such as were used in the Midtown Manhattan Study) or of point-prevalence would have been much lower.

All these phenomena lack concreteness of definition, and the causal nature of any relationship between them and psychiatric disorder is unproved. Absence of feeling of affiliation is equivalent to the concept of *anomie*, originally proposed by Durkheim, which refers to failure of social integration in the collective rather than the personal sense, with values and norms being weak or absent; anomie and social disintegration are sometimes used synonymously. If anomie could lead to suicide (as Durkheim believed), then it might also lead to psychiatric disorder in general. From their studies in northern Spain, Barquero et al (1982) suggest that the tendency of more advanced societies to organise themselves into urban communities involves a series of sociological changes which are capable of transforming the interactions of individuals, not only in their work and external environment, but also through their internal family dynamics. The negative aspects of these changes involve factors such as isolation, dehumanisation, loss of pride in work, and breaking up of family ties, which 'are at at the roots of social disorganisation and contain as a consequence the origins of mental illness' — a view which must inevitably be overstated.

Srole (1956) regarded anomie as representing 'deterioration in the social and moral ties that bind, sustain and free us'; but it will be clear that objectification and quantification of any aspect of the process of 'social disintegration' is extraordinarily difficult, so that the concept cannot be regarded as resting on firm scientific ground, though it is a fruitful heuristic source of ideas and hypotheses. However, the fact that groups which are in a minority in any area tend to have a higher rate of psychiatric disorder there, but not necessarily in areas where they form the majority — the 'social fit' hypothesis — may be seen as lending some support to the disintegration theory (see Chapter 5).

Similar findings came from Barquero et al (1982) when they surveyed the population of a Spanish valley, which had three contrasting cultures: an urban area, undergoing profound social and cultural changes; an area of rural villages; and an area of isolated farms, whose culture was primitive and very traditional. In the previous 40 years, the urban population had increased by 21.5 per cent, while that of the isolated area had fallen by 28.5

per cent. The overall psychiatric morbidity was 23.8 per cent, which was similar to the median rate reported by the Dohrenwends (1974) from their review of 22 community surveys. Rates of neurosis were highest in the urban area and lowest in the isolated part, with the rural area intermediate; females showed a positive lowering of morbidity in the isolated area, whereas for males there was simply an absence there of the urban increment. For both sexes, a very significant relationship was found between place of residence and neurotic morbidity, but none with different types of neurosis. The urban excess of morbidity was associated with young, single people of low social, educational, and occupational level; this might be because they were more susceptible to the disintegrating mechanisms of urbanisation, or because of the type of people who migrated, i.e. social 'selection'.

On the other hand, in the case of the Hutterites in North America, there was no evidence that a very high degree of social integration was associated with freedom from psychiatric disorder (Eaton & Weil 1955), while the preceding part of this chapter referred to evidence that Hebridean women were relatively protected from depression by the strong social integration of their isolated communities, though at the cost of higher levels of anxiety. The difference between these and the Spanish data indicates that no definite conclusion can yet be reached on the relationship between social integration/disintegration and psychiatric disorder, while Leighton (1982) accepts that disintegration could account for only a part of the variance of psychiatric disorder in populations. Social disorganisation theory is closely allied to the 'breeder' hypothesis, which was originally proposed by Faris & Dunham (1939) in the case of schizophrenia (see Chapter 14).

Social rigidity

The reverse of social disintegration is social rigidity. This is described as the overall social structure of a society having become so inflexible that individuals have no choice but to conform to the prescribed social norms. Typically, this occurs in small communities, dominated by traditional values and by a social structure that imposes specific statuses and roles on people. Those unable to conform to the situation will either migrate away, or feel so constrained that they experience various forms of psychological or emotional disturbance, or else turn to delinquent behaviour. Newman (1980) states that such societies are 'characterised today by a commonly shared problem: their young people are fleeing to distant cities to find the freedom and opportunity their parent societies cannot give them'. Whilst this process has always occurred to some extent, modern communication media and transport have turned it into a huge, world-wide migration. Social rigidity was also to be found to be in the closely knit working class communities of industrial England; community pressure strongly discouraged behaviour or interests which deviated from the accepted norm, while kindhip networks could result in a whole urban micro-environment being dominated by a single 'Mum' of strong personality (Roberts 1978).

In sociological terms, communities showing social rigidity can be described as 'closed and integrated', their social structure having often been reinforced by well established patterns of work in docks, mines, garment making, etc. They are characterised by a very efficient human communication system, operated mainly by women and sometimes centered on an individual one; this is associated with control of values and opinion, and of access into and out of the social network (see Chapter 7).

Social isolation

Other social processes, in addition to disintegration, are likely to be related to psychiatric disorder and to have important environmental implications. Faris & Durham's view (1939) was that the improverishment and transient life style conditions of central city slums had the effect of minimising positive and enduring social contacts and relationships. Thus social isolation was originally put forward as an aetiological factor in schizophrenia, though it is almost certainly a result of the condition, rather than a cause of it, as Kohn & Clausen (1955) first pointed out. This is not to deny that social isolation is stressful, and that it may have adverse psychological effects, which could contribute to a worsening or recurrence of schizophrenic illness; Gruenberg (1974) describes it as 'a specific set of distortions of interpersonal communication, embedded in the structure of human communities'. Investigation of institutional environments showed that schizophrenics had an increased sensitivity to social deprivation, leading to further withdrawal; if this situation was altered too quickly, the resulting stress would be likely to provoke a relapse (Wing & Brown 1970). In a study in Austin, Texas, Jaco (1954) found five factors of social isolation, which were characteristic of areas with high rates of admission for psychosis: limited contact with neighbours, friends, etc; more people renting than owning their homes; less participation in occupational or voluntary organisations; greater occupational mobility; and fewer visits to other parts of the city or away from it. The effect of social isolation, as thus identified, on psychiatric disorder was thought to be precipitating rather than predisposing, but such effects may possibly be more significant in neuroses and personality disorders than in schizophrenia. Furthermore, the characteristics of a neighbourhood may tend to promote social isolation or such related effects as alienation, which in turn may contribute to general dissatisfaction or psychological separation from the local environment. These outcomes could be regarded as stress-related, and it is possible that they also have effects on aspects of health, e.g. lack of social ties making it more difficult for a person to cope with health-related stress. However, such cause–effect relationships have not yet been scientifically established (Taylor 1982). (See also Chapter 14 for discussion of social isolation).

Social stress

'Social stress' is a concept which grew partly out of wartime experience, such as that of Dunkirk survivors (Leighton 1982). The Midtown Manhattan Study (Srole et al. 1962), the Stirling county work, and Hollingshead & Redlich's (1958) investigation of social class and mental illness agreed in showing a consistent relationship between indicators of social stress and rates of psychiatric morbidity. Though there is little agreement in the literature as to which factors should be included, the concept of social stress assumes that such phenomena as stigmatisation, effects of poverty, role disturbance (e.g. one-parent families), or high parity are of aetiological significance in psychiatric disorder. In Mechanic's view (1973), evidence of some relationship between social stress and psychiatric disorders, as well as with other diseases, has been inconsistent, but since such stress appears to be a factor contributing to medical consultation, it is essential to separate the role of stress in the aetiology of a condition from its influence on seeking professional help. In spite of some strong statistical associations, the aetiological significance of social stress in psychiatric disorder remains to be clearly established, but this work does provide a possible basis for focussing preventive and therapeutic inventions more effectively within defined areas (Regier 1982).

Most studies which have attempted to investigate social causes of mental illness have used social stress as a frame of reference; Murphy (1976) conceptualises this as including social forces or events which threaten psychological well-being through the failure to satisfy needs. These needs include creature comforts, affiliation with others, coherence in values, social role training, self-expression, and recognition of the individual as a unique and valued person. Stress theories used in psychiatric epidemiology reflect the view that mental health is promoted by social situations in which there are adequate resources for such needs, and though these theories remain controversial, they have not yet been replaced by others which are more solidly founded. (Stress as a general concept of mediating processes in the study of environmental effects on individuals has been referred to earlier in this chapter). Since research on cultural differences has produced very little evidence of a relationship with differences in levels of psychiatric morbidity (though the expression of this morbidity may vary), Murphy concludes that if social stress has anything to do with mental illness, it must be of a type which is ubiquitous in human populations. It appears, in fact, that no group of people large enough to be self-perpetuating as a culture is free from psychiatric disorder or lacks a view of mental illness.

If social stress is a useful concept, it is almost certainly relevant to the situation of these living in the inner city areas of Britain (about four million

people) and of other older industrialised countries. Such areas are characterised by:

> falling population, increasing concentration of the poor and those of lower status in society,
> a predominantly poor housing stock and neglected environment, subjected to large-scale
> physical change, and virtual abandonment by economic activity and productive investment
> (Liverpool Inner Area Study 1975).

These processes are part of a cycle which began with the Industrial Revolution, 200 years ago, and which now involves the collapse of the economic
base which led to the establishment of these cities as places where people
came to work. The long-standing residents of inner cities undoubtedly feel
powerless to influence such overwhelming changes in the economic pattern
of their society, as well as 'the uncertain and deteriorating future of their
area' (Exit Photography Group 1982).

Whether a useful distinction can be made in these circumstances between
social stress and social disintegration is uncertain, and it should also be
remembered that similar processes can be seen in rural areas which are
affected by migration, economic decline, etc. Ridley (1981) regards young
people in inner city areas as subject to passive alienation — 'A generation
idle and frustrated because unemployed; rejected by employers, thus alienated; concentrated in certain districts where the environment itself is grim';
they must inevitably be at high risk of involvement in crime, extremist
politics, or simply random violence.

Social change, especially if rapid, has often been considered a form of
social stress, though Ruesch's (1965) opinion still has validity, that 'the
tolerance limits for social change show great individual variation, and what
causative role social change plays in the aetiology of mental disease has not
yet been clearly established'. Selye (1956) had proposed that the phenomenon of change itself, beyond the capacities of the organism to adapt —
irespective of the results of the change — is the critical precipitant of stress-
related pathology, whether physical or psychiatric. However, Brenner
(1979) added that deleterious life changes should be regarded as more
harmful because they are capable of producing stresses which in turn lead
to other life changes and stresses ('accleration of stress'). From analysis of
data at the national level, he concluded that abrupt economic changes,
regardless of direction, are stress-provoking, but that undesirable changes
such as unemployment and income loss are substantially more pathogenic.
This appeared to confirm Selye's view that extremely high stimulation has
an overall stressful effect, though the whole issue remains a controversial
one.

There is also the likelihood that social changes may become cumulative
and self-accelerating; Myrdal (1957) states that it is usual for supporting
processes to emerge, rather than countervailing ones, thus moving the
change further in the same direction. Involuntary moves of residence may
represent an important example of social change which is likely to have

adverse mental health consequences (see Chapter 7). Socio-cultural change may or may not disrupt the integration of a society, depending on the relevance of this change to the self-esteem of its individuals; if demoralisation is caused, e.g. through damage to the symbols representing that society's dominant sentiments, then distress is likely to be widespread (de Figuerido, 1983).

Reviewing the social stress concept, Dohrenwend (1975) emphasised highly consistent relationships between the estimated prevalence of various psychiatric disorders and three sociocultural factors — sex, urban/rural residence, and social class. These relationships might be explained if the factors caused people to be exposed to stress, but there were great gaps in the evidence linking variation in these factors to variations in the stress to which people are exposed, and in the evidence on how types of stress are related to disorders in individuals. Some support for this view of the effects of environmentally induced stress can be seen in the sequelae of extreme situations (e.g. disaster victims, see Chapter 10) and in the relationship of stressful life events to psychiatric disorder. Also, evidence for genetic effects in the genesis of schizophrenia leaves much of the variability still to be explained, but this argument by subtraction does not prove that environmentally-induced stress is important aetiologically in its own right. Dohrenwend concluded that existing evidence failed to demonstrate that sociocultural and social-psychological factors are important in the aetiology of functional psychiatric disorders, but in view of the complexity of the issue and the often insidious onset and long duration of the conditions involved, this was not surprising. Much more detailed investigations would be needed, for instance to separate the influence of biological from social differences in variations of morbidity between the two sexes.

This impressive analysis is rather flawed, however, by the fact that one of the three main props of the argument — differences between overall urban and rural psychiatric morbidity — no longer seems valid (Chapter 6). Cassel (1974) suggests that those involved in rapid social change become unfamiliar with the cues and expectations of their society, find that their actions are unlikely to lead to anticipated consequences, and experience stress, which leads to neuro-endocrine disturbances, and so to increased susceptibility to disease.

Social class

Closely related to social stress is the possible influence of social class. From their survey of the literature, the Dohrenwends (1974) concluded that a higher rate of psychiatric symptoms was to be found in the lower socio-economic classes, and that it resulted from the response of their members to relatively frequent and severe stresses, which are an inevitable part of life at that level; but this was mainly an urban phenomenon. Working-class people are particularly subject to stresses of a developmental nature, e.g.

disruptive effects from high rates of births, family deaths, and marital disruption. In addition, they have to adjust to stress without the resources and social support available to the middle class; for instance, the family unit's being often broken or discordant may make it a stressor rather than a resource. In fact, any excess in rates of psychiatric morbidity is concentrated in the very lowest socio-economic class, and it is there also that a higher prevalence of weak and unstable social network ties is found (Mueller 1980). In Leighton's view (1982), life in the lower social classes is associated with stress, which is essentially that of living in a socioculturally disintegrated environment, though once again, this would only apply to the bottom of the socio-economic scale.

From the point of view of social networks, Hammer (1983) suggests that although few firm data are yet available about class differences, it appears that people of lower social class in industrialised societies generally have smaller overall networks, but are in frequent contact with the individuals contained in them. If their normal situation should be disrupted for any reason, they would be left with very little support on which to draw, in terms of an extended network. Also, the patterns of socialising which were involved in their small network of very familiar people might not be helpful in developing the skills required for relating to new situations. There is evidence (Horwitz, 1978) that when a person suffers from a psychiatric disorder, a fairly dispersed social network is generally more helpful than a closely-knit homogeneous one in providing information and practical advice; if so, it would also be a factor tending to associate lower social class with higher rates of psychopathology. Related to this is the generally greater dependence of working-class people, compared with those higher up the social scale, on a particular geographical milieu (see Chapter 7).

Although it has become a form of conventional wisdom that low socio-economic status is associated with a higher prevalence of psychiatric disorder (Brenner (1979) describes this as 'the single most consistent empirical regularity in the field of psychiatric epidemiology'), there is no agreement as to whether social stress or selection would provide the primary explanation for this. In other words, do genetically vulnerable individuals accumulate in the laver socio-economic groups, or do the effects of adverse environmental and social factors correlate with low socio-economic status? The Midtown Manhattan study concluded that both social stress (childhood deprivation) and social selection (inter-generational mobility) contribute to the strong inverse relationship between psychopathology and social class, but it would be just as plausible to substitute genetic predisposition for childhood deprivation (Dohrenwend 1975). There are also diagnostic differences; schizophrenia and personality disorder are consistently found to be at their highest rate in the lowest socio-economic class, but this is not the case for neurosis or for manic-depressive psychosis. For personality disorder, it is not clear how important is social selection, relative to environmentally-induced stress, in determining the relationship with social class.

Evidence from Sweden (Leighton et al. 1971; Hagnell 1966) suggests that if lower status is not associated with financial deprivation, there may in fact be no correlation between it and excess psychiatric disorder; if anything, those in lower occupational groups had a lower rate. Similarly, Leighton et al. (1963) did not find in either Canada or Nigeria that poverty or socio-economic factors in themselves were significantly related to psychiatric morbidity, unless accompanied by sociocultural disintegration. An epidemiological study in India (Nandi et al. 1980) found that the rate of psychiatric morbidity in the higher socio-economic classes of all three groups of that population was greater than that in the lower classes (see Chapter 14). Studies on the relationship of depression and social class in Britain have been referred to above, as well as the fact that social network may take different forms at different socio-economic levels. Eaton (1980) showed from a probability model that social selection and social drift (see below) together form a sufficient explanation for the recorded excess of schizophrenia in the lowest social classes; furthermore, if some kinds of stress are concerned in the development of schizophrenia, they are not necessarily related to social class, but would be constant over the socio-economic scale.

In several American studies (e.g. Dunham 1961); *prevalence* of psychiatric disorders was found to be greater in lower social classes, whereas *incidence* was the same throughout; the difference was therefore due to the longer persistence in more disadvantaged groups of conditions which arose at the same rate throughout the population, and this was attributed to less adequate treatment. A prevalence study in New Haven (Myers et al. 1973) showed that when the factor of life stress was controlled, there was no association between psychiatric symptoms and social class; therefore, the class difference in level of symptoms was attributed to the differential distribution of life stress. However, an incidence survey of psychiatric symptoms amongst an urban population in Oakland (Uhlenhuth et al. 1974) found an association between intensity of symptoms and demographic characteristics — age, marital status, and race; since there was also an association between symptom intensity and life stress, it was concluded that differences in the rate of reporting symptoms could be accounted for (at least partly) by the way stress is distributed within sub-groups of the population. Higher symptom intensities were also found in those of lower social class, which it was suggested 'may be reflections and instruments of a life style'; but this rather cryptic comment is not explained any further.

There is also the question of diagnosis. The Dohrenwends (1974) concluded that the various types of psychiatric disorder show markedly different relationships to social class, as well as to urban versus rural settings. For instance, rates of schizophrenia and personality disorder are highest in the lowest social class, (though less so in rural areas for personality disorders), whilst neurosis and manic-depressive psychosis show no inverse relationship to social class. Further understanding of this question would require a separation between symptoms and disabilities which are either situation-generated, or which derive from personality defects, since the first type are more likely to be related to social stress and the second to social selection. Neither is there reliable information on differences between ethnic groups, when social class is controlled.

Marxist writers, not surprisingly take a rather different view of the significance of social class and environmental factors in relation to all aspects of health, as well as to other forms of social behaviour. Whitelegg (1982) complains that:

> the explanation of inequalities in housing or health care merely takes one item of consumption, temporarily abstracted from the context of the capitalist mode of production, and attempts an analysis independent of the social and class structures within which the particular act of consumption is taking place.

He adds that the patterning of cities into 'good' and 'bad' areas 'is a primary structural feature of a capitalist society organised around unequal access to resources'. Similarly, Peet (1975) states that:

> inequality may be passed on to the next generation via the environment of opportunities and services into which each individual is implanted at birth . . . the hierarchy of resource environments which make up the social geography of the modern city is a response to the hierarchical labour demands of the urban economy; just as the capitalist system of production must lead to a hierarchical social class structure, so it must provide differentiated social resource environments in which each class reproduces itself.

In Harvey's view (1973), 'created space in the modern city . . . reflects the prevailing ideology of the ruling group and institutions in society . . . We fashion our sensibilities, extract our sense of wants and needs, and locate our aspirations with respect to a geographical environment that is in large part created'.

Such statements are naive in their failure to acknowledge that non-capitalist cities also have a pronounced spatial patterning which is related to status and to the relative disirability of different environments; the hierarchy and mode of access to better living situations there are simply organised differently. Also, the Marxist view leads to a condemnation of 'spatial reformism', based on the strange logic that improving people's environmental conditions is harmful to them, through reducing their revolutionary ardour. The fact that revolution itself is ostensibly supposed to have the aim of improving those conditions leads to the suspicion that its actual purpose is to replace one ruling group by another. So far as 'created space' is concerned, this is a non-specific concept which can be applied to any society. Reliable epidemiological data of psychiatric morbidity from societies with varying political and economic systems would allow these questions to be approached more scientifically and would throw further light on the relationship of mental health and environment, but there seems little possibility of such a comparison being achieved, since only 'capitalist' societies are so far open to objective enquiry.

Social drift and residue

The final aspect of social factors to the discussed here consists of a pair of opposite tendencies, which are both varieties of the social selection hypothesis. 'Social drift' is the migration of those affected by psychiatric morbidity to areas of a particular kind, where social demends on them may be less; it is considered to be particularly relevant to schizophrenics, though alcoholics, drug addicts, people with marked personality disorders, and others with reduced social competence and fewer affiliative bonds show the same tendency. Inner city areas are the ones to which such affected individuals are most likely to migrate, since these tend to contain cheap, single-person accomodation and opportunities for casual but lowly paid work, whilst they lack any well-knit social structure which would make the deviant feel unwelcome. At the same time, though, there is an absence of social support, and this may operate as an adverse factor on mental health for some people.

The reverse of this process is 'social residue', i.e. that the mentally healthy migrate away from socially and environmentally undesirable areas, leaving the relatively incompetent behind. One example of this is to be found in British new towns, where there seems to be a relatively low rate of serious psychiatric morbidity, at least in the earlier years (Taylor & Chave 1964), due to the processes by which their residents are selected (see Chapter 7). Another, showing the opposite aspect of the process, is in the dramatic population fall of the industrial city of Salford, beginning in 1928, which was the sharpest for any local authority in England (Freeman 1984a), and which resulted predominantly from the movement of smaller family groups containing employed adults. Such a differential fall tends to leave behind those who are below average in social mobility, including the mentally and physically disabled, single-parent families, the elderly, etc. Thus, Lei et al. (1974) found in a Californian city that the highest concentrations of mental retardation were in areas where the population had been longest established.

Migration is a difficult issue in relation to psychiatric morbidity (Chapter 12), not least because there is evidence that both good and bad mental health may provoke a higher rate of mobility than the average, though for different reasons. The two concepts of drift and residue make this dichotomy clear, and both may operate at the same time and place. Possibly resulting in part from differential migration, a high prevalence of schizophrenia has been recorded both for inner city Salford (Freeman 1984b) and for rural areas of Ireland. In Salford, a study of the treated prevalence of schizophrenia for 1974, based on the Psychiatric Case Register, showed that the annual rate was 6.43 per thousand of the adult population (4.87 per thousand total population), excluding borderline cases, whilst the point-prevalence rates were 4.33 and 3.28 respectively. A summary of 15 surveys for 12 countires, dating from 1929 to 1972, gave one-year prevalence rates of schizophrenia of between 1.5 and 4.2 per thousand total population, but most were in the range 2.0–3.5 (Cooper 1978).

So far as Ireland is concerned, the one-day prevalence figure of schizophrenia for three mainly rural counties was 8.3 per thousand of the adult population, compared with 2.36 for the Camberwell area of south London (Walsh et al. 1980). This study suggests that in addition to the possible differential effect of migration, another factor 'may derive from historic-cultural characteristics such as an over-generous provision of in-patient facilities, a passive/submissive tendency on the part of patients to accept hospitalization . . . a paternalistic attitude and practice on the part of psychiatric personnel, and a lack of involvement of primary health care personnel'.

However, a different view of the Irish data is that of Murphy & Vega (1982), who found that first addmissions for schizophrenia in Northern Ireland are significantly higher for Catholics than for the rest of the population, although not as high as in the Republic. This excess of Catholic cases affects only the never-married, and derives much more from the rural west of the territory than from the industrial east; except in Tyrone, the overall rate of schizophrenia declines as one moves from south-west to north-east (as it does in the Republic), but this relationship of geography to schizophrenia applies mainly to Catholic males. thus, being a Catholic in Northern Ireland implies a considereably greater risk of schizopherenia for the unmarried person than being a non-Catholic does.

The same is true in the Republic, which has a comparatively high celibacy rate and a late average age at marriage. Rates of schizophrenia there are little higher among Catholics than non-Catholics for the married; but for the unmarried, rates of illness are much higher, except in young women. If more limited employment possibilities in the western counties were a significant factor, they should also affect non-Catholic males, but this is not the case. The ratio of single to married schizophrenics declines as one moves from west to north-east.

Murphy & Vega suggest that if these geographical differences in rates for Catholic males are not due to migration, they might be due to an unidentified organic factor or to a sociocultural factor, such as the marked sex imbalance in some areas, or the degree to which cultural traditions (which are much stronger in the west) have become out of harmony with modern life. In fact, the percentage of unmarried males in the western Irish counties is double that in the eastern; the high rate of celibacy in the west is not due to unmarried women leaving the region, since the percentage of them in the population is higher there than in the east. Thus, it is nore probable that the western women leave because the men there are not ready for marriage than that the men remain single because too many women have left. Social anthropoligical studies indicate that mothers' dominance over their sons and interference with their marriages had been most marked in the west, but weakens as families move to the east. However, accelerating cultural change, the virtual cessation of external emigration in recent years, and the rapidly rising proportion of young people in the population seem very likely to result in the prevalence rates of schizophrenia in rural areas falling to nearer average levels over the course of time.

Murphy (1976) points out that discovering the social causes of psychiatric disorder means not only developing case-finding methods for the dependent variables, but also locating those events in human societies which are genuinely antecedent to the disorders, and are therefore independent variables. The Irish situation might provide such an opportunity, but it would be as well to heed the warning of Hammer et al. (1978) that 'migration, social class and ethnic marginality are too gross as social variables and too complex as social phenomena to implicate any particular mechanism that would account for their association with psychopathology'. These authors do, however, see a possible common mechanism underlying the processes, which is adverse change in people's social networks, and this suggests a direction for further investigation.

ECOLOGY

The final aspect to be referred to in this survey of the scientific background is ecology, which studies the relationship between organisms and their environment, and seeks to correlate the spatial distribution of behaviour with environmental conditions in defined geographical areas. All work of this kind, however, runs the risk of the 'ecological fallacy' (see Chapter 12) so that results which relate to the structures of communities should not be assumed to apply to individuals. For instance, an excess of both schizophrenia and juvenile delinquency might be found in one area, but this does not mean that most delinquents are schizophrenic, or vice verse; and even if the same people show two abnormal phenomena, the correlation between them is not necessarily evidence of some common underlying process in the social structure. Nevertheless, ecology can be of great heuristic value, as with the early Chicago studies of mental hospital admissions, and it also provides important information for planning services, in revealing local concentrations of particular types of illness and social problems.

A sophisticated example of such studies is that on suicide and parasuicide in Edinburgh by Buglass & Duffy (1978). Four previous British investigations of the ecological correlates of parasuicide had shown population mobility and overcrowding to be the most consistently associated social factors; in this case, considerable overlap was found between the distributions of suicide and parasuicide, and some central areas had high rates of both, but two peripheral housing estates showed an excess of parasuicide only. Social factors correlating with parasuicide alone characterised lower-class districts with high rates of unemployment, overcrowding, poverty, juvenile delinquency, and demands for social aid (but not hospitalisation). Here, the population structure contained the highest proportions of children under 15 (whereas the central areas had many elderly people) and dwellings tended to be taken by families whose need for accommodation was only one of their problems, after other people on the Council's waiting list had refused them.

Ecological studies of suicide have shown a correlation with other 'problem' variables, which tends to be explained in terms of concepts such as anomie or social disintegration (see above), on the assumption that suicide would occur more often in societies where rules which had provided restraint and cohesion are no longer generally accepted. But although these concepts are seen as attributes of social groups, their presence can only be inferred from the behaviour of individuals, or from the way individuals relate to each other, and the argument may then become circular. Sainsbury (1955) saw anomie in terms mainly of people living alone, and disintegration as high rates of divorce, illegitimacy, and juvenile delinquency, but he did not find suicide associated with poverty. Buglass & Duffy point out that this argument as to aetiological relationships has never been satisfactorily resolved. Suicide may occur in certain areas because certain types of people (who are at risk through some characteristics of their own) come to live there, or suicide rates may be high because features of the area intensify people's feelings of isolation and worthlessness, or both factors may operate together (the environment aggravating their existing difficulties). Similarly, disorganisation and poverty may occur in the same areas of some cities, but may be separated elsewhere. Thus, the extent to which the environment — seen in either social or physical terms — causes either suicide or para-suicide remains uncertain, but it may well have more effect on the frequency of suicidal attempts than on that of completed suicide.

A method of investigation based on the ecological approach is that of social area analysis, which attempts to explain certain behaviours of residents through characteristics of the district in which they live, e.g. social factors which are related to high levels of psychiatric disorders. Theoretically, this would be valuable both in investigating such disorders and in measuring the effects of mental health intervention strategies, but it requires population areas to be sub-divided into units which are relatively homogeneous for such characteristics as social class, urbanisation, or ethnicity. Since categorisation of this kind is likely to be very difficult, social area analysis is a technique needing much further development (Goodman et al, 1982). In contrast to the ecological approach, the socio-cultural one focusses on cultural responses and behavioural adaptations to objective situations which are characteristic of life in particular settings; these situations are regarded sociologically as stemming from factors such as size, density, and social variety (Allen, 1982).

An example of the application of the ecological method to the eighth largest urban area in Britain is to be found in a study of psychiatric admissions from the city of Bristol (Ineichen et al, 1984; Harrison et al, 1984). This took place 25 years after Hare's survey of schizopherenics (1956), which confirmed American findings that high rates of admissions were derived from run down central areas, containing a high proportion of single-person accommodation. In the intervening period, there had been considerable shifts of population in the working-class inner areas of Bristol, with the arrival of substantial numbers of ethinic minorities, nearly half of whom were to be found in four electoral wards. Surprisingly enough, though, the pattern of distribution of admissions across the city remained largely unchanged over this time.

The highest admission rates (three times the lowest) occurred in a contiguous group of nine central wards, though these also had a low rate of referral of psychiatric out-patients, and even when their residents were referred, they often defaulted. Compulsory admissions for the city showed a clustering in central districts (in which lower social class vulnerable groups predominate) and in the immigrant wards, with a rate more than four times that of some peripheral middle-class areas. White patients from the inner city often had poor social networks, and a tendency for the police to be involved in their compulsory admissions — not because of increased violence or threatening behaviour, compared with suburban patients, but because of a tendency for them to become publicly disturbed, in a way which attracts police attention. Similar patients in suburbia are either coped with by their families, are seen by the GP at an earlier stage, or at least escape involvement with the police, whose presence in the area is at a lower level, compared with the inner city.

That these differences were socially determined was confirmed by the finding that after admission, there was little difference between the behaviour of inner-city and suburban white patients respectively. In spite of the central location of the immigrants, the social profile of West Indian patients was very similar to that of suburban whites. Harrison et al (1984) state that in the whole sample, very few patients were geographically mobile, e.g. living in hostels, or of no fixed abode.

Related findings come from a study of schizophrenic patients aged under 65, in Southampton in 1981–2, which found that those living with a supportive relative or friend were fairly evenly distributed throughout the city, whereas patients without such support were over-represented in the inner city area. The two inner city wards contained 45 per cent of unsupported patients, but only 14 per cent of supported ones, reflecting the geographical distribution of hostels and lodging houses, where very many of the unsupported patients were accommodated (Gibbons et al, 1984).

If there is one outstanding conclusion, though, which can be drawn from this survey of a highly complex subject, it is that both individual and environmental factors must be regarded as equally important. Further knowledge of the social contribution to the aetiology of psychiatric disorder can only be obtained by examining the processes of their interaction in much greater depth than has been the case up to now.

REFERENCES

Abbott N F 1979 The density pathology hypothesis in comparative perspective: density, status and pathology in pre-revolutionary Moscow. Internation Journal of Comparative Sociology 23: 17–33

Allen I 1982 Exploring the city (review). Society 19: 90–91

Altman I 1975 The environment and social behavior. Brooks Cole, Monterey

Amato P R 1981 The impact of the built environment on prosocial and affiliative behaviour: a field study of the Townsville city mall. Australian Journal of Psychology 33: 297–303

Anderson E N Jr 1972 Some Chinese methods of dealing with crowding. Urban Anthropolgy 1: 141–150

Ashmore R D, McConahay J B 1975 Psychology and America's urban dilemmas. McGraw Hill, New York

Bain S M 1974 A geographer's approach in the epidemiology of psychiatric disorder. Journal of Biosocial Sciences 6: 195–220

Barker R 1968 Ecological psychology. Stanford University Press, Stanford

Barquero J L V, Munez P E, Jaurequi V M 1982 The influence of the process of urbanization on the prevalence of neurosis. Acta Psychiatrica Scandinavica 65: 161–170

Bebbington P 1978 Epidemiology of depressive disorder. Culture, Medicine & Psychiatry 1: 297–341

Booth A 1976 Urban crowding and its consequences. Praeger, New York

Bornstein M H, Bornstein H G 1976 The pace of life. Nature 259: 557–559

Brenner M H 1979 Influence of the social environment on psychopathology: the historic perspective. In Basset J E (ed) Stress and mental disorder. Raven Press, New York

Brown G W 1979 A three-factor causal model of depression. In: Barrett J E (ed) Stress and mental disorder. Raven Press, New York

Brown G W, Davidson S, Harris T, MacLean U, Pollock S, Prudo R 1977 Psychiatric disorder in London and North Uist. Social Scinece & Medicine 11: 367–377

Brown G W, Harris T 1982 Social class and affective disorder. In: Al-Issai I (ed) Culture and philosophy. University Park Press, Baltimore

Brown G W, Prudo R 1981 Psychiatric disorder in a rural and an urban population: 1, aetiology of depression. Psychological Medicine 11: 581–599

Buglass D, Duffy J C 1978 The ecological pattern of suicide and parasuicide in Edinburgh. Social Science & Medicine 12: 241–253

Campbell E A, Cape S J, Teasdale J D 1983 Social factors and affective disorder: an investigation of Brown and Harris's model Br J Psychiatry 143: 548–553

Cappon D 1975 Designs for improvement in the quality of life in downtown cores. International Journal of Mental Health 4: 31–47

Carey G W 1972 Density, crowding stress and the ghetto. American Behavioral Scientist 15: 495–509

Cassel J C 1970 Physical illness in response to stress. In: Levine S, Scotch N A (eds) Social stress. Aldine, Chicago

Cassel J C 1971 Health consequences of population density and crowding. In: National Academy of Science (ed) Rapid population growth: consequences and policy implications, Volume 1. John Hopkins University Press, Baltimore

Cassel J C1974 Psychiatric epidemiology. In: Caplan G (ed) American handbook of psychiatry, Second edition, Vol. 2. Basic Books, New York

Choldin H M 1978 Urban density and pathology. Annual Review of Sociology 4: 91–113

Chombard de Lauwe P M 1959 Famille et habitation. Centre National de la Recherche Scientifique, Paris

Cooper B 1978 Epidemiological aspects. In: Wing J K (ed) Schizophrenia: toward a new synthesis. Academic Press, London

Cohen S, Weinstein N 1982 Nonauditory effects of noise on behavior and health. In: Evans G W (ed) Environmental stress. Cambridge University Press, Cambridge

Dabbs J M Jr, Stokes N A 1975 Beauty is power. The use of space on the sidewalk. Sociometry 38: 551–557

Dohrenwend B P 1975 Sociocultural and sociopsychological factors in the genesis of mental disorders. Journal of Health & Social Behavior 16: 365–393

Dohrenwend B P, Dohrenwend B S 1974 Psychiatric disorders in urban settings. In: Caplan G (ed) American handbook of psychiatry, Second edition, Vol 2. Basic Books, New York

Downes D M 1966 The delinquent solution: a study of subcultural theory. Routledge & Kegan Paul, London

Dunham H W Social structures and mental disorders: competing hypotheses of explanations. Milbank Memorial Fund Quarterly 39: 259–311

Dye T R 1975 Population density and social pathology. Urban Affairs Quarterly 11: 265–275

Eaton J W, Weil R J 1955 Culture and mental disorders. Free Press, Glencoe

Eaton W W 1980 A formal theory of selection for schizophrenia. American Journal of Sociology 86: 149–156

Eisenthal S 1979 the sociocultural approach. In: Lazare A (ed) Outpatient psychiatry. Williams & Wilkins, Baltimore

Evans G W 1982, General introduction. In: Evans G W (ed) Environmental stress. Cambrige University Press, Cambridge

Exit Photography Group 1982 Survival programmes in Britain's inner cities. Open University Press, Milton Keynes

Faris R E L, Dunham H W 1939 Mental disorders in urban areas. Chicago University Press, Chicago

Fisher C S 1973 Urban malaise. Social Forces 52: 221–235

Fischer C S 1975 The study of urban community and personality. Annual Review of Sociology 1: 67–89

Fischer C S 1976 The urban experience. Harcourt, Brace, Jovanovich, New York

Frankenheauser M 1975 Experimental approach to the study of catecholamines and emotions. In: Levy L (ed) Emotions; their parameters and measurement. McGraw-Hill, New York

Freedman J L 1975 Crowding and behavior. W H Freeman, San Francisco

Freedman J L, Heshka S, Levy A 1975 Population density and pathology: is there a relationship? Journal of Experimental Social Psychology 11: 539–552

Freeman H L 1984a Mental health services in Salford up to 1974. Medical History (in the press)

Freeman H L 1984b A study of the treated prevalence of schizophrenia in Salford 1974 (awaiting publication)

Fried M, De Fazio V J 1974 Territoriality and boundary conflicts in the subway. Psychiatry 37: 47–59

Gans H 1968 People and Plans. Basic Books, New York

Gath D, Cooper B, Gattoni F, Rockett D 1977 Child guidance and delinquency in a London borough. Oxford University Press, London

Gibbons J S, Horn S H, Powell J M, Gibbons J L 1984 Schizophrenic patients and their families. Fritish Journal of Psychiatry 144: 70–77

Giggs J A 1979 Human health problems in urban areas. In: Herbert D T, Smith D M (eds) Social problems in urban areas. Oxford University Press, London

Gove W R, Hughes M, Galle O R 1979 Overcrowding in the home: an empirical investigation of its possible pathological consequences. American Sociological Review 44: 59–60

Goodman A B, Rahav M, Popper M M 1982 A social area analysis of Jerusalem: implications for mental health planning and epidemiologic studies. Israel Journal of Psychiatry and Related Sciences 19: 185–197

Goldstein J M, Caton C L M 1983 The effects of the community environment on chronic psychiatric patients. Psychol Med 13: 193–199

Greenblatt M, Becerra R M, Serafetinides E A 1982 Social networks and mental health: an overview. American Journal of Psychiatry 139: 977–984

Gruenberg E M 1974 The epidemiology of schizophrenia. In: Caplan G (ed) American handbook of psychiatry, Second Edition, Vol 2. Basic Books, New York

Gurland B J 1976 The comparative frequency of depression in various adult age groups. Journal of Gerontology 31: 283–292

Gutlsnf B Gurland B, Copland J, Kuriansky J, Kelleker M, Sharpe L, Dean L L 1983 The Mind and Mood of Aging. Croom Helm, London

Gutmann D 1980 Observations on culture and mental health in later life. In: Birren J E, Sloane R B (eds) Handbook of mental health and aging. Prentice Hall, Englewood Cliffs N J

Hagnell O 1966 A prospective study of incidence of mental disorder. Norstedts-Bonniers, Stockholm

Hall E T 1968 Proxemics. Current Anthropology 9: 83–95

Hammer M, 1983 Social networks and the long term patient. In: Barofsky I, Budson R D (eds) The Chronic Psychiatric Patient in the Community. MTP, Lancaster

Hammer M, Makiesky-Barrow S, Gutwirth L 1978 Social Networks and schizophrenia. Schizophrenia Bulletin 4: 522–545

Harrison G, Ineichen B, Morgan H G, Smith J 1984 Psychiatric hospital admissions in Bristol. 2. Social and clinical aspects of compulsory admission British Journal of psychiatry (in press)

Harvey D 1973 Social justice and the city. Edward Arnold, London

Henderson S 1980 A development in social psychiatry: the systematic study of social bonds. Journal of Nervous & Mental Disease 168: 63–9

Horowitz M J, Duff D F, Stratton L O 1964 Body-buffer zone. Archives of General Psychiatry ii: 651–656

Horwitz A 1978 Family, kin and friend networks in psychiatric help seeking. Social Science and Medicine 23: 297–304

Ineichen B, Harrison G, Morgan H G 1984 Psychiatric hospital admissions in Bristol. 1. Geographical and ethnic factors. British Journal of Psychiatry (in press)

Jaco E G 1954 The social isolation hypothesis and schizophrenia. Americal Sociological Review 19: 567–577

Kahn R L, Perlin S 1967 Dwelling unit density and use of mental health services. Proceedings of the 75th Annual Convention of the American Psychological Association. Washington D C

Kasl S V 1972 Physical and mental health effects of involuntary relocation and institutionalisation on the elderly — a review. American Journal of Public Health 62: 377–384

Kasl S V 1977 The effect of the man-made environment on health and behavior. Center for Disease Control, Atlanta

Kasl S V, Harburg E 1975 Mental health and the urban environment: Some doubts and second thoughts. Journal of Health and Social Behaviour 16: 268–282

Kasl S V, Rosenfield S 1980 The residential environment and its impact on the mental health of the aged. In: Birren J E, Sloane R B (eds) Handbook of mental health and aging, Prentice Hall, Englewood Cliffs N J

Killilea M 1982 Interaction of crisis theory, coping strategies and social support systems. In: Schulberg H C, Killilea M (eds) The Modern Practice of Community Mental Health. Jossey-Bass, San Francisco

Kirmeyer S L 1978 Urban density and pathology: a review of research. Environment & Behavior 10: 247–269

Klein D C, Fencil-Morse E, Seligman E P 1976 Learned helplessness, depression, and the attribution of failure. Journal of Personality & Social Psychology 33: 508–516

Kohn M L, Clausen J A 1955 Social isolation and schizophrenia. Americah Sociological Review 20: 265–273

Korte C D 1976 The effects of an urban environment on social behaviour. University of St Andrews, St. Andrews

Korte C D, Ypma I, Toppen A 1975 Helpfulness in Dutch Society as a function of urbanization and environmental input level. Journal of Personality & Social Psychology 32: 996–1003

Lawton M P 1970 Assessment, integration, and environments for the elderly. Gerontologist 10: 38–46

Lee T 1976 Psychology and the environment. Methuen, London.

Lei T J, Butler E W, Rowitz L, McCallister R J 1974 An ecological study of agency labelled retardates. American Journal of Mental Deficiency 79: 22–31

Leighton A H 1959 My name is legion. Basic Books, New York

Leighton A H 1981 Culture and psychiatry. Canadian Journal of Psychiatry 26: 522–529

Leighton A H 1982 Caring for mentally ill people. Cambridge University Press, Cambridge

Leighton D C, Harding J S, Macklin D B, Macmillan A M, Leighton A H 1963 The character of danger; psychiatric symptoms in selected communities. Basic Books, New York

Leighton D C, Hagnell O, Harding J S, Kellert S R, Donley R A 1971 Psychiatric disorder in a Swedish and a Canadian community: an exploratory study. Social Science & Medicine 5: 189–201Levy L, Herzog A N 1974 Effects of population density and crowding on health and social adaptation in the Netherlands. Journal of Health and Social Behaviour 15: 228–240

Lipman A 1968 Territorial behaviour in the sitting rooms of four residential homes for old people. (Unpublished) Quoted by Mercer (1975)

Lipowski Z J 1975 Sensory and information inputs overload: behavioural effects. Comprehensive Psychiatry 16: 199–221

Liverpool Inner Area Study 1975 Third study review: issues and policies. HMSO, London

McCarthy D, Saegert S 1976 Residential density, social control and social withdrawal. Human Ecology 6: 253–272

Mechanic D 1973 The contribution of sociology to psychiatry. Psychological Medicine 3: 1–4

Mehrabian A, Russell J A 1974 An Approach to Environmental Psychology. MIT Press, Massachusetts

Mercer C 1975 Living in cities: psychology and urban environment. Penguin, Harmondsworth

Milgram S 1970 The exoerience of living in cities. Science 167: 1461–1468

Miller W B 1974 Psychological and psychiatric aspects of population problems. In: Caplan G (ed) American Handbook of Psychiatry. Second edition, Vol 2. Basic Books, New York

Mitchell R E, Trickett E J 1980 Task force report: Social networks as mediators of social support. Community Mental Health Journal 16: 18–27

Monahan J, Vaux A 1980 Task force report: the macro-environment and community mental health. Community Mental Health Journal 16: 14–26

Morris R N 1968 Urban sociology. Praeger, New York

Mueller D P 1980 Social Networks. Social Science & Medicine 14A: 147–161

Mueller D P 1981 The current status of urban-rural differences in psychiatric disorder. Journal of Nervous & Mental Disease 169: 18–27

Murphy H B M, Vega G 1982 Schizophrenia and religious affiliation in Northern Ireland. Psychological Medicine 12: 595–605

Murphy J E 1976 Social causes; the independent varuable. In: Kaplan B H, Wilson R N, Leighton A H (eds) Further explorations in social psychiatry, Basic Books, New York

Murray R, Boal R W 1979 The social ecology of urban violence. In: Herbert D T, Smith D M (eds) Social problems and the city: geographical perspectives. Oxford University Press, London

Myers J K, Lindenthal J J, Pepper M P 1973 Social class, life events and psychiatric symptoms (Quoted by Uhlenhuth et al. 1974)

Myrdal G 1957 Economic theory and underdeveloped regions. Methuen, London

Nandi D N, Mukherjee S P, Boral G C, Banerjee G, Ghosh A, Sarkar S, Ajmany S 1980 Socio-economic status and mental morbidity in certain tribes and castes in India — a cross-cultural study. British Journal of Psychiatry 136: 73–85

Newman O 1975 Reactions to the 'defensible space' study and some further findings. International Journal of Mental Health 4: 48–70

Newman O 1980 Community of interest. Anchor, Doubleday, New York

Peet R 1975 Inequality and poverty: a Marxist-geographic theory. Annals of the Association of American Geographers 65: 564–571

Piha J, Lathi J A, Aaltonen J 1979 Family psychiatric background for the study of mental health and housing environment. Man-environment systems 9: 175–179

Prudo R, Brown G W, Harris T, Dowland J 1981 Psychiatric disorder in a rural and an urban population: 2. Sensitivity to loss. Psychological Medicine 11: 601–616

Rapoport A 1975 Toward a redefinition of density. Environment & Behavior 7: 133–158

Regier D A 1982 Research progress 1955–1980. In: Wagenfeld O, Lemkau P V, Justice B (eds) Public mental health: perspectives and prospects. Sage, Beverly Hills

Ridley R F 1981 Unemployment in Liverpool. Political Quarterly 52: 1–22

Rodgers W L 1981 Density, crowding, and satisfaction with the residential environment. Social Indicators Research 10: 75–102

Roncek D W 1981 Dangerous places: crime and the residential environment. Social Forces 60: 74–96

Ruesch J 1965 Social psychiartry: an overview. Archives of General Psychiatry 12: 501–509

Rutter M 1981 The city and the child. American Journal of Orthopsychiatry 51: 610–625

Rutter M, Quinton D 1977 Psychiatric disorder — ecological factors and concepts of causation. In: McGurk H (ed) Ecological factors in human development. North Holland, Amsterdam

Sainsbury P 1955 Suicide in London. Chapman & Hall, London

Selye H 1956 The stress of life. McGraw-Hill, New York

Shaw C R, McKay H D 1942 Juvenile delinquency and urban areas. University of Chicago Press, Chicago

Silberman I 1979 Mental transitional spheres. Psychoanalytie Quarterly 48: 85–92

Simmel G 1950 The metropolis and mental life. In: Wolff K (ed) The sociology of George Simmel. Free Press, Glencoe

Sommer R 1969 Personal space. Prentice Hall, Englewood Cliffs, N J

Srole L 1956 Social integration and certain corollaries; and exploratory study. American Sociological Review 21: 709–716

Srole L 1972 Urbanization and mental health: some reformulation. American Scientist 60: 576–583

Solomon Z, Bronet E 1982 The role of social factors in affective disorder: an assessment of the vulnerability model of Brown and his colleagues. Psychol Med 12: 123–130

Srole L, Langner T S, Michael S T, Opler M K, Rennie T A C 1962 Mental health in the mentropolis. McGraw Hill, New York

Stokols D 1978 Environmental psychology. Annual Review of Psychology 29: 253–95

Taylor R B 1982 Neighbourhood environment and stress. In: Evans G W (ed) Environmental stress. Cambridge University Press, Cambridge

Taylor S (Lord), Chave S P W 1964 Mental health and environment. Longmans, London

Trichopoulos D, Katsauyanni K, Zavitsanos X, Tzonou A, Dalla-Vorgia P 1983 Psychological stress and fatal heart attack: the Athens (1981) earthquake natural experiment. Lancet i: 441–444

Tuan Y 1979 Landscapes of fear. Blackwell, Oxford

Uhlenhuth E H, Lipman R S, Balter M B, Stern M 1974 Symptom intensity and life stress in the city. Archives of General Psychiatry 31: 759–764

Vaughan C, Leff J P 1976 The influence of family and social factors on the course of psychiatric illness. British Journal Psychiatry 129: 125–137

Walsh D 1968 Hospitalized psychiatric morbidity in the Republic of Ireland. British Journal of Psychiatry 114: 11–14

Walsh D, O'Hare A, Blake B, Halpenny J V, O'Brien P F 1980 The treated prevalence of mental illness in the Republic of Irelan — the three county case register study, Psychological Medicine 10; 465–470

Webb S D, Collette J 1975 Urban ecological and household correlates of stress-alleviating drug use. American Behavioural Scientist 18: 750–769

Webber M 1963 Order in diversity, community without propinquity. In: Wing L (ed) Cities and Space. Johns Hopkins Press, Baltimore

Werry J S, Carlielle J 1983 The nuclear family, suburban neurosis and iatrogenesis in Auckland mother of young children Journal American Acadamic Child Psychiatry 22: 172–179

Whitelegg J 1982 Inequalities in health care. Straw Barnes, Retford
Windley P G, Scheidt R J 1982 An ecological model of mental health among small-town rural elderly. Journal of Gerontology 37: 235–42
Wing J K, Brown G W 1970 Institutionalism and schizophrenia. Cambridge University Press, Cambridge
Young M, Willmott P 1957 Family and kindhip in east London. Routledge & Kegan Paul, London

Crowding and territoriality: a psychiatric view

Like most creatures, man has the capacity to adapt to a wide variety of social contacts, partly by using internal homeostatic devices to control cortical arousal and partly by controlling the external environment. He does this not only directly, by erecting barriers, but indirectly by sharing with his peers a concept of space and privacy — of *territory*. In ethological terms, territory has been divided into total range, home range (familiar ground), core area (sleeping area), and individual distance, i.e. that which moves around with the animal (Wilson 1975). The territory can serve different functions, from the nesting area of the herring gull (Tinbergen 1955) to the food source of the grouse (Wynne-Edwards 1962). Although inter-specific competition for territory is not uncommon in birds, intra-specific competition is always stronger. The rival of man is man, and the maintenance of his territory will be most threatened by human crowding.

MEANING OF CROWDING

Crowding has been defined by Stokols (1972) as a condition where the demand for space exceeds supply. Such a definition is almost a tautology, but correctly emphasises that crowding is a subjective sensation and cannot be measured simply by demographic data; Stokols proposed that it should only be used to describe the internal perceptual and motivational states resulting from the interaction of spatial and personal factors, but such states cannot yet be fully identified or measured. One of the the more subtle means of estimating this demand is to measure personal space. Hall (1966) distinguishes four types of space: 'intimate', ranging from skin contact to a distance of 6–18 inches, in which the individual is subject to the sensations of smell and temperature; personal (1.5–4 ft), which is within the range of contact by outstretched arm, but sufficiently distant to take in a face by macular vision; 'social' (4–12 ft) where contact is restricted to the verbal; and 'public' (12–20 ft) where contact is usually with several individuals. Kinzel (1970) has measured personal space in prisoners by asking them to tell the experimenter to stop when his approach made the subject feel uncomfortable. He found not only that this measure was consistent for the individual, but that violent prisoners in particular required more space, especially behind, than non-violent ones; solitary confinement might increase this dimension.

Hall also described how perception of crowding varied between cultures, English and Northern Europeans requiring more space than, for example, Arabs. When such different cultures come into contact, the former see the latter as over-familiar, whilst the latter interpret the distance maintained by the English as dislike. Similarly, a fairly consistent difference has been found between the sexes, men requiring a larger space than women, at least when relating to their own sex. Thus, Freedman et al. (1972), using groups of four high school students of the same sex, compared their response to a game in which they could either cooperate or compete with one another. The latter condition allowed one of the four to win more than he or she could by sharing the proceeds of the cooperative strategy, although the group as a whole would win less. In a small room (6 square feet per person), males were more competitive than in a large one (20 sq. ft. per person), but females were more competitive in the large room. These studies did not, however, directly compare the personal space of males and females, bearing in mind that the Kinzel method would be invalidated by the different effect that the sex of the experimenter would have on the two sexes.

Freedman (1975) also studied games and mock trials in small and large rooms respectively; women were said to respond more 'positively' than men in crowded rooms, in the sense of showing signs of well-being. However, some findings contrary to this have been described by Baron (1977), while Paulus et al. (1978) pointed out that the brief and relatively benign conditions of the laboratory setting make such findings of limited generalisability to intense, inescapable, and long-term crowding in actual living situations. Ashmore and McConahay (1975) state that no experimental studies have been able to examine independently the three factors of crowding, density, and number of persons or interactions involved. Unlike correlational studies in populations, which deal with long-term crowding, laboratory investigations can only examine short-term situations; yet crowding effects may only emerge in chronic situations, or people who live amongst long-term crowding may react differently to acute crowding situations.

Surprisingly little investigation has been done into the effect of personality on personal space, though Cozby (1973) showed a close correlation between the size of personal space and dislike of crowding. Introversion, as might be expected, was found by Vandeveer (1973) to be associated with an active avoidance of crowding in public space. Similar results were obtained by Williams (1971), Cook (1970), and Patterson and Holmes (1966). In one of the first experiments on personal space, Horowitz et al. (1964) asked patients with either schizophrenia or affective disorder to imagine that a hat-stand was a person, and were told to approach as close to the stand as they felt comfortable. This distance constituted the 'body-buffer zone'. As in most experiments with schizophrenics, they were found to be the most variable group; but in general, they maintained a larger personal distance than those with affective disorders, and both groups reduced this distance after recovery.

Whilst one may assume that crowding occurs when the personal space of the individual is invaded, the nature of that stress is yet to be determined. The body-buffer zone of the individual is a mobile territory — the equivalent of the individual distance in ethology — though this use of the term 'territory' is by analogy, and may tend to reify it to a greater extent than is justified. The invasion of this personal space, however, is likely to provoke a more intense response than that caused by invasion of the core area, as typified by the home. Personal space is indicated by decreasing eye contact as proximity increases (Argyle & Dean 1965), followed by an increased sensation of discomfort and probability of flight. Explanations for the effect of crowding include: sensory overload (leading to dominance hierarchies); a reduction in choice; humiliation from the lack of a fulfilling role (as there is competition for the few tasks available); and anxiety caused by invasion of instinctive boundaries. Schmidt & Keating (1979) regard crowding as an attribution of settings in which there is a loss or lack of personal control. Implicit in most of these theories is the view that crowding in itself does not cause the stress, but provides an environment where these stresses are more likely to impinge; however, this view is not universally shared (e.g. Paulus et al. 1978). If a prison houses one man to a cell and communal activities are forbidden, the stresses of crowding are likely to be replaced by those of isolation, in this extreme situation. Baron (1977) states that field studies provide no indication of a link between crowding and crimes of violence, but the failure to find this may result from the complex nature of environment–behaviour interactions.

Stokols (1976), discussing this issue, divides crowding experiences firstly into personal, or neutral, where the stress is seen as an inevitable consequence of restraints within the environment, and secondly into those taking place in the primary environment, like the home or place of work, or in the secondary environment, such as the train, street, or theatre. This would separate four stress areas, e.g. marital conflict (occurring in the personal primary area); conflicts over the sharing of rooms, baths, etc. (in the neutral primary area); mugging (in the personal secondary area); and queuing (in the neutral secondary area). High density would exacerbate the latter two conditions, whilst crowding within the home would do so with the former. It is likely that such stresses would have different effects on different individuals, eliciting emotions ranging from fear to anger, or even resignation. At this point, however, the huge variation between individual personalities and coping skills makes questionable the attempt to relate such specific stress to individual effect.

Subjective and social factors are nearly always crucial in these matters. The presence of another individual on a mountain may evoke a feeling of crowding in a sole mountaineer, whilst the same individual may feel isolated at a party where only five people remain in the room. A hostile encounter in a railway compartment is stressful, a discussion over a crossword is not; a single bed may be too big at the beginning of a marriage and separate beds too close by the end. Paulus et al. (1978) propose that there is a difference between 'social density', which may be the primary factor when moderate numbers are involved, and 'spatial density', which becomes more potent at high levels of occupation.

Stress occurs when an antagonistic encounter takes place, and the restriction on space prevents a retreat; such encounters between animals in the wild, though, are usually resolved without injury. Evidence for territoriality as a human characteristic, however, has been derived mainly from studies of the social organisation of primitive tribes. For instance, Eibl-Eibesfeldt (1974) claimed that the ! Kung bushmen show territoriality of the band (association of extended families), and even areas of defined activity within the band. Bands belonging to the same nexus (grouping) are readily granted access to hunting grounds or water holes, though this is denied to bands of another nexus. However, this cannot be taken to prove that territoriality is an inescapable characteristic of *Homo sapiens*. The concept is also used politically, referring to conflict between nations; but biologically, this use does not seem valid, having little in common with the animal phenomenon, which is a property-defensive strategy (see also Chapter 2). Gove et al (1979) regard the conceptualisation of crowding as focussing on two distinct but inter-related concepts, excess of stimulation and lack of privacy; when these are combined, the experience of crowding involves an excess of social stimuli, generally in the form of demands, combined with an inability to regulate either them or the need to respond to them. In the study of crowding within the home, neither factor has so far been measured, but there are very marked cultural variations in the way they are regulated. It seems plausible, though, that the norms of a given culture would tend to regulate social interaction in such a way that people in typical situations would experience an optimal level of such interaction; crowding would thus be experienced by those who receive the most demands and have the least privacy (as understood by each society). Culture determines what are the appropriate demands and responses in any particular case, but socially defined role obligations seem to be the key variable underlying these. Gove et al. put forward a general model in which the subjective experience of crowding (excess demands and lack of privacy) acts as an intervening variable between an objective measure of crowding (persons per room) and dependent variables (some moderately pathological states and behaviours).

ANIMAL STUDIES

Findings in animal studies cannot be transposed directly to human populations, but they do provide a means by which the effects of crowding can be studied in isolation from other stressors, and may thus indicate possible consequences. Studies in the wild, such as that of chimpanzees by Jane Goodall

(1971), showed that whilst animals low in the hierarchy have a lower expectation of life, they rarely die as a result of intra-specific conflict. This
contrasts with the effect of imposing artificial conditions on the colony, as
on Monkey Hill (Zuckerman 1932); 94 male baboons and six females were
enclosed in a space measuring 100 × 60 ft, while a further 35 animals were
added two years later (30 female). In the first six years, 61 males died
(eight from injuries) and 33 females (30 from injuries); of the 15 births, 14
died before reaching adult life. Such slaughter was the result not only of
crowding, but of sexual imbalance. Southwick (1967) showed that aggressive
encounters almost doubled when the cage holding a troop of rhesus
monkeys was cut to half its original size. However, the introduction of a
strange monkey into the cage had an even greater effect, and since crowding
increases all interactions, the increase in aggressive encounters must be kept
in perspective. In the wild, the response to increasing density is dispersal,
especially by the less dominant animals who are unable to gain a central
territory. An extreme response of this kind is the migration of lemmings to
the sea (Cluff 1971), but if dispersal is prevented, the social structure breaks
down. Russell & Russell (1968) write: 'a key part in the whole response
to (population) crisis is the switch in attitude and behaviour to females and
young . . . chivalrous protection of the female is transformed into brutal
domination'.

The physical effects of crowding on animals have been well documented
by Thiessen & Rodgers (1961) and by Christian (1964). They include lower
body weight, delayed maturation, increased adrenal weight, glomerulo-
nephritis, thymic involution, infertility, reduced resistance to infection,
increased sensitivity to alloxan-induced diabetes, and lower antibody
response to antigen challenge (Vessey 1964). In 1962, Ratcliffe & Snyder
described the arteriosclerosis of animals of Philadelphia Zoo, compared to
those in the wild, and attributed this to excessive stimulation from other
animals and humans. Mckissock et al. (1961) reported that the degree of
arteriosclerosis in chickens was directly related to both the distance apart
of the cages and the sexes of the birds; the greatest effects were produced
in crowded males, the least in isolated birds of both sexes. Myers et al.
(1971) found that increased death rates were associated with crowding in
rabbits, and that this increased mortality continued, even in animals who
were no longer crowded. The psychological effects of crowding on animals
are more difficult to assess, although it is not unreasonable to attribute the
physical changes mentioned above to psychological stress initially.

Calhoun (1962) studied the behaviour of the Norwegian rat in colonies
of about 80, occupying an area measuring 10 ft × 4 ft, divided into four
pens, and with adequate space for at least 50 if the space had been evenly
divided. One dominant male would take over one of the pens with his harem
of about six females, leaving the rest to share the remainder of the space,
often three-quarters of the males and 40 per cent of the females occupying
the same pen. He attributed the formation of this behavioural sink to the

method of feeding, which forced the animal to stay at the hopper for several minutes to obtain enough food, and broke down the normal inhibition of rats to eat together. A second experiment, where the food was more quickly available, resulted in a more even distribution and less severe social pathology.

The dominant males were generally the least affected by these changes, although in the crowded pens, there were frequent changes of hierarchy; apart from occasionally going berserk and attacking all and sundry, their behaviour was generally appropriate. However, there were three other groups of males: a pansexual group, who retained their sexual drive without their discrimination; the somnambulists who opted out of all sexual and dominance behaviour, thereby remaining sleek but infertile; and the hyperactive, who mounted females in oestrus without any of the normal courtship and despite attack from the dominant males. The females lost their ability to build nests and would abandon their litters. As on Monkey Hill, many females died in pregnancy and most of their progeny perished. Before attributing all behavioural changes to crowding, however, one should consider the possibility that they were due to the social stresses in expanding the colony, and that if the colony were to be crowded but remain in this state for several months without further increase, behaviour would return to normal.

This explanation would also fit with the survey of Henry & Cassell (1969) into hypertension in humans; they concluded that blood pressure rises in response to social change, rather than to specific social conditions. In the wild, however, animals control the density of their populations either directly, as with the Arctic Skua which needs to present its mate with a fish before mating and is therefore prevented from breeding at times of food shortage, or indirectly by obtaining a territory sufficient to provide food for the progeny before attracting a mate, as in the grouse (Wynne-Edwards 1962). In general, however, ethological theories which explain stress at the individual level, in terms of physiological and psychological properties of the animal concerned, are not appropriate to human settlements (Choldin 1978). Combining such theories with urban spatial analysis, for instance, leads to introduction of the ecological fallacy; in that case, it is no longer possible to posit a direct connection between stress and environmental factors such as population density, though this has not uncommonly been done. Gove et al. (1979) consider that overcrowding in the micro-environment of the home is much more analogous to that found in animal studies than is high density at the macro-environmental level.

EFFECTS IN HUMANS

The effects of crowding on humans can usefully be divided into: alterations of behaviour in normal individuals during psychological experiments; effects on mortality; and effects on the prevalence of psychiatric illness. Psycho-

Table 3.1   Hypotheses supported by current research evidence

Hypothesis	Findings Supportive	Total
Small room size (high spatial density) produces a feeling of crowding, discomfort, or other negative moods/states	18	29
In brief exposures to a constant-sized area, increases in group size are associated with feelings of crowding or discomfort	6	9
In prolonged exposures to a constant-sized area, increases in group size are associated with feelings of crowding or discomfort		9
A feeling of crowding is more likely when a group works together or interacts than when members work alone	4	6
In brief exposures to high room density in same-sex groups, males react more negatively to others than in low room density, but females react more positively to other in high than low room density	9	18
A person with a history of intense or frequent social stimulation shows greater tolerance for high density than does a person with a history of relative isolation (adaptation-level effect)	4	5
Performance of complex tasks is poorer during brief exposures to high room density than to low room density	3	6
Prolonged exposure to high room density is associated with poor health	11	15
Prolonged exposure to high household density is associated with crime or aggression	4	5
Prolonged exposure to high neighbourhood density is associated with withdrawal from interaction among males	4	5

logical experiments on normal subjects to study the effect of crowding have been comprehensively reviewed by Sundstrom (1978). Table 3.1 summarises his conclusions, but does not consider data where there are less than five studies, and does not, therefore, cover studies which attempt to isolate the effects of crowding in thwarting goals, through increasing unpredictability and thereby arousal. Reference has been made earlier to the different effects that crowding has on the sexes, but this might fit with the findings of the Stirling County study (Leighton et al. 1963) that males were more vulnerable than females to the effects of living in a socially unstable community, as defined in that research (see Chapter 2). It is also clear that humans can adapt to the effects of crowding. Gruchow (1974), for example, found a correlation between the urinary excretion of VMA (vanylmandelic acid, the breakdown product of adrenalin and noradrenalin, hormones released in response to arousal or physical exertion) and the perception of crowding by the individual. However, this was only marked in subjects who had grown up in small families, and were therefore less used to crowding. D'Atri & Ostfeld (1975) found that prison inmates who were housed in a dormitory had higher blood pressures than those who were housed in one-man or two-man cells; this was confirmed by Paulus et al. (1978).

The importance of territory for man was emphasised by the classic study of Sommer & Becker (1969), who observed the manner in which students avoided intruding into the space of others when selecting their seat in a library. They also showed that personal belongings had a similar, though less severe effect on the use of the surrounding space than another individual. A long experience of crowding, though it makes crowding more tolerable, has a less beneficial effect on behaviour; Rodin (1976) showed that children from crowded environments were less willing to exert choice and scored less well on a soluble task after being exposed to an insoluble one. This suggested that they were more easily discouraged, and she concludes that children from overcrowded homes are less persistent, and adopt an attitude of relative helplessness, which in turn might lead to a greater vulnerability to depression. Murray (1974), in a sophisticated study on the effect of crowding in the home, found that children from crowded homes were more aggressive and impulsive, boys being more neurotic and girls less. The most sensitive demographic measure was the Family Interaction Density Index, which divides the floor area into a number of possible pair relationships (Bossard 1960).

One of the more imaginative studies on the physiological effects of crowding was by Middlemist et al. (1976), who observed the delay in passing urine by an unsuspecting subject in a three-man urinal, under varying conditions. These were when alone, when separated from the stooge by the middle urinal, and when next to the stooge with the far urinal 'out of order'. The results were in the expected direction, increasing proximity leading to increasing delay. Stark (1973) studied behaviour in supermarkets, finding that the behavioural norms of shoppers changed, according to whether conditions were quiet, crowded, or intermediate; increased crowding led to greater abandonment of acceptable standards of good behaviour. Similarly, a prison study showed that overcrowding resulted in more negative responses to the physical environment and tended to be followed by destruction of property (Paulus et al. 1975). A further study (Paulus et al. 1978) found that rates of death and psychiatric commitment increased with population density, as did blood pressure and complaints of crowding in more crowded areas. The lack of choice, potential hostility of others, and degree of physical proximity here might be seen as approaching the conditions of some animal studies. Its findings were interpreted as showing that long-term, intense, inescapable crowding can produce high levels of stress, which can lead to physical and psychological impairment. The number of individuals in a housing unit, stability of population, possibilities of privacy, etc., would probably all be involved in producing these effects.

Although not directly related to mental health, some of the most reliable data are those of mortality, but as death is a relatively rare event (compared with, for example, the rate of medical consultation) one must sample a very large population, or a smaller population over a long time to provide valid conclusions about the effects of crowding. However, the use of a large unit for the analysis leaves the possibility that an association with crowding is erroneous, in that the individuals who die may be atypical for the district. Many other pathogenic factors are often associated with crowding, but cultural and possibly genetic factors tend to modify the stress induced in a population from this source. The respect for privacy shown by the Chinese in Hong Kong tends to minimise crowding effects, whilst the gregariousness of Egyptians might be expected to exaggerate them (Hall 1966). Under these circumstances, one should not be surprised that international comparisons fail to show any relationship of mortality to either crowding or density; this applies both to mortality as a whole and to that from individual diseases (Factor & Waldron 1973; Giel & Ormel 1977).

Galle et al. (1972) examined the relationship between mortality and various measures of density for census tracts in Chicago; they attempted to disentangle the effects of social class, ethnicity, and of a combined index of crowding based on four measures (persons per room, rooms per dwelling unit, dwelling units per structure, and structures per acre). They were unable to decide which was the most lethal variable, but persons per room accounted for 60 per cent of the variance in mortality ratios and correlated best with such measures of social pathology as juvenile delinquency and people receiving public assistance; mental hospitalisation rates correlated best with rooms per housing unit, ie. the rates were high where many people were living alone. However, Freedman et al. (1975) state that this study used highly questionable techniques, combining the measures in different ways for each analysis, but that even if the findings are accepted at face value, density — however measured — explains only a small amount of the variance beyond that accounted for by income and race.

Unlike Chicago, density in Holland (measured by population per acre) and crowding (persons per room) are inversely related, density being positively correlated with income per head, due to the tendency of wealthy Dutch to live in flats. Levy & Herzog (1974), using as their units the 125 economic/geographical regions of Holland, found that total mortality, and male deaths from heart disease (both age-adjusted) bore a significant relationship to density, even when they controlled for the effects of crowding and economic status. In Rotterdam, however, a relationship was found between death rates and crowding, 1 per cent increase in persons per room producing 1.2 per cent increase in death rates (Herzog et al. 1977); the discrepancy between these findings and those of Giel & Ormel (1977) in a random sample of the Dutch population may be because the former relate to a central city area. Schmitt (1966) found that density was the most important variable to be related to mortality in the city of Honolulu; however, he had previously shown (1963) that in Hong Kong, though measures of density and crowding were extremely high, so was the expectation of life.

Studies in London

On the other hand Kellett (in preparation), using as his unit the 33 London Boroughs and cumulative mortality from 1969 to 1973 inclusive, had sufficient numbers to relate the demographic indices not only to overall mortality in males and females aged 15–54 and 54–64, but also to specific causes in those groups. The results of this study, some of which are displayed in Tables 3.2 and 3.3, showed that overall mortality was closely related to crowding, as measured by people per room, and to a lesser extent to density (people per hectare), especially for the older age groups. In the latter, this correlation remained significant at the .0001 level, even when controlling

Table 3.2 Correlations of mortality (by London boroughs) with indices of crowding and density (controlled for social class). Male

	Age	Pop/room	Pop/hect	N
Total	15–54	.37	.16	24,123
	55–64	.64	.47	44,933
Cancer – large intestine	15–54	(−.22)	−.41	359
– pancreas	55–64	.38	.21	689
– lung	15–64	.27	.36	2,093
	55–64	.43	.58	7,095
Rheumatic heart disease	15–54	.36	.28	517
	55–64	.31	.30	581
Hypertension	55–64	(.25)	.35	719
Acute myocardial infarction	55–64	.45	.43	12,850
CVA	15–54	.51	.38	1,269
Venous thrombosis & embolism	55–64	.44	.46	403
Pneumonia	55–64	.31	.11	1,307
Bronchial asthma	15–54	.31	(.08)	847
	55–64	.74	.63	3,139
Chronic bronchitis	55–64	.76	.61	2,805
Motor vehicle accidents	15–54	−.34	−.31[a]	1,427
Poisoning	15–54	.80	.71	307
Suicide	15–54	.64	.78	1,336

Not reaching significance:

Cancer stomach (15–54) (55–64), large intestine (15–54), prostate (55–64), bladder (55–64); hypertension (15–54); acute myocardial infarction (15–54); chronic ischaemic heart disease (15–54) (55–64); CVA (55–64); subarachnoid haemorrhage (15–54) (55–64); pneumonia (55–54; chronic bronchitis (15–54); motor vehicle accidents (55–64); suicide (55–64)

N.b. Diseases whose mortality was less than 300 were excluded from this analysis

19/36 possible correlations significant at <.05 or more

Levels of significance: r = >.30   p <.05
                              r = >.40   p <.01
                              r = >.50   p <.001

Table 3.3 Correlations of mortality (by London boroughs) with indices of crowding and density (controlled for social class). Female

	Age	Pop/Room	Pop/Hct.	N
Total	15–54	Not significant		16,600
	55–64	.74	.70	24,172
Cancer – lung	55–64	.56	.58	
– cervix	15–54	.52	.50	624
	55–64	.44	.57	709
– ovary	15–54	.39	−.45	700
Ischaemic heart disease	55–64	.32	(.25)	4,007
Acute myocardial infarction	15–54	.35	(.03)	983
	55–64	.49	.41	3,306
Venous thrombosis & embolism	55–64	(.20)	.38	342
Bronchitis & asthma	55–64	.43	(.28)	798
Bronchitis	55–64	.40	(.21)	616
Motor vehicle accidents	15–54	(.15)	.37	497
Poisoning	15–54	.70	.70	1,390
	55–64	.34	.53	541
Suicide	15–54	.54	.76	
				951
	55–64	(.10)	.30	

Not reaching significance:

Cancer stomach (55–64), rectum (55–64), breast (15–54) (55–64), pancreas (55–64), ovary (55–64); hypertension (55–64); chronic ischaemic heart disease (55–64); strokes (15–54) (55–64); subarachnoid haemorrhage (15–54) (55–64)

16/30 possible correlations were significant at the <.05 level or more

N.B. Diseases whose mortality were under 300 were excluded from this analysis.

Levels of significance: $r = >.30$ $p = >.05$
                              $r = >.40$ $p = >.01$
                              $r = >.50$ $p = >.001$

for the effects of social class (male $r = .73$ [.64 controlling for social class], females $r = .82$ [.74]). In London, although the indices of crowding and density correlated closely, $(r = .79)$ there was less relation to social class $(r -.59$ and $-.23$ respectively). Cancers, apart from lung and cervix, generally showed little correlation with these indices, and cancer of the large intestine in males and ovary in females seemed more common in less crowded boroughs. This contrasted strongly with vascular and respiratory diseases, which were closely correlated with crowding, and violent deaths, which though correlated with crowding, seemed to relate more to density in females.

Whilst data for total mortality by residence in a London borough are likely to be accurate, the accuracy of death certification is open to doubt (Royal College of Physicians 1978). However, this inaccuracy is only apparent when diseases are broken down into small categories; in the broad categories used in this analysis, they are likely to be correct. Whilst the association of mortality with crowding or density is probably a direct result of the social stresses caused by these social conditions — especially when these associations are controlled for the effects of social class — there remains a possibility that crowding is associated with a more obviously lethal influence, such as smoking or softness of water. Though smoking habits appeared to be evenly distributed in London and across the classes (Tobacco Manufacturers Standard Committee 1967), there were no data giving the prevalence of smoking by borough. Similarly, climate and water supply, though not identical for each London borough, are broadly similar.

MORBIDITY AND ENVIRONMENT

Morbidity is yet more difficult to define and measure than mortality, and if measured by rates of consultation, is likely to reflect factors unrelated to the severity of the disease, such as cultural concern with illness, hypochondriasis, proximity to the surgery, and trust in and approval of the doctor concerned. Furthermore, the finding of a correlation between morbidity and housing conditions leaves the possibility that the chronic illness has led the individual to accept a lower standard of housing, which becomes the result rather than the cause of illness. Two investigations have, in fact, succeeded in escaping these strictures, in that the allocation of housing was truly random, and the same practice served both types of housing and was equidistant from them. Fanning (1967) compared the rates of attendance at a GP surgery during a ten-week period for 558 service families, comprising 1163 women and children living in three- to four-storey blocks of flats, and 445 in terrace houses of the same age and standard. Expressed as rates of first attendance per 1000 people at risk, there were 599 from the flat dwellers and 382 from the terrace dwellers. This difference was reflected in all the diagnostic categories except diseases of the musculoskeletal system (including back strain), which were more common in the terrace dwellers. Much the commonest conditions were diseases of the respiratory system, comprising one-third of all consultations, but these and diseases of the endocrine, metabolic, nervous and genito-urinary systems, as well as allergies, were all more than twice as common in the flat dwellers. Psychiatric disorders were also twice as common in the flat dwellers, but comprised only 42 of the 696 first attendances, suggesting that they may have been subsumed under other categories. Fanning also noted that the rate of consultation for non-medical reasons, e.g. immunisation and witnessing documents, were equal in the two groups, suggesting that differences between flat and terrace dwellers were not due to ease of consultation.

A similar study was performed by Moore (1974) which, though coming to a negative conclusion, actually supports the findings of Fanning. Comparing flat and house dwellers, 12 per cent of the flat dwellers were psychiatric cases (by scoring 50 or more on the questionnaire of the Cornell Medical Index), compared with 7 per cent of the house dwellers. Using attendance at the GP, and controlling for length of residence, rank, age, and size of family (which might well remove the effect of crowding), the figures were 23 per cent for flat dwellers and 17 per cent for house dwellers, but the sample size became too small to achieve statistical significance. Moore (1976) did, however, find significant differences in case numbers between those scoring high on neuroticism living in flats and similar subjects in houses, suggesting that it is only those who have high emotional liability who are likely to suffer from the flat environment.

In another study of the same sample (1975), Moore found that flat dwellers were significantly less content with their housing, had an inferior social life within their housing, and made fewer visits out of the flat. Bearing in mind that these conclusions came from low-rise blocks, they reinforce the findings of Fanning, who suggested that a neutral territory, such as a garden, provided an essential component in making friends and continuing social communication. These studies are also discussed in Chapter 7.

Rates of consultation for physical illness as a measure of morbidity in the community are open to question, although there is no *a priori* reason why house dwellers should be more reluctant to attend a doctor. Psychiatric illness, on the other hand, may well not only reduce insight, such that the illness is unrecognised by the sufferer, but may produce so profound a pessimism that the idea of a remedy seems beyond belief: Brown et al. (1977) have demonstrated the frequency of unrecognised 'endogenous' depression in women who had not seen a psychiatrist. Even more erroneous are estimates based on rates of psychiatric referral and of admission to mental hospital. Referral to a psychiatrist is more likely if one is young and of higher social class, whilst in-patient admission tends to occur if one is socially isolated, poor, and female. Bearing these strictures in mind, the earliest studies were all based on rates of admission to mental hospitals, a measure which may be more valid if restricted to serious psychotic illnesses like schizophrenia.

The effects of environment on mental health have been reviewed by Freeman (1978) and Kirmeyer (1978). The original classic study was that by Faris & Dunham (1939) who found an excess of admissions for schizophrenia from the central areas of Chicago, which had a high proportion of rented lodgings, high density, and often a high degree of crowding. Hare (1956) confirmed these findings in Bristol, but concluded that the prodromal symptoms of the illness often caused the patient to seek the anonymity of the behavioural sink in the centre of the city, where social isolation might then make the condition worse (see Chapter 14).

Dohrenwend (1975), on the other hand, argues that the high rates of mental illness in New York blacks are more easily explained by a response to their poor social conditions than by genetics or drift. Assuming that they are not genetically more loaded for schizophrenia, which is unlikely in view of the relatively low prevalence of this condition in their countries of racial origin (Jablensky & Sartorius 1975), the drift hypothesis would predict a higher rate in whites, who typically migrate into the city centre as they fall ill. Blacks, forced by discrimination in job opportunities to share the same poverty, are found to be equally vulnerable to schizophrenia, but this conclusion must be tempered by the knowledge that schizophrenia may be over-diagnosed by psychiatrists unfamiliar with black culture, and that blacks might be more readily admitted to hospital when they become ill (see also Chapter 5).

CROWDING AND PSYCHIATRIC DISORDER

Before considering the evidence relating crowding to psychiatric illness as a whole, it may be interesting to consider whether schizophrenia is partic-ularly likely to be induced by excessive social interaction (Brown & Birley 1968). Certainly, relapse in schizophrenia is more likely if the subject is exposed to a high degree of expressed emotion in the home, and is least if he is relatively isolated from this kind of influence. Paykel (1974), comparing the type of life events before depression or schizophrenia, found that the former was most frequently precipitated by loss of a relationship ('exit events'), whereas the latter showed more sensitivity to the effects of a new person on the scene. The possible difference between the effects of crowding on schizophrenia and depression respectively has been built into a hypothesis by myself (Kellett 1973). This suggests that the personality type prone to schizophrenia evolved in a situation where territory formed an essential part of social organisation. Such an environment would be unable to sustain more than small groups of humans, and such individuals would have to cope with the stress of isolation. The cyclothymic personality, on the other hand, would be likely to evolve in a rich environment, where people congregated in larger numbers. In this sort of environment, the social order would be maintained more through the effects of hierarchy formation, and affective disorder could be seen as a means of stabilising this hierarchy (a fall in the hierarchy causes depression and thereby stops the individual from trying to regain his position, whilst hypomania enables the victor quickly to establish an unassailable status).

   This hypothesis cannot explain the disastrous effects of schizophrenia on the organism, but could explain why the personality traits which are associ-ated with this condition were originally selected. If indeed schizophrenia could be shown to be due initially to a viral infection, as some evidence has suggested (Crow et al. 1979), one might expect that such constitutions, being adapted to isolation, would be more susceptible to diseases trans-mitted by droplet infection, which are sustained by large groups of humans living in close proximity. There is some support for this view in the study by Machon et al. (1983).

   Also, as applied to affective disorders, this hypothesis does not explain the relatively high prevalence of depression in females, and its explanation might be better restricted to bipolar disorder, where the incidence in males and females appears to be equal. Unipolar depression could perhaps then be seen as a response to starvation, the male reacting by becoming more active as he seeks food for his family (in modern civilisation, this activity would present as anxiety, and perhaps result in seeking solace in alcohol), whilst the female would preserve her energy, reducing her physical activity to a minimum. Such a constellation might explain the genetic group delineated by Winokur (1972) as depression spectrum disease. The original hypothesis was that communal life would exaggerate sexual differences by allowing the luxury of specialisation and increasing the pressures on sexual selection. However, a prediction from this — that sexual dimorphism would be greater in humans adapted to communal living, has not been supported. In this study, (Kellett, unpublished) women between the ages of 15 and 30 were somatotyped and in addition, measures of bust size taken. These measures were compared to measures of personality, based on the Eysenck Personality Questionnaire and and the schizoid scale of the MMPI. No significant associations between physical measures distinguishing male and female were found to be associated with these personality measures, although it may be argued that relationships between personalities and somatotypes of females have always been much less impressive than those recorded for males.

Certainly, marked differences remain between the social structure of institutionalised schizophrenics and that of people with normal personality. Kellett & Rowe (unpublished data) compared the behaviour of long-stay schizophrenics in a mental hospital with patients institutionalised for physical injuries in a hospital for ex-soldiers. Many schizophrenics were ignorant of even the name of the patient who had slept in the next bed for the last 10 years. The physically disabled, on the other hand, knew every detail of the lives of their companions, and maintained a lively interest in their visitors, hobbies, and communal activities. Lack of privacy in these open wards was compensated for by the genuine interest of the physically disabled in each other, compared to the indifference which greeted the suicide of a patient in the ward for schizophrenics.

Demographic studies relating to psychotic disorder include that of Galle et al. (1972), who found that admissions to mental hospital in Chicago correlated better with indices of crowding than with those of density, though class and race seemed more important variables than either; this has been referred to above. Bagley et al. (1973) used rates of both in-patient stay and out-patient attendance to assess the incidence and prevalence of psychiatric illness in the 19 electoral wards of Brighton. Psychiatric illness in general correlated with a wide variety of social variables, of which the strongest was the percentage of rented, furnished rooms ($r = .88$, $p < .001$); crowding — as measured by the percentage of households with more than 1.5 persons per room — also correlated ($r = .66$, $p < .01$. However, persons per room correlated most strongly with alcoholism ($r = .74$) and parasuicide ($r = .75$), though here the correlations were equally high with the proportion of single-person households, which was hardly an indication of crowding! Once again, it becomes impossible to separate the effects of one variable from another, although it is not unreasonable to postulate that areas with both overcrowded homes and single-person bedsitters are likely to contain the least well controlled social interactions (see Chapter 2).

However, not all studies show the same effects. Bloom (1968) correlated rates of admission to mental hospitals with demographic data from 33 census tracts in Pueblo, Colorado. He found that admission rates were inversely related to indices of overcrowding (persons per household and more than one person per room), but were strongly related to indices of isolation and marital disruption. These indices, though, are the ones that might be expected to be related to hospitalisation, rather than to psychiatric illness itself. Schmitt (1966) concluded, after studying the 42 census tracts of Honolulu, that density was more important than crowding for all the pathological variables (mortality ratio, infant death, TB, VD, illegitimate births, juvenile delinquency, imprisonment, as rates of admission to mental hospital) except suicides. Possibly, intakes of crowding Rove more effect in temperate climates, where most time is spent indoors, whilst density would have more effect in warmer climes. Freedman et al. (1971), however, criticised this study on the grounds that the controls used for education and income were such as to minimise their effect, so that the remaining relationships between density and pathology were considered to be highly suspect.

One step away from hospital admission statistics are case registers, which record all patients coming into contact with psychiatric services in a particular area. Although little differential effect of crowding has been shown by the Camberwell register, possibly because the wards within the borough show few differences in levels of overcrowding (Hurrey, personal communication), the Aberdeen register covers both an area of urban population and a highly dispersed rural population in the North-East of Scotland. Bain (1974) found that rates of psychiatric referral were higher in Aberdeen than in the other urban areas, and 77 per cent higher than in the rural areas. However, within the small burghs, referral rates did not relate to levels of crowding, although such a relationship did apply in the case of the rural areas and coastal burghs, and in Aberdeen itself.

Unfortunately, most surveys of psychiatric illness have either failed to use sophisticated methods of case identification or have not tried to record crowding and density. On the other hand, the relationship between expressed levels of satisfaction and the environment depends to some extent on the values expressed by society as a whole. Thus, an early study on the effects of high-rise housing in Baltimore (Wilner et al. 1962) came out with results diametrically opposed to a more recent one in Oldham, an industrial town in the North-West of England, which showed that householders nearly all preferred a house to a flat (Department of the Environment 1970). The

Baltimore investigators compared levels of psychological health in families that had been rehoused in high-rise flats with those of similar housing priority who remained in their old terraced housing. The high-rise dwellers were significantly more optimistic about the future and satisfied with the present than either themselves before the move or the controls. A new flat, in what was then considered prestigious architecture, not surprisingly rated higher than the previous slum, but later studies are less sanguine about the effects of high-rise housing. As with the Hawthorn effect, innovation will usually meet with approval, but the proof of architecture is in its occupation for more than 20 years. High-rise blocks may now be in their nadir, though, and could perhaps rate more highly with their residents in a few years' time, particularly if these residents are selected differently from the earlier ones (see Chapter 7).

Hare & Shaw (1965) found that family size was crucial in determining the 'expressed satisfaction' of female adults about the home, while adult males had more opportunity to escape the confusion of the house. Baldessare (1979) suggests that crowding is only likely to affect the health of those such as children, mothers of young families, and the elderly, who are unable to find ways of alleviating the stress. He was not surprised to find little relationship between levels of satisfaction and crowding in large surveys of individuals in the United States. However, he did record that high densities were associated with depression and loneliness in the elderly and with dissatisfaction in the middle-aged; power was regarded as the key variable in relation to crowding within the home. Similarly, Gillis (1977) showed that only females were distressed by increasing height from the ground in high-rise housing.

Gove et al. (1979) interviewed people, selected to minimise any correlation of socio-economic status and persons per room, from each of 80 census tracts of Chicago. They found that the number of persons per room correlated significantly with levels of psychiatric symptoms, 'alienation', irritability, and rates of nervous breakdown in the preceding year, and negatively with happiness, self-esteem, positive effect, and mental health balance. These relationships remained significant when the effects of sex, race, marital status, education, age, and family income were controlled; and the effects of room crowding were linear, i.e. not primarily due to extreme reactions at very high levels. Furthermore, 61 per cent of the variance of nervous breakdowns could be explained by the effects of crowding, while more of the variance of nervous breakdown, happiness, and irritability was explained by the crowding variables than by the others. Similarly, the crowding variables (persons per room, felt demands, and lack of privacy) accounted for more than 60 per cent of the variance in marital relations, closeness to spouse, and getting along with other people, though other demographic variables accounted for more of the variance in frequency of arguments. Thus, crowding showed a relationship to poorer marriage, and was also important in determining lack of sleep and dissatisfaction with child care. This important study largely succeeded in separating the effects of crowding from those of other factors, and concluded that the influence of objective crowding, as measured by persons per room, is largely mediated by a feeling of excessive social demands and of lack of privacy. Since room crowding was shown to have substantial effects, particularly on mental health, Gove et al. proposed that research should now be directed towards factors which may alter its effects, e.g. though norms of privacy vary, effects of household composition, and the interaction of household crowding with the macro-environment.

Taylor & Chave (1974) investigated the suggestion of 'New Town Blues', a concept which would detract from crowding theory, by comparing the prevalence of psychiatric illness in a suburban estate, a new town, and an old London borough. Far from confirming this hypothesis, they found higher rates in the inner borough. Surprisingly, the prevalence of neurosis was similar in all three environments, but psychosis less frequent in the new town, and they concluded that 'good social planning . . . may be expected to reduce the incidence both of the psychoses and the environmental neuroses but increase somewhat the incidence of mixed neuroses'. They attributed the rise in recorded mixed neurotic states to the ease with which medical attention and support could be obtained in the new town, and thus saw them as being largely iatrogenic. Unfortunately, like most of the more sophisticated community studies of psychiatric illness, this one included no direct measures of crowding. The same applies to the Stirling County study (Leighton et al. 1963) and to the Midtown Manhattan study (Rennie et al. 1957). Taylor & Chave also seem to have failed to appreciate that a new town population, consisting almost entirely of young married adults and children, would be likely to show a low rate of psychosis; the longer they remained there, however, the more this population would approximate to the average in this respect (see Chapter 7).

Baldessare (1979) has suggested that children would be more vulnerable than adults to the effects of crowding, and this is supported by studies showing a strong relationship between large family size on the one hand and delinquency, low verbal IQ, and poor reading skills on the other (Clausen 1966; Douglas 1968). Rutter et al. (1975), comparing the incidence of psychiatric disorder in the Isle of Wight and in the London Borough of Camberwell, estimated that 12 per cent of 10 year-olds had disorder of this kind in the Isle of Wight, compared with 25 per cent in Camberwell. This excess could not be explained by drift, since disorder was as frequent in the families of parents born and bred in Camberwell as in immigrants, but clearly, there are many differences between these two environments which might account for it. However, looking first at factors which relate to variation within each environment, marital discord and malaise of the mother were important in this respect. Of the demographic factors, large families and crowding seemed particularly important in the Isle of Wight, and social class in Camberwell. Rutter et al. suggest that a large family leads to delayed language development, through lack of verbal stimulation by adults, and quote from their earlier Isle of Wight study where, in families of six or more, 27 per cent of fathers had not spoken to each child as often as once a week (compared to 14 per cent in smaller families) and for mothers the figures were 10 per cent and 2 per cent respectively. Poor language development tends to lead to delayed reading, dissatisfaction at school, truancy, and finally delinquency. This family size effect also applies at the upper end of the educational scale; Poole & Kuhn (1973) showed that amongst university students, first and second class degrees were significantly more frequent amongst first-born children.

Although a survey of the type carried out by Rutter appears to provide a reasonably accurate measure of the prevalence of psychiatric illness in a particular population group, there are also indirect measures. Webb & Collette (1975), for example, looked at the prescription of psychotropic drugs in 45 urban areas of New Zealand and found — contrary to prediction — that though crowding provided the best predictor of drug use, this was in the opposite to the expected direction, i.e. the more crowded the area, the lower the amounts of psychotropic drugs prescribed. The authors attribute this finding to an association between drug taking and single-person households. There remains the possibility that ethical drugs are taken more in that situation and social drugs in the crowded environments, but nevertheless, this negative result does emphasise the danger of assuming a simple relationship between crowding and psychiatric illness (see Chapter 8).

Another indirect measure of such illness is the rate of suicide. Although this is an all-or-none event, and so might be expected to be a reliable statistic, there is a wide variation in the willingness of coroners to pass the verdict, especially where any element of doubt exists. Furthermore, one may question whether suicide is primarily a measure of psychiatric illness, or rather an indication of cultural attitudes to this means of escape. The same uncertainties attach to figures for parasuicides, many of whom never reach a doctor, and therefore go unrecorded. Sainsbury (1955), in his classic study of suicide in London, found no relationship of rates of suicide to crowding, but did find a relationship to other indices of social pathology, such as rates of divorce. Others, like Stengel (1964) have implicated urban-isation and social isolation; he maintained that homicide increases with urbanisation, the isolated killing themselves, the crowded others.

Studying 216 consecutive suicides in Edinburgh, McCulloch et al. (1967) found that crowding and a previous history of self-poisoning or injury were the two most powerful ecological correlates, the former correlating ($r = .73$, $p < .001$) with the rates of suicide in different kinds of accommodation. They suggest that suicide rates are high in the single elderly, living in old tenement blocks and in the young living in council accommodation, where there are high levels of juvenile delinquency and social breakdown. This latter crowded environment also produced large numbers of attempted suicides (McCulloch & Phillip 1971). Bagley et al. (1973) also found that rates of suicide in Brighton correlated significantly with crowding (r = .58), as did parasuicide (r = .75), although the strongest correlations of crowding were with the number of psychiatric cases (r = .82), rates of alcoholism and personality disorder (r = .89), and proportion of dwellings which were furnished rooms (r = .89). In a later paper (1976), Bagley et al. distinguished three groups — older middle-aged with physical illness, young sociopathic, and a chronically depressed group characterised by isolation, only the latter being associated with residence in the crowded wards of the town (see Chapter 6).

In my study of London boroughs, there were few significant correlates for the older groups, aged 55–64, but as can be seen from Table 3.4, rates of suicide in younger groups are closely related to such indices of social disintegration as divorce, furnished accommodation, unmarried women, population density, indictable offences, and assaults. The index of crowding, on the other hand, showed little such correlation (.45 for younger males, .19 for younger females). The figures thus mirrored the findings of Sainsbury twenty years earlier. Although these results confirm the importance of isolation in producing suicide, it is likely that it is only when psychiatric disturbance and isolation come together that suicide is successful, and that psychiatric illness in crowded conditions is more likely to be dealt with by other means.

Table 3.4 Correlations with rates of suicide

Males aet 15–54		Females aet 15–54	
Divorce rate	.82	Divorce rate	.85
% rented furnished	.79	% rented furnished	.81
% unmarried women	.76	indictable offences	.74
population per hectare	.72	population per hectare	.61
indictable offences	.68	% unmarried women	.54
car ownership	−.66	assaults	.54
assaults	.64		

All correlations above .5 significant at the .001 level

CONCLUSION

The maintenance of personal space depends not only on the extent of crowding, but on the space required per person, the social skills of the individual, the use of markers and barriers which help to maintain the integrity of boundaries, and on the nature of the personalities involved. Demographic indices are an inexact measure of such events since, for instance, the effects of the proximity of friends is very different from that of strangers (Fisher 1974). One of the effects of crowding is to increase the unpredictability of one's world.

Like all social animals, man is particularly sensitive to the behaviour of his own species. As a result, crowding can only be tolerated in one of two ways — either the individual opts out of human contact, becoming impervious to the behaviour of others, or society imposes rules on its subjects to control that interaction. The more the crowding, the more rigid become these rules, as the risk of anarchy increases. The stress arising from the restriction of choice is increased by formal demands, whose origin and purpose may become unclear, while unwritten taboos arise to further constrain behaviour.

Ashmore & McConahay (1975) propose that an important aspect of these matters is perceived personal control; the cost of adjustment to noise is lower when the individual perceives that he can control it, (Glass & Singer 1972) and Milgram's analysis (1970) suggested that the diminished social responsibility, etc., of urban dwellers resulted from attempts to exert control over social overload. The possibility of privacy or escape which is provided by an uncrowded home, even in densely populated areas, may be what accounts for the differential effects of crowding and density on people; therefore, social and political institutions ought to be developed which will allow individuals to control those aspects of the urban environment over which they have no control at present unless they are very rich or can exercise the option of leaving altogether.

Personal space is not identical to territory; it will vary in size according to the circumstances. Enduring relationships will require more definite formulation of space than casual ones (Rosenblatt & Budd 1970), while males and those with aggressive or introverted personalities will require more space than others. Transient crowding can be tolerated or even enjoyed (e.g. pop festivals and football matches), but continuous exposure is damaging. Life events, as described by Rahe & Homes (1967), by Brown & Birley (1968), and by Paykel et al. (1969) are closely related to the onset of psychiatric illness, and are likely to be increased by crowding. However, the use of demographic data to test the effect of crowding cannot take full account of the actual experience. The number of persons per room reveals nothing of the size of the room, the presence of territorial boundaries within it, the size of the household (possible interactions increase almost exponentially with that figure), the nature of the individuals, the opportunities for escape, or the surrounding environment. Under these circumstances, it is likely that many features of the environment conspire together to increase the effect of crowding, and attempts to isolate that effect by controlling for the influence of other factors seem doomed to failure. Thus Booth & Cowell (1976), after scrupulously controlling not only for economic variables, but also for the other three of their four indices of crowding, conclude that crowding has little effect on health; however, they did find that a subjective experience of being crowded correlated with a lower blood pressure, when controlling for the objective measures of crowding — a finding contrary to the prison studies mentioned earlier. Before concluding that crowding is a remedy for hypertension, though, one should consider the possibility that when actual levels of crowding are held constant, the subjective experience is likely to be felt most by the schizoid personality, which is well known to relate to an asthenic physique and to be less likely to develop hypertension than his pyknic cousin. Drawbacks of these Toronto studies have been refered to in Chapter 2.

Clearly, one cannot assume that a correlation between crowding and physical or psychiatric illness indicates a causal effect. Crowded populations are often disadvantaged in other ways, and may attract those who in themselves are more vulnerable to psychiatric illness. Nevertheless, most studies have attempted to control for socio-economic factors, and the service samples reported by Fanning (1967) and Moore (1974) cannot be interpreted in terms of the drift hypothesis.

Both human beings and their social structures are amazingly adaptable. Exposed to high levels of crowding, a society may degenerate into anarchy, or may retain its social order by the imposition of a strict hierarchy, Japan being an example of the latter. Reference was made earlier to the Chinese in Hong Kong who have evolved rigid rules of courtesy, placing special emphasis on the preservation of personal space; they are thus spared many of the consequences of disordered interaction (Schmitt 1963). Even here, however, emotional disturbance occurs when crowding forces contact with non-family members, or where escape from the crowding is prevented (Mitchell 1971). Similarly, the repression of many South American regimes might be related to a rate of population growth of over three per cent per annum, with massive migration to the cities.

One should not be surprised that adaptation to urban life exacts a cost. *Homo sapiens* first emerged half a million years ago, while his hominid precursors like *Australopithecus* were present five million years ago. The social and technological developments that have taken place over the last ten thousand years, since the change from hunter gatherer to farmer, have been possible largely as a result of the cultural learning of the human, as against the rigid genetic programming found in birds. Genetically, man is almost identical to the savage in the savannah, ten thousand years before the birth of Christ. Our genetic programmes were formed to suit a hunter-gatherer life style, very different from that of a city commuter (see Chapter 1).

Hunter-gatherers generally lived in small bands of around 25–50 people, limiting births to make sure that the last child was mobile before the mother could cope with another. Within this extended family would be the immediate family of about ten members, and beyond this group, the tribe of about 300. Each group would differ in their spatial arrangements; the immediate family would enjoy the intimate space described by Hall, where touch and smell would predominate. The extended family could not enter intimate space, nor the tribe into personal space, except on special occadions, such as a tribal dance. Similarly, the immediate family would maintain few secrets from one another, the extended family would all be familiar and known by name, whilst the tribe would share facial recognition. Anthropological evidence for different dimensions of territory has been referred to earlier. The ! Kung bushmen choose to site their camp in such a way that the 30 to 40 in the group are forced to sit touching one another (Draper 1973), so that such apparent crowding must be more a comfort than a stress. In the modern city, on the other hand, man is expected to relate to many total strangers, who may be invading his territory and threatening his dominance there.

It is no coincidence that private housing schemes seek to create the village in the town, i.e. groups of houses containing the number of people similar to that of a primitive tribe, whilst municipal housing schemes seem more concerned to celebrate the skills of the architect than the needs of those who are to live in them. Such forced interaction with strangers is very likely to lead to a distortion of social responses and to attempts to avoid physical and emotional contact (Milgram 1970). Man is not, however, at the mercy of his environment. His urban surroundings are largely of his own making, and instead of seeing expenditure on urban design as competing for money with health services, it would be more sensible to see this as a part of preventive medicine. It is far too precious a commodity to leave in the hands of 'experts', even if they were expects in human behaviour, rather than in housing sculpture. Humans differ not only in earning power, but in styles of life, so that the ideal city would be one of small housing schemes, differing widely one from another, and allowing each family to choose its tribe. Monkey Hill must never find a counterpart in the human city.

REFERENCES

Argyle M, Dean J 1965 Eye contact, distance and affiliation. Sociometry 28: 289–304
Ashmore R D, McConahay J B 1975 Psychology and America's urban dilemmas. McGraw Hill, New York.
Bagley C, Jacobson S, Palmer C 1973 Social structure and the ecological distribution of mental illness, suicide and delinquency. Psychological Medicine 3: 177–187
Bagley C, Jacobson S, Palmer C 1976 Ecological variation of three types of suicide. Psychological Medicine 6: 423–427
Bain S M 1974 A geographer's approach in the epidemiology of psychiatric disorders. Journal of Biosocial Science 6: 195–220
Baldessare M 1979 Residential Crowding in Urban America. University of California Press
Baron R A 1977 Human aggression: perspectives in social psychology. Plenum, New York
Bloom B L 1968 Ecological analysis in psychiatric hospitalisations. Multibehavioural Research 43: 423–463
Booth A, Cowell J 1976 Crowding and health. Journal of Health and Social Behaviour 17: 204–220
Bossard J H, Ball E S 1960 The sociology of child development, 3rd edn. Harper, New York
Brown G, Harris T, Copeland J 1977 Depression and loss. British Journal of Psychiatry 130: 1–8
Brown G W, Birley J L T 1968 Crises and life changes and the onset of schizophrenia. Journal of Health and Social Behaviour 9:·203–214

Calhoun J B 1962 Population density and social pathology. Scientific American 206: 139–148
Choldin H M 1978 Urban density and pathology. Annual Review of Sociology 4: 91–113
Christian J J 1964 Physiological and pathological correlates of population density. Proceedings of the Royal Society of Medicine 57: 169–174
Clausen J A 1966 Family structure, socialisation and personality. In: Hoffman L W, Hoffman M L (Eds) Review of clinical development research Vol. 2. Russell Sage Foundation, New York
Cluff G C 1971 Behavioural responses of Norwegian lemmings to crowding. Bulletin of Ecological Society of America 52: 38–42
Cook M 1970 Experiments on orientation and proxemics. Human Relations 23: 61–76
Cozby F 1973 Effects of density, activity and personality on environmental preferences. Journal of Research Personality 7: 45–60
Crow T J, Tyrell D A J, Parry R P, Johnstone E C, Ferrier I N 1979 Possible virus in schizophrenia and some neurological disorders. Lancet i: 839–842
D'Atri D A, Ostfeld A 1975 Crowding: its effects on the elevation of blood pressure in a prison setting. Preventive Medicine 4: 550–558
Department of Environment 1970 Living in a slum: a study of St Mary's Oldham. Design Bulletin 19: HMSO, London
Dohrenwend B P 1975 Sociocultural and social psychological factors in the genesis of mental disorder. Journal of Health and Social Behaviour 16: 365–392
Douglas J W B, Ross J M, Simpson H R 1968 Allow futures. Peter Dovies, London
Draper P 1973 Crowding among hunter gatherers: the! Kung bushmen. Science 182: 301–303
Eibl-Eibesfeldt I 1974 The myth of the aggression-free hunter and gatherer society. In: Holloway R A (ed) Primate aggression territoriality and xenophobia: a comparative perspective. Academic Press, New York
Factor R, Waldron I 1973 Contemporary population densities and human health. Nature 242: 381–384
Fanning D M 1967 Families in flats. British Medical Journal 4: 382–386
Faris R E L, Dunham H W 1939 Mental Disorders in Urban Areas. Chicago University Press, Chicago
Fisher J D 1974 Situation-specific variables as determinants of perceived environmental aesthetic quality and perceived crowdedness. Journal of Research in Personality 8: 177–188
Freedman J L 1975 Crowding and behaviour. W H Freeman, San Francisco
Freedman J L, Klevansky S, Ehrlich P R 1971 The effect of crowding on human task performance. Journal of Applied Social Psychology 1: 7–25
Freedman J L, Levy A S, Buchanan R W, Price J 1972 Crowding and human aggression. Journal of Experimental Social Psychology 8: 528–548
Freedman J L, Heshka S, Levy A 1975 Population density and pathology: is there a relationship? Journal of Experiment Social Psychology 11: 539–552
Freeman H L 1978 Mental Health and the environment. British Journal of Psychiatry 132: 113–124
Galle O, Gove W, MacPherson J 1972 Population density and pathology, what are the relationships for man? Science 176: 23–30
Giel R, Ormel J 1977 Crowding and subjective health in the Netherlands. Social Psychiatry 12: 37–42
Gillis A R 1977 High-rise housing and psychological strain. Journal of Health and Social Behaviour 18: 418–431
Glass D E, Singer J E 1972 Urban stress. Academic Press, New York
Goodall-Lawick J van 1971 Introduction of man. Collins, London
Gove W R, HughesM, Galle O R 1979 Overcrowding in the home — an empirical investigation of its possible pathological consequences. American Sociological Review 44: 59–80
Gruchow H W 1974 A study of the relationships between catecholamine production, crowding, and mortality. PhD dissertation, University of Wisconsin
Gruchow H W 1978 Too close for comfort
Hall E T 1966 The hidden dimension. Bodley Head, London
Hare E H 1956 Mental illness and social conditions in Bristol. Journal Mental Science 102: 349–357
Hare E H, Shaw G K 1965 A study in family health: (1) Health in relation to family size. British Journal of Psychiatry iii: 461–465

Henry J P, Cassell J C 1969 Psychosocial factors in essential hypertension. American Journal of Epidemiology 90: 171–200

Herzog A, Levy L, Verdonk 1977 Some ecological factors associated with health and social adaptation in the city of Rotterdam. Urban Ecology 2: 205–234

Horowitz M J, Duff D F, Stratton L O 1964 Body buffer zones. Archives of General Psychiatry 11: 651–656

Jablensky A, Sartorius N 1975 Culture and schizophrenia. Psychological Medicine 5: 113–124

Kellet J M 1973 Evolutionary theory for the dichotomy of the functional psychoses. Lancet i: 860–863

Kinzel A F 1970 Body buffer zones in violent prisoners. American Journal of Psychiatry 127: 59–64

Kirmeyer S L 1978 Urban density and pathology: A review of research. Environment and Behaviour 10: 247–269

Leighton D C, Harding J S, Macklin D B, Hughes C C, Leighton A H 1963 Psychiatric findings in the Stirling County Study. American Journal of Psychiatry 119: 1021–1026

Leutenegger W 1978 Scaling of sexual dimorphism in body size and breeding system in primates. Nature 272: 610–611

Levy L, Herzog A N 1974 Effects of population density and crowding on health and social adaptation in the Netherlands. Journal of Health and Social Behaviour 15: 228–240

Machon R A, Mednick S A, Schulsinger F 1983 The interaction of seasonality, place of birth, genetic risk and subsequent schizophrenia in a high risk sample. British Journal of Psychiatry 143: 383–388

McCulloch J W, Philip A E 1971 Acta Psychiatrica Scandinavica 43: 341–346

McCulloch J W, Philip A E, Carstairs G M 1967 The ecology of suicidal behaviour. British Journal of Psychiatry 113: 313–319

McKissock W, Fliesinger G L, Ratcliffe H L 1961 Federation Proceedings 20: 81

Middlemist R D, Knowles E S, Matter C F 1976 Personal space invasions in the lavatory: Suggestive evidence for arousal. Journal of Personal Social Psychology 33: 541–546

Milgram S 1970 The experience of living in cities. Science 167: 1461–1468

Mitchell R E 1971 Some social implications of high density. American Sociological Review 36: 18–29

Moore N C 1974 Psychiatric illness and living in flats. British Journal of Psychiatry 125: 433–516

Moore N C 1975 Social aspects of flat dwelling. Public Health Reports 89: 109–115

Moore N C 1976 The personality and mental health of flat dwellers. British Journal of Psychiatry 128: 259–261

Murray R 1974 The influence of crowding on children's behaviour. In: Canter D, Lee T R (eds) Psychology and the British environment. Architectural Press, London

Myers K, Hale C, Mykytowyez R, Hughes R 1971 The effects of varying density and space on sociality and health in animals. In: Esser A H (ed) Behaviour and environment. Plenum Press, New York

Patterson M L, Holmes D S 1966 Social interaction correlates of MMPI extroversion scale. American Psychologist 21: 724–725

Paulus P B, McCain G Cox V C 1978 Death rates, psychiatric commitments, blood pressure and environment. Journal of Applied Social Psychology 5: 91

Paulus p B, McCain G Cox V C 1978 Death rates, psychiatric commitments, blood pressure, and perceived crowding as a function of institutional crowding. Environmental Psychology and Nonverbal Behaviour 3: 107–116

Paykel E S 1974 Life stress and psychiatric disorder: application of the clinical approach. In: Dohrenwend B S, Dohrenwend B P (eds) Stressful life events, their nature and effects. John Wiley, New York

Paykel E S, Myers J K, Dienselt M N, Klerman G L, Lidenthal J J, Pepper M P 1969 Life events and depression: a controlled study. Archives of General Psychiatry 21: 753–760

Poole A, Kuhn A 1973 Family size and ordinal position — correlates of academic success. Journal of Biosocial Science 5: 51–59

Rahe R H, Holmes T H 1967 The social readjustment rating scale. Journal of Psychosomatic Research 11: 213–218

Ratcliffe H L, Snyder R L 1962 Patterns of disease controlled population and experiments design. Circulation 26: 1352–1357

Rennie T A C L, Srole L, Opler M K, Langner T S 1957 Urban life and mental health. American Journal of Psychiatry 113: 831–837

Rodin J 1976 Density, personal choice and response to controllable and uncontrollable outcomes. Journal of Experiment Social Psychology 12: 564–578

Rosenblatt P C, Budd L G 1975 Territoriality and privacy in married and unmarried cohabiting couples. Journal of Social Psychology 97: 67–76

Ross M, Layton B, Erickson B, Shopler J 1973 Affect, facial regard and reactions to crowding. Journal of Personality Social Psychology 28: 69–76

Royal College of Physicians 1978 Medical Services Group. Death certification and epidemiological research. British Medical Journal 2: 1063–1065

Russell C, Russell W M S 1968 Violence in monkeys and man. Macmillan, London

Rutter M, Tizard J, Whitmore K 1970 (eds) Education, health and behaviour. Longmans, London

Rutter M, Yule B, Quinton D, Rowlands O, Yule W, Berger M 1975 Attainment and adjustment in two geographical areas II: some factors accounting for area differences. British Journal of Psychiatry 126: 520–533

Saeger S, Mackintosh E, West S 1975 Two studies of crowding in urban public spaces. Environment Behaviour 7: 159–184

Sainsbury P 1955 Suicide in London, Chapman & Hall, London

Schmidt D E, Keating J P 1979 Human crowding and personal control: an integration of the research. Psychological Bulletin 86: 680–700

Schmitt R C 1963 Implications of density in Hong Kong. Journal of American Institute of Planners 29: 210–217

Schmitt R C 1966 Density, health and social disorganisation. Journal of American Institute of Planners 32: 38–40

Sommer R, Becker F D 1969 Territorial defence and the good neighbour. Journal of Personality and Social Psychology 11: 85–92

Southwick C H 1967 Experimental study of intra-group antagonistic behaviour in rhesus monkeys. Behaviour 28: 182–209

Stark C A 1973 The effects of crowding on one aspect of social behaviour. Journal of Behavioral Science 1: 367–368

Stengel E 1964 Suicide and attempted suicide. Penguin, London

Stokols D 1972 A social-psychological model of human crowding phenomena. Journal of American Institute of Planners 38: 72–84

Stokols D 1976 The experience of crowding in primary and secondary environments. Environment and Behaviour 8: 49–86

Stokols D, Rall M, Pinner B, Schopler J 1973 Physical, social and personal determinants of the perception of crowding. Environment and Behaviour 5: 87–115

Sundstrom E 1978 Crowding as a sequential process: review of research on the effects of population density on humans. In: Baum A, Epstein Y M (eds) Human responses to crowding. Lawrence Erlbaum, New Jersey

Taylor S, Chave S 1974 Mental health and the environment. Longman, London

Thiessen D D, Rogers D A 1961 Population density and endocrine function. Psychological Bulletin 58: 441–451

Tinbergen N 1955 The herring gull's world. Collins, London

Tobacco Manufacturers Standard Committee 1967 Todd G S (ed) Research Paper No 1, London

Vandeveer R B 1973 Privacy and the use of personal space. Unpublished dissertation, Temple University

Vessey S H 1964 Effects of grouping on levels of circulating antibodies in mice. Proceedings of the Society of Experimental Biological Medicine 115: 252–254

Webb S D, Collette J 1975 Urban ecological and household correlates of stress alleviative drug use. American Behavioural Scientist 18: 750–770

Williams J L 1971 Personal space and its relation to extroversion-introversion. Canadian Journal of Behavioural Science 3: 156–160

Wilner D M, Walkley R D, Pinkerton T C, Tayback M 1962 The housing environment and family life. Johns Hopkins Press, Baltimore

Wilson E D 1975 A new synthesis. Harvard University Press, Cambridge, Mass

Winokur S 1972 Types of depressive illness. British Journal of Psychiatry 120: 265–266

Wynne-Edwards V C 1962 Animal dispersion in relation to social behaviour. Oliver and Boyd, Edinburgh

Zuckerman Z 1932 The social life of monkeys and apes. Routledge, London

Human aggression and the physical environment

INTRODUCTION

The topic examined here is potentially enormous, and bound to prove contentious; it is also inevitable that different accounts would be generated by, for instance, a biologist or a sociologist. A distinction has been made in the analysis of human behaviour between 'emic' and 'etic' statements (Harris 1976). The first of these refers to phenomena built up out of constructs and discriminations regarded as appropriate by the actors themselves, while the second refers to phenomena regarded as appropriate by the community of scientific observers. Biologists have a tradition of etic statements, but these may not always be appropriate in man (Marsh et al. 1978).

One initial problem concerns the definition of the terms 'aggression' and 'environment'; another is that any relationship between environment and aggression is an interactive one — the environment changes behaviour and behaviour changes the real or perceived environment. Uni-directional relationships are often implied between these factors, and though it might have been appropriate to present these effects of environmental factors on the probability of humans being victims of aggressive acts, the discussion here will concentrate on the propensity to attack other individuals.

Aggression

'Aggression' is a value-laden term, employed in both popular and scientific writings; one indication of the size of the problem is the 106 definitions of aggression compiled by Van der Dennen (1980). A useful view is that of Buss (1971) — 'the attempt to deliver noxious stimuli (whether or not that attempt is successful)'. Stimuli may be physical and/or psychological and the definition implies that the attempts to deliver them are intentional (not accidental) and/or are perceived as such by the potential victim. Many workers also favour including emotional arousal as a feature of 'true' aggression, since this eliminates various forms of predatory attack from the definition. Some of the complications involved in defining an interaction as aggressive in humans (particularly the effects of perceived appropriateness, degree of harm involved, and intentionality) are detailed by Mummendey et al. (1982). They concluded that 'identical acts may be differently rated (as aggressive or non-aggressive) depending on the surrounding situational context'.

Even within 'simple' animal studies, a number of workers (notably Moyer 1968) have emphasised the non-unitary nature of harm-doing behaviours. More recently, Blanchard and Blanchard (1977) and Brain (1979a, 1981a), have argued that a major distinction should be made between essentially offensive and essentially defensive forms of attack, though these may change in the course of encounters. Brain (1979a) suggests three broad categories of animal aggression: social (competitive attack including inter-male and territorial forms of aggression); self-defensive; and parental (property defensive) forms of attack. It now seems unreasonable to extrapolate too freely between the different animal models of attack — a strategy that is certainly unreliable when dealing with diverse human situations. Humans are adept at both symbol manipulation and substitution, which gives us an enormous range of potentially aggression-provoking and aggression-inhibiting stimuli. We are also trained to accept 'appropriate' circumstances for aggressive responses, and conditioned to give a 'reasonable' response in different circumstances. Overt expressions of aggression in man are less predictable than those seen, for example, in rodents, though even these are not as fixed as was formerly believed.

There are a wide range of views, from Freud's psychoanalytical model to Bandura's learned social response view, concerning the nature and origins of aggression in man, and these have induced much variation in interpretation of the effects of the environment on behaviour (Baron 1977; Kutash et al. 1978; Van der Dennen 1980; Brain 1982). According to instinctive (Lorenz 1966) and frustrated drive (Dollard et al. 1939) views of aggression, individuals are seen as being impelled to attack by either internal forces or all-pervasive external stimuli. In contrast, the social learning view (Bandura 1973) suggests that violence occurs, at least in part, because of learned associations or expectations between aggression and environmental factors. None of these views offers a complete explanation of the genesis of behaviours that are described as aggression in humans. Any behaviour, whether we call it aggression or not, is a result of complex interplay between biological factors, situational elements, and the effects of prior experience.

'Violence' refers to physical aggression with an attached value judgement that the intensity of the response transcends any reasonable standard, but the dangers of such a term should be immediately obvious, since what is regarded as 'reasonable' varies from subject to subject and from situation to situation. Indeed, the situation is made worse by the fact that the evaluation is often made by a third party, rather than by the participants in the encounter. Also, there is something inherently artificial about considering aggression in isolation, since such activities often account for a relatively small proportion of behaviour, and all the activities of individuals should be considered to get a clear idea about behavioural change.

Classification of human aggression

Any attempted classification of harm-related behaviours in humans cannot hope to be precise, since the variety of aggressive acts available to *Homo sapiens* seems virtually limitless. Berkowitz and Frodi (1977) state that there are two major identifiable divisions of human aggression — 'intentional' (or premediated) and 'involuntary' (or impulsive) behaviour, and that involuntary components may be the general source of most excessive violence. One should note that this distinction runs counter to the device of removing non-aroused activities (such as predation) from the category of aggression in infrahuman studies. If this is done, the behaviour of psychopaths would not qualify for inclusion in the concept of aggression.

Table 4.1 The different types or categories of aggression proposed by Buss (1971)

Physical – active – direct	Punching, stabbing, or shooting another person
Physical – active –indirect	Setting a booby trap or hiring an assassin to kill someone
Physical – passive – direct	Physically preventing another person from obtaining a desired goal or performing a desired act (as in picketing, ostracising, etc.)
Physical – passive – indirect	Refusing to perform necessary tasks (e.g. refusal to move during a sit-in)
Verbal – active – direct	Insulting or derogating another person in face-to-face confrontations
Verbal – active – indirect	Spreading malicious rumours or gossip about another individual
Verbal – passive – direct	Refusing to speak to another person or answer questions
Verbal – passive – indirect	Failing to make specific verbal comments (e.g. failing to speak up in another person's defence when he or she is unfairly criticised)

It may be instructive to list some of the very diverse situations in which aggression is studied in man (Brain 1978, 1981a, b). Although the methodologies employed are often comparable in different studies (e.g. use of particular questionnaires or reliance on specific physical acts), one must be pessimistic about finding a common basis for these activities, and many of the situations studied in humans are far removed from animal examples. They include studies on:

1. Behaviour of children in pre-school play groups (Haug et al. 1982), playground interactions (Olweus 1977, 1979) and summer camps (Savin-Williams 1977). Many such studies appear concerned with the development of proposed dominance/subordination relationships and territoriality (Esser 1973a) as in primates.
2. Reactions to films (Geen & O'Neil 1969), television programmes (Tannenbaum 1973) or to written accounts differing in their 'violence content'

3. Response to hostile criticism or actions by a stooge of the experimenter, in a variety of structured situations (Frodi 1977).
4. The willingness of subjects to deliver electric shocks to another human being (Milgram 1974); this is perhaps more correctly viewed as an index of compliance to authority rather than aggression (see Chapter 11).
5. 'Natural' stressful situations, such as long-term isolation in caves (Zubeck 1973) or on the Ra raft expeditions across the Atlantic (Genoves 1977).
6. Violence on the field of play in sport (Russell 1981).
7. Violence off the field of play in sport, e.g. football hooliganism (Marsh et al. 1978)
8. War, military training, and riot situations (Bourne 1971)
9. Individuals charged with or convicted of violent crimes, including studies on factors predisposing individuals towards rape (said by Groth & Birnbaum (1979) to be 'the sexual expression of power and anger') and homicide (Lunde 1975). The distinctions between impulsive and premeditated actions, and between sexually motivated and nonsexual crime are thought by many workers to be of great importance
10. Persons exposed to real or imagined threat to their person or property (Steinmetz & Straus 1974)
11. Clinical populations suffering from overt psychiatric disorders (e.g. schizophrenia) in which hostility may be a feature (Depp 1976) or mainly somatic disorders accompanied by psychiatric changes, such as the 47 XYY syndrome (Hunter 1977) and endocrine dysfunctions (Brain 1977, 1978, 1979a)
12. Natural physiological variations which may be related to behaviour e.g. increased rates of violence amongst American youth at puberty (Earls 1978) and the premenstrual tension syndrome, with its claimed associated changes in hostility, in various groups of institutionalised women (Bardwick 1976)
13. Violence within the home; Gelles (1974) and Straus (1974) maintain that one is much more prone (at least in the United States) to suffer violence in the home than in any other location.
14. Questionnaire experiments on normal subjects (Feshbach 1979) to assess attitudes or personality.

One should note that the above categories are by no means a complete list, are not mutually exclusive, and are based on different aspects of the described category (in some, the subjects specify the category, whereas in others it is the situation itself).

There is a similarity between the above list and Durant's (1981) account of the Victorian view that 'the legacy from man's brutish past was held to be revealed in the behaviour of children, criminals, idiots, savages and rioting mobs'. Things are undoubtedly not so simple.

Environment

There are also considerable problems associated with the use of the term 'environment', which is taken by some workers to be synonymous with sociological explanations of violence; indeed, other humans are the most important environmental factors in the case of man. A complete account should include reference to interpersonal relationships (Feshbach & Fraczek 1979; Kutash et al. 1978), but this is not possible here. Environmentally orientated scientists, however, employ the term as a collective word for the extrinsic factors of the habitat that modify behaviour; that is how it is used in the present chapter. Some of these factors influence the development of systems, others change mood or physiology, (which can in turn alter responsiveness to situations), and the remainder are situational predisposers.

INTERACTIONS BETWEEN ASPECTS OF THE PHYSICAL ENVIRONMENT AND HUMAN AGGRESSION

The importance of the environment has been stressed by Kiritz & Moos (1974), who state that 'the most efficient predictor of a person's physiological behaviour in a given environment may consist of how he perceives that environment'. Of course, physiological responses may result in behavioural change (as emphasised by Freeman 1975). Figure 4.1 is intended to express some of the problems associated with attempts to relate environmental factors to human aggression. This emphasises the multiple actions of environmental factors on both physiology and behaviour, which are much influenced in our species by prior experience. An interaction involving two individuals is illustrated, though this may be varied, and the figure suggests that aggression is only a part of activity which can be classed as social behaviour. The environment may influence the body's functioning by changing motivation (itself a difficult concept), perception of the context or other individuals, and the real or perceived social signals passed between the interactors. Actions may be directed through the central nervous system (CNS) or through the intimately related endocrine system, and real or imagined experiences feed back to the participants to modify their subsequent behavioural tendencies; factors such as personality are important here. The diagram shows that environmental factors may also serve as parts of the situational determinants which are essential for the appropriate expression of behaviour. However, the traditional medical distinction between body and mind does not fit easily into this scheme. An indication of current clinical trends is provided by Looney et al. (1978), who suggest that the concept of psychosomatic disease is of limited utility, since actual disease consists of a spectrum of somatic and psychological changes. One must add to this construct, though, an extra layer of confusion by re-emphasising that the application of the term 'aggression' to interactions is

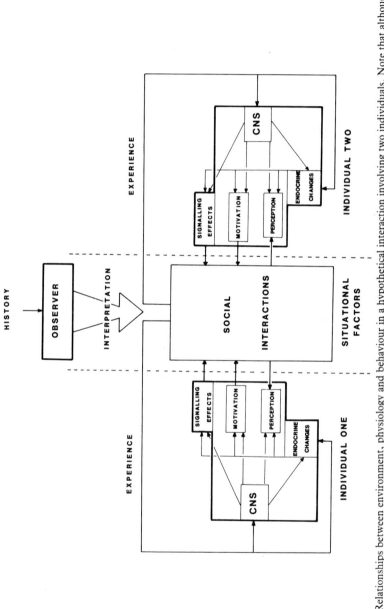

Fig. 4.1 Relationships between environment, physiology and behaviour in a hypothetical interaction involving two individuals. Note that although a symmetrical device is employed, this condition is unlikely as most of the features change as the encounter progresses. 'Aggression' in the diagram is simply a portion of social behaviour or a value-judgement applied to these activities by an external observer. 'Motivational systems' are the internal systems that change an organism's predisposition to behave in particular fashions, 'perceptual systems' refers to the senses and the interpretation of this input and 'signalling effects' are the cues (e.g. postures, expressions, odours, or words) which pass information between the participants.

generally via an external observer, whose value judgements are influenced by his own development, environment, and prior experience.

External environmental variables are generally complexes, and cannot simply be dubbed physical or social factors; when group size is changed, variations may be produced in availability of resources, number of inter-personal contacts, noise, body heat, and a host of other variables, as well as the intended change in physical density (Rusbult 1979). An example of this complexity is provided by Lunde (1975), who found correlations between homicide in the United States and possession of guns, drinking alcohol, the economy, the incidence of suicide, retention of capital punish-ment, age, chromosomal complement, mental illness, the lunar cycle, magnetic fluctuations, weather and latitude. Esser & Deutsh (1975) provide a bibliography of references on the relationship of psychiatric disorder to environmental factors; but drawing conclusions from this about individuals obviously requires great caution.

RATIONALE FOR THIS REVIEW

Why should one consider environmental influences on human aggression separately from aspects of the organism's biology? One reason is that a considerable body of information on the claimed role of physiological factors on animal and human aggression (Brain & Benton 1981; Brain 1984) has been recently attempted. Also, Eibl-Eibesfeldt (1979) has examined these phenomena from a human ethology viewpoint, and it seems appropriate to counterbalance this by a greater emphasis on the environment. Another reason is that environmental manipulations may offer more appropriate and ethical means of modifying human aggression than biological manipulations, in view of the considerable debate generated by even investigations of such associations (Gaylin et al. 1981). These may be sanctioned only in a percentage of clinical conditions — perhaps those where some lesion or dysfunction is established. There are also extreme views, such as that of Jeffrey (1971), who claimed that 'there are no criminals, only environmental circumstances that result in criminal behaviour', which must be examined.

Categories employed in this review represent defined areas of interest in an extensive literature. Although the account is largely limited to human data, reference will be made to appropriate animal studies, where they seem likely to provide enlightenment, as well as to some popular books, as these often influence general opinion.

STUDIES ON AGGRESSION AND THE ENVIRONMENT

Pain

Pain is a psychological concept, generally referring to sensations fed into the organism by the sympathetic portion of the nervous system, when responding to potentially physically harmful agents. Crabtree & Moyer (1977) review the effects of a wide variety of presumably painful situations, e.g. exposure to electroshock, pinching, and physical attack, on aggression in both humans and infra-humans. Tullar (1977) claims that 'the causes of human aggression are undoubtedly related to fear, pain and frustration brought about both by environmental situations and physiological state of the individual'. Pain is a factor associated with aggression in some situations, but one can take issue with Tullar's failure to recognise that aggression may be appetitive in some circumstances. For example, Lagerspetz (1979) notes that aggression can act as a reward in some situations, and that one can reduce it by punishing its appearance. Hartup & de Wit (1978) go so far as to maintain that 'neither the child who lives in the poorest ghetto nor the child who lives in the most affluent circumstances can survive unless he acquires a harm-doing repertoire and some capacity for coping with, aggressive affect'.

Temperature

It has been repeatedly suggested (e.g. Ginsburg & Allee 1942) that environmental temperature influences fighting in rodents, and the association between this environmental variable and human aggression has been examined by Bell & Baron (1981). They argue that research has been stimulated by the suggestion that the earth may be entering a period in which the 'greenhouse effect' will become important in relation to aggression. Many studies of this kind seem to have been prompted by the claimed association of rioting in US ghettos and 'the long, hot summer'. Laboratory evidence suggests, however, that the correlation of aggression with environmental temperature follows an inverted U-shaped function. Moderately uncomfortable heat increases aggressiveness, whereas extreme discomfort suppresses it and makes flight a dominant response (this is the *negative affect-aggression* hypothesis). Baron (1977) notes that 'the frequent occurrence of riots, looting and similar events during the hot summer months does not stem directly or exclusively from the presence of uncomfortable heat during such periods'. The conditions could simply result in there being more people on the streets, an effect which is likely to be more obvious in ghetto populations than amongst the air-conditioned middle classes. Harries (1980) states that, although it is 'intuitively obvious' that hot humid weather provokes people to be violent, analytical evidence for this view is lacking.

Light

Lunde (1975) describes a study conducted between 1956 and 1970 in Florida, showing that more murders tended to occur at the full moon.

Rather than hypothesising 'tides' in the ventricles of the brain, he suggests that the improved visibility at the full moon produces the correlation, also reporting a slight positive correlation between the incidence of murder and day-time visibility. Rockwell et al. (1976) found that sudden time-shifts of light/dark cycles elevated questionnaire-assessed aggressiveness in groups of three men, who were experimentally isolated. It was suggested that disruptions of the normal circadian rhythm of adrenocortical activity changed irritability.

Diet

There are many reports, both anecdotal and scientific, suggesting that diet influences aggression in populations. Hypoglycaemia has been linked with hostility in clinical, criminal, and anthropological situations, and even in normal male undergraduates (Benton et al. 1982). Low blood sugar may increase irritability, accounting for changes in behavioural predisposition. A variety of ingested materials including caffeine, alcohol, and tryptophan have been implicated in changes in aggression in both animals and man (Valzelli 1980, 1981). Brain (1982) has, however, examined some of the complications of assessing the involvement of alcohol's known physiological actions on aggression, concluding that 'the physiological correlates of alcohol ingestion (which are acutely and chronically somewhat different) are also very diverse and there seems no easy way to currently relate these to behavioural changes'. The situation is even more complex when the material administered via the environment is difficult to monitor (e.g. the debate concerning the lasting effects of environmental lead).

Odour

A study by Rotton (!) et al. (1977) suggests that the intensities of foul odours to which laboratory populations are exposed have effects on aggressiveness. An inverted U-shaped function described the relationship, as in the case of variations in environmental temperature.

Noise

Exposure of individuals to presumably irritating noise may sometimes facilitate aggression in angered or annoyed subjects (Baron 1977). Indeed, Hutchinson et al. (1977) found that loud noise produced transducer-measured jaw-clenching in humans, a response that they correlated with aggressiveness. Sabini (1978) notes that although noise may intensify aggressive responses, 'these experiments do not touch on the question of people's ability to discount irritations when they are chronic, such as living near an airport'. (This subject is discussed more fully in Chapter 9.)

Density and number

This subject is also discussed in Chapters 2 and 3, but here the overt and covert extrapolations from animal studies to associations between density and human aggression are initially examined. In many examples, though, density would not be viewed as the key variable; few social scientists who studied ghettos, for example, would put crowding near the top of their list of problems. Factors such as: social deprivation; lack of adequate jobs; lack of suitable schooling; deviant subcultural norms; and the high proportion of physically and mentally disadvantaged individuals deservedly receive more attention.

Relevance of animal studies on crowding to man

Brain & Benton (1983) have reviewed animal studies on this topic and concluded that current investigations do not assess effects of isolation and crowding as such, but merely look at differential housing. The effects of this are dependent on the prior history, age, sex, and 'natural' social organisation of the species studied (Archer 1970). However, the social organisations of rodents may change with density or with the distribution of resources within the environment (Parmigiani et al. 1981). Brain (1971, 1975a) and Brain & Benton (1977, 1983) have stressed the multiplicity of physiological (e.g. hormones and neurotransmitters) and behavioural consequences of differential housing in rodents.

The most influential animal studies on environment and aggression are those of Calhoun (1962, 1967, 1971a, b, 1973a, b). In his view, studies on rats and mice confirm that abnormal behaviour (including aggression) seen in confined populations can lead to extinction. Sorenson (1974) adds that 'with the tragic misuse of the environment and the tardy realisation that overpopulation increases rivalry for the quality aspects of the environment, man now studies other animal societies to understand the inherent values of organised competition', Calhoun (1973a) also suggests that 'for an animal so complex as man, there is no logical reason why a comparable sequence of events should not also lead to species extinction', though there is equally no logical reason why it should. In fact, Calhoun has only described local extinction, when animals in his 'universe' are prevented from migrating. Freedman (1975, 1980) provides tentative support for this evaluation, but emphasises that numbers of individuals rather than their density may be the crucial factor, finding little current evidence that mechanisms of response to population are qualitatively different in man and rodents (Freedman 1979). Brain (1972, 1975b) has also reviewed the apparent contribution of rodent studies to a consideration of the effects of density in man; their most obvious utility seems to be in drawing attention to the possible consequences of environmental change.

So-called r-strategists such as mice (characterised by features of reproduction in which the potential rate of population increase is maximised at the expense of intensive nurture of the offspring and efficient resource utilisation) may not be good models for population effects in a K-strategist such as man (with relatively small numbers of offspring and a heavy parental investment in the offspring). Baron & Needel (1980) state that 'the ability of humans to almost endlessly transform the meaning of physical events provides ample justification for proposing that, at least on occasion, human responses to density rest on very different foundations than those of other species'. However, animal studies are revealing in predicting associations between the physiological and behavioural consequences of environmental stressors. Although most studies have concentrated on the apparently deleterious effects of crowding, some have been concerned with the allegedly dire consequences of isolation. Brain & Benton (1977) challenged the view that 'isolation-induced aggression' in rodents is simply a consequence of stressful social deprivation, and note that evidence for such a phenomenon is much stronger in developing primates (Hebb 1947) than in mature rodents.

General studies of the effects of density on human aggression

Treshow (1976) speculates that 'possibly crowding would lead to international conflict and nuclear war but it could just as readily lead to epidemics of disease and frustration in life'; in Freedman's view (1975), 'sometimes people seem to respond positively to crowding, sometimes negatively and often they do not respond one way or the other'. He proposes that crowding, rather than being intrinsically beneficial or deleterious, merely intensifies the individual's typical reactions to particular situations. Rusbult (1979) confirms that physical density is not always aversive in humans, but suggests that the negative aspects of short-term exposure to crowded settings, including increased aggressiveness and punitiveness, are well documented.

Studies of ghettos and building design

There have been many attempts to relate aggression in field studies of western societies to factors such as overcrowding and social disruption. Beames (1852) said of the notorious Rookeries of London that 'they are not only the haunts where pauperism recruits its strength — not only the lurking places, but the nurseries of felons. A future generation of thieves is there hatched from the viper's egg, who shall one day astonish London by their monstrous birth'. A more recent example of hyperbole is provided by Morris (1969) claiming that, in contrast to city dwellers, 'under normal conditions in their natural habitats wild animals do not mutilate themselves, masturbate, attack their offspring, develop stomach ulcers, become fetishists, suffer from obesity, form homosexual pair-bonds or commit murder'. However, he subsequently feels free to maintain that captive animals are a valid comparison for the city dweller, which would not be regarded as sound from the zoological point of view.

Territoriality

There have also been attempts to relate violence in societies to the concept of territoriality. Shuttles (1968, 1972) says of Chicago slums that 'in slum neighborhoods territorial aggregation usually precedes a common social framework for ensuring orderly relations'. Whilst conceding that humans do not possess exact replicas of the types of territory evident in animals, he feels that the competitive structures are similar, even though attempts to symbolise status differences by aggressive displays seldom achieve unqualified submission, but 'often end in an escalation of retaliatory acts in a vicious circle far more destructive than aggressive displays among non-humans'.

The concept of territoriality in human society is most strongly associated with Ardrey (1966). Noble (1939) defined a territory as any defended area, and territories have been described in a wide variety of infra-human vertebrates where a single male or mated pair generally attack conspecifics that intrude into a defined geographical area. The fact that conspecifics are excluded seems an important distinction; Charles-Dominique (1974) states that a territory is 'that area occupied by an animal or group of animals, and which is defended against intrusion by others of the same species', which also recognises that territories may be held by groups. Most workers would now maintain that the above definitions are too wide, as they do not distinguish 'genuine' territoriality from defence of a nesting or sleeping site.

Territoriality was seen by ethologists as a method of parcelling up the limited available environment into units which could support breeding animals and their offspring. Verner (1977) has critically examined this concept in animals, and concludes that 'defence of a disproportionate share of space/resources by more aggressive individuals reduces the possibility of survival and/or reproduction of less aggressive conspecifics'. It could be argued that this statement does not necessarily limit the concept of territory to a geographical location, and the problem of relating fitness to 'aggressiveness' has already been mentioned. Because of its relationships to breeding, possession of territories may be a seasonal phenomenon in some species. The 'resident' is generally viewed as having a distinct advantage on its location over intruders, only being supplanted when a large size difference operates against it or the animal becomes diseased or injured. This is stressed in Willis' definition of territory (cited in Silberbauer 1973) as 'a space in which one animal or group dominates others which become dominant elsewhere', though this definition also involves problems in relation to the activities of members of social hierarchies. Territoriality is seen by many workers as a strategy for reducing potentially physically injurious activities between members of the same species. The view has also developed that intraspecific displays (threat or submission) and other forms of communication, such as odour marking and bird song, serve to reduce over fighting in such situations. In this connection, Maynard-Smith & Parker (1976) have proposed a games theory, in which the costs and benefits of different behavioural strategies are computed.

In spite of the above-mentioned problems, Henry & Stephens (1977) considering territoriality in mice, infrahuman primates and man, simply state that the described phenomena have 'common physiological and evolutionary bases'. There are many references to the tendency in our species to become attached to particular geographical locations and objects, though some statements are highly contentious, e.g. Morris (1977), who states that 'at the centre of this space, there is the nest — the bedroom — where, tucked up in bed, we feel at our most territorially secure'.

Possible evidence for human territoriality is derived from two distinct areas. Firstly studies of the social organisations of primitive tribes, e.g. Eibl-Eibesfeldt (1974), leading to claims such as that of Wilson (1978) that 'the biological formula of territorialism translates easily into the rituals of modern property ownership', and Morris (1977) that 'in the broadest sense, there are three kinds of human territory: tribal, family and personal'. There are even anecdotal claims that certain aborigines may employ urinary marking of territories in a manner similar to mice! However, demonstration of territoriality in a particular group (particularly one that is non-mainstream) does not mean that it is an inescapable characteristic of *Homo sapiens*. In spite of this, Wilson (1975) confidently maintains that 'primitive men lived in small territorial groups, within which males were dominant over females'.

Secondly, evidence for human territoriality is said to be contained in statements and assumptions concerning conflict between nations. Sorensen (1974) notes that 'as nations expand, their borders push against those of their neighbours and individuals fence their territorial lines'. States attacking others are often accused of 'territorial aggression', but the term 'territoriality' is used here in a sense which does not seem to be biologically valid. Relative success by resident humans against invaders could equally be attributed to familarity with the terrain and lines of communication and to their greater corporeal and emotional investment in it, rather than to hypothetical 'territorial advantages'. Classical studies on animal territoriality may have had a particularly profound effect on interpretations of human behaviour because of Noble's (1939) publication immediately prior to World War 2. Even the concept of an immutable, exclusive territoriality of certain animal species is currently less valid. Many species seem capable of changing their social organisations in response to changing environmental needs (Ehrlich et al. 1976) such that they can exploit a range of environments. Further, the idea of a territorial imperative (i.e. an instinct or drive to form such organisations) in animals is not supportable. Most laboratory studies of man (e.g. Ellis 1974) have failed to obtain clear evidence of a tendency for power and influence to be defined in terms of spatial or territorial boundaries. Comments concerning body buffer zones (p. 29) use the term 'territory' by analogy, which is a dangerous device. Schmidt & Keating (1979) conclude that crowding is an attributional label, applied to settings where density results in a loss or a lack of personal control. Esser (1971a, 1973b, c) also sees crowding as an inability to handle information input and suggests that it is coped with in human societies by the formation of dominance hierarchies and by territoriality; he sees man–environment interactions as complicated by man's 'triune' brain. This view (MacLean 1964) holds that the human brain is a chimaera of that of his primitive reptile, lower mammal, and higher mammal ancestors, the different 'brains' interacting, but operating on different levels. Esser (1973b) regrets that 'our perceptions of the structures of withdrawal and violence (as reactions to insurmountable feelings of crowding) make us in turn feel crowded'.

Territoriality has, however, proved a very appealing concept, and seems to have played a part in the genesis of Newman's (1975, 1976) concept of defensible space in building design, similar to Jeffrey's (1971) call for the control of crime through urban planning and design. Newman recognises that appropriate building designs may differ for different populations (e.g. families with young children and retired pensioners) but maintains that design of housing developments can alter the vulnerability of populations to crime. Noting the great increase in US crime between 1964 and 1974, he commented that 'some of these high-density environments (evident in the high-rise developments of the period) bring people into contact with each other in totally new ways — some of which have been found to be disturbing'. Placing individuals in featureless boxes might abolish aggression, but says little about the normal influences of the environment on human aggression. Rusbult (1979) advocates intervention strategies for high density settings, which may involve changing the physical setting, facilitating attempts of individuals to adapt, and altering the individual's perception of the situation, emphasising positive rather than negative features. This seems a potentially fruitful approach. (See also Chapter 11).

Other workers, however, have different explanations of behaviour in crowded ghettos and other situations. Clark (1964) says of Harlem that 'random hostility, aggression, self-hatred, suspiciousness, seething turmoil and chronic personal and social tensions also reflect self-destructive and nonadaptive reactions to a pervasive sense and fact of powerlessness'. Baron (1977) notes that field studies provide 'no indication of a link between crowding and the incidence of crimes of violence — such as murder, rape or aggravated assault', but this may be a consequence of the complex nature of environment–behaviour interaction, rather than of the absence of influence of crowding on this diverse group of activities.

Studies on young children

Freedman (1975) reviewed the effects of crowding on aggression in children in rooms and playgrounds of different sizes, concluding that 'the more extensive and controlled work has found no negative effect of crowding'. Earlier work (e.g. Hutt & Vaisey 1966) had suggested that more aggression could be observed in larger rather than smaller play-groups of normal or brain-damaged children. The effect was said to be most marked in the latter, though normal children showed progressively fewer nonaggressive social interactions with increasing crowding. More recently, Olweus (1978) has revealed that larger schools have a higher level of playground 'mobbing behaviour' than smaller ones.

Studies on vandalism

Vandalism (criminal damage) has been regarded as aggression against property, and Clarke (1978) suggests that complex interactions between groups of variables contribute to the aetiology of this phenomenon. Factors said to influence degrees of vandalism include: early environment and upbringing of the subjects, heredity, criminal personality, socio-economic and demographic status, current living circumstances, crises and events, situation, and personal factors. A study of high and low vandalism schools in Houston, (Pablant & Baxter 1975) concluded that quality of maintenance and neatness of the buildings and grounds was the greatest protective factor against vandalism, and this has been confirmed elsewhere.

Studies on criminal populations

The most violent delinquents in a Californian study were males from large (four or more children), intact (as opposed to broken) families (Andrew 1978), whereas the least violent males and the most violent females were from small, intact homes. However, 'violent' may mean different things when applied to these two genders. As well as apparently predisposing individuals towards some forms of violent crimes, density in prison appears to alter this factor within the institution. Hokanson et al. (1976) concluded, on the basis of a study on the behavioural, emotional and autonomic reactions to stress in two hundred youthful, male prison inmates, that 'institutional pressures dictate reactions in the helpless-depressive direction and temporarily suppress aggressive modes of response'. McCain et al (1980) describe a wide variety of negative psychological and physiological effects of sustained crowding in US prisons. Large institutions showed proportionately more aggression (reflected in deaths due to violence), but partitioning of dormitories had an ameliorative effect; great individual differences were evident, which may be partially determined by differing perceptions of crowding by different ethnic groups.

Studies on personal space or body buffer zones (said with little justification by Curran et al. (1978) to be analogues of territoriality) have been attempted in prisoners. Personal space is reflected by decreasing eye contact as spatial proximity increases (Argyle & Dean 1965) and an increased sensation of discomfort and probability of flight as it is invaded (Sommer 1969). Kinzel (1974) and Curran et al. (1978) found that the violent prisoner's body buffer zone was much larger than individuals from a nonviolent group (see also Chapter 3).

Miscellaneous

Russell & Drewry (1976) found no clear association between crowd size and 'competitive aspects of aggression' (by players) in an archival study of the Alberta Highwood (Ice) Hockey League records for 1970–1971. Conversely, patients in psychiatric wards, institutionalised psychotic boys, and emotionally disturbed children have all been said to show clear territoriality, which could lead to unpredictable aggressive behaviour (Esser 1971b, 1977). Esser feels that 'understanding of our powerful territorial and dominance structures will lead to a change of consciousness that will equal the impact of the psychodynamic account of our sex drive.'

Social stress

The effects of social 'stress' (including fighting/defeat) on the adrenal gland are well documented (Brain 1977, 1979b). However, concentration on this gland as an indicator of stress now seems inappropriate, as many endocrine variables are altered by such exposures. For example, Rose (1969) and Rose et al. (1969) provide good evidence that the gonadal system is modified by the presumed stresses of basic military training and imminent combat. They suggested that threats inhibited testosterone secretion, which may have an influence on aggressiveness, but noted that such changes may be consequences of lowered sexual activity.

Murphy (1977) recorded that war stress produced long-lasting effects similar to clinical depression in evacuees from a battlefront in (then) South Vietnam. Changing the degree of emotional disturbance will inevitably modify aggressiveness, even if this is reflected in extreme passiveness (see Seligman's 1975 concept of 'learned helplessness'). One must also note that some human data from military situations provide strong evidence that man can 'decide' what is and is not stressful (Bourne 1971).

Social status

Variations in social rank in infrahuman animals may be associated with different levels of chronic stress (Brain 1977, 1978, 1979a). 'Dominance' also has hidden complexities; it is a difficult term to define, but usually describes a condition where an animal is likely to threaten or attack another member of its species in the context of a particular commodity (food, a mate, water, social status) over which it takes precedence when the latter challenges that right. This is said to be in contrast to territoriality, where the relationship is determined spatially (Brain 1977). Different methods of attempting to determine social status in rodents and infrahuman primates do not necessarily generate identical results (Bernstein 1981). Dominance appears dependent on the commodity competed for, so that an animal may be of high status when food is involved, but have low priority in its access to water or receptive females. The status of particular animals is governed by their social relationships (Bernstein & Gordon 1980) — an alpha rhesus monkey is only an alpha with respect to its particular group, and not all hierarchies are like chicken peck orders. Thus, animals may have separate or combined male and female social structures, show nonlinear (despotic dominance) relationships, or have complex relationships in which animals subordinate to one individual may dominate that individual's superiors.

Biologists generally hold that hierarchy formation is another method of reducing overt fighting between cohabiting conspecifics, at the same time enabling favoured animals to monopolise limited substrates (food or mates). Brain (1981a) has argued that both territoriality and social dominance are best viewed as variants on a strategy which utilises intraspecific aggression to enhance Darwinian fitness.

What of the evidence for dominance hierarchies in man? This explanatory device has also been much utilised in both scientific and nonscientific discussion (Tiger & Fox 1974). An extreme view is presented by Ardrey (1970), that 'strong' (in the sense of being suited to survival) social organisations or nations are those in which there are clearly defined leaders and followers. This simple natural hierarchy view of society is countered by Reynolds (1980), who points out that the use of different infrahuman primate models for man generates different views of our basic social organisation. The Hamadryas baboon (much favoured as a model for human society by Ardrey) has a well established male dominance hierarchy, but our closer relative the chimpanzee exhibits a much more fluid social organisation, with females showing promiscuity. There is no reason to assume that hierarchies are a preprogrammed part of human nature, but they may prove useful strategies in a variety of situations.

As in the case of territoriality, the evidence for human hierarchies is largely circumstantial (Brain 1981b). Eibl-Eibesfeldt (1974) has described how the oldest prepubertal girl in Bushman groups may sometimes attack other children without obvious reason, and suggests that 'the function of this aggression is to achieve and keep rank and respect, which is a prerequisite for functioning as a mediator and soothing quarrels between other playmates'. There are, however, some quite bizzare statements, such as Ehrlich et al.'s (1976) that Cadillacs may be a dominance symbol among American physicians. The point at issue is whether these social arrangements are homologous, or merely analogous to the now recognisably hetero-genous animal hierarchies.

In spite of the drawbacks of dominance as a concept in humans, Shenkin (1973) has applied ethological principles to the analysis of nonclinical exam-ples of human behaviour, particularly in committees, and contrasted the approach with more typical sociological analyses. He concluded that his examples were best understood in terms of the ethological concepts of dominance/subordination. Zaleznik et al. (1977) studied bureaucratic organ-isations in Canada, and noted that 'the environment, particularly, the frus-trations and deprivations associated with bureaucracy and the lack of power, activates the defences against anger and rage that in turn lead to symptom formation', i.e. stress-related disease. These workers found that managers showed less stress-related illness than more lowly ranked staff, which runs counter to the observation on the high incidence of stress-related ulcers in 'executive monkeys'. It is, of course, debatable whether one should equate the dominance of the animal studies with human social status, though this is not to deny that social status has a considerable effect on the type of environmental pressures to which anyone is exposed.

CONCLUSIONS AND SUMMARY

Some of the problems of attempting to relate human aggression to a variety of physical environmental variables have been explored in this chapter. It has been noted that 'aggression' and 'the environment' are difficult concepts, and that the interplay between them is extremely complex. Indeed, recent evidence suggests that one should attempt to distinguish subdivisions within these concepts, noting that the terms are used in different ways by different writers. The diversity of situations in which 'aggression' is introduced as an intervening variable suggests that few unifying principles will be evident at the present primitive state of the art.

Terms such as 'territoriality' and 'dominance' may be applied to portions of the repertoire of human responses which include aggression, but this does not prove that there is a basic human tendency to assume territorial or hierarchical social organisations. Such organisations may be 'selected' as strategies when environmental factors make them appropriate, and it is argued that historical traditions or even genes may also predispose societies towards assuming such structures. It is revealing, however, that the only major selection role of aggression seen in infrahuman animals which has not been strongly postulated as a human characteristic (in a largely western literature) is that of mate selection. Perhaps this is because of the fashion in our societies to form pair bonds, though the fact that such unconscious selectivity exists should give pause for thought.

It seems appropriate to emphasise that the traditional separation between physiological and cognitive effects of the environment is arbitrary, and this is especially important in medical sciences, in connection with the mental health consequences of the environment. However, there is an obvious element of subjectivity in the designation of particular behavioural conditions as 'pathological', and even if the biological technologies for controlling aggression were available (Brain 1983), their appropriateness and the ethics of their use would cause concern. A variety of environmental factors do alter neural events (e.g. firing of particular constellations of neurones), hormonal levels (especially of sex steroids, adrenal steroids, and medullary catecholamines), neurotransmitters, and enzyme concentrations. These changes may or may not be easily associated with behavioural alterations, especially since behaviour can alter the actual or perceived environment.

Extrapolations from the deceptively 'simple' findings on rodents to man have to be undertaken with great care. Indeed, it is rarely possible with complete intellectual honesty to identify areas where simple statements are possible. Also, current research effort has suggested that the analysis of environment/physiology/behaviour interactions in infrahuman vertebrates is much more complex than has been hitherto admitted and that many of the old concepts have limited utility.

Environmental factors seldom appear to have immutably positive or negative influences on aggression, so that each individual example of apparent behavioural disturbance must be considered on its merits. The great variability in responses also means that useful information is only likely to be gathered by using large and diverse samples, a variety of situations, and a number of methods of behavioural assessment. This reinforces the desirability of enlightened interdisciplinary work in the essential area of environment/physiology/behaviour. A balanced integration of evidence from a variety of perspectives is needed, especially as the consequences of being wrong may be translated into human misery and conflict.

Finally, the impact of popular biology on debates similar to the present one needs comment. These volumes do provide readable accounts, which stimulate interest and awareness of current problems and perhaps solutions. However, their inevitable but unfortunate tendency to oversimplify and to illustrate by analogy can create major problems. A medical scientist whose only exposure to ethology is *On Aggression* or *The Territorial Imperative* is likely to form a distorted view of the current consensus in this area. If he finds it difficult, what then of the planner or politician? Cross-disciplinary dialogue can be both disappointing and exasperating, but it is necessary, and there should be a serious attempt to encourage such activities further. In this respect, the recent formation of societies with members from multiple specialisms seems a most desirable trend.

ACKNOWLEDGEMENTS

I would like to thank Drs David Benton and John Durant for commenting on a draft version of this account.

REFERENCES

Andrew J M 1978 Violence among delinquents by family intactness and size. Social Biology 25: 243–250

Archer J 1970 Effects of population density on behaviour in rodents. In: Crook J H (ed) Social behaviour in birds and mammals. Academic Press, London, pp 169–210

Ardrey R 1966 The territorial imperative. Collins, London

Ardrey R 1970 The social contract. Collins, London

Argyle M and Dean J 1965 Eye contact, distance and affiliation. Sociometry 28: 289–304

Bandura A 1973 Aggression: a social learning analysis. Prentice Hall, Englewood Cliffs, NJ

Bardwick J 1976 Psychological correlates of the menstrual cycle and oral contraceptive medication. In: Sachar E J (ed) Hormones, behaviour and psychopathology, Raven Press, New York

Baron R A 1977 Human aggression: perspectives in social psychology. Plenum, New York

Baron R M, Needel S P 1980 Toward an understanding of the differences in the responses of humans and other animals to density. Psychological Review 87: 320–326

Beames T 1852 The rookeries of London, 2nd edn. Thomas Bosworth, London

Bell P A, Baron R A 1981 Ambient temperature and human violence. In: Brain P F and Benton D (eds) Multidisciplinary approaches to aggession research, Elsevier North-Holland, Amsterdam

Benton D, Kumari N, Brain P F 1982 Mild hypoglycemia and questionaire measures of aggression. Biological Psychology 14: 129–135

Berkowitz L, Frodi A 1977 Stimulus characteristics that can enhance or decrease aggression: association with prior positive or negative reinforcements for aggression. Aggressive Behavior 3: 1–15

Bernstein I S 1981 Dominance: the baby and the bathwater. The Behavioral and Brain Sciences 4: 419–457

Bernstein I S, Gordon T P 1980 The Social component of dominance relationships in rhesus monkeys (Macaca mulatta). Animal Behaviour 28: 1033–1039

Blanchard R J, Blanchard D D 1977 Aggressive behaviour in the rat. Behavioral Biology 21: 197–224

Bourne P G 1971 Altered adrenal function in two combat situations in Vietnam. In: Eleftheriou B E, Scott J P The physiology of aggression and defeat. Plenum, New York

Brain P F 1971 The physiology of population limitation — a review. Communications in Behavioral Biology 6: 115–123

Brain P F 1972 Stress as an urban pollutant. Journal of Environmental Planning Pollution Control 1: 28–35

Brain P F 1975a What does individual housing mean to a mouse? Life Sciences 16: 187–200

Brain P F 1975b Studies on crowding; a critical analysis of the implication of studies on rodents for the human situation. International Journal of Mental Health 4: 15–30

Brain P F 1977 Hormones and aggression, vol 1. Eden Press, Montreal

Brain P F 1978 Hormones and aggression, vol 2. Eden Press, Montreal

Brain P F 1979a Hormones, drugs and aggression, vol 3 Eden Press Montreal

Brain P F 1979b Effects of the hormones of the pituitary-adrenocortical axis on behaviour. In: Brown K, Cooper S J (eds) Chemical influences on behaviour. Academic Press, London

Brain P F 1981a Diverse actions of hormones on 'aggression' in animals and man. In: Valzelli L, Morgese L (eds) Aggression and violence: a psychobiological and clinical approach, Edizioni St Vincent

Brain P F 1981b Classical ethology and human aggression. In: Brain P F, Benton D (eds) The biology of aggression, Sijthoff/Noordhoff, Alphen aan den Rijn

Brain P F 1982 Alcohol and aggression: some notes on the presumed relationship between the physiological and behavioural correlates of man's oldest drug. British Journal on Alcohol and Alcoholism 17: 39–45

Brain P F 1984 Biological explanations of human aggression and the resulting therapies offered by such approaches: a critical evaluation. In: Blanchard R J, Blanchard D C (eds) Progress in aggression research vol 1. Academic Press, New York

Brain P F, Benton 1977 What does individual housing mean to a research worker? IRCS Journal of Medical Science 5: 459–463

Brain P F, Benton D (eds) 1981 The biology of aggression. Noorhoff/Sijthoff, Alphen aan den Rijn

Brain P F, Benton D 1983 The environment, hormones and aggressive behaviour. In: Svare B (ed) Hormones and aggressive behavior. Plenum, New York

Buss A H 1971 Aggression pays. In: Singer J L (ed) The control of aggression and violence. Academic Press, New York, pp 7–18

Calhoun J B 1962 Population density and social pathology. Scientific American 206: 139–146

Calhoun J B 1967 Ecological factors in the development of behavioral anomalies In: Zubin E (ed) Comparative psychopathology. Grune and Stratton, New York

Calhoun J B 1971a Space and the strategy of life. In: Hesser A H (ed) Behaviour and the environment. Plenum Press, New York

Calhoun J D 1971b Psychoecological aspects of population. In: Shepherd and McKinley (eds) Environmental essays and the planet as a home, Houghton-Mifflin Co. 111–133

Calhoun J B 1973a Death squared: The explosive growth and demise of a mouse population. Proceedings of the Royal Society of Medicine 66: 80–88

Calhoun J B 1973b From mice to men. Transactions & Studies of the College of Physicians of Philadelphia 41: 92–118

Charles-Dominique P 1974 Aggression and territoriality in nocturnal prosimians. In: Holloway R L (ed) Primate aggression, territoriality and xenophobia: a comparative perspective. Academic Press, New York

Clark K A 1964 Youth in the ghetto: a study of the consequences of powerlessness and blueprint for change. Haryou, New York

Clarke R V G 1978 Tackling vandalism. Home Office Research Study No 47, Her Majesty's Stationery Office, London

Crabtree J M, Moyer K F 1977 Bibliography of aggressive behavior: a reader's guide to the research Literature. Alan R Liss Inc, New York

Curran S F, Blatchley R J, Hanlon T E 1978 The relationship between body buffer zone and violence as assessed by subjective and objective techniques. Criminal Justice & Behaviour 5: 53–62

Depp F C 1976 Violent behaviour patterns in psychiatric wards. Aggressive Behavior 2: 295–306

Dollard J, Boob L, Miller N, Mourrer O H, Sears R R 1939 Frustration and aggression. Yale University Press, New Haven, Connecticut

Durant J 1981 The beast in man: a historical perspective on the biology of human aggression. In: Brain P F, Benton D (eds) The biology of aggression, Nordhoff/Sijthoff, Alphen aan den Rijn

Earls F 1978 The social reconstruction of adolescence: towards an explanation for increasing rates of violence in youth. Perspectives in Biological Medicine 22: 65–82

Ehrlich P R, Holm R W, Brown I L 1976 Biology and society. McGraw-Hill, New York

Eibl-Eibesfeldt I 1974 The myth of the aggression-free hunter and gatherer society. In: Holloway R L (ed) Primate aggression territoriality and xenophobia: a comparative perspective. Academic Press, New York

Eibl-Eibesfeldt I 1979 The biology of peace and war. Thames and Hudson, London

Ellis K R 1974 An exploratory experiment on human territoriality. Dissertation

Esser A H 1971a Toward a definition of crowding. Guest editorial in The Sciences, October

Esser A H 1971b A psychopathology of crowding in institutions for the mentally ill and retarded. Paper presented at 5th World Congress of Psychiatry, Mexico City

Esser A H 1973a Cottage fourteen: dominance and territoriality in a group of institutionalized boys. Small Group Behavior 4: 131–146

Esser A B 1973b Experiences of crowding: illustration of a paradigm for man-environment relations. Representative Research in Social Psychology 4: 207–218

Esser A H 1977 Expressions of territoriality and human psychopathology. Comments to VI World Congress of Psychiatry, Honolulu, Hawaii

Esser A H, Deutsch R D 1975 Environment and mental health. Man Environment Systems 5: 333–348

Feshbach N D 1979 Empathy training: A field study in affective education. In: Feshbach S and Fraczek A (eds) Aggression and behavior change, Praeger, New York

Fesbach S, Fraczek A (eds) Aggression & behavior change, Praeger, New York

Freedman J L 1975 Crowding and behavior. W H Freeman & Co., San Francisco

Freedman J L 1979 Reconciling apparent differences between the responses of humans and other animals in crowding. Psychological Review 86: 80–85

Freedman J L 1980 Responses of humans and other animals to variations in density. Psychological Review 87: 327–328

Freeman H 1975 The environment and human satisfaction. International Journal of Mental Health 4: 6–14

Feshbach S, Fraczek A (eds) 1979 Aggression and behavior change. Praeger Publishers, New York

Frodi A 1977 Sexual arousal, situational restrictiveness and aggressive behaviour. Journal of Research in Personality 11: 48–58

Gaylin W, Macklin R, Powledge T M (eds) 1981 Violence and the politics of research. The Hastings Center, New York

Geen R G, O'Neal E C 1969 Activation of cue-elicited aggression by general arousal. Journal of Personality and Social Psychology 11: 289–292

Gelles R J 1974 The violent home: a study of physical aggression between husbands and wives. Sage Publications Inc., Beverley Hills

Genoves S 1977 Acali, Ra 1 and Ra 2: Some conclusions and hypotheses concerning human friction under isolation and stress, with special reference to intelligence and personality assessment. Aggressive Behavior 3: 163–172

Ginsburg B E, Allee W C 1942 Some effects of conditioning on social dominance and subordination in inbred strains of mice. Physiological Zoology 15: 485–506

Groth A N, Birnbaum J J 1979 Men who rape: the psychology of the offender. Plenum Press, New York

Harries K D 1980 Crime and the environment. Thomas, Springfield

Harris M 1976 History and significance of the EMIC/ETIC distinction. Annual Review of Anthropology 5: 329–350

Hartup W W, de Wit J 1978 The development of aggression: problems and perspectives. In: Hartup W W, de Wit J (eds) Origins of aggression, Mouton, The Hague

Haug G, Hemminger H, Schumacher A 1982 Aggressive interactions in a kindergarten group. Aggressive Behavior 8: 238–241

Hebb D O 1947 Spontaneous neurosis in chimpanzees: theoretical relations with clinical and experimental phenomena. Psychosomatic Medicine 9: 3–16

Henry J P, Stephens P M 1977 Stress, health and the social environment: a sociobiological approach to Medicine. Springer-Verlag, New York

Hokanson J E, Megaree E I, O'Hagen S E, Perry A M 1976 Behavioural, emotional and autonomic reactions to stress among incarcerated, youthful offenders. Criminal Justice & Behaviour 3: 203–234

Hunter H 1977 XYY males: some clinical and psychiatric aspects deriving from a survey of 1811 males in hospitals for the mentally handicapped. British Journal of Psychiatry 131: 468–477

Hutchinson R R, Pierce G E, Emley G S, Proni T J, Sauer R A 1977 The laboratory measurement of human anger. Biobehavioral Reviews 1: 241–259

Hutt C, Vaizey M J 1966 Differential effects of group density on social behaviour. Nature, London. 209: 1371–1372

Jeffrey C R 1971 A new model: crime control through environmental engineering. Sage Publications, Beverley Hills

Kinzel A F 1974 Syndromes resulting from social isolation — 3. Abnormalities of personal space in violent prisoners. In: Cullen J H (ed) Experimental behaviour: a basis for the study of mental disturbance. Irish University Press, Dublin

Kiritz S, Moos R H 1974 Physiological effects of social environments. Psychosomatic Medicine 36: 96–114

Kutash et al (eds) 1978 Violence: Perspectives on Murder and Aggression. Jossey-Bass, San Francisco

Lagerspetz K M J 1979 Modification of aggressiveness in mice. In: Fesbach S, Fraczek A (eds) Aggression and Behavior Change. Praeger, New York

Looney J G, Lipp M R, Spitzer R L 1978 A new method of classification for psychophysiologic disorders. American Journal of Psychiatry 135: 304–308

Lorenz K 1966 On Aggression. Harcourt Brace Jovanovich, New York

Lunde D T 1975 Murder and Madness. Stanford Alumni Association, California

MacLean P D 1964 Man and his animal brains. Modern Medicine 32: 95–106

Marsh P, Rosser E, Harre R 1978 The Rules of Disorder. Routledge and Kegan Paul, London

Maynard-Smith J, Parker G A 1976 The logic of asymmetric contests. Animal Behaviour 24: 159–175

McCain G, Cox V C, Paulus P B 1980 The effect of prison crowding on inmate behavior. Report from the Department of Psychology, University of Texas at Arlington, Texas

Milgram S 1974 Obedience to authority. Harper & Row, New York

Morris D 1969 The human zoo. Jonathan Cape, London

Morris D 1977 Manwatching. Jonathan Cape, London

Moyer K E 1968 Kinds of aggression and their physiological basis. Communications in Behavioral Biology 2: 65–87

Mummendey A, Bornewasser M, Loschper G, Linneweber V 1982 Defining interactions as aggressive in specific social contexts. Aggressive Behavior 8: 224–228

Murphy J M 1977 War stress and civilian Vietnamese: a study of psychological effects. Acta Psychiatrica Scandinavica 56: 92–108

Newman O 1975 Reactions to the 'defensible space' study and some further findings. International Journal of Mental Health 4: 48–70

Newman O 1976 Design guidelines for creating defensible space. National Institute of Law Enforcement and Criminal Justice, US Government Printing Office, Washington, DC

Noble G K 1939 The role of dominance in the social life of birds. Auk 56: 263–273

Olweus D 1977 Aggression in schools. Hemisphere Publishing Co, Washington, DC

Olweus D 1978 Personality factors and aggression: with special reference to violence within the peer group. In: Hartup W W, de Wit J (eds) Origins of aggression, Mouton, The Hague

Olweus D 1979 Stability of aggressive reaction patterns in males: a review. Psychological Bulletin 86: 852–875

Pablant P, Baxter J C 1975 Environmental correlates of school vandalism. Journal of American Institute of Planners 41: 270–279

Parmigiani S, Mainardi D, Pasquali A 1981 A comparison of aggressiveness in dominant, subordinate and isolated house mice. In: Brain P F, Benton D (eds) The biology of aggression, Noordhoff/Sijthoff, Alphen aan den Rijn

Reynolds V 1980 The biology of human action, 2nd edn. W H Freeman & Co, Oxford

Rockwell D, Hodgson G, Beljan J R, Winget C M 1976 Psychologic and psychophysiologic response to 105 days of social isolation. Aviation Space and Environmental Medicine 47: 1087–1098

Rose R M 1969 Androgen responses to stress 1. Psychoendocrine relationships and assessment of androgen activity. Psychosomatic Medicine 31: 405–417

Rose R M, Bourne P G, Poe R O, Mougey E H, Collins D R, Mason J W 1969 Androgen responses to stress 2. Excretion of teststerone epitestosterone, androsterone and etiocholanolone during basic combat training and under threat of attack. Psychosomatic Medicine 31: 418–436

Rotton J, Frey J, Barry T, Milligan M, Fitzpatrick M 1977 Modelling, malodorous air pollution and interpersonal aggression. Paper presented at meeting of Midwestern Psychological Association, Chicago

Rusbult C E 1979 Crowding and human behavior: a guide for urban planners. Environment and Planning A 11: 731–744

Russell G W 1981 Aggression in sport. In: Brain P F, Benton D (eds) Multidisciplinary approaches to aggression research. Elsevier North Holland, Amsterdam

Russell G W, Drewery B R 1976 Crowd size and competitive aspects of aggression in ice hockey: an archival study. Human Relations 29: 723–735

Sabini J 1978 Aggression in the laboratory. In: Kutash I L et al (eds) Violence: perspectives on murder and aggression. Jossey Bass, San Francisco

Savin-Williams R C 1977 Dominance in a human adolescent group. Animal Behaviour 25: 400–406

Schmidt D E, Keating J P 1979 Human crowding and personal control: An integration of the research. Psychological Bulletin 86: 680–700

Seligman M E P 1975 Helplessness. W H Freeman and Co, San Francisco

Shenkin L I 1973 An application of ethology to aspects of human behaviour. British Journal of Medicine and Psychology 46: 123–134

Silberbauer G B 1973 Sociobiology of the G/Wi Bushmen. PhD Dissertation, Monash University, Australia

Sommer R 1969 Personal space; the behavioral basis for design. Prentice Hall, Englewood Cliffs, NJ

Sorensen M W 1974 A review of aggressive behavior in the tree shrews. In: Holloway R L (ed) Primate aggression, territoriality and xenophobia: a comparative perspective. Academic Press, New York

Steinmetz S K, Straus M A (eds) 1974 Violence in the family. Harper and Row Inc, New York

Straus M A 1974 Levelling, civility and violence in the family. Journal of Marriage and the Family 36: 13–29

Shuttles G D 1968 The social order of the slum: Ethnicity and territoriality in the inner city. The University of Chicago Press, Chicago

Shuttles G D 1972 The social construction of communities. The University of Chicago Press, Chicago

Tannenbaum P H 1973 Studies in film — and television — mediated arousal and aggression: a progress report. In: Television and Social Behavior Vol 5, Washington, DC

Tiger L, Fox R 1974 The imperial animal. Paladin, St. Albans

Treshow M 1976 The human environment. McGraw-Hill, New York

Tullar R M 1977 The human species: its nature, evolution and ecology. McGraw-Hill, New York

Valzelli L 1980 An approach to neuroanatomical and neurochemical psychophysiology. C G Edizioni Medico Scientifiche, Torino

Valzelli L 1981 Psychobiology of aggression and violence. Raven Press, New York

Van der Dennen J M G 1980 Problems in the concepts and definitions of aggression, violence, and some related terms. Publication of the Rijksuniversiteit Groningen, Polemologish Instituut, The Netherlands

Verner J 1977 On the adaptive significance of territoriality. American Naturalist 111: 769–775

Wilson E O 1975 Sociobiology. Harvard University Press, Cambridge, Mass

Wilson E O 1978 On human nature. Harvard University Press, Cambridge, Massachusetts

Zalenznik A, De Vries M F R, Howard J 1977 Stress reactions in organizations: syndromes, causes and consequences. Behavioral Science 22: 151–162

Zubek J P 1973 Behavioral and physiological effects of prolonged sensory and perceptual deprivation: a review. In: Rasmussen J E (ed) Man in isolation and confinement. Aldine Publishing Co., Chicago

Geographical approaches to mental health

INTRODUCTION

Until recently, few people seriously considered the possibility that psychiatric illness is infectious (Hare 1979; Schwab & Schab 1978; Crow 1983). This may account for the fact that it has not received much attention in human geography, which is dominated by the notions of proximity and contagion. The simplest and oldest geographical truth — that all things are related to all other things, but more so at close distances — has predetermined most analysis. Those geographers inclined towards medicine have concentrated on disease aetiology, where hypotheses about spatial contagion and diffusion could be tested for a variety of illnesses (Pyle 1979). Traditionally, no such data have been available for the study of psychiatric disorder, and it has been necessary to look elsewhere for relevant hypotheses and methodologies. In spite of this, recent geographical literature shows evidence of a small but steady trickle of interest in mental health (Giggs 1979; Smith 1977). However, this work cannot yet be classified rigorously, and a 'geography of mental health', i.e. a body of work with unique characteristics, is simply non-existent (Smith 1978), while evidence as to the possible infectious aetiology of some psychiatric illness has not yet aroused geographical interest.

This chapter describes some existing work; outlines possibilities for the future; and documents the contributions that can be made by adding a geographical perspective to the existing social science research on mental health. Three paradigms will be identified within human geography (Herbert 1979):

1. Areal — identification of spatial patterns and differentiation of environmental characteristics from one location to another
2. Ecological — aggregation at the locality level of social and environmental characteristics which are thought to have causal influences on human outcomes
3. Spatial/behavioural — focusing on the individual and group processes which help to determine the spatial patterns observable in society

AREAL ASSOCIATIONS AND THE SEARCH FOR REGIONAL PATTERNS

Using maps and regionalisation techniques, geographers have spent much time searching the world for spatial patterns. In mental health, the most typical approach involves identification of such patterns in prevalence rates, and usually of socio-demographic indicators that co-vary spatially with that pathology. The simplest and one of the most useful applications of this work is in assessment of mental health needs.

Epidemiological studies and needs assessment

Numerous socio-demographic correlates of psychiatric illness have been identified (Longest et al. 1976; Dohrenwend & Dohrenwend 1969; Schwab and Schwab 1978; Redick et al, 1971) and a geographical analysis of prevalence rates and socio-demographic indicators, using spatially disaggregated data, can be very useful. One application of simple descriptive analysis is in programme planning and the identification of regions where the demand for services exceeds the supply, in relation to national norms. In the US, comparing distribution of needs and location of community mental health centres (CMHCs), should allow the identification of catchment areas where prevalence rates are above the State mean, but which still have no MHC to act as a focus for services.

   Another application is in assessing consumer response to the provision of services; Fig. 5.1a shows that admissions to mental hospitals for alcoholism from Oklahoma are highest in three areas — the northwestern part, the central area, and the northeast. The State's three mental hospitals are also located in these areas (Fig. 5.1b), and the use of such facilities is probably related, in part, to their availability and proximity — a phenomenon referred to as 'Jarvis's Law' (Shannon & Dever 1974; Sohler & Claphis 1972).

   A third application of the regionalisation approach is in the identification of specific socio-demographic variables that are spatially correlated with psychiatric prevalence rates. The value of such a technique is to highlight those groups within the population whose mental health needs are greater than the norm for the State. With such data, health planners can assess needs amongst special populations more effectively. Table 5.1 shows the results of a survey to assess the prevalence of emotional problems amongst 2638 families in Oklahoma. Respondents were asked: 'how many members of your household, including yourself, now have an emotional problem for which help is needed; whether or not help is being received'? Prevalence was highest amongst Indians and Blacks (7.8 per cent and 7.5 per cent) and lowest amongst white males, especially those living in rural areas; rates amongst women, the elderly, and urban dwellers were all higher than the mean for the entire sample. Though the survey question asked about

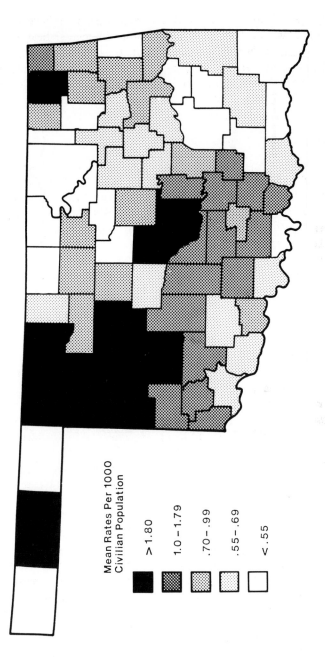

Fig. 5.1a DMH alcohol admission rates, 1975–1979

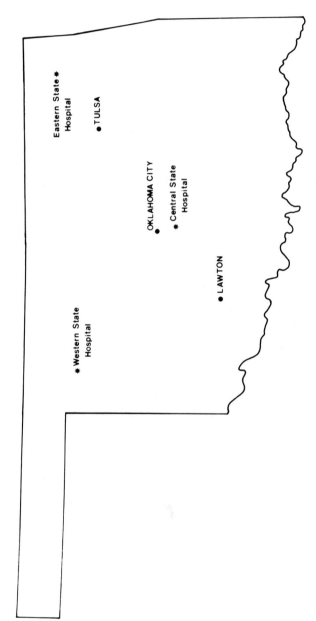

Fig. 5.1b Oklahoma's public mental hospitals

Table 5.1 Prevalence Rates for 'emotional problems'

	Respondents[a]	Sample Size[b]	Number experiencing emotional problems	%
Total population	2638	7197	328	5.0
Blacks	186	559	31	7.5
Native Americans	80	234	19	7.8
Women	1472	3670[c]	194	6.2
Elderly	949	383[d]	25	5.9
Rural[e]	1394		137	3.9
Urban	1244		191	6.2

   [a] Number of respondents (families) surveyed
   [b] Number of individuals represented by all the families surveyed
   [c] Estimated as 51% of the total number of individuals in the sample
   [d] Number of families with no persons less than 60 years old
   [e] Defined as persons not living in the 5 most urbanised Oklahoma counties (Cleveland, Oklahoma, Canadian, Tulsa, and Comanche;

'emotional problems', rather than hospitalised psychiatric illness, the relatively low rates recorded indicate that respondents were only including fairly serious problems.

A combination of these techniques provides a graphic representation of the comprehensiveness of alcoholism programmes in Oklahoma (Smith 1980a). The first map (Fig. 5.2a) was constructed by scoring each county according to the services it provides for alcoholics (Longest et al. 1976; Glaser et al. 1978). Counties providing a full range of in-patient, out-patient, and residential facilities score the highest (6) on comprehensiveness, one with no facilities scores the lowest (1), and suitable cut-off points were assigned for the intermediate categories. When the levels of need in each county were also measured, those with a surplus of alcoholism services could be identified (Fig. 5.2b).

This illustrates another application of regionalisation techniques: analysis of the geographical patterns of service delivery and of the corresponding needs for services suggests some deviations in the equity of the existing system. The graphs in Fig. 5.3 show the relationship between prevalence rates of alcoholism and the comprehensiveness of treatment programmes; they also illustrate the extent to which service delivery is 'progressive' in response to different measures of need. This is most clearly the case in relation to the absolute numbers of people in treatment for alcoholism at State facilities (Figs. 5.3a and b). Thus, the counties that have more people in treatment have the most comprehensive services; this relationship may either be trivial, i.e. true by definition, or a result of Jarvis's Law (Shannon & Dever 1974). In other words, we cannot be sure that the demand for services has 'created' the supply, and is therefore a *bona fide* example of a progressive delivery system, because there is substantial evidence that the process often works in reverse.

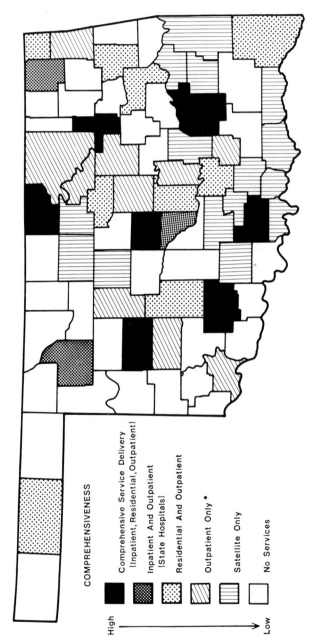

*Delaware And Washita Counties Have One Residential Facility (Halfway House) Each, But No Outpatient Facility

Fig. 5.2a Alcoholism treatment comprehensiveness, 1980

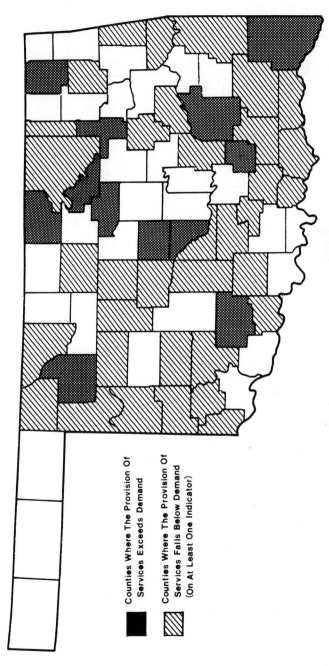

Fig. 5.2b Alcohol Services: equating supply and demand factors

Counties Where The Provision Of Services Exceeds Demand

Counties Where The Provision Of Services Falls Below Demand (On At Least One Indicator)

PROGRAM   COMPREHENSIVENESS   AND THE   DEMAND   FOR
ALCOHOL   SERVICES

A. ALCOHOL ADMISSIONS TO MENTAL HOSPITALS

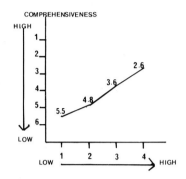

B. ALCOHOL INTAKE TO ALL STATE FUNDED PROGRAMS

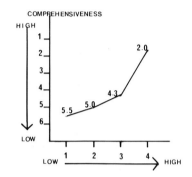

C. ADMISSION RATES TO MENTAL HOSPITALS
(PER 1000)

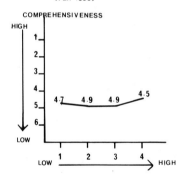

D. INTAKE RATES TO ALL STATE FUNDED PROGRAMS
(PER 1000)

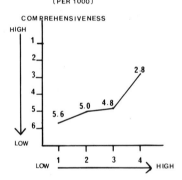

E. DRUNKENNESS ARRESTS (PER 1000)

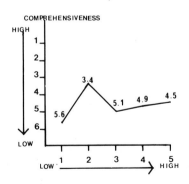

F. D.U.I. ARRESTS (PER 1000)

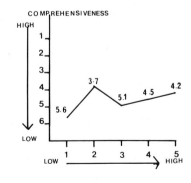

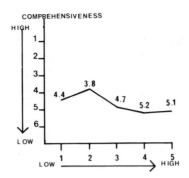

Fig. 5.3 Programme comprehensiveness and the demand for alcohol services. A Alcohol admission to mental hospitals. B Alcohol intake to all state-funded programmes. C Admission rates to mental hospitals (per 1000). D Intake rates to all state-funded programmes (per 1000). E Drunkenness arrests (per 1000). F DUI arrests (per 1000). G Drinking driver ratio

Figs. 5.3c and d show the relationships between prevalence and comprehensiveness, using the same treatment data, but this time they are transformed into rates per 1000 of the civilian population. Both curves appear flatter, which suggests a lesser degree of responsiveness of provision to increases in needs. Therefore, the spatial pattern of service delivery for alcoholics in Oklahoma may be more closely linked with, and responsive to, absolute numbers of people in treatment than to *per capita* rates of the condition. It is conceivable that programme planners respond more readily to the visibility of the problem within their communities than to the rate at which it occurs; the presence of 20 alcoholics in a small community may create a public demand more directly than the presence of hundreds or even thousands, spread across a large city.

Finally, Figs 5.3e, f, and g show the relationships between comprehensiveness and the need for services, measured by non-treatment indicators of problem drinking (drunkenness arrests; arrests for driving under the influence; drinking drivers involved in accidents). The graphs show only slightly higher levels of comprehensiveness with higher levels of demand for service, and in fact for the drinking-driver ratio, the service delivery pattern is 'regressive', with more comprehensive services located in areas with low demand.

Regional patterns in mental health policy

The search for geographical patterns at the regional level has only recently begun, but one of its most fruitful areas is the inter-relationship of deinstitutionalisation and the implementation of community mental health (CMH)

programmes. These policies are implemented in the US at the State level — usually by departments of mental health — or at the substate level, by groups of counties or city governments. There have been hypotheses of two kinds about the geographical implementation of these policies. The first, primarily from political science, has identified regional patterns in the adoption of policy innovations (Foster 1978; Walker 1969). From these, it has been possible to test a variety of explanations for regional clustering of 'innovativeness', ranging from simple proximity and contagion effects to more complex ecological assumptions that states with similar environmental, economic, or political characteristics will adopt innovations at the same rate.

Walker (1969) found that regional patterns could be explained fairly well with four variables — urbanisation, industrialisation, population size, and the equitable political apportionment of urban areas. It was clear that a state's innovativeness was more closely related to the characteristics of the state than to the policy in question, and that certain states are typically early adopters in many areas of policy. The second hypothesis suggests that some of these same states had also been leaders in the psychiatric deinstitutionalisation and CMH movements (Bloom 1977; Bachrach 1976). Specific studies have investigated the correlates of particular patterns of implementation in mental health policies, and the results demonstrate that such states as California, New York, Texas, and Illinois have consistently been innovators (Langsley et al. 1978; Aviram et al 1976: Hogben et al. 1979).

In general, these studies imply that deinstitutionalisation policies, and corresponding attempts to provide mental health services in the community, occur in response to a number of factors operating at the national level, with geographically variant factors superimposed at the local (state) level to bring about faster or slower rates of change. In New York State, Aviram & Syme (1976) noted that in 1968–1969, there was a nine per cent decline in the number of resident patients, which was more than twice the annual decline in any other year; but during 1968, a strike in several state hospitals forced administrators to release more patients than would have otherwise been the case. In California, Langsley et al. (1978) attributed much of the push toward greater provision of community services to the passage of the Lanterman-Petris-Short (LPS) Act in 1968, which brought about an unprecedented shift in the locus of treatment. There is also some evidence that rates of admission to mental hospitals are inversely related to downturns in the economy (Brenner 1973; Dear et al. 1979), which might be generalised to suggest that the overall prevalence of psychiatric disorder at both the national and the local level is greater during times of economic hardship. To date, this is not clearly established, although Brenner (1979) has applied his arguments to explain the relationship between unemployment and a variety of mortality rates. Marshall & Funch (1979) have seriously questioned Brenner's findings, largely because admission rates to mental hospitals appear to be related more closely to hospital capacity than to the economy. Therefore, we might expect states with the greatest investment in such facilities to continue having the highest admission rates, which appears to be the case (Smith & Hanham 1981a).

Deinstitutionalisation: a spatial – temporal analysis

Since the mid-1950s, most American states have significantly reorganised their mental health services. This process of 'deinstitutionalisation' has resulted in a reduction in the number of resident patients in public mental hospitals from 558 922 in 1955 to 170 619 in 1976. Each state operates its policies differently, and presumably encounters a unique set of circumstances, but it would be reasonable to expect the process to have some geographical pattern. To test this hypothesis, Smith & Hanham (1981a) collected data for the lower 48 contiguous states and the District of Columbia on three major indicators of deinstitutionalisation: resident patients in mental hospitals (1955–1975); admissions (1955–1975); and discharges (1958–1975). The data were analysed by time-path analysis, which identifies a number of factors to represent the patterns in the data over time. The first factor approximates to the mean trend in the deinstitutionalisation data, while subsequent factors act as correction terms. For each of the three deinstitutionalisation rates, there was a dominant trend, accounting for 91 per cent, 79 per cent, and 81 per cent of the variance for residents, admissions, and discharges respectively; secondary trends accounted for 6 per cent, 13 per cent, and 12 per cent (Fig. 5.4).

For resident patients, the dominant curve shows a pattern of gradual reduction, accelerating after 1962 and slowing down in the 1970s. The secondary component shows the rate increasing gradually until 1968, and then falling gradually. For admission rates, the dominant component shows a pattern of slow, steady increases until the middle 1960s, followed by a period of rapidly rising admissions. The secondary trend also shows a pattern of slow increase until 1971, followed by a rapid reduction. For discharge rates, the major trend suggests a dramatic increase after 1964; the secondary component shows an increase until 1971, followed by a sharp deceleration.

The scores for any given state indicate the extent to which its pattern of deinstitutionalisation can be described by either of the components. If it has a high score on the dominant one, this indicates that its deinstitutionalisation policies closely followed those of the aggregate for the US. A state with a low score on the dominant component, but high on the secondary one, would have a deinstitutionalisation trend similar to the secondary trend. Each state's scores on both components were subsequently used to search out regional patterns in the three indicator rates, to determine which states had similar trends for residents, admissions, and discharges, through the period. A six-group classification was the most suitable for each of the three rates, and its spatial distribution for resident patients is shown in Fig. 5.5. This reveals some regionalisation, e.g. states in group 6 cluster in the southeast and the northwest (Montana, Wyoming, and South Dakota); and group 4 includes five states in the northeast; Rhode Island, Massachusetts, Connecticut, New Jersey, and New Hampshire. The distributions for admissions and discharges are illustrated and discussed by Smith & Hanham (1981a); the time path of one representative state in each group is shown in Fig. 5.6. Several basic patterns can be seen in these hospitalisation rates during the last two decades.

A first pattern is one of rapid decline, characteristic of New York and Washington, DC (group 5), which differ from all others in that both began

RESIDENTS:

TIME COMPONENTS

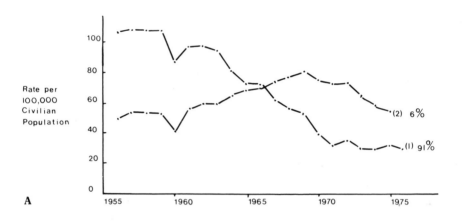

A

ADMISSIONS:

TIME COMPONENTS

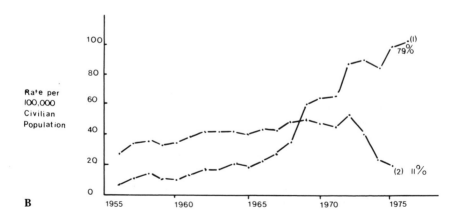

B

RELEASES:
TIME COMPONENTS

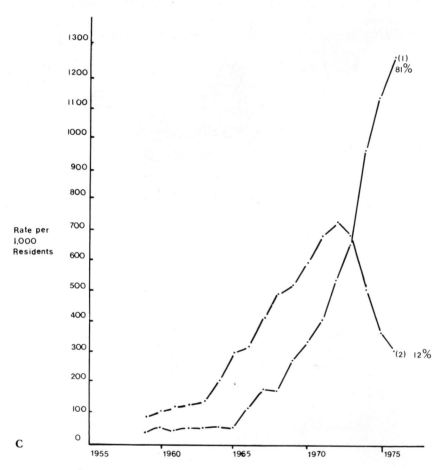

Fig. 5.4 Deinstitutionalisation in the District of Columbia. a Residents: time components. b Admissions: time components. c Releases: time components

the period with high rates of hospitalisation (870 per 100 000 in Washington, DC; and 600 in New York), but subsequently reduced the rates substantially. By 1975, however, their in-patient rates were still absolutely higher than the 1955 rates in many other states, e.g. those in groups 2 and 6. Two groups of states (1 and 3) experienced a moderate decline by reducing their in-patients more gradually, but these states began and ended the period with substantially lower rates than those in New York and Washington. In two states in group 1 (Minnesota and California), hospitalisation rates had stabilised and even slightly increased by the mid-1970s, which

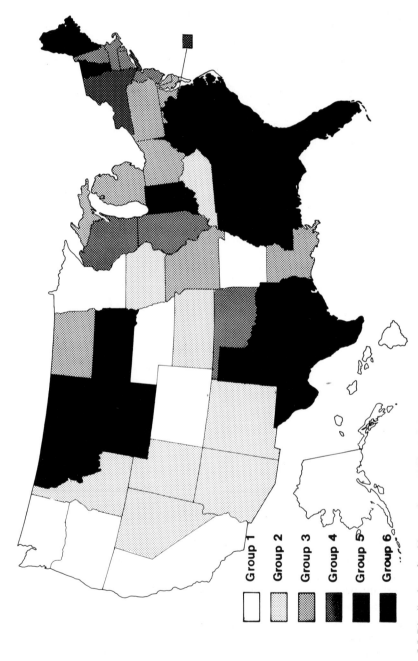

Fig. 5.5 Distribution of resident patients, 1955–1975, by six-group classification

suggests a reversal of previous deinstitutionalisation policies. In California, it is possible that the adverse publicity surrounding the closure of some state hospitals and subsequent effects on communities like San Jose may have been partly responsible for this re-evaluation (Wolpert & Wolpert 1976). It is also interesting that in both groups 1 and 3, there is evidence of regionalisation — a west coast cluster in group 1 (California, Oregon, Washington); and northern/eastern in group 3 (Ohio, Michigan, Pennsylvania, Delaware, Maryland).

Another pattern, one of slow decline, is evident in groups 2 and 6, where the states appear to have implemented deinstitutionalisation gradually. Two regional clusters are evident: one in the west (group 2 — Idaho, New Mexico, Nevada, Arizona, Utah), where in-patient rates have traditionally been much lower than in other parts of the country; and another in the south/southeast (group 6 — Florida, Georgia, Alabama, Mississippi, S. Carolina, N. Carolina, Tennessee, Virginia, W. Virginia). In general, group 6 states began the period with higher rates than those in group 2, but were consistently conservative in reducing their hospital population in 1955–1970. In the 1970s, several of these states began to speed up the process, perhaps as their local treatment facilities started to offer viable alternatives to hospital care, and as the CMH movement spread.

In group 4, it is more difficult to detect clear-cut trends. Thus in Rhode Island, there was a gradual decline in hospitalisation rates in the 1950s, followed by a rapid decline after 1963 and a return to a slower decline in the early 1970s. Other states on the east coast exhibited similar trends, e.g. New Hampshire, Massachusetts, Connecticut and New Jersey; however, they began the period with high rates of hospitalisation, i.e. usually 400–500 per 100 000.

These and the others in group 4, exhibit time paths that most clearly resemble the dominant curve for the country as a whole (Fig. 5.4a). Deinstitutionalisation began gradually in the early 1950s, partly as a result of the increased use of medication, which helped patients function more effectively in the community. After the passage of the Community Mental Health Centers (CMHC) Act in 1963, a determined effort was made to reduce the emphasis on state hospitals, but the rate of reduction slowed considerably in the 1970s, as states evaluated the wisdom of rapid deinstitutionalisation.

The purpose of the time path analysis was exploratory, but three possible explanations for the regional pattern could be investigated. Firstly, spatial diffusion of policies; it is plausible that the implementation of a policy in one state might be conducive to its implementation in another. This might be based on proximity or spatial contagion, which could have a 'snowball' effect within a particular region, or be aspatial, when a politically progressive state implements a model programme adopted from another, equally progressive state.

Secondly, regional administrative homogeneity for administrative purposes; the National Institute of Mental Health (NIMH) divided the US into ten regions. It is possible that policies are filtered down from the Federal level, and reinterpreted at the regional level to suit local circumstances. If so, it would be reasonable to anticipate some homogeneity between the policies adopted by states in the same region. Within each region, one or more states probably act as a leader in innovativeness (Walker 1969).

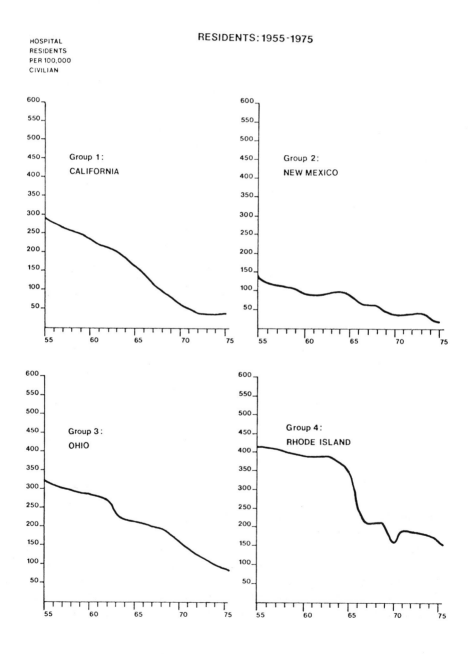

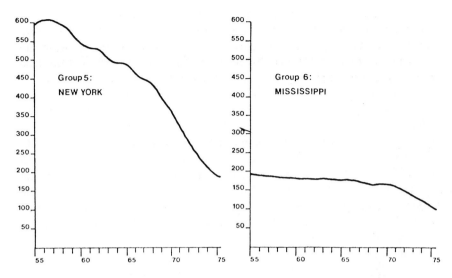

Fig. 5.6 Time path of deinstitutionalisation, 1955–1975, in six representative states

Thirdly, uniform regions: this explanation involves the most fundamental geographical hypothesis, i.e. that states with similar social, economic, and demographic characteristics will adopt uniform policies. Thus, northeastern states might be expected to have higher hospitalisation rates than western and mountain states, perhaps because of their higher population densities, or as a result of regional differences in fiscal policies and cultural traditions.

Community mental health: An innovation in mental health policy

Deinstitutionalisation is a two-stage process, involving a shift away from traditional institutional care and concurrent expansion of community-based services (Bachrach 1976). As the research described above indicates, many states have substantially reduced their emphasis on institutions, but the provision of community-based care has not proceeded as well as was hoped (Bassuk & Gerson 1978; Rose 1979).

In 1963, the CMHC Act made federal funds available for the construction and staffing of comprehensive CMHCs in each of 1499 catchment areas. Over time, federal funds were to be matched by state and local monies, but this was the first formal attempt to establish a national policy in the US.

CMHCs were intended to be much more than new buildings; they were to provide a coordinated system of preventive, treatment, and rehabilitative services within the community. It was hoped that they would provide access to comprehensive mental health services for all Americans by 1980; but by 1978, only 718 of the 1499 centres had been funded, and less than half of the population was being served (NIMH 1979). In evaluating the spread of the movement and its effectiveness, geographical contributions are possible in three overlapping areas: utilisation of services under the catchment area concept; the provision of comprehensive services; and the diffusion of the new policy across the country. To date, only a modest start has been made in this, however, and most of it not by geographers.

States wishing to apply for federal funds were required to divide themselves into non-overlapping tracts ('catchment areas'). Each tract was defined as 'a geographical section within which a CMHC may be reached in one hour's travelling time, and having a population of 75 000 to 200 000' (Regester 1974). As Tischler et al (1975) have observed, this was simply a geographical entity, containing individuals and groups who, after the drawing of a boundary, were defined as a population. Guidelines from the NIMH left determination of the catchment areas to the discretion of each state, but the boundaries were expected to be based on such factors as existing neighbourhoods, planning areas, physical environment, and existing resources. It became obvious, however, that areas could be delimited by a wide range of characteristics, and that they would vary tremendously in size, shape, and in the population served.

Regester (1974) argued that many of the characteristics of the centres would be determined by how the planners and professionals defined the term 'community'. Table 5.2 presents a number of alternative conceptual models of this term, each of which has different implications for determining the target population, the staff characteristics required, the needs to be served, and the effects of the centre on the host community. Different conceptions of 'community' may have resulted in some of the subsequently reported geographical inequities in service delivery patterns.

In Oklahoma City, for example, the built-up area is cross-cut by four catchment areas, that look as though they might have been created in the best spirit of political gerrymandering. The effect of such a pattern, assuming adoption of the Geographical Area model is that some of the people living in the long tentacles of certain catchment areas may have an illogically long journey to reach their centre. Dear (1977a) also observed this phenomenon in Lancaster County, Pennsylvania, where the catchment rule produced serious distortions in the geographical patterns of usage; it was calculated that more than half of the clients visiting a particular centre had to pass a closer one along the way, and that if all clients were assigned to their closest centre, there could be as much as 25 per cent saving in travel distances. This consideration is likely to be increasingly important in future times of higher travel costs.

Huffine & Craig (1973) described an attempt to define a catchment area boundary in Baltimore by plotting the residential locations of individuals receiving psychiatric care at the Johns Hopkins Hospital, and thus allowing the consumers to define a 'natural' catchment area, which was a relatively small part of Central Baltimore, with about 140 000 inhabitants. However, in spite of the obvious advantages of this self-definition in terms of accessi-

Table 5.2 Different conceptions of 'community' and their service-related implications

Conceptual model of 'community'	Criteria determining target population (demographic definition)	Staff characteristics	Awareness of community needs	Effect on target population
1. Geographical area	Specific catchment area based on residence in a certain area	Must live inside catchment area	Produces territorial behaviour, client 'dumping', jurisdictional squabbling	Creates 'putative' boundaries, alienates some clients who must travel long distances
2. Majority	The greatest number of people in a given region	Must live inside catchment area and be continually active in the community	Impossible goal of responding to all needs	Creates a 'numbers game,' depending on quantity not quality
3. Vocal minority	The voice of the economically and politically most powerful	Requires specialist staff member	Political influence on the running of the agency, produces unequal services	Discriminatory and prejudicial service delivered
4. Society at large	Focus on all people and on all problems	Requires complete diversity of staff	Should enhance awareness at all levels	Enhances positive mental health
5. Common body	Focus on specific attributes, e.g. life-style, race	Allows homogenous staff	Lack of recognition of some types of problems, e.g. minorities	In-fighting between community factions, decreasing tolerance for individual difference
6. Feeling of belongingness	A group of people who share feelings and accept others	Staff functions should mirror conception of community	Staff should become aware of community needs	Promotes positive mental health
7. Elitist	Determined mainly by staff attitudes about who they want to serve	Hiring of specialists, researchers, others with elitist views	Usually detracts from consideration of community needs	Authoritarian staff, suspicious of 'grass roots' organisations

Source: Adapted from Regester (1974)

bility, the area was extremely diverse demographically. This diversity was thought to imply markedly different patterns of need across the catchment area, so that an access-based definition of a community may be valid, but it is by no means the only or necessarily the most effective one.

Several studies have provided evidence that the establishment of catchment areas has helped to satisfy needs that in the past have not been met through traditional services. Tischler et al. (1972) argued that in catchment populations, there is increased accessibility to and use of services, and a shift towards service by a comprehensive network, rather than more fragmented and episodic resort to emergency facilities. Secondly, out-patient services in a catchment area are generally more accessible and comprehensive than those offered in a traditional setting; intakes are briefer, referrals more successful, waiting lists shorter, and greater use is made of crisis intervention services (Tischler et al. 1975). Patients are also more satisfied with the services they receive (Goldblatt et al. 1973). Thirdly, catchmented services sometimes ensure greater representation of socially disadvantaged groups in the population (Tischler 1977). However, in spite of these positive results the issue is far from determined, and for every report documenting the advantages to be gained, there is a rebuttal. Particularly vociferous was the so-called Nader report (Chu & Trotter 1974) and even Tischler et al. (1975) admitted that catchmenting had had almost no impact on the provision of indirect services, such as consultation with community groups and public education, though opinions may vary about the importance of these.

Mollica & Redlich (1980) suggest that the findings of the Tischler group may not be representative of all MHCs. They investigated treatment patterns for psychiatric patients in New Haven, Connecticut and compared their findings with the results reported for 1950 in Hollingshead & Redlich's book *Social Class and Mental Illness* (1958). A number of significant changes were identified for the 25-year period, e.g. expansion in the overall availability of psychiatric services, and a vast proliferation in out-patient provision. However, the state hospital had continued to provide the primary source of in-patient care, in spite of its decreasing size and the growth of other public and private services. This was particularly true for groups such as the elderly (90.6 per cent of the in-patient services for this group in the mental hospital), alcoholics (95.1 per cent), and minority patients (95 per cent for blacks, 100 per cent for Hispanics).

Since a lack of equity in service provision for different sub-groups is probably associated with care of a lower quality, in spite of the expansion of CMH services, there are serious doubts whether the goals of the 1963 legislation can be met. As Mollica and Redlich observed, it is a common error to equate equity with accesibility. Other variables should be considered, particularly quality of care and respect for each individual in treatment; 'if readily accessible services are for some reason dehumanising or of inadequate quality, these services would be considered inequitable . . . (and) if the delivery of these services is primarily determined by patients' demographic characteristics and not by patients' need, the situation would also be inequitable'. In both the United Kingdom and France, however, mental health services are being planned and developed nationally on a catchment area basis (Freeman 1983).

Due to falling financial support, a number of CMHCs have had to reduce their commitments in recent years. Weirich & Sheinfeld (1982) report that one centre in Philadelphia had to close a peripheral out-patient clinic and 'recentralise' services; the total hours of service offered were reduced by 40 per cent, and 45 per cent of the clients were discharged, mostly at their own request. However, this fall was differential between the sexes and racial groups, Hispanic men being most affected. Although longer distances, need to cross major routes, and unfamiliar public transport were relevant to this, they appeared less important than crossing of community boundaries, loss of cultural supports through the move, uncertainty of travelling in unknown areas, and identification of the new service with another community and racial group. Careful planning of such changes is therefore advised, though many CMHCs may well be unable to undertake this in the way they believe to be right.

Examining comprehensiveness of MHC services, Longest et al (1976) attempted to match resources with needs in each of the 1499 catchment areas in the United States. Needs were assessed using the Mental Health Demographic Profile System (MHDPS), on the assumption that there is a relationship between socio-demographic conditions in a catchment area and the prevalence of psychiatric disorders (both treated and untreated). The service capabilities of each area were assessed by an inventory of the services defined as essential in the initial CMHC Act: in-patient, out-patient, partial hospitalisation, and 24-hour emergency provision. A typology of five categories of comprehensiveness was created by determining whether the four services were both available and accessible in each area.

The summarised data in Table 5.3 analyse the areas by need and by comprehensiveness; only 253 (16.9 per cent) had services that were adequate by the originally defined standards, whereas of the remaining 1246, 807 (53.8 per cent) required major structural modifications, and 439 (29.3 per cent) minor ones. Major modifications were required if any of the essential services were absent, and minor if any service was deficient in availability or accessibility. These results indicate that to some extent, catchment area services are responsive to levels of assessed needs — 40 (30.8 per cent) areas in the high-need category had fully comprehensive services, and another 34 (26.1 per cent) required only minor modifications. This compared favourably with the situation in low-need areas, where only 24 (8.9 per cent) had fully comprehensive services, and 165 (60.9 per cent) were in need of major modifications. Longest et al. argue that it may not be urgently necessary to provide additional CMHC services in these low-need areas, partly because the sociodemographic data indicate low prevalence rates for psychiatric illness, and partly because the population is likely to be mobile, and therefore

Table 5.3 Levels of need and the provision of community mental health services

Catchment area level of need	Structural modification	Some structural modification[a]	Minor structural modification only[b]	Major structural modification[c]	Number of catchment areas in need category
Low need	8.9% (24)	91.1% (247)	30.2% (82)	60.9% (165)	271
Moderate need	17.2 (189)	82.8 (909)	29.4 (323)	53.4 (586)	1098
High need	30.8 (40)	69.2 (90)	26.1 (34)	43.1 (56)	130
All catchment areas	16.9 (253)	83.1 (1246)	29.3 (439)	53.8 (807)	1499

[a] A service structure requires structural modification if one or more of its services are: deficient in resource quantities, deficient in accessibility; deficient in availability.

[b] A service structure requires minor structural modification if the necessary modifications are limited to (1) eliminating deficiencies of quantity and/or (2) eliminating deficiencies of accessibility. All such service structures are at least complete.

[c] A service structure requires major structural modification if there are any of the essential services absent in the catchment area. Such a service structure may also suffer from any or all other forms of deficiencies in remaining services.

Source: Adapted from Longest et al. (1976)

able to travel to nearby facilities in higher need/higher comprehensiveness areas. In general the low-need areas are in suburbs, from which it may be easier to reach the facility-rich central city areas. In comparison, the moderate-need catchment areas are in a much worse situation, with 909 (82.8 per cent) requiring additional services (323 or 29.4 per cent needing minor changes, and 586 or 53.4 per cent major changes). It was concluded that the service situation in high-need areas is not as responsive to needs as it could be; there, residents have both the least mobility and the greatest demand for low-cost services. To find that 69.2 per cent of the areas need additional services, and that 43.1 per cent need major improvements (including seven that have no services at all) indicated that the CMHC programme was far short of its goals, and the situation since then has probably become worse rather than better.

Although these authors did not attempt to present their data geographically, they examined the relationships between needs and services in urban as opposed to rural catchment areas. As might be expected, central city areas have the highest service levels; but non-metropolitan urban areas (where a large proportion of the population live) were considerably worse off than non-metropolitan rural areas. When poverty levels were entered into the analysis, it was found that those areas with more than one-quarter of their population living below the poverty level were, in general, well endowed with services, but not in terms of professional manpower. However, cross-tabulating with urban-rural status showed that metropolitan poverty areas were in a worse situation than non-metropolitan poverty areas in the provision of services and manpower. (For a general discussion of urban-rural differences, see Chapter 8.)

To explain why non-metropolitan areas have fallen behind would require analysis of the factors that determine accessibility to federal funds for the establishment of CMHCs. Longest et al. (1976) note that the areas that began with a high level of services, including urban poverty areas, have been able to achieve the CMHC goals with a minimum of additional cost and effort. The sheer magnitude of the task in non-metropolitan catchment areas, with sparsely settled communities, may have amplified the difficulties. The same situation of differential levels of service in different areas continuing for many years is to be found in Britain, even though health service costs have been paid by the Government since 1948 (Freeman 1983).

In this connection, Wilkinson (1982) points out that contemporary changes have resulted in an expansion of the geographical area needed for meeting human needs in rural areas, i.e. to retain the numbers of people, organisations, and facilities required for a relatively complete community. This results in a shift away from people having their various needs met by one geographically close reference group to different needs being met by formal hierarchical organisations, e.g. large employers, schools, or hospitals. Though small places tend to become parts of larger regional communities in terms of these functions, several studies have shown that people's identity remains with their immediate locality of residence, and this disjunction could have unfavourable implications for the cohesion of communities and perhaps for individual psychological well-being. In the UK, opposition to the closure of village shops, schools, and cottage hospitals indicates widespread dissatisfaction with this trend. Another possible explanation is that non-metropolitan areas may lack the political power and organisational ability to obtain, or even apply for the services they need. Hence, although demand remains high, the supply remains low.

A useful contribution by the geographer here would be to investigate the spatial and temporal patterns in the adoption of CMHC programmes, in a similar way to that of deinstitutionalisation time paths (Smith & Hanham 1981a). If clear regional patterns could be identified, it would be possible to test a series of hypotheses, in which adoption of the CMHC innovation was explained in terms of one of the following:

1. Responses to deinstitutionalisation policies in particular states or regions
2. Hierarchical diffusion of the innovation from large urban areas downward to smaller places
3. Underlying similarities in socio-demographic and political characteristics
4. Proximity to catchment areas that were early adopters of the new policy

The present author is in fact currently investigating the geographical diffusion of mental health policy, by analysing the distribution of federal funds for the construction and staffing of CMHCs.

ECOLOGICAL STUDIES AND THE SEARCH FOR NEIGHBOURHOOD EFFECTS

The areal analysis described above involves mapping mental health statistics, a search for spatial patterns, and speculation about possible relationships between two or more patterns. Ecological studies, on the other hand, are more concerned with relationships between the presence of problems and the specific environments in which they occur. Most of this work has been done in urban areas, where data describing social and demographic characteristics, usually collected from census materials, have been averaged for particular spatial subdivisions. Census tracts have been popular for this purpose, but in recent years smaller and smaller units, such as city blocks or enumeration districts, have been used to characterise the specific local features. Extensive reviews of the ecological studies performed by geographers and others have been prepared by Giggs (1979), Herbert (1979, 1976), Freeman (1978), and Schwab and Schwab (1978), so that this section will simply describe two groups of investigations that illustrate the range and potential of the ecological approach.

Prevalence rates and locality studies

The studies initated by Faris & Dunham (1939) to identify the social correlates of psychiatric disorders are well known (for reviews see Schwab & Schwab 1978; Dohrenwend & Dohrenwend 1969; Daiches 1981; Chapters 12 & 14 of this book). In most of them, higher hospitalisation rates for psychiatric disorders are shown to be concentrated in low income groups, characteristically located in inner city areas. Other potential aetiological influences are also chiefly found in inner city locations: e.g. where the population is predominantly elderly and where mobility rates are highest (Bagley et al. 1973); where there is a high proportion of social disorganisation and unstable families (Srole et al. 1962); and where a majority of the population is either foreign-born or members of ethnic minorities. Other studies have shown some relationships with the physical aspects of the environment, (Taylor 1974); and a substanital literature refers to the still elusive relationship between housing density and pathology (Giggs 1979).

However, the establishment of specific causal links between physical and social aspects of the environment and psychiatric illness has so far proved uncertain; at best, we can conclude that such problems are multi-causal. Several researchers have favoured the 'breeder' hypothesis (Giggs 1979), in which a poor social climate and the inadequate housing typical of inner city areas somehow produces psychiatric disorders. This explanation literally blames the environment, and its exponents suggest various solutions, including urban renewal and relocation schemes, though there is no evidence so far that such measures are helpful in this respect. A second view, however, tends to blame individuals by suggesting that those who are vulnerable move (or drift) down the social ladder, and eventually cluster in inner city neighbourhoods. In this explanation, the locality's characteristics are not necessarily influential, but offer cheap housing and an environment where deviance of all kinds is more typical than is usually the case in suburban neighbourhoods, for instance. It is not accidental that many of the patients discharged from mental hospitals through deinstitutionalisation end up in such neighbourhoods (Dear 1977b; Wolpert & Wolpert 1976). However, there may be several advantages there for individuals who are service-dependent, in that their accessibility to welfare, treatment, and residential services may be improved (Smith 1981; Wolch 1979).

A third possible explanation for the strong relationship between ecological characteristics and psychiatric illness has been suggested by Smith (1980b) and by Rabkin (1979). It is possible that local demographic characteristics may have an important but indirect influence, on the way mental health problems are identified and subsequently treated. This involves a 'contextual' effect, in which a locality or group characteristic tends to alter an individual effect. Smith (1980b) observed the relationship between ethnicity and various domains of life satisfaction; blacks reported lower levels of satisfaction with their residential neighbourhood than whites, and this was consistent with findings in nation-wide studies, showing that minority status in American cities is typically associated with lower life satisfaction (Campbell et al. 1967). Thus, in a comparison of blacks with whites, we can infer that being black is associated with feelings of dissatisfaction (the individual effect); but the overall racial composition of the neighbourhood (the contextual effect) revealed substantial differences in levels of satisfaction. In general, whites living in integrated settings are less satisfied with their neighbourhood, community, neighbours, and residence, than whites living in all-white or mostly white neighbourhoods (Fig. 5.7). This might have been expected, but those whites are also less satisfied than blacks living in the same neighbourhoods. The individual adverse effect of ethnic status on satisfaction seems to be either non-existent or reduced for blacks who live in integrated neighbourhoods, so that the advantage of being white appears to diminish there.

Thus, an individual's ethnic status may not be as important in this respect as the overall ethnic characteristics of the locality. A study by Rabkin (1979) has shed further light on this type of contextual effect; she investigated first admission rates to mental hospitals for whites, blacks, and Puerto Ricans in 338 areas of New York City. For the city as a whole, blacks and Puerto Ricans were shown to have substantially higher admission rates (the individual effect), but when the racial characteristics of the localities (the contextual effect) were investigated, there were some startling deviations. Rabkin's data show that admission rates for a particular ethnic group fall as the ethnic density of the locality increases in favour of that group. Thus whites, blacks, and Puerto Ricans have lower admission rates than non-whites, non-blacks, and non-Puerto Ricans, when they are in a residential majority; i.e. admission rates are higher for all ethnic groups that comprise a minority of a locality's population, regardless of ethnicity.

Rabkin offers a number of hypotheses to explain this. One is a breeder hypothesis — feelings of being an alien or being insecure in times of need might result in higher admission rates. Another is a drift explanation — people in better mental health move out of minority areas, or people with worse health move in. Another comes from community labelling theory (Dohrenwend & Chin-Shong 1969); there is some evidence that black community leaders define deviance differently from their white counterparts, and the norms for admission to a mental hospital may reflect such differences. Thus, in a largely black or Puerto Rican community, psychiatric illness may be more accepted, or defined more rigorously for purposes of admission; whereas in predominantly white communities, members of other ethnic groups might be noticed, and hospitalised, more quickly. Theoretically, this explanation might also hold for whites living in predominantly non-white areas, but this point is unresolved.

Another possibility is that the higher rates of admissions for minorities in largely white areas are simply artefacts of the attitudinal and behavioural responses to the treatment of psychiatric illness there. In a predominantly white area, a black person may feel there is less stigma attached to seeking out psychiatric care, or may simply find there are more services available.

INDIVIDUAL AND CONTEXTUAL EFFECTS OF RACE ON SATISFACTION

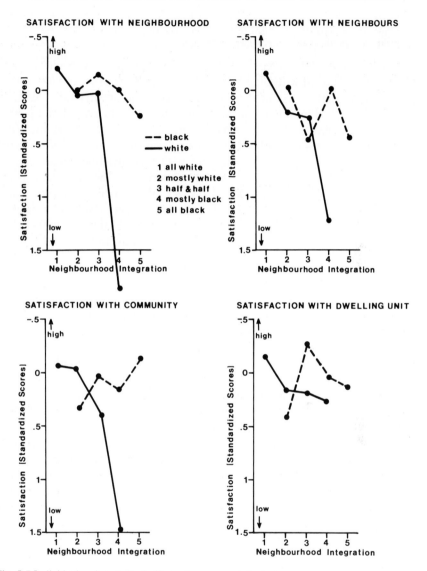

Fig. 5.7 Individual and contextual effects of race on satisfaction.

Huffine & Craig (1973), reported that in some of the integrated neighbourhoods in Baltimore, prevalence rates of psychiatric illness were higher than in either predominantly white or black areas, and suggested that individuals in integrated areas may not express their desire for services strongly enough:

the needs of this vulnerable population are not apt to be articulated. By the very nature of their environment, residents here will have attenuated senses of identity with their neighbourhood and neighbours. Since it is such identity that provides the base for organised action, these populations are apt to lack both effective political power and the means to make their needs known to providers of service.

Finally, there is the possibility that lack of congruence with one's neighbours may be linked with higher rates of psychiatric disorder because incongruent groups have fewer network ties and experience greater social isolation (Mueller 1980). This phenomenon applies not only to race, but to other social characteristics such as occupation, age, and marital status. The relatively high rates of morbidity that have been found in ecological studies among sub-groups who are incongruent with their neighbourhood in such ways suggests that the nature of social networks may be important in the aetiology of psychiatric disorder. However, this relative minority status concept is not supported by findings in Ireland, where the highest rates of schizophrenia for Catholics do not occur in areas where they are numerically the weaker, but where they are the stronger (Murphy and Vega 1982).

Community adjustment and therapeutic neighbourhoods

Another direction of research — into the possible influence of locality characteristics on the recuperation of formerly hospitalised individuals — can help to evaluate deinstitutionalisation policies. However, most geographers have been unwilling to embark on it, perhaps because of the need to identify actual patients and collect data on their progress after discharge. As a result, community follow-up studies have rarely considered locality effects to be important. This is particularly unfortunate because US Census data have been scrutinised by NIMH, and a rich source of ecological data at the census tract level is available there (Redick et al. 1971)

One consistent exception has been the work of Segal & Aviram (1978), who have identified some of the community characteristics that facilitate the integration of former patients living in sheltered care. Predictors of external integration (independent involvement outside the facility) or internal integration (social involvement within it) include: the efforts of neighbours to interact with residents on an individual basis; acceptance of the facility by neighbours; urban, as opposed to rural locations, especially those close to community resources and medical services; and availability of transport to those resources. In an earlier attempt to identify some of the social and demographic correlates of such community factors, Trute & Segal (1976) examined census data in Saskatchewan and California for the tracts in which care facilities were located; they suggest that the communities most conducive to social integration were midway between the extremes of social cohesion and social disintegration. In rural locations, the supportive areas had a higher percentage of people living alone and in transient accommodation, while in urban areas, they had many older people and a substantial proportion of rented and overcrowded dwellings:

> These community characteristics may be reflective of social groupings whose attitudes toward, and association with, the mentally incapacitated are structurally determined . . . The census predictors may describe 'supportive communities' whose socio-environmental circumstances create a community social structure that enhances integration of the 'mentally ill' and provides a neighbourhood atmosphere that reduces the exclusion of socially deviant individuals.

In a study using neighbourhoods much smaller than census tracts, Smith (1976) identified some of the spatially variant ecological characteristics that appear to be significantly related to positive community prognoses for former patients. A group of discharged patients was followed-up for 18 months to assess community adjustment, levels of stress, and readmissions; also, an attempt was made to isolate the effects of the residential environments, while controlling for the traditional social, psychological, and institutional predictors of community recuperation. Data from photographic and cartographic sources, and from the Housing Census were used to describe visual, functional, and demographic dimensions of the neighbourhoods; ten statistically independent dimensions were identified (Table 5.4), and several could significantly predict adjustment, stress, and readmissions. These were: *commercial/industrial* (the amount of non-residential land in the neighbourhood); *low-unit density* (a large proportion of single and elderly residents); *transience* (a neighbourhood with much traffic and non-permanent residents); *low housing density* (large houses on large lots); and *recreational* (a large amount of recreational space) (Table 5.5)

Although there is a danger in leaping to ecological inferences, three general conclusions emerged. Firstly, neighbourhood characteristics can predict community outcomes at least as accurately as the hospital staff. Therefore, staff should consider the patient's community environment seriously, if only because it is often one of the few variables that can be manipulated. Secondly, the visual characteristics of residential neighbourhoods were important to former patients, but the positive effects of living in visually pleasing and/or quiet neighbourhoods were stronger than the negative effects of ugly and/or noisy neighbourhoods. It is possible that pleasing districts can be therapeutic, whereas the characteristics of less wholesome ones can be disregarded. This makes sense intuitively, because so much of the modern urban environment appears visually and functionally unpleasing to people in general, through overcrowding or pollution (Freeman 1978).

However, former mental hospital patients are among an increasingly large group of service-dependent individuals who seem destined to inhabit such urban areas for the foreseeable future (Scott & Scott 1980; Dear 1977b). If they can effectively adapt to these settings, without adding to their existing problems, then one additional burden has been overcome. Thirdly, a neigh-

Table 5.4 Intercorrelations between residential neighbourhood dimensions

	CL	RL	CW	AL	LH	BO	ER	TE	LD	SF
Commercial/Industrial (CL) — amount of non-residential land use	—	-0.56	0.04	-0.29	0.05	0.10	-0.26	0.25	0.19	-0.34
Recreational (RL) — amount of recreational space		—	0.15	0.18	-0.03	0.11	0.15	-0.27	0.01	-0.25
Close to water (CW) — proximity to rivers, lakes etc.			—	0.18	0.05	0.14	-0.13	-0.03	0.05	-0.12
Arboreal (AL)				—	0.30	-0.11	0.24	-0.12	-0.12	0.01
Low housing density (LH) — space occupied by each dwelling unit					—	-0.21	0.17	-0.37	-0.13	0.35
Black overcrowded (BO) — minorities, large families, female heads of household						—	-0.21	0.10	-0.06	0.04
Expensive real estate (ER) — large, expensive houses, large lots							—	0.03	-0.20	-0.01
Transience (TE) — non-permanent residents, major traffic routes								—	0.21	-0.59
Low unit density (LD) — older residents, living alone and at low density									—	-0.44
Single family uniform housing (SF) — uniform houses and family types, single family units										—

Source: Smith (1980b)

bourhood characteristic labelled 'low unit density' — a measure of the number of old people and the proportion of people living alone — was a significant predictor of two of the outcome measures; readmissions and stress. Patients living in such neighbourhoods seemed to perform well and were less likely to return to hospital, even though it is difficult to imagine how loneliness and old age could, *per se*, be conducive to psychological well-being.

Two conclusions can be offered. The first is that a clear linear relationship could not be shown between well-being and features of population density, such as isolation and crowding, which is not surprising (Stokols 1973; Galle et al. 1972). Secondly, the 'old and lonely' neighbourhoods are not totally negative as residential environments; they may provide familiar settings for former in-patients, where more than the usual amount of deviance from prevailing norms is acceptable, containing communities in which relatively few normative demands are made.

A number of large-scale studies of readmission support this contention (Freeman & Simmons 1963; Levy & Rowitz 1973; Wing & Brown 1970; Trute & Segal 1976). A strong sense of community may not always be necessary, and the best intentioned efforts to create an old-fashioned neighbourly type of community may be inappropriate for ex-patients. The city provides for everybody, including the mentally ill: 'The impersonality of city life breeds its own tolerance for the private lives of the inhabitants. Individuality and even eccentricity can flourish more readily . . . . Stigmatized persons may find it easier to lead comfortable lives, free of the constant scrutiny of neighbours' (Milgram 1970). As Jones (1982) comments: 'Among the rapidly changing population of the apartment blocks and rooming houses, the clientele of the mental health services (pass) almost unnoticed'.

The notion that inner city neighbourhoods, with a high proportion of service-dependent individuals and much social disorganisation, can provide therapeutic living environments needs to be taken seriously, while the attempts of professionals to recreate 'normal' family and neighbourhood situations for former patients may often be simply unrealistic. The realities of psychiatric illness and the demand for urban accommodation may imply that many former patients can never be assimilated successfully into more normal parts; to accept this might free some time and energy for effort in other directions, including public education and attempts to involve community residents more positively.

SPATIAL ANALYSIS AND THE SEARCH FOR BEHAVIOURAL EXPLANATIONS OF GEOGRAPHICAL PATTERNS

It is in this third area that most work by geographers has been done, and although relatively little is related to mental health, it reflects the diversity of the discipline. The geographical perspectives that have been applied to one particular problem area — the deinstitutionalisation of the mentally ill and the provision of CMH services for them — can be categorised under two headings. Firstly, residential segregation, and secondly, external effects on geographical localities of deliberate policies to decentralise services and to discharge patients.

Residential segregation of the mentally ill

Geographers have observed that service-dependent populations, including the mentally ill, elderly, and poor are becoming increasingly concentrated in the core areas of American cities (Golant 1980; Wolch 1979). A corresponding tendency has been detected among service agencies for these populations, including welfare offices, treatment and residential centres, hostels, and rooming houses (Wolpert et al. 1975; Wolch 1980). The most obvious explanations include the following:

1. The residential and commercial abandonment of inner city areas has left vacant many old offices, apartments, and schools that can readily be converted into treatment or residential facilities. Many patients who have no families to live with are likely to be assigned to these areas.
2. Community opposition to the introduction of facilities has often resulted in agencies discarding their original plans, and instead selecting inner city sites, where either nobody lives or nobody cares who moves in.
3. The mentally ill population includes many who are poor and unemployed; they tend to gravitate towards the cheap and transient sections of the city, in a process described as 'residential filtering' (Dear 1977) or 'drifting' (Daiches 1981).

Observers are tempted to view these concentrations negatively, in that they appear to sentence the poor and the inept to a lifetime of imprisonment in the inner city. On the other hand, there may be benefits, such as opportunities for mutual aid and for the development of effective social support networks among handicapped people (Smith 1981). The advantages of accessibility, when the location of services coincides with where the mentally ill actually live, have also been noted (Dear 1979). For them and for others dependent on welfare and public services, the location of State and Federal offices may be more important than possible places of employment (Wolch 1980). Cohen and Sokolorsky (1978), studying a single-room-occupancy hotel in Manhattan, of which the residents were mostly discharged mental hospital patients, stated that the hotel's location had one major advantage for the schizophrenic tenants — there was no permanent residential population nearby which could serve as a stigmatising force against them.

Attempts to interpret and evaluate these phenomena are only recent, but in a structural explanation at the societal level, Dear (1979) suggests that the increasingly 'public city' has not resulted from the aggregation of individual locational decisions by members of the dependent groups, but from a series of widespread economic, political, and geographical forces. As the

Table 5.5 Neighbourhood dimensions predicting community recuperation in discharged mental patients

Dimension	% correct prediction (discriminant analysis)	d^2	F-statistical significance	
(a) Discrimination between return/non-return to hospital (n = 71)				
Commercial/Industrial	53.5	0.21	3.77	0.05
Low unit density	64.8	0.46	3.97	0.02
Transience	64.8	0.65	3.71	0.01

Overall correct classification (46/71 = 65%, p > 95%)

	No return	Return	Total
Correct group	25	21	46
Incorrect group	10	15	25
Total	35	36	71

	% correct prediction	d^2	F-statistical	
(b) Discrimination of good adjustment/poor adjustment (n = 71)				
Low housing density	53.5	0.23	3.59	0.06
Recreational	59.2	0.41	3.08	0.05

Overall correct classification (42/71 = 59.2%, p>95%)

	Good adjustment	Poor adjustment	Total
Correct group	20	22	42
Incorrect group	7	22	29
Total27	27	44	71

	% correct prediction	d^2	F-statistical	
(c) Discrimination of low stress/high stress (incidence of problem events)				
Arboreal	59.2	0.21	3.04	0.08
Commercial/Industrial	60.6	0.48	3.50	0.03
Low unit density	64.8	0.68	3.25	0.02
Transience	69.0	0.86	3.02	0.02

Overall correct classification (49/71 = 69%,p>95%)

			Total
Correct group	20	29	49
Incorrect group	9	13	22
Total	29	42	71

Source: Smith (1980b) p 401

cycle of residential and commercial abandonment became contagious in many American cities, the deinstitutionalisation of mentally ill, mentally retarded, elderly, and criminal individuals partly filled the vacuum. This was accelerated by public choices, made at the neighbourhood level, to keep members of such groups residentially segregated. For the residents of stable, single-family-dominated neighbourhoods, the concentration of service-dependent groups in inner city areas was, and still is highly desirable.

Relevant to this situation is 'Public Facility Location Theory' — a technique of public decision-making which involves balancing considerations such as ease of access, the availability and cost of land, and maximisation of demand.

Smith (1980c) has suggested a complementary analysis of individual residential decision-making among the mentally ill, and models of residential mobility have been popular (e.g. Brown & Moore 1970; Adams & Gilder 1976), but because of the particular needs of the mentally ill and the community opposition they encounter in resettling, traditional models of locational decision-making are not appropriate. Discharged patients are at a considerable disadvantage in the housing market; many need to look for a new home, as an alternative to returning to hospital or living with their families, while others who have no families may have had to give up their old dwellings on admission. The champions of deinstitutionalisation gave little thought to the magnitude of the housing problem they would create, but at a conservative estimate, more than five million people have left institutions in the United States since 1955 (Bassuk & Gerson 1978). In central Oklahoma, 90–100 patients were released from one hospital every week in 1979, most returning to live in nearby Oklahoma City. This trend seems likely to continue in many states, especially with the climate of fiscal austerity that is sweeping the country at the time of writing.

To identify some of the behavioural factors involved in the relocation of former patients, Smith (1980c) described a choice-constraint model of residential selection. An individual exercises residential choices within a constrained social, geographical, and economic environment (Fischer et al. 1977), but one must begin with some assumptions about individual decision-making and the housing market. The two most important of these are: (1) former patients are goal-orientated and largely rational in the conduct of their affairs; (2) the housing market sets limits on the search process, but does not completely determine either the type of residence, or the neighbourhood to be selected. These assumptions, however, represent a break with traditional ways of thinking, both about the nature of psychiatric illness and about the modern city. The former patient is not seen as a helpless and passive individual, to whom things are done; a viable alternative is suggested to the geographical determinism implicit in the notion of downward filtering amongst service-dependent individuals, and the assumption that residential locations are influenced primarily by the location of service facilities is questioned (Dear 1979; Wolch 1980; White 1979). This model assumes that former patients are just like anyone else in the housing market; they have preferences and exercise choices, but their searches and ultimate selections are seriously constrained by lack of resources; by the socio-economic characteristics of the neighbourhoods in which they search; and by the attitudes of the individuals with whom they then come into contact.

However, this refers only to patients going through the private market, usually as tenants; it is not concerned with those who return to a setting arranged for them, e.g. with their families or in a half-way house, nor with agency selections for residential facilities, such as hostels. Once a decision has been made to live independently, the choice of a location will be influenced by four general constraints: the availability of properties for rental in suitable places and at reasonable prices; awareness of what is available, as well as its location and price; the acceptability of a particular unit, and of its neighbourhood; and the accessibility of the location, which is important both during the selection process and after moving in. Fig. 5.8 suggests that any or all of these could influence an individual's selection or (as will often be the case) his decision to end the search and return either to his family or to an institution.

During the evolution of neighbourhoods within the city, different physical, social, and attitudinal characteristics are developed, ranging from the availability of units for renting and their price, to relative willingness to accept strangers. Thus a neighbourhood, by the actions of its individual and group decision-makers, presents a residential environment whose characteristics will either discourage or facilitate the search process. A neighbourhood that has fought for public bus routes in the past will be more accessible to a poor person than one that has decided public transport is not necessary, e.g. because of a high rate of ownership of private cars. One which is mostly zoned for single-family dwellings, and where the average family income is high, is likely to be unavailable to a former patient simply because it does not offer any cheap housing, to buy or rent (and very few ex-patients will be in the market as buyers). We might also expect that where most people own their own homes, and where there are many children, ex-patients would be unacceptable as neighbours. Therefore, the constraints on residential selection are set partly by the existing residents and partly by the circumstances of those looking for a new place to live.

An empirical study based on this model would require a longitudinal design, following patients on discharge. As an initial exploration, census tract data for Oklahoma City were used to test the availability and acceptability constraints. The first relevant factor is neighbourhood acceptance. Assuming that a patient's decision where to live is constrained both by his perceptions of neighbourhood acceptance and by the collective expressions of this, we would expect most searches to be in areas not dominated either by house owners or by nuclear family residents. Neighbourhoods with a high proportion of rental units are most likely to be acceptable, both to the patients and to the existing residents. The distribution of rental units as a percentage of total residential units showed a concentric pattern, very familiar to urban geographers, with many of the inner tracts having more than 50 per cent of their units rented (Smith 1980c). The fact that acceptance of the mentally ill is greatest in neighbourhoods that have a high

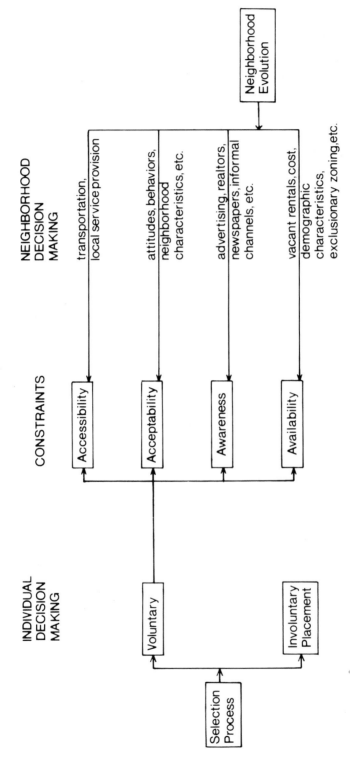

Fig. 5.8 A model of residential selection for service-dependent groups

proportion of rental units suggests that residents there do not choose to exercise much discretion over the future of their community, perhaps because many of them are transients in it (Segal et al. 1980).

The second factor is the number of available units; the distribution of rental properties that are vacant, and therefore (theoretically) available for occupancy, gives a pattern that is much less concentrated. Assuming that former patients are more likely to search where there are more available units, their search will be more widely spread throughout the city than was implicit from the overall distribution of rental properties. The third factor is that of low cost; assuming that most of the patients are close to the bottom rung of the socio-economic ladder, the price of vacant units becomes an important constraint. Oklahoma City has a rental distribution similar to that of many American cities, with the most expensive and exclusive properties concentrated in one sector (Smith 1980c), and former patients would be unlikely to find accommodation there.

When acceptance (measured by the proportion of all housing units that are rentals), availability, and cost are combined into a simple index, the neighbourhoods theoretically most available to the mentally ill are in the urban core and immediately to the south and southeast of it. Thus, using only the residential selection model and some census data, it appears that if the process were voluntary, and if individual patients and residential neighbourhoods acted in predictable ways, ex-patients would locate themselves in a highly concentrated area.

The neighbourhoods most likely to be selected will contain many low-cost units and a high proportion of non-permanent residents. Otherwise, we know little about whether they will be good, bad, or indifferent places for former patients. However, the area of highest rental availability and lowest cost overlaps only partly with that with the highest concentration of disadvantaged residents (blacks and other ethnic minority groups). Thus, although we might expect residents of this part of the city to be least able, politically and economically, to avoid the encroachment of individuals and facilities they find 'undesirable', the model of residential selection does not isolate only the black neighbourhoods as potential hosts. Also, only nine of the 33 census tracts in the area of greatest rental availability have more than 10 per cent of the residential units defined as overcrowded (1.01 persons per room); and only five have more than 10 per cent of the units lacking adequate plumbing. Thus, this area is not necessarily the most run down, delapidated, and socially disorganised. It may not be the 'best' place to live, if by that we mean an area of comfortably placed, intact, nuclear families, but it may not be the 'worst'. This tentative conclusion fits with the findings of Trute & Segal (1976), which suggested that optimum neighbourhoods may well fall somewhere between the most coherent and the most disorganised.

Considering the implications for deinstitutionalisation policies, the data suggest that although cheap and available rental units were plentiful (13 per cent of the total market of rental units were vacant then), they were spatially concentrated in the urban area, although not restricted to the most disadvantaged neighbourhoods. If large numbers of patients or other service-dependent people were left to seek out their own homes, they could probably be accommodated easily, but the ultimate residential pattern would be highly concentrated. The original goals of deinstitutionalisation included provision of community alternatives to hospital treatment and residence, which it was hoped would be dispersed throughout the catchment area. After about two decades, it appears that these policies have substantially reduced the numbers in hospital, but the distribution of the psychiatrically ill in the community may be as concentrated now as before, and possibly more so.

An even greater concern is the implication for the location of group homes and other CMH facilities. Although vacant units for rental in Oklahoma City are plentiful, they are in a minority of its census tracts, so that potential host neighbourhoods should be approached cautiously. A recent study concluded that 'the room for error is small ... each unit of suitable housing that is lost through community opposition diminishes by that amount the possibility of achieving the goals of ... deinstitutionalisation and community care' (Scott & Scott 1980). If a neighbourhood successfully opposes the introduction of a group home for the mentally ill, it is extremely unlikely that similar facilities can be located nearby. In Pennsylvania, it has been estimated that for every facility that was successful in overcoming local opposition, two or three failure had occurred (Baron 1981). If this were to happen in Oklahoma City, the supply of potential host neighbourhoods would rapidly be used up.

External effects of community mental health facilities

Much of the research reported here has been concerned with finding optimum residential environments for the mentally ill and locations for their treatment facilities. The goals of the studies varied — those on service utilisation analysed provision of equitable and accessible services; the residential neighbourhood studies defined optimum environments for recuperation; and the residential mobility studies considered how patients find cheap and decent housing in the community. However, all share concern for the well-being of individual patients.

In most existing research, though, the response of the neighbourhoods that would be affected by deinstitutionalisation programmes has only been considered peripherally. There has been an implicit tendency to assume that neighbourhoods will act like sponges, providing locations for new facilities as the needs arise. But in recent years, substantial opposition from residents in neighbourhoods thus targeted has shaken such complacency (Baron 1981; Armstrong 1976; Cupaiuolo 1977). Yet only rarely has it been seriously suggested that local opposition (or support) should be included in the overall cost–benefit analysis of deinstitutionalisation policies (Bachrach 1976). A balanced approach should try to complement patient-orientated studies with those that consider neighbourhoods' responses. The relevant research can be grouped into three categories: the impact of community-based programmes on public attitudes toward mental illness; community perceptions of residential and treatment facilities for the mentally ill; and the reciprocity between neighbourhoods' reactions and patients' prognoses for social integration in the community.

Public attitudes towards mental illness

Much has been written about public attitudes towards the mentally ill (Rabkin 1974; Segal 1978), but few attempts made to assess the impact on these attitudes of deinstitutionalisation programmes. Some recent geographical studies have tried to assess the influence of proximity to mental health facilities on the public's acceptance or rejection of the mentally ill (Dear et al. 1980; Dear & Taylor 1979); small-scale facilities appear to have little impact on their host neighbourhoods and equally little effect on the attitudes of the residents. In fact, only a small percentage of the residents surveyed were even aware of one facility's existence (Dear et al. 1979). These are encouraging signs, but they do not explain the substantial community opposition that has surfaced in many American neighbourhoods when new facilities have been proposed (Armstrong 1976; Baron 1981). Smith & Hanham (1981b) investigated public attitudes toward the mentally ill in a neighbourhood that contained a large and very visible psychiatric hospital.

A version of Kirks' (1974) Social Rejection Index was used to determine how the residents felt about people described as mentally ill; 72 respondents in the adjacent neighbourhood were matched with 68 from a similar neighbourhood, over half a mile away. It appeared that acceptance of severe psychiatric illness was significantly higher near the hospital than in the control neighbourhood, and although there was some evidence of lower acceptance in the houses that actually overlooked the facility, proximity to both the facility and its clients seemed to result in a higher level of acceptance, as Dear & Taylor found (1979). The proximity effect was greater than most of the traditional predictors of attitudes toward the mentally ill, which include education, age, income, family size, and length of residence (Rabkin 1974), and it remained significant when the effects of these were controlled.

It was also evident that the residents did not think of the facility as a threat to themselves or the neighbourhood. Although they reported seeing someone they thought was a client two to three times a week on average, 76.4 per cent of the residents said they either rarely or never thought about the facility *per se*; and 80.6 per cent said its proximity did not bother them. Combined with the greater acceptance close to the building, these results are encouraging for deinstitutionalisation, suggesting that even when such a facility has a massive impact on a neighbourhood, there is no evidence of greater rejection — in fact, the opposite. The effect of proximity also proved to be independent of length of residence, so that the increased acceptance nearby cannot be explained as a gradual process, in which residents become resigned to its presence. Nevertheless, it is possible that once the facility begins its operations, the presence of patients in the community may help to create a more favourable local climate of opinion, which may be important to future success.

In locational policy, this conclusion may provide a rationale for further decentralisation, because it suggests that residents in that community will eventually accept their new neighbours, even if they do not do so at first. On the other hand, the same conclusion could also be used to favour further centralisation. Possibly, the optimum location for a new facility is one where attitudes are already favourable, since this will reduce the need for advance publicity and education.

In these terms, the argument for further centralisation may make the most sense, because in spite of the evidence of community acceptance, most neighbourhoods, if they have a choice, will opt not to share their residential space with mental health or other 'undesirable' facilities (Baron 1981; Smith & Hanham 1981c). However, the issues surrounding community acceptance of the mentally ill are complex; Dear & Taylor (1982) point out that community facilities in accepting areas are often 'effectively invisible', and suggest that this quality may sometimes usefully be increased, e.g. by building a screening wall. If the invisibility is of such an extent, though, it does raise the question of how much benefit the residents are then gaining from being situated in the general community, rather than in an institution.

Community perceptions of mental health facilities

To determine how people feel about the possible introduction of new mental health facilities in their localities, 90 respondents were asked to evaluate a list of public facilities, half of which provide human services and the rest urban services (Smith & Hanham 1981c). They were asked how close they would prefer to live to each facility. Using Rothbart's (1973) hypothesis, the purpose of the study was to determine whether groups of individuals use distance as a counter to the perceived 'noxiousness' of mental health facilities (Dear et al. 1977). A joint space multidimensional scaling procedure (MDSCAL) was used, with the mean preferred distance to each facility as data for each of three groups: 'liberals' (n = 14), 'conservatives' (n = 28), and 'middle-of-the-roaders' (n = 48) — based on their self-avowed political leanings. A configuration of points represented both the facilities and the three political groups in a k-dimensional space, corresponding to the rank ordering of preferences. An ideal point for each group was determined within the facility space, and the facilities located closest to this point are the most preferred.

A two-dimensional solution was the most appealing, and the overall good-

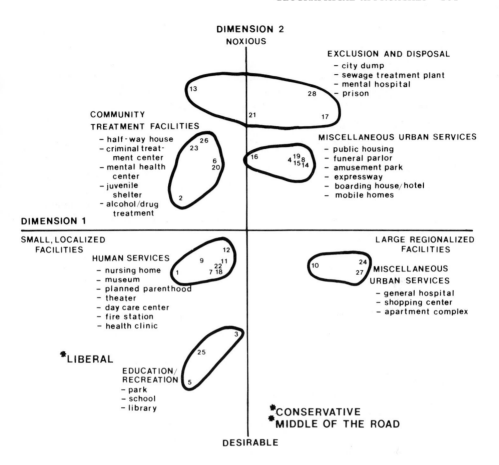

Fig. 5.9 Two-dimensional facility space and group locations (MDSCAL)

ness-of-fit was 0.009 (Fig. 5.9). Facilities that appear in clusters are similarly preferred in terms of distance, and boundaries and labels have been added for identification. Dimension 1 describes the size and centrality characteristics of the public facilities, while 2 appears to describe their desirability or 'noxiousness'. Six facility clusters are clearly visible; using the liberal group for comparative purposes, the preferred distances between individuals in this group and each cluster of facilities can be shown in a linear graph (Fig. 5.10). Only the park had a mean score of less than two, indicating that in general, the respondents preferred to have *no* public facility encroachment on their blocks. Naturally, educational and recreational facilities are the most desirable as neighbours, while the next are small-scale human services, such as a nursing home, planned parenthood clinic, theatre, day nursery, fire station, or health clinic. For 'liberals', the next most desirable group included the small-scale mental health and

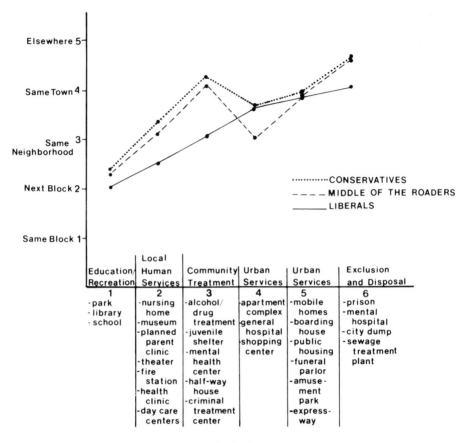

Fig. 5.10 Preferred distances: mean scores for facility clusters

correctional facilities (community treatment), which had a mean distance score of 3.08, indicating agreement to have such facilities located in their neighbourhoods. However, the 'conservative' and 'middle' groups found these facilities far less acceptable.

Fig. 5.10 also shows that both the urban service clusters are more acceptable to the 'conservative' and 'middle' groups than community treatment facilities. For these two groups, which represent the majority (84.4 per cent) of the sample, CMH facilities are clearly undesirable as neighbours, the only ones considered less desirable being those labelled 'exclusion and disposal' in Fig. 5.9, ie. prisons, mental hospitals, sewage plants, and dumps; even motorways, shopping centres, public housing projects, and apartment complexes are thought more desirable. The only optimistic conclusion from this study was the willingness of those individuals describing themselves as 'liberals' to have mental health facilities in their neighbourhoods.

Obviously, it would be extremely difficult to shift public attitudes towards such facilities in a positive direction, but the above results indicate that visibility and contact may help to bring about a substantial improvement. However, this can only occur if the facilities are able to find suitable locations. If local opposition is too great and the planners have to look elsewhere, the community education process will be set back even further. At present, no obvious mechanisms are available to equate the overall benefits of community care for the mentally ill with the loss of local community discretion (Dear 1978). One possible solution would involve some compensation to the affected neighbourhoods (Wolpert et al. 1972), which already exists in the form of local kickbacks and patronage, but which generally favours the most influential and vocal areas of the city.

Community reactions and integration of the mentally ill

In one of the rare discussions of the relationship between community reactions and the social integration of former psychiatric patients, Segal et al. (1980) examined the characteristics of 'accepting environments' and found that adverse reactions from neighbours have a negative influence on integration into sheltered accommodation. Such reactions were most easily identified in 'conservative middle class' neighbourhoods, which are typically white (95 per cent), with high income families, living mostly in single-family units. Surprisingly, communities with a moderate degree of adverse reaction seemed to be conducive to social integration. This was the case in 'liberal, non-traditional' areas, which are racially mixed, low-income districts having a high proportion of households with unrelated persons (15 per cent, versus 2 per cent for the state of California as a whole); and also in 'conservative working class" neighbourhoods, which are mainly white (89 per cent), low-income areas. In these communities, the mildly negative public attitudes may exert pressure on the service providers to promote greater social integration amongst their clients. Again, it appeared that the elusive optimum environment for former patients lies somewhere between the poles of coherence and disorganisation. Segal et al. concluded that the identification of such environments may be beneficial for patients, but that in the not-too-distant future, these communities may simply run out of steam: 'There are significant social costs involved in becoming a community that is safe for madness' (Segal and Baumohl 1980); 'No community, no matter how good-hearted, can long suffer the accumulation of society's wounded and outcast without exhausting its resources and patience' (Segal et al. 1980).

They suggest that the solution is to try to understand and remove intolerance, rather than seek out sanctuaries within the community, but another possibility involves community action to mobilise a locality's latent resources (Warren and Warren 1977). Either way, the key is a combination of research at the local level to identify accepting environments, with community intervention to expand the potential for support in localities that are currently passive about, but not completely averse to, the influx of service-dependent individuals like the mentally ill.

CONCLUSIONS

This chapter has considered some of the recent mental health research that is geographical in nature. Much of it has been conducted by non-geographers, which is a mixed blessing for the profession. On the one hand, it is encouraging to see some of the spatial aspects of mental health problems being studied seriously; but at the same time, geographers may be understandably nervous about entrusting what they perceive to be their 'turf' to other social scientists, some of whom have begun to realise that mental health issues can usefully be considered from a spatial perspective, and that they share with geographers a common interest in the influence of forces operating at a larger scale than that of the individual. Recent trends in mental health may also help to bring the work of geographers more into the forefront — particularly the increasing emphasis on a community-based systems approach to problem solving.

There are, however, important conceptual problems within the discipline that need to be tackled before geographers can argue unequivocally about the contribution they can make to the study of social problems such as mental illness. It is useful, in this connection, to focus on three areas of concern.

1. The *pattern/process debate* — much of the work conducted within the areal association tradition simply describes spatial patterns in the phenomenon being studied. However, most modern goegraphy attempts to go considerably beyond observing patterns, either to identify causal ecological pathways, or to uncover the underlying social and spatial processes. Unfortunately, the demarcation between pattern and process is not always clear. In fact, the two are often interdependent: for example, the physical and demographic characteristics of a residential neighbourhood (pattern variables) might influence, directly or indirectly, the attitudes of residents towards the influx of newly discharged patients (process variables). Successful opposition to residential change might result in a rezoning of the neighbourhood, specifically to exclude non-single-family units. In this way, the spatial patterns will have influenced the spatial processes, which, in turn, help to determine the future pattern. As this example illustrates, any parcel of land within the city needs to be considered carefully in both its historical and geographical context.

2. The problem of *ecological inference* — this is familiar to all social scientists, but particularly geographers, who attempt to isolate the unique effects of localities on particular behaviours.

Caution is warranted in conducting ecological studies, but it ought not to supress all attempts to undertake such research. Options are available for it, particularly if such possibilities as multiple causality and the existence of interaction between different causal agents are considered, but the research discussed here has pointed out some of the dangers involved in leaping to conclusions from apparent causal connections in data. In the case of hospital admissions from different ethnic areas, for example, the variations in admission rates were not necessarily a result of the interaction of ethnic status and psychiatric illness, or of the effect of ecological characteristics on the prevalence rate. It was clear that at least as important were institutional and artefactual variables that vary sharply by locality, such as rates of arrests, and the availability of services. These are geographical variations, but they obviously need to be considered in a wholly different category from the ethnic and ecological variables.

3. The question of *scale* — geographers have long been torn between the desire to provide general explanations and the much easier task of describing the unique combinations of circumstances that prevail at particular localities. At the smallest scale, it is possible to detect scores of attributes, any of which may be validly related to the phenomenon in question. A search for higher levels of generality would, on the other hand, obscure much of the richness of such fine-scale analysis; and we find many criticsms, therefore, of investigations conducted at the neighbourhood or census tract level. To extend this scale problem even further, as in the discussion of residential location among former mental hospital patients, it may also be necessary to consider the influence of macro-level forces operating in the political and economic realm.

Geographers have begun to consider such forces, partly in search of a 'more relevant' research agenda, and partly as a way of increasing their ability to communicate effectively with other social scientists. In doing this, they run the risk of diluting their impact, by abandoning their uniquely spatial approach to the study of social problems. However, it should be possible to offer a geographical perspective that is general enough to be of interest to other social scientists, and yet unique enough to contribute a new dimension to the study of mental health problems.

REFERENCES

Adams J S, Gilder K A 1976 Household location and intra-urban migration. In: Herbert D T and Johnston R J (eds) Social areas in cities, Vol I, spatial processes and form. Wiley, London,

Armstrong B 1976 Preparing the community for the patient's return. Hospital and Community Psychiatry 27: 349–356

Aviram U, Syme S L, Cohen J B 1976 The effect of policies and programs on reductions & mental hospitalizations. Social Science & Medicine 10: 571–584

Bachrach L L 1976 Deinstitutionalization: analytical review and sociological perspective. National Institute of Mental Health Series D No 4: US Government Printing Office, Washington DC

Bagley C, Jacobson S, Palmer C 1973 Social structure and the ecological distribution of mental illness suicide and delinquency. Psychological Medicine 3: 177–187

Baron R C 1981 Changing public attitudes about the mentally ill in the community. Hospital and Community Psychiatry 32: 173–177

Bassuk E L, Gerson S 1978 Deinstitutionalization and mental health services. Scientific American 238: 46–53

Bloom B L 1977 Community mental health: general introduction. Brooks Cole, Monkerey

Brenner M H 1973 Mental illness and the economy. Harvard University Press, Cambridge, Mass

Brenner M H 1979 Mortality and the national economy: a review and the experience of England and Wales 1936–76. The Lancet September 15: 568–573

Brown L A, Moore E 1970 The intra-urban migration process: a perspective. Geografiska
Annaler B 51: 1n13

Campbell A, Converse P, Rodgers W L 1967 The Quality of American life: perceptions,
evaluations and satisfactions. Russell Sage, New York

Chu F D, Trotter S 1974 The madness establishment: Ralph Nader's study group report on
the national institute of mental health. Grossman, New York

Cohen C I, Sokolorsky J 1978 Schizophrenia and social networks: ex-patients in the inner
city. Schizophrenia Bull 4: 546–560

Crow T J 1983 Is schizophrenia an infectious disease? Lancet: 173–5

Cupaiuolo A A 1977 Community residences and zoning ordinances. Hospital and
Community Psychiatry 28: 206–210

Daiches S 1981 People in distress: a geographical perspective on psychological well-being.
The University of Chicago Department of Geography Research paper No 197

Dear M 1977a Locational factors in the demand for mental health care. Economic
Geography 58: 223–240

Dear M 1977b Psychiatric patients in the inner city. Annals of the Association of American
Geographers 67: 588–594

Dear M 1978 Planning for mental health care: a reconsideration of public facility location
theory. International Regional Science Review 3: 93–111

Dear M 1979 The public city. Paper, presented at a conference on residential mobility and
public policy. Mimeo, University of California, Los Angeles

Dear M, Fincher R, Currie L 1977 Measuring the external effects of public programs.
Environment and Planning A 9: 137–147

Dear M, Clark G, Clark S 1979 Economic cycles and mental health care policy: an
examination of the macro-context for social service planning. Social Science and Medicine
13: 43–53

Dear M, Taylor S M 1979 Community attitudes toward neighbourhood public facilities. A
research report submitted to the social science and humanities research council of Canada
grant #410-77-0322

Dear M, Taylor S M, Hall G B 1980 External effects of mental health facilities. Annals of
the Association of American Geographers 70: 342–352

Dear M, Taylor S M 1982 Not on our street: community attitudes to mental health care.
Pion Ltd, London

Dohrenwend B P, Chin-Shong E 1969 Social status and attitudes toward behavioral
disorder; the problem of tolerance of deviance. In: Kolb L C, Bernard V W,
Dohrenwend B P (eds) Urban Challenges to Psychiatry, Little Brown and Co, Boston

Dohrenwend B P, Dohrenwend B S 1969 Social status and psychological disorder: a causal
inquiry. Wiley-Interscience, New York

Faris R E L, Dunham H W 1939 Mental disorders in urban areas. University of Chicago
Press, Chicago

Fischer C S, Jackson R M, Steuve C A, Gerson K, Jones L M, Baldassare M 1977
Networks and places: social relations in the urban setting. The Free Press, New York

Foster J L 1978 Regionalism and innovation in the American States. The Journal of Politics
40: 179–187

Freeman H L 1978 Mental health and the environment. British Journal of Psychiatry
132: 113–124

Freeman H L 1983 District mental health services. In: Bean P (ed) Mental illness: changes
and trends. Wiley, Chichester

Freeman H E, Simmons O G 1963 The mental patient comes home. Wiley, New York

Galle O R, Gove W R, McPherson J M 1972 Population density and pathology: what are
the relations for man? Science 176: 23–30

Giggs J A 1979 Human health problems in urban areas. In: Herbert D T, Smith D M (eds)
Social problems and the city: geographical perspectives. Oxford University Press, Oxford.

Glaser F B, Greenberg S W, Barrett M 1978 A systems approach to alcohol treatment
Addiction Research Foundation, Toronto

Golant S 1980 Locational-environmental perspectives on old-age segregated residential areas
in the United States. In: Herbert D T, Johnston R J (eds) Geography and the urban
environment Vol III progress in research and applications. Wiley, Chichester

Goldblatt P B, Berberian R M, Goldberg B, Klerman G L, Tischler G L, Zonana H 1973
Catchmenting and the delivery of mental health services. Archives of General Psychiatry
28: 478–482

Hare E H 1979 Schizophrenia as an infectious disease. British Journal of Psychiatry 135: 469–473

Herbert D T 1976 Social deviance in the city: a spatial perspective. In: Herbert D T, Johnston R J (eds). Social areas in cities Volume 2: spatial perspectives on problems and policies. Wiley, Chichester

Herbert D T 1979 Introduction: geographical perspectives and urban problems. In: Herbert D T, Smith D M (eds) social problems and the city: geographical perspectives. Oxford University Press, Oxford

Hogben G L, Critelli T, Hoffman R 1979 The impact of political process on hospital psychiatry. American Journal of Psychiatry 136: 201–204

Hollingshead A B, Redlich F C 1958 Social class and mental illness. Wiley, New York

Huffine C L, Craig T J 1973 Catchment and community. Archives of General Psychiatry 28: 438–488

Jones K 1982 Realities of community mental care. Lancet: 1210–1211

Kirk S A 1974 The impact of labelling on rejection of the mentally ill: an experimental study. Journal of Health and Social Behavior 15: 108–117

Langsley D G, Barker J T, Yarvis R M 1978 Deinstitutionalization: the Sacramento story. Comprehensive Psychiatry 19: 479–493

Levy L, Rowitz L 1973 The ecology of mental disorder. Behavioral Publications, New York

Longest J L, Konan M, Tweed D 1976 A study in deficiencies and differentials in the distribution of mental health resources in facilities. National Institute of Mental Health Series B No 15. US Government Printing Office, Washington DC

Maddox J F, Desmond D P 1982 Residence relocation inhibits opioid dependence. Arch Gen Psychiatry 39: 1313–1317

Marshall J R, Funch D P 1979 Mental illness and the economy: a critique and partial application. Journal of Health and Social Behavior 20: 282–289

Milgram S 1970 The experience of living in cities. Science 167: 1461–1468

Mollica R F, Redlich, F C 1980 Equity and changing patient characteristics 1950–1975. Archives of General Psychiatry 37: 1257–1263

Murphy H B M, Vega G 1982 Schizophrenia and religious affiliation in Northern Ireland. Pschological Medicine 12: 595–605

National Insitute of Mental Health 1979 1979 Directory of Federally Funded Community Mental Health Centers, DHEW Publication No (ADM) 79–258

Pyle G F 1979, Applied medical geography, V H Winston and Sons, Washington DC

Rabkin J G 1974 Public attitudes toward mental illness: a review of the literature. Schizophrenia Bulletin, Fall: 9–33

Rabkin J G 1979 Ethnic density and psychiatric hospitalization: hazards of minority status. American Journal of Psychiatry 136: 1562–1566

Redick R W, Goldsmith H F, Unger E L 1971 1970 Census data used to indicate areas with different potentials for mental health and related problems. Mental Health Statistics Series C No 3 US Government Printing Office, Washington DC

Regester D D 1974 Community mental health: for whose community? American Journal of Public Health 64: 886–893

Rose S M 1979 Deciphering deinstitutionalization: complexities in policy and program analysis. Milbank Memorial Fund Quarterly/Health and Society 57: 429–460

Rothbart M 1973 Perceiving social injustice: observations on the relationship between liberal attitudes and proximity to social problems. Journal of Applied Social Psychology 3: 291–302

Schwab J L, Schwab M E 1978 Sociocultural roots of mental illness: an epidemiologic survey. Plenum, New York

Scott N, Scott R A 1980 The impact of housing markets on deinstitutionalization Administration in Mental Health 7: 210–222

Segal S P 1978 Attitudes toward the mentally ill: a review. Social Work 23: 211–217

Segal S P, Aviram U 1978 The mentally ill in community-based sheltered care. Wiley, New York

Segal S P, Baumohl J 1980 Engaging the disengaged: proposals on madness nad vagrancy. Social Work 25: 358–365

Segal S P, Baumohl J, Moyles E W 1980 Neighborhood types and community reaction to the mentally ill: a paradox of intensity. Journal of Health Social Behavior 21: 345–359

Shannon G W, Dever G E A 1974 Health care delivery: spatial perspectives. McGraw Hill, New York

Smith C J 1976 Residential neighborhoods as humane environments. Environment and Planning A 8: 311–326

Smith C J 1977 Geography and mental health. Commission on college geography, resource paper no 76–4, Association of American Geographers. Washington DC

Smith C J 1978 Problems and prospects for a geography of mental health. Antipode 10: 1–12

Smith C J 1980a Planning comprehensive community facilities for alcoholics. A report prepared for the Division of Alcohol Services, Oklahoma Department of Mental Health unpublished, mimeo

Smith C J 1980b Neighborhood effects on mental health. In: Herbert D T, Johnston R J (eds) Geography and the urban environment Vol III. Progress in research and application. Wiley, Chichester

Smith C J 1980c Residential needs of the deinstitutionalized mentally ill. In: Frazier J W, Epstein B J (eds) Applied geography conferences Vol 3. Kent State University, Kent, Ohio

Smith C J 1981 Urban structure and the development of natural support systems for service dependent populations. The Professional Geographer 33: 457–465

Smith C J, Hanham R Q 1981a Deinstitutionalization of the mentally ill: a time path analysis of the American States, 1955–1975. Social Science & Medicine 15: 361–378

Smith C J, Hanham R Q 1981b Proximity and the formation of public attitudes towards mental illness. Environment & Planning A 13: 147–165

Smith C J, Hanham R Q 1981c Any place but here! Mental – health facilities as noxious neighbours. Professional Geographer 33: 326–334

Sohler K B, Clapis J A 1972 Jarvis's law and the planning of mental health services. HSMHA Health Reports 87: 75–80

Srole L, Langner T S, Micheal T, Opler M K, Rennie T A C 1962 Mental health in the Metropolis. McGraw-Hill, New York

Stokols D 1973 Psychological social and personal determinants of the perception of crowding. Environment and Behavior 5: 87–115

Taylor S D 1974 The geography and epidemiology of psychiatric disorders in Southamptom. Unpublished PhD thesis, University of Southampton

Tischler G 1977 Ethnicity and the delivery of mental health services. In: Serban G (ed) New trends of psychiatry in the community. Ballinger, Cambridge, Mass

Tischler G L, Henizz J, Myers J K, Garrison V 1972 Catchmenting and the use of mental health services. Archives of General Psychiatry 27: 389–392

Tischler G L, Aries E, Cytrynbaum S, Wellington S W 1975 The catchment area concept. In: Bellak L, Barren H (eds) Progress in community mental health Vol III. Brunner/Mazel Inc, New York

Trute B, Segal S P 1976 Census tract predictors and the social integration of sheltered-care residents. Social Psychiatry 11: 153–161

Walker J L 1969 The diffusion of innovations among the American States. American Political Science Review 62: 880–899

Warren R B, Warren D I 1977 The Neighborhood organizer's handbook. Notre Dame University Press, Notre Dame, Indiana

Weirich T W, Sheinfeld S N 1982 The effects of recentralizing mental health services. Community Ment Health Journal 18: 200–209

White A N 1979 Accessibility and public facility location. Economic Geography 55: 18–35 Wilkinson

Wing J K, Brown G W 1970 Institutionalization and schizophrenia: a comparative study of three mental hospitals 1960–1968. Cambridge University Press, Cambridge

Wolch J 1979 Residential location and the provision of human services. The Professional Geographer 31: 271–276

Wolch J 1980 Residential location of the service-dependent poor. Annals of the Association of American Geographers 70: 330–341

Wolpert J, Mumphrey A, Seley J 1972 Metropolitan neighborhoods: participation and conflict over change. Commission on college geography resource paper No 16, Association of American Geographers, Washington, DC

Wolpert J, Dear M, Crawford R 1975 Satellite mental health facilities. Annals of the Association of American Geographers 65: 24–35

Wolpert J, Wolpert E 1976 The relocation of released mental hospital patients into residential communities. Policy Sciences 7: 31–51

Urban delinquency: ecological and educational perspectives

Urban ecology is concerned with the relationships between people and their physical environment, studied — in spatial terms — in the context of city growth and change. This discipline, which evolved from ecological studies in biology, concerned with the complex relationships of flora, fauna, and terrain, is one of the pivotal points at which geography, sociology and social science interact. The utility of urban ecology in fields such as psychiatry is becoming increasingly acknowledged (Wilkinson & O'Connor 1982), while the study of social networks and mental health (Greenblatt et al. 1982) and of ecological psychology (Wicker 1979) is allied to it. I will consider here some of the theoretical, methodological and substantive work in this field, paying particular attention to British studies of juvenile delinquency and of various kinds of disturbed behaviour in urban school children. Finally, I will review recent studies which have compared the relative influences of school, family, and urban neighbourhood upon variables such as deviant behaviour and under-achievement in these children. The relationship of these problems to psychiatric disorder will also be considered.

Studies of the ecology of cities in both North America and Europe have shown that deviant or maladaptive behaviours of various kinds (adult and juvenile crime, psychiatric illness, scholastic under-achievement, school absenteeism, children taken into care, child guidance referrals, etc.) tend to have particularly high rates in certain districts. Usually these are areas of poor housing, overcrowding, poverty, and of migrant or unstable populations. They are often in the decaying parts of city centres; but this coincidence of multiple deprivation and multiple pathology can also occur in outlying districts of poor quality public housing (Buglass & Duffy 1978). The existence of such areas poses problems for urban planners and educators, since the schools in such areas are intimately involved with many of the behaviours and social conditions found there. How can schools compensate, if at all, for such conditions and incipient behaviours? Can some schools, by virtue of their depressed conditions and ethos, actually make the problems of these areas worse instead of better? What kinds of changes in the organisation of such schools might influence pupils in a positive rather than a negative direction? And to what degree do such changes have to be accompanied by wider programmes of urban renewal and community regeneration?

CRIME AND DELINQUENCY IN THE CITY

An excellent review of the concept of social ecology in the study of delinquency, and of earlier British and American work in this field has been presented by Morris in *The Criminal Area* (1957). His own study of Croydon identified seven quite small areas with very high delinquency rates; the distribution of these 'criminal areas' and their relationship to other features of city life led him to criticise some aspects of the theories of the Chicago school, whose work in the 1920s in America had done much to stimulate such research. There was in fact more continuity in his work with the studies of nineteenth century London (by Mayhew, etc.) than with the models of delinquency and social conditions which had emerged in America. Moreover, town planning and relocation of slum-dwellers had distorted the 'natural' growth of the city, which was so important in the Chicago model (Burgess 1926). What was important, stressed Morris, was the survival of a culture of delinquency, involving a set of norms about relationships to property and wealth, which were transmitted within families. Sons followed their fathers' delinquent example, and were supported in this behaviour by mothers and sisters. Nevertheless, there was also much disorganised behaviour in these families; fathers left, not only for prison, but for other women; over-crowding and illness were common, unemployment (in a time of labour shortage) was frequent, and psychiatric problems seemed to be above average in extent.

A striking feature of ecological studies of delinquency in Britain has been the finding of continuity: delinquent sub-cultures survive generations, moves from poor to reasonable public housing, and the transfer of the younger generation from slum schools to new secondary schools. This persistence of delinquent norms emerged clearly in a study in Exeter (Bagley 1965), which had extremely high rates of juvenile delinquency in the 1960s, in contrast to other city areas in England and Wales, and indeed only Liverpool and Grimsby had higher levels. The rates of juvenile delinquency were plotted in the 16 electoral wards in Exeter, using a sample of court offenders obtained from probation records. Forty per cent of delinquents appearing before the courts over a 6-month period came from one ward — a relatively small council estate, built in the 1930s, where the inhabitants had been relocated from decaying housing in the inner city area. Both that housing, and the deviant and lawless behaviour of its population seemed from historical accounts to be medieval in origin. The normative sub-culture which favoured the opportunist thieving of unattended goods had survived for centuries, and seemed not to have been much influenced by a move to public housing.

Why had the rate of delinquency in Exeter remained so high, while in other, geographically similar cities it had declined over time? To answer this question, the crime rate was compared with various social indices in 22 similar 'isolated conurbations' (Freeman 1959). In these conurbations, both social class and amount of education received had linear relationships with juvenile delinquency rates: the lower the social class profile of a city, and the fewer who stayed on at school, the higher the crime rate. Moreover, the amount spent on youth facilities and clubs had a strong negative correlation (–0.58) with delinquency rates, which remained significant when all social factors were controlled. Therefore, a causal connection was inferred between youth service provision (including school-based) and high delinquency rates, implying that some kinds of social intervention can counteract the long-standing norms of the delinquent sub-culture.

It was significant that in Exeter, youth services were entirely absent in the high-delinquency Wonford ward, and that the amount spent on these services in the city was the lowest in any of the 22 conurbations considered, except Grimsby. Subsequent research by Farrant (1963) confirmed this picture, following ethnographic work with delinquent gangs in Exeter: 'Many of the members of these delinquent groups and quasi-groups were failures in terms of the education system and had low status jobs as well as low status at work'. However, later research in Sheffield (Baldwin & Bottoms 1976) did not find evidence to support a negative association between juvenile delinquency on council estates and adequacy of leisure provision for youth.

Studies of the ecology of delinquency in British cities continue. Wallis & Maliphant (1967) took samples from detention centres, prisons, and borstals serving the London area, and plotted rates of crime for the population aged 17 to 20 for all London boroughs. The highest rates were in Kensington and in Islington, followed by a number of East London Boroughs. These crime rates co-varied significantly with indicators of over-crowding, poor housing, rented accommodation, density per acre, low social class, population change, high birth rates, children in care, early school leaving, and unemployment. What was remarkable was the degree to which delinquency rates, and their social correlations, remained stable in London over a 40-year period, despite considerable social change, just as the distribution of suicide rates in London remained remarkably stable over an equivalent length of time. In 1973, the Greater London Council identified 155 'high stress' wards, that would be the target of special programmes of action. The areas in North Kensington and Islington identified by Wallis and Maliphant, using 1961 census data, were precisely those of high stress identified by the GLC from 1971 census data.

Knight et al. (1971), in their longitudinal study of 411 males born in a working class district of London, found that delinquency at age 22 could be predicted with some degree of accuracy from data available when the child was aged eight. A potent factor was the history of crime in the family; various aspects of behaviour, including unemployment, point to the possibility that the 'culture of delinquency' in various families (who are particularly likely to live in certain areas) contributes in large measure to the delinquency rate; i.e. the majority of cases of juvenile crime have their origins in delinquent families, which reside by and large in delinquent areas. As Mack (1963) has shown in Glasgow, many adult and professional criminals are recruited from these delinquent sub-cultures, while somewhat similar implications can be drawn from Willmott's (1966) study of adolescent boys in East London, where there are strong sub-cultural traditions of delinquency and crime (Downes 1966). In such areas crime is not deviant, but is normatively sanctioned or easily tolerated behaviour in family and neighbourhood groupings, whose values are often at variance with those of the major society. In Rutter's view (1981), the evidence suggests an ecological effect in areas with high rates of disorder, which is not just a function of the aggregation of vulnerable families. Herbert (1979) analysed delinquency data for Cardiff, in relation to enumeration districts (EDs), and found high, stable rates in areas with reputations as problem zones and with characteristics of poor social environments; as the reputations of schools in areas became fixed, a filtering process occurred, whereby vacancies in them were only accepted by those with low aspirations. Though delinquency showed localised clustering within certain housing estates, it was not closely coincident with small sub-territories within them.

From a survey of public housing estates in Sheffield, Bottoms & Xanthos (1981) tentatively concluded that an explanation for the differing rates recorded in them might be a combination of: (1) indirect effects of the city's allocation system of tenancies; (2) the reputation of each estate, as 'respectable', 'rough', etc.; (3) a sub-cultural value system on one estate, closely linked to poverty; (4) socialisation into this value system, including deviant norms; and possibly (5) a differential influence of the schools on two estates. These interacting social aspects had to be seen within a broader societal context of a national shortage of homes for low-income families, and a public sector of housing which is internally differentiated in terms of dwelling type and built environment.

Studies from Northern Ireland and Liverpool provide further examples of continuity in social deprivation and delinquent sub-cultures. Bagot (1941), describing ecological studies of delinquency in Liverpool in the 1930s, reported a clearly differentiated pattern of delinquency rates, with a particular concentration in the central and dock areas — resembling that observed in the earlier Chicago studies. High rates of delinquency were associated with overcrowding and extreme poverty.

When Mays (1963) carried out ecological work in the late 1950s, the pattern of delinquent areas had hardly changed. The most detailed study of delinquent areas in Liverpool is that of Flynn et al (1972). This pointed to the multiple coincidence of social disadvantage and behavioural pathology or handicap; the rate of theft was strongly associated, on an area basis, with: educationally subnormal children, possession orders for rented housing, welfare conference cases, court debtors, children deloused, adults mentally ill, job instability, unemployment, school absenteeism, violent crime, illegitimacy, school clothing grants, adults of subnormal intelligence, children in care, vandalism, and physically handicapped children. The ward with the highest rate, on a principal component representing these indices, was a central one, while the adjacent ward also had a high rate.

But a notable change from the earlier pattern was the high rate in Speke, an outlying estate of council housing, which accommodated people rehoused after massive slum clearance in the central area. This finding paralleled those in Exeter (Bagley 1965) and in Edinburgh (Buglass & Duffy 1978): rehousing a population from slums into indifferent public housing, whether a pre-war estate or modern high-rise, does little to counteract the underlying patterns of behaviour which prevailed within families and neighbourhoods, and which educational and social services have largely failed to counteract (Herbert 1979). Bush (1981) has undertaken research in the comprehensive school serving the area in Toxteth, Liverpool, where serious civil disorder occurred in 1981, showing that the exact location of these riots could have been predicted from Bagot's (1941) ecological work on social disorganisation, some 40 years earlier; and that this recent picture of social deprivation in the area has many similarities to May's (1963) description. The picture, as in other ecological studies, is one of continuity of deprivation and deviant reaction.

The evidence from Northern Ireland is also also salutary. Dell (1962) examined the areal distribution of juvenile delinquents in Belfast, using the school as the unit of analysis. There were large differences in the rates of delinquency between schools, and those serving the old central and socially declining areas of the city (both Catholic and Protestant) had particularly high rates.

Clearly, the facts of deprivation and their counterparts in delinquency and crime in deprived inner city areas of Belfast were known long before the outbreak of sectarian violence. Spencer (1973) identified areas from which young terrorists were likely to come, and found them to be precisely the same areas which Dell had identified a decade earlier. In Ballymurphy, rates of overcrowding were extremely high, just under half of the population living in dwellings at a density of 1.5 persons per room or more; there was also chronic unemployment and ill-health in its residents, 27 per cent of males being unemployed. A further study (Northern Ireland Housing Executive 1976) identified similar areas of disadvantage, in which poverty, poor housing, and crime in children and adults all went hand in hand, while the Community Organisations of Northern Ireland (1979) found that in certain inner areas of Belfast, including Ballymurphy, unemployment rates have reached 50 per cent amongst males, and the incidence of poverty is four times greater than elsewhere in the province. These findings show that the areas of deprivation, from which both criminals and terrorists are disproportionately drawn, were known well in advance. Although the root causes of sectarian strife in Ulster lie deep in history and social structure, the stimulus for recruitment to terrorist organisations has, it seems, been extreme poverty and deprivation, which was largely remediable.

Comparable results, involving suicide, have been obtained in Greater Cleveland, USA. Hirsch et al. (1973) examined rates of both homicide and suicide for the period 1940–1970, during which the white population of the city fell from 90.3 per cent to 61.0 per cent, whereas the suburban areas changed only from 99.2 per cent to 95.4 per cent. Homicide rates increased greatly in the later 1960s, mostly involving guns, and suicide rates also increased, though only slightly compared to the dramatic rise in homicides; both increases were almost entirely within the city. Throughout the period, suicide rates in the city remained significantly higher than those in the suburbs, but this difference was entirely in respect of men. In Cleveland as elsewhere, homicides correlated strongly with poverty.

METHODOLOGICAL PROBLEMS

There are various methodological problems in ecological studies of crime and delinquency — principally of statistical inference, the validity of data, and of developing a relevant model of areal influences (Chilton and Dussich 1974).

A major pitfall to be avoided is that of drawing naive conclusions about cause from ecological correlations. For example, Levy and Rowitz (1971), in a study of rates of mental illness in Chicago, found that there was a high correlation between the percentage in an area who were black, and the percentage who were schizophrenic. A naive interpretation would be that blacks are particularly likely to be schizophrenic. But an examination of individual cases showed that schizophrenics were predominantly white; because of failure to hold jobs, they tended to drift into low-rent areas, where the majority of tenants were black. It is interesting that these areas were, with few exceptions, the ones identified as high-rate areas by the Chicago studies (Burgess 1926; Shaw & McKay 1942).[1] A caveat, then, in interpreting ecological correlations is that they should always be checked on a sub-sample of individuals. Choldin (1978) points out that although crowding and delinquency may correlate at the neighbourhood level, this does not prove that the residents of the relatively few crowded households there are the ones who have become delinquent.

Similarly, the Psychiatric Rehabilitation Association (1973), finding that rates of schizophrenia were highest in decaying areas of London, suggested that poor social conditions played a major causal role in the emergence of the illness. But, as comparison of individual and ecological correlations of schizophrenia and other psychiatric illness has shown, the picture is by no

(1) Cf. Brown & Frank (1971) on ecological change in Chicago in the decade 1950–1960.

means so simple (Bagley 1975). A major factor is the predominant type of housing, with the possibility that marginal individuals drift into areas of poor accommodation. Nevertheless, poor housing and its associated stresses do most likely represent a factor exacerbating relapse in such individuals.

A second problem in ecological work is that of spatial auto-correlation. Ecological correlations tend to be much higher than individual ones, since they measure at the same time both co-variation in the dimensions involved and the resemblance of the relevant rates due to spatial contiguity of the 'cases' studied. For example, the characteristics of Wandsworth and Lambeth have many similarities simply because these two London Boroughs are contiguous. Because the units of analysis are not independent of one another, conventional tests of significance ought not be used, although they frequently are, in the educational and biomedical fields. A variety of solutions to this problem have been proposed (Cliff & Ord 1973); one useful technique seems to be factor or principal components analysis (Slatin 1974; Clark et al. 1974), which can divide patterns of correlations according to their source (e.g. co-variance or contiguity). Controversies continue to rage in this area (see Herbert and Johnston 1976; and Bogue and Bogue 1976 for reviews), and the researcher is faced with a choice of methodologies. My preference is to calculate normal correlation coefficients, without attributing statistical significance, and adding a principal components analysis; if possible, a sub-sample of individuals is examined also, to check whether or not factors (such as delinquency and overcrowding) which go together in a particular area also coincide in individuals (Bagley et al 1973). If the same people are involved in two forms of behaviour, ecological correlations will not reveal anything about the underlying social structure, but if people who are at risk are obliged to live in situations which intensify their problems, then both individual and ecological factors may operate simultaneously (Buglass & Duffy 1978).

A third problem concerns the validity of data about delinquents, gathered in area surveys. Labelling theorists (Schur 1971) suggest that the police may have a selective perception of who is delinquent, and who should be arrested and processed by the penal system. Potential delinquents may be perceived in symbolic terms, rather than in terms of their 'real' characteristics. Thus, certain areas and families may have the reputation for delinquency, so that when crimes are committed, police may automatically seek suspects there. Ultimately, high rates may be artefacts of the perception which the police have of certain areas, and the particular action they take; thus, the correlation between delinquency and poor social conditions in particular areas could be a tautologous one. Therefore, as a result of police action, and not perhaps of the poor social conditions, these areas would come to have a high crime rate. In the Exeter research (Bagley 1965), we were unacquainted with labelling theory, and had not considered this possibility.

However, in Brighton, in the early 1970s, we attempted to avoid this problem, first by taking a sample of delinquents not from court convictions, but from the police incident book. The police record the name of a suspect after a report of crime, but often release him with a warning, rather than a court summons. It has been claimed that children of middle class families are much more likely to be let off in this way. However, using this source probably avoids the possibility that the delinquency data might reflect police disposal procedures, which are in turn based on selective perception of children from particular class or area backgrounds.

We asked the police from what area criminals were most likely to come, and there was unanimity in nominating Falmer ward, which contains a high proportion of pre-war council houses; but the ecological study (Bagley et al. 1973) indicated that although Falmer had the highest number of delinquents, this was a function of the large size of the population at risk. By contrast, the highest *rate* of delinquency was found in the relatively small central wards. None of the authorities — police, social services, and psychiatric hospitals — from whom we obtained data had anticipated this, so we concluded that labelling effects had been unlikely to contribute to these results.[2]

Fourthly, there is the problem of interpreting ecological work in the context of wider studies of social deprivation and action. It is clear from the Liverpool work of Flynn et al. (1972) for example, that a wide range of social and behavioural variables have to be considered, as have aspects of the wider social structure (Green 1971). Further, the reasons for areal differences and the accompanying correlations have to be related to wider models of inequality (Craig & Driver 1972). The most comprehensive critique of existing area studies has been advanced by Edwards (1975), who argues that they are carried out with an assumption that there is value consensus about both the parameters and cause of urban deprivation, and that identifying areas of deprivation ('social pathology') will lead to appropriate remedial action to cope with delinquency, poverty, and poor housing. This often implies some kind of minor structural alteration, which leaves the existing social order untouched. But without first defining power and class systems in the city, the empirical analysis and the remedies proposed are unlikely to achieve any major change or alleviation in social deprivation. The degree to which areas of some cities remain socially deprived over decades, and even half a century, lends some force to Edwards' criticisms.

Finally, there is the point made by Herbert (1979) that 'Ecologists yield to the temptation to progress from observations on characteristics of urban life to theories, which view offenders as products of particular environmental features. What is not understood is how these environments look to the offenders themselves'.

(2) In ongoing work on the ecological distribution of delinquency, mental illness, and suicide in Calgary, we are using Police data on all delinquent cases, regardless of court appearance. Work on these 4000 young 'delinquents' again does not support the labelling hypothesis.

In fact, the researcher has two roles. One is basically taxonomic — simply describing patterns of social variation in the city, and identifying types of city which have common patterns. The second is not to engage in political action or debate as such, but to present the results of this research to political scientists and decision makers, for their own analysis and action.

THE COMPLEX PATTERNING OF BEHAVIOURAL DEVIANCE AND SOCIAL DISADVANTAGE IN CITIES

The Chicago school in the 1920s, paralleling British work, had identified social disorganisation in areas of change and decay, which would develop in communities where social solidarity and controls were weakened. It was hypothesised that the condition would have many manifestations, including physical and mental illness, family disintegration, criminality, juvenile delinquency, and poverty. Giggs (1970), however, found from his work in Barry, South Wales, that the patterning of social pathology and disadvantage bore little consistent resemblance to the major formulations built into the Burgess (1926) concentric and zonal arguments.[3] However, he was unable to explain his results with a satisfactory alternative theory — 'the development of a satisfactory formal theory of the structure and distribution of social disorganisation in urban areas lies a long way in the future'. Relevant factors are not only the 'natural' patterning and relationship of industry, people, and housing, but the values which people bring to particular areas, and which develop through structurally and spatially determined interaction; there are also the effects of social planning, of industry, amenities, transport, and access to various types of housing, as well as the wider patterns of stratification and income distribution. In nearby Cardiff, Herbert (1979) found that high delinquency rates were more strongly related to poor social environment (high levels of unemployment, shared dwellings, and overcrowding) than to poorly built environment (lack of amenities and fixed baths). A further important variable, (see below) may be the influence of schooling on the values, motivation and orientation of urban adolescents.

(3) Burgess (1964) from his ecological studies of Chicago, argued that most modern cities develop 'natural areas', which can form the basis for social planning and action. The areas identified in Chicago were categorised in terms of five concentric rings, each within the other. At the centre of the city was the loop, or central business district. Surrounding this was the 'zone in transition', containing ghetto slums, ethnic underworlds, a roomers' quarter, and a centre of vice. Surrounding this was a zone of working-men's homes, surrounded in turn by a residential zone of apartments and residential hotels, surrounded again by a commuter bungalow section. Despite the many critics of the assumptions made in arriving at this model and its applicability to urban areas outside Chicago (Timms 1971), the Chicago model still seems to have relevance for many large cities, such as London. Sainsbury's work (1955) on the ecology of suicide in London, and Timms' (1965) on the distribution of social pathology in Luton seem fully explicable in terms of the Chicago model, as Timms himself avers (1971).

Ecological studies of social and behavioural disadvantage (reflecting the general trend in urban and residential differentiation work — see Timms 1971) have moved to the development of indicators, using factorial methods developed from urban geography. Work in Edinburgh over several years (e.g. Buglass & Duffy 1978) showed that many different indicators of social pathology are inter-related, and have high rates in two contrasted areas — the centre of the city, and an older peripheral council estate (which rehoused people from the worst of the inner-city tenements in the 1930s). A comparison of the ecological patterning of psychiatric illness and suicidal behaviour in Edinburgh and Brighton showed, however, that the patterns which emerged in Brighton had some significant differences from Edinburgh, probably relating to the fact that Brighton attracts an unstable, migrant population, as well as a stable but elderly migrant group (Bagley & Jacobson 1976).

Our work there (Bagley et al. 1973) utilised data on serious psychiatric illness (900 cases), suicide (150 cases), serious crime (1300 cases), and child welfare problems (800 cases). Addresses of the individuals concerned were plotted by ward and ED, and rates for a variety of sub-indicators (e.g. type of offence, type of psychiatric illness, type of hospital admission) were calculated for each urban area, using census data to estimate the populations at risk in various sex- and age-groups. Census data for these areas (on social class, housing type and conditions, amount of open space, immigration, population stability, car ownership, etc.) were also utilised in correlation, cluster, and component analyses.

The census-derived (non-behavioural) data showed a patterning of variables along two orthogonal axes (Bagley & Jacobson 1976), both of which were bipolar. The first represented at one extreme, low social class, single-person households, shared facilities, furnished rented accommodation, a high proportion of immigrants (from the rest of the UK and Ireland, but not from the Commonwealth), and a high proportion of the elderly; and at the other extreme of the axis, individuals in council housing. The second axis represented at one extreme middle-class owner-occupiers, and at the other, working-class people in poor quality, owner-occupied housing. The 19 Brighton wards were fitted (through factor scores) into the space defined by these two components, and this patterning proved to be strongly predictive of the way in which behavioural pathologies clustered in further ecological analyses. Three central wards had very high rates on all the indicators of social pathology, and these behavioural rates had strong correlations with one another. These correlations clearly represented ecological, rather than individual relationships; thus, the rate of schizophrenia in a ward correlated 0.72 with the percentage of Sussex University students who were living there. This link does not mean (presumably) that Sussex University students were particularly likely to be schizophrenic, but that they were living in low-rent accommodation to be found in cheap, rooming house areas, and which

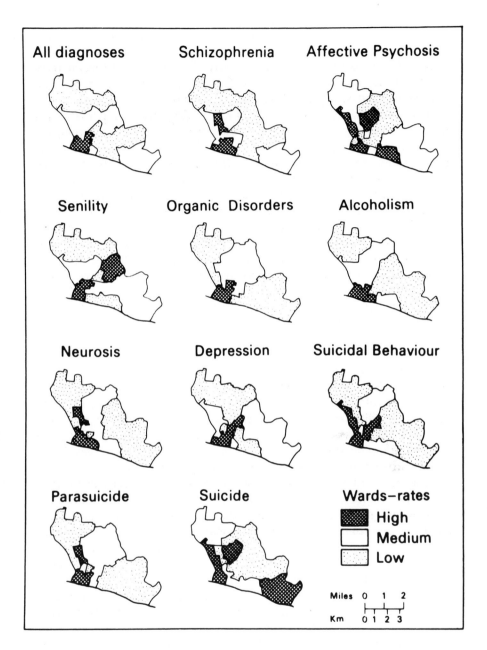

Fig. 6.1 The distribution of psychiatric morbidity and mentality in Brighton (Bagley et al. 1973)

also served a variety of disadvantaged individuals, including the elderly, the mentally ill, and socially disorganised and disadvantaged families. Four apparently phenomenologically distinct kinds of suicide (depressive, socio-pathic, physical illness, and residual) were examined in relation to three ecologically contrasted areas in Brighton — four central wards, four middle class wards, and 13 intermediate. Analysis revealed that two of the four categories of suicide varied significantly across the ecologically contrasted areas, 'sociopathic' suicide occuring predominantly in the central wards and 'physical illness' suicide in the middle-class ones.

An attempt to measure the influence of housing stress on residents in the high-rate areas was made by a study of 100 individuals, randomly selected there, compared with 100 psychiatric patients with an address in the three central wards (Bagley 1975). Data from the neuroticism scale of the Eysenck Personality Inventory were examined. As hypothesised, people with psychiatric illness were much more likely to have experienced poor quality and overcrowded housing, but in addition, housing stress was related to degree of neuroticism, even in those who had never had any treatment for psychiatric illness. The hypothesis that patients and controls will differ according to the incidence of various types of housing conditions was sustained at a significant level, and there were significant correlations between in-migration, housing conditions, and psychiatric admission. The relationship between the time that had elapsed since migration into the city and the appearance of psychiatric symptoms, in patients who had moved into Brighton in the past 5 years, suggested that both stress and selection factors were at work. In other words, vulnerable individuals did not have the means to command adequate or securely tenured housing, and drifted into these cheap, rooming house areas, which forced interaction with other, often undesirable people. The stress of this poor housing added to their initial problems, and led in a significant number of cases to further psychiatric breakdown. There was a clear tendency for a group of individuals to break down shortly after migration, but following this, the rate of breakdown was fairly evenly distributed over time, and a majority of these later cases experienced housing stress. When this happened in a one-parent family, children often had to be taken into care, and the delinquency rate in the children of these families (both one- and two-parent) was particularly high, as were referrals to other agencies, such as child guidance clinics. Thus, social problems in Brighton were found to be distributed in non-random ways in parts of the city characterised by poor quality and overcrowded housing.

Similarly, Landini et al. (1973) have shown that child guidance referrals are related ecologically to high levels of delinquency in Lausanne, the two rates of referral coinciding in areas marked by poverty and social disorganisation. In Britain, there was a detailed ecological study of delinquency, child guidance referrals, and related social conditions in Croydon by Gath et al. (1977). Wide variation in clinic referral rates (which were strongly correlated with delinquency rates) was found in a comparison of the various wards; these rates were low in the residential suburbs, and high in the central wards. Both child guidance and delinquency rates were related to a number of social indices; in particular, to the proportion in lower social classes, poor housing, high population density, and lack of owner-occupied houses. A multiple regression analysis found that the best predictor of child guidance referral in secondary school children was the school probation rate (implying some 'school effect', see below). The next three indices, in order of importance, were all ecological: proportion of persons living in shared households, proportion of foreign-born residents, and rates of in-migration to the borough. Although high-rate delinquency areas tended to be in the central parts, this was not universally so, and the pattern bore a significant resemblance to that identified by Morris (1957) 20 years earlier.[4] Both McCulloch et al. (1967) and Buglass & Duffy (1978) found that juvenile delinquency correlated with suicide and parasuicide in Edinburgh; the latter authors point out that it is difficult to believe that delinquency 'causes' suicide, and that such variables are more likely to be 'markers' of some underlying malaise in the society concerned. However, these associations were not confirmed in either London or Brighton.

Kirmeyer (1978) has suggested a number of possible theoretical linkages between population density, at the level of the home, and juvenile delinquency: overcrowding may make parents more irritable and the home environment less attractive; children may then seek relief by staying away; parents may also try to increase privacy and reduce crowding by encouraging children to spend more time outside the home, thus diminishing their supervision and control over the children's activities. The long-term consequences of reduced surveillance of children may not be foreseen by parents whose energies are taken up in coping with the everyday demands of an overcrowded home environment. (See also Chapter 1).

MIGRATION, MOBILITY AND SOCIAL CHANGE

It is thus clear that planned social change can disperse individuals from traditional sub-cultures of delinquency and disadvantage, but that these same patterns often reappear in tenants of public housing, which itself may be environmentally depriving, and does not break the 'cycle of deprivation' or transmission of delinquency within families. But it is difficult to say how

(4) It is interesting to compare the study by Morris with that of Hare & Shaw (1965) in the same area, a decade later. They showed that relocation in new council housing had no influence in improving mental health, in comparison with similar residents in slum housing. This result is consistent with studies showing the persistence of deviance and social pathology, despite marked environmental changes.

much the survival of pockets of delinquency is the expression of a normative pattern, reflecting a viable sub-culture — in the terms defined by Valentine (1968) — or of an underlying social disorganisation, manifested in various forms of instability, of which crime is only one (Morris 1957). Labelling theorists (Schur 1971) would assert that multiple rates of behavioural pathology simply reflect the interventions of a variety of professional social agencies (whose main function is social control) with groups who have been symbolically or ritually stigmatised.

This latter hypothesis has some attraction, and some empirical verification, for example Okely and Adams' study (1976) of gypsies in Britain. Most plausibly, the coincidence of rates of behavioural deviance in areas characterised by environmental disadvantage as well as material poverty reflects both the activities of the authorities, and the rather anarchistic set of values in the communities involved. Probably, socialisation is lax there, in the sense of failing to inculcate the major normative standards of society; there is some evidence for this in the study by Wilson and Herbert (1978) of areas of social deprivation in Birmingham. A further possibility is that there are different types of sub-culture. It seems likely that the isolated council estate with high delinquency rates identified in Exeter (Bagley 1965) is fundamentally different from the kind of sub-culture identified in central Brighton (Bagley et al. 1973) in terms of housing type, inward migration, and range of pathological behaviours encountered. Thus, there is a clear need for taxonomic work (using cluster analysis), comparing and classifying types of areas, both within and between cities.

Migration into these central areas of Brighton was of the 'drift' type, and featured very few people from outside Britain (e.g. from the New Commonwealth). Rather, poor and socially inadequate people were attracted from other parts of the country, but the effect of New Commonwealth immigration into areas of cheap housing, which may well be also of delinquency and counter-culture values, is likely to be different. Lambert (1970), in his study of criminal neighbourhoods in Birmingham, found that young West Indians had very low rates of delinquency (despite the generally high rates in the indigenous population) in the areas of poor quality housing which they had to inhabit. He thought that succeeding generations of this group would have higher rates of delinquency, to the extent that they became absorbed in the delinquent sub-cultures in which they grew up. However, the apparently high rates of delinquency in young West Indians at present may have causes in the general pattern of race relations, rather than in more traditional factors (Humphry & John 1972). Wallis and Maliphant (1976) had identified North Battersea (now part of Wandsworth) as a traditional delinquent area; the worst of the slum terraces near the river were pulled down, however, and many of the families rehoused in high-rise flats in Roehampton. A school-based survey of delinquency rates (Metcalfe & Leggett 1970) found that the highest rates in the Borough were now in schools serving the virtually all-white population in Roehampton, and the remaining white indigenous population in North Battersea.

Finally a possible cause of social change in areas of disadvantage is intervention by social agencies. For example, in Islington, the identification of 'social priority areas' by means of ecological indicators (poor housing, psychiatric illness, delinquency, vandalism, changing population) led to the re-siting of local authority social work offices, and input of additional resources (Deacon & Cannan 1970). A similar policy was initiated in Brighton, following our identification of areas with high rates of social deviance in the centre of the city. Gill's study (1977) of a delinquent area in Liverpool ('Luke Street') makes it clear that innovations in housing policy must be accompanied by comprehensive programmes of social action and social support. His pessimistic conclusion is that:

> Techniques of social intervention are not enough to counteract the creation of the delinquent area. The economic disadvantages of those families that are forced to move to the least desirable areas will not be changed by piecemeal local tinkering, nor will the drastically severe employment difficulties of young school leavers . . . be affected in this way. Indeed, the increased rationalisation of urban life and work may mean that in the future there are more rather than less Luke Streets.

Halsey (1973) initiated experimental projects, aimed to combat such structural deprivation, but the effectiveness of these is in doubt, since they have been directed mainly at the infant and primary school level, with little carry-through to secondary schools or to the deprived neighbourhoods from which children in 'educational priority areas' usually come. Only in Liverpool were home–school links systematically built into a programme of community action, but for the reasons which Gill (1977) advanced, these efforts were almost certainly ineffective in the long term.

Halsey (1975) has acknowledged the possible tensions between two approaches: concentrating on areas which are socially deprived; and concentrating on individuals from both deprived and non-deprived backgrounds. The study by Wilson and Herbert (1978) of deprived children (in terms of parental income, home circumstances, under-achievement in school, and delinquent histories) in inner areas of Birmingham suggests that such children, identified in the school context, and their families may benefit from *individual* casework. Putting resources into individual families, rather than spreading them more thinly may be a more cost-effective method of intervention; a small sample in our Brighton study did suggest that individual counselling, combined with social work for the families of these adolescents, is a fairly effective method of changing attitudes and orientations (Bagley et al. 1979). Similar conclusions were drawn by Rose and Marshall (1975) on the basis of their study in Manchester: individual counselling and linked social work, based on the school rather than on the community, was likely to lead to non-delinquent careers, in comparison with control children, who were not given such counselling.

THE SCHOOL EFFECT

Writers about area-based delinquency often refer to the role of the school. Sometimes, educational institutions are seen as having a passive role, reflecting the high rates of delinquency in the areas they serve; or the school may be seen as offering remedies, both social and psychological, for the deleterious influences of family, neighbourhood, and poor housing (Dell 1962); or as having an influence on delinquency, sometimes negative, which is independent of the neighbourhood effect (Morris 1966). More complex explanations are sometimes offered, and in the study of Exeter (Bagley 1965), I attempted to utilise theories of Cloward and of Ohlin on opportunity structure, arguing that lack of opportunity for occupational advancement was one factor which facilitated the continued existence of a delinquent sub-culture. The local school offered a curriculum which was not related to local needs or conditions, and was seen as largely irrelevant by many adolescents from the delinquent area.[5]

Liazos (1978), suggests that providing better schools in delinquent areas may make the problem worse, since schools create delinquents because of their success, not their failure. Under the present economic system, schools must prepare youths (especially of the working class) for 'alienated' work and lives; they become delinquent, therefore, when they reject their destiny. 'The society and economy must change first, since they demand alienated labour, before schools can prepare people for liberated lives'. Whether those who do the same kind of work under different economic systems are less 'alienated' is an issue not discussed, though.

A somewhat similar view of the school is suggested by Willis (1977) in his ethnographic study of a counter-cultural group of boys in a north of England comprehensive school. He sees the school as conniving, albeit implicitly, in the under-achievement of working-class boys; it is a dispiriting ('alienating') experience, which prepares the adolescents for the alienating world of work and unemployment that they have to enter. The 'real' world of these boys, however, is in their sub-culture, which is living, rich, and independent. However, the more statistical approach of epidemiologists in London's East End has provided rather a different picture (Morris 1966; Power 1965; Power 1972). In Tower Hamlets, comparison of area-based delinquency with rates calculated for schools showed that differences between schools, in delinquency rates amongst pupils, could not be fully accounted for by the characteristics of the areas from which the pupils were drawn. In the 20 schools studied, the highest rate was 11 times that in the lowest. A comparative ecological study had shown that the 300 EDs in the Borough had marked variations in delinquency rates, ranging from zero to 73 per cent of those at risk over a 3-year period. But even when these ecological differences

---

(5) Cf. the criticism by Hamnett (1979) of my Exeter work. He suggests that I placed too much emphasis on areal, and not enough on structural influences.

were taken into account, differences between schools still remained significant, leading Morris to conclude that: 'Schools . . . are only one part of the picture. The individual boy, the family, school and community need to be considered together'. Such a study could not be done, however, because the schools, alarmed at the prospect of being identified as 'delinquent', would not grant entry, though this was later granted to others, leading to an important report on school effects (Rutter et al. 1979).

Cannan (1970) compared the delinquency rates for five schools in Islington with those for the districts from which their pupils were drawn, and concluded that there was sufficient mismatch to infer the existence of a significant school effect on delinquency. Some schools may have a specific sub-cultural influence, which socialises pupils into delinquent activity, e.g. fostering particular kinds of offence, such as receiving stolen property. In this model, schools as formal organisations are seen as often irrelevant to the lives of their pupils, merely allowing the growth of sub-cultural values, which are more or less congenial to the emergence of delinquent activities and careers: 'Some schools seem to be carriers of delinquent cultures — not only because of children's home values, which are brought into the school, but because particular interactions which occur within the school network of relationships and rules continually create and enforce oppositional attitudes and actions'.

Carroll (1971) found in a study in Swansea that schools appeared to be more to blame for high truancy rates than the home backgrounds of pupils. Reynolds et al. (1976), also in South Wales, studied nine secondary schools in a homogenous, economically deprived, working-class community, all taking the lower two-thirds of the ability range. Data were collected on three outcome measures — delinquency, attendance, and attainment — over a 6-year period, and significant variations between schools on these indicators were observed, which remained systematically from year to year. Furthermore, schools with high delinquency rates had poor achievement in pupils, and high truancy rates, while pupils from the 'best' schools were those most likely to obtain employment when leaving school. This provides very clear evidence for the school effect, particularly the positive aspects.

Farrington (1972), reporting results of the Cambridge longitudinal study of 411 boys born in a working-class district of London, argues in contrast that 'delinquency begins at home'. Family factors, identified when the child was aged eight, proved the most powerful predictors of delinquent behaviour in the teenage years. The 13 secondary schools attended by most of these boys could not be shown to have delinquency rates which were significantly high, compared with those of neighbouring and feeder schools. Schools did differ markedly in their delinquency rates, but this could be explained by the characteristics of the pupils entering them. Family characteristics (particularly a history of criminal behaviour) were the most powerful predictors of delinquency, and this type of family tended to cluster in certain areas, which fed certain schools. Farrington criticises the results of

Power and of Morris on the grounds that parental choice for a particular school was not sufficiently taken into account. When a school is known to be 'bad', non-delinquent families will do their best to have their children sent to others; thus the comparison of neighbourhood and school delinquency rates may give false results, because the true catchment area of the school is ill-defined. These criticisms may also apply to the work of Reynolds et al, while Baldwin (1972) has also criticised the Power and Morris results because the procedures for separating school from area influences were apparently inadequate.

Finlayson and Loughran (1976) showed that pupils' perceptions of school, learning, and teachers differ significantly between high and low delinquency schools, but this could have been due to the parental choice effect, rather than to that of school culture which socialises negative perceptions of authority. The work by Gath et al. (1977) in Croydon has thrown further light on this problem. Rates of delinquency in the 27 secondary schools were calculated, and compared with the rates in the wards which served these schools. Multiple regression, controlling for socio-economic aspects of the neighbourhoods, showed that at least some of the variance in school delinquency rates could be explained by the characteristics (including their sub-cultures) of the neighbourhoods from which the schools drew their pupils. Nevertheless, the possibility remained open that schools themselves might contribute to delinquency rates.

Heal (1978) tried to solve this problem by a longitudinal study of individual pupils from 13 primary schools, going on to a single secondary school. He argued that if a school effect existed, the differential characteristics of the pupils from the feeder schools would be to some extent homogenised by their experiences in the secondary school. At the primary level, the 470 pupils studied showed significant variations, by school attended, on a self-report measure of delinquent behaviour. Pupils from four of the primary schools with contrasting delinquency rates were then followed-up in the secondary school. After some months, the self-reports showed the same rank order by primary school attended, but the rates were now much closer together than previously, and were converging on a grand mean. Nevertheless, this school effect was small enough for many other factors to be involved in explaining delinquency. Heal observes that:

> The effect of the school upon misbehaviour has been found to be relatively small, and therefore only by understanding precisely how this effect is brought about will there be any chance of identifying characteristics of the school which, on one hand are *amenable* to control, yet on the other are associated with misbehaviour sufficiently strong to *warrant* control.

Rutter et al. (1979) made a longitudinal analysis of children first studied at the age of ten, when they were attending primary schools in the former Borough of Camberwell. These children were initially followed-up into their first year at 21 secondary schools, which were found to have markedly different rates of delinquency, truancy, high and low achievement, and behaviour disorder. Twelve schools were then studied on the basis of the contrast in the rates of the various indices, some 2000 children being followed-up for a further 3 years. In attempting to explain school differences, a range of institutional processes in the schools were examined, as well as the characteristics of the pupils coming to each. The initial differences were maintained, and were reflected in the fourth and fifth years by differences in attendance, delinquency, success in public examinations, and numbers staying on. Although schools often took in different types of pupils, in terms of initial rates of delinquency and behavioural deviance, these differences did not wholly account for the variations between schools in their pupils' later behaviour and attainment, i.e. schools appeared to have an independent influence on pupils' progress. The variations were stable over a 5-year period, and rates on all indicators varied together in a systematic way — schools with high rates of delinquency had much truancy and behaviour disorder, poor achievement, and many early leavers, and vice versa. Differences between schools were not due to physical factors, such as the size of the school, age of buildings, or space, nor to broad differences in administration or organisation, but were systematically related to their characteristics as social institutions. The degree of academic emphasis, teacher actions in lessons, availability of incentives and rewards, and the extent to which children were able to take responsibility, were all significantly associated with outcome differences between schools.

All these factors appear open to modification by staff, rather than being fixed by external constraints, but there were other school influences on pupils' outcomes, which were beyond staff control. The academic balance in intake, which was independent of the other measures of school climate, was particularly important: the greater the proportion of intellectually less able children, the higher the delinquency rates, so that delinquency and low achievement seemed to have some intrinsic connection, independently of other influences. Not surprisingly, combining these independent associations with outcome had a cumulative effect in explaining variance in factors such as delinquency. Although 'school ethos' clearly had an important independent effect on delinquency and related measures, other factors including home background (as evidenced by initial lack of ability or motivation) and neighbourhood effects (higher rates of delinquency and behavioural deviance at the outset) were also important. What cannot be determined is the exact magnitude of neighbourhood and family effects, but it is quite possible that the school effects explain only a relatively small proportion of the outcome measures — a similar finding to that of Heal (1978).

This research attracted much public attention, for it seems to show that schools can exercise a considerable, and autonomous, influence on pupil outcomes, but subsequent analyses (Wragg 1980; Heath & Clifford 1980) make it clear that generalisations from it may be difficult, and the exact degree of school influence hard to quantify, although it still has many valid implications for school practice and future research (Maughan et al. 1980). Marjoribanks (1982) showed in Australia that schools differ markedly in the proportion of interested parents they attract, and the failure to control for such a variation could be a serious source of error in school-effects research. In addition the individual influence of families on children has yet to be controlled for adequately.

SCHOOL AND NEIGHBOURHOOD EFFECTS IN THE BRIGHTON STUDY

Though we collected data on juvenile delinquency in Brighton, those on school effects have not been analysed previously, and the results below are presented for the first time. In the early 1970s, there were six non-selective schools in Brighton (two were co-educational, two for boys, and two for girls). There are data on 340 pupils of secondary age, who were known to the police in connection with an act of delinquency. A random sample of these was interviewed, giving data including family circumstances, home background, and school attended for 140 boys, aged 11 to 16; 135 of these attended one of four secondary schools.[6] Rates of delinquency were calculated for these schools, on the basis of the information gathered on the 135 boys. In Rutter et al.'s study (1979), rates of delinquency in the 12 selected schools ranged from 45 per cent to 18 per cent, but the range in our four unselected schools was much less — their delinquency rates were 8.4 per cent, 10.9 per cent, 14.6 per cent and 21.8 per cent respectively. Simple analysis of variance shows that this difference is significantly different from a random distribution, yet this tells us nothing about whether the schools themselves have a causal influence on delinquency rates. To answer this question, we employed complex analysis of variance to see whether the variation in delinquency rates across schools remained significant, when family background and neighbourhood delinquency rates are controlled. In fact, the unadjusted school effect explains a relatively small amount of the variance in delinquency rates: the value of Eta squared in 0.19, indicating that less than 20 per cent of the variance is explained. Using standard ANOVA programmes in the SPSS, it became clear that this school effect failed to explain any significant proportion of the variance in delinquency rates, when neighbourhood rates were controlled; the latter consisted of the rate, adjusted by the population in the age- and sex-group at risk in the EDs, using data on delinquency for all 340 boys. The variance

(6) Results of this individual enquiry strongly support the results of the previous ecological enquiry (Bagley et al. 1973).

of delinquency rates across EDs was much stronger than that between schools, the ED rate varying from zero to 67 per cent (cf. Morris 1966). Another measure gathered in the personal interviews — a family history of delinquency — also explained a significant amount of the difference in delinquency rates, both between schools and between EDs. Just under half the delinquent boys had a sibling or parent who had been convicted or warned by the police for an offence in the previous 5 years, a finding which is in accord with those of Farrington (1972). Thus, in statistical terms, schools in Brighton did not have a significant influence on delinquency rates in their pupils; rather, these were fully explained by the neighbourhood and family influences. One reason could be that delinquency there is often highly localised; there are several pockets of a few streets with very high rates of delinquency, adult crime, and other indicators of social disorganisation. These pockets are between the catchment areas of the two schools with the highest rates of delinquency. The 'deviant' pupils are few enough not to upset the ethos of the schools they attend, but neither is the school's ethos particularly successful in influencing them. Whether this pattern is relatively unique, is difficult to say at present, but there may be several different types of relationship between school, delinquency patterns, and family and neighbourhood influences.

CONCLUSIONS

The literature clearly indicates that delinquency and associated behaviours can have high prevalence in certain urban areas. Although often associated with poor, decaying, or changing housing conditions, such behaviour can survive rehousing. There are grounds for believing that this delinquency may be based on a set of sub-cultural norms, although the reasons for this and for the continuance of the delinquent sub-culture are not clear. Possibly, as Hamnett (1979) suggests, these pockets of disadvantage, with norms which run counter to those of the mainstream society, are reflections of the class system, and have to be analysed in those terms. Whatever the merit of such a Marxian approach, there is much to be found in a more micro-level analysis of spatial patterning of behaviour and of its relationship to local institutions, examining also the cognitive and affective characteristics of their individual participants. Although we were unable in the Brighton work to identify a significant influence of schools in moulding their pupils' delinquent behaviour, such effects — both negative and positive — do exist. The work of Rutter et al. (1979), which appears to demonstrate a school climate that can affect pupils' behaviour and attitudes to society, seems to be in the tradition of Durkheim's educational sociology (1961). In this, institutions and social structures have an existence and a social reality which precedes and profoundly influences individuals, whatever their personal or individual characteristics. Rutter (1981) also draws attention to the 'considerable disadvantages in an educational system that allows such an uneven distribution of children that some schools have intakes with a heavy preponderance of the intellectually less able'.

At the same time, it is clear that the effect of school climate is never total, and explains a relatively small amount of the variance in the observed behaviour. Delinquency, like many other social actions, has multiple causes. It seems that both neighbourhood climate and family background, including normative support for delinquency, can explain some of the variance in delinquency rates. Whether the effect of these is additive or interactive is not clear, but multiple-variable studies of deviant behaviour of this kind are extremely important (Bagley 1971). Choldin (1978) also points out that if it is assumed that social structure determines the distribution of negative phenomena such as delinquency or psychiatric disorder, than that structure must be seen and investigated in very complex terms.

Another important strand of work links schooling and school sub-cultures to the alienation experienced by many working class adolescents in city schools. These mainly ethnographic studies (e.g. Hargreaves 1967; Willis 1977; Gill 1977) see patterns of deviance as reactions to, or fulfillment of the kinds of role for which lower class youth are prepared in the wider society. Corrigan (1979) regards soccer violence, truancy, vandalism, and other delinquent behaviour as expressions of the lack of power experienced by working-class youth in cities; but no firm theoretical propositions about this can be made on the basis of the existing evidence (Tanner 1978), and the same may be said of sub-cultural theory in general. However, to the extent that phenomena such as alienation or anomie occur in urban populations, they may indicate significant mental health, as well as law enforcement problems. Scott (1972) points out that, although delinquents and criminals include many people sharing personal maladjustment, who may be more likely to be apprehended by the police, there are many others who are psychologically more normal, and less likely to be caught. But since most of the literature on the spatial analysis of deviant behaviour relates to those who have been apprehended, it may not give a fully representative picture of people who exhibit such behaviour.

In his heroic synthesis, Timms (1971) suggests that:

> Given present knowledge no attempt to produce an integrated theory of residential differentiation is likely to be successful . . . (this) involves both the overall structure of society and the decision-making activities of individual households. The attempt to understand the resulting urban structures must encompass aspects of both micro-sociology and social psychology.

Timms is writing about all aspects of urban residential differentiation and behaviour, but as Giggs (1979) makes clear in his comprehensive review of the literature on behavioural ecology, similar problems of synthesis face workers in the field of health and deviant behaviour. Finally, Morris & Hawkins (1970) warn that:

Although attempts have been made to relate general psychiatric/sociological explanations to the individual case and to explain how it comes about that certain children and adults in certain environments do in fact come to behave in an anti-social manner, none of them has been formulated in terms susceptible of empirical verification.

Much research has yet to be done.

REFERENCES

Bagley C 1965 Juvenile delinquency in Exeter: an ecological and comparative study. Urban Studies 2: 39–50

Bagley C 1971 The social psychology of the child with epilepsy. Routledge and Kegan Paul, London

Bagley C 1975 The built environment as an influence on personality and social behaviour: a spatial study. In: Canter D (ed) Psychology and the built environment. The Architectural Press, London

Bagley C, Jacobson S, Palmer C 1973 Social structure and the ecological distribution of mental illness, suicide and delinquency. Psychological Medicine 3: 177–187

Bagley C, Jacobson S 1976 Ecological variation of three types of suicide. Psychological Medicine 6: 423–427

Bagley C, Verma G, Mallick K and Young L 1979 Personality, self-esteem and prejudice. Saxon House, Farnborough

Bagot J 1941 Juvenile delinquency: A Comparative study of the position in Liverpool and England and Wales. Jonathan Cape, London

Baldwin J 1972 Delinquent schools in Tower Hamlets: a critique. British Journal of Criminology 12: 399–401

Baldwin J, Bottoms A E 1976 The urban criminal: a study in Sheffield. Tavistock, London

Bogue D, Bogue E 1976 Essays in human ecology. University of Chicago Press, Chicago

Bottoms A E, Xanthos P 1981 Housing policy and crime in the British public sector. In: Brantingham P J Brantingham P L (eds) Environmental criminology. Sage, Beverley Hills

Brown L, Frank F 1973 Social change in Chicago. Urban Studies 7: 271

Buglass D, Duffy J 1978 The ecological pattern of suicide and parasuicide in Edinburgh. Social Science and Medicine 12: 241–253

Burgess E 1926 The Urban community. University of Chicago Press, Chicago

Burgess E 1964 Natural areas. In: Gould J (ed) A dictionary of the social sciences. New York

Bush T 1981 Youngsters who refuse to be sacrificed. The Guardian July 7: 12 London

Cannan C 1970 Schools for delinquency. New Society December 12: 1004

Carroll H 1971 Absenteeism in South Wales: studies of pupils, their homes and their secondary schools. University College, Department of Education, Swansea

Chilton R, Dussich J 1974 Methodological issues in delinquency research: some alternative analyses of geographically distributed data. Social Forces 53: 73–82

Choldin H M 1978 Urban density and pathology. Annual Review of Sociology 4: 91–113

Clark·D, Davies W, Johnston R 1974 The application of factor analysis in human geography. The Statistician 23: 259–281

Cliff A, Ord J 1973 Spatial autocorrelation: a review of existing and new measures with applications. Economic Geography 46: 269–292

Community Organisations of Northern Ireland 2979 Poverty, the B.A.N. Answer? Belfast

Corrigan P 1979 Schooling and the Smash Street Kids. Macmillan, London

Craig J, Driver A 1972 The identification and comparison of small areas of adverse social conditions. Applied statistics 21: 25–35

Deacon B, Cannan C 1971 Social priority areas and Seebohm. Social Work Today 44–53

Dell G 1962 Social factors and school influence in juvenile delinquency. British Journal of Educational Psychology 33: 312–322

Downes D 1966 The delinquent solution. Routledge and Kegan Paul, London

Durkheim E 1961 Moral education: a study in the theory and application of the sociology of education. The Free Press, Glencoe

Edwards J 1975 Social indicators, urban deprivation and positive discrimination. Journal of Social Policy 4: 275–287

Farrant M 1963 Inside the delinquent gang. MA Thesis, University of Exeter

Farrington D 1972 Delinquency begins at home. New Society September 14: 495–497

Finlayson D, Loughran J 1976 Pupils' perceptions in high and low delinquency schools. Educational Research 18: 138–145

Flynn M, Flynn P, Mellor N 1972 Social malaise research: a study in Liverpool. Social Trends 3: 42–52

Freeman T 1959 The conurbations of Great Britain. Manchester University Press, Manchester

Gath D, Cooper B, Gatonie F, Rockett D 1977 Child guidance and delinquency in a London Borough. Oxford University Press, London

Gill O 1977 Luke Street: housing policy, conflict and the creation of the delinquent area. Macmillan, London

Giggs J 1970 Socially disadvantaged areas in Barry. In: Carter A, Davies W (eds) Urban essays. Longman, London

Giggs J 1979 Human health problems in urban areas. In: Herbert D T, Smith D M (eds) Social problems and the city. Oxford University Press, London

Green B 1971 Social area analysis and structural effects. Sociology 5: 2–19

Greenblatt M, Becerra R, Serafetinides E 1982 Social networks and mental health: an overview. American Journal of Psychiatry 139: 977–984

Halsey A 1973 Educational priority: EPA problems and policies. HMSO, London

Halsey A 1975 The juxtaposition of social and individual approaches in compensatory educational projects. In: Compensatory education. Council of Europe, Strasbourg

Hamnett C 1979 Area based explanations: a critical appraisal. In: Herbert D T, Smith D M (eds) Social problems and the city. Oxford University Press, London

Hare E, Shaw G 1965 Mental health on a new housing estate. Routledge and Kegan Paul, London

Hargreaves D 1967 Social Relations in a Secondary School. Routledge and Kegan Paul, London

Heal K 1978 Misbehaviour among school children: the role of the school in strategies for prevention. Policy and Politics 6: 321–332

Heath A, Clifford P 1980 The seventy thousand hours that Rutter left out. Oxford Review of Education 6: 3–19

Herbert D, Johnston R 1976 Social areas in cities, Vol 1. Spatial processess and form. Wiley, Chichester

Herbert D 1979 Urban crime: a geographical perspective. In: Herbert D T, Smith D M (eds) Social problems and the city. Oxford University Press, London

Hirsch C S, Rushforth N B, Ford A B, Adelson L 1973 Homicide and suicide in a metropolitan county: I Long-term trends. Journal of the American Medical Association 223: 900–904

Humphry D, John G 1972 Police power and black people. Panther Books, London

Kirmeyer S L 1978 Urban density and pathology: a review of research. Environment & Behaviour 10: 247–269

Knight B, Osborn S, West D 1971 Early marriage and criminal tendency in males. British Journal of Criminology 17: 348–360

Lambert J 1970 Crime, police and race relations. Oxford University Press, London

Landoni G 1973 Étude de la clientèle d'un service de guidance infantile. Social Psychiatry 8: 1–15

Levy L, Rowitz L 1971 Ecological attributes of high and low rate mental hospital utilisation areas in Chicago. Social Psychiatry 6: 20–28

Lewis D O, Balla D A 1976 Delinquency and psychopathology. Grune and Stratton, New York

Liazos A 1978 Schooling, alienation and delinquency. Crime and Delinquency July: 355–374

Mack J 1963 Full-time miscreants, delinquent neighbourhoods and criminal networks. British Journal of Sociology 15: 38–53

Marjoribanks K 1982 Fifteen thousand hours: a related study of family–school differences. Oxford Review of Education 8: 45–52

Maughan B, Mortimore P, Ouston J, Rutter M 1980 Fifteen thousand hours: a reply to Heath and Clifford. Oxford Review of Education 6: 289–303

Mays J 1963 Crime and the social structure. Faber and Faber, London

McCulloch J W, Philip A E, Carstairs G M 1967 The ecology of suicidal behaviour. British Journal of Psychiatry 113: 313–319

Metcalf M, Leggett M 1970 A report of the Wandsworth Council for Community Relations. London

Morris J 1966 Young offenders. The Guardian December 23: 1

Morris N, Hawkins G 1970 The honest politician's guide to crime control. University of Chicago Press, Chicago

Morris T 1976 The criminal area. Routledge and Kegan Paul, London

Northern Ireland Housing Executive 1976 Poverty in Ulster. New University of Ulster, Coleraine

Okely A, Adams B 1976 Gypsies and government policy. Heinemann, London

Power M 1965 An attempt to identify at first appearance before the courts those at risk of becoming persistent juvenile offenders. Proceedings of the Royal Society of Medicine 58: 704–705

Power M 1972 Delinquency. New Society September 28: 634

Psychiatric Rehabilitation Association 1973 Poverty and schizophrenia. PRA, London

Reynolds D, Jones D, St. Leger S 1976 Schools do make a difference. New Society July 29: 223–224

Rose G, Marshall T 1975 Counselling and school social work: an experimental study. Wiley, London

Rutter M, Maughan B, Nortimore P, Ousten J 1979 Fifteen thousand hours. Open Books, London

Sainsbury P 1955 Suicide in London. Chapman & Hall, London

Schur E 1971 Labelling deviant behaviour. Harper & Row, New York

Scott P 1972 The spatial analysis of crime and delinquency. Australian Geographical Studies 10: 1–18

Shaw C, McKay H 1942 Juvenile Delinquency and Urban Areas. University of Chicago Press, Chicago

Slatin G 1974 A factor analytic comparison of ecological and individual correlations: some methodologic implications. Sociological Quarterly 15: 507–520.

Spencer A 1973 Ballymurphy — A Tale of Two Estates. University of Belfast Press, Belfast

Timms D 1963 The spatial distribution of social deviants in Luton, England. Australian and New Zealand Journal of Sociology 1: 38–52

Timms D W G 1965 The Spatial distribution of social deviants in Luton, England Australia and New Zealand Journal of Sociology 1: 38–52

Timms D 1971 The Urban Mosaic. Cambridge University Press, Cambridge

Valentine C 1969 Culture and Poverty University of Chicago Press, Chicago

Wicker A 1979 An Introduction to Ecological Psychology. Brooks-Cole, Monterey, California

Wilkinson C, O'Connor W 1982 Human ecology and mental illness. American Journal of Sociology 139: 985–990

Willis P 1977 Learning to Labour. Saxon House, Farnborough

Wilmott P 1966 Adolescent Boys in East London. Routledge & Kegan Paul, London

Wilson H, Herbert M 1978 Parents and Children in the Inner City. Routledge & Kegan Paul, London

Wragg E 1980 The Rutter Research: Perspectives I. Exeter University School of Education, Exeter

SPECIFIC ISSUES

Housing

From the common-sense point of view, housing seems to represent that part of the physical environment which is most important for any person's mental health and, since it usually contains the immediate family, also relates to the most significant aspect of the social environment. Propositions can easily be offered about housing that people will agree with, as readily as they will condemn sin: it should contain all the basic amenities that are generally available in an industrialised society; it should not have structural defects that will let in cold or damp; it should include enough space to avoid overcrowding, as judged by the prevailing norms of the community; it should not be subject to such unpleasant outside influences as noise or smoke. Though people obviously prefer good accommodation to bad when there is a choice, relatively little is known about the specific effects of any of these aspects of housing on psychiatric morbidity.

However, it is an over-simplification to assume that there is a dichotomy whereby unsatisfactory physical conditions impair only physical health, whilst poor psychological or social conditions impair mental health, since all these constantly interact (Carstairs & Brown 1958). Therefore, this subject would be best considered primarily in relation to some of the social processes such as rapid change, referred to in Chapter 2. At the same time, the relationship of any housing to its own environmental context is certainly most important, and this needs to be examined in both social and structural terms. Much of the research undertaken in this field has focussed on residential movement, which is then a point of reference for investigating changes in mental health status; it is not ideal as such since, as Kasl & Rosenfield (1980) point out, what is being studied then is not a selected and well defined housing variable, but 'a broad-based socio-residential experience with uncertain components and boundaries'. For instance, a move to the suburbs is accompanied by changes which were the reasons that the move were made, and not its effects, so that it is very difficult to analyse and assess the specific impact of a particular residential experience.

Both in the UK and US, residential mobility since World War Two has been predominantly out of cities and into new communities — expanded towns, new towns, and suburbs or peripheral housing estates; amongst these, new towns are a particularly British development, and the failure to examine the effects of moving to them nothing short of disastrous, since there is still hardly any information in human terms as to whether or not the whole effort was worthwhile (see Introduction). Enormous numbers of people have moved out of the central areas of British cities; in the decade 1966–1976, half a million left London, 200 000 Glasgow, 150 000 Liverpool, and 100 000 Manchester; Salford, at the heart of the Greater Manchester conurbation, fell from a population of 247 000 in 1928 to 131 000 in 1971. In this process, the great inward migration of the Industrial Revolution was to some extent reversed; but at the same time, part of the vacated inner city accommodation was then re-occupied, mostly by minority races or those with socially marginal characteristics. In this process, the nature of urban communities changed fundamentally, and in such a way as to produce a whole series of major social problems, particularly as it began to coincide with economic decline and deindustrialisation (see Chapter 11).

The present topic is also important because of sociological and anthropological evidence of the significance of 'community structure', which may well play a significant part in shaping individual attitudes, values, and behaviour patterns. Communities can be defined in various ways, but one useful classification is in terms of two dimensions: open/closed, and integrated/non-integrated. Because of the speed of contemporary social and structural changes, physical communities within cities may go through several of these categories within a single generation, so that urban residents may have to adjust more than once to this restructuring around them, causing obvious risks to mental health (Howes 1983).

NEW COMMUNITIES

Expanded towns

Examining the different types of new communities primarily in a British context (see also Freeman 1972), the category of expanded towns mainly relates to London and Liverpool. Whilst something like a doubling in size must have had profound effects on a provincial community, its basic identity still remained intact, and some of the changes involved — such as replacement of old-established local businesses by multiple stores — were taking place throughout the country in any case. One can assume that some tensions existed between the original residents and the newcomers, though never becoming a major public issue, and it is known that a significant number of the latter went back (Evans et al. 1969); but otherwise there is no definite evidence of specific adverse effects on people in this situation, at least from the psychiatric point of view. This does not mean, however, that the expanded town policy was right. It grew out of the planning clichés of the time, which were embodied in legislation of the 1940s, and assumed that conurbations were grossly overcrowded, that they had a severe shortage of land for development, and that it was economically and socially desirable to move business and industry out of the cities. Because of reaction to the urban sprawl of the inter-war period, it was also believed that new development should occur well beyond the 'green belt', and not become an extension of some existing conurbation.

There were certainly strong arguments in favour of this last point, but much anecdotal evidence suggests that people who moved to expanded towns would generally not have done so if they could have found reasonable accommodation within the city, and that they preferred to remain there, especially if it would have been possible to have houses rather than flats. The same seems to be true of many of those, somewhat higher up the social scale, who moved to newly developed private housing well outside the city; in the case of London, this process caused large increases of population in parts of Berkshire, Buckinghamshire, Hertfordshire, and Essex. Ironically enough though, it now appears that the whole phenomenon was largely unnecessary; there was in fact always much unused land, e.g. from obsolete railways and docks, and this amount increased steadily throughout the 1960s and 70s. There were also many adequate houses available, which could have been rehabilitated, rather than demolished as 'twilight areas', but this was not politically acceptable then. Finally, the dispersal of business and industry should have been resisted rather than encouraged, if the enormous problems of urban social and structural decay were to have been avoided. So far as mental health is concerned, kinship and other social networks would then have been preserved, much stressful daily travel would not have been necessary, many long established urban communities would have remained in being instead of disappearing, and employers who went out of business when they lost their premises would often have continued if left alone.

It would also have been much better if grandiose road developments had not been ruthlessly imposed on communities, bringing them few benefits and enormous costs; Ward (1981) describes this as 'official vandalism', whose victims are usually well down the social scale. These changes make it much more difficult for pedestrians and cyclists to move around, since they now often have to negotiate subways, ramps, footbridges, or several 'pelican' crossings, whilst previously compact neighbourhoods may become broken up and dispersed. Existing communities and residential units are ignored by highways, whose vastness and flow of vehicles cause the subdivision of urban areas into artificial, segregated cells; those who move along the roads may not even be aware that local centres or amenities exist around them, in contrast to the congested but vital and human atmosphere of what has been cleared away. A wiser principle for public authorities would have been one of improvement, but of minimal interference with people and places (see Chapter 1). Willmott (1982), from his immense knowledge of London's East End, believes that the decline of British cities would not have gained the momentum it did, nor its effects have been as tragic, if public policy had been more soundly based on what people themselves so clearly wanted.

New towns

Most of the above considerations also apply to the new towns, though these embodied a much more conscious element of social engineering, and were designed to become balanced and self-sufficient communities, with their own sources of employment, as opposed to being merely dormitory areas. In this, they were the successors of the Garden City movement, which was inspired by Ebenezer Howard, and produced not only Letchworth and Welwyn, but the industrial estate villages of Port Sunlight and Bournville; all were imbued with a high moral tone, though the restrictions this imposed tended to wither over the course of time. They remain today aesthetically pleasing to the eye, and (from most points of view) good places in which to live, yet clearly offering no general solution to the problem of working-class housing. The new towns of the 1950s and 60s in practice continued a selective choice of residents, which protected them from the worst social problems of the inner cities, and from the burdens of the elderly and chronicly sick, including those with psychiatric disabilities.

The new towns were built on the principle of the neighbourhood unit, making the assumption that this would establish social values, and that residents would have a positive feeling of relationship towards it. To some extent, this view was supported by Lee's (1976) concept of the socio-spatial schema, which is personal to each individual; most people construe their neighbourhood in a territorial sense of about 100 acres, with patterns of friendship, in residential areas at least, perceived as part of a spatial framework. Nicholson (1961) stated that planned neighbourhoods:

> have come nearest to success (where) they are either based on natural features, which would probably have created some degree of a sense of belonging anyhow, or are strongly reinforced by locally grouped services. If they are seen to have a meaning and a function, they can become a reality (but) they must first satisfy felt needs — including the need to belong to some place which is recognisably different from the places where other men belong.

How that requirement can be met is a problem that has continued to plague all large-scale contemporary developments, and may be unanswerable without at least a return to the use of local building materials. Silver (1968) believed new towns must be unsatisfactory because 'there is no built-in steady change of state, just an all-at-once end state'; they have also suffered from planners' obsession with the compartmentalisation of functions, in contrast with the human muddle of organic communities, which tends to give their environments a ghostly quality even during the day. However, we have no means of knowing whether or not this neighbourhood formula achieved what was expected of it, because it has never been investigated; the new towns were alien implants so far as the surrounding rural areas were concerned, and it is likely that something of a cultural gulf existed between the two, though this also must remain a matter of speculation.

In the first group of new towns, the character of the incoming population was affected by the low birth rates of the early 1950s, but in the next decade, parents came with more children, and continued to be affected by the 'baby boom'. This time of young parenthood often strained the personal and financial resources of married couples, particularly when they were separated from previous family and friendship networks. The new towns failed, in fact, to become balanced communities of the kind that was originally planned, and this failure was mainly the result of current housing arrangements, whereby young married couples who were establishing new households had special difficulties in getting accommodation anywhere else, particularly when their housing requirements changed with each new child. Yet these needs could generally have been accommodated by very local moves, if housing policy had been organised along suitable lines (Thomas 1969).

New towns contained few middle class people, since there was little private housing available, few of the lowest socio-economic groups, and very little special housing for the elderly. During the 1960s, their populations showed a marked degree of upward social mobility, but the communities were socially unbalanced, through having a high proportion of the population within a narrow income range. It was assumed then (as is human nature) that this economic advance would go on indefinitely, and the new city of Milton Keynes was designed for a working population that would be relatively affluent and car-owning; the circumstances of recent years, though, have made these assumptions completely invalid. One alarming aspect of the skewed age-structure of new town populations came to light during 1967 in Crawley, which then had 41 per cent of its population of 62 000 aged under 20 (comparable with a developing country); de Alarcon & Rathod (1968) found 92 cases or possible cases of heroin abuse, aged 15–20, of whom nine out of ten were males, representing 2.7 per cent of the entire male population in this age-group.

Soon after the first new towns were established, there were reports of 'New town blues', mainly among women with small children at home, whereas the men had generally moved as part of a group of employees, and benefited from the social support of the work-place. This was confirmed to some extent in a study of psychiatric out-patients from Crawley by Sainsbury & Collins (1966). However, the first major investigation was that by Taylor & Chave (1964); collecting a remarkable amount of information with very limited resources, they compared measures of mental ill-health in Harlow New Town with data from a peripheral housing estate (Martin et al. 1957), and also with those of an inner area of London, from which many of the Harlow people had come. They distinguished a constitutionally vulnerable group (described as having the 'sub-clinical neurosis syndrome'), which was found to be of about the same size in all three areas. In the new town, this group made relatively more demands upon both general practice and hospital care, needed more help from Housing and other authorities, and generally showed much more difficulty in adapting to the local conditions than the rest of the population. Their symptoms of psychiatric ill-health, which tended to be found in association, were 'nerves', depression, excessive irritability, and poor sleep.

However, in contrast to the peripheral estate, fewer people from Harlow than in the general population were under specialist psychiatric care. Taking general practice consultation rates for neurosis, Harlow gave a higher figure than the national average, but this level of treated prevalence was not taken to mean that neurotic illness was more common in the new town; the explanation accepted was that Harlow had an exceptionally good family doctor service, which people were more ready to consult than they would have been in their old city area. It was also found that neurotic illness did not become less with length of residence in Harlow, which was held to confirm the view that such illness is mainly of constitutional origin, rather than a product of the immediate environment. The neurotic group showed a greater tendency to be dissatisfied with their environment and to complain of loneliness, which was considered to result from their vulnerable personalities; an association was also found between physical and emotional ill-health. Finally, the rate of psychosis was found to be well below the national average (in contrast to the peripheral estate) and this was held to remain true even when corrections were made for the age- and income-structure of the Harlow population, and for a possible loss of schizophrenics in social class V, as a result of differential class migration to the new town. Hooper & Sullivan (1979) consider that if a more refined measure than 'over/under 2 years' had been used, the whole study would have gained considerably.

Throwing epidemiological scruples to the winds, Taylor and Chave postulated that environment has a markedly determining effect on the manifestation and course of psychotic illness (though not neurosis), and that 'good social planning can reduce the incidence of psychosis'. This highly optimistic view ignored the fact that schizophrenia is a long-term disorder, with a low rate of incidence, but relatively high prevalence in settled populations. However, they were on firmer ground in pointing out that 'The full measure of the success or failure of a new town will come only in the next generation, in the children who have been born and brought up in an environment which differs markedly from that which their parents knew in childhood'. It would have been even more interesting to look at this next generation if any of the new towns had experimented boldly with medical, social, or educational services; apart from Harlow's particularly good GP service, though, this did not take place, partly because the administrative structure of the National Health Service at that time neither encouraged joint planning nor gave anyone the overall responsibility to coordinate services for each new community.

New towns, in fact, present an almost unique population laboratory for systematic research, as well as a fairly concrete social situation, within which various parameters can be manipulated. In the US, however, new towns were limited to a few private developments, which have not been notable for any particular innovations, except in Columbia, Maryland (Klein & Adelson, 1978). Satellite communities have also been developed on the periphery of Paris and Stockholm, and several countries have created new capitals, of which Brasilia is the best known. There does not seem to be any systematic information about mental health available from any of these situations, though anecdotal reports from the French and Swedish new communities speak of malaise and rootlessness in them, perhaps best expressed in Jean-Luc Godard's film 'Alphaville'.

Housing estates and suburbs

Peripheral housing estates or suburbs have received by far the largest proportion of people moving to new homes, and this has been the case in virtually every industrialised country, as well as in many developing ones. The process began on a large scale after World War One, and in the UK resulted in four million houses being built within 20 years, taking over eight million people, predominantly of upper working- or lower middle-class status. Though these mostly semi-detached houses seem highly conventional today, they offered, in fact, a totally new living situation for people who had generally come from nineteenth century terraced houses within the city, which were without such amenities as bathrooms and hot running water. The density of the new environment was on average about one-third that of the old. The greater part of this huge resettlement was carried out by private enterprise, making little use of architects or planners, though there were also some large municipal schemes, such as the LCC's at Dagenham and Manchester's at Wythenshawe. Building was all by conventional methods, and that of the local authorities has generally stood the test of time very well, though some private developers had lower standards.

One significant fact, though, from the psychological point of view, was that local materials and styles were almost completely abandoned in this period, so that a residential road or shopping parade anywhere from Land's End to John O'Groats took on an almost identical appearance, particularly as 'Modern' and Art Deco styles filtered down in the 1930s. The other important feature of these developments was that they were profligate in their use of land, compared with previous forms of mass housing; the built-up area of London doubled between 1919 and 1939, with only a one-fifth increase in population. Landmarks tended to become submerged in the tide of 'semis', and the combination of large built-up areas with unrelieved uniformity of style and layout produced a peculiarly disorientating effect.

Considering the size of this migration, it would seem that the suburb and peripheral estate offered people in Britain what they wanted — usually a separate family house with a garden (Oliver et al. 1981) — though once again, we do not know whether or not many of them might have preferred a decent home nearer the urban centre. The significance of these developments, though, was overshadowed at the time by the Great Depression, yet the standard of housing being provided compared very favourably with that in almost any other country — a fact rarely acknowledged within Britain itself — and it was not until 20 or 30 years later that people of comparable socio-economic level in other parts of Western Europe generally gained a similar level of amenity.

The dormitory suburb has generally had a poor press; Lewis Mumford called it 'an asylum for the preservation of illusion' and said it was based on a childish view of the world, while Dyos (1982) referred to it as 'a supremely ambivalent invention . . . a gesture of non-commitment to the city in everything but function'. The values of its society were described by Willmott (1982) as 'a blend of class-consciousness, patriotism, conservatism, ambition . . . and basic decency'; it is despised by Marxists because it represents a myriad of individual choices and private ownerships, rather 'democratically controlled public housing' (whatever that might be). In sociological terms, the suburb can be described as an open and integrated community, in which 'control' mechanisms are not induced by a web of kinship ties, but by prescribed patterns of work and leisure, and by a set of social expectations, e.g. on the role of women in the home or on children's educational achievements. Unlike the closed and integrated community, there are no networks of communication, because domestic privacy and 'keeping oneself to oneself' are part of the required social conformity (Frankenberg 1964).

In the US, mass migration has occurred mainly since World War Two; in Newman's view (1980), the problem is that:

> new suburban communities house few extended families and facilitate little contact with one's neighbours or between different ethnic and income groups. They are spread over too large areas and provide little incentive (for) residents in one group to seek out the community or institutions of another, when both are identical. Each . . . is intentionally designed to be self-contained, and because of the small size of its population, each can support only the most mundane of communal and commercial facilities.

Also, each family has to spend a large percentage of its earnings to provide on its own property what should be the community's collective amenities. Suburban residential areas become fluid and transient, rather than developing firm social networks, whiie the immediate family takes on an increasingly important role and inward focus, replacing the traditional role of the community. Newman states that flight to the suburbs involves a loss of belief in that urban culture which had provided a ladder of upward mobility in the past for the poor and for members of minorities; there is also loss of the 'rich interactive milieus' of social and economic heterogeneity which occur in cities.

Interest in the mental health aspects of suburban and peripheral communities really began with Taylor's now classic paper on 'Suburban Neurosis' in 1938; he recorded the stresses which commonly occurred after removal from a central city area to a housing estate, i.e. higher expenses, social isolation, distance from employment, and loss of familiar surroundings, and noted that these seemed to result in a higher incidence of neurotic disturbances, particularly in women. In 1957, Martin et al. surveyed a housing estate about 12 miles from London; they found that the mental hospital admission rate there was higher than the national average at all ages, but particularly for females aged 45 and over; that consultation rates with GPs for neurosis and similar conditions greatly exceeded those found in a national sample, and that the proportion of persons with nervous symptoms found in interviews with a sample of the estate population was nearly twice that found in a nation-wide survey. Taking into account other data, such as those for juvenile delinquency and the use of child guidance clinics, the rate of mental ill-health (particularly neurosis) in the estate population appeared to be higher than the national average. Martin et al. suspected that this was partly due to the shock of rehousing and partly to the poor social facilities on the estate, which led to a degree of loneliness and social isolation considered incompatible with good mental health.

However, it could not necessarily be assumed that these apparently rather high rates of psychiatric morbidity were the result of the social conditions peculiar to new housing estates. For instance, GP consultation rates for neurotic disorders vary, being generally much higher in urban areas than outside them, and though many studies had shown that people in good houses tend to have better physical health than those in bad ones, this did not necessarily mean that the good housing was responsible for the better health; it might be due to one or more of a number of factors, such as income, age, or heredity, which tend to cluster in a positive or negative direction. Also, comparison of morbidity rates from the estate with national rates might be less valid than a direct comparison of it with a nearby population in a comparable urban setting.

Such a comparison was carried out by Hare & Shaw (1965) between a peripheral housing estate in Croydon and an older, central area of the town. Their positive findings were a marked association between mental ill-health and physical ill-health, and a similar association between nervous disturbance and attitudes of general dissatisfaction with the neighbourhood. Although more people in the new estate made complaints about lack of amenities than in the old area, attitudes of general dissatisfaction with the environment were no commoner. In the central area, in fact, over half the sample complained of the physical discomforts associated with industrialisation and old housing. It was concluded that every population contains a vulnerable group, who are more prone to the development of illness, both mental and physical. This group will tend to complain of their surroundings — wherever they are — probably because such complaints are mostly a projection of their poor health; such a view is very similar to the one developed by Taylor & Chave in their survey of Harlow.

Subsequently, Hare (1966) suggested that mental health might be expected to improve from moving to a new development, since the houses there would be better designed and easier to run, and the greater space and privacy should reduce fatigue, irritability, and resentments within the family (see discussion of household crowding, Chapter 2). On the other hand, housewives who have grown up amongst a tradition of neighbourliness, with ready help and advice available from relatives and others, may be bewildered to find these missing in the artificially derived population of a new town or peripheral estate. On the whole, Hare believed that the conditions of new town life have no long-term influence on the mental health of adults who move there, though the process of moving (i.e. rapid cultural change) might cause a temporary exacerbation of symptoms in those who were already neurotic. However, children in the new towns already seemed to be showing evidence of improved physical health, and this gave grounds to hope that when they grew up, their mental health also might be better than that of their parents.

Hare's conclusion was that the apparent precipitants of mental ill-health in new communities might be no more than fairly small additional influences, which could tip the scales over to illness, when other conditions were equally balanced. Since it is a vain hope to prevent neurosis by trying to exclude minor misfortunes from life, he suggested that the really weighty causal factors of neurosis must be looked for in the human constitution, and that the only feasible way of improving this in future adults would be by reducing environmental factors that may damage it in infancy. Support for this view was claimed in evidence of an association between complications of pregnancy and childbirth on the one hand and later ill-health or maladjustment on the other. Thus, children with a congenitally impaired nervous system might be vulnerable not only to common ailments, but also to the effects of a disturbed family life. The argument, however, seems somewhat complicated by the fact that 'constitution' and 'environment' are not clearly separable in respect of early life, yet unless they are rigorously defined, comparison with other statements becomes difficult. Hare's view of the role of the residential environment is somewhat similar to that of Kasl & Rosenfield (1980), who consider that it is best seen as a facilitator, permitting certain outcomes to take place, but not initiating or stimulating them. A recent survey of young mothers in Auckland, New Zealand (Werry & Carlielle 1983) showed little evidence of 'suburban neurosis' in the conventional sense of social isolation, chronic dysphoria, consumption of tranquillisers, and dissatisfaction with their current lot; their level of perceived ill-health was low. While the circumstances of life for this population were more favourable than those for many others, the findings suggest that many currently unfavourable views of family, motherhood, and medical practice should not be generalised too widely.

REDEVELOPMENT AND REHOUSING

As pointed out earlier in this book, recent times have been marked by massive world-wide processes of population growth, spread of industrialisation and urbanisation to previously under-developed regions, decline of central city areas, and migration of urban residents to dispersed suburbs. Cooper & Sartorius (1977) have put forward some intriguing hypotheses as to how industrialisation, with these accompanying processes, could lead to a greater prevalence of chronically handicapped schizophrenics in a community. Urbanisation clearly involves some form of migration, which in itself is likely to be associated with an increased risk of psychiatric disorder, though the underlying conditions for this are extremely complex (Chapter 12). It should not be assumed, though, that the full effects of urbanisation are necessarily seen in the short term, and an incubation process could extend over several generations, during which the environment continues to change, so that there could be a persisting cultural lag (Swedish Government 1971).

Another form of migration, though over relatively short distances, is the enforced rehousing or 'relocation' resulting from clearance and redevelopment of old urban areas. This has occurred on an enormous scale in Britain since World War Two, displacing three million people in the period 1955–1975, but it is most regrettable that there has hardly been a single research study of possible adverse psychological and emotional effects of it on individuals. That such adverse effects might occur is quite likely, considering that many of the cleared areas were long-established communities, with a characteristic culture of their own and important networks of kinship and mutual help, which can never be reproduced artificially.

The demolition of a neighbourhood, in fact, is not just the destruction of buildings, but also that of a functioning social system: 'slum areas not only provide cheap housing but also offer the kinds of social support that poor people need to keep going in a crisis-ridden existence' (Gans 1967). Furthermore, 'most of the social problems found in slums cannot be traced to the area itself' — a point which might now seem obvious, but which has often been forgotten in over-enthusiastic planning and redevelopment. Kasl (1977) concluded that 'rehousing represents to many individuals a major life change which, as the recent developments in psychosomatic medicine suggest, can be stressful and can have definite health consequences', while Willmott (1974) has emphasised that the whole process of redevelopment can take as long as 10 years, during which time people are worried about their future, watch the decay of the neighbourhood around them, and may finally be compulsorily moved to a home they do not want. He added (1982) that 'Redevelopment inside the cities has been a disaster, destroying established communities and creating a kind of housing that is almost universally detested'. In this process, the boundaries and spatial arrangements which different ethnic or social groups have established over time are wiped out, and with them often their *modus vivendi* with society in general. At the same time, the decline of both religious and civic rituals, which, as Durkheim said 'affirm the moral superiority of the community over its individual members', may mean that there is eventually no 'community' with any values to affirm (Howes 1983).

One of the few systematic accounts of the social effects of moving people from one spatial milieu to another is Young & Willmott's (1957) study of the Bethnal Green area of east London, from which large numbers were then being rehoused in the new peripheral estate of 'Greenleigh'. Like most others, this development was designed on the assumption that undesirable features of the old community could be planned away, and that life would be better in an environment consisting only of adequate housing, together with a few essential shops. But as Hansen & Hillier (1984) point out, virtually none of the anticipated benefits of achieving this 'spatial correspondence to social grouping' have actually been shown to occur — 'the spatial hierarchy completely failed in its purpose of supporting social integration'. They relate this to the fact that 'it was only possible to go *to* Greenleigh, not *through* it . . . it is a physically discrete spatially identifiable enclave, not well-embedded in a more global system of space. The layout . . . seemed to have engendered suspicion, rather than sociability, and the pattern of hostility was repeated at the level of integration of the estate into the wider community'. So far as social networks were concerned, 'Kin ceased to play the vital role . . . of making relationships carry across space, while the local neighbour network, so characteristic of the old way of life, seemed to have disappeared entirely'.

This view contrasts, however, with the more medical one of Hare & Shaw (see above), which emphasised the benefits of good physical accommodation. In the case of nearly every peripheral estate, provision of essential services lagged far behind the building of houses or flats, so that there was sometimes not even a post box; this resulted in severe stress for residents in the earlier years of the development, much of which would have been avoidable. Hird (1965) refers to a high rate of suicide in one estate outside Birmingham, which, in the fifth year, was nine times the national average; there was also a disproportionately high rate of night calls in the early years, often reflecting the panic of isolation more than medical emergencies.

The first specific study of the consequences of relocation for mental and physical health was that of Wilner et al. (1962) in Baltimore. Out of 600 families who were very poorly accommodated, half were to be rehoused on a new estate; the health of both groups was then observed for a follow-up period of 2 years. At the end of this time, the children who had moved showed less physical ill-health than those who had not, and as a result, their school attendance was more regular and their results rather better. Some benefit (though less) was seen in the case of young adults who had moved, but no difference in the physical health of those aged over 35. Adults in the new housing area were more ready to invite friends into their house, to form friendships with neighbours, and to help them in practical ways; they were also more interested in caring for their houses and gardens, and were more optimistic in their outlook on life. On the other hand, there was no difference between the two groups in the amount of friction and quarrelling among family members or in the amount of irritability, nervousness, and depression in individuals, so that in terms of mental health, the effects of rehousing over this period of time were relatively unimpressive. Since the study dealt with a group of people living in an unusually poor environment, its results may not be generally applicable, and it is possible that non-housing variables such as poverty may have prevented the relocated residents from gaining as much benefit from the move as they might otherwise have done. Marris (1974) suggests that 'We should not burden ourselves with so many simultaneous changes that our emotional resilience becomes exhausted'.

Commenting on this Baltimore study, Kasl & Rosenfeld (1980) point out that it has been criticised for using too limited a notion of housing, and for not broadening the investigation to include better dimensions of the social environment. But if the operational definition of the residential environment combines physical and psycho-social components, it may no longer be possible to tell how the two interact with each other, or whether the observed impact of change may not be due solely to the social dimensions. The problem of negative evidence about effects of the physical-residential environment on mental health and behaviour is then merely sidestepped. Finally, there is the problem that it may be much more difficult to implement interventions in the psychosocial environment than in the physical one.

Probably the first psychiatric report relating to this problem was by Thorpe (1939) from Sheffield, where slum clearance was beginning to displace long-settled city residents into new peripheral housing areas. He observed a number of cases of severe depression in which the onset seemed clearly related to a compulsory move, and attributed this to 'a profound emotional shock when elderly people are compelled to leave a residence in which they may have lived for twenty years or more (to be) rehoused in a new estate of lonely roads', which they find strange and empty. The main aetiological factors, affecting particularly women and older people, were considered to be: firstly, dispossesion from a home to which a strong emotional attachment had often developed; and secondly, inability of older people to adapt to new surroundings, where the neighbours were strange and the cost of living higher.

However, the most important study of the psychiatric sequelae of relocation is that of Fried (1963) on people who had been moved from the West

End of Boston, a long-established, mainly Italian working-class community. It was found that among 250 women, 26 per cent reported that they still felt sad and depressed 2 years after moving, and another 20 per cent reported having had these feelings, related to the move, for at least 6 months. Among 316 men, the percentage showing long-term grief reactions was only slightly smaller. These affective reactions had most of the characteristics of grief and mourning for a lost person, but in addition, many other men and women indicated less severe depressive responses in their answers to questions. The two most important components of the grief reaction were found to be fragmentation of the sense of spatial identity, and dependence of group identity on stable social networks. These components, with their associated affective qualities, were critical foci for the sense of continuity which, in such a working class community, appears to be dependent on the external stability and familiarity of places and people.

Fried goes on to point out that any severe loss disrupts a person's sense of continuity, which is a framework for functioning in a universe with temporal, social, and spatial dimensions. In old-established working class communities of Europe and North America, the local area around the dwelling unit is seen as an integral part of home, and contains interlocking sets of social networks — in marked contrast to the 'transpatial' orientation of the middle class person. Greenbie (1974) suggests that 'For sophisticated urban men, conceptual territories may be provided by professions, hobbies, and religious or political organisations, which can substitute for physical territory. The poor and cultural minorities will be most likely to need secure physical-cultural boundaries'.

The Boston study showed that following enforced removal from the area, marked grief was the more likely, the more a person had been committed to that community, in terms of liking it, feeling that it had been his real home, and having an extensive familiarity with it. An integrated sense of spatial identity seems to be fundamental to human functioning and, in the working class at least, to be tied to a specific place — 'largely because of the importance of external stability, dislocation from a familiar residential area has so great an effect on fragmenting the sense of spatial identity' (Fried 1963).

A related study (Fried & Gleicher 1961) showed that slum areas have many sources of satisfaction for their residents, but these are mostly invisible to outside people, who do not share the culture and value-system, and Marris (1974) concludes that 'It is in situations where slum clearance is confused with broader ambitions of social reform that it characteristically provokes reactions akin to bereavement, for it is then that it threatens the sense of identity'. But this would presumably not apply to areas which are undergoing rapid social change of an adverse kind, or where there has been a breakdown of law and order. There have also been some methodological criticisms of Fried's main study (Key 1967) on the grounds that his sample of Italian-Americans were given to emotionality in verbal expression, that he used non-neutral language in his questions, and that comparative techniques were missing.

Rather different conclusions about intra-urban migration were reached by Hall (1966) from a study of 122 patients in Sheffield who had attributed their symptoms to a change of home. These included a sub-group of 54 young women, who mostly had depressive or hysterical symptoms, and uniformly poor marital relationships, often with severely neurotic reactions to the birth and care of children; whilst their clinical features seemed to have no relationship to the kind of new housing, complaints about it were numerous, usually vague, and almost invariably a projection of other problems. A second sub-group of 16 male patients complained mainly of obsessional symptoms, and mostly reported a married life characterised by sexual inadequacy, hostility, and lack of stability. A third group of 23 older women presented depressive symptoms, and in 18, complaints about their new housing ceased when the depression had been treated. Finally, there were small numbers suffering from schizophrenia and other specific disorders, but the actual conditions of the new housing did not seem to be aetiologically significant for any of them.

Hall suggests that a new housing environment forms a more suitable matrix than a well structured one for the projection of personal difficulties by neurotic patients. Complaints about housing usually disappeared in the course of psychotherapy, however, and there was no case of illness being clearly precipitated by moving house, in anyone of previously well adjusted personality. Though social planning of new public housing schemes ought to be concerned with relieving the unhappiness and isolation felt by certain incoming tenants, the psychiatric contribution might be in identifying such vulnerable individuals, and providing support and counselling at an early stage of their migration — preferably before the move. Yet any intervention of this kind would be extremely difficult in practical terms, unless the people concerned were already under medical care; these difficulties would probably be rather less, though, in cases where there is attachment of mental health professionals, such as clinical psychologists, social workers, and psychiatric nurses, to the general practice concerned.

Similar results were obtained by Johnson (1970), who analysed applications for rehousing on psychiatric grounds to the local authority in Salford, and followed-up the individuals concerned. In respect of their necessity for psychiatric treatment, no difference was found between the group who were actually rehoused and those who were not, and the same was found for change in severity of symptoms. Irrespective of whether rehousing had occurred or not, the clinical changes that were measured could have been predicted from the usual prognostic indications, and psychiatric treatment seemed to be more important in obtaining symptomatic improvement than this form of social manipulation. It is difficult to reconcile these findings with those of Fried, for instance, but they do suggest that whatever contribution environmental factors may make to psychiatric disorder, clinical diagnosis and treatment along established lines remain worthwhile, and should certainly not be regarded as irrelevant in any patient.

Hooper & Ineichen (1979) conclude that research on the effect on mental health of moving one's home has so far failed to produce a clear picture; the reasons may be, as Kasl & Rosenfield (1980) suggested, that nearly all studies have been opportunistic, resulting in 'sporadic and spotty accumulation of scientific knowledge', and that the effect of a particular physical residential parameter probably varies with different sub-groups of residents. Their own study of the impact of the residential environment on the mental health of the elderly concluded that this did not seem to be overwhelming; it was greatest in respect of housing satisfaction (not surprisingly), less on social and leisure activities, and least on the more traditional indicators of mental health. Since many housing interventions are also, in fact, social interventions, the strongest negative impact of the residential environment seemed to be associated with certain life experiences, which have a residential change embedded in them. Social and physical environmental variables were seen to interact most prominently in the joint influence of physical proximity and social homogeneity on social interaction. Generally, residential moves for the elderly are likely to be stressful, even if the new home is of a better standard, unless the move is away from an urban area with great social stress. Hooper and Ineichin's own research confirmed the picture suggested by earlier studies that after an initial phase of difficulty, most families adapt to a new residential environment, though there are circumstances in which adverse practical problems become overwhelming (see Chapter 13).

Physical structure

A general characteristic of new communities is their relatively low density of population compared to older urban areas; this may be significant in the development of neurotic disorders because of the greater amounts of open space and unfamiliar visual patterns in new districts. Ethological evidence on this point has been summarised by Marks (1969) who states that 'agoraphobic behaviour in hamsters is mainly a response to illumination above the level optimal for the animal, rather than a response to the openness of the situation'. Normally, excessively bright light causes avoidance responses, which are dissipated by searching behaviour; but if the latter is blocked, the animal shows evidence of increased stress. Similarly, human agoraphobics tend to feel easier in the dark and, if crossing an open space, feel less anxious if they can skirt the edge. Marks suggests that innate mechanisms probably do not produce phobias of themselves, but rather select as targets certain situations, which may then be affected by other conditions, e.g. space and light perception, through optokinetic reflexes. This is also seen in the fact that many people feel uncomfortable in high flats with exterior walls of glass, whilst Hayden (1978) reports that agoraphobics are likely to find pedestrian bridges over main roads terrifying, particularly when a corner has to be turned, high in the sky. The same situation occurs when a lift in a high block of flats opens on to a dimly lit balcony; stepping out of this may give the phobic person the feeling that he is walking straight into space.

Whilst there is no firm evidence yet for direct connections between particular forms of urban development and the emergence of neurotic illnesses, it does seem likely that there are advantages in more traditional forms, such as arcaded streets or enclosed markets; Gradidge (1981) refers to the pleasure obtained from 'the sense of enclosure given by a small room . . . warmed with a great wood fire, womb-like and protective while outside the storms howl or the fog drips'. In fact, people will often find ways of re-creating a sense of cosiness in circumstances where this would seem almost impossible, such as open-plan offices; in this way, there is a kind of constant guerilla warfare against the designs of architects and planners, perhaps indicating that stable behaviour and social institutions must rest on an innate biological basis. Leyhausen (1965) suggests that 'the human species is adapted to social life in a small group . . . having need for larger social gatherings from time to time . . . feeling a need to be by himself quite often, and reacting to continued over-socialisation with all sorts of frustrations, repressions, aggressions, and fears'.

Such a view perhaps ignores cultural differences, but those who plan and build should surely have a greater sense of humility, which would prevent them, for instance, from simply abolishing such a fundamental aspect of human society as the street, particularly when this change is imposed on people who have no choice as to where they live. Hillier & Hudson (1984) point out that the arrangement of built space determines to a large extent the degree to which people are made aware of the presence of others, both neighbours and strangers; thus, if people are likely to be in a place because of its relationship to other places, then it will probably remain busy (and so probably safe) for no apparent reason. But new environments, which have generally broken away from established patterns of movement, tend to consist mostly of dead space — 'urban wastelands, through which people dash between their homes and places of work or leisure'. Disappearance of the street was primarily associated in Britain with the spread of high-rise blocks of flats; Gardiner (1982) considered that:

> The street is the most important single element in neighbourhood design . . . its loss produced a desert; (it) performs so many useful duties you scarcely notice it, and only appreciate its importance when it's not there . . . It establishes continuity, connects different parts of a neighbourhood and provides a link in a network of varying heights, materials, activities and landmarks. Streets which bring people together in terraces, or on the sides of a square looking across a garden, probably make the ideal community form.

However, this question of urban form now requires consideration of the high-rise issue as a whole.

HIGH RISE

How it happened

The tide of high-rise blocks of flats, which began to sweep over Britain in the late 1950s, and which house over a million people, has to be seen against the historical background of housing in the country; town walls had largely lost their importance by the sixteenth century, so that a growing population did not have to be squeezed into very small areas after that, as was still the case in most of Europe. Also, since the cost of building land in the nineteenth century was very much lower than that in Germany, for instance, instead of urban housing in England and Wales consisting of dense blocks of tenements and apartments, with detached houses elsewhere, the terraced home became almost universal, housing almost 90 per cent of the population at the beginning of this century (Muthesius 1982). For all its drawbacks, it had the virtue of compactness; in 1914, the half-million people of Leeds were mostly housed within 2.5 kilometers of the city centre, and nearly four out of five lived in terraced houses. The tenement was fairly common in Scotland, though, up to a height of four storeys, and not unknown in English cities; but it always seems to have been considered something of an aberration, so that when high-rise blocks began to appear, they were generally regarded as quite foreign to the accepted tradition of urban housing in Britain — as indeed they still are.

Between the two World Wars, local authorities started to build homes for the working class, the great majority being single-family houses, and usually semi-detached. When this process began, in 1919, 90 per cent of British homes were privately rented, yet this figure was to fall to 14 per cent in 1971, and even further since then. The remaining Council homes in this period were walk-up flats, usually not exceeding four floors and following in the tradition of the Victorian philanthropic tenements, such as those of the Peabody Trust; in this period, the benefits of craftsmanship, good quality materials, and traditional methods produced 'the last generation of multi-storey housing to weather well' (Esher 1981). Very large numbers of urban houses were destroyed or damaged during World War 2, and many more fell into disrepair as a result of wartime neglect, rent control, or simply the ageing of poor quality building. Great demand for new housing then resulted not only from these factors, but also from the large number of new households that were being formed in the post-war period, and from higher expectation about standards of accommodation; working class couples no longer accepted, as their parents had done, that they should bring up a family in four rooms, with no bathroom, inside WC, or running hot water, and no garden. Nor did young adults of any social class continue to expect to remain in the parental home until marriage.

This great demand for new homes coexisted with a climate of opinion in local authorities and the professions which was governed by the architectural and planning clichés referred to above, particularly regarding a 'shortage of land' in urban areas. It came to be felt that traditional building methods, based on brick or stone, were too slow, too expensive, and in any case out of date; furthermore, there was little satisfaction for the new generation of architects and engineers in further variations on the endlessly repeated semi. In the immediate post-war period, single-storey prefabricated houses helped to meet some of the most urgent need for homes, and although small, they did contain the most essential modern conveniences. Their success, in the short term at least, turned attention to the possibility of a 'quick techno-logical fix', which would be in tune with the general ethos of the period and solve a problem that otherwise seemed likely to go on indefinitely. Yet at the same time, successive social surveys had shown that between 80 per cent and 98 per cent of the working population preferred a house to a flat, it the rents were the same (Self 1957).

Waiting in the wings was the architectural Modern Movement, repre-sented particularly by Le Corbusier and by Walter Gropius and the Bauhaus; their ideas had reached Britain in the 1930s, but had only resulted in the appearance of a relatively small number of structures, mostly in or near London. When building resumed after World War 2, the neo-Georgian and Arts and Crafts traditions which had strongly influenced local authority designs up to then were largely discredited. Instead, Le Corbusier taught that there could be vertical garden cities in the sky, surrounded by plentiful open space, and containing pleasant and efficient living accommodation, which would be the setting for a better life for all. These would not only put an end to the squalid housing of the last century, but also to the urban sprawl of the inter-war period, while the visual effect of towers rising from the ground was considered altogether more aesthetically exciting than that of a cottage estate, and could be a source of pride to both local authority officers and their political masters. The combination seemed irresistible, and to add to it, large building contractors promised the enormous benefits of new prefabricated systems, which would both discard the structural limi-tations of traditional methods and speed up the delivery of homes ready to be occupied. Because everything was so new, such claims could be made 'in the absence of experience or of any firm theoretical basis for prediction' (Cooney 1974). In the prevailing euphoria, Glasgow's city fathers promised that the notorious Gorbals slums would be replaced by something more akin to the Hanging Gardens of Babylon. The situation was clinched when the Ministry of Housing became convinced that high-rise building was the only practical answer to large-scale housing needs, and arranged its policy on subsidies accordingly; the higher a housing authority built, therefore, the more money it received relatively.

Not everyone was convinced, though; most local authority housing managers knew well enough that flats were unpopular as homes for families, but they were ignored as being men of little faith. Before long, it became clear that very large sites were needed for the new construction methods, and this usually required clearing them of existing buildings, most of which were not unfit for futher use, by any reasonable standards. So 'Twilight Areas' was the slogan devised to provide an excuse for demolishing huge tracts of existing housing and of industrial or commercial premises; when the occupants of these naturally protested at what was being done, they were told that they were being 'selfish' or 'behind the times'. Before long, the whole process had become a juggernaut that seemed to have gone totally out of control and that was wiping out a large proportion of the urban structure of Britain. A corresponding process was going on in relation to shops and offices, whereby the familiar high streets and small office blocks were being demolished to make way for large new structures, often occupying much of the central area of a town. With few exceptions, these new developments were tasteless, shoddy, and totally without character; their effect on many of Britain's historic towns was devastating and, in the case of one cathedral city, rightly described as 'the sack of Worcester'. As one urban area after another disappeared under a forest of tower blocks, 'many architects stood appalled . . . in the position of the sorcerer's apprentice' (Cooney 1974). However, by then it was too late.

At no point in the story had there been any attempt to examine the needs or wishes of those who were to occupy this new Babylon; the whole political process, in so far as it purported to represent the views of the public, had in fact failed to operate, both at national and local levels (Dunleavy 1981). Neither did the medical profession cover itself in glory, since Medical Officers of Health almost invariably declared as 'unfit' any houses that their authority wanted to demolish, even when this was clearly a travesty of the facts. It was not long, however, before both GPs and psychiatrists became aware of the ill-effects of what was going on, as a result of the dispersal of well integrated communities and through the unsuitability of the new flats for families with young children. It did not help that wider social and cultural changes were happening at the same time, leading to a situation that could be described in many areas as 'social disintegration' (see Chapter 2). The consequences in one city were described by Gardiner (1981) as 'a panoramic picture of towers and slabs looming above an eerie wasteland of unkempt grass. Their designs' total loss of contact with people shows in acres of grey concrete and black tarmac and in the seemingly arbitrary location of identical blocks . . . (with) horrific vandalism, graffiti, violent crime, abandoned buildings'.

On the personal level, many people felt remote in high flats, cut off from the general life of the community, having no real neighbourly contact, yet at the same time lacking privacy because of the failure to provide sound insulation (Lowenstein 1982); radio and television were then a poor substitute for real-life interactions. Such disadvantaged groups as the elderly and physically handicapped found the situation hazardous and stressful because of their dependence on lifts, rubbish chutes, or other services which did not always work, because of their isolation (compared with conventional housing), and because they were often harrassed or even terrorised by gangs of adolescents who tended to hang around the communal areas and surroundings (Cook & Morgan 1982).

Many social disabilities result from the fact that a multi-storey flat is excessively self-contained. Jephcott (1977) points out that it has none of the neutral areas, such as doorsteps, backyards, or gardens 'which help people to build up their dossiers on each other without necessarily exchanging a word. And it is blind in that its windows afford no two-way link with the outside world. This turns the block and estate into eventless places, short of those goings-on of life that tempt people out of their homes, give them shared interests and help them strike up acquaintance should they so wish'. She adds that 'Any community needs some spots that lend themselves to a bit of gossiping', but the usually inhuman atmosphere of entrance lobbies and landings removes them from this category, and such new outside assets as lawns and relative freedom from traffic are not made use of unless there is positive encouragement to do so.

Medical and psychiatric research

One of the first medical attempts to examine the question scientifically was that of Fanning (1967), who compared the health of service families living in low-rise flats in Germany with similar families living in houses. Measured by consultation rates, both with family doctors and with specialists, flat-dwellers showed 57 per cent more morbidity than people in houses. The higher rates were most marked in the case of allergic, neurological, respiratory, dermatological, genito-urinary, and neurotic conditions, the latter especially for young married women. The largest group of cases was that of respiratory illness in the flat-dwellers, which might have been due to lack of open-air exercise, or (perhaps more likely) to emotional stress. From the subjective standpoint, boredom, isolation, and difficulty in coping with young children were certainly reported to a significant extent by those living in flats, and it is quite likely that the threshold for medical consultation was lower in this group because their life was less satisfactory. However, living in flats was only one of the stresses affecting these subjects, representing an addition to those which arose from disruption of the extended family through service overseas. Ineichen (1979) criticised this study on the grounds that wives of servicemen in flats were generally younger than those in houses, had more recently moved to Germany, and had husbands of lower rank, so that what appeared to be an effect of dwelling type might be reduced largely to a difference in population.

Comparisons of similar groups, but also including residents of one tower block, were made by Moore (1974, 1975, 1976), who found that the indoor, but not the outdoor social life of the flat-dwellers was inferior, but that psychiatric illness was no more prevalent among them, even when evidence of Cornell Medical Index scores was added to that of consultation rates. For those of neurotic personality, flat dwelling was sufficient stress to cause some increase in clinical psychiatric illness, but this did not produce an overall level which was significantly greater than that of all house-dwellers. As in Fanning's investigation, though, the flats were mostly low-rise, and the subjects did not cover an age range comparable to that of the general population. However, Reynolds & Nicholson (1969) investigated the prevalence of neurotic symptoms in women living on six council estates in London and Sheffield, most of whom were in high-rise dwellings; although these symptoms were very frequent, their distribution showed no relationship to building form, height above the ground, or estate density.

A similar study in Bristol by Ineichen & Hooper (1974), found that women living in houses in a redeveloped central area reported more neurotic symptoms than those in high-rise flats, or in maisonettes (which had the lowest rate). The wives in houses generally had poor health — both mental and physical — as well as relatively the largest number of children, often including a problem child; their dissatisfaction with the environment centred around derelict buildings, inflow of immigrants, noisy neighbours and children (often resulting in conflict between the parents), high rents, and the powerlessness of tenants to get anything done. So far as the families in flats were concerned, the number of children considered by their mothers to present behaviour problems was almost double that in any of the other groups; loneliness and isolation were significant complaints amongst these women. Families in any kind of accomodation in the central area who had no car (50 per cent) found difficulty in maintaining contact with their relatives, when these had been rehoused in outer suburbs, while environmental 'problems', as these central area families perceived them, were many-layered, the 'solution' of one often merely revealing the next beneath it.

Bagley (1973) compared a random sample of women living in a 12-storey block of flats with a control group living in houses on a pre-war council estate; as measured by the Eysenck Personality Inventory, the house dwellers were significantly less neurotic, and they consulted their general practitioners significantly less often for 'nervous illness'. The control women also complained significantly less about housing and environmental matters, including adequacy of play space.

Freedman (1975) concluded from his studies of crowding that if a social situation is initially unfavourable, living in a high rise building with hundreds of other families is likely to exaggerate feelings of fear, suspicion, and isolation. Similarly, Jephcott (1971) suggested that high-rise living is particularly hard on those who are below average in social assets, since the support which they might expect from neighbours and friends in a traditional street is much less likely to exist, in view of the large numbers of people involved, and the isolation of individual flats. It is probably unreasonable to expect them to show the methodical habits, self-restraint, and social competence required to make satisfactory use of multi-storey housing, whereas those who are better off can afford such compensations as the use of a car, seaside holidays, or outdoor sports.

It has been suggested that young children in high flats tend to lead a passive existence, cooped up with their mothers, who are often socially isolated themselves, and tend to develop compulsive fears (by no means unreasonable) about the children falling out of windows or off balconies (Stewart, 1970); in fact, Coroner's records for 1973–1977 show that children living above the first floor were 57 times more likely to be killed by falling from their homes than other children, in England and Wales. Such restrictions of stimuli and personal interactions, together with those imposed outside by traffic dangers and urban sprawl, could well hinder children's social and perceptual development, which may now largely occur at second hand, through television. For school-age children, the high-rise estate is lacking in environmental interest, is deprived of the supervisory care of adults, and is more vulnerable to damage, compared with the traditional street; because of this, play and sport facilities are particularly important, yet exist hardly anywhere in the way that is needed. Stewart also found that mothers in high flats with young children were particularly likely to show symptoms of psychiatric disorders, though this was not true of mothers with teenage children.

Three matched groups of families, each with two very young children, living respectively in high-rise flats, low-rise flats, and houses, all rented from the council in the same London borough, were compared by Richman (1974). She found that the children might spend most of the day isolated in a flat with their mother, so that the resulting boredom and irritation could well lead to tension and strained relationships; this was particularly the case when children were at the toddling stage or able to run about, but could not safely be left on their own. Since contact with neighbours might only be by chance, when entering or leaving, flat life seemed to exacerbate the inherent difficulties of women who were poor mixers, and to increase the problems of isolation and restriction to the home experienced by many mothers of young children. Depression of moderate to severe extent was found in 41 per cent of the mothers, and was more marked among those living in flats; surprisingly, though, the highest prevalence was amongst the women in low-rise flats, which did not necessarily allow the mother more mobility or the children more freedom than high-rise accomodation (whose residents produced the most complaints). Psychiatric problems in the mothers tended to be associated with behaviour problems in the children. Richman concluded that depression, loneliness, and dissatisfaction with accomodation affect a high proportion of mothers with young children who live in flats; she also suggested that some of the differences between families in different kinds of accomodation might have been obscured by the number of those who had moved out of high-rise flats in the previous year. This view was confirmed by Ineichin and Hooper (1974), who re-interviewed their sample after 18 months, finding that 40 per cent of the total, but 60 per cent of the flat-dwellers, had moved by then, thus causing an ironing-out of the differences between the groups in prevalence of symptoms — at least temporarily.

A study in Edinburgh by Gilloran (1968) concluded that the outstanding problem of family life in high flats was isolation: 'to have forgotten a couple of items in a shopping list may produce a major crisis'. Though 'A safe place in which to play . . . outside the dwelling has been part of small children's natural environment for many centuries', there is usually no possibility of this in tower blocks, while the usual separation from relatives and established friendship networks means that young mothers are never free of the responsibility of child-minding — 'Never previously anywhere have mothers been expected to undertake this task entirely alone.'

In Canada, Gillis (1977) carried out a statistically sophisticated study of parents with children, living in rented public flats; he found that women, but not men, showed more psychological stress, the higher up they lived. A possible explanation of this sex difference was that women might be constantly aware of their failure to occupy a detached house, which would be an important goal to those whose role was that of the traditional wife-mother — a role which might be difficult to fulfill in such a modern, man-made environment. Gillis has also suggested that those on the ground floor might feel vulnerable in respect to crime, though this would not necessarily be true in private housing schemes. In Glasgow, Hannay (1980) found a significant correlation between residence in high flats and an increased prevalence of psychiatric symptoms; in particular, those on the fifth floor and above had twice the prevalence compared to those on the lower floors or those living in houses. Controlling for the effects of age and sex did not affect this association (see Chapter 15).

Ineichen (1979) concludes that there is a fundamental difference in respect of high-rise living between single people, who generally like it — as do many childless couples — and families, who generally do not. It is often difficult, though, to disentangle the effects of a particular kind of home from the effects of moving (which, in itself, is unlikely to produce psychiatric disorder in a hitherto stable personality). However, the fact that so many high-rise tenants vote with their feet may have prevented some research from arriving at positive conclusions, because those showing evidence of adverse effects may not remain long enough to appear in a sample. Also, Jephcott (1971) points out that with working-class people, 'it is easy to drum up an opinion on the fitness of a new bathroom, but less so to weigh up and then put into words such a nebulous matter as the influence of life in a high flat on one's social contacts'. Almost all research material, in fact, is derived from residents of the public housing sector, and Ineichen believes that 'This is a group whose status in society is falling rapidly. Sixty years ago (they) were the favoured segment of the working classes, enjoying for the first time reasonable housing standards, and rescued from their weak market position vis-a-vis the private landlord . . . Today they are a vulnerable minority'. This tends to result in a feeling of powerlessness to control their immediate environment, and the fact that many high-rise developments are often drab, impersonal, or brutal worsens the feeling, as do bad design or maintenance.

An unique report, which might be very significant for high-rise, and indeed all forms of high-density housing, is that of Kazanetz (1979) on inceptions of schizophrenia in 41 apartment buildings within a sub-area of Moscow. Out of 2392 tenants who had regular and prolonged contacts with primary schizophrenia patients, 1.58 per cent developed schizophrenia within a 7-year period, whereas 2875 tenants in the same blocks who had no such contact with the patients showed an inception rate of only 0.10 per cent. This was thought to provide evidence for an infectious agent in the aetiology of schizophrenia, which would be consistent with the accepted clustering of the disease in families. Further studies along the same lines would be very valuable.

The basic problem of all such research, though, is that large effects from changes in housing variables could only be expected 'If the whole package of poverty, illness, and social problems could be unravelled into a single long causal chain with housing as one of the early links', but instead, 'residential variables (are) richly embedded in a large matrix of individual and social variables that condition and attentuate the impact of the residential environ ment' (Kasl et al, 1982). These authors point out that the 'meaning' of housing needs to be understood in the experiential, rather than just in the physical sense, and that 'poor housing is an obstacle to well-being and self-fulfillment, but remedying only poor housing is not enough'. They also consider it undesirable to take a particular residential parameter, such as persons per room, translate it into a specific psychological construct, and so commit us to a single intervening process between that and behavioural outcomes or human experiences. Because of the many ways in which different psycho-social variables can alter the effects of these processes in sub-groups of the population, Kasl et al consider that the main effort of research should be directed towards disentangling these various influences and outcomes.

Maintaining the structure

One of the fundamental points about tower block accomodation, in fact, is that it is a high-technology environment, involving large maintenance costs (mostly ignored in the original calculations), and only successful when there is money to ensure that all the mechanical aspects are working, and that the communal areas are clean and free from crime. But most housing authorities in Britain, like public housing bodies in many other countries, built large developments on a scale which went far beyond their capacity to maintain these satisfactorily. It was not long before essential services were breaking down, while the many faults that occurred with new and sometimes untried building systems might stay uncorrected for months or even years. Some, like dampness, have remained incurable, yet the complexity of the problem means that the tenant himself can do nothing about it; his personal freedom and opportunities for choice and self-expression are also restricted in such matters as keeping pets, making adaptations to the home, and having any outside space in which to potter about. Even the prototype of high-rise public housing — Le Corbusier's Unite' d' habitation at Marseilles — deteriorated over the years so that almost all the special features for which it was promoted fell into disuse. Vint & Bintliff (1983) point out that if there are risks associated with technical change and new building methods, then the costs of these should be accepted by housing authorities or by the building industry — not by the tenants, as has usually been the case.

Quite apart from the lack of resources for maintenance, the administrative structure of many Housing Departments, with their rigidly bureaucratic habits, virtually collapsed under the weight of complaints and of appeals for things to be put right. Yet as soon as any chill economic wind blew (which seemed to happen frequently, from the time these developments were finished) maintenance, cleaning, and repairs invariably bore the first brunt of any financial cuts. As the quality of these services fell, so vandalism, crime, and despoiling of the environment escalated, increasing further when respectable working class families with young children began to find more suitable accomodation elsewhere, and to be replaced by 'difficult' people on the waiting list. A vicious circle of environmental deterioration began, in which the chief sufferers were those already disadvantaged, whose plight was now compounded by being trapped in often dirty, dangerous, noisy, and incomprehensible living situations; old houses certainly had their problems, but this was something on a different scale. A survey of Housing Departments (Littlewood & Fisher 1981) found little evidence of attempts by them to alleviate the problem of high-rise tenants; three-quarters of mothers with children under five were unhappy living above ground level, but after rehousing, two-thirds reported their own emotional health to be better, and most said that their children were better behaved.

Finally, there is the question of how an environment looks. Though this has not generally been regarded as significant from the point of view of health, and though virtually impossible to study scientifically, it has certainly been dramatically affected by the advent of high-rise buildings. The previously familiar British townscapes of terraced housing or suburban semis, like comparable areas of many North American and European cities, were not on the whole aesthetically pleasing, yet still had some very positive aspects — for instance, the intimate scale of a traditional street, or flowering trees of a suburb in the spring.

But tower blocks and other megastructural forms of housing, as well as giant shopping centres, overwhelm the human environment in ways which seem almost wholly bad. Jephcott (1971) describes how tower blocks:

mostly rear up fortuitously and in unrelated chunks. Traditionally . . . the tall, eye-catching building . . . has been an expression of the community's concept of something pre-eminent, a church, town hall, or university. Apart from deliberately introduced landmarks of this nature, buildings have mostly flowed close to the contours of the ground. Moreover the lofty silhouette has normally had some affinity with natural forms (but) . . . The rearing rectangular outline of the multi-storey block is hard on the eye. And it is inescapable. (These towers) dwarf everything, important public buildings, trees, humans. They also shut off and shut in. A single block can become a giant stopper, keeping out what used to be a pleasant glimpse of the sky at the end of a dull street. Or a line of blocks may slash across a dramatic view of snow-capped hills. They also diminish the pleasantness of city parks and public gardens since their prodigious height dispels the illusion of rural things . . . They likewise steal the nearer sky, lessening the chance of small pleasures like a fine sunset or a new moon. And any house or garden lying alongside a multi-storey block suffers drastically from the overshadowing of this cold and concrete wing.

What is more, none of the claimed advantages of high-rise housing proved to be true in practice. It did not save land (if one excludes special cases such as Hong Kong, where separation between buildings is minimal); it was not necessarily quicker, especially when new building methods went wrong; it was certainly not cheaper — both construction and maintenance turned out to be enormously more expensive than for low-rise homes; and finally, the idea that it would bring a better quality of life was the opposite of most residents' experience. Perhaps most fundamental of all is a widespread feeling among people, not to be dismissed because it is difficult to define, that tower blocks are somehow an offence against the traditional or natural order of human habitation. When very large numbers are gathered into one settlement, there has to be a trade-off between the benefits of proximity and the costs of overcrowding; but the answer to this dilemma is not to be found in high-rise housing. Kennan (1974) asks 'How long will it take city planners to realize that what people want in an urban community is . . . variety and intimacy? The search for grandeur . . . attempts to remove man from the reassuring disorder of nature, in which he once had his habitat, and in which he was accustomed, over millions of years, to look for his security'.

REFERENCES

de Alarcon R, Rathod N H 1968 Prevalence and early detection of heroin abuse. British Medical Journal i: 549–551

Bagley C 1973 The built environment as an influence on personality and social behaviour: a spatial study. In: Canter D, Lee T R (eds) Psychology & the built environment. Architectural Press, Tonbridge

Carstairs G M, Brown G W 1958 Census of psychiatric cases in two contrasting communities. Journal of Mental Science 104: 72–80

Cook D A G, Morgan H G 1982 Families in high-rise flats. British Medical Journal 284: 846

Cooney E W 1974 High flats in local authority housing in England and Wales since 1945. In: Sutcliffe A (ed) Multi-storey living: the British working class experience. Croom Helm, London

Cooper J E, Sartorius N 1977 Cultural and temporal variations in schizophrenia: a speculation on the importance of industrialization. British Journal of Psychiatry 130: 50–55

Dunleavy P 1981 The politics of mass housing in Britain 1945–1975. Clarendon Press, Oxford

Dyos J 1982 In: Cannadine D, Reeber S (eds) Exploring the urban past. Cambridge University Press, Cambridge

Esher L (Lord) 1981 A broken wave. Allen Lane, London

Evans J W, Lovel J W I, Eaton K K 1969 Social workers and general practice. British Medical Journal i: 44–46

Fanning D M 1967 Families in flats. British Medical Journal iv: 382–386

Field M 1963 Grieving for a lost home. In: Duhl L J (ed) The urban condition. Basic Books, New York

Field M, Gleicher P 1961 Some sources of residential satisfaction in an urban slum. Journal of the American Institute of Planners 27: 305–315

Frankenberg R 1969 Communities in Britain. Routledge & Kegan Paul, London

Freedman J L 1975 Crowding and behavior. W H Freeman, san Francisco

Freeman H L 1972 Mental health and new communities in Britain. In: Nossiter T J, Hanson A H, Rokkan S (eds) Imagination and precision in the social sciences. Faber, London

Gans H J 1967 Planning and city planning for mental health. In: Eldredge H W (ed) Taming megalopolis, Vol 2. Doubleday, New York

Gardiner S 1981 Slabs in a wasteland. The Observer, August 2nd

Gillis A R 1977 High-rise housing and psychological strain. Journal of Health and Social Behavior 18: 418–431

Gilloran J L 1968 Social health problems associated with 'high living'. The Medical Officer 120: 117–118

Greenbie B B 1974 Social territory, community health and urban planning. Journal of the American Institute of Planners 40: 74–82

Gradidge R 1981 Dream houses. Constable, London

Hall P 1966 Some clinical aspects of moving house as an apparent precipitant of psychiatric symptoms. Journal of Psychosomatic Research 10: 59–70

Hannay D R 1981 Mental health and high flats. Journal of Chronic Diseases 34: 431–432

Hare E H 1966 Mental health in new towns: What next? Journal of Psychosomatic Research 10: 53–58

Hare E H, Shaw G K 1965 Mental health on a new housing estate. Oxford University Press, London

Hayden E W 1978 Agoraphobia and the role of the architect. Building Design, March 31, 1

Hillier W, Hudson J 1984 Creating life: the relation between people and space in urban localities. Architecture & Behaviour (In press)

Hird J F B 1965 Planning for a new community. Journal of the Royal College of General Practitioners: 33–41

Hooper D, Ineichen 1979 Adjustment to moving: a follow-up study of the mental health of young families in new housing. Social Science & Medicine 13D: 163–168

Howes G A K Policing and social policy in multi-ethnic areas in Europe — the social context. Paper to Sixth Cranfield conference, Cambridge

Ineichen B 1979 High rise living and mental stress. Biology & Human Affairs 44: 81–85

Ineichen B, Hooper D 1974 Wives' mental health and children's behaviour problems in contrasting residential areas. Social Science & Medicine 8: 369–374

Jephcott P 1971 Homes in high flats. Oliver & Boyd, Edinburgh

Johnson D A W 1970 Rehousing and psychiatric illness. The Medical Officer 124: 225–228

Kasl S V 1977 In: Hinkle L E, Loring W C (eds) The effect of the man-made environment on health and behavior. Center for Disease Control, Atlanta

Kasl S V, Rosenfield S 1980 The residential environment and its impact on the mental health of the aged. In: Birren J E, Sloane R B (eds) Handbook of mental health & aging. Prentice Hall, Englewood Cliffs

Kasl S V, White M, Will J, Marcuse P 1982 In: Baum A, Singer J E (eds) Advances in environmental psychology, Vol 4 (environment and health). Lawrence Erlbaum, Boston

Kazanetz E F 1979 Ways to define the role of environmental factors in the initiation of schizophrenia (preliminary report). Rivista di Psicologia Analitico 10: 193–202

Kennan G F 1974 The New Yorker, April 29th

Key W H 1967 When people are forced to move. Menninger Foundation, Topeka

Klein D C, Adelson D (eds) 1978 Psychology of the planned community: the new town experience. Human Sciences Press, New York

Lee T R 1976 Psychology and the environment. Methuen, London

Leyhausen P 1965 The sane community — a density problem. Discovery 26: 27–33

Littlewood, Tinker 1981 Families in Flats. HMSO, London

Lowenstein L F 1982 Psychological effects of high-rise living. British Journal of Clinical & Social Psychiatry 1: 39–41

Marks I M 1969 Fears and phobias. Heinemann, London

Martin F M, Brotherston J H F, Chave S P W 1957 The incidence of neurosis in a new housing estate. British Journal of Preventive & Social Medicine 11: 196–202

Moore N C 1974 Psychiatric illness and living in flats. British Journal of Psychiatry 125: 500–507

Moore N C 1975 Social aspects of flat dwellings. Public Health 89: 109–115

Moore N C 1976 The personality and mental health of flat dwellers. British Journal of Psychiatry 128: 259–261

Marriss B 1974 Challenging rubbish. New Society, August 29th

Muthesius S 1982 The English terraced house. Yale University Press, London

Newman O 1980 Community of interest. Anchor Doubleday, New York

Nicholson J H 1961 New communities in Britain. National Council of Social Service, London

Oliver P, Davis I, Bestley I 1981 Dunromin. Barrie & Jenkins, London

Reynolds I, Nicholson C 1969 Living off the grounds. Architects Journal 34: 150–154

Richman N 1974 Effects of housing on preschool children and their mothers. Developmental Medicine & Child Neurology 10: 1–9

Sainsbury P, Collins J 1966 Some factors relating to mental illness in a new town. Journal of Psychosomatic Research 10: 45–51

Self P 1957 Cities in flood. Faber, London

Silver N 1968 Against new towns. New Statesman, August 2nd: 149

Stewart W F R 1970 Children in flats — a family study. NSPCC, London

Swedish Government 1971 Urban conglomerates as psycho-social human stressors. A report to the UN Conference on the Human Environment, Stockholm

Taylor S 1938 Suburban neurosis. Lancet i: 759–761

Taylor S (Lord), Chave S P W 1964 Mental health and environment. Longmans, London

Thomas R 1969 Aycliffe to Cumbernauld. PEP, London

Thorpe F T 1939 Demolition melancholia. British Medical Journal ii: 127–128

Vint J, Bintliff J 1983 Tower blocks: the economics of high rise housing. Social Policy & Administration 17: 118–129

Ward C 1981 Pitfalls of punditry New Society, August 27: 357–358

Werry J S, Carlielle J 1983 The nuclear family, suburban neurosis, and iatrogenesis in Auckland mothers of young children. J American Academy of Child Psychiatry 22: 172–179

Willmott P 1974 Population and community in London. New Society 30: 206–209

Willmott P 1982 Support for Suburbia. Times Higher Education Supplement, March 12: 13

Wilner D M, Walkley R P, Pinkerton T C, Tayback M 1962 The housing environment and family life. Johns Hopkins Press, Baltimore

Young M, Willmott P 1957 Family and kinship in east London. Routledge & Kegan Paul, London

Rural–urban differences in mental health

The conventional wisdom of both the scientific community and the lay public is that psychiatric disorders occur at a much higher rate in cities than in small towns or rural areas. Noise, congestion, impersonality, and the general speed of urban life are thought to contribute to the anxiety and stress which supposedly characterise urban living. On the other hand, small town life is often idealised in terms of neighbourliness, tranquillity, and a style of living more in tune with the 'natural' needs of man. Social and medical scientists also have provided many findings in support of the 'city as hell' hypothesis, and while there have been occasional discrepant reports, these have been largely ignored and quickly forgotten. In fact, the history of social, political, religious, and even scientific thought is replete with references to the city as an environment inimical to the physical and mental health of its inhabitants (White & White 1962; Ericksen 1954). It has appeared that in cities:

> our reckless disregard of standards of efficiency, resource conservation, health, and esthetics reaches its fullest expression. Cities, we are told, are cancerous growths. They occupy space where wildlife once lived, they overlay arable land with ugly structures that soon will be reduced to blight, they pollute the atmosphere, the soils and the streams, they foster mean, antisocial and materialistic behaviours, and they harbour the poor, the lawless and the underprivileged. The indictment is sweeping. It is strange, indeed, that so many people live in cities (Hawley 1972).

These anti-urban sentiments can be traced back to some of the earliest literature. The Book of Genesis gives us Sodom, Gomorrah, and the whore city of Babylon, while the agrarian Thomas Jefferson was constrained to write that, 'I view great cities as pestilential to the morals, the health and the liberties of man'; similar views were expressed by Emerson, Thoreau, and others. It is unlikely, of course, that these have been purely a product of the imagination. Cities of earlier times were generally offensive and unhealthy places, and Shelley may have been close to the truth at the time when he wrote, 'Hell is a city like London'. But the undesirable qualities of urban life were not the sole source of anti-urban attitudes. Equally important is the fact that society was agriculturally dominated, and that the majority of the population lived in rural areas. Thus, rural life was seen as 'natural' and cities as 'unnatural' environments, in which people were not 'meant' to live. Tuan (1979) also suggests that 'Every major human achievement appears to be attended by a feeling of unease, as though success might inflame the envy of the gods who alone have the right to create; as though it had been forged at the expense of nature, which might then take revenge. The city is one such major achievement'.

Today, however, approximately 70 per cent of the population of developed nations live in urban areas, and a large proportion of the remainder are highly dependent on the city. This is a dramatic reversal of residential trends prevalent as little as 50 years ago. Given the urban dominance of contemporary industrialised society, then, we might expect that sentiments of anti-ruralism would prevail in it, yet the pastoral ideal has continued to govern much thinking in regard to both rural and urban lifestyles. Thus, when even the flimsiest evidence has been offered in support of anti-urban views, it has often been accepted as a confirmation of what everyone knew already.

The idea that rural life is somehow more natural to man, coupled with these feelings, has had at least two unfortunate consequences. The first is that a major focus of urban research has been the 'urban pathologies', concentrating on crime, vice, gang behaviour, suicide, and other forms of deviancy as particularly phenomena of cities. Indeed, the Chicago School of Sociology brought the prestige of science to these studies, and thereby reinforced the pre-existing anti-urban tradition. Srole (1972) states that they 'Betrayed an uncritical tendency to interpret the immediate social setting of the city dweller as a primary etiological determinant of behavioral and mental disorders', and exceeded the reach of their data, e.g. in generalising about the pathogenicity of social factors in the general population from the social characteristics of mental hospital patients. Secondly, since it is almost universally assumed that urban is more stressful than rural or small town life, it is also assumed, by extension, that urban areas would 'naturally' show a higher incidence of psychological disorders. This view has been reinforced by certain research studies, while those providing counter-intuitive findings have received less attention.

However, it is to be noted that for his part, Kraepelin did not accept the conventional wisdom of his time that increasing urbanisation, with the 'mental over-exertion' that it was said to cause, was responsible for dementia praecox. He came to this conclusion after travelling to Singapore and examining the population of the mental hospital there, which was made up of various Asian races; he observed a remarkable homogeneity of symptoms and history among them, and in comparison with European patients, drawing the conclusion that race, climate, food, and any other general circumstances of life such as urbanisation or method of child rearing should be excluded as causes of psychosis (Gottesman & Shields 1982). Similarly, two long-term studies of mental hospital admissions — in Massachusetts by Goldhammer & Marshall (1953) and in Norway by Astrup & Ødegard (1960) — showed remarkable stability of rates of severe psychosis over periods of 100–150 years. In spite of the many limitations of this method, it would be surprising not to find major changes in these rates if processess such as industralisation and urbanisation were significant factors in the aetiology of the psychoses, particularly schizophrenia.

On the level of anthropological observation, Lewis (1951) found in a small Mexican village that violence, cruelty, suffering, and conflict were common, both in its internal life and in its relationships with other villages. Thus, residents of such rural communities might be subject to degrees of anxiety and personal maladjustment as great as those of most urban areas. The classicist Peter Green (1984) states that life in a remote Greek village 'abounds with fear, crude superstition, insensate cruelty, jealousy, back-biting, and the most hair-raising neuroses', while Gutmann (1980) reports of the villages of the Highland Maya that 'Corrosive envy is the major undertone of human relationships there'. Other anthropologists, though, took a more favourable view, and Carstairs (1983) suggests that there is fairly general agreement about some key values of village life in developing countries: these include love of the land, respect for manual toil in the fields, subordination of the self in deference to obligations to one's family, the exercise of domestic authority, and suspicion of city folk.

ENVIRONMENTAL STRESS

Rural and urban environments are generally thought to differ widely in terms of their stress-inducing potential, and chronic stress to be closely linked with various forms of impairment, especially psychiatric. However, virtually every type of stress can be said to be environmentally engendered, i.e. resulting from an imbalance between the demands of the environment and the individual's ability to adjust to them. Assuming that an organism strives to maintain a state of homeostasis with the demands of his natural, social, and cultural environments, should these demands exceed his ability to adjust to them, he will experience a stress reaction or disequilibrium. This can take many forms, including anxiety, fear, defensiveness, and avoidance behaviour. Thus disequilibrium implies a threat situation, which the individual will endeavour to reduce to the point where the environmental field is seen as 'problem-free', and these adaptive reactions of the organism, in response to a stimulus overload from the environment, may embody stress. As Howard & Scott (1965) suggest, 'Stress occurs if the individual does not have available to him the tools and knowledge to either successfully deal with or avert challenges which arise in particular situations', but unfortunately, the stress concept has seldom been rigorously defined in a scientific sense (Hinkle 1973). Rather, it operates as a heuristic device to provide a framework within which to study emotional disturbance (and other behaviour) from diverse perspectives (Lehman 1972).

Demands or threats, and the stress to which they give rise, derive from the interaction of the individual and environment, but whether a particular situation is conducive to stress depends on the individual's emotional health, vulnerability, and personality structure. Continued exposure to the wear and tear of even mild stressors can result in development of one of the emotional, behavioural, or physiological 'diseases of adaptation' because of the natural reaction of the human organism to prepare for fight or flight when faced with a threatening stressor. If he flees or fights, the physiological system will afterwards return to normal, and the stressful situation has been coped with. This allows for a natural cycle of reaction followed by re-adjustment to any unusual demands. The problem in contemporary society, however, is that very few stressful situations allow for either fight or flight; the stress is not dissipated and the physiological reactions accumulate, to the detriment of the organism. For example, increased blood pressure and heart rate, release of hormones, and increased blood sugar, if prolonged, may play a part in the aetiology of cardiovascular disease, peptic ulcer, diabetes, and probably psychoneurosis.

Both life-threatening and more chronic psychosomatic disorders have been linked to stress, and in particular to job stressors. Though it would be ideal to be able to associate each stressor with a specific problem or condition, the phenomenon appears at present to be largely non-specific, in both its determinants and its consequences. The syndrome can be activated by any number of factors, and the reactions to stress vary over a wide range of social and psychophysical problems and diseases (Selye 1973). Rebkin & Struening (1974) stress the degree of evidence for the aetiological re-lationship of excessive stress to pathology, and consider that the stress itself is the product of socially structured situations and environmental factors. They state that the aetiological model of the onset of illness is generally associated with a number of potential factors, which include 'stressful environmental conditions, perception by the individual that such conditions are stressful, the relative ability to cope with or adjust to these conditions, genetic predisposition to a disease, and the presence of a disease agent'. They regard stress as a general concept, describing the organism's reaction to environmental demands, and its utility as deriving from its role in iden-tifying productive lines of research on the aetiology of disease, which encompass external events that influence individuals and populations.

In Detroit, Kasl & Harburg (1975) devised an Ecological Stress Index, based on socio-economic level and measures of instability — disorganisation, for each census tract. Differences in stress levels were not found to be related to differences in indicators of mental health and well-being, though these latter did have some relationship to variations in perception of the urban environment. However, limitations in the experimental design reduce the significance of these findings.

It is widely recognised that chronic stress is normally engendered, not by a single traumatic event, but rather by a series, any one of which may be temporarily annoying, but which together combine to induce a state of morbid anxiety or depression. Thus it would be advisable to concentrate on those potentially stressful factors which endure over time, and from which there is little possibility of escape. Amongst these, environmental conditions may be an incessant source of irritation, are often difficult to avoid, and concomitantly less amenable to improvement.

An example is rapid social change; Brown et al. (1977) concluded from their comparative studies of Inner London and Hebridean islands that the main psychiatric impact of industrialisation and urbanisation has been in causing a very high rate of depression among working-class city women. Middle-class women there have largely avoided this, though they experience more depression than women in a traditionally structured community. Within the Hebrides, there is a higher rate of depression among certain groups of women, who have moved further from a traditional way of life, and this seems to be linked to the same kind of provoking agents that are found in the inner city, particularly among working-class women (Brown & Prudo 1981). However, it was concluded that 'a simple urban/rural dichotomy does not give an accurate picture of the differing rates of depression within the two populations'. (Social stress is discussed in Chapter 2). Another illustration of the effects of rapid social change comes from a longitudinal study of drinking practices in two communities of the Shetland Islands since the development of the oil industry there (Caetano et al. 1983). Increases in mean alcohol consumption were found to be twice as large in an area directly affected by the oil developments as in a central area, which was in a protected zone, where any such developments were banned. However, in both communities, increases in drinking were largely concentrated among those aged under 30.

Another important aspect is in relation to population density (see Chapter 3). Miller (1975) concludes that for each individual, there is an optimum range beyond which, in either direction, he begins to experience stress. This range varies according to such factors as personal characteristics of the individual, cultural aspects of his group, and sociological characteristics of his environment. The distruptive effects of extreme density occur within a narrower range for some psychological — behavioural dimensions (e.g. affective interpersonal behaviour) than for others (e.g. task performance), while for a given individual or sub-population, the range of non-stressful densities is more restrictive than that for a large population. Moving an individual or sub-population along the density dimension to a point outside the usual experience creates stress, which is relieved by adaptation over time. Miller concludes that the exact relationship between stress and feeling crowded, or between feeling crowded and pathological behaviour is unresolved.

Miller has also used a stress model to analyse the psychiatric implications of geographical mobility in terms of four main stress points: antecedent events, which have not been significantly studied; separation, which is unlikely to have serious psycho-social sequelae if the migration is unforced, and if the lost social organisation can be replaced; the process of moving, which is relatively tolerable intranationally, but may be associated with greater stress internationally; and re-establishment, when the degree of stress depends on many factors, both in the individual, his family, and the host community. Miller concludes that the relationship between psychiatric morbidity and mobility behaviour is a complex one, and that the two main explanatory hypotheses are both much too simplistic; these are *social causation* (that migration is more stressful than non-migration) and *social selection* (that the mentally ill migrate in greater numbers than the non-mentally-ill). (See also Chapter 12).

A dramatic illustration of the effects of stress on physical and mental health came with the Athens earthquake of 1981 (Trichopoulos et al. 1983). Though several lines of evidence had linked fatal heart attacks, and particularly sudden deaths with acute psychological stress, there had not previously been an adequately controlled epidemiological study, demonstrating the association in a human population. In this case, a very large population, with adequate health and registration services, was suddenly and simultaneously exposed to events that invoked the danger of death or serious injury. It was found that earthquake-related stress increased the short-term probability of a fatal cardiac event by about 50 per cent, and the short-term probability of death from atherosclerotic heart disease as underlying cause by about 100 per cent. The peaking of the excess of cardiac deaths during the third, rather than the first day after the major earthquake, was thought to be related to lesser quakes having occurred on the second and third days. The symbolic danger of these may have generated stress as effectively as the real danger, because conditioned reflex pathways had become established. The facts that deaths from quake-related cardiac events were more common among men than women, and among subjects aged 69 or less than among the older, were also thought to confirm the general interpretation of the findings.

Though there has been a general tendency to regard stress as primarily an urban phenomenon, Keller & Murray (1982) point out that:

> Rural people have always been stressed by the environment in which they live. Lack of control over (it) is keenly felt . . . (they are) ultimately dependent on the weather for their success or failure. Even without bad weather, isolation may lead to loneliness, depression, a sense of helplessness, and loss of interpersonal skills.

They add that further emotional stress may result from the challenges which modern communication media bring to rural values and life-styles, particularly causing conflict in the young, and that 'rural life is complicated by many significant social, economic, and environmental problems that take a heavy toll on those who live there'. It would therefore be simplistic and misleading to regard environmental stress as particularly characteristic of either urban or rural life alone. Devos (1974) states that one of the main difficulties of theories which regard the transition to urban life as stressful is not so much an incorrect view of city life as 'a mistaken and romanticized image of what village, rural, or tribal life is typically like'.

PHYSICAL HEALTH

From the physical point of view, urban populations generally enjoy a level of health and medical care superior to that of their rural counterparts. Cross-nationally, the most widely used index is the infant mortality rate (i.e. the number of infant deaths per 100 live births), which is seen as being sensitive to changes in the health status of large population groups, as well as reflecting the quality of health services. With few exceptions, rural areas have persistently higher levels of infant mortality, and this is usually coupled with higher mortality rates. Similarly, non-urban populations show a higher incidence of chronic illness, disability and injury rates, and of accident fatalities (Heald & Cooper 1972; Rogers & Burge 1972; Wan & Tarver 1972; Hassinger & McNamera 1971; Doherty 1970; Weinstein 1980). Even in terms of self-evaluation of health status, the ratings of poor health, number of disorders, and severity of physical limitations increase as one moves from large cities to farm populations (Rosenblatt 1981). But the interaction of health status with other demographic factors is of considerable importance. Because differences of age, sex, and race predispose to and interact with illness, it might be assumed that these factors provide the 'real' explanation for rural–urban health differences. Yet this does not appear to be the case. The relative disadvantage of the non-urban population persists, even after controls for these factors are introduced (Rosenblatt 1981).

In general, urban populations are known to make more visits to doctors, have higher *per capita* expenditures for health care, and greater access to doctors and hospitals, as well as much higher ratios of health professionals to population. As Rosenblatt (1981) has said of the United States, 'the relative deficiency of health resources in non-metro areas is dramatic, pervasive, and unequivocal . . . medical care services are distributed along gradients other than need'. However, these differences in quantity and quality of services are diminished or absent in developed countries where there is a state-financed national health service; Book et al. (1978) report that the community which they investigated in the most remote part of northern Sweden had social and medical services which were at least as good as the national average.

Of greater interest here, however, is the impact that physical health has on mental, since it is generally agreed that a close relationship exists between the two (Markush & Favero 1974; Reeder et al. 1973; Seiler & Summers 1974), though the actual mechanisms are not always clear. Most explanations posit that while one is neither a necessary nor sufficient condition for the other, they are often linked by the concept of stress; physical illness engenders in many persons a morbid state of stress, as the body attempts to cope with the condition, and should this persist, psychiatric impairment may be one of the results. It has also been hypothesised that an environment which promotes the improvement of a population's physical health will eventually achieve the improvement of its mental health also (Chapter 7).

MENTAL HEALTH

Though rural–urban contrasts are consistent and well-documented in relation to the incidence and prevalence of somatic illness, the same cannot be said for psychiatric disorders. Among the reasons for this is the fact that the comparative psychological well-being of rural and urban populations has not been subject to adequate systematic investigation. Most studies are of limited application because of serious methodological and conceptual deficiences.

Measurement issues

One major problem is that most studies have focused largely on urban areas, and/or comparative rates of disorders between areas of a single city, or between cities. Those which have attempted rural–urban comparisons have been largely restricted to 'twin' investigations, comparing a single rural with a single urban area, and the external validity of such comparisons is limited. Another problem is the difficulty of defining and measuring mental health or illness within a population. The difficulties surrounding the use of the term 'mental health' have been referred to earlier in this volume (see Chapter 1), but even in the case of psychiatric illness, everything from minor self-reported psychosomatic symptoms to gross functional incapacity has been used at times to define it.

The measurement of psychiatric illness in epidemiological studies has traditionally followed either of two general strategies. The first relies on institutional rates, usually admissions to mental hospitals, clinics, etc. or the proportion of the population resident in them. Case records of agencies or doctors dealing with the psychiatrically impaired have also been used to derive a rate of illness for a particular area, for instance, through case registers. However, this strategy of using institutional and treatment rates has severe limitations, if we are to make comparisons between different locales. For example, as mentioned above, access to mental health facilities and practitioners is much better for the urban dweller, and this alone could account for significant differences. There are also major variations between the characteristics of rural and urban populations that would directly affect treatment rates, independently of the actual prevalence of impairment. Among these are the greater likelihood of family rather than institutional care in rural areas, as well as differences in socio-economic level, and in health beliefs which differentially predispose persons to seek and utilise psychiatric assistance. As Leacock (1957) has pointed out, 'research has shown that the ratio of hospitalisation incidence to true prevalence is by no means constant throughout different sections of the population. Further, cross-comparability of hospitalisation data is seriously limited by the inconsistency and uncertain validity of diagnostic categories that have been employed'.

A second strategy relies on respondents to report their experience of psychological and psychosomatic symptoms, associated with psychiatric impairment. The number and frequency of symptoms reported is then used as an index of the degree of impairment in the group tested. Although not without drawbacks, this method may have more validity in measuring the overall psychiatric health of a population than data derived from the use of institutions or services. However, the symptom indices usually tap only the milder forms of disorders, and because they provide a single measure, do a disservice to the multi-dimensional nature of psychiatric morbidity. There is also the important issue of whether persons who manifest symptoms of stress are in fact psychiatrically impaired in the clinical sense. In other words, is the concept of psychiatric disorder, as used in studies relying on the reporting of symptoms and signs, in fact valid?

There are a number of other questions closely related to this: 'Do the symptom patterns or mental health ratings of various kinds really constitute dependable entities? To what extent would they be recognised by competent clinical psychiatrists as identical with diagnostic entities? Do they have a predictable life history? Are they influenced in a regular way by improvement or deterioration in the socio-cultural climate? What level of impairment can be used to discriminate those who require treatment? How do persons rated at various points on the scales appear to a clinician?' (Leighton & Leighton 1967). Unfortunately, the answers to these questions are still very much unresolved; (for a review of this and other measurement problems see Seiler 1973; Schwartz et al. 1973; Reeder et al. 1973; Goldberg & Huxley 1980). Some studies include psychiatric disorders with definite organic bases, e.g. dementia or epilepsy, whilst others exclude them; it is unlikely, though, that social and cultural factors are aetiologically important in these conditions.

A third model was used in the Midtown Manhattan Study by Langner & Michael (1963), who demonstrated a strong association between the incidence in the area. The stresses analysed were: broken home in childhood, parents' character negatively perceived, parents' quarrels, parents' poor physical health, poor physical health as an adult, poor interpersonal relationships, socio-economic status worries, marital worries, and parental worries. The dependent variable was a rating of mental health, based on the clinical judgements of two psychiatrists, which in turn were based on psychological information obtained in interviews with respondents. However, this method has been criticised on grounds of the validity of the ratings, the concept of 'mental health', and its amenability to unitary measurement by means of survey research (Berkman 1971).

Thus, most studies which have compared rural and urban areas for the prevalence of psychiatric disorder have been of limited scope, both in terms of the populations studied and of the criterion of measurement. Nevertheless, a number of investigations have attempted to do this.

The first studies

One of the earliest studies of rural and urban differences in psychiatric disorder was by Sorokin & Zimmerman (1929), who reviewed data from a variety of sources and, while finding exceptions according to the type of disease concerned, concluded that overall, morbidity was greater in urban districts. Rose & Steel (1956), summarising the literature, stated that a preponderance of persons in psychiatric institutions consistently come from urban areas, and that there is a direct association between city size and the quantity of such illness. Numerous other studies, most of them utilising hospitalisation rates, have reached the same general conclusion (e.g. Clinard 1964; Mann 1970; Rutter et al. 1974).

There have been two comparisons of rates of psychiatric disorder from a small town and from rural areas with those reported by Srole et al. (1962) in the Midtown Manhattan project. Laird (1973), using records from rural areas in Minnesota, estimated the prevalence of severe disorder as 1 per cent, whereas a rate of 10 per cent was reported for Manhattan. Summers et al. (1971) compared the frequency of self-reported psychiatric impairment between Manhattan and a small town in Illinois. Although their sample was not comparable to the Manhattan one on the dimensions of sex and age, they concluded that 'the prevalence of psychiatric impairment symptoms (is) lower in rural communities than in previously studied urban areas'.

While it might be assumed from the above that most evidence favours urban areas as places of greater mental illness and stress, there are equally persuasive arguments and data indicating otherwise. A number of studies have documented the relatively high rate of certain types of impairment in rural areas, and though confined to these areas, and therefore not comparative, they nevertheless provide important data. Probably the best known, and certainly one of the most ambitious studies began in 1952 in 'Stirling County', a rural district of Nova Scotia (Leighton et al. 1963). A major goal was to estimate the overall prevalence of pyschiatric disorder for the county. Utilising data from 1010 respondent interviews, research observations, doctors' impressions, and institutional records, it was estimated that 31 per cent of the men and 33 per cent of the women showed significant impairment in functioning due to psychiatric disorder.

The Stirling County survey is one of a number of psychiatric epidemiological studies that have been conducted in isolated communities. Others in Sweden (Essen-Moller 1956), Norway (Bremer 1951), Canada (Seimens 1973) and Australia (Burvill 1975) reached a similar conclusion: isolated rural areas, and especially the small resource or boom towns, show psychiatric impairment rates substantially higher than those found in other, more diversified and settled communities. The advantage of isolated areas is that they are relatively little affected by population mobility and migration, which often make it almost impossible to provide a denominator in epidemiological studies of larger communities; on the other hand, they tend to be atypical in many ways of even rural areas of the country concerned, so that findings from them may have limited generalisability.

Another source of evidence on this issue comes from data on the Republic of Ireland, a country composed largely of rural areas and small towns, which has the highest rate of hospitalised psychiatric morbidity in the world. This is true for both the overall 'treatment' rate and for the first admission rate, and applies particularly to schizophrenia; the lowest levels of this condition are in the Dublin area, which is more similar to the rest of western Europe (Walsh 1968; Walsh & Walsh 1968), while rates increase steadily from east to west in the country. Emigration of younger and more economically active members of the population has very likely been one factor in producing this picture, though the effects of migration are complex. A fascinating report by Dawson (1911) stated that 59 per cent of the population was then agricultural, and the hospitalisation rate for mental illness was 5.52 per thousand, compared with 3.61 for England and Wales. However, the more industrial province of Ulster had a rate of 4.2, whereas the eight Irish counties with the highest rates were all agricultural, and also had high rates of pauperism; this general picture continues to hold good (see Chapter 2).

In South Wales, Ingham et al. (1972) used two methods to obtain estimates of the prevalence of psychiatric disorder in different communities. The first relied on the referral of cases to psychiatric services: 'A case was defined as any person seen by a psychiatrist at lest once during the period (five years) either in a psychiatric clinic or hospital, or on a domiciliary visit. The period prevalence rate was the number of cases, divided by the population at risk'. The second part was based on a sample survey, using a single interview to determine whether the respondents were disordered, impairment being measured by a modified version of the Cornell Medical Index and related scales. This allowed for the calculation of a point-prevalence rate, which could be compared with the period-prevalence rate from the first part of the study. It was concluded that 'factors other than the symptoms assessed by the Cornell Medical Index contribute to whether people become psychiatric patients or not and they operate differentially for different combinations of area and sex'. Overall, the urban respondents revealed many more psychiatric symptoms, but were less likely to become psychiatric patients than the rural.

Similar evidence is provided by Srole (1977) in a comparison of psychiatric morbidity rates between 'Stirling County' and Midtown Manhattan. The former, an isolated area dependent upon fishing, lumbering, and subsistence farming, with a population density of only 20 people per square mile, provides an extreme comparison for Manhattan, with 750 000 inhabitants per square mile. The two studies had been carried out independently, by different research teams, yet shared many similarities, particularly in their interview instruments for psychological signs and symptoms. Srole roughly matched the two samples to achieve 'a foundation of demographic comparability in race, nativity, age, sex and socio-economic class', and concluded that the Manhattan sample showed a lesser prevalence of psychiatric impairment than the rural one. However, Mueller (1981) has criticised this comparison on the grounds of 'problematic assumptions', e.g. that the definitions of psychiatric caseness were equivalent in the two studies. Srole also states (1972) that many of the functionally impaired adults as well as a majority of those with non-impairing symptoms were actually migrants to the city, where the tolerant climate and more available psychiatric resources may be a more therapeutic milieu than that of smaller communities from which these people originated. However, this migration effect cannot be quantified because, as Dohrenwend (1975) points out, no studies have taken pre-migration measures of 'true' prevalence of psychiatric disorder and followed these up by post-migration measures in the urban destination; such an undertaking would clearly be enormously difficult.

Brunetti carried out two prevalence studies of psychiatric morbidity in a rural commune in the south of France; the first (1964) showed significant impairment in 25 per cent of the sample , the most frequent conditions being anxiety neuroses, usually with marked somatic symptoms, and only 2 per cent being psychotic. The topographical distribution of cases was uneven, with relatively high concentrations in the village and one of the three hamlets. Then, Brunetti et al. (1978) compared two rural samples of married women with three in Paris; one rural sample (farmers' wives) showed the lowest level of psychiatric impairment, while the other (non-farming rural residents) showed the highest. The better mental health of farming women was attributed to the rewarding interactions they experienced with both the human and material aspects of their environment, since they continuously cooperated with their husbands in a working group and characteristically liked their work, in spite of the hardship. On the other hand, non-farming women lived in considerable isolation, with limited social contacts outside the family.

Following an extensive review of European, Asian, and American research, Leacock (1957) concluded that 'Urban living *per se* is not more conducive to mental illness than rural living'. A number of subsequent studies, using a variety of methodologies, have come to a similar conclusion (Inkeles & Smith 1970; Kato 1969; Kasi & Harburg 1975; Fischer 1973a, b; Freeman & Giovanni 1969). However, a departure from these arguments is provided by Engelsmann et al. (1972) as a result of their survey of 875 persons in two rural, two suburban, and two inner city populations. They found that the suburban sample showed the highest scores for psychiatric impairment, while the lowest scores were obtained by the rural.

Wagenfeld (1982) reviewed the literature on psychopathology in rural areas and concluded that evidence from both the United States and other countries suggested that rates of psychiatric disorder are actually higher in rural than in urban areas. A possible explanation for this excess was that greater stress associated with poverty, unemployment, poorer physical health, and the inability of traditional institutional structures and value systems to satisfy needs and aspirations might be aetiologically associated with psychiatric morbidity. Rural areas may also contain barriers to the receipt of services because the delivery of these tends to be based on urban models, and because practitioners are trained in urban centres. However, the extent to which rural areas may be affected by any of these adverse factors will obviously vary greatly from country to country and from place to place.

It is therefore difficult to come to any firm conclusions about the differential prevalence of psychiatric morbidity in rural and urban environments respectively, but the lack of congruence in research findings should not be very surprising, given the diversity of methodologies used and of areas investigated. Srole (1977) pointed out that previous studies of general populations in either urban or rural areas had generally been done by different investigators, using diverse kinds of methods, data, and diagnostic criteria. There had therefore not been sufficient comparability to make firm generalisations about urban–rural differences.

More recent studies

In the past few years, a number of well designed studies have been published, and constitute an important contribution to knowledge in this area. One of the most widely cited is that of Bruce & Barbara Dohrenwend (1974), in which they re-analysed a series of nine independent 'twin' investigations of impairment rates in matched rural and urban areas. These were carried out between 1942 and 1969, in such diverse settings as Taiwan, Finland, Nigeria, and Iceland. Because the concepts, methods, and criteria for determining disorder in each of the studies were inadequately reported, we must presume they were identical in each pair of communities.

In their summary judgement on this set of intra-pair divergences, the Dohrenwends focus on:

> The consistency in direction of most of the urban–rural differences in these studies, despite the diversity of time, place and method of assessing disorder (which) suggests that the results be taken seriously ...... on the basis of this evidence, there appears to be a tendency for total rates of psychiatric disorder to be higher in urban than in rural areas

This consistency of direction is shown in the fact that seven of the nine studies give a plus value, i.e. a higher urban disorder rate. While this is certainly the case, the Dohrenwends' conclusions regarding the significance of these findings are open to considerable question. As Fischer (1976) pointed out, each of the studies is limited with regard to samples, procedures, and controls for spurious relationships and for drift. Even more important, however, is the fact that most of the differences between rural and urban areas are minuscule, and if we examine the magnitude of the rate differences, rather than their direction, we come to a rather different conclusion. In the first six studies, the differences are actually so slight that they could be chance variations, based on sampling error alone. The three remaining investigations showed higher urban disorder rates by 5 per cent, 5.1 per cent, and 13.9 per cent respectively, so that the question is how valid are these findings, and how representative of other rural and urban areas?

For a start, the Nigerian urban sample is drawn from Abeokuta, then a 'city' of only 80 000 residents in south-west Nigeria; the urban sample consisted of only 64 persons and was conceded by the researcher to be a faulty, non-random sample. The second study in Poland relied on Plock, a small town of only 37 000 people, as its 'urban' site; the Icelandic study used Reykjavik, a fishing and shipping town of only 65 000. Given these considerations, it is doubtful that the urban–rural differences presented by the Dohrenwends are in any way representative of what we would expect to find in modern industralised countries. Furthermore, the observed differences would, for most cases, not fall outside the range of possible chance variation. Thus, the most appropriate conclusion to be drawn from these nine twin investigations seems to be that overall, there is little or no difference in rates of psychiatric disorders between the rural and urban areas studied. Also, Helgason (1978) showed that whereas his earlier study, based on cases of neurosis recognised by doctors, gave a lower rate for rural areas, this no longer held when a psychiatric screening questionnaire was sent to a random sample of the whole population.

Barquero et al. (1982) maintain that different methods are needed to measure neurotic illness in general communities from those used to record severe mental illness in them. They regarded seven studies as having satisfactorily compared urban and rural areas by the same methods for prevalence of neurosis, and of these, four showed a higher prevalence in the rural area. Their own study (which involved screening the whole population with the General Health Questionnaire and then interviewing of selected persons by a team of psychiatrists) revealed significantly higher levels of neurosis in an urban area than a neighbouring rural one; the prevalence was lower still in an area of isolated farms with a traditional, fairly primitive way of life (see Chapter 2).

Another major source of information is a large study carried out by the US National Center for Health Statistics between 1960 and 1962. A sample of 6672 adults were medically examined and interviewed in mobile clinics, and the respondents asked to report the degree to which they suffered symptoms of psychological distress. The study relied on twelve self-reported symptoms, of the kind used in the Stirling County and Midtown Manhattan studies. Ten of these symptoms were validated against the other two, which were based on those experienced in or perceived as an impending 'nervous breakdown'. All ten symptoms showed moderate to high correlations with the two items representing 'nervous breakdown'.

The sample respondents were identified by the size of the community in which they resided, which ranged from large metropolitan areas of over three million population to rural areas with less than 2500. While these data were not specifically collected for the purpose of examining psychiatric impairment across the rural–urban continuum, Srole (1977) was able to obtain and re-analyse the data to provide the breakdown shown in Table 7.1. With these, he demonstrated that when age, gender, and race were controlled, residents of smaller communities reported more symptoms than persons living in the larger urban areas.

There are, however, a couple of problems in interpreting these data. The first (Table 7.1) is that the mean symptom scores range only between 1.53 to 1.98 for men and 2.70 to 3.26 for women, with a possible range of 0–11. Thus, the differences are not great, and since Srole did not report standard deviations, it is impossible to determine the statistical significance of these findings — are the rural–urban differences due to chance, or large enough to warrant closer attention? A second problem is that socio-economic status was not controlled in this study, so that the variations observed could have been due to socio-economic differences, which obviously may occur in relation to rural–urban location. Overall, it would appear that the most appropriate interpretation of these data is that there are only marginal rural–urban differences in reported psychiatric symptoms, and that these may be due to artefacts, unassociated with actual variations in morbidity.

A third major study was carried out in New Zealand; in this, we followed a similar methodology, assessing the self-reported symptoms of a large sample of respondents from across the rural–urban continuum.

Table 8.1 White age-adjusted mean symptom scores by sex and population size

Population size of area	Mean symptom score	
	Men	Women
Over 3 000 000	1.53	2.73
500 000–3 000 000	1.65	2.77
50 000–500 000	1.63	2.70
2500–50 000	1.98	3.26
Less than 2500	1.90	3.14
Farm	1.81	3.25

Source: Srole 1977.

A questionnaire was posted to 6500 households; it included a composite index of 23 symptom items, taken largely from the Langner 22-item index of psychiatric impairment and from the Gurin Medical Index, to measure degree of psychological impairment in the respondents. As shown in Table 8.2, a comparison of symptom rates for each type and size of community, ranging from farms to cities of over 100 000 population, revealed virtually no differences. It was concluded that the most outstanding characteristic of these data is the degree of homogeneity between the population sub-groups in their reported rates of impairment. Further substantiation is provided by the correlation coefficient between population size and

Table 8.2   Mean psychiatric symptom scores for persons residing in rural and urban environments

Type of locality	Female Average symptom score	Number sampled	Male Average symptom score	Number sampled
Farm	34.4	56	32.5	100
Rural non-farm	34.1	35	33.8	64
Small-town fringe	36.3	18	32.8	12
Small towns-under 5000 population	34.7	46	34.4	97
Towns 500–10 000	34.3	69	33.0	163
Towns 10 000–25 000	35.1	124	33.2	287
Towns 25 000–100 000	35.4	238	33.7	559
Cities 100 000 and over	35.3	205	33.5	436
All localities	35.1	791	33.5	1718
Standard deviation (ungrouped data)	6.0		5.5	
Variance (ungrouped data)	36.2		30.6	
Correlation between population size and symptom scores (ungrouped data)	$r = .04$		$r = .01$	

Source: Webb, 1978

symptom scores for ungrouped data. There is virtually no statistical relationship between the two variables (Webb 1978). It was also found that variations in sex ratios, socio-economic status, ethnicity, and marital status could not explain the lack of mental health differences across the rural–urban continuum.

A further source of information comes from a major US study carried out in 1976 (Veroff et al. 1981) on people's view of their mental health. Using a multi-stage probability area design, the investigators interviewed 2267 respondents throughout the country. A wide variety of variables, including perceived happiness, morale, experience of nervous breakdown, and psychological anxiety were used as indices of mental health. The authors concluded that 'City dwellers do not show more symptoms than those from rural areas. They worry and report somewhat less happiness in their current lives, but on psychological anxiety and physical ill-health, city dwellers are more symptom-free than their counterparts in rural settings'.

The final study to be reviewed here was also part of our New Zealand investigations; it employed a research strategy different from, and possibly more valid than those previously used in most epidemiological studies of this kind. Rather than recorded contacts with mental health agencies, or disorder rates as measured through perceived symptoms, the prevalence of psychotropic drug use was taken as an empirical indicator of illness. We obtained nationwide data from pharmacists on all prescriptions dispensed for psychotropic drugs, including tranquillisers, hypnotics, antipsychotics, and antidepressants. In addition to type of drug prescription, information was also obtained on dosage, client sex, and total number of prescriptions. These data were adjusted and aggregated for each locality to provide a general index for that community.

To date, this is the only study to have obtained such data on so useful an index of psychiatric disorder. On the other hand, drug use is probably a mid-range indicator of severity, i.e. measuring the milder forms of impairment, severe enough for a doctor to prescribe pharmacological treatment, yet not severe enough to result in hospitalisation.

Our analyses of these data (Webb & Collette 1979) provide a striking illustration of the pitfalls inherent in ecological or epidemiological investigations. The first analysis relied on the number of prescriptions as a measure of impairment in each locality, and used the population of the administrative area to determine prescription rates. A significant inverse relationship was found here between community size and drug use, but subsequent analyses clearly demonstrated that using administrative areas rather than general ecological areas introduced significant bias, because the rural and urban localities differed dramatically in the hinterland populations they served. Further analyses, using counties as the unit of analysis, showed that the rate of drug prescriptions varied directly, rather than inversely, with locality size. However, as shown in Table 8.3, additional analyses of total milligrams of drug prescribed, as well as of the total daily dosages in milligrams, revealed that there were only marginal differences between rural and urban areas. That is, in terms of the amount of drugs and daily dosage — rather than number of prescriptions — there were virtually no rural–urban differences.

Thus, while a greater number of prescriptions are issued in the larger towns, the strength and dosages of the prescriptions are slightly smaller than

Table 8.3 Mean monthly rates[a] of prescribed milligrams, milligram dosage and total drug prescriptions by county and urban area population size (New Zealand, 1973)[c]

County size	Pharmacists N	Mean number of mg	Mean mg per day	Mean total prescriptions	Per cent of all prescriptions for psychotropic drugs
1000–2499	4	47 601	1 595	491	9.6
2500–4999	8	36 713	1 348	546	9.2
5000–9999	26	93 589	3 530	692	11.0
10 000–24 999	65	42 073	1 410	572	10.8
25 000–99 999	166	33 699	1 183	648	10.6
Urban areas over 100 000	274	35 472	1 211	870	10.6
All localities	543	48 781	1 736	626	10.5
		$r = -.11$[b]	$r = -.12$	$r = .46$	
		$p = .24$	$p = .21$	$p = .001$	

[a] Per 1 000 population
[b] Pearson product moment correlations were calculated on ungrouped data.
[c] Source: Webb S D, Collette J 1979

those in rural districts. Possible explanations for this include the following: the rural populace suffers more serious illness, and thus is in need of greater dosage; rural doctors are busier, and thus write fewer but larger prescriptions; the urban populace has greater access to doctors and may seek assistance for more minor or non-existent illnesses, resulting in more but weaker prescriptions; or some combination of these or other factors.

Table 8.3 also presents the rates of all prescribed pharmaceuticals, as well as the percentage of all prescriptions which is for psychotropic drugs. These data lead to two conclusions: first, that urban residents receive almost double the number of all drug prescriptions as do the rural residents; second, that the percentage of all pharmaceuticals which are psychotropic drugs varies only marginally across the rural–urban continuum. As pointed out, it is very unlikely that urban residents suffer a higher rate of somatic illness, so that it appears most likely that the higher urban rate of prescriptions is due to doctor access and/or differences in 'illness behaviour' between the two populations. If access and illness behaviour are reasonable explanations for the fact that urban residents receive more total prescriptions, then they are equally useful in explaining any psychotropic drug use difference in rural and urban populations. Thus, it was concluded that impairment levels, as measured by prescribed psychotropic drugs, vary little across the rural–urban continuum.

Discussing surveys which show higher rates of depression in inner London than in the Hebrides, but even higher in Ugandan villages (Orley & Wing 1979), Goldberg & Huxley (1980) state that the factors which produce such differences need not be social or environmental, but could equally be genetic or selective migration. They add that 'the reason for the different rates cannot be determined by a simple cross–sectional survey, and the range of possible explanations is very wide . . . (but) it is no longer possible to involve urban/rural factors to account for the differences'.

Although total rates for all forms of psychiatric disorder have failed to show significant urban–rural differences, Mueller (1981) suggests that this may be partly due to the masking of contrasting relationships for different diagnostic groups. The Dohrenwends (1974) found that the rates for specific disorders varied, although the differences were small, diagnostic criteria were not uniform, and there was no clear trend for schizophrenia. However, a fairly clear trend did emerge for non-psychotic depression to be at a higher rate in urban areas, particularly among females; this was confirmed in later studies (e.g. Brain et al. 1977; Rutter et al. 1974; Sethi et al. 1973). Mueller proposes an explanation for this difference, linked to the level of interpersonal or social support which is characteristic of different environments (see Chapter 2).

Conclusions

Thus it appears that earlier research on rural–urban differences in mental health suffers from a number of limitations, and that the findings were inconsistent, so that firm generalisations cannot be made from them about such differences. More recently, however, a number of well designed studies have been completed, and although they have used very different research strategies, the findings are relatively consistent. In each case, it was found that rural and urban areas differed very little in terms of the prevalence of psychiatric impairment, while in the four largest and most comparative studies, the marginal differences which were observed all showed highest rates of disorder in the rural population. Moreover, these findings coincide with those of Leacock (1957), following her extensive review of earlier research in Asia, Europe, and North America. The most comprehensive studies to date therefore arrive at the same conclusion — that the prevalence of mental impairment varies little across the rural–urban continuum — though depression may be at a somewhat higher rate in cities. There is also the possibility of a complex interrelationship between place of residence, diagnosis, and social class; for instance, though rates of personality disorder are consistently highest in the lowest class, this is less marked in rural areas (Dohrenwend & Dohrenwend 1974). Finally, irrespective of the amount of psychiatric morbidity in different types of area, there is the possibility that its manifestations may vary; this seemed to be confirmed by a study in (Chu et al. 1982). In a sample of 275 consecutively admitted schizo-phrenics, significant differences were found, in that rural patients were more frequently apathetic, blunted, labile, angry, aggressive, negativistic, and uncooperative, while urban patients were more often anxious, rigid, ambivalent, disorientated, conceptually disorganised, and asocial.

The present state of knowledge has been well summarised by Gold (1982):

> the amount of nervous illness in any society or population will depend upon the genetic composition of the population, the prevalence of certain types of trauma or pathogenic processes in early family life, the kinds of stresses to which adults are exposed late in life, cultural definitions of mental illness and the exercise of potential controls, which may limit the development of symptoms. The relative weights and particular forms of factors and the degree to which the various urban and non-urban environments are contributing factors have not yet been conclusively established.

DISCUSSION

The perspective taken in this chapter is that of the ecology and epidemiology of psychiatric disorder, attempting to find the broad distribution of morbidity within a population, and to establish and compare rates of illness for segments of the population characterised by their rural–urban residence. This approach has great heuristic value for establishing initial relationships, but also significant limitations, particularly that because the units of analysis are ecological rather than individual, and therefore deal with averaged rates of pathology, there is a tendency to obscure individual differences (Bagley et al. 1973). However, the rural–urban variable holds great fascination, and because of the often dramatic differences between the two environments, it seems only natural that the populations residing there would also contrast sharply. If the environment is somehow a cause of illness or health, this should be most apparent when the environments contrasted are radically different. Yet, as Freeman (1978) points out, 'Direct cause-and-effect relationships are very unlikely to be found between specific features of the environment and abnormal mental states or forms of psychological malfunctionings. The intervening processes must be extremely complex'.

As far as the differential prevalence of mental disorder is concerned, though, the rural–urban variable has little utility; this may be partly due to conceptual and measurement problems, but is more likely a function of the fact that it is simply too global. It is inadequate to define an area as a city, or suburb, or farm, and expect that the population that lives in that environment will manifest differential degrees of impairment just because they reside there. Rather, the area being studied must be defined in terms of more relevant criteria, especially the detailed composition of the population. Bastide (1972) points out that large cities harbour religious or ethnic communities that are stable and relatively harmonious, whilst anomie exists among migrant agricultural workers or in isolated rural regions with declining villages, which are socially disorganised.

Variables such as age, gender, income, education, migration status, mobility, and ethnicity are much more likely to affect psychological outlook and the utilisation of the health care system than are any differences based solely on place of residence. Even though the overall degree of impairment might be very similar across the rural–urban continuum, the causes of that impairment may be substantially different in the various communities. Murphy (1976) points out that the lack of evidence for significant rural–urban differences in psychiatric morbidity may not mean that the hypothesis of additional social stress (e.g. alienation) in cities is wrong, but rather that the usual rural–urban dichotomy does not represent it. This is because each large rural or urban area is too diverse to have the same impact on all its inhabitants, whereas smaller units may be more specific in terms of the fabric of human interactions within them.

Earlier studies, relying largely on hospitalisation rates, appeared to show that psychiatric disorders were more prevalent in urban areas. Subsequent work on the urbanism–mental health relationship had mixed findings, and was generally of limited validity because of a number of problems: (a) the types of data used (first admission to mental hospital, treatment records, self-report scales, etc.) differ widely; (b) major differences may have existed previously, but have declined as contemporary changes broke down the self-sufficiency and isolation of rural areas; (c) many persons live in areas different from those in which they grew up, so that urban rates may be artificially inflated by migrants whose disorders originated in rural settings; (d) sampling methods and definitions of rural and urban areas vary from one study to another, making comparisons difficult; (e) differences in types of disorder may be obscured by the tendency to deal with total rates of impairment; (f) age, sex, education, income, occupation, mobility, ethnicity, etc. may affect psychological outlook, coping strategies, and utilisation of health services, which may be more important than differences based solely on place of residence.

In this connection, Srole (1972) states that present-day mobility (an average American changes his residence 13 times during his life) means that 'an adult's current residential position loses its claim to being a unidirectional aetiological input factor, relative to his present and subsequent mental health as output'. Because of motor transport and the mass media, a village may be merely a suburban dormitory satellite of a city, while there has been a homogenisation of what used to be 'contrasting psycho-sociological continents, that seemed fixed and culturally unbridgeable'.

More recent studies have both overcome many of the earlier limitations and arrived at relatively consistent conclusions, in spite of their use of different research strategies. We can cautiously conclude, therefore , that in general, urban and rural populations now differ only marginally in regard to the prevalence of psychiatric impairment, but this is not to say that specific communities might not have exceptionally low or high rates, for any number of reasons — for instance, the farmers' wives studied by Brunetti (see above) or the resource towns of Australia and Canada, in which impairment rates seem to be substantially higher than those in more diversified and settled communities (Burvill 1975). Although these rates may be similar across the rural–urban continuum, the aetiology of the disorders in each community may of course be very different; a specific form of illness might be related to either the crowding and congestion of the large city or the isolation and deprivation of the small town.

However, Selye (1973) has hypothesised that the causes of chronic mental disease are in fact non-specific, so that the simple fact of rural–urban impairment rates being similar should neither mislead us to believe that their causes are the same, nor dissuade us from continuing to seek the aetiology — environmental or otherwise — in each type of community.

REFERENCES

Adebimpe V R, Chu C C, Klein H E, Lange M H 1982 Racial and geographic differences in the psychopathology of schizophrenia. American Journal of Psychiatry 139: 888–891
Astrup C, Ødegard Ø 1960 The influence of hospital facilities and other local factors upon admission to psychiatric hospitals. Acta Psychiatrica Scandinavica 25: 289–301
Bagley C, Jacobson S, Palmer C 1973 Social structure and the ecological distribution of mental illness, suicide and delinquency. Psychological Medicine 3: 177–187
Barquero J L V, Munez P E, Jaurequi V M 1982 The influence of the process of urbanization on the prevalence of neurosis. Acta Psychiatrica Scandinavica 65: 161–170
Bastide R 1972 The sociology of mental disorder Routledge & Kegan Paul, London
Berkman P L 1971 Life stress and psychological well-being: a replication of Langner's analysis in the Midtown Manhattan Study. Journal of Health and Social Behaviour 12: 35–45
Book J A, Wetterberg L Modrzeurska K 1978 Schizophrenia in a North Swedish geographical isolate, 1900–1977. Epidemiology, genetics and biochemistry. Clinical Genetics 14: 373–394

Bremer J 1951 A social psychiatric investigation of a small community in northern Norway. Acta Psychiatrica et Neurologica Scandinavica: supp 62

Brown G W, Davidson S, Harris T, Maclean U, Pollock S, Prudo R 1977 Psychiatric disorders in London and North Uist. Social Science and Medicine 11: 367–377

Brown G W, Prudo R 1981 Psychiatric disorder in a rural and an urban population: 1. Aetiology of depression. Psychological Medicine 11: 581–599

Brunetti P M 1964 A prevalence survey of mental disorders in a rural commune in Vaucluse. Acta Psychiatrica Scandinavica 40: 323–358

Brunetti P M, Dacher M, Sequeira S 1978 Prevalence of psychological impairment in city and in country samples. Acta Psychiatrica Scandinavica 58: 369–378

Burville P W 1975 Mental health in isolated new mining towns in Australia. Australia and New Zealand Journal of Psychiatry 9: 77–83

Caetana R, Suzman R M, Rosen D H, Voorhees Rosen D J 1983 The Shetland Islands: longitudinal changes in alcohol consumption in a changing environment. British Journal Addiction 78: 21–36

Carstairs G M 1983 Death of a witch. Hutchinson, London

Chu C C, Klein H E, Lange M H 1982 Symptomatology differences between urban and rural schizophrenics. International Journal of Social Psychiatry 2814: 251–255

Clinard M B 1974 Deviant behaviour: urban-rural contrasts. In: Elias C E Jr, Gillies J, Reimer S (eds) Metropolis: values in conflict. Wadsworth, Belmont, Ca

Dawson W R 1911 The relation between the geographical distribution of insanity and that of certain social and other conditions in Ireland. Journal of Mental Science 57: 571–597

De Vos G A 1974 Cross-cultural studies of mental disorder. In: Caplan G (ed) American Handbook of Psychiatry, Vol. II, 2nd edition. Basic Books, New York

Doherty N 1970 Rurality, poverty and health: medical problems in rural areas. Agricultural Economic Report 172, US Government Printing Office, Washington, DC

Dohrenwend B P, Dohrenwend B S 1974 Psychiatric disorders in urban settings, In: Caplan G (ed) American handbook of psychiatry, Vol II, 2nd edn. Basic Books, New York

Engelsmann F, Murphy H B M, Prince R, Leduc M, Demers H 1972 Variations in responses to a symptom check list by age, sex, income, residence, and ethnicity. Social Psychiatry 7: 150–156

Ericksen E G 1954 Urban behaviour. Macmillan, New York

Essen-Moller E 1956 Individual traits and morbidity in a Swedish rural population. Acta Psychiatrica Scandinavica: supp 100

Fischer C S 1973a On urban alienation and anomie: powerlessness and social isolation. American Sociological Review 38: 311–326

Fischer C S 1973b Urban malaise. Social Forces 52: 221–235

Fischer C S 1976 The urban experience. Harcourt Brace Jovanovich, New York

Freeman H E, Giovannoni J M 1969 Social psychology of mental health. In: Lindzey G, Aronson E (eds) Handbook of social psychology. Addison-Wesley, Reading, Mass

Freeman H L 1978 Mental health and the environment. British Journal of Psychiatry 132: 113–124

Gold H 1982 The sociology of urban life. Prentice Hall, Englewood Cliffs, NJ

Goldberg D P, Huxley P 1980 Mental illness in the community. Tavistock, London

Goldhammer H, Marshall A 1953 Psychosis and civilization: Two studies in the frequency of mental disease. Academic Press, New York

Gottesman I I, Shields J 1982 Schizophrenia: The epigenetic puzzle. Cambridge University Press, Cambridge

Green P 1984 The furies of civil war Times Literary Supplement No 4216, 20th January

Guttmann D 1980 Observations on culture and mental health in later life. In: Birren J E, Sloane R B (eds) Handbook of mental health and aging. Prentice Hall, Englewood Cliffs, NJ

Hassinger E W, McNamara R J 1971 Rural life in the United States. In: The quality of rural living: proceedings of a workshop, National Academy of Sciences. Washington, DC

Hawley A H 1972 Population density and the city. Demography 9 November: 521–529

Heald K A, Cooper J K 1972 An annotated bibliography on rural medical care. Rand Corp, Santa Monica

Helgason T 1978 Prevalence and incidence of mental disorders estimated by health questionnaire and a psychiatric case register. Acta Psychiatrica Scandinavica: –266

Hinkle E Jr 1973 The concept of stress in the biological and social sciences. Science, Medicine and Man 1: 31–48

Howard A, Scott R A 1965 A proposed framework for the analysis of stress in the human organism. Behavioral Science 10 April: 141–160

Ingham J G, Rawnsley K, Hughes D 1972 Psychiatric disorder and its declaration in contrasting areas of south Wales. Psychological Medicine 2: 281–292

Inkeles A, Smith D H 1970 The fate of personal adjustment in the process of modernization. International Journal of Comparative Sociology 11: 81–114

Kasl S V, Harburg E 1975 Mental health and the urban environment: some doubts and second thoughts. Journal of Health and Social Behaviour 16: 268–282

Kato M 1979 Psychiatric epidemiological surveys in Japan: the problem of case findings. In: Caudill W, Lin T Y (eds), Mental health research in Asia and the Pacific. East-West Center Press. Honolulu

Laird J T 1973 Mental health and population density.The Journal of Psychology

Langner T S, Michael S T 1963 Life stress and mental health. Free Press, Glencoe

Leacock E 1957 Three social variables and the occurrence of mental disorder. In: Leighton A H, Clausen J A, Wilson R N (eds), Explorations in social psychiatry. Basic Books, New York

Lehman E C 1972 An empirical note on the transactional model of psychological stress. The Sociological Quarterly 13: 484–495

Leighton D C, Leighton A H 1967 Mental health and social factors. In: Freedman A M, Kaplan H I (eds) Comprehensive textbook of psychiatry, Williams & Wilkins, Baltimore, Md

Leighton D C, Harding J S, Macklin D B, MacMillan A M, Leighton A H 1963 The character of danger: psychiatric symptoms in selected communities. Basic Books, New York

Lewis O 1951 Life in a Mexican Village: Tepoztlan restudied. University of Illinois Press, Urbana

Mackon R A, Medrick S A, Schulsinger F 1983 The interaction of seasonality, place of birth, genetic risk and subsequent schizophrenia in a high risk sample. British Journal of Psychiatry 143: 383–388

Mann P H 1970 An approach to urban sociology. Routledge & Kegan Paul, London

Markush R, Eavero R V 1974 Epidemiologic assessment of stressful life events, depressed mood, and psychophysiological symptoms — a preliminary report. In: Dohrenwend B S, Dohrenwend B P (eds), Stressful life events: their nature and effects. John Wiley, New York

Miller W B 1974 Psychological and psychiatric aspects of pouplation problems. In: Arieti et al. (eds) American handbook of psychiatry, 2nd Edn. Basic Books, New York

Mueller D P 1981 The current status of urban-rural differences in psychiatric disorder. Journal of Nervous and Mental Disease 169: 18–27

Murphy H B M, Wittkower E D, Fried J et al 1963 A cross-cultural survey of schizophrenic symptomatology. International Journal of Social Psychiatry 9: 237–249

Murphy J E 1976 Social causes: the independent variable. In: Kaplan B H, Wilson R N, Leighton A H (eds) Further explorations in social psychiatry. Basic Books, New York

Orley J, Wing J K 1979 Psychiatric disorders in two African villages. Archives of General Psychiatry 36: 513–520

Rabkin J E, Struening E L 1974 Life events, stress and illness. Science 194: 1013–1020

Reeder L G, Schrama P G M, Dirken J M 1973 Stress and cardio-vascular health: an international cooperative study. Social Science and Medicine 7: 573–584

Rogers E M, Burdge R J 1972 Social change in rural societies. 2nd edn. Appleton-Century-Crofts, New York

Rose A M, Stub H R 1956 Summary of studies on the incidence of mental disorders. In: Rose A M et al. (eds) Mental health and mental disorder. Routledge & Kegan Paul, London

Rosenblatt R A 1981 Health and health services. In: Hawley A H, Mazie S M (eds) Nonmetropolitan America in transition, UNC Press, Chapel Hill

Rutter M, Yule B, Quinton D, Rowlands O, Yule W, Berger M 1974 Attainment and adjustment in two geographical areas. British Journal of Psychiatry 125 520–533

Scheper-Hughes N 1979 Saints scholars and schizophrenics: mental illness in rural Ireland. University of California Press, Berkeley

Schwartz C C, Myers J K, Astrachan B M 1973 Comparing three measures of mental status: a note on the validity of estimates of psychological disorder in the community. Journal of Health and Social Behavior 14: 265–273

Selye H 1973 Stress in health and disease. Butterworths, Boston

Seiler L 1973 The 22-item scale used in field studies of mental illness: a question of method, a question of substance, and a question of theory. Journal of Health and Social Behavior 14: 252–264

Seiler L H, Summers G F 1974 Toward an interpretation of items used in field studies of mental illness. Social Science and Medicine 8: 459–467

Seimens L B 1973 Single enterprise community studies in northern Canada. UNESCO seminar on man and the environment: new towns in isolated settings. Kambalda

Sethi B B, Nathawak S S, Gupta S C 1973 Depression in India. Indian Journal of Social Psychology 91: 3–13

Sorokin P, Zimmerman C C 1929 Principles of rural-urban sociology. Henry Holt, New York

Srole L 1972 Urbanization and mental health: some reformulations. American Scientist 60: 576–583

Srole L 1977 The city vs town and country: new evidence on an ancient bias In: Mental health in the metropolis (Revised Edition). Harper, New York

Srole L, Langner T S, Michael S T, Kirkpatrick P, Opler M K, Rennie T A 1962 Mental health in the metropolis. McGraw-Hill, New York

Summers G F, Seiler L H, Hough R L 1971 Psychiatric symptoms: cross validation with a rural sample. Rural Sociology 36: 367–378

Trichopoulos D, Katsayanni K, Zavitsanos X, Tzonai A, Dalla-Vorgia P 1983 Psychological stress and fatal heart attack: the Athens (1981) earthquake natural experiment. Lancet I: 441–444

Tuan Y 1979 Landscapes of fear. Blackwell, Oxford

Wagenfeld M O 1982 Psychopathology in rural areas: issues and evidence. In: Keller P, Muray J D (eds) Handbook of rural community mental health. Human Sciences Press, New York

Walsh D 1968 Hospitalized psychiatric morbidity in the Republic of Ireland. British Journal of Psychiatry 114: 11–14

Walsh D, Walsh B 1968 Some influences on the intercounty variation in Irish psychiatric hospitalization rates. British Journal of Psychiatry 114: 15–20

Wan T T H, Tarver J D 1972 Socioeconomic status, migration and morbidity. Social Biology 19: 51–59

Webb S D 1978 Mental health in rural and urban environments. Ekistics 266: 37–42

Webb S D, Collette J 1979 Rural-urban stress: new data and new conclusions. American Journal of Sociology 84: 1446–1452

Weinstein M S 1980 Health in the city. Pergamon Press, Toronto

White M, White L 1962 The intellectual and the city: from Jefferson to Frank Lloyd Wright. Harvard University and M I T Press, Chicago

Environmental noise and mental health

Research into the effects of environmental noise has become particularly important because of increasing road, rail and air transport. The effects of industrial noise on the individual have received much attention, but it is only relatively recently that the impact of general environmental noise on the community became a cause for concern. Ward and Dubos (1972) state that 'of all forms of pollution, noise is perhaps the most inescapable for the urban dweller. It pursues him into the privacy of his home, tails him on the street and quite often is an accompaniment of his labour'. The planning of new airports and motorways demands answers to the question of whether noise contributes to, or even causes ill-effects in the individual. Research has been extensive, ranging from physiological experiments on laboratory animals to interviews with respondents in community surveys. It is impossible to do justice to the entire field, and so this chapter will focus on the effects of aircraft noise on mental health.

For this, we will draw on a series of surveys conducted around Heathrow Airport, which grew out of both government and public concern about the socio-medical consequences of exposure to environmental noise, particularly in relation to the possible construction of a fourth London Airport, or a fourth terminal at Heathrow. The questions to be answered were manifold: does noise, as experienced by ordinary dwellers in usual circumstances, impair mental health? Is it associated with defined psychiatric disorders? Or does it produce mild, non-specific symptoms or stress? Is there a higher consumption of medicines, in particular psychotropic drugs, in areas of high noise? Do people exposed to environmental noise place burdens on health and social agencies more than residents of quieter areas?

The results were obtained in two major studies. One consisted of an analysis of admissions to psychiatric hospitals, aimed at testing the controversial view that aircraft noise is associated with an increase in psychiatric admissions. The second, an equally large community survey, collected first-hand information from city dwellers on their health (both physical and psychiatric), their symptoms, reactions to noise, and the use they made of medicines and services. However, in our current work, we have moved away from assessing the presence or absence of specific effects to studying the individual vulnerability and personality features that predispose some people to suffer psychologically from noise.

SOUND AND NOISE

Some general features of this subject need to be considered here. Firstly, there is a distinction to be made between sound and noise. Sound intensity is commonly expressed in decibels (dB). As a rough guide, 0 dB is about the level of sound that a person can detect if he has very good ears and is in a very quiet environment. 70 dB corresponds to a vacuum cleaner at 10 feet, and 120 dB to a jet take-off at 200 feet. The decibel scale is logarithmic, and so intensity doubles with each additional 3 dB of sound level. The maximum exposure recommended is 90 dB for 8 hours per day (HMSO 1963), and similarly for every 3 dB increase in sound, the duration of exposure must be halved — 93 dB for 4 hours, 96 dB for 2 hours, etc.

Noise may be defined as types of sound that are unwanted by the listener and perceived as being unpleasant, bothersome, interfering, and possibly harmful (Kryter 1970). Tighter definition of noise is precluded by the consideration of its different qualitative aspects — loud music may be a source of pleasure to the enthusiast, but an annoying noise to his neighbours. A sound does not have to be loud to become an annoying noise, e.g. the constant dripping of a tap. Sounds may become an annoying noise by token of their meaning or significance to the subject, in terms of his own personal experience or the message they convey (Tarnopolsky and McLean 1976). Therefore, by definition, noise is unwanted and constitutes an undesirable feature in the environment; the extent to which it can damage health, both psychologically and physiologically, will be discussed below.

HEARING LOSS, DEAFNESS AND THEIR PSYCHIATRIC IMPLICATIONS

It is customary to describe the effects of noise as auditory and extra-auditory. Partial or total loss of hearing capacity is the best documented medical consequence of noise, and was already identified as an occupational hazard in the nineteenth century (Shepherd 1974). The extent of hearing loss is dependent on the level and duration/frequency of exposure to noise (Fearn 1972, 1973, 1974), but it does not necessarily affect the entire auditory spectrum. For example, aircraft maintenance crews show hearing loss at 5000 Hertz, whilst exposure to loud music at pop concerts may cause hearing loss at 1000 Hertz. As the normal speech frequency range is about 600 to 4800 Hertz, the latter case may constitute a greater disability than the former. Hearing loss may also affect other processes, e.g. communication, which in turn is detrimental to the individual and therefore of interest to psychiatrists.

Psychological and social handicaps of deaf people have been reviewed by

Mykleburst (1964). In a community study, Kay et al. (1970) interviewed a representative sample of people over 65 years-old; six out of the seven people with paranoid psychoses had some degree of hearing loss, but all three subjects with endogenous depression had normal hearing. The association between deafness and psychiatric morbidity has also been confirmed in ENT units (Mahapatra 1974; Singerman et al. 1980), in psychiatric hospitals, and in the general population. Two large-scale surveys in mental hospitals have shown age-specific hearing loss in in-patients to be four times the age-expected rates found in the general population (McCoy and Plotkin 1967; Jeter 1976). Kay and Roth (1961) found that 40 per cent of a paraphrenic population suffered hearing loss, compared with only 7 per cent in a control sample of patients with affective disorders, while Cooper et al. (1976) found that deaf paraphrenics had significantly increased percentages of normal premorbid personality characteristics. In other words, the deafness appeared to have increased their liability to develop paranoid illness above the level that would otherwise have been expected. Finally, in the community, we found that subjects with impaired hearing capacity complain more frequently than normals of mild psychiatric symptomatology (unpublished findings of the Heathrow survey).

However, general environmental noise is not so relevant in relation to hearing loss, which is caused by disease, trauma, and industrial noise, but the levels of noise in the community rarely reach damaging levels. Noise exposure from an airport will more frequently give rise to direct emotional effects (e.g. annoyance) due to loudness, lack of predictability, and other characteristics of the noise stimulus. Indirect effects due to hearing loss are infrequent, but annoyance is in fact the major social consequence of environmental noise. The research to be reported below shows annoyance to be the most significant mediator between noise exposure and medical consequences (e.g. symptoms, drug use).

PHYSIOLOGICAL EFFECTS OF NOISE

As with any perceived stimulus, noise registers physiologically, psychologically, and physically. A sound will register physically against the eardrum, will effect physiological changes in certain systems, and may register cognitively in the person. For the purpose of this chapter, it is probably best to consider these three aspects at the same time (see also Chapter 2).

In general, response to a stimulus, may be categorised into orientation reactions (OR) and startle or defensive reactions (DR) (Sokolov 1963). Orientation is a sitting up, alerting, what is it?' reaction, as if the organism were primed to receive information from the environment. Defensive reactions are caused by intense stimuli, and consist of a flinching, cowering response, as if the organism is shrinking from an environmental threat. The psychophysiological concomitants of both reactions are similar, and have been described by Lynn (1966):

1. Increase in sense organ sensitivity
2. Changes in skeletal muscles that direct sense organs
3. Arrest of current activity, changes in electromyogram tonus
4. Electroencephalogram changes indicative of arousal
5. Autonomic responses, e.g. changes in electrodermal activity, slowed respiration, slowed heart rate in humans.

A major difference between ORs and DRs is that peripheral vasoconstriction occurs in the OR, but dilatation in the DR. Habituation to intense stimuli causing DRs is slow, if it occurs at all. These are all normal adaptive responses to novel or significant stimuli, and as such are not pathological.

Physiological changes produced by noise consist of non-specific responses, often associated with stress reactions (Glorig 1971; Selye 1956). These include changes in electrodermal activity, cardiovascular activity, and hormone secretions; they can affect respiratory and digestive systems. An extensive review of relevant studies is given in McLean and Tarnopolsky (1977); it should be borne in mind that the majority of these studies have involved short-term exposure to relatively high sound levels in the laboratory, so that extrapolation to environmental noise effects must be tentative.

In the cardiovascular system, humans show peripheral vasoconstriction in response to noise (Falk 1972; Jansen 1969; Anticaglia and Cohen 1970). However, this is normally compensated for with a reduced stroke volume, and so there are no hypertensive reactions to noise in normal subjects. On the other hand, hypertensive patients do show repeated and persistent hypertensive reactions to noise in experiments. Richter-Heinrich and Sprungh (1969) found that hypertensives had lower acoustic thresholds, and showed attenuated habituation to noise; the evidence also suggests that chronic exposure to noise can be a causal factor in hypertension. Cohen et al. (1980) found that children from schools in noisy areas had higher blood pressure, while Knipschild's (1977) evidence suggests that in areas of high aircraft noise, there are more people with heart trouble or hypertension. Jansen (1969) found a positive significant correlation between blood pressure and hearing loss to noise exposure.

Other physiological effects are that noise can cause increased recovery time for the GSR (Atherley et al. 1970) and increased arousal, as shown by EEG desynchronisation and hyper-reflexia (Anticaglia and Cohen 1970). In a study carried out on people living near Paris-Roissy airport, one year after it opened, to assess sleep disturbance by aircraft noise, EEG recordings showed a moderate response rate, indicating limited habituation to the noise (Vallet and Francois 1982).

At very high intensities (>100 dB), noise impairs balance (Anticaglia and Cohen 1970) and can produce vestibular nystagmus (Dickson and Chadwick 1951). High levels of industrial noise are associated with EEG abnormalities and with cardiac dysrythmias, which probably occur via coronary vasoconstriction (Cohen 1963; Shatalov et al. 1962; Anticaglia and Cohen 1970).

Studies of the endocrine system have concentrated on adrenocortical and medullary function, but the general results are unclear. Noise of sudden onset causes slowing or arrest of alimentary functions, salivation, gastric secretion and digestive functions. However, in spite of all this laboratory evidence, direct links between noise exposure and either definite psychosomatic disorders or any other disease entity are not conclusive (Tarnopolsky and McLean 1976). Some studies (e.g. Drettner et al. 1975) fail to confirm the association between blood pressure and noise exposure, and this is an area where more evidence is needed.

In a small minority of apparently normal people, habituation of the physiological response to noise consistently fails to occur (Glass and Singer 1972); this phenomenon has not been systematically investigated. It could be explained by the presence in the noise of some 'meaning' which was perceptible only to these people but adequate to ensure a continuing OR. Alternatively, some people may be constitutionally disposed to react to noise with repeated attention, and so fail to gain the protection which rapid habituation affords to the rest of us. If so, it would be important to develop simple standard techniques for identifying this group of people.

Atherley et al. (1970) showed that when experimental noise exposure is held constant, and subjects go about their normal business during the exposure, the effects of the noise, in terms of adrenocortical activity and minor mental distress, are dependent on the presence or absence of meaning in the noise. This importance of meaning in relation to distress would be predictable from evidence about the OR; this shows that a repeated sensory stimulus would provoke an OR that reappears at each repetition, without habituation, if the stimulus had novelty or learned significance, signified conflict, or was the subject of an instruction to pay attention to that stimulus. The same criteria determined the waking power of sensory stimuli for a sleeping subject. Thus, when individual responses are being assessed, noise measures need to be combined with measures of meaning for the individual subject; however, this involves major methodological problems, which are not yet solved, and it is not easy to see how reliable techniques could be developed which could embrace the enormously wide individual variations in meaning (McLean and Tarnopolsky 1977).

Some categories of neurotically ill patients show responses to noise that are markedly different from those of normal subjects. Hysterical patients fail to habituate to repeated noise, and anxious patients show much greater responses of adrenal cortical and medullary activity (reviewed by McLean and Tarnopolsky 1977).

NOISE AND SYMPTOMS

The association between noise and certain symptoms has frequently been documented, both in industrial settings and in social surveys. Industrial surveys report that noise exposure can result in increased anxiety and

emotional stress. Increased incidence of nervous complaints, nausea, headaches, instability, argumentativeness, sexual impotence, changes in general
mood, and anxiety have been reported in workers exposed to high-intensity
noise (110 dB or above) by Cohen (1969), Granati et al. (1959) and Miller
(1974). However, there may be other contributory factors in both the work
and social environment of factory workers, and so the noise may not be the
only cause. It has also been shown that it is not always possible to disentangle the relative contributions of personal disposition and selection for
particular employment. No control groups were available for comparison
with the highly exposed groups, nor were clinical impressions of them
expressed in any systematic way.

Noise from traffic, airports, and railways tends to be far less intense, but
at the same time less avoidable by the ordinary citizen. McLean and
Tarnopolsky (1977) report on a number of community surveys, indicating
an association between noise and various symptoms. In most of these,
respondents were asked explicitly whether aircraft noise was responsible for
any symptoms reported. OPCS (1971) found that in the higher noise areas,
higher percentages of people reported headaches, restless nights, or being
tense and edgy. Finke et al. (1974) found that irritability rose with the level
of exposure to noise. Kokokusha (1973) studied community samples of
housewives around Osaka airport, and found that those in the high-noise
area reported higher percentages of many symptoms, in particular nervousness, sleep problems, and headaches. However, the validity of these results
is in question because of a possible response bias, due to the direct association of the symptom with aircraft noise.

In a large community survey of the population around three Swiss
airports, Grandjean (1974) used a symptom questionnaire that did not
mention aircraft noise and was distributed separately from sections dealing
with noise annoyance. Whilst the object of the questionnaire may have been
apparent, this source of bias was reduced, and it is noteworthy that Grandjean then found no significant association between aircraft noise and symptoms. Similarly, we (Barker and Tarnopolsky 1978) found that more
affirmative answers were received when aircraft noise was mentioned than
when the questions made no reference to it.

The issue of bias is further illustrated by Kokokusha's observation that
many other symptoms were volunteered by the respondents, who felt that
the noise was also responsible for pregnancy problems, lactation, and
impaired school performance. A survey of GPs' records in high- and low-
noise areas around Amsterdam's airport (Knipschild 1977) reports more
frequent complaints of low back pain and spastic colon in the high-noise
area, although social class differences may play a role in determining these
results. A conservative approach to all these data is the interpretation that
aircraft noise creates strong feelings in people, rather than actually causing
those particular symptoms. On methodological grounds, only symptoms
obtained from subjects who were not informed of the noise aspects of the

interview should be considered. Another possibility is to consider the symptom simultaneously with the subject's reaction to noise (i.e. annoyance). In our own research, we did both.

In areas of different aircraft noise exposure in London, we investigated the presence of 27 common symptoms of psychological and physiological disturbance, each classified as chronic and acute. Only two chronic items were more common in high-noise areas, and both were understandable consequences of exposure: ear problems and ringing in the ears (tinnitus). Instead, the majority of the acute symptoms were more frequent in high-noise areas, although only seven reached an acceptable level of statistical significance: waking at night, irritability, depression, difficulty in getting to sleep, swollen ankles, burns/cuts/minor accidents, and skin troubles. The most evident conclusion of the study was that relationships between noise exposure and symptom prevalence were complex and difficult to investigate. A straightforward comparison of rates, even with the usual epidemiological safeguards, does not suffice (Tarnopolsky et al. 1981). Many chronic symptoms, for instance, were more common in the low-noise area, suggesting a baseline of worse general health there, possibly due to migration or other selective processes. Equally remarkable was the fact that people exhibiting general annoyance by noise also showed greater prevalence of most symptoms, both chronic and acute. The relationships of this finding with exposure levels were very complex, and suggested that some of the effects of noise are mediated by psychological factors (e.g. annoyance) and personal vulnerabilities. The latter may be attributed to the interplay of genetic predisposition, noise sensitivity, personality traits, etc. The next area to be considered, then, is the extent and characteristics of annoyance reactions.

Annoyance

The capacity of noise to bother or disturb is widely recognised in the work of acousticians, sociologists, and psychologists, and is generally termed 'annoyance'. Annoyance may be regarded as a reaction to the intrusion of unwanted stimuli into our private life space. It is, in fact, the most usual community reaction to noise from traffic, railways, aircraft, industry, etc. Noise is unavoidable; it invades the privacy of the home and detracts from the enjoyment of leisure, the satisfaction of work, and the possibility of rest. Control over its sources is limited, and very often involves political activities, e.g. opposition to the development of industries or motorways — in itself a controversial issue.

Vast numbers in the community are disturbed by noise, but not necessarily all, nor to the same degree. Taking the example of aircraft noise, nearly everybody hears it, and some 70 per cent of the population is distinctively affected by it, but only 15 per cent complain that aircraft noise is unbearable. However, these people are not evenly distributed; they range from about 10 per cent 'very annoyed' in relatively quiet areas to more than

50 per cent in the proximity of the airports. Annoyance is present among people of both sexes and all ages. Three different components of it can be identified from the literature:

1. Feelings of being bothered or disturbed, the most general and basic experience
2. The effect of interference with common activities, communication, relaxation, or work
3. Symptomatic aspects such as headaches, tension, irritability.
   The last of these is strikingly similar to emotional reactions that occur under environmental, familial, or social 'stress', but which usually fall short of receiving formal psychiatric diagnosis.

The three layers tend to 'telescope', i.e. people who suffer symptoms are also likely to report interferences and to feel bothered, but exceptions do occur.

In community and occupational surveys, in schools, and in some experimental work, headaches, insomnia, tiredness, irritability, and an increased sensation of pain were found to be associated with noise annoyance (Grandjean 1974; Finke et al. 1974; McKennel 1971; Bryan and Tempest 1973; Crook and Langdon 1974). This symptomatic component is, of course, of the utmost interest to psychiatrists, who have argued that its features may represent a stress reaction, a mild neurotic state, a forerunner of another clinical entity, or a specific form of disorder. Bryan and Tempest (1973) have described 'the classic symptoms of annoyance, i.e. irritability, headaches, depression and a desire to escape from the noise'. Similar temporary conditions have been studied in non-medical frameworks, and described as the consequence of 'transient difficulties in living that beset individuals in the ordinary course of their lives' (Bradburn 1969).

Contemporary interest in the epidemiology of these reactions is witnessed by Wing (1975), who coined the expression 'mental ill health' to describe the condition of large numbers of people who 'complain of less severely disabling psychological conditions, such as a degree of depression or anxiety, nervous or muscular tension, irritability, sleeplessness, or self-consciousness, and these may also be expressed in bodily symptoms, headaches, dyspepsia, and so on'. Shepherd (1974) has drawn attention to the problem of classifying those cases, and to the convenience of placing them outside section V (Mental Disorders) of the International Classification of Diseases. He finds them more akin to 'symptoms and ill-defined conditions' together with nervousness, debility, headaches, and ambiguous depressions. The character and classification of annoyance, e.g. the issue of whether it leads to a definite neurosis or is self-limiting, cannot clearly be solved in the absence of long-term follow-up of relevant cases. Ideally, data should be obtained in situations where noise exposure was withdrawn and later reinstated, in a manner similar to an experiment.

The association between noise, annoyance, and symptoms has been studied in cross-sectional studies, whose results are more interesting than those obtained from looking at noise in isolation. Some time ago, Fog and Jonsson (1968) reported that the proportion of persons with headaches, insomnia, and nervousness increased strongly in the highest annoyance category. In our own work, we found that most symptoms, both chronic and acute, tend to be more frequent in the highest annoyance class, or as annoyance increases, both in high- and in low-noise conditions. Of the 27 symptoms investigated, 21 showed a higher prevalence in the highest annoyance category, and ten were significantly related to annoyance. The indicators of psychological distress were irritability, difficulty in getting to sleep, night waking, depression, and undue tiredness; joint/muscular pains and tinnitus also ranked high in this respect.

The case of irritability demonstrates some of the complexities of the issue (Fig. 9.1). Acute irritability shows an intuitively clear relationship with noise and annoyance; prevalence increases with annoyance, and at any given annoyance level, the rate in high-noise situations exceeds that in low-noise ones. A simple additive model, with both noise and annoyance tending to increase prevalence, accounts for these findings. As a chronic symptom, however, the rates are higher in low-noise situations, so that the highest prevalence is seen in the low-noise/high-annoyance group, and the lowest prevalence in the high-noise/low-annoyance group.

This ordering was examined at length elsewhere (Tarnopolsky et al. 1980), introducing the notion of a personal vulnerability to stress, which would be paramount among those who exhibit intense annoyance in low-noise conditions, and would also justify their high prevalence of symptoms. The lowest prevalence of irritability is seen among those who are not annoyed despite severe noise stress (low annoyance in high noise), i.e. those resilient to stimuli, with lower reactivity than the rest. It is necessary to

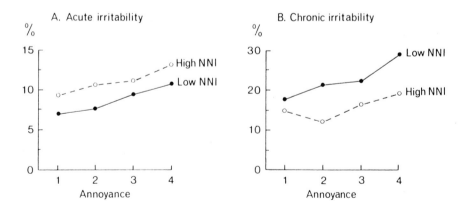

Fig. 9.1 Prevalence of irritability by annoyance, noise, and time of onset of symptom

examine next how this hypothesised vulnerability can be defined and assessed.

There is much evidence that a person's preconceived ideas about an event alter his response to it; this holds for psycho-social responses such as annoyance, as well as for psychophysiological phenomena such as perception. Patterson and Connor (1973) showed that the amount of discussion of aircraft noise indulged in by a person was a predictor of his individual annoyance to the noise. Sorensen (1970), making quantitative measures of annoyance and self-reported sleep disturbance due to aircraft noise, showed in a community survey that both these reactions were significantly altered by propaganda which aimed to alter people's attitudes in favour of the airplanes involved; these changes in response were stable at 3-year follow-up. Several investigators (e.g. Grandjean 1974) have found that employment connected with an airport or with the aircraft industry was a predictor of low individual annoyance towards aircraft noise. Thus, while it seems that propaganda and other influences affecting an individual's attitude towards aircraft noise are capable of altering his risk of annoyance, it is not clear that they alter his risk of morbidity (McLean and Tarnopolsky 1977). The study on residents near Paris-Roissy, using questionnaires, found high levels of annoyance from aircraft noise at night for the first 2 years after the airport opened, after which it decreased to a moderate level, as did the evidence of EEG disturbance (Vallet and Francois 1982).

Sensitivity

Annoyance tends to vary according to the level of noise exposure, but there remain some individuals who report high annoyance under conditions of low noise (hypersensitives), as well as individuals who report little or no annoyance under high-noise conditions (imperturbables) (McKennel 1971). These data introduce the concept of sensitivity, which may be regarded as a predisposition or susceptibility towards becoming annoyed. Bregman and Pearson (1972) proposed describing sensitive people operationally, as follows: 'given two persons rating the same sound, if one person rates the sound higher on any annoyance scale, it is assumed that the person is more sensitive to noise'.

Sensitivity is characterised as a relatively stable personal characteristic, while annoyance is possibly only a temporary reaction to environmental factors (Anderson 1971). Different combinations of personal threshold and intensity of stimulus are possible, and the analogy that an 'anxious' person does not necessarily need major mishaps to precipitate his anxiety may illustrate this point.

It is not clear, however, what sensitivity is about, and different writers have pointed to its relationship with psychological, physiological, and psychiatric variables. Some have shown that noise sensitivity is associated with attitudes towards the environment, and is more marked in subjects who are concerned about or aware of changes in the milieu, who feel frightened of air crashes, or who believe noise may injure their health. Other writers have assessed personality traits, and suggested that the person sensitive to noise is likely to show a fairly high level of empathy, creativity, and intellectual ability (Bryan and Tempest 1973). Broadbent (1972) pursued a different avenue of research when he found a correlation between neuroticism and sensitivity, while Nystrom and Lindegard (1975) incorporated sensitivity to noise in a scale of predisposition to psychiatric disorders. Some psychiatrists may feel justified in arguing that noise sensitivity is an expression of neurotic illness, or of a predisposition to it, or of neuroticism. However, data from our own surveys show that considerable numbers of sensitive subjects are also found among psychiatrically 'well' people. People who score high on sensitivity measures are not invariably found to show higher annoyance measures than the rest (exposure being constant). However, definition and measurement of noise sensitivity have not generally been satisfactory (McLean and Tarnopolsky 1977).

It is possible to hypothesise the existence of different types of sensitivity: one type may be part of psychiatric disorder, but another seems to exist independently of morbidity. A possible way to validate the concept is to search also for physiological concomitants of noise reactivity, e.g. skin conductance, heart rate, and blood pressure — a line of work we are developing now. However defined, sensitivity classifies subjects not only in terms of their annoyance, but also in terms of their health response. Thus annoyance responses to noise are not only dependent on the characteristics of the source of noise, but are also rooted in personality characteristics of which very little is known. There is a minority of people — perhaps 4–6 per cent — who do not show physiological habituation to meaningless noise, but it is not clear whether this is a constitutional trait, or is due to some undetected meaning in the noise (see Addendum).

NOISE AND PSYCHIATRIC DISORDERS

The next question to consider is whether noise is associated not just with some symptoms, but also with the more complex and stable aggregate usually termed 'neurotic disorders'. The evidence from previous research was unsatisfactory, and thus the central aim of the Heathrow survey was to examine this issue.

The identification of psychiatric illness is a very controversial issue (Williams et al. 1980) and diagnosis by an experienced psychiatrist is usually the accepted criterion. This method is impractical for community surveys, and so a screening questionnaire — the General Health Questionnaire (GHQ) (Goldberg 1972), developed to identify non-psychotic disorders in the community — was adopted for use in our studies. Respondents to the GHQ can be classified into those scoring 5+, called 'possible psychiatric cases', and those scoring 0–4, 'possible normals'. A correction factor was used to estimate the proportion of 'confirmed cases' (i.e. those that would be given a diagnosis if assessed in a psychiatric interview).

Both in the pilot and final surveys, we found no overall association between noise exposure and psychiatric morbidity; the percentage of 'possible' and 'confirmed' cases was essentially the same in all noise zones (Table 9.1). Therefore, noise could not be postulated to be a major, clear cause of psychiatric disorders. However, an association between noise and morbidity may be restricted to a sub-group of the population, or masked by the interplay of social and demographic variables.

Table 9.1 Percentage of GHQ scores and of estimated confirmed psychiatric cases by noise exposure

	Noise	and	number	index	
	−35	35–44	45–54	55+	Total
	%	%	%	%	%
Low GHQ scores	78	78	80	77	79
High GHQ scores	22	22	20	23	21
Total	1396	1634	2093	778	5900
	$x^2 = 5.833$, 3 of df (n.s.)				
Estimated confirmed psychiatric cases	27	27	26	27	26

Adapted from Tarnopolsky and Morton Williams 1980

Among a very well defined group (who finished full-time education at age 19+ and/or were in professional occupations) there was a progressively increasing proportion of high GHQ scores as aircraft noise increased (Table 9.2). The fact that a clear positive trend of increasing numbers of cases with

Table 9.2 Percentage of GHQ scores and of estimated confirmed psychiatric cases by noise exposure for respondents who finished full-time education at age 19+ and/or were in professional occupations

	Noise	and	number	index	
	35	35–44	45–54	55+	Total
	%	%	%	%	%
Low GHQ scores	85	79	77	73	79
High GHQ scores	15	21	23	27	21
Total	246	313	345	83	987
	$x^2 = 8.180$; d.f : 3; sig − 5% level				
	x^2 trend; G.98; df: 1 − sig 1% level				
Estimated percentage of psychiatric cases	14	17	18	20	(n.s)

Modified from Tarnopolsky and Morton Williams 1980

increasing noise is restricted to just one population group makes it evident that interactions with socio-demographic variables are to be explored further, and that personal sensitivity and vulnerability factors may play a role in producing these effects. This middle-class phenomenon appears to be largely a social attitude to noise, 'related to the higher standard of amenity that they expect in their home environment, since they are only marginally more sensitive to noise in general' (OPCS 1971). However, 'high GHQ scores' is an heterogeneous measure, made up partly by confirmed cases and partly by people whose symptomatology is not severe or precise enough to be labelled 'neurosis'. The distinction between these two tiers is important, as it seems likely that the latter, less conspicuous phenomenon may be related to annoyance. The statistical and temporal relationships between the two are discussed in detail in Tarnopolsky and Morton-Williams (1980).

Use of medicines and health services

Whilst the GHQ has been shown to be a valid instrument for the screening of morbidity, other indicators speak of the 'illness behaviour' of the individuals, i.e. their ways of seeking and obtaining assistance for their complaints. Indicators such as the consumption of medicines, visits to GPs, or admissions to hospital complete a picture of the morbidity in a population.

Several investigations have related the use of drugs and the contact rate with GPs to the level of aircraft noise. Grandjean (1974) found that the proportion of the population taking drugs was higher in areas with high levels of aircraft noise. Knipschild and Oudshoorn (1977) monitored drug use in two villages, one of which was a control with low aircraft noise, and another where exposure increased after some time. They found that there was no clear change in the low-noise village, but the purchase of sleeping pills, sedatives, antacids, and antihypertensive agents increased with continued exposure in the high-noise village. Both Grandjean and Knipschild found an association between the GP contact rate and the level of aircraft noise exposure. Relster (1975) found that various indicators of morbidity and use of health services were related to complaints of road traffic noise (i.e. annoyance), but few were related to the noise level itself. Our findings are in accordance with the latter. In the Heathrow airport survey (Watkins et al. 1981), various health care indicators were used, namely the use of any drug, of psychotropic drugs, or of self-prescribed drugs in the last two weeks; visits to a GP in the last two weeks; attendances at an out-patient clinic or in-patient episodes in the last three months; and the use of various community health and social services in the last month (e.g. meals on wheels, health visitors). There was no clear trend for any of these six indicators in relation to differing levels of noise, and where any departures from uniformity occurred, they were generally in the direction opposite to that predicted, i.e. greater use in lower-noise zones.

Mention has already been made of a baseline of worse general health in low-noise environments, and it can be argued that this has concealed the hypothesised noise effects. This impression is supported by the discovery of some associations between health care and annoyance, (results akin to the relationship between annoyance and symptoms, or GHQ score): the use of psychotropic drugs increases significantly with increasing annoyance, while out-patient attendance and the GP contact rate are highest among those at the top of the annoyance scale, but are not always statistically significant.

The relationships between health care indicators and annoyance were different in high- and low-noise environments. Use of medicines or services increases with annoyance in high noise; but in low noise, they are sometimes stable and sometimes rise with annoyance. Watkins et al. (1981) examined the complex interaction found, and warned that when assessing environmental effects on health, it is crucial to consider not only the physical stressor, but also the subjective response to it (in this case, the annoyance). They contend that acute symptoms and self-medication rates reflect a low level of disturbance, which is directly produced by environmental stress.

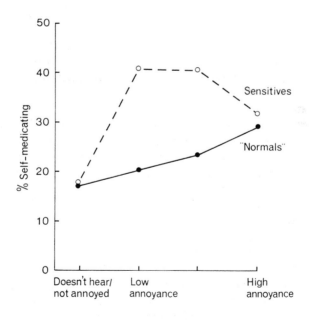

Fig. 9.2 Proportion self-medicating in high noise

Chronic symptoms of psychiatric disorders as measured by the GHQ, and use of health services demand another explanation, which must include the role of personal vulnerabilities to disease and to the milieu (as explained before in relation to chronic irritability).

It is opportune to illustrate now how noise sensitivity is a factor that potentiates not only the noise annoyance, but also the health response, using the case of self-medication (Fig. 9.2). In low-noise situations, self-medication rates do not change as annoyance increases. (and were omitted from the figure), while in high noise, self-medication rises with annoyance. However, people sensitive to noise react more intensely and more quickly: their rates are not only higher than those of the non-sensitive, they also reach their peak at lower levels of noise disturbance.

Noise and admissions to psychiatric hospitals

Several studies investigated the controversial effects of noise on admission to psychiatric hospitals. Both Abey-Wickrama et al. (1969) working in the environs of Heathrow Airport, and Meecham and Smith (1977) near Los Angeles airport, reported that high exposure resulted in more hospital admissions. However, other researchers have been critical of many methodological aspects of these studies. Gattoni and Tarnopolsky (1973) repeated the Abey-Wickrama study around Heathrow airport, using data from the same psychiatric hospital (Springfield), but covering a larger catchment area, for the two-year period from 1970. They found small increases in admissions from higher-noise areas, which were statistically non-significant; the postulated noise effects faded away when the methodology of the study was tighter. Frerichs et al. (1980) attempted a complete re-analysis of the results obtained by Meecham and Smith (1977), but the data were not available; they noted, however, that failure to control for any confounding variables made the results particularly suspect.

In an attempt to clarify this muddled issue, we analysed data from 9000 admissions to three large psychiatric hospitals over a period of four years. The admissions were classified according to the aircraft noise exposure of their home address, using the Noise and Number Index. Age-standardised rates were calculated, divided by sex and marital status; stringent sampling techniques were used and were controlled for possible confounding variables. Data from Springfield Hospital gave the disconcerting result that rates actually increased as noise became lower (Jenkins et al. 1979). In this case, the low-noise areas were also central urban districts, where high admission rates would in any case be expected, and it became evident that noise could not override other variables affecting admission.

In the final study, Springfield Hospital was compared with the other two, St. Bernard's and Holloway Sanatorium. In these latter two, aircraft noise was associated with higher admission rates. We concluded, however, that in all three hospitals, the trends of admission could be attributed to non-noise factors characteristic of the population; we held to the view that the effect of noise, if any, could only be a moderate one, influencing other causal variables but not overriding them.

We searched then for interactions with socio-economic characteristics of the areas of residence, using log-linear models. These produced ample evidence of complex effects between noise, admissions, and demographic and social features of the subjects and of the population. It was characteristic that findings in one district were not substantiated in another; the associations between noise and admissions were only present in some population groups and in some districts. Noise was more likely to affect admissions of those aged 45 and older (Springfield) and 45+ not-married (Holloway), in the highest exposure zone. Districts prone to show noise effects had high proportions of people living alone (St Bernard's), or of immigrants (Springfield), or of professionals and managers (Holloway). These features describe the areas rather than the subjects, and any interpretation of the results should avoid the ecological fallacy of attributing the same characteristics to the individuals admitted.

TERATISM AND MORTALITY

An issue that was investigated with similar techniques is the effect of aircraft noise on births and mortality rates. Increased aircraft noise has been associated with pregnancy complications and with decreases in the health and survival of newborn infants (Ando and Hattori 1973, 1977; Edmonds et al. 1979; Jones and Tauscher 1978).

Meecham and Shaw (1979) report an association between increased aircraft noise levels and increased death rates due to strokes and cirrhosis of the liver, but Frerichs et al. (1980) re-analysed the data, controlling for the effects of age, race, and sex, and found no differences in the mortality rates of the airport and control areas respectively. Whilst studies have investigated relationships between teratism, mortality, and aircraft noise, the evidence is in no way conclusive that there is any association between them. The need for caution in formulating conclusions from exploratory research, emphasised earlier à propos the initial studies on psychiatric admissions, should perhaps be repeated here.

OVERVIEW

This chapter has been concerned with the effects of noise, in particular aircraft noise, on mental health. The evidence reviewed has ranged from the impact of noise on organisms in controlled laboratory conditions to community surveys and studies of hospital admissions. It is hardly surprising that the picture which emerges is complex.

Noise causes a number of physiological reactions, well documented in laboratory experiments, which typically are short-term adaptive responses, and the extent to which these can develop into pathological reactions is unknown. It also causes a psychological reaction, termed 'annoyance'. Whilst a strong association exists between noise exposure and annoyance, there remain individuals who are highly annoyed by low levels of noise. Such people have been termed 'sensitive'. Noise-sensitive and noise-insensitive people show broadly different patterns of reaction to noise, their reactions being correspondingly high or low at identical levels of exposure.

Though intense industrial noise has long been known to cause deafness, the effects of environmental noise on the general population's mental health has only been explored recently. The general pattern is that fewer health variables are associated with noise *per se* than with annoyance, so that whilst noise may contribute directly to the development of some acute symptoms and to self-medication, most other effects are only evident in the presence of annoyance. Thus, people who report high annoyance also exhibit both acute and chronic symptoms, consume more psychotropic drugs, and also probably attend GPs and out-patient clinics more frequently than those who are not annoyed.

The results from a general population sample, examined with a psychiatric screening instrument, show that noise *per se*, in the community at large, does not seem to be a frequent, severe, pathogenic factor in causing psychiatric illness. However, the data do suggest that certain groups within the community are at greater risk than others, and annoyance remains the main social and medical problem produced by noise, being strongly related to noise exposure. The components of annoyance, i.e. feeling bothered, activity interference, and common psychosomatic symptoms, are not easily classifiable, belonging in an area which is 'minor' compared with other psychiatric problems. Also, little is known about the evolution of annoyance; the idea that it may develop into neurotic disorders is only hypothetical at this stage. These facts should not be used to belittle the problem though, since the subjects who exhibit annoyance reactions certainly suffer from them and require attention and, if possible, relief; further research should be directed into the structure and origin of annoyance and sensitivity. Such research should aim to link tightly controlled laboratory experiments to community research, in such a way as to provide information about high-risk groups, and to provide validation for the concepts of annoyance and sensitivity.

As far as more severe disorders are concerned, noise is not a major influence on hospital admissions; some initial studies, which showed a very strong positive relationship, were not confirmed, or were questioned on methodological grounds. Recent surveys have shown that the association between noise and admissions was restricted to specific sub-groups; interactions were found between noise and different social factors in different districts. The relationship between mortality, teratism, and noise is similarly obscured by lack of necessary control groups and by inadequate methodology. However, people who are already affected by a psychiatric disturbance react more intensely than normals to noise, just as they would also probably suffer more from many other adverse personal and social circumstances.

It seems clear that whatever relationships do exist need to be investigated further. Noise occasionally appears to affect health directly, but generally it operates through the mediation of psychological and constitutional factors of which little is known. Nevertheless, it may be significant that in the psychoanalytical literature, references to the communicative value or symbolic meaning of noise are broadly associated with threatening experiences.

REFERENCES

Abey-Wickrama I, a' Brook M F, Gattoni F E G, Herridge C F 1969 Mental hospital admissions and aircraft noise. Lancet ii: 1275–1277
Alexandre A 1973 Decision criteria based on spatio-temporal comparisons of surveys of an aircraft noise. In: Ward W D (ed) Proceedings of the International Conference on Noise as a Public Health Problem, EPA 550/9-73-008, Washington DC
Anderson C M B 1971 The measurement of attitude to noise and noises. National Physical Acoustics report, Ac 52
Ando Y, Hattori H 1973 Statistical studies on the effects of intense noise during human fetal life. Sound & Vibration 27: 101–110
Ando Y, Hattori H 1977 Effects of noise on human placental lactogen (HPL) levels in maternal plasma. British Journal of Obstetrics & Gynaecology 84: 115–118
Anticaglia J R, Cohen A 1970 Extra-auditory effects of noise as a health hazard. American Industrial Hygiene Association Journal 31: 277
Atherley G R C, Gibbons S L, Powell J A 1970 Moderate acoustic stimuli: the interrelation of subjective importance and certain physiological changes. Ergonomics 13: 536–545
Barker S M, Tarnopolsky A 1978 Assessing bias in surveys of symptoms attributed to noise. Journal of Sound and Vibration 59: 349–354
Bradburn N M 1969 The structure of psychological well-being. NORC Monograph, Aldine, Chicago
Bregman H L, Pearson R G 1972 Development of a noise annoyance sensitivity scale. NASA Report CR, Washington DC
Broadbent D E 1972 Individual differences in annoyance by noise. Sound 6: 56–61
Bryan M E, Tempest W 1973 Are our noise laws adequate? Applied Acoustics 6: 219–232
Bugard P, Souras H, Valade P, Coste E, Salle J 1953 Le syndrome de fatigue et les troubles auditifs des metteurs au point d'aviation. La Semaine des Hopitaux 29: 65–70
Cohen A 1969 Effects of noise on psychological state. In: Noise as a Public Health Hazard, Report No 4, American Speech and Hearing Association, Washington DC
Cohen H H et al 1973 Noise effects, arousal, and human processing task difficulty and performance. Human Factors, North Carolina State University Publication
Cohen S, Evans G W, Krantz D S, Stokols D 1980 Physiological, Motivational, and cognitive effects of aircraft noise on children. American Psychologist 35: 231–243
Cooper A F, Curry A R, Kay D W K, Garside R F, Roth M 1974 Hearing loss in the paranoid and affective psychoses of the elderly. Lancet ii: 851–854
Crook M A, Langdon F J 1974 The effects of aircraft noise in schools around London Airport. Journal of Sound and Vibration 34: 221–232
Dickson E D, Chadwick D L 1951 Observations on disturbance of equilibrium and other symptoms induced by jet engine noise. Journal of Laryngology & Otology 65: 154–165
Drettner B, Hedstrand H, Kolckhoff I et al 1975 Cardiovascular risk factors and hearing loss. A study of 1000 fifty-year-old men. Acta Otolaryngol, Stockholm 79: 366–371
Edmonds L D, Layde P M, Erickson J D 1979 Airport noise and teratogenesis. Archives of Environmental Health 34: 243–247

Falk S A 1972 Combined effects of noise and ototoxic drugs. Environmental Health Perspectives 2: 5–22

Fearn R W 1972 Noise levels in youth clubs. Journal of Sound and Vibration 22: 127–128

Fearn R W 1973 Pop music and hearing damage. Journal of Sound and Vibration 29: 396–397

Fearn R W 1974 Level limits on pop music. Leeds Polytechnic Department of Architectural Studies Report A5 74/12

Finke H O, Guski R, Martin R, Rohrmann B, Schumer R, Schumer-Kohrs A 1974 Effects of aircraft noise on man. Proceedings of the Symposium on Noise in Transportation, Section III, paper 1, Institute of Sound & Vibration Research, Southampton

Fog H, Jonsson E 1968 Traffic noise in residential areas. National Swedish Institute for Building Research Report 36E

Frerichs R R, Beeman B L, Coulson A H 1980 Los Angeles Airport noise and mortality — fault analysis and public policy. American Journal of Public Health 70: 357–362

Gattoni F, Tarnopolsky A 1973 Aircraft noise and psychiatric morbidity. Psychological Medicine 3: 516–520

Glass D C, Singer J E 1972 Urban stress. Academic Press, New York and London

Glorig A 1971 Non-auditory effects of noise exposure. Sound & Vibration 5: 28–29

Goldberg D P 1972 The detection of psychiatric illness by questionnaire. Oxford University Press, London

Granati A, Angelepi F, Lenzi R 1959 L'influenza dei rumori sul sistema nervoso. Folio Medica 42: 1313–1325

Grandjean E 1960 Physiologische und psycho-physiologische Wirkungen des Larms. Menschen Umwelt 4: Quoted in Cohen A 1968, Transactions of the New York Academy of Sciences 30: 910–918

Grandjean E 1974 Sozio-Psychologische Untersuchumgen vor den Fluglarms. Eidgenossisches Lustamt, Bundeshaus, Berne

HMSO 1976 Occupational deafness. Cmnd 5461, London

Jansen G 1969 Effects of noise on physiological state. American Speech and Hearing Association Report No 4: 89–98

Jenkins L M, Tarnopolsky A, Hand D J, Barker S M 1979 Comparison of three studies of aircraft noise and psychiatric hospital admissions conducted in the same area. Psychological Medicine 9: 681–693

Jeter I K 1976 Unidentified hearing impairment among psychiatric patients. American Speech & Hearing Association 18: 843–845

Jones F N, Tauscher J 1978 Residence under an airport landing pattern as a factor in teratism. Archives of Environmental Health 33: 10–12

Jonsson E, Arvidsson O, Berglund K, Kajland A 1973 Methodological aspects of studies of community response to noise. In: Proceedings of the International Congress on Noise as a Public Health Problem, Dubrovnik, 611–617, US Environmental Protection Agency Publications 550/973–008, Washington DC

Jonsson E, Sorensen S 1973 Adaptation to community noise — a case study. Journal of Sound & Vibration 26: 571–575

Kay D W K, Bergmann K, Foster E M, McKechnie A A, Roth M 1970 Mental illness and hospital usage in the elderly: a random sample followed up. Comprehensive Psychiatry, 11: 26–35

Kay D W K, Roth M 1961 Environmental and hereditary factors in the schizophrenias of old age. Journal of Mental Science 107: 649–686

Knipschild P, Oudshoorn N 1977 Medical effects of aircraft noise. General practice survey. International Archives of Occupational and Environmental Health 40: 191–196 & 197–200

Kokokusha D 1973 Report on investigation of living environment around Osaka International Airport. Association for the Prevention of Aircraft Nuisance, Japan

Kryter K D 1970 The effects of noise on man, part III. Academic Press, New York

Lynn R 1966 Attention, arousal and the orientation reaction. Pergamon, Oxford

Mahapatra S B 1974 Psychiatric and psychosomatic illness in the deaf. British Journal of Psychiatry 125: 450–451

McCoy D F, Plotkin W H 1967 Audiometric screening of a psychiatric population in a large state hospital. Journal of Audio Research 7: 327–334

McKennel A C 1971 Measurements of annoyance due to aircraft noise. In: OPCS 1971 Second Survey of Aircraft Noise Annoyance Around London (Heathrow) Airport, HMSO, London

McKennel A C 1973 Psycho-social factors in aircraft noise annoyance. In: Proceedings of the International Congress on Noise as a Public Health Problem, Dubrovnik, 627–644, US Environmental Protection Agency Publication 550/973-008, Washington DC

McLean E K, Tarnopolsky A 1977 Noise, discomfort and mental health. Psychological Medicine 7: 19–62

Meecham W C, Shaw N 1979 Effects of jet noise on mortality rates. British Journal of Audiology 13: 77–80

Meecham W C, Smith H G 1977 Effects of jet aircraft noise on mental hospital admissions. British Journal of Audiology II: 81–85

Miller J D 1974 Effects of noise on people. Journal of the Acoustical Society of America 56: 729–764

Mykleburst H R 1964 The psychology of deafness. Grune & Stratton, New York

Nystrom S, Lindegard B 1975 Predisposition for mental syndromes. Acta Psychiatrica Scandinavica 51: 69–76

OPCS 1971 Second Survey of Aircraft Noise Annoyance around London (Heathrow) Airport. HMSO, London

Patterson H P, Connor W K 1973 Community responses to aircraft noise in large and small cities in the US. In: Proceedings of the International Congress on Noise as a Public Health Problem

Relster E 1965 Traffic noise annoyance. Polyteknisk Forlag, Lyngby

Richter-Heinrich E, Sprungh 1969 Psychophysiological untersuchungen un anfangestadium der essentiellen hypertonie. Zutschrift fur die Gesamte Innere Medizin und Ihre Grenygebiete 24: 17–21

Selye H 1956 The stress of life. McGraw-Hill, New York

Shatalov N N, Saitanov A, Glotova K 1962 On the problem of the state of the cardiovascular system during the action of continuous noise. Laboratory of Hygiene and Occupational Diseases 6: 10–14

Shepherd M 1974 Pollution and mental health, with particular references to the problem of noise. Psychiatrica Clinica 7: 226–236

Singerman B, Riedner E, Folstein M 1980 Emotional disturbances in hearing clinic patients. British Journal of Psychiatry 137: 58–63

Sokolov Y N 1963 Perception and the conditioned reflex. Pergamon, Oxford. p 46

Sorensen S 1970 On the possibilities of changing the annoyance reaction to noise by changing the attitudes to the source of annoyance. Nordisk Hygicasc Tidshrift, suppl 1, 1–76

Tarnopolsky A, Barker S M, Wiggins R D, Mclean E K 1978 The effect of aircraft noise on the mental health of a community sample: a pilot study. Psychological Medicine 8: 219–223

Tarnopolsky A, Hand D J, McLean E K, Roberts H, Wiggins R D 1979 Validity and uses of a screening questionnaire (GHQ) in the community. British Journal of Psychiatry 134: 508–515

Tarnopolsky A, McLean E K 1976 Noise as psychosomatic hazard. In: Hill O (ed) Modern trends in psychosomatic medicine. Butterworth, London

Tarnopolsky A, Morton Williams J 1980 Aircraft noise and prevalence of psychiatric disorders. Social and Community Planning Research, London

Tarnopolsky A, Watkins G, Hand D 1980 Aircraft noise and mental health: I Prevalence of individual symptoms. Psychological Medicine 10: 683–698

US Bureau of Census 1973 Annual housing survey: 1973 US and regions: Part B. Indicators of housing and neighbourhood quality. Current Housing Report Series H-150073-B, US Government Printing Office, Washington

Vallet M, Francois J 1982 Evaluation physiologigue et psychologigue de l'avion sur le sommeil. Travail Humain 45: 155–168

Ward B, Dubos R 1972 Only one earth. Norton, New York

Watkins G, Tarnopolsky A, Jenkins L M 1981 Aircraft noise and mental health II: use of medicines and health care services. Psychological Medicine 11: 155–68

Weinstein N D 1976 Human evaluations of environment noise. In: Craik K, Zube E H
(eds) Perceiving environmental quality. New York
Williams P, Tarnopolsky A, Hand D 1980 Case definition and case identification in
psychiatric epidemiology: a review and assessment. Psychological Medicine 10: 101–114
Wing J 1975 The nature of psychiatric morbidity in general population samples.
Unpublished contribution to World Psychiatric Association Symposium on Social Causes
of Psychiatric Disorders, Yugoslavia

ADDENDUM

Two further studies on noise sensitivity have recently been completed. Stansfield et al (1984a) interviewed a sample of women, of varying noise sensitivity, 3 years after the subjects had participated in the 1977 West London survey. Groups of high, intermediate and low noise sensitivity respectively were compared for psychiatric disorder, personality, and reactivity to other sensory stimuli; the highly noise-sensitive women showed significantly more psychiatric symptoms, higher neuroticism scores, and greater reactivity to the other stimuli than those of low noise sensitivity. Secondly, high, intermediate and low noise-sensitive women were compared on measures of blood pressure, heart rate, skin conductance, hearing threshold, level of loudness which they found uncomfortable, and magnitude estimation of six tones (Stansfield et al, 1984b). These physiological measures did not clearly distinguish groups of different noise sensitivity, except that highly noise-sensitive women had consistently slower heart rates; noise sensitivity was not related to auditory threshold. In the area with high exposure to aircraft noise, there were significantly more skin conductance responses than in the area with low aircraft noise, irrespective of subjects' noise sensitivity; this may be the result of chronic exposure to high aircraft noise.

REFERENCES

Stansfield S A, Clark C R, Jenkins L M, Tarnopolsky A (1984a) Measurement of psychiatric
disorder and personality. Psychological Medicine (in press)
Stansfield S A, Clark C R, Turpin G, Jenkins L M, Tarnopolsky A (1984b) Measurement of
psychophysiological indices. Psychological Medicine (in press)

Mental illness and urban disaster

> The Paris slums are a gathering-place for eccentric people — people who have fallen into solitary, half-mad grooves of life and given up trying to be normal or decent. Poverty frees them from ordinary standards of behaviour, just as money frees people from work.
>
> George Orwell, 1933.

The Big City is a unique institution; it is the nest in which concepts and ideas are laid and events hatched. Civilisation, government, progress, structure and ferment, riot, epidemic and revolution are all characteristics of big cities, rather than of other modes of living. However, our attitude towards and expectations of the Big City have changed. In mediaeval, and especially renaissance times, the social ideal of perfection was contained in living in a beautiful city, as exemplified by Cannaletto's Venice. This was based on a number of models: Jewish imagery — Zion, the city of God; the Greek concept of the well-ordered city state; Rome as the cultural, administrative, military, and later, ecclesiastical centre of the known world; and the Christian ideal — the description in the book of Revelation of Heaven being a 'city four-square'. The Renaissance idyll always contained order and architecture — an urban Elysium, quite unlike our modern idea of bliss, which is almost always rural.

There was an important practical reason behind these dreams concerning the planning of the city. Its physical structure was a visual symbol of the state of society; it conveyed the ideal in religion, culture and social order, so that a magnificent and beautiful city became the permanent legacy from a ruler who could both impose his will and be creative. The material character of the city is designed to produce an emotional climate; it is inevitable that cities will create a distinctive atmosphere, and if planning does not aim at harmony, then the resultant structural and architectural discord will form a background mood of hopelessness and confusion.

Architectural dreams were portrayed, for example, in Canaletto's depiction of the magnificence of Venice, or in Lorenzetti's picture, 'The effects of good government in the city'. There was no demarcation between the artist and the craftsman or builder, for the artist's vision became actuality in the city. Such idealism has not been confined to the past; in our century also, planners have devised their own ideal for social order. An example,

271

is Le Corbusier's building, the *Unité d'habitation*, to house 1600 people in rectangular interlocking flats, each on two storeys, with shared facilities such as shops, day nurseries, cafeteria, gymnasium, and roof garden (Hitchcock 1963). The expressed intention was that the physical structure should produce social benefits; the relationships and quality of life of the residents should be enhanced by the design of the building.

The planner's dream so easily became a nightmare, however. Quarry Hill Flats in Leeds was an experiment in which the occupants of working-class slums were rehoused in high blocks, surrounded by open spaces; 3250 people lived on 26 acres in 938 Units, with 29 shops on the site; 82 per cent of the total area was devoted to open space. This housing scheme, built in 1935 and heralded with international acclaim, was a bold and brilliant failure (Johns 1965). Its forbidding castle walls dictated the lifestyle of the inhabitants, who felt themselves to be prisoners in their little flats; the open area did not belong to anyone and became vandalised. It became an intolerable place in which to live, and was eventually razed to the ground by a courageous City Council.

In her detailed case history of Quarry Hill Flats, Ravetz (1974) showed that the estate was uniquely typical of large housing projects of its age. The Flats began as a mechanistic expression of social engineering — mass housing to replace 19th century back-to-back slums. The original population of the Quarry Hill area was entirely dispersed, and all the old housing razed to the ground before the new estate was built. If any of the original inhabitants subsequently returned to the new Flats, it was quite fortuitous; there was therefore no established community for people to join as they moved into the estate. Neither was there flexibility in the design of the project; it was assumed that the original plan with crèche, health centre, recreation ground and community hall would function satisfactorily from the start, and not need to be changed. When the flats were occupied, the greatest problems were those in the public realm, to do with shared facilities such as playspace and rubbish disposal; the bureaucratic machinery of the Local Authority was found to be poor at solving such crises, which arise suddenly and need rapid attention. The inhabitants found the estate much too big to identify with and individual tenants only 'colonised' a restricted area. This whole project was imposed upon the inhabitants as a *model* environment and was therefore very difficult to modify, renew, or personalise; it could not function as a *natural* habitat. The problem for the future is to convert such bureaucratic enterprises into a community which is administered locally, and to allow individuals to create their own living space.

The city as a concept, though, has long since lost its idealism; pestilence and infective epidemics have been replaced by social and psychological problems, so that many aspects of housing become relevant for mental health. Emotional distress is common in women living in big cities who have pre-school children at home; in a survey in London, Moss and Plewis (1977) found that 52 per cent of such mothers described significant distress in the 12 months prior to interview. Women living with young children, especially if lacking a supportive relationship from a man, have serious limitations of their social freedom and interactions. If there is also a history of early bereavement, and the social and financial constraints of not going to work, an urban woman is highly likely to demonstrate significant depressive symptoms (Brown & Harris 1978). In another study, women in an urban environment showed higher scores than men for anxiety, depression, and such vegetative symptoms as loss of appetite, somatic preoccupation, sleep difficulties, and fatiguability (Benfari et al. 1972).

Development of modern cities is often piecemeal, and commercial in its aspirations, so that they become at best a convenience, and at worst a dangerous slum; the most conspicuous social feature is conflict of interest and of objectives, at all social levels, and between all types of social groupings. A further characteristic is the presence of minority groups, who can establish a foothold in cities, whereas they may not be able to do so in the country, but once established, may provoke more or less violent opposition. The centrality of conflict in sociological groupings was recognised at the beginning of this century by Simmel (1908), who saw hostility as part of the primary nature of human beings living in groups, and conflict over opposed causes as a necessary sequel to the human characteristic of espousing different political parties.

How big is a 'big city' though? This is not just determined by the size of population or surface area, but more by psychological factors. A big city is large enough in which to lose one's identity; large enough to create, in Durkheim's sense (1897), a state of 'anomie'. This concept, implying a society which had lost its capacity for social restraint or regulation, has been closely linked to a state of moral poverty (Lukes 1973). Anomie, overcrowding, and poverty appear to be three of the most destructive elements of big cities in which lifestyle, political affiliation, range of work, leisure activities, and often predominant beliefs show a different distribution from those found in a market town or rural community. A significant proportion of people living in inner areas of our major cities continue to suffer from multiple deprivation — that is, problems of poverty, unemployment, poor housing, ill-health, and low educational attainment (Bor 1973).

MENTAL HEALTH AND BIG CITIES

The inhabitants of big cities are prone to epidemic psychopathology. For example, Cohn (1957) describes how floridly disordered and highly contagious millennial movements spread like forest fires through the dispossessed urban proletariat of central Europe during the late middle ages. This was closely associated with the growing population of these cities, as landless labourers were forced out of rural habitation to seek work in the developing commercial centres. In our century, an association has been found between living in a big city on the one hand and certain patterns of pathological behaviour and/or distribution of psychiatric illnesses.

A classical demonstration of spatial patterning for physical illness in the city was the work of Snow on the epidemiology of cholera in London in 1849 (Snow 1965). For psychiatric illness, not only is the process of spatial patterning important, but a satisfactory methodology for the identification of cases must precede the geographical aspects. When case identification was standardised, about 2 per cent of urban populations in both the UK and the USA were found to have been in touch with psychiatric services during one year (Wing 1976). The distribution of pathological behaviour has been examined within cities: for suicide, in London by Sainsbury (1955), and in England & Wales by Whitlock (1973); and for milder categories of behaviour, in Brighton by Bagley et al. (1973). Statistical and spatial relationships have been elicited between the presence of major social problems, such as crime and delinquency, and the rates for ill-health and mortality in cities (Castle & Gittus 1957; Giggs 1979). Relationships have also been derived between the quality of housing and other social variables, and the frequency of depressive illness in Plymouth (Dean & James 1980; see Chapter 14). Where studies have been carried out on the prevalence of major psychiatric illnesses and mental retardation in different areas of big cities, an association has usually been found between higher rates for such pathology and living in inner city areas characterised by lower income and a greater degree of social disorganisation (Faris & Dunham 1939; Hare 1956; Bagley et al. 1973; Lei et al. 1974). For manic-depressive psychosis, however, no such socio-economic association has been found (Faris & Dunham; Bagley et al.; Levy & Rowitz 1968; Weissman & Myers 1978). Rowitz & Levy (1968) commented, from their work in Chicago, that 'a relationship exists between urban social structure and social disorganisation. Areas of high social disorganisation also tend to be the ones where the highest rates of mental illness, as measured by reported admissions to public or private mental institutions, occur'.

What are the pathoplastic factors, then, if such exist in modern cities? Overcrowding, poverty, submersion in a counter-culture from which there is no escape, loneliness, isolation from peers and relatives — all these and many more have been implicated. It is difficult to argue with Durkheim's concept of anomie — that it is not just isolation but also separation from traditional social mores that is destructive.

> The shame of our cities today is the priority given to material over human values, the price that we pay for this is planning where joy is no consideration; it is fear, it is the maldevelopment of our people. The shame of our cities is greater because here are created our alienated and our dispossessed, our superfluous ones, our aged, our poor, our infirm, our deserted, our drug addicts, our derelicts, our criminals, our outcasts of all kinds (Duhl 1968).

Such views would imply that to improve mental health, there must be concern with the structure of society in the city, rather than merely with the provision of treatment facilities, yet the resources required for this are economic and political, more than medical (Greenblatt 1970).

The mental health problems of the inner city would therefore be not so much technological, as fundamentally socio-psychological in nature, and in response, all sorts of structures have been proposed to improve the condition of the community; for example, in New York, the following: Family Centres, Child Centres, Neighbourhood Council, a Black American League, a Spanish-American League, and a Therapeutic Agency for Mental Illness. 'An inner city is much like a colonised country. The native is exploited by outer factions for his manpower, money, and in some instances, his political influence' (Scagliola 1971). According to this view, not only are individuals mentally disordered, but the community itself is ill, and therefore social and legislative reforms are needed to change living conditions, remove health hazards, and prevent disease by improved education.

Srole (1972) considered that the poor circumstances of inner city life were results rather than causes, and that the pathogenic factor was the immobility of society, in which its members were held as 'local captives'. The present institutional rigidities of American society were depriving people of the option of moving upward economically and outward in social space, so that the central thrust in urban society should be to allow greater social mobility. However, social mobility may be a consequence of better-than-average mental and physical health, and the lack of mobility found associated with psychiatric illness may be a manifestation of the 'learned helplessness' found as a feature of reactive depression (Seligman 1975).

Although this approach of finding associations between psychiatric illness and the major deficiencies of cities, together with the search for major political and social solutions, is important, in practice the links are often unproved, and improvements in the state of those living in the inner city have more often been based on social argument than psychiatric service planning. Therefore, it seems most profitable to concentrate upon more specific psychiatric disorder in urban settings (Dohrenwend & Dohrenwend 1974). The remainder of this chapter is devoted, therefore, to two more specific issues which it is hoped will serve as models both of the social precipitation of urban mental health problems, and also for ways of looking at practical measures which may be used to redress them. These issues are a study of the referrals in cities to psychiatric services from the police, and an examination of the psychological effects and management of major urban disaster.

PSYCHIATRIC REFERRALS TO THE POLICE

For two reasons, looking at those individuals who show behaviour in a public place is relevant for the study of psychiatric illness in the big city — disorder in public is a common manifestation of such illness, and it is most likely to occur in the disorganised but densely populated areas of the inner city. One accessible method of examining such public disorder makes use of information concerning the referral of disturbed individuals by the police to social and psychiatric services. Patients reaching treatment facilities in this way are often amongst the most acutely disturbed admissions to psychiatric hospitals. A high rate of police referral for the mentally disordered occurs with urban disorganisation, and characteristically occurs in the decaying parts of big cities, which have poor housing and multi-occupation, and among lonely isolated people, often from minority communities (Sims and Symonds 1975). The patient population is in many ways similar to those people, admitted to psychiatric hospitals, who are of 'no fixed abode' (Berry & Orwin 1966). This is also a problem characteristically occurring in big cities and much less common in smaller cities and towns — relatively much more common in Birmingham (population 1 000 000) than Coventry (population 340 000). Disturbance in the patient may reflect conditions of social disorganisation; an upset in the internal balance of forces in the individual is often closely related to disturbances in the field of forces by which he is surrounded (Caplan 1969).

Park & Burgess (1925) described how a city (based upon Chicago) may be represented diagramatically in concentric circles, with different functions of the city and types of residence occurring as one proceeds peripherally

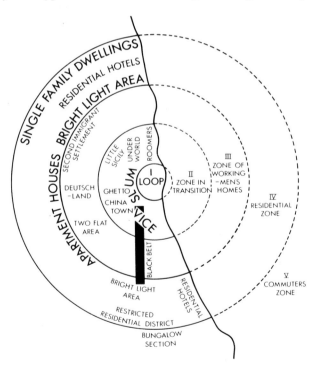

Fig. 10.1 Zoning of a city, based on Chicago (Park and Burgess 1925)

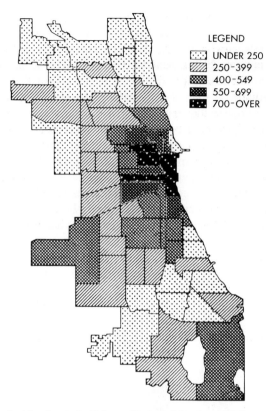

LEGEND

- ⬚ UNDER 250
- ▨ 250-399
- ▦ 400-549
- ■ 550-699
- ▩ 700-OVER

Fig. 10.2 Rates of schizophrenia in Chicago (Faris and Dunham 1939)

through the different zones. This is illustrated in Fig. 10.1. Faris & Dunham (1939) carried out a study of illness according to this model, and their rates for schizophrenia in Chicago are shown in Fig. 10.2. This demonstrates that people suffering from schizophrenia in Chicago were overwhelmingly concentrated (in terms of their residence) in the 'transitional zone', described by Park & Burgess. The distribution of mental illnesses in Chicago over 40 years has changed according to Levy & Rowitz (1973), but some of the same phenomena can be generalised to other large cities.

Psychiatric referrals from the police in the city of Birmingham, UK over a 12-year period were studied by Sims &Symonds (1975). The police may either invite the person whom they believe to be mentally ill into the police station for further investigation informally, or they may use Section 136 of the Mental Health Act, 1959 (Kelleher & Copeland 1972). The former was the method used in Birmingham, and the number of such referrals from the police to psychiatrists was found to rise steadily over a decade. In one year, 224 patients were referred by the police; of these, 20 individuals were referred on a total of 48 occasions. The mean age for males was 39 years and for females 40 years. Using Park & Burgess's model, as in Fig. 10.3, all police referrals were zoned by place of residence; 70 per cent of patients lived in Birmingham, 20 per cent were described as of no fixed abode, 7 per cent were resident outside the city, and 3 per cent lived in a hostel or hospital. Zoning for the city of Birmingham was based upon postal district. When data for those living in the city were examined, 52 per cent of the police referral patients were resident in the inner zone at the time of the referral, whereas only 7 per cent of the city population lived in that zone; 29 per cent of patients and approximately 22 per cent of the city population lived in the middle zone; 18 per cent of the police referrals lived in the outer zone, compared with 70 per cent of the city population; very few people lived in the city centre (1 per cent of patients and about 1 per cent of the city population). The police referral patients were overwhelmingly concentrated in the 'inner' or transitional zone.

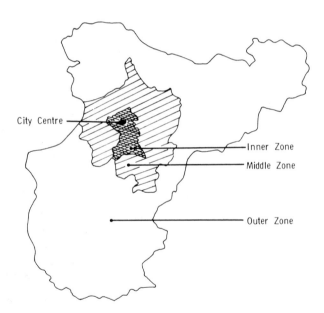

City Centre

Inner Zone

Middle Zone

Outer Zone

Fig. 10.3 Zones of the city of Birmingham based on postcode districts

Disordered persons are usually taken to the police station nearest to where they are found. There is a high concentration of police stations in the city centre, and it is higher in the inner zone than more peripherally. Despite this, there was a tendency for most cases to have occurred at City centre police stations (9.0 cases per station), and progressively less at inner zone stations (6.7 cases per station), middle zone (6.6) and outer zone (2.9 cases per station). The trend was, therefore, for mentally disturbed individuals living predominantly in the inner city to move centripetally before committing their act of public disorder, which resulted in police intervention and referral. For reasons of 'social drift' (Hare 1967), mentally disturbed people tend to live in the transitional zone of big cities. For other reasons, perhaps associated with the 'social magnetism' of metropolitan centres, such people often demonstrate their abnormal behaviour when they are out of their home in the city centre.

When these police referrals were examined diagnostically, at subsequent admission to psychiatric hospital, psychoses predominated; 40 per cent were found to be suffering from schizophrenia, 12 per cent from manic-depressive psychosis, and 5 per cent from organic psychosyndromes. Conditions associated with alcohol comprised a further 8 per cent. Transient situational disturbance and problems associated with personality disorder made up rather less than a quarter of the sample. Foreign-born people were considerably over-represented in the police referral sample, when compared with the general population of the city; this was especially so for those born in the West Indies (relative risk 4.0), or the Irish Republic (relative risk 2.3). Police referrals showed a marked downwards skew for social class, with a gross preponderance of unemployed and disabled, and an under-representation of Social Classes I, II and III. There was a marked trend for these police referrals to be living on their own — 26 per cent compared with 5.7 per cent of the general population in the West Midlands. The police referral subjects tended either to be living on their own or, if female, with one other person; they were less often living in family groups than the general population, but more likely to be in multi-occupied accommodation.

It would appear that police referral is one particularly prominent symptom of urban disorganisation. It is more frequently found in those who are living in a state of anomie, and it reflects a marked breakdown in ordinary social communications. In this example, the deleterious features of the big city interact with pre-existing mental disorder and social deprivation in the individual to result in public disorder. The isolation of a mentally disordered person in an urban setting may be extreme (Mitchell-Bateman 1970), but in the next example, massive public disorder is shown to provoke individual adverse psychological reaction especially in those who are already vulnerable and predisposed.

PSYCHOLOGICAL CONSEQUENCES OF MAJOR DISASTER

With an apparently increasing climate of violence, man-made as opposed to natural disaster is an important problem in big cities. However, where disaster is defined as 'a situation of massive collective stress (Kinston & Rosser 1974), the psychological aspects of disaster are often overlooked. For example, when ten major English teaching hospitals were asked recently what plans they had for dealing with the short-and long-term psychological consequences of a major accident, none of them had formulated any effective stratagem. Some of them viewed this situation with complacency; others recognised a need to have plans in readiness, though they had not actually done so. It is, of course, human nature that one hopes such disasters will not happen, but the evidence suggests that it very well may. In a recent series of articles, discussing practical planning in hospital to deal with disaster, only one paper of the three had one short paragraph on anything related to psychological consequences and their management; this was simply a short reference to the 'sorrowful ... who do not appear to be physically injured and yet are in need of support' (Williams 1979; Yates 1979; Evans 1979).

The degree of human involvement in a disaster is represented diagrammatically in Fig. 10.4; with increasing distance from the centre of disruption, there is decreased involvement. At the epicentre, all may die; slightly further from the source of the damage, serious physical injury is likely to occur; further away still, people will consider themselves to have been involved in the catastrophe, but they are not seriously injured physically. Beyond that is the community in which the disaster occured, and this community will produce a distinctive reaction to disaster; a major disaster also has repercussions nationally. There is a greater feeling of involvement if the catastrophe is very great, or if the experience of those involved differs very markedly from those in the same community who are not involved; i.e. there is a sharp boundary between those caught up in the disaster, who may feel themselves to be isolated from the rest of society, and that society. For example, the 'hibakusha' or survivors of the Hiroshima bombing felt themselves to be isolated from, and discriminated against by the rest of the community; they were made to feel guilty for being alive (Lifton 1967).

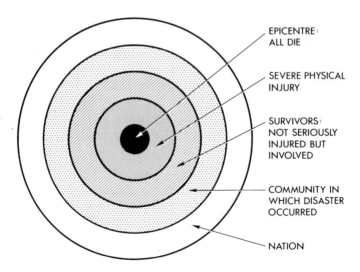

Fig. 10.4 Degree of human involvement in a disaster

Lifton has stressed the extent to which these survivors differ from other people; having been so close to death yet survived sets them apart. Such a person comes to believe that his survival was at the expense of those who died, and this precipitates feelings of guilt and shame. The blame which the survivor directed towards himself was shared by the local community, who regarded the survivor as in some way culpable for the death of the victims. The survivors expect special treatment because of their involvement in disaster, but then feel persecuted when they are, in fact, treated as different.

Theories of attribution can make an important contribution to the understanding of those involved in disaster. Causal responsibility and culpability are associated with the ability to cope effectively (Brewin 1981). In a study of patients with spinal injuries, Bulman & Wortman (1977) found that the tendency to blame oneself for the outcome of the accident predicted successful coping with disability. Paradoxically, however, perceiving the accident to be avoidable was associated with a poor ability to cope. Bulman & Wortman suggested that a more successful reaction to disability followed an accident when the subject had chosen to take part in the activity during which the accident occurred. Then the behaviour was by no means exceptional, and yet the accident could be seen as resulting from the subject's actions; e.g. a sports injury in an active sportsman. Being the victim of man-made disaster is in many ways the extreme opposite of this situation; many victims repeatedly bemoan, 'Why did it happen to me?' The disaster was dramatically different from 'normal' experience, so that no connection could reasonably be made between the victim's actions and being involved in disaster.

It has long been known that adverse life events are powerful precipitants of neurotic illness, and disaster is a situation of catastrophically adverse life events. There are two possible mechanisms by which neurotic illness may be precipitated in such situations. The first is the experience of loss due to physical injury, loss of loved ones through death, damage to property, or loss of status. The second is the subjective experience of being involved in catastrophe. We know that loss may be followed by symptoms (Parkes 1972), but there is also some evidence to support the view that involvement in disaster without personal experience of loss is also associated with the development of neurotic symptoms. This may be associated with the feelings of guilt experienced by those involved, and to some extent thrust upon them by those in the community not involved. It may also be associated with aspects of attribution; those involved see themselves as 'not causally responsible' and yet to some extent 'culpable'.

Features were demonstrable of this 'aftermath neurosis' in a follow-up investigation of those involved in the Birmingham bomb disaster in November, 1974 (Sims et al. 1979). Bomb explosions occurred in two city centre public houses in Birmingham during a late shopping evening, a few weeks before Christmas; 21 people were killed, 43 detained in hospital with serious injury, and 116 others taken to hospital casualty departments but allowed home later that evening. This latter group of 116 people who were involved but not seriously injured were investigated at 2-year follow-up.

Then, it was found that these people had shown prolonged symptomatic disability and disturbance in social relationships. Many had experienced phobic symptoms, chronic anxiety, feelings of depression, and hypochondriacal symptoms to a conspicuous extent over the 2 years since the disaster. Several ascribed both marital breakdown and severe employment problems, which they had experienced since the disaster, at least partly to it. They felt that it had had a markedly deleterious effect upon their lives, the consequences of which they were still suffering two years later. Thus, 70 per cent of those involved who were interviewed at 2-year follow-up described prolonged emotional symptoms; 40 per cent had required psychotropic medication, and some had become dependent upon it. Several people who had been moderate to heavy drinkers before their experience had shown an alcoholic drinking pattern subsequently. Nearly half of the sample who were interviewed at follow-up ascribed long-term problems in employment to the nervous effects from the bombing; this included unemployment that had followed severe anxiety since the explosion, moving to an inferior job in the suburbs because of 'bad nerves', and performing their work less satisfactorily. These people, involved but not severely injured, described a change in their social and political attitudes. Many commented that they were generally less sociable than before the explosion, and specifically that they had become antagonistic and prejudiced against innocent citizens of Irish extraction. A woman informant said that she had not spoken to her (Irish) neighbour for 2 years after the bombing, having enjoyed good relations previously.

These victims of the bombing who were not seriously injured were compared with an age- and sex-matched sample of casualty patients, not associated with major disaster, but who also were allowed home from hospital without admission. This comparison group was formed from those attending the two casualty departments to which the bomb victims were taken, on the three Thursday evenings previous to the disaster. Incapacity, in terms of number of days off work due to sickness, is shown for the two samples in Table 10.1. These samples were: (1) bomb victims — those people with adequate documentation who were inside one of the public houses at the time of the bombs, taken to a casualty department, found not to be seriously injured and allowed home that evening; and (2) attenders — previous attenders at a casualty department, not admitted to hospital, age- and sex-matched with the bomb victim group. In the 6 months before their accident, the comparison group of casualty attenders had more days off work than the bomb victim group. This was probably because some regular casualty attenders, with chronic or recurrent disability were included within this group. In the 6 months after the accident, there was an 8-fold increase in days off work due to sickness for the bomb victim group, but

Table 10.1 Work incapacity in bomb victims compared with casualty attenders recorded in number of days off work per person.

	6 months before accident	Days off work per person 6 months after accident	% incapacity increase 6 months after accident
Bomb victims n = 62	1.6	15.6	+857%
Attenders n = 70	2.9	3.1	+4%

only a minimal increase for the control attender group. Experience of involvement in a major disaster, even without serious physical injury, appeared to be a potent factor in the precipitation of neurotic symptomatology; this occurred to a much greater extent than in subjects with similar physical disability, where there was no major disaster involved.

There have been many papers describing the psychological sequelae to natural disaster; for example, Cobb & Lindemann (1943) studied the survivors of a serious fire at the Coconut Grove Nightclub, Popovic & Petrovic (1964) described the psychological reactions of those involved in the first 24 hours after the Skopje earthquake, and Bennet (1970) has described aspects of the long-term outcome following the Bristol floods of 1968. The effects of a natural disaster (severe winter storm) in children have been described by Burke et al. (1982). The course of adjustment to the Darwin cyclone of 1974 has been charted by Parker (1977), pointing out the gradual lessening of psychological dysfunction over the subsequent 14 months, and the effects of the Athens earthquake have been referred to in Chapter 8. With respect to the sequelae of man-made disaster, Lifton (1967) gave an important description to which referral has already been made of the victims of Hiroshima. A totally different situation, in which the physical damage was relatively slight, but the feeling of involvement very great was the Dutch train siege, in which there was considerable psychological disturbance in the victims (Bastiaans et al. 1979).

Daly (1983) has examined the diary of Samuel Pepys for evidence of reactions to the Great Fire of London, and concludes that:

After his initial reaction of disbelief, Pepys showed the constructive coping qualities . . . which were eventually to bring him to high public office . . . He found that his constructive behaviour allayed his anxiety. Nevertheless . . . he described subjective fear and showed an understandable irritability and tendency to criticize others. He also personalized the menace that faced him. His considerable anxiety was accompanied by insomnia and mild depersonalization. He showed some evidence of memory impairment and self-defence against guilt and about saving himself and his property. His diary records the tendency for rumours to spread easily during times of public disquiet. He also had nightmares of the Fire, and various ideas and physical situations brought forth anxious feelings associated with the Fire: these are recorded as persisting for at least eight months, after which there appears to be no further mention of such symptoms.

Daly considers that this pattern corresponds with the category of post-traumatic stress disorder in the American Psychiatric Association DSM III of

1978. The essential feature of this category is the development of characteristic symptoms after experiencing a psychologically traumatic event or events, outside the range of human experience usually considered to be normal; the symptoms involve re-experiencing the traumatic event, numbing of responsiveness to or involvement with the external world, and a variety of other autonomic, dysphoric, or cognitive symptoms.

Tyhurst (1951) has classified five phases of disaster, which are useful for classifying reactions and for planning antidotes: pre-impact (threat), warning, impact, recoil, and post-impact. The pre-impact or threat may exist for months or years and often provokes both denial and anxiety in the society in which it occurs. For the Birmingham bombing, the 'threat' consisted of several bombs, discovered in the city over months, with one death when an attempt was made to defuse the device; macabre jokes had become the standard response to bomb scares, but also many precautions sometimes irrational, were taken. The 'warning' occurs minutes or hours before the event, and may result in fear or denial; in the Birmingham disaster, this was the air of tension and foreboding that surrounded the arrangements for the funeral, earlier on the same day, of an Irish Republican who accidentally blew himself up whilst attempting to explode a telephone exchange. The 'impact' stage is the immediate response to the disaster. According to Glass (1959) about 75 per cent of those involved appear stunned, apathetic, and emotionless; the rest respond either with anxious coping, or with panic, inappropriate behaviour, and hysteria. These behaviours and emotions were seen in the bomb victims when they were in the Casualty Departments. The 'recoil' stage is the immediate adjustment to disaster, when a healthy victim shows extreme garrulousness, dependence on others, and emotional release. This was seen in Birmingham in the days that followed the bombing; for example, a girl who made a good adjustment subsequently said that when she went back to work, she 'talked and talked and talked'. It is recognised that the reactions of the 'post-impact' stage go on for a long time — perhaps the rest of the victim's life; following the bombing, marked symptoms were certainly present at 2-year follow-up.

Lindemann & Cobb (1943) made the important observation that it is previous personal conflicts which are highlighted and exacerbated by the stress and psychological trauma associated with involvement in a major disaster. Thus, the person whose marriage is already unstable before being involved in catastrophe may well experience the final breakdown of his marriage in the aftermath; the established problem drinker is likely to increase his consumption to the level of definite alcohol dependence, while a person with existing anxiety symptoms may manifest a disabling phobic neurosis.

Accidents are frequently followed by more or less prolonged neurotic symptoms. Non-organic post-accident syndromes may, according to Robitscher (1971), be one of three types: (1) true traumatic neurosis (to which the neurotic reaction of the unimpaired victims of Birmingham bomb disaster appeared to conform); (2) compensation neurosis; or (3) ma-lingering. There is a plethora of terms used to describe the neurotic sequelae of accidents, unfortunately accompanied by a paucity of research obser-vation. Compensation neurosis was described by Kennedy (1946) as 'a state of mind, born out of fear, kept alive by avarice, stimulated by lawyers, and cured by verdict', but this is a considerable over-simplification; the complex-ity of the issue is well recognised by Trimble (1981). Is compensation neuro-sis a euphemism for malingering; is it the malignant effect of an excessively bureaucratic judicial system upon the individual victims of calamity, or is it the result of abnormal attitudes developing in the predisposed through person-ality disorder? There is no clear answer to such questions, though it is likely that neurotic constitution or premorbid personality disorder predicts those who are more likely to suffer from post-traumatic neurosis. The contention that compensation neurosis is invariably alleviated by a settlement of the claim acceptable to the patient is clearly mistaken; many sufferers continue with neurotic symptoms for many years after settlement; yet the obverse is probably true — it is unlikely that the symptoms will remit until the legal issues have been completed.

MANAGEMENT OF URBAN DISASTER

When introducing psychiatry into disaster planning and relief work, it should be seen as 'a means of increasing awareness of and sensitivity to the way people react to extreme environmental stress and as an adjunct to the overall management of survivors' (Edwards 1976). Plans, of course, have to be adapted to the nature and size of a disaster, and to the geographical and social conditions in which it occurs. But planning is vital for the smooth management of all major disasters; the police, ambulance services, and major hospitals in cities clearly need to have detailed schedules, prepared in advance, in the event of a major civil catastrophe (Williams 1979). Within the hospital, the initial emphasis is upon surgical triage, with rapid assess-ment of the extent of the injury in each of many victims, and direction of the casualty to appropriate treatment services (Yates 1979). In many disas-ters, there will be a large number of uninjured victims brought into hospital from the site of the accident at the same time as the severe casualties. These need to be separated from the physically injured patients at the triage stage; in the Birmingham bombing, for example, 65 per cent of the victims were not seriously injured.

In the psychological aspects of planning, attention needs to be given to several different dimensions; medical rescue and human service support systems, as well as personal, family, and community needs, and public policy (Singer 1982). A notable failure in the Buffalo Creek disaster, with long-term consequences for affected individuals, was the lack of adequate attention to the severely disrupted social network of victims (Gleser et al. 1981). Plans for dealing with disaster should include a stratagem for that potentially large number of uninjured victims who have to be separated from those requiring surgical management at the triage stage. Failure to do so may result in psychological distress and even mass panic at the time, as well as severe psychological trauma in a large number of people later.

At the impact stage (Tyhurst 1951), the uninjured should be taken to a large hall or waiting area near the casualty department; they should not be discharged immediately from the hospital, because there is still a risk from delayed manifestations of serious physical injury, and also some of these people will require skilled psychological help. About 75 per cent of such people are likely to be emotionally numbed and unresponsive; they need to be with others. They can carry out automatic activities under instruction, but are too dazed to initiate anything themselves. They can be interviewed, and greeted by close relatives in the waiting rooms, but are not likely to make spontaneous social contact. If they remain at the site of the disaster, they would be able to remove rubble or carry blankets under supervision. There will be a small proportion of victims demonstrating 'anxious coping' behaviour and their restlessness needs to find expression, e.g. telephoning relatives or helping other people. The small minority of victims experiencing acute panic and manifesting disturbance of behaviour need to be out of sight of the majority whom they will frighten, and will require individual care from a relative or a professional. Isolating them from the rest of the victims will diminish their symptoms and prevent the spread of mass panic.

There is often plenty of time at this stage, and the emotionally disturbed victims need to mix with people who were not involved. Professional interviewers, called to the hospital in accordance with prearranged disaster plans, should be available to interview these uninjured victims for the recording of basic data, and also to carry out an initial assessment as to whether further psychological support is likely to be necessary. This will depend upon the stability of the social environment from which the victim comes, i.e. his relationship with and attitudes towards members of his family and those with whom he works, and his present emotional reaction to the disaster. For the identification of those who are vulnerable, evidence of previous conflict in life situations is more important than the severity of the present emotional distress.

During the recoil stage, ventilation of feelings should be encouraged, without censoring or interpretation. The survivors need to be with other people (Edwards 1976), need people to talk to, and describe their experiences to; they also need to be dependent, and to be cared for (Tyhurst 1951).

As mentioned above, survivors of Hiroshima were often exposed to hostility from the rest of the community, who were not personally involved. An important part of management in the post-impact stage, therefore, is to diminish the difference between those involved but not seriously injured, and those who were not involved at all. Inclusion of uninjured victims into closely knit supportive human groupings, which allow the uncensored expression of emotion but do not explore psychopathology, are highly beneficial. The ideal would be to include such people in groups of volunteers, helping physically with the effects of a disaster; it is important to allow these victims to integrate fully with those who were not involved. Those who made a successful psychological adjustment to the disaster in Birmingham described talking exhustively about their experiences in the early post-impact stage, and this was found to be cathartic. A rapid return to work facilitated this process. It was considered that for children, following involvement in a natural disaster, school was important for supporting coping skills (Burke et al. 1982). Skilled psychiatric help during this state of social disequilibrium, that occurs in the recoil stage, will be beneficial for those who have been found at initial interview to be vulnerable (Caplan 1963). In the case of the Athens earthquake of 1981, a peak of fatal heart attacks occurred on the second and third days, generating as much stress as the real danger of the first in sensitised victims (Trichopoulos et al. 1983).

Where practicable, some sort of follow-up by a skilled professional, e.g. a social worker, would be beneficial for all victims of a major disaster, perhaps at 1 month, 6 months and a year. This would be most important for those identified as already experiencing severe conflict before the disaster. Where such follow-up has taken place, it is usually seen by the victim himself to be evidence of care by the authorities, and not as an unjustifiable intrusion upon his privacy. It enables those with neurotic problems in the aftermath to be advised about available treatment. Amongst a sample of previously treated neurotic patients, a research follow-up interviewer was generally welcomed, and absence of routine follow-up was interpreted as lack of interest by the hospital (Sims 1976).

Advice to providers of primary care would also be beneficial following a disaster. In the United Kingdom, virtually every person is registered with a family doctor, whose name would be recorded as part of the routine information collected at interview on arrival in hospital, after the disaster. Advice to the GP could be provided as part of the follow-up plan. Many GPs did not treat psychological symptoms which occurred in the victims of the Birmingham bombing, except by putting the patient off work with a sickness certificate. Nor did they refer such patients for psychiatric help, because they considered the causes of these patients' symptoms as understandable: 'You were in the pub that was bombed; of course, you will feel upset'. It is probable, though, that many of these subjects would have benefited from skilled help at an earlier stage. Anniversary dates may be particularly difficult for the victims of disasters, and may be the occasion for morbid remembrance, which results in further anguish.

The psychological consequences of severe disaster may be very prolonged, and out of all proportion to the extent of physical injury. Detailed planning for major urban disaster, with careful attention to psychological management, may prevent short-term panic and long-term psychiatric disability. This has not been generally recognised, nor incorporated into disaster plans for civilian catastrophes in British hospitals, nor in most areas elsewhere. From an American perspective, Cohen (1982) states that a mental health team should give priority to three modes of action in a disaster situation: first, linking into the network of assisting staff, e.g. giving them brief instructional sessions on psychiatric reactions; second, rapidly assessing the characteristics of the affected people, to determine their needs; third, establishing collaborative procedures with both government and voluntary agencies who are already involved. There are also three types of people who need most immediate help: patients on continuous medication, who have been deprived of it; those dependent on drugs or alcohol, and without their usual supplies; and people decompensating under the intense stress of the disaster.

CONCLUSIONS

Big cities show distinct patterns for many types of psychiatric illness, e.g. schizophrenia, alcoholism, and suicidal behaviour (Giggs 1979). The transitional zone of big cities has become a magnet for certain people with psychiatric illnesses, especially those with schizophrenia, and the social disturbance resulting from such illness is more common in these areas. Police referrals are a particular example of urban disorganisation, and patients referred by them are likely to be mentally ill people who are also the victims of social isolation. Man-made disaster is more likely to occur in big cities; and the psychological consequences of such catastrophe are severe, even for those involved but not seriously injured. Thus, consideration should be given in all such areas to planning services to cope with the seriously injured, to deal with the psychological consequences of disaster, and to prevent long-term disability from it.

There is a need to pay greater attention to the psychological aspects of conservation in cities and to preserve local communities (Freeman 1978). Big cities are far too extensive for natural laws of territoriality or feelings of belonging to exist. The individual needs to identify with a smaller unit than a massive conurbation; a traditional inner-city back street, a small suburban housing estate, or a rural village will serve. However, for those living in vast amorphous overspill estates, or cooped in with young families in tower blocks, the alternatives may be either no social group with which to identify, or some potentially violent minority with a strong sense of group cohesiveness. Urban planning and architecture ought to take into account the psychological needs of both individuals and social groups — something they have manifestly failed to do up to now.

Although the psychiatric services for the community are usually provided in hospitals and units which are within the city, there has been very little attention paid to the specific needs of the cities themselves, or to problems which are typically urban. There is an inequality of provision for health care in the UK between those of higher and those of lower social class (DHSS

1980), inner city working-class areas being often particularly deprived in the quality of treatment services available. New day-patient and out-patient facilities should be sited in the inner city, accessible to public transport and near where people live, rather than in large old mental hospitals often inappropriately situated at the extreme edge of the big cities.

Greenblatt (1970) has outlined plans for action in managing what he calls the 'troubled mind in the troubled city':

(1) Designate a catchment area and a target population
(2) Citizen representation, participation, and sanction are necessary for any programme
(3) A survey should be done of needs and resources
(4) A master plan for the mentally ill in each area must be developed
(5) Services should be available promptly when needed, where the individual resides, and without stigma or threat of removal
(6) Research and evaluation are essential.

Services for coping with the psychological effects of urban disaster, for dealing with psychiatric consequences of urban disorganisation, and for providing an adequate range of facilities for those living in big cities who suffer from psychiatric illness or emotional disturbance require coordination, in a manner which has not so far occurred in the UK. Urban psychiatric services need to be planned jointly by the local authority and health authorities for the entire city, with the needs of the whole community taken into account; too often, big cities have been divided — for generally excellent reasons — into small areas for the administration of hospital services, and those for one district may bear no relation to the facilities enjoyed by its neighbour. It is the exception rather than the rule that services for a city are planned on a city-wide basis. Too often, social services have not been taken into account in health authority planning, so that they do not complement health services, nor are the areas served by the two coterminous.

It is very rare for the citizens themselves to have any direct say in the provision of their psychiatric services, except in the rather negative sense that they may have opportunity to make public protest against the siting of a psychiatric hostel or regional secure unit. There is much that needs to be done, but planning cannot start until an administrative structure is created to produce realistic, multi-disciplinary cooperation; when that has been achieved, the results will depend more than anything on the financial backing that is provided.

REFERENCES

Bagley C, Jacobson S, Palmer C 1973 Social structure and the ecological distribution of mental illness, suicide and delinquency. Psychological Medicine 3: 177–187
Bastiaans J, Jaspers J P C, Van Der Ploeg H M, Van Den Berg-Schaap Th E, Van Den

Berg J F Rapport: Psychological Onderzoek naar de Gevolgen van Gijzelingen in Nederland 1977. Ministerie van Volksgezondheid en Milieuhygiene Leidschendam

Benfari R L, Beiser M, Leighton A H, Mertens C 1972 Some dimensions of psychoneurotic behaviour in an urban sample. Journal of Nervous and Mental Disease 155: 77–90

Bennet G 1970 Bristol Floods 1968 Controlled survey of effects on health of local community disaster. British Medical Journal 3: 454–458

Berry C, Orwin A 1966 'No fixed abode': A survey of mental hospital admissions. British Journal of Psychiatry 112: 1019–1025

Bor W 1973 Problems of inner city areas, with special reference to the Brimingham Study. Housing Review 22: 5–7

Brewin C 1981 Coping with accidental injury: Adaptive and maladaptive aspects of self-blame. In: Antaki C, Brewin C (eds) Attributions and psychological change London. Academic Press, London

Brown G W, Harris T 1978 Social origins of depression. Tavistock, London

Bulman R J, Wortman C B 1977 Attributions of blame and coping in the 'real world': Severe accident victims react to their lot. Journal of Personality and Social Psychology, 35: 251–365

Burke J D, Borus J F, Burns B J, Millstein K H, Beasley M C 1982 Changes in children's behaviour after a natural disaster. American Journal of Psychiatry 139: 1010–1014

Caplan G 1963 Principles of preventive psychiatry. Basic Books, New York

Castle I M, Gittus E 1957 The distribution of social defects in Liverpool. Sociological Review 5: 43–64

Cobb S, Lindemann E 1943 Neuropsychiatric observations during the Cocoanut Grove fire. Annals of Surgery 117: 814–824

Cohen R E 1982 Intervening with disaster victims. In: Schulberg H C, Killilea M (eds) The modern practice of community mental health. Jossey-Bass, San Francisco

Cohn N 1957 The pursuit of the millenium. Secker & Warburg, London

Daly R J 1983 Samuel Pepys and post-traumatic stress disorder. British Journal of Psychiatry 143: 64–68

Dean K G, James H D 1980 The spatial distribution of depressive illness in Plymouth. British Journal of Psychiatry 136: 167–180

Department of Health & Social Security 1975 Better services for the mentally ill. HMSO, London

Department of Health and Social Security 1980 Inequalities in health. HMSO, London

Dewhurst K, Reeves M 1978 Friedrich Schiller: medicine, psychology and literature. Sandford Publications, Oxford

Dohrenwend B P, Dohrenwend B S 1974 Psychiatric disorders in urban settings. In: Caplan G (ed) American Handbook of Psychiatry, Vol III: Child and adolescent psychiatry, sociocultural and community psychiatry. Basic Books, New York

Duhl L J 1968 The shame of the cities. American Journal of Psychiatry 124: 1184–1189

Durkheim E 1897 Le suicide (translated 1952: Suicide, a study in sociology) Routledge & Kegan Paul, London

Edwards J G 1976 Psychiatric aspects of civilian disaster British Medical Journal 1, i: 944–947

Evans R F 1979 The patient with multiple injuries British Journal of Hospital Medicine 22: 329–333

Faris R E L, Dunham H W 1939 Mental disorders in urban areas. Hafner, Chicago

Freeman H L 1978 Mental health and the environment. British Journal of Psychiatry 132: 113–24

Giggs J A 1979 Human health problems in urban areas. In: Herbert D T, Smith D M (ed) Social problems and the city. Oxford University Press, London

Glass A J 1959 Psychological aspects of disaster. Journal of American Medical Association 171: 222–225

Gleser G L, Green B L, Winget 1981 Prolonged psychosocial effects of disaster: A Study of Buffalo Creek. Academic Press, New York

Greenblatt M 1970 The troubled mind in the troubled city Comprehensive Psychiatry 11: 8–17

Guze S B 1967 The diagnosis of hysteria: What are we trying to do? American Journal of Psychiatry 124: 491–498

Hare E H 1956 Mental illness and social conditions in Bristol. Journal of Mental Science 102: 349–357

Hare E H 1967 The epidemiology of schizophrenia. In: Coppen A, Walk A (eds) Recent developments in schizophenia. Headly Brothers, Ashford

Hitchcock H R 1963 World architecture. Paul Hamlyn, London

Johns E 1965 British townscapes. Edward Arnold, London

Kelleher M J, Copeland J R M 1972 Compulsory psychiatric admission by the police: A study of the use of Section 136. Medicine Science and the Law 12: 220–224

Kennedy F 1946 Mind of injured worker: its effect on disability neurosis. Compensation Medicine 1: 19–30

Kinston W, Rosser R 1974 Disaster: effects on mental state and physical state. Journal of Psychosomatic Research 18: 437–456

Lei T-J, Rowitz L, McAllister R J, Butler E W 1974 An ecological study of ageing labelled retardates. American Journal of Mental Deficiency 79: 22–31

Levy L, Rowitz L 1973 The ecology of mental disorder. Behavioural Publications, New York

Lifton R J 1967 Death in life: survivors of Hiroshima. Random House, New York

Lukes S 1973 Emile Durkheim. Allen Lane, London

Mitchell-Bateman M 1970 The urban setting III Mental health services and the isolated citizen. Rhode Island. Medical Journal 53: 263–266

Moore N C 1974 Psychiatric illness and living in flats. British Journal of Psychiatry 125: 500–7

Moss P, Plewis I 1977 Mental distress in mothers of pre-school children in Inner London. Psychological Medicine 7: 641–652

Orwell G 1933 Down and out in Paris and London. Gollancz, London

Park R E, Burgess E W 1925 The city. University of Chicago Press, Chicago

Parker G 1977 Cyclone Tracy and Darwin evacuees: On the restoration of the species. British Journal of Psychiatry 130: 548–555

Parkes C M 1972 Components of the reaction to loss of a limb, spouse or home. Journal of Psychosomatic Research 16: 343–349

Popovic M, Petrovic D 1964 After the earthquake. Lancet ii: 116–117

Ravetz A 1974 Model estate: planned housing at Quarry Hill Leeds. Croom Helm, London

Robitscher J 1971 Compensation in psychiatric disability and rehabilitation. Thomas, Springfield

Rowitz L, Levy L 1968 Ecological analysis of treated mental disorders in Chicago. Archives of General Psychiatry 19: 571–579

Sainsbury P 1955 Suicide in London. Chapman and Hall, London

Scagliola M H 1971 Mental and physical health in the American inner city. Lancet ii: 1415–1417

Seligman M E P 1975 Helplessness. W H Freeman, San Francisco

Simmel G 1908 Conflict in Sociology 3rd ed (translated Wolff K 1955). The Free Press, Glencoe

Sims A C P 1976 The consequences of severe neurosis Practitioner 216: 321–329

Sims A C P, Symonds R L 1975 Psychiatric referrals from the police. British Journal of Psychiatry 127: 171–8

Sims A C P, White A C, Murphy T 1979 Aftermath neurosis: psychological sequelae of the Birmingham bombings in victims not seriously injured. Medicine, Science & the Law 19: 78–81

Singer T J 1982 An introduction to disaster: Some consideration of a psychological nature. Aviation Space and Environmental Medicine 245–250

Snow J 1965 Snow on cholera: being a reprint of two papers. Hafner, London

Srole L 1972 Urbanization and mental health: A reformulation. Psychiatric Quarterly 46: 449–460

Tricohopoulos D, Katsayanni K, Zavitsaros X, Tzonau A, Dalla-Vorgia P 1983 Psychological stress and fatal heart attack: The Athens (1981) earthquake. Natural experiment. Lancet 1: 441–444

Trimble M R 1981 Post-traumatic neurosis. John Wiley, Chichester

Tyhurst J S 1951 Individual reactions to community disaster. American Journal of Psychiatry 107: 764–769

Weissman M M, Myers J K 1978 Affective disorders in a U.S. urban community Archives of General Psychiatry 35: 1304–1311

Whitlock F A 1973 Suicide in England and Wales 1959–63. Part 2: London Psychological Medicine 3: 411–420

Williams D J 1979 Disaster planning in hospitals. British Journal of Hospital Medicine 22: 308–322

Wing J K 1976 Mental health in urban environments. In: Harrison G A, Gibson J B (eds) Man in urban environments. Oxford University Press, London

Woodruff R A 1968 Hysteria: An evaluation of objective diagnostic criteria by the study of women with chronic medical illness. British Journal of Psychiatry 114: 115–9

Yates D W 1979 Surgical triage. British Journal of Hospital Medicine 22: 323–328

K. Keith Wedmore & H. L. Freeman

Social pathology and urban overgrowth

When I first came to New York it seemed like a nightmare. As soon as I got off the train at Grand Central I was caught up in pushing, shoving crowds on 42nd Street. Sometimes people bumped into me without apology; what really frightened me was to see two people literally engaged in combat for possession of a cab. Why were they so rushed? Even drunks on the street were bypassed without a glance. People didn't seem to care about each other at all.

Stanley Milgram's hypothetical tourist in
The Experience of Living in Cities.

OVERALL URBAN SIZE

Instinct tells us to convert our need for comfort and security into terms of size and scale, and though we sometimes say 'This thing is too big for me', it is odd that such a statement of the obvious is not carried into the study of social pathologies such as crime. The comparison of smaller places with larger confirms in general what might be suspected: things get worse as human settlements get bigger. Even in countries which are relatively crime-free, the rate is still markedly higher in their larger towns than elsewhere; but where even the smaller towns have a substantial amount, it gets entirely out of hand in larger ones. In fact, public safety crime shows a tendency to rise exponentially with the size of the associated community in Western countries (Harries 1973), though this relationship is complicated by the usual excess in large cities of other social pathologies, and it may well be further increased both by commuting to work and by large, impersonal structures. The triple hypothesis — that urban growth, commuting, and inhuman buildings exacerbate crime — is examined in this chapter.

It forms part of the present book because of the inter-relationship of different forms of social pathology in specific environments, and because fear of crime and distress about its consequences are significant aspects of mental health for Western city dwellers, who now form a high proportion of the populations of their countries. Urbanisation has generally been seen as crucial to the development of increasingly complex societies, though urban and rural communities depend on each other, and have very varied economic, political, and cultural relationships. This chapter does not

293

attempt to examine the reasons for variations in urban size, which depend, to varying extents, on market and political factors in different countries. However, Tuan (1979) draws attention to the paradox that 'Although human beings create order and society by acting cooperatively, the mere fact of amassing in the same place sets off a situation that can result in violence', and Fischer (1975) states that the pivotal question about cities today is how can the moral order of society be maintained and the integration of its members achieved, within social structures which are increasingly huge, differentiated, and technologically complex.

International comparisons

From Fig. 11.1, it will be seen that the US Serious Crime rate (FBI Index crimes) per 100 000 people increases from 2229 for rural areas to 7629 for cities of over one million. In 1975, the FBI violent crime index went from 176 per 100 000 for rural areas to 1419 per 100 000 for these cities. French experience is very much the same; between cities of 150 000 and those of 500 000 the rate actually quadrupled, in 1977, and the take-off point was at around 220 000 inhabitants (Fig. 11.2). For this reason, the Peyrefitte Committee recommended that towns which have not already passed the

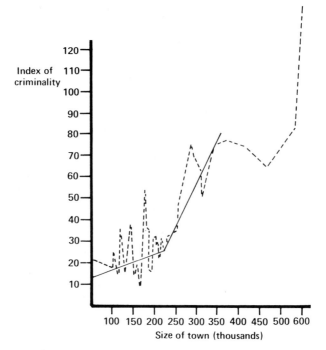

Fig. 11.1 Index of urban criminality related to size of town (US) (derived from Réponses à la Violence, 1977)

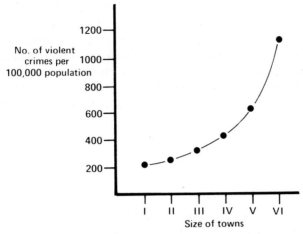

I   : 4327 towns with < 10,000 inhabitants
       (average rate 231.5)

II   : 1314 towns with 10,000 to 25,000 inhabitants
       (average rate 267.8)

III : 538 towns with 25,000 inhabitants
       (average rate 343.0)

IV   : 253 towns with 50,000 to 10,000 inhabitants
       (average rate 450.7)

V   : 100 towns with 100,000 to 250,000 inhabitants
       (average rate 631.6)

VI   : 58 towns with > 250,000 inhabitants of which
       6 have more than a million

Fig. 11.2 Incidence of violent crime related to size of towns (France)
(derived from Reponses à la Violence, 1977)

200 000 mark should be permitted to stop there (Réponses a la Violence, 1977).

English data are similar. For 1979, serious offences per 100 000 can be analysed by police authority; the rate for Avon and Somerset, whose largest town is Bristol (population some half million) was 3832, while that for Metropolitan London was 7667. The rate in West Wales which contains no towns bigger than Cardigan (60 000), was only 2716 (Criminal Statistics 1979). These figures show rates spread over an entire regional police authority, but to compare places of differing sizes within a particular authority, figures were obtained from individual Chief Constables. In Avon and Somerset, the serious crime rate in Yeovil and Frome (a largely rural area) was less than half that of the Central Division of Bristol; and for violent crime, the rate of the former in 1980 was less than one-tenth. County towns in the rural areas show a not much worse record; one's chances of being robbed in Taunton and Bridgewater were less than one-seventh of what they were in central Bristol. Similarly, in Devon and Cornwall,

Okehampton (15 000) and Tavistock (25 000) were compared with Plymouth (240 000), whose size is just above the point at which the French report says crime begins sharply to take off. In 1980, there were no robberies at all in the small places, whereas the rate per 100 000 in Plymouth was 30, and violent crime in general was $2\frac{1}{2}$ times as common there as in Tavistock or Okehampton. McClintock (1968) found that indictable crimes in 1965 were 1670 per 100 000 in 17 large counties of the UK (more rural than urban), but were 3378 per 100 000 in London. As the detection rate in London was then hardly more than one-third of that in many rural places, the city rates are probably under-reported, and the real difference in fact even greater.

Between 1970 and 1980, the population of Calgary, Alberta, grew from 385 000 to 561 000; the burglary rate rose by 70 per cent and robberies by 45 per cent, though assaults declined slightly. Should Calgary get to its projected population of a million before the end of the century, (and it is currently growing at 2500 a month) then it is likely to become, by Alberta standards, a dangerous place. There is evidence that fast-growing metropolises have higher crime rates than slowly growing ones (Phillips & Brunn 1978). If the hypothesis of this paper is right, then the citizens of Calgary are on as near infallible a course to increase crime as could have been achieved, without actually dismantling the police force. The figure of 500 000 may have other significance; Kohn (1974), reviewing published data on the relationship between schizophrenia and lower social class, observed that this holds for larger cities, but weakens with decreasing populations, half a million being the critical level. Kohn believes that this relationship is not accounted for by social drift, or by methodological deficiencies in the studies.

Though there are problems about comparing one country's criminal statistics with another, Clinard (1978) reported that Switzerland has a far lower rate than Sweden, with little public concern about crime; 60 per cent of the population live in the cantons where they were born, and those average a quarter of a million population each. In 1973, in the whole of Switzerland (population $6\frac{1}{2}$ million), there were only nine towns of above 50 000 and the biggest of these was Zurich with 671 500. On the other hand, Sweden (population $8\frac{1}{2}$ million) is wholly centralised politically, and more urbanised; 56.5 per cent of the population live in towns of above 10 000, and the major cities are significantly bigger, Stockholm having some 1.3 million people. Clinard concludes that the strong Swiss sense of local responsibility has had an important bearing on their strikingly low rate of crime, and that whereas for countries, size is not an important variable, cities should not exceed 250 000–500 000 population, if there is concern about this aspect of life in them. He also found that whereas rural offenders tend to be of the individual rather than group type, urban offenders are often enmeshed in elaborate patterns of criminal relationships.

Christie (1965) compared the criminality of men in the cities of Oslo and Bergen with those in rural areas; this was a survey of self-reported crime, where one would expect the more serious offences to be, if anything, under-reported. Respondents born in Oslo and Bergen and still there were twice as likely to be involved in serious crime as those who had come from a rural area. This rate, in turn, was about the same as that in rural areas of people who were not born there, but in Oslo or Bergen. In each case, this rate (half that of the city-born residents) was twice that of those born in, and staying in the rural areas. It would seem that one reduces one's criminality by moving into the country, although not entirely losing the city taint. Thus, the crime rate of those in the city at all times was (by their own confession) four times that of the male public who had never left the countryside. It is also likely to be relevant that a comparative study of adolescents in central Oslo with others in a rural area of Southern Norway showed that psychiatric problems were much more frequent in the inner city (Lavick 1977). Simi-larly, Rutter (1981) reports that psychiatric disorders in children, which are related to serious family difficulties, are at a much higher rate in inner London than in Aberdeen or an industrial area of South Wales, which are far smaller communities.

When Scott reviewed the subject in 1972, he observed that whilst the rates for most crimes varied with the order of size of cities, the nature of the relationship varied markedly by the type of offence and over time. From the 1940s to the 1960s in the US, the peak incidence for several types moved up through the urban hierarchy from the medium sized to the largest cities, where all major crimes except burglary then predominated. In Britain, the relationship between incidence of overall crime and size of towns did not emerge as statistically significant until the 1960s, but the distribution of offences against the person was very different from the American one. Similarly in Denmark, the incidence of rape varied inversely with popu-lation size, probably because of intervening opportunities. Scott concluded that correlations between crime rates and any crude index to urbanisation, such as the proportion of a population in towns of 50 000 or more, were unlikely to be meaningful.

Sigvardson et al. (1982), examining the inheritance of criminality in the Stockholm Adoption Study, found a sex difference in the social experiences that contribute to this behaviour in adult life; urban rearing and prolonged institutional care both increased the risk of criminality in women, but not in men. However, in less socially homogeneous countries, such as Britain and the US, environmental variability may have a more powerful influence on the emergence of criminal behaviour.

From a public safety point of view, variations in the rate of robbery or mugging are particularly noticeable; for instance, central Paris has a rate 36 times that of the surrounding countryside (Réponses à La Violence 1977). Cressey (1964) stated that 'In 1958, robberies known to the police increased from a rate of 14.1 in American towns of less than 10 000 population to 112.4 in cities with populations over 250 000 . . . the urban rate generally so far exceeds the rural that it is reasonable to conclude that there is in fact a great excess of crime in urban places. Moreover, a large proportion of urban crime is overlooked'. However, criminal statistics do not always refer to comparable offences, and words like 'towns' or 'cities' have to be used with caution when discussing them. Also, most larger towns include a number of police districts, which may report separately; Calgary includes five. Though the population of 'Calgary' may be 560 000, that of its extended metropolitan area may be larger, and it is that overall population which is significant from this point of view. Yet the overall size of a metropolis may also be misleading — especially taking into account its total area of human interaction — when one may on the whole be visually and socioculturally homogeneous, whereas another is divided into fairly autonomous areas, each with a sense of local identity. Such reservations must not be forgotten, though they are difficult to quantify.

While it appears that bigger places have most crime, there must be profounder reasons than mere size for the difference, and though there are many other explanations for crime in cities, it seems probable that size and scale alone do account for a significant factor, perhaps acting as a catalyst. The hypothesis proposed here is not that without excessive size there would be no crime; rather that it has a base rate, accounted for by other variables such as national culture or level of industrialisation, and that size is a way of exaggerating this. For example, the murder rate in England, including cities, is about a tenth of that in the USA (Mulvihill & Tumin 1969). If the English base rate is x, an important magnifier, e.g. freely available guns, may increase the base rate in the USA sevenfold to $7x$. But the city size magnifier may increase it another ten times to $70x$; in fact, some big American cities score nearer 100 times the English average. Since most Americans do not live in the largest cities, though, the national average will be not $70x$, but perhaps nearer $10x$. This hypothesis may be related to Freedman's (1975) density–intensity theory of the effects of crowding (Chapter 2). However, Hoch (1976) states that the association of city size with raw crime rates in the US overstates the risks associated with size; he attributes much of the difference to other factors which are incidentally correlated, but not intrinsically connected with them, e.g. minority ethnicity, unemployment, crowded housing, and proportion of people living alone.

Characteristics of urban life

City dwellers are often heard to report how much more friendly or relaxed villages are, while those from country areas complain of the confusion and tension of cities, whose anonymity confuses and frightens, so that one may become conscious of a sense of background menace. That all this often goes with a breakdown in standards of law enforcement may not be really surprising.

Anonymity, lack of certainty that one's outlook is shared by others, tends to contribute to crime, and to worsen in relation to very large size of community. Merton (1964), who defined anomie as the gap between culturally prescribed goals and culturally available means for reaching them, suggested that urban life lacks the senses of place, of status, of class, of family links, of recognition that give people elsewhere a feeling of identity. These are a rein on irresponsible, let alone criminal behaviour; both the feeling that you are 'somebody' and the recognition that if you behave badly, others will recognise you. Social alienation has been widely regarded as a form of stress that is specific to urban life and injurious to personality functioning (Murphy 1976); it refers to absence of affiliative supports which are necessary for psychological well-being in indifferent and atomistic social settings. The term, however, has been much abused by Marxist writers.

In the western world, and especially the US, the accent is on success, which may involve not being too squeamish about how it is obtained, even if only because — unlike other and older societies, and smaller places in modern times — there are few other ways of being recognised. This felt need for success, which seems to be strongest in cities, comes up against an obstacle: people do not have equal access to the opportunity structure, and in a society that promises them in principle what they are denied in reality, appreciable numbers are likely to become estranged. Briggs (1982) states that the four features of the industrial city which have been particularly subject to criticism are: deterioration of the physical environment, social segregation, impersonal human relationships, and excessive materialism. James Baldwin (1961) makes this same point: 'The American equation of success with the big time reveals an awful disrespect for human life and human achievement. This equation has placed our cities among the most dangerous in the world and our youth among the most empty and bewildered'. In contrast, Clinard (1978) described informal mechanisms of social control which regulate behaviour in rural areas; where social visibility is high, fear of negative public recognition promotes conformity, i.e. there is a stronger bond to society.

Though smaller English towns, especially in the North, generally show a significant level of social coherence, the move of people to larger cities further South may cause this quality to be lost. One ex-Scot who moved to Coventry said 'Our neighbours informed us when we moved in, 'We don't want any of that Northern nonsense, popping in and out of each other's houses' (Observer, 10 May 1981), while a character in a Coventry-based play (*Risky City*) commented 'You've got a town full of people who are here because they are nowhere else; because their old man got off the train at Coventry station'. Reporting similar changes in the US, Newman (1980) points out that traditional communities were composed of large, extended families or of those who shared common interests and vocational pursuits, and who provided each other with support and friendship. However, increased social mobility, the growth of urban areas, change in the structure of the family, and separation of residential areas from places of work have together rendered this old concept of community meaningless. Harries (1980) states that urban systems may affect crime patterns through social flux and complexity, which are facilitated by the same mobility that enhances the system's economic efficiency — 'Migration and intensified spatial sorting are two of the most critical processes enhancing the potential for crime'. He adds that though the role of urbanisation in promoting criminality is often acknowledged, urbanisation is an amorphous and complex process, and there is a lack of predictive theory about its sub-processes which might be related to crime. The Chicago School first reported in the late 1920s that higher rates of recorded crime occurred near the centre of a metropolis, but there is little agreement as to whether this is best explained in terms of poverty, unemployment, poor housing, family status, anomie, segregation, social rank, ethnic composition, or degree of urbanisation (Gold 1982).

Jane Jacobs (1961) observed that 'The public peace — the sidewalk and street peace — of our cities is not kept primarily by the police, as necessary as the police are, but by an intricate, almost unconscious, network of voluntary controls and standards among the people themselves, and enforced by them'. She suggests that no place larger than 200 000 operates like a district and if that is so, then the maintenance of the public peace in such a situation would become problematic, unless there was an unusual degree of social cohesion — a quality now absent in many city areas.

Clinard (1978) notes the 'citizen responsibility and personal honesty' in Switzerland, a small country, and one of small places. In Berne, when he had stopped to clean the windscreen of his car, several people told him he should not stop there, and waiting in a parking lot with his engine running on a cold day, a woman passing asked him to turn it off, as it was polluting the air. Similarly, a Geneva car owner, whose licence had expired, was reported to the police by persons living in his apartment building. In large cities, though, people are generally less responsive to the apparent difficulties of others; they find endless excuses for non-intervention, for which the primary reason is that they are too inundated by numbers to be able to make exceptions, too menaced by uncertainty as to the attitudes of others to take steps at variance with their own immediate aims. Thus, in ceasing to feel community, we cease to be police; yet if the community does not do the policing for itself, the police cannot do it for them.

Clifford (1976) says of the Japanese that they 'may talk less about the public ideals of service to the community, but they do more by instinct and by habit to inhibit crime; by the only method that (short of total suppression and tyranny) has ever been made to work — the use of community pressure and involvement at the local level'. In Western countries at least, it seems likely that this kind of community involvement is inconsistent with great size and with 'concrete canyons, filled with dangerous torrents of vehicles', but rather, that it is associated with 'the alleys and courts, the small squares and cosy bars and cafes that were the best aspects of urban centres in the past' (Freeman 1975). Community consciousness goes with the sense of place, where there are 'chances for accidental encounters to occur, all within an identifiable area'.

Milgram (1970) has analysed the hypothesis that inundation of relationships leads to social irresponsibility in terms of systems overload, which:

> refers to a system's inability to process inputs from the environment, because there are too many to cope with, or because successive inputs come so fast that A cannot be processed when B is presented. When overload is present, adaptations occur. The system must set priorities and make choices. A may be processed first while B is kept in abeyance, or one may be sacrificed altogether. City life, as we experience it, constitutes a continuous set of encounters with overload, and of resultant adaptations. Overload characteristically deforms daily life on several levels, impinging on role performance, the evolution of social norms, cognitive functioning, and the use of facilities.

On a more poetic level, Wordsworth (Quoted by Briggs 1982) pointed to the association of cities with dissolute behaviour, and with 'a perpetual whirl of trivial objects melted and reduced to one identity'. (This subject is also discussed in Chapter 2).

In Nassau County, a New York City suburb, Milgram calculated that one can meet 11 000 people within a 10-minute radius; in Newark (a small city) 20 000 people; in mid-town Manhattan 220 000. Having to come into contact with these vast numbers, the big city man avoids making any real contact with them; he conserves psychic energy that way, becomes closely acquainted with an infinitely smaller proportion of people, and more readily accepts a superficial relationship with those. Otherwise, the contacts of the first half hour would take up the entire day — the late Gerald Hoffnung, in a humorous series of malicious hints to foreigners in England, urged that on entering a London underground train, one should greet each occupant and shake him by the hand! However, Rutter's view (1981) is that 'the issue of city anonymity remains a vague one, with both its components and its effects ill understood', and as far as increased stresses and life changes are concerned, 'the suggestion remains speculative in the absence of systematic empirical evidence'.

Milgram concludes that our adaptive response to overload is in fact the allocation of less time to each input, to form: 'new norms of non-involvement (which) are so well defined and so deeply a part of city life that people are reluctant to violate (them). Men are actually embarrassed to give up a seat on the subway to an old woman . . . everyone realises that, in situations of high population density, people cannot implicate themselves in each others' affairs, for to do so would create conditions of continual distraction, which would frustrate purposeful action'. Therefore, personal relationships are adjusted to a high level of input from the social field by the use of interpersonal screening and inhibitory processes.

This view does not conflict (as it might at first appear to) with concern at the emptiness of modern cities, particularly those of the US. The large city–high-rise buildings–commuting triad has the effect of removing people from the streets much of the time, particularly when suburban shopping centres cause the deterioration of downtown retail business. Though 'the idea of the 'life' of cities has rarely been defined, much less analysed in terms of its relationship to built form' (Hillier & Hudson 1984), these contemporary processes which have the effect of eliminating most pedestrians, seem very destructive of any such phenomenon.

In fact, mixing up millions of people without demarcation has only happened within the last 100 years, more especially since the widespread use of the motor car — for about 0.0025 per cent of the history of man. Hamburg (1971) draws attention to the fact that 'No society was urbanised before 1800 and only one by 1900 (Great Britain). In the Europe of 1600, about 1.6 per cent of the population lived in cities of 100 000 or more population . . . and in 1800 about 2.2 per cent . . . In a few generations, then, with very little time for change in man's biological equipment — and not even much time for change in customs — a drastic transformation in man's environment has occurred'.

It is hardly surprising that we have not really adapted to this. It is even conceivable that we cannot, and that the basic integrity of society is under threat from the increasingly large numbers gathered in any one place, amongst whom many cause disruption by obeying no particular code. That is somewhat Hamburg's own conclusion:

> While there is no doubt that urbanisation has provided remarkable opportunities for economic development, intellectual stimulation, and other valued experiences, it would be truly miraculous if there were not also unintended consequences and unwanted side-effects. In general, the speed and magnitude of this environmental transformation has been so great, so truly unprecedented, that it is altogether unlikely that effective adaptation to the new conditions has yet been achieved . . . Urbanised societies, in which a majority of the people live crowded together in towns and cities, represent a new and fundamental step in man's social evolution.

These unintended consequences include, in many Western and especially American cities, uncontrollable crime. Another feature of large cities is that their inner areas contain an over-representation of the unmarried and of those who have experienced such traumatic circumstances as divorce, bereavement, or unstable family backgrounds; these people are at greater risk that the average for developing psychiatric disorder.

Furthermore, since World War 2, the cities of North America, Britain, and other West European countries have received a tidal wave of immigrants, mostly with darker skins. Settling in areas around the commercial centre, they have provoked two major forms of displacement — of the white working class to more peripheral housing estates, and of the middle class to distant suburbs. Both these movements were already occurring in the inter-war period, especially in Britain, but it was the great new inward migration which gave it momentum and which totally altered the character of inner residential areas. The only major exceptions to this pattern are to be found, e.g. in London, New York, Chicago, and Paris, where the wealthiest section of the population continues to live in certain parts of the city centre, though other central districts have followed the same deteriorating process as elsewhere. That rapid and massive changes in cities cause stress because people feel they have no control over their environment is quite likely, and deserves investigation.

Surveys in the US (e.g. Department of Housing 1978) have shown that fear of crime is the strongest force behind the outward movement of white residents, though desire for more space and for separation from the unpleasantness of city traffic and industrial processes have also played their part. It has been, as Newman (1980) points out, a process of seeking stability and community through the creation of new residential areas in which the poor and minority races are generally absent, but 'A very high price has been paid for putting increasing distance between whites and blacks, in abandoned residential neighbourhoods, business areas and social and cultural institutions, and in the high cost of commuter travel ... an even higher price in the disappearance of urban life-style'. In this way, the middle class have 'forsaken the environments which once provided them with the nourishment essential to their own development. They have left behind the decaying remnants of a once rich urban environment to shelter the last generation of urban migrants'. The devastation resulting from this, in areas such as the South Bronx in New York City, is almost unbelievable; Harries (1980) describes this — as 'one of the most hyperbolic examples' of inner city decline. Elisenberg (1982) points out that such differential migration also makes the problem of the deprived child even more pressing, since suitable foster homes become very difficult to find, while group homes are very expensive for cities whose revenues are declining for the same reason. Hunter (1978, quoted by Taylor 1984) has introduced the concept of 'incivilities' as clues to the underlying decay of the social order in city areas; physical forms include abandoned housing, vandalism, vacant lots, and profuse litter, while social forms include public harrassment, loitering groups, and drinking or drug use in public. Incivilities may be particularly prevalent in neighbourhoods undergoing social change, and are likely to be more effective in arousing fear than crime itself. In urban areas generally, fear is much more prevalent than crime, and does not necessarily show a direct correlation, district by district, with the rate of offences.

Newman also shows that the whole downward spiral tends to go out of control, as the 'respectable' population is increasingly replaced by those of lower income, living more in multi-occupancy dwellings, and with a much higher proportion of children and young people, often truanting or unemployed. The flight from crime is eventually self-defeating, though, since it results in previously stable neighbourhoods being successively eaten away by social malaise. Newman sees the long-term stability of all residential areas, including the suburbs, as being dependent eventually on a planned integration of lower-income and minority-race people into them. In this process, he hopes that middle-income values, including respect for the law, will prevail, though it would be a vast social experiment, with little margin for error. However, Harries (1980) states that when a compact urban area in Oklahoma known as the 'combat zone' was demolished, and its inhabitants dispersed throughout the suburbs, an intractable law enforcement problem was created as a result.

GIGANTISM OF DESIGN

The Peyrefitte Committee recommended in 1977 that further tower blocks should be avoided for residential use, and the building of individual houses encouraged. It concluded that the instabilities of urban life tend to be worse in an environment of large blocks, and that the size of these, their height, and the length of facades should be reduced to a more human scale. Comparative studies of public housing in Sheffield, however, (Bottoms & Xanthos 1981) found that the ages and other personal factors of residents had more influence on their attitudes to the environment than the height of the building. Some multi-storey developments had lower crime rates than more 'defensible' cottage estates with private gardens, but one high-rise estate was marked by lack of adequate social controls (especially over youth) which seemed to have been somewhat worsened by the design features of the environment. There was a marked fear of crime in the area, which had a self-feeding effect because people spent as little time as possible in the public spaces, leaving them effectively unpoliced by normal informal community controls.

It does appear, though, that high-rise can theoretically be a satisfactory living situation for sections of the population such as single adults, childless working couples, and non-disabled retired people. On the whole, they do not require space outside the dwelling unit, such as is needed for children's play, and may be glad to leave the responsibility for communal areas to others. In the absence of children and teenagers, vandalism is unlikely, and the quality of the environment may remain high, at least within the block.

However, much remains uncertain about the psychological significance of height and mass in housing, though they are believed to be capable of causing loneliness and isolation through straighforward physical factors. High-rise office buildings could tend to produce the same effects, in that they are nearly always associated with commuting, since their development causes the destruction of inner residential buildings. The difference between the human scale of the terraced street, and the tower block of flats in the middle of an empty space, is only too obvious. Rapoport (1975), who regards density as an experience greatly influenced by perception, believes that large building heights may create a feeling of high density, even when spaces and other perceptual cues indicate low density (See Chapter 7).

Newman (1972) found that crime, and fear of crime, were directly related both to the height of buildings and to the size of individual housing developments. His views were criticised, for instance by Mawby (1977) and by Mayhew (1979), who suggested that not enough allowance had been made for the fact that high-rise blocks tended to house the sort of people who were inclined to crime. However, Newman (1975) said he had never proposed that 'the forms of the built environment directly affect the social structures and values of society . . . or create 'moral' attitudes', nor had he ever claimed that crime is inevitable if certain design conditions are present. Social and management problems usually co-exist with deficiencies of design, and it would be unreasonable to expect life in a particular environment to improve greatly if all these are not tackled together (Wilson & Hunter 1978). Gillis & Hagan (1982) found in a suburban area of Toronto that the number of households per building was related to frequency of marijuanha use by adolescents, but not to their deviant behaviour in general. Multiple-family dwellings were also found to attract police presence, since they were regarded as likely trouble spots. Therefore, increased formal control might have more effect on recorded rates of delinquency than reduced informal control, but in the area studied, variations in socio-economic status and in the overall rates of offending were relatively low.

In a major study of working class housing schemes, Newman & Franck (1980) found that the rates of crime, fear of crime, and instability of resident population were related to four major factors. These were: the size of the building; its accessibility for unauthorised entry; a combined factor of low incomes and proportion of one-parent families; and the ratio of teenagers to adults. The tenets of 'defensible space' theory were confirmed in the indirect effects of building size on rates of burglary, personal crime, and fear of crime, for which residents' control of the space outside their apartment was found to be an important intervening variable. Another major factor, related to both volume and type of crime, is the number of families using the same entry to a block; the larger the number, the more difficult it is for people to identify it as being theirs or to feel they have any right to control the activities taking place in communal spaces, through an established code of behaviour. A complex, anonymous environment, poor maintenance, and social instability of the resident population will all tend to have adverse effects on the quality of life for people living in any development. This view is confirmed to some extent by the study of Timms (1965) in Luton; both schizophrenia and serious crime were found to be concentrated in areas of the town marked by low residential status and high population turnover — the rooming house area, slums and older council estates (see Chapter 6). That Newman's hypotheses are relevant to less serious measures of social pathology than crime, and to environments outside the US has been shown in an inner London study by Coleman (1983). However, one design feature which Newman did not investigate, because it is rare in North America, is the overhead walkway in blocks of flats, which represents an important alternative escape route for criminals; as many as 81 blocks were linked in this way, allowing 2268 dwellings to be reached from any one entrance. Walkways are extremely unpopular with residents, greatly increasing the number of vertical routes, of interconnected exits, and of dwellings accessible from one entrance. When the results were adjusted for the influence of walkways, abnormal user behaviour (rubbish, graffiti, vandalism, excrement) was found to be related to design variables of the flats, in almost the same way as Newman's results for crime.

In Britain, the precepts of defensible space were enthusiastically taken up, when a reaction set in to the high-rise mania of the 1960s; the answer that emerged was the 'neo-vernacular' urban village — 'high-density low-rise schemes often with brick and timber facades to the houses, pitched roof and winding walkways' (Hansen 1983). Its purpose was to combine domestic privacy with a more human scale — 'front doors are clustered around a few small and well separated spaces deep in the heart of the estate, well away from the public streets. The buildings are laid out to minimise visual contact with the outside world and between clusters of dwellings . . . (but) the much vaunted small scale of such spaces only increases their isolation from public view, and their sense of segregation'. As a result, the dangers of the walkways and staircases of tower blocks have been re-created; it is very difficult for anyone walking through the area to know where and when they are likely to meet anyone else (and) because the spaces are so axially fragmented and generally short, (he) usually encounters other people very suddenly . . . in contrast to traditional street systems, where strangers can be approached, and weighed up from a distance' (Hillier & Hudson 1984). Because of the way that space is broken up, and because of the absence of a 'global' structure, it is very difficult for anyone to interpret where they are, in relation to the area as a whole.

The reason for this failure in practice is:

> a fundamental misunderstanding among architects about what makes a community work. It has been a cardinal belief for years that communities can only flourish if they are small and well defined; and if architecture creates separation as a way of establishing identity (through) small, highly localised living areas. But traditional urban communities were never like this . . . They were unstructured and diffuse . . . what made them safe was the fact that you never knew who you would meet in the street — but that you could be fairly sure you would meet someone. Strangers . . . policed public space, while inhabitants knew each other well enough to police the strangers. (Hansen 1983)

In other words, people will tend to be found in a particular spatial location because of its relationship to others, and to the area or city as a whole; they are there going about their daily business. But once this traditional street pattern has been disrupted, the throughput of people falls, and 'The modern estate appears to exist in a state of 'perpetual night' . . . the experience of walking around such areas can be quite frightening, whether or not any real danger exists' (Hillier & Hudson 1984).

COMMUTING: THE TRANSIENT CITY

Commuting seems a harmless enough activity, but it is enforced by great urban size, and itself further encourages size; Los Angeles is an extreme example. Jane Jacobs (1961), stressing that it is the community which in the end does the policing, says the mechanism of this consists of the 'eyes upon the street', and that those eyes are largely removed by commuting, which is generally on the increase. It is actually encouraged by city authorities — the Golden Gate bridge into San Francisco is free if there are two passengers with the driver — yet this deprives the environment of caring eyes. For it is responsible and present eyes which are needed, not people only concerned to travel through, whose contact is transient and irresponsible. Commuters lose effective contact with their place of residence, and in any event, during the day are simply not there. Nor are they any better as police when arrived at their office blocks; they care little for those surroundings, and usually vacate them the moment work stops. As Jacobs points out, the sprawl 'creates cars, creates smog, creates more sprawl', while security lies in going by car; 'Think what the crime figures might be if more people without metal shells were helpless upon the vast, blind-eyed reservations of Los Angeles'. But there are already 1200 homicides a year there — four times those in the entire UK. It seems reasonable to suggest that a city of a given gross size with less commuting will also be less crimogenic.

Once one is forced to commute to work, there are commercial temptations to make the mechanised part of the journey a few minutes longer, so that the length becomes quite disproportionate to its original necessity, and the 'advantage' is increased. To spend 15 to 20 hours each week journeying in and out of London or New York is not uncommon, and high-rise buildings, especially offices, are likely to exaggerate this tendency. French studies (Quoted in Baldwin & Bottoms 1976) have shown that for matched groups of workers, time spent playing with children, and hence the children's relationships with their parents, the conjugal relationship, and the amount of leisure time are all directly affected by the length of the journey to work. This matters, for as another Baldwin has said (1961): 'Children have never been very good at listening to their elders, but they have never failed to imitate them . . . they have no other models'. Commuting has a directly destructive effect — on the home area, which is not worked in; on the business locale, which is not lived in; and on the areas in between, which, used as passageways, inevitably cease to be 'places'. 'Public areas which were once intensively used have been reduced to mere arteries, mechanisms to get us from one place to another' (Newman 1980).

Jennings (1962) emphasises the difficulties caused by separation of home from workplace and draws attention to the problems of anonymity in the over-large urban environment, following insensitive urban renewal, which reverses the low crime rate associated with old, varied populations. She describes the fate of those now living in more impersonal areas; 'since they were not (now) known as persons, they could only assert their status through their material possession . . . Thus, debt, sometimes linked with increased matrimonial disharmony, became more common. Many were young and for the first time in their lives were removed from the restraining influence of parents' and neighbours' codes'. This situation can be interpreted in terms of the disturbance of social networks (see Chapter 2). Similarly, about 10 per cent of families who had moved from London to an overspill development in Andover returned, often after only a few months; in many cases, this resulted from financial difficulties due to such changes as higher rent, more expensive heating, hire purchase debts, lack of cheap street markets, and reduced earnings (Evans et al. 1969).

In the case of new communities, produced by commuting and urban dispersal, the distorted age-structure of new suburbs or towns may represent a significant disruption in networks of advice and assistance. It is quite likely that the emotional development of the young will therefore proceed less well than in a multi-generational setting. There are also likely to be acute social problems when very large numbers reach adolescence or leave school within a short period of time.

A recent study of Russian crime (Shelley 1980) found that a significant amount was committed by youngsters who commuted long hours to their schools and jobs, and who carried out offences not in their home suburban areas, but in the inner city communities to which they travelled. Similarly, Gardiner (1976) identified the intrusion of strangers into traditional community focal points, such as parks, schools, or small shopping areas as the source of significant amounts of American crime. Newman (1980) describes residential areas which were formerly part of an integrated amalgam with places of work, shopping, and entertainment as being now uni-functional zones, distantly located from the others; they are mainly 'a haphazard assembly of families of diverse ages and backgrounds, sharing little more than an occasional similarity in incomes, race or religious origin'. In such circumstances, increased crime is hardly surprising.

THE TRIPLE HYPOTHESIS

The hypothesis has been advanced above that the physical environment may be a magnifier of crime on three counts — urban overgrowth; dispersal created by or causing commuting; and gigantism of individual structures. The major factor is overall size, but as a crime precipitant, this is generally ignored by planners; it is as if we looked out on a world of crime so large that nobody can dare to notice it. Most discussion about large cities almost ignores the crime factor altogether (e.g. Gilbert 1976). It is hardly surprising, then, that the popular view of crime control tends to favour simply more police or tougher sentences, or that the American public buys more guns. The alternative would be to 'develop crime prevention programmes based on a new model of man and his environment' (Jeffery 1976).

There are, of course, other attributes of cities than size, and scale (i.e. a combined factor of size and density) but the views of planners and politicians, and even of most criminologists, would suggest that those attributes alone explain the criminality of large communities. It has not been suggested here that size alone causes crime, and that factors such as poverty or oppression are irrelevant, but rather that these latter take effect as magnified by the size/scale factor. But could the crimogenicity of cities be nothing to do with their size and only to do with the fact that they contain a high proportion of poor or unemployed people — or at any rate, a higher proportion than in other parts of industrialised countries? Investigation of these factors is made difficult by the phenomenon of clustering or colinearity, which requires complex statistical procedures to isolate the influence of any one of them.

SITUATIONAL AND TRANSPERSONAL VARIABLES OTHER THAN SIZE

The first of these variables is poverty. Bigger cities contain more poor, and the poor often tend to drift into cities; by and large, the poorer areas of a city are the more crime-ridden ones. In American cities generally, the distribution of crime is inversely related to income; in Minneapolis, this has been true recently of all the city except the central business district, where the rate is as high as in the lowest-income areas elsewhere, but most of this crime is against commercial and entertainment establishments. During the 1970s, though, crime in the US shifted steadily from commercial to residential areas (Newman 1980). Myers (1982) points out that the low-income, high-turnover secondary labour market can provide easy access to criminal work, and moving such workers into better paid jobs might be an effective way of reducing crime — unless they were replaced by others, even lower down the social scale at present.

However, the worst parts of Oakland or Harlem have inhabitants richer than those in the Himalayan foothills or some south sea islands, which are virtually crime-free. Smith (1974) points out that in Pennsylvania, some of the least affluent cities have the lowest recorded crime rates. Clinard (1978) compared Switzerland with even richer (and more crimeful) Sweden and says 'the pronounced differences in the extent of crime in these highly affluent countries indicate that ordinary crime basically is far from being produced by economic disadvantage, or poverty'. Sutherland and Cressey (1966) concluded that 'in poor communities most people do not steal . . . Poverty as such is not an important cause of crime'. Even the Marxist

Castells (1977) agrees that crime actually went down in the Depression of the 1930s. Carstairs (1969) believes that:

> The mere juxtaposition of wealth and poverty is not sufficient by itself to excite a spirit of revolt. The stimulus to develop impossible expectations seems to come from a sense of inner insecurity and helplessness, a total loss of confidence in one's own future . . . The situation is aggravated when, as a result of uncontrolled population increase, standards of living actually begin to decline at the very time when, by marginal, vicarious participation in a 'consumer culture', a people's material aspirations have been raised to new levels.

Either way, poverty may be crimogenic, but is not incapable of being magnified as a variable by urban oversize, though Hoch (1976) reports that in the US, with increasing city size, there is an increase in wage rates for the same work, which is stable over time; this of course is not relevant to the unemployed.

Secondly, there is the belief that some urban crime — especially street robbery — is associated with black skin. This is not wholly without statistical foundation, for blacks tend to congregate in cities, and the crime rate associated with them in the US is higher than for other groups. Silberman (1978) points to areas where blacks account for four or five times as many robberies per head as Hispanics, while Hoch (1972) concluded that as blacks tend to live in large cities, their crime figures get distorted, but that there is some relative increase in overall crime with greater city size and density, for a given racial mix. Blau & Blau (1982), from a study of urban criminal violence in the US, found this to be related to socio-economic irregularities between races, though within races, the picture was more complex. Thus, relative deprivation seemed to be more significant than poverty, and inter-racial inequality was considered to have a direct influence on violence against strangers. Hoch (1976) points out that American blacks have much higher heroin addiction rates than whites, and are therefore more likely to engage in robbery on that account. Since a well developed heroin market appears to be a function of city size, it may thus be reflected in higher rates of robbery.

Homogeneous ethnic areas may be better than mixed ones, in this respect at least. Interstitial areas, says Jeffery (1971), have always had high crime rates; 'in Baltimore the high rate area was the mixed Negro–white one, not the homogeneous ethnic areas (which) often have a very low crime rate because of their community organisation and informal controls'. Similarly, there is evidence that prevalence rates of psychiatric illness may be higher in racially integrated neighbourhoods than in either predominantly white or black areas (see Chapter 5). Jane Jacobs points out that in New York City, the Cross-Bronx Expressway created a vacuum area, which is dangerous; in 'West Side Story', the setting for the 'rumble' was under an expressway and the hero was killed in a playground. Oscar Newman has also repeatedly emphasised the dangers associated, under current conditions with such unused public spaces in large cities.

The third variable might be discrimination. Tensions lead to discontent;

are they therefore the real cause of public safety crime? Three examples argue against this. The working class in England in Victorian times was discriminated against in every conceivable way, yet the period after the introduction of a police force (1829) was not noted for public safety crime. Secondly, while the experience in America of blacks, whose crime rate is high, might support such a theory, that of the Japanese, whose crime rate is low, refutes it (Wilson 1975). Finally, in rural places, is discrimination — whether on grounds of race, class, or sex — less than in the city? Probably not, except that smaller numbers are involved, yet the two kinds of areas have very different crime rates. Harries (1980) points out that though it is possible to identify the correlates of crime, these are always imperfect; 'To say that poverty is often associated with crime is not to say that poverty causes crime. If that were the case, poverty would be linked to crime universally ... But only a minority of the poor, or victims of discrimination, of the insane, or the retarded become criminals, suggesting that criminality is a probabilistically arrived-at condition'.

Or is it just that our cities are badly laid out? There is Newman's (1972) concept of defensible space, focussed on crime control in specific housing schemes, though the localisation of crime control might have no more than that result. However, other favourable social consequences are possible, e.g. in improved neighbourly relationships, if previously unusable public space can be reclaimed for legitimate use. Research continues into whether buildings and projects which are better 'eye-patrolled' are both feasible and effective, in the terms proposed by Newman. But according to Gardiner (1978), 'the defensible space concept risks the danger of becoming a fortress within a neighbourhood', and perhaps the safer you make the fortress, the more unsafe you make its surrounding. Mayhew (1979) states that such solutions do little to reduce the overall levels of crime, and may be little more than displacement of anti-social activity or 'target hardening' — a view which Newan refutes. It has also been suggested that urban design theory such as Newman's represents 'pacification', as an alternative to structural reforms in society, though this is to confuse objectives, and recalls Rutter's warning (1981) about failure to attain practical goals because of an unreal search for 'basic causes'. However, there appear to be two clusters of behaviour intervening between environmental design and behavioural outcomes such as crime; these are residents' own behaviour and the perceptions of the environment by potential offenders, neither of which have been assessed fully (Taylor 1982). Hillier & Hudson (1984) conclude that spatial configuration strongly influences the apparent 'life' of residential areas, though this does not imply that it has any direct causative relationship with states of consciousness.

Another aspect might be protection; dungeons or iron-backed windows are effective, in their way, at keeping people in or out. Alistair Cooke once described his stay in the apartment of a rich friend; at two in the morning, feeling the need of air, he sought to open the window. The block had been designed on the assumption that the only person who would try to open a window would be a burglar; alarms were set off within and without. In a few minutes, he was confronted in his room with the local police, the apartment block's security service, the neighbours, and his astonished host. In fact, what happens in general when a neighbourhood fills with protection devices, alarms, dogs, and posted warnings is counter-productive. Far from residents coming to feel safer, they perceive more danger, and feel less able themselves to tackle any that may arise. 'Eventually this perception can lead to a breakdown of the community's social structure by resident withdrawal from neighbourhood life and indifference to problems and thus a relegation to the police of total responsibility for neighbourhood control' (Gardiner 1978). The idea that the high crime rates of cities are due to poor physical protection would be an odd one if one were to compare city with country, the grilles and guards of big city stores with the open door of the little country post office.

The public, however, usually sees crime in cities as an offshoot of the failure of another kind of protection — that of the criminal justice system itself. Militant criminologists also, of both left and right, commonly share this view; from the left maintaining that the system is a pompous irrelevance, and that there should be a return to the 'root causes', while from the right, there is a demand for harder sentences or for more police. As Alderson (1979) puts it:

> There are many people with a vested interest in perpetuating the myth that society is made up of the criminals and the non-criminals, and that if the police and criminal courts and penal institutions are only given sufficient resources, the time will come when all the criminals will be caught and sentenced, and all will be well ... it is an important symbolic act for society to indicate its abhorrence of serious crime and its disapproval of crime generally, (but) misleading to suggest that crime can be properly controlled in this way.

Neither is manpower or technology and equipment apparently the answer. The British police are almost entirely unarmed, and the policing ratio for London around half as many per resident as it is for New York. In 1971, rape and murder figures were, for London, 135 and 113 respectively; for New York, 3271 and 1691; the two populations are about the same size. Only recently have British police acquired any helicopters at all, whereas the Oakland (California) police force alone has two, for a population of about 330 000, as well as 100 squad cars and every possible aid in computers, forensic medicine and technology. Yet the numbers of murders in Oakland alone equals that of the entire UK annually, and would be higher, had local hospitals not become peculiarly expert in bringing the bullet-ridden back to life.

These comparisons of similar-sized New York and London, and (below) of New York with even bigger Tokyo, might seem to refute a relationship of urban size to crime. On that simple basis, London would be as dangerous as New York, and Tokyo worse than either, but that is not the hypothesis. Any person lives in an environment within which he regularly has to meet, make contact with, and react to a certain number of people. If this reactive field is too big, then it appears to become one crimogenic factor which is a magnifier of others — a burner to heat up an unpleasant mix or base rate, determined by historical, social and cultural forces. The mix in Tokyo and in London is at present a mild one; in the US, it appears to be generally more dangerous and unstable. Accordingly, one could expect to find that the ratio of public safety crime in New York City is to that in the rural upstate area as that of Greater London is to rural Kent. Haynes (1973) hypothesised that if everyone in a population other than the actual criminal is a potential victim for a given crime, crime opportunity would be a function of the square of the population. But in fact, only a fraction of the theoretically available opportunities are realised, so that density of opportunities may be the key crime indicator; this is related to the sociological concept of social density (Webb 1972). Harries (1980) suggests that the key concept of an urban system is interaction, and that the potential for this — including criminal interaction — is increased in a system with numerous effective linkages. Thus, density of opportunities for crime might be more significant than their actual number, and more closely related to overall crime rates than either population size or density. When Haynes examined the 1960 data for six different forms of crime in 86 US cities of varying size, the density–opportunity model corresponded closely to rates of assault and car theft, whereas other crimes were below expectation. These data are now very old, but Choldin (1978) reports that studies of three American cities, which he carried out with Roncek, showed no relationship between crime rates and 'population potential' — a combination of the population per area at a particular location and the accessibility of individuals throughout the area to a person at a given point.

It is not surprising therefore that Alderson (1979) as a practising policeman, urged that since 'all the indications are that reintegration should begin with the creation of smaller communities . . . the pattern of the rural village should be introduced and strengthened within the city'. Clifford (1976) compared crime in Japan with that in the US, and called for 'community alternatives . . . for simpler social solutions to crime than repression by helicopters, electronics, computerisation of records, and armed policemen'. Unfortunately, the 'communities' referred to are often not in existence, and American figures may actually understate the problem, since city crime has been somewhat reduced by the unwillingness of people there to go out more than they have to. This behaviour, though, must have very adverse effects, both on their personal lives and relationships and on the social and cultural life of the urban society, not to mention its economy.

SIZE AND DENSITY

High crime rates in relation to population pressures are often vaguely thought of as due to overcrowding or excessive density, and much misplaced 'urban renewal' has resulted. The confusion between size and density is very frequent, but places can be small and highly dense, large and dense, or large and not at all dense (see Chapter 2). Hong Kong has 150 times the density of the US, yet its homicide rate is one-sixth as high (Scherer et al. 1975). Tokyo is hardly less dense than New York City, yet it has some 350 robberies a year compared to 15 000, and one-tenth the number of rapes; New York records nearly as many murders as the whole of Japan (Bayley 1976). The research of Freedman (1975) provided no evidence that high density was bad for people: 'Those crimes most related to aggressive feelings, which should be the best indication of the effects of crowding, show absolutely no relation to population density', while high density also results in a greater degree of surveillance by others. Scherer et al. (1975) point out that cities in the US have been getting less dense as they have become more violent; Los Angeles is an example. Yet in parts of Nepal, whole small communities are said to go into a kind of hibernation all winter, the inhabitants often sleeping ten to a room to keep warm; the crime rate there has been described as nil!

If density is taken to mean overcrowding, which is to some extent a subjective standard, then like any other chronic misfortune, it may contribute to crime (Roncek 1975). However, in the non-pejorative sense, density has been shown to be related to crime, but negatively (Harries 1980). Kvalseth (1977) found unemployment to have a magnifying effect on the crime rate, but density, if significant at all, again a negative one. Hoch (1974) predicted that some causes of crime may be associated with urban scale, defined as embracing both size and density. He found that in fact, the introduction of other independent variables attenuates, but does not eliminate the positive effect of population size on crime; 'contrary to initial hypothesis, density generally tends to have a negative effect on crime, and this persists even with the introduction of other variables. Because density is positively related with population size, the negative density effect is an offset to the positive effect of size on crime rates'. In other words, as a crimogenic variable, size would have an even more pronounced effect, were it not commonly accompanied — perhaps mercifully — by high density. However, Harries (1980) concludes that 'definite studies of the relationships between crime, density and crowding have yet to be performed'.

Mixing up millions of people without demarcation has only happened in the very recent history of man.

> The preindustrial cities of medieval Europe and those which still exist in some parts of the world have certain common features . . . The buildings were crowded together and there was a high density within them . . . (there was) strict social segregation, exemplified in sharply delineated 'quarters' or 'wards' . . . Each ethnic group tended to live separately and to utilise a distinct occupation niche . . . The cramped living quarters encouraged the development of well-defined neighbourhoods. Such groups provided a cohesive social unit with clear guidelines for behaviour among its members, and extensive opportunity for children to observe the activities of adults. Bonds among the members of each group tended to be strongly reinforced through common religious beliefs and activities (Hamburg 1971)

These characteristics have almost totally disappeared from present-day cities in industrialised countries.

High density which is not shiftless and transient can still go with togetherness and sharing; the poorer parts of London for many years were relatively safe and friendly. Scherer et al. (1975) give an account of post-war Bethnal Green, a crowded London East End district, which was also predominantly a close ethnic group (Jewish):

> Family ties were close and everyone seemed to know everyone else. A spirit of warmth and familiarity pervaded the area. Most people had lived in the borough for a long time and shared a background of school or gang or pub with their neighbours. Relatives were apt to live close by. A man had only to stand at his front door to find someone out of his past who (was) also in his present. Relatives provided a link with the larger community. A person was friends with his brother's friends and was likely to be acquainted with his uncle's neighbours. Those who lived on the same street enjoyed a special feeling of community. Each 'turning' made up a sort of village, with its own meeting places, shops, pubs, and occasional parties. Thus, the Bethnal Greener was surrounded not only by his own relatives and their acquaintances, but also by his acquaintances and their relatives'.

However, Rutter (1981) states that although such milieux may be becoming less frequent, 'cohesive homogeneous communities with a substantial sharing of values, a high level of social interaction and support, and a feeling of distinctiveness from other areas have probably always been rather atypical of cities'.

An alternative argument might be canvassed that criminals tend to congregate in cities, but that urban size is no more relevant here than is the size of a whole field to a bee seeking nectar. Therefore, to urge that hugeness causes crime is ingenuous; criminals go there on purpose. This is certainly realistic, since many offences, such as white collar crime and complicated frauds can only be carried out in a sophisticated and massive environment, where the targets for other 'touches' may also be more numerous. Professional criminals show mobility; over 50 per cent of the already low crime rate of Italian-speaking Switzerland is due to Italians who come especially to commit crime, and who regard the Swiss as a soft option (Clinard 1978). This self-selection effect is described by Fischer (1975) as a 'third factor explanation', in which the significance of ecological factors is indirect, rather than aetiological.

City size *per se*, however, may still be a crimogenic factor. One common reason for going to cities for certain kinds of crime (and especially public safety crime, such as burglary and robbery) is because the surveillance may be expected to be low and detection unlikely. Streets may be so thronged with both people and vehicles as to maximise pockets to be picked and minimise pursuit.

Keim (1981) believes, however, that the relationships between spatial organisations and urban ways of life may actually be much more complex than those on which classical social ecology has focussed, and which fail to come to grips with structural relationships. The thesis that larger cities have more crime was derived from the selective nature of social contacts there, leading to less social control, together with greater opportunities for deviant behaviour, e.g. from concentrations of property. Keim proposes three possible structural relationships between cities and criminal violence: actualising — social conditions are affected by urban structure so that deviant behaviour which would otherwise have remained latent now takes place; symbolic — elements of the urban structure are chosen as suitable objects against which violence is directed, e.g. semi-public entrances and lifts; productive — elements of the urban structure contain forms of violence which are directed at the spatially organised inhabitants. All three relationships are likely to operate, though to varying extents in different places. Keim studied three different types of housing areas in German cities, and did not confirm Newman's findings that in high-rise buildings, the rate of violent crime increased with the number of storeys. Since 1976, the cities with the highest relative number of offences have been Frankfurt, Berlin and Hamburg — the three largest — but in the period 1971–1979, the total rate of criminality in cities with more than 100 000 people (accounting for 34 per cent of the national population) changed little. The rate of juvenile delinquency has not shown any marked relationship to the size of cities, and though inner city areas contain relatively large numbers of foreigners, their rate of offending is lower than that of German males. However, the presence of some institutional buildings, such as railway stations and barracks, will tend to result in more aggressive offences occurring in their districts, whilst new housing areas may encourage delinquency through failing to allow for the needs of young people; such environmental factors must be remembered, in considering criminal statistics for cities.

WHY SHOULD SIZE MATTER?

Unless there is a real community, there can be no feeling of community; without a feeling of community, there will be no eyes in the street, none of the 'public figures' who note the vandalised parking meter, report a suspicious entry, stop a teenage vandal, hand in a found wristwatch. To create a community, it is not enough merely to label places, as newly built houses which have never been slept in are labelled 'homes' (Gardiner 1978). A community is somewhere with a sense of place, a sense of identity, and able to give its members (many of whom will work, as well as live there) a feeling of these qualities. But a sense of place is not achieved overnight. Gertrude Stein, born in Oakland, when asked if she would ever go back, answered 'Go back there? There is no *there* there'. Barnes (1980) says that 'A community can only persist in a wholesome way if it has an objective well beyond itself', while Leighton (1982) points out that many geographically defined populations today are little more than crossroads for regional or national networks, and are largely devoid of the kind of autonomy and competence required to run their own mental health service, for instance.

Storr (1985) as a psychiatrist, believes that:

It is principally in big cities that the individual can easily feel that he is a mere cog; an expendable element in a vast machine which could just as easily do without him. In a village, hostile tensions between people may be extreme. Gossip, back-biting, and malice flourish just as much, if not more, in small communities. But they at least feel that they exist; even if their place is only that of the village idiot, it is better than feeling one is nothing.

Also, as is pointed out in Chapter 5, human problems will generally be much more visible in a smaller community, and it will be more difficult to neglect them, even though they may actually be less common, as a proportion of the general population.

From the point of view of a zoologist, Desmond Morris (1979) considers a certain degree of size as beyond man's inherent scope. In the course of the history of man, 'Super-tribal clashes became bloodier . . . As human relationships, lost in the crowd, become even more impersonal, so man's inhumanity to man is increased to horrible proportions . . . (since) an impersonal relationship is not a biologically human one, this is not surprising'.

He defines our over-large societies in historic terms as 'super tribes':

> It has often been said that the law forbids men to do only what their instincts incline them to do. It follows from this that if there are laws against theft, murder and rape, then the human animal must, by nature, be a thieving, murderous rapist. Is this really a fair description of man as a social biological species? Somehow, it does not fit the zoological picture of the emerging tribal species. Sadly, it does fit the super-tribal picture. Theft, perhaps the most common of crimes, is a good example. A member of a super-tribe is under pressure, from all the stresses and strains of his artificial social condition. Most people in his super-tribe are strangers to him; he has no personal, tribal bond with them. The typical thief is not stealing from one of his known companions. He is not breaking the old, biological tribal code. In his mind, he is simply setting his victim outside his tribe altogether.

Sociologically, Marris (1974) described the bereaving effect of slum clearance, and how profoundly discontinuity of old associations disrupts individuals: 'Since people cannot assimilate change without continuity they are bound to evade the purposes of slum clearance in any way they can. The outcome can be destructive: not only for the residents, but for society at large'. He adds that:

> tribal associations help reconcile the need to identify with the nation without being overwhelmed by strangers, who rob you not only of your livelihood but of a sense of your own being. Here, the tribal boundaries which protect the integrity of each group are sensitive to any disturbance of this delicate balance. Once upset, the hostility towards others latent in tribal self-consciousness breaks out in violent denunciation. The more secure a tribal group, the more confident of its collective identity, the less fear will be projected upon its stereotypes of other tribes.

'Tribal' may be seen as a concept relevant to long-established urban communities, usually of the working class, though it should not be taken in a pejorative sense. Rapaport (1975) believes that the destruction of social networks and homogeneous enclaves leads to feelings of crowding and possibly stress, because the presence of strangers requires more attention and information processing, with a higher perceived density in the area.

Hamburg's study of aggression (1971) stresses our tendency to label and group people as 'they' or 'us'. 'The outgroup is classified as essentially non-human . . . Groups under stress respond by blaming their difficulties on other groups . . . The strange group, not well known or 'understood', is a likely target of animosity. Such relations represent one of the great dangers of our era, perhaps even greater than most diseases'. Larger communities are also more likely to experience a separation into sub-areas with different social characteristics, where the disadvantaged may be left to themselves, out of sight of those higher in the social scale; Clausen & Kohn (1959) found that in a medium sized town, schizophrenics were fairly uniformly distributed whereas in large cities, they tend to be concentrated in areas of lower status.

It may be that the community is the only responsible society, and that from living in it, people will feel that in looking after others around them, they are looking after their own. Neighbourhoods and urban regions may require 'legitimate sovereignty' for their inhabitants as a basic requirement for crime control (Nieburg 1974); this is seen both in terms of physical and of legal urban design, of environment and autonomy. Thus, big cities are inimical to concern with those around us, so far as crime is concerned, and while urbanisation involves movement and migration, relocation involves loss; severe loss disrupts the continuity which appears to be essential as a framework for effective functioning.

Finally, it should be re-emphasised that the discussion here has mainly related to urban settlements in Western industrialised countries. East European countries do not publish sufficient data to make valid comparisons, though it may be assumed that cities in which private market forces are largely absent, and in which population mobility is much reduced will have rather different patterns of criminal behaviour. The huge new cities of Asia, Africa, and South America are also not directly comparable with the older ones of North America and Western Europe, though it would be almost inconceivable that they did not have relatively much higher rates of crime than the villages and small towns from which most of their present inhabitants have migrated.

EXPERIMENTS RELATING TO URBAN SCALE

Experiments (quoted by Milgram 1970) have been carried out into people's reactions to circumstances of differing environmental scale; for instance, to test the difference in helpfulness between subjects in small and large towns respectively. In one, researchers, as anonymous strangers, telephoned subscribers with a series of requests for help which were increasingly onerous in scale. The urban subjects were more helpful than expected, expectation being rather low, though it is possible that they felt more secure in giving help or advice over the phone than in other situations. Nonetheless, people in the city were found to be less helpful and informative than those in small towns.

Another experiment investigated willingness to admit strangers. Experimenters (total strangers to those on whose door they knocked) asked if they could come into the house to use the phone, claiming to have mislaid the address of a nearby friend; they were between twice and five times as likely to be admitted in small towns. The women were far more successful than the men, but each investigator did at least twice as well in towns as in cities. Milgram concluded that 'the city–town distinction overrides even the predictably greater fear of male strangers than of female ones'.

Experiments in differences between city and town behaviour were also conducted by Zimbardo (1973); in one, cars were abandoned in the Bronx and in Palo Alto respectively. In each case, the bonnet was left up, so that the car appeared to have been temporarily left because of some mechanical distress. Within 10 minutes, the New York car was visited by a family, who removed the radiator, battery, and contents of the glove compartment and boot. There were 22 other separate visits by evildoers over the next 3 days, at the end of which time the car was a 'battered, useless pile of junk'. The Palo Alto car was left unmolested for a week without incident, though one old man stopped to put the bonnet down, murmuring that 'the motor shouldn't be allowed to get wet'. At the end of the week, the despairing research team removed the car, at which two members of the public promptly phoned the police to complain that the car was being stolen.

In April 1964, a New Yorker called Kitty Genovese was set upon by a mentally disturbed man, on her return home. He took over half an hour to stab her to death, leaving and returning twice to get a sharper knife. Thirty-eight of her neighbours in this high-rise building not only heard her terrified and persistent screaming — persisted in until her death — but actually were able to watch, and did so. Not one of them even called the police.

This event prompted studies by Latane & Darley (1970). They concluded that the conscious presence of others in a situation inhibits action, and that if these others are seen to do nothing — perhaps because they are considering whether the matter is serious, or what should be done — the impassivity is (circularly) seen by the others as an indication that it is not serious, or that there is some other objective reason for not interfering. In effect, a 'stranger group' situation inhibits helping out in emergency, but perhaps even more significantly, it was shown that people have no real conception that this is how they behave — that they do not in fact take independent decisions.

In one experiment, subjects had to listen to the sound of an apparently injured woman calling for help; 30 per cent did not respond. When a coauditor stooge, who did nothing, was placed with them, 90 per cent did not respond. Yet subjects almost always claimed that in a 'real' emergency, they would be among the first to help a victim. They also remained inert, although next to noises of children seriously hurting each other, yet then assured the interviewer that had the fight been real, they would have immediately intervened; in fact, the noises sounded entirely real. When bogus bystanders, who had instructions to be inactive, were introduced as onlookers to an emergency, this 'seeded' the result, since subjects then became even more disproportionately apathetic. The most significant finding was that people were quite unwilling to admit that their perceptions are influence by others present, but it also emerged that for a bystander in New York chancing to witness distress or crime, the smaller the size of the community in which he grew up, the more likely he was to help the victim.

These factors may affect police perceptions, morale, and in turn their efficiency. According to Wilson (1975) 'the police are convinced that lack of citizen cooperation and support is a major barrier to crime control. Any patrolman can recount many stories of an investigation being frustrated because bystanders claimed they saw nothing, witnesses refused to testify, victims dropped charges, and no one would come to an officer's aid when he was being overpowered in a scuffle'. If people's behaviour, their urge to crime, is powerfully affected by their position, by the complexity of numbers around them, rather than by character, upbringing, morals, or even attitude to the police; if the urban situation has as persistent and terrible an effect as here described, would we not have noticed the fact? Possibly not.

Milgram (1974) conducted a series of now well known experiments into behaviour, when the subject perceived himself as under command; however, there was no sanction if the subject disobeyed, and he even knew he would get paid. The discipline, then, fell a good deal short of that in armies, where disobedience might result in being court martialled and shot. However, subjects did in fact perceive themselves as under direction, when they were confronted with what was presented as 'an experiment in teaching and punishing'. They were instructed to give shocks of increasing severity for each wrong answer, and understood from the machine, with its warnings of 'extreme shock' or 'danger' at the top end, that this would be eventually lethal. This was reinforced by the grunts, groans, and ultimately (as shocks increased) the screams, and then silence of the victim. Yet about two-thirds of the subjects were prepared, with only verbal coercion from the experimenter, to give the victim what they must have thought were fatal shocks. However, when two stooges who were seen as peers, and who did object to the treatment, were placed with them, 36 out of 40 subjects defied the experimenter, i.e. were not prepared to give 'lethal' shocks.

In the present context of urban environments, the significant point is that a majority of 'defiant' subjects denied that the confederates' action was the critical factor in their own defiance, although it clearly was. Another group then had the experiment and its object explained to them, and were asked to guess the results. They predicted that virtually all the experimental subjects would refuse to obey the experimenter to the end, and that only a pathological fringe would have gone so far. Thus, people have a distorted perception of how far their behaviour is controlled by their immediate situation, rather than by their past beliefs and training. However, investigations have shown that behaviours stemming from social relationships are highly patterned to fit a particular setting; this phenomenon of 'behaviour setting' is composed of three highly interlinked parts — places, people, and actions (Murphy 1976).

Darley & Batson (1973) told theological students to go off and deliver a sermon on the Good Samaritan. Some were told they were late, others that they had plenty of time; the situation was rigged so that each had to pass an alleyway, which contained a moaning man, covered in blood. Only 10 per cent of those who thought they were in a hurry stopped. Zimbardo attributes the amazing behaviour quite 'respectable' people will exhibit when they sense they are free of controls to 'deindividuation', and therefore suggests the need for 'neighbourhoods where people are recognised by others and are concerned about the social evaluation of those others'.

In behavioural matter, it seems, people largely deceive themselves, and this is highly relevant when huge numbers of people are gathered into urban settlements. Situational influences must be less influential in small communities, where it is much more likely that individuals will be personally known to each other, or at least have something in common. Rutter (1981) comments that 'People behave in the way that they do not only as a result of individual predisposition but also through ecological or group predisposing factors (such as the neighbourhood and school influences), through current circumstances (in terms of stresses and crises, protective factors and sources of support), and also through opportunities and situation'.

BACKGROUND FOR RESEARCH

If urban size if crimogenic, then we would have a monstrous society, and be in the process of making a worse one — actually building crime. Through the level of expansion now reached, we may threaten whole cities as places to live — even the integrity of society itself. Yet if this is right, how strange that social scientists have been so little concerned with a 'process which claims to underlie all human organisation and forms the very basis of human tragedy' (Zimbardo 1969). Moreover, the evidence on urban size is subject to argument about the extent to which other variables operate which are colinear with it; solid evidence is also lacking about gigantism in structures, while the effect of commuting is so far speculative.

There are signs, though, that criminologists are moving towards a livelier interest in this question. 'Since crime rates seem to differ so much between town and country, and since urban theory has devoted so much energy to themes of contrast, one might expect that criminologists would have made extensive use of such themes. This, however, is decidedly not the case'

(Baldwin 1976). 'Decisions on transportation, residential and commercial development, parks and recreation, planning and zoning are being made without realisation that they can directly result in the opportunity for crime and fear of crime. While it is the avowed purpose of city planning to coordinate such impact decisions, all too often this is not done' (Gardiner 1978).

'Criminological themes have been little concerned with situational determinants of crime. The main object . . . has been to show how some people are born with or come to acquire a 'disposition' to behave in a consistently criminal manner' (Clarke 1980). 'Criminology must shift from a *service* orientation to a scientifically based *research* orientation . . . A major research project should be undertaken to determine the ways in which urban design contributes to crime' (Jeffery 1971). Yet a multi-author book on environmental criminology (Brantingham & Brantingham 1981) does not deal specifically with the question of urban size at all.

This kind of situational criminology must be inter-disciplinary, whereas most investigators have a narrow professional focus. Relevant work may appear in a bewildering variety of publications — geographical, psychological, urban studies, sociological — but the need for joint programmes is becoming recognised. Herbert (1979) says that: 'Urban crime, perhaps more than any other single theme, has demonstrated the need for an interdisciplinary view', and Reppetto (1976) that:

> the criminological community has tended to reject or ignore design theory . . . key obstacles are the nature of the discipline of criminology (and) incorrect perceptions of what crime prevention via urban design involves . . . The proponents of urban design largely come from the field of planning and architecture . . . a discipline that has no traditions of interaction with criminology. If the response of criminologists is to ignore them, then the discipline is likely to become increasingly irrelevant to real-world considerations of crime.

If indeed criminology exists to explain and reduce crime, it has so far failed. Any real progress will require much longer-term perspectives, as well as consideration of how to make an impact on the public with the findings that may emerge from research.

If there were a sincere desire to tackle public safety crime, it might be possible to manipulate existing cities so as to create within them fairly independent areas, within which most people would both work and live. There, they could feel themselves identified and at home, living in a real place, and might therefore regard themselves as in a community, keep an eye on things, and so be in effect the police. A start could be made by converting empty city centre buildings for residential use, at reasonable prices. It may be that this would be a return to the only kind of large city situation man has ever coped with adequately, and imaginitive sub-division might be the kind of approach that could save cities like Los Angeles from uncontrollable social pathologies. Newman (1980) advocates the 'community of interest', consisting of people of similar age and life-style but with a mixture of income-groups and races; they would be denser, and smaller in size and scale than suburban communities, but in combination, would make possible the investment in public facilities that can serve a large and varied population. In that way, the mostly abandoned belief in urban culture would be restored. Leroy (1974) has proposed that there is a relationship between mental health and the potential for local decision making, so that if communities were dealt with by governments as groups of responsible citizens , alienation might be reduced and personal identity enhanced.

RESEARCH SUGGESTIONS

More comparisons are needed of crime rates for populations of differing sizes. This information is not usually available , however, from published police reports, which tend to give figures for areas covered by that force, rather than for whole communities. As well as more detailed data from the police, this would require alternative sources , such as courts, self-reported crime, or victim surveys. Results for a number of other variables also need to be compared , e.g. the rise or fall of serious crime on a national basis. For instance, it could not be claimed that the doubling of crime rates in a settlement that has grown by 50 per cent over 10 years is associated with that growth, if there was a national doubling of crime in the same period.

It might also be useful to select a particular public safety crime, such as robbery, and see if the rural/city rate increases are broadly the same in different societies, or to compare cities which started with the same population, but then had either rapid growth,none, or a decline. Do cities of the same size, but differing in the time they have been so, vary in their effects on social pathology? Some which have little commuting could be compared with similar-sized ones which are strongly affected by the commuting process. Another variable which needs investigation is that of high-rise structures; it might be possiible to compare towns which differ mainly in having low profile and informal buildings on the one hand, or high-rise and massive structures on the other. Similarly, those with a grid-iron street pattern might be compared with others, which have irregularly directed roads, influenced by geography and topography. Kasl & Rosenberg (1980) state that studies of victimisation and fear of crime among the elderly generally do not extend to an examination of the empirical link to mental health and well-being. This clearly needs to be done ,and there is also the question of how to achieve feedback since such information as exists about consequences of urban size has up to now had virtually no impact on planners or policy makers. Much might also be learnt from the experience of a pilot scheme of 'community policing' in Devon and Cornwall (Blaber 1979).

The evidence which has been discussed here can leave little doubt as to the importance of the subject, whether seen primarily from the point of view of social stability, or in terms of the mental health of city residents. As Chapter 2 pointed out, cities characterise the extreme aspects of any society; the best, in terms of cultural and economic opportunities,and the worst, in terms of environmental pollution, overcrowded housing, and social pathology such as crime. Dicken & Lloyd (1981, quoted by Whitelegg 1982) state that city size appears to be a key influence in the large variations in social well-being which are found between urban areas of both the US and Britain — 'Increasingly . . . the big city is regarded as a 'bad' rather than a 'good', as the focus of many of the problems facing modern society, particularly social and environmental problems. In fact, it is extremely difficult to separate problems which occur *in* the city, and simply reflect the fact that a majority of the population live there, from problems which are intrinsically *of* the city in the sense that they are produced by urban processes'. The problem of resolving this dichotomy remains to be answered by future research — but research on a different scale from that of the past.

REFERENCES

Alderson J 1979 Policing freedom. Macdonald & Evans, Plymouth
Baldwin J 1961 Nobody knows my name. The Dial Press, New York
Baldwin John 1979 Ecological and areal studies in GB and the US. In: Morris M, Tonry M (eds) Crime and justice: an annual review of research Volume 1, Chicago University Press, Chicago
Baldwin J, Bottoms A E 1976 The urban criminal. Tavistock, London
Barnes K 1980 Unpublished address to London Yearly Meeting of the Religious Society of Friends
Bayley D H 1976 Forces of order: police behaviour in Japan and the US. University of California Press, Berkeley
Blaber A 1979 The Exeter Community Policing Consultative Group. A study of the first year. NACRO, London
Blau J R, Blau P M 1982 The cost of inequality: metropolitan structure and violent crime. American Sociological Review 47: 114–129
Bottoms A E, Xanthos P 1981 Housing policy and crime in the British public sector. In: Brantingham P & P (eds) Environmental criminology. Sage, New York
Briggs A (Lord) 1982 The environment of the city. Encounter 59: 25–35
Carstairs G M Overcrowding and human aggression. In: Gurr G (ed) The history of violence in America. Praeger, New York
Castells M 1977 The Urban question: A Marxist approach. Edward Arnold, London
Choldin H M 1978 Urban density and pathology. Annual Review of Sociology 4: 91–113
Christie N, Andenaes J, Skorbetch S 1965 A study of self-reported crime. In: Scandinavian studies in criminology, Volume 1. Munksgard, Copenhagen
Clarke R V G 1980 Situational crime prevention: theory and practice, British Journal of Criminology, 20: 136–141
Clifford W 1976 Crime in Japan. D C Heath, Lexington, Mass
Clinard M B 1978 Cities with little crime. Cambridge University Press, Cambridge
Coleman A 1983 Defensible space on the map. Urban Design Quarterly February: 3
Cressey D R 1964 Delinquency crime and differential association. Nijhoff, The Hague
Criminal Statistics for England and Wales 1979. HMSO, London
Darley J M, Batson C O 1973 From Jerusalem to Jericho: a study of situational variables in behavior. Journal of Social Psychology 27: 100–108
Department of Housing and Urban Development (US) 1978 A survey of citizen views and concerns about urban life, Final Report, Part 1. Louis Harris, Washington, DC
Dicken P, Lloyd P 1981 Modern Western Society: a geographical perspective on work, home and well-being. Harper & Row, London
Eisenberg L 1962 The sins of the fathers: urban decay and social pathology. American Journal of Orthopsychiatry: 5–17
Evans J W, Lovel J W I, Eaton K K 1969 British Medical Journal i: 44–46
Fischer C S 1975 The study of urban community and personality. Annual Review of Sociology 1: 67–89

Freedman J L 1975 Crowding and behavior. Viking Press, New York

Freeman H L 1975 The environment and human satisfaction. International Journal of Mental Health 4: 6–14

Freeman H L 1978 Mental Health and the environment. British Journal of Psychiatry 132: 113–124

Gardiner R A 1976 Crime and the neighbourhood environment. HUD Challenge 8: 9–13

Gardiner R A 1978 Design for safe neighbourhoods. National Institute for Law Enforcement, Washington DC

Gilbert A 1976 The arguments for very large cities reconsidered. Urban Studies 13: 17–35

Gillis A R, Hagan J 1982 Density, delinquency and design. Criminology 19: 514–529

Gold H 1982 The sociology of urban life. Prentice Hall, Englewood Cliffs, NJ

Gurr R T, Grabusky P N, Hula R C The politics of crime and conflict: A comparative study of four cities. Sage, Beverley Hills

Hamburg D A 1971 Crowding, stranger contact and agressive behaviour. In: Levi L (ed) Society, stress and disease. Oxford University Press, Oxford

Hansen J 1983 Out of touch with front doors. The Guardian, July 27

Hansen J, Hillier W E G 1984 The architecture of community. Architecture and Behaviour (In the press)

Harries K D 1973 Spatial aspects of violence and metropolitan population. Professional Geographer 25: 1–6

Harries K D 1974 The Geography of crime and justice. McGraw-Hill, New York

Harries K D 1980 Crime and the environment. Charles C Thomas, Springfield, Illinois

Haynes R M 1973 Crime rates and city size in America. Area 5: 162–165

Herbert D 1979 Urban crime: A geographical perpsective. In: Social problems and the City. Oxford University Press, London

Hillier W E G, Hudson J 1984 Creating life. Architecture and behaviour (In press)

Hoch I 1972 Income and city size. Urban Studies 9: 299–328

Hoch I 1974 Factors in urban crime. Journal of Urban Economics 1: 184–229

Hoch I 1976 City size effects, trends and policies. Science 193: 856–863

Jacobs J 1961 Death and life of great American cities. Random House, New York

Jeffery C R 1971 Crime prevention through environmental design. Sage, Beverley Hills

Jeffery C R 1976 Criminal behaviour and the physical environment — a perspective. American Behavioural Scientist 20: 171–5

Jennings H 1962 Societies in the making. Routledge & Kegan Paul, London

Kasl S V, Rosenfield S 1980 The residential environment and its impact on the mental health of the aged. In: Birren J E, Sloane R B (eds) Handbook of mental health and aging. Prentice Hall, Englewood Cliffs, NJ

Keim D 1981 City and criminality. Paper to International Criminological Congress, Thessaloniki

Kohn M L 1974 Social class and schizophrenia: A critical review and reformulation. In: Ronen P M, Trice H M (eds) Explorations in psychiatric sociology. Davis, Philadelphia

Kvalseth T O 1977 Note of the effects of population density and unemployment on urban crime. Sage, Beverley Hills

Latane B, Darley J M 1970 The unresponsive bystander: why doesn't he help? Prentice-Hall, Englewood Cliffs, NJ

Leighton A 1982 Caring for mentally ill people. Cambridge University Press, Cambridge

Leroy C 1974 Housing et santé mental. Psychiatrica Clinica (Basel) 7: 237–270

McClintock F H, Avison N H 1968 Crime in England and Wales. Heinemann, London

Marris P 1974 Loss and change. Routledge & Kegan Paul, London

Mawby R I 1977 Defensible space: a theoretical and empirical appraisal. Urban Studies 14: 169–179

Mayhew P 1979 Defensible space: the current status of a crime prevention theory. The Howard Journal 18: 150–159

Merton R K 1964 Anomie, anomia and social interaction. In: Clinard M B (ed) Anomie and deviant behaviour. The Free Press, Glencoe, NY

Milgram S 1970 The experience of living in cities. Science 167: 1461–8

Milgram S 1974 Obedience to authority. Tavistock, London

Morris D 1969 The human zoo. Jonathan Cape, London

Mulvilhill D J, Tumin M M 1969 Crimes of violence. US Government Printing Office, Washington, DC

Murphy J E 1976 Social causes: the independent variable. In: Kaplan B H, Wilson R N, Leighton A H (eds) Further explorations in socail psychiatry. Basic Books, New York

Newman O 1972 Defensible space. Macmillan, New York

Newman O 1975 Reactions to the 'Defensible space' study and some further findings. International Journal of Mental Health 4: 48–70

Newman O 1980 Community of interest. Anchor Doubleday, New York

Newman O, Franck K A 1980 Factors influencing crime and instability in urban housing developments. US Department of Justice, Washington, DC

Nieburg H L 1974 Crime prevention by urban design. Society 12: 41–47

Phillips P D, Brunn S D 1978 Slow growth: a new epoch of American metropolitan evolution. Geographical Review 68: 274–292

Rapoport A 1975 Toward a new definition of density. Environment and Behaviour 7: 133–158

Réponses à la Violence 1977: Rapport du comité national de prevention de la violence. Presses Pochek, Paris

Reppetto T 1976 Crime prevention through environmental policy. American Behavioral Scientist 20: 275–80

Roncek D W 1975 Density and crime: a methodological critique. American Behavioral Scientist 18: 843–860

Scherer K R, Abeles R P, Fischer C S 1975 Human aggression and conflict: interdisciplinary perspectives. Prentice-Hall, Englewood Cliffs, NJ

Scott P 1972 The spatial analysis of crime and delinquency. Australian Geographical Studies 10: 1–18

Shelley L S 1980 Geography of Soviet criminality. American Sociological Review: 45: 111–122

Sigvardson S, Claninger R, Bohman M, Von Knorring A L 1982 Predisposition to petty criminality in Swedish adoptees. III Sex differences and validation of the male typology. Archives of General Psychiatry 39: 1248–1253

Silberman C E 1978 Criminal justice, criminal violence. Random House, New York

Smith D M 1974 Crime rates as territorial indicators: the case of the United States. Department of Geography, Queen Mary College, London

Søtensen T 1979 Commuting, local milisse and mental health. Unpublished MD thesis, University of Oslo, Norway

Srole L, Langner T S, Michael S T, Opler M K, Rennie T A C 1962 Mental health in the metropolis. McGraw-Hill, New York

Storr A 1985 What makes men violent. (publication pending)

Sutherland E H, Cressey D R 1966 Principles of criminology. Lippincott, Philadelphia

Taylor R B 1982 Neighbourhood physical environment and stress. In: Evan G W (ed) Environmental stress. Cambridge University Press, Cambridge

Timms D W G 1965 The spatial distribution of social deviants in Luton, England. Australia and New Zealand Journal of Sociology 1: 38–52

Tuan Y 1979 Landscapes of fear. Blackwell, Oxford

Webb S D 1972 Crime and the division of labor; testing a Durkheimian model. American Journal of Sociology 78: 543–656

Whitelegg J 1982 Inequalities in health care. Straw Barnes, Retford

Wilson J Q 1975 Thinking about crime. Basic Books, New York

Wilson S, Hunter J 1978 Updating defensible space. Architects Journal: October II

Zimbardo P 1969 The human choice: individuation, reason and order versus deindividuation, impulse and chaos. In: Nebraska Symposium on motivation. University of Nebraska Press, Lincoln

Zimbardo P 1973 Psychology for our times. Scott Foresman, Glenview, Illinois

Residential mobility and mental health

Today, *Homo sapiens* is the most widely distributed and fastest growing species on earth. Although the precise time and place of his beginnings are uncertain, the available archaeological evidence suggests that the new species probably developed in several separate centres, located in tropical-subtropical latitudes in Africa and Asia. From these focal areas, man has spread out to colonise an enormous range of environments (Pfeiffer 1969).

Mobility — variously described as spatial, geographical, or residential — has therefore always been an important feature of human life. During the past 200 years, however, the scale, variety, and tempo of man's residential mobility have all increased enormously. Since the early decades of the nineteenth century, investigators from several disciplines have examined the effects of residential mobility on the mental health of the movers (Plog 1969; Bastide 1972), but research findings in this important area appear to be conflicting. The present chapter therefore attempts to identify the major problems involved, the current 'state of the art', and relevant topics which require further investigation.

Many of the problems that have emerged in attempting comparative reviews of the available evidence stem from contrasting interpretations of the phenomenon 'residential mobility'. Although it comprises numerous different types, demographers customarily classify changes in residence according to the distance involved in the move and the kinds of political boundary lines (if any) that are crossed (Petersen 1969). In the present context, three important types of mobility will be considered: international migration, internal (or intra-national) migration, and local (or intra-community) moving. It will be shown that there are substantial differences between these three kinds of residential move, which have important implications for the analysis and interpretation of comparative levels of psychiatric illness in both movers and host populations.

INTERNATIONAL MIGRATION AND MENTAL HEALTH

Today, few countries have populations that are composed entirely of native-born persons. Most have sizable immigrant minorities, which differ from

327

the host populations not only in terms of birthplace, but also by other important variables such as race, language, and religion (Peach 1983). Some countries are true 'melting pots', having attracted settlers from all over the world; thus the USA has grown from a sparsely settled area to the fourth largest nation in the world chiefly as a result of sustained, massive immigration between 1840 and 1920 (US Bureau of the Census 1981). In Australia, the impact of international migration has been even more recent and obvious, with 20.2 per cent of the total Australian population of 12.8 million registered as foreign-born in 1971; and Borrie (1975) has estimated that 'directly and indirectly, immigration since 1946 has been responsible for 57 per cent of the Nation's growth'. Even those European countries which traditionally experienced net outflows of people for protracted periods have received quite substantial numbers of immigrants in recent decades. Thus, the coloured immigrant population of the UK — drawn chiefly from the countries of the New Commonwealth and Pakistan — grew from circa 50 000 in 1951 to an estimated 2.2 million in 1980 (Peach 1982).

The mental health implications of international migration began to attract the attention of pioneer social psychiatrists in the 1840s (Plog 1969). However, large-scale comparative scientific investigations of the relative incidence of psychiatric disorders among native and foreign-born populations began much later, in the early years of the present century (Malzberg 1969). The past 80 years have witnessed a sustained scientific interest in the subject, and it would therefore be impracticable to attempt to present here an exhaustive review of the entire literature. For several countries, it has in fact been documented and reviewed quite recently — notably for the US (Gaw 1982), the UK (Littlewood & Lipsedge 1982), Continental Europe (Friessem 1974; Ramon et al. 1977; Binder & Simoes 1978), and Australia (Giggs 1977; Burvill et al. 1982). Sanua (1969) pointed out that two major theories have been developed to explain the apparently high admission rates of immigrants to mental hospitals, particularly in the US. Firstly, there is the *social causation* theory, which assumes that a change of environment, with its ensuing problem of social and cultural adaptation, may cause psychological stresses. Secondly, the *self-selection* theory presumes that those who are predisposed to psychiatric disorder are more prone to migrate than the average for their population. A third possibility (Gordon 1965) is that migrants may not actually have a higher prevalence of this disorder, but may be more likely than the native-born to be hospitalised and diagnosed as such (see below).

The present discussion therefore focusses upon the main research findings concerning the relationship of international migration to psychiatric illness, and especially upon the associated analytical and interpretive problems. The available evidence suggests that many forms of psychiatric disorder are commoner among immigrant minority groups than among native-born populations. In some studies, (e.g. Gaw 1982) the results have apparently been contradictory and inconsistent, but much of the variation between them can probably be attributed to the difficulties involved in trying to determine mental illness rates among immigrants accurately. These difficulties arise from several sources. One set relates specifically to the concept of psychiatric illness itself. In many investigations, the incidence and prevalence rates for psychiatric disorders understate the true levels in both foreign-born and native-born populations because they have been derived exclusively from mental hospital admission records. Furthermore, there is ample evidence to show that considerable temporal and spatial variations still exist in the definition and classification of such disorders among psychiatrists, both within and between countries (WHO 1973; Giggs 1977). This issue is particularly important in the context of immigrant minorities, because native-born psychiatrists frequently assign diagnoses for several mental disorders more readily to immigrants than to native-born referrals (Gaw 1982; Littlewood & Lipsedge 1982).

The problems of identifying and classifying accurately the numbers suffering from psychiatric disorders are compounded by those relating to the denominators, or the populations at risk. Accurate incidence and prevalence rates can only be calculated if appropriate population census data are available. Ideally, these should distinguish the immigrant minorities from the host populations in terms of such key variables as birthplace, race, colour, age, sex, marital status, social class, and length of residence in the host country (Sanua 1969). However, very few countries publish census data in a form which is suitable for calculating accurate illness rates for all these important population subgroups. The UK population censuses are particularly unsatisfactory with respect to the identification of most immigrant groups (Peach 1982, 1983). In many cases, it is also recognised that the published census statistics seriously understate the true number of immigrants living in specific countries. This problem is particularly acute in the UK, where there are many illegal immigrants, (Peach 1982, 1983) and in the USA, which now has possibly millions of illegal Hispanic immigrants (Gaw 1982).

Even in those countries where reasonably detailed demographic data are available, accurate epidemiological research can only be undertaken if analyses are restricted to the few years straddling each decennial census. During the intercensal years, the direction and scale of changes in many important population traits can only be estimated. This issue is of critical importance when relatively small but fluctuating and mobile population subgroups (such as immigrants) are the objects of analysis. The problem can be exemplified by reference to Faris & Dunham's (1939) classic study of psychiatric disorders in Chicago. Here, mental hospital admissions for the periods 1922–1931 and 1922–1934 were aggregated, and rates calculated for the total population, foreign-born persons, negroes, and other races, using the 1930 population census as the primary source for the denominator populations. However, during the period 1920–1930, these major population sub-groups increased substantially in size (Table 12.1).

Table 12.1 Chicago's population, by race and nativity

	1920	1930	% change
		(1000)	
Total population	2702	3376	+24.9
Native white			
of native parentage	643	943	+46.7
of foreign/mixed parentage	1141	1332	+16.7
Foreign-born white	805	842	+ 4.6
Negro and other races	113	259	+129.2

Source: Bureau of the Census (1941) Statistical Abstract of the United States 1940 (62), Washington DC.

The Chicago example also raises other important issues, which require greater recognition and undoubtedly influence the rates of psychiatric disorder that have been calculated for immigrant minorities. The majority of immigrants in most countries during the present century have tended to settle in the larger cities. In the UK, most of the coloured immigrant population came from rural parts of the New Commonwealth and Pakistan, but in 1971, only 0.3 per cent of them were enumerated in rural districts, and 72 per cent were concentrated in cities larger than 250 000, compared with only 35 per cent of the total UK urban population (Jones 1978). Such marked environmental changes, combined with the greater availability and use of psychiatric services in large cities, undoubtedly combine to inflate the rates of hospital admission for many immigrant minorities.

The levels of psychiatric illness among immigrant groups within large cities like Chicago are influenced not only by rapidly changing numbers, but also by their changing spatial distributions. For several decades, social scientists have analysed the varying spatial patterns of immigrant settlement and dispersal within cities. Some immigrant groups form temporary residential clusters, and then quickly become culturally assimilated and spatially dispersed within cities. Other groups form spatially segregated ethnic clusters which persist for much longer periods of time, due to the interaction between external discrimination (from native born populations) and internal cohesion. Boal (1976) has identified several distinctive spatial patterns in relation to the varying spatial/temporal outcomes of the interaction of these processes. Although the spatial patterning of immigrant groups undoubtedly influences levels of group cohesiveness and mental health, this subject has not been examined in sufficient detail from the psychiatric point of view.

Given the scale and range of these problems, it is scarcely surprising that many of the studies of psychiatric disorders among international migrants have yielded variable and sometimes apparently conflicting results. However, despite the many methodological problems inherent in this kind of research, the carefully corrected results of several investigations do suggest that the incidence levels of several forms of such disorder are generally higher among some groups of immigrants than among native-born, non-migrant, populations (Gaw 1982; Littlewood & Lipsedge 1982), though simple and all-embracing testable explanations of these higher rates have yet to be offered. The actual move itself probably does not generally precipitate psychiatric illness, since modern transport systems ensure that this is usually accomplished both quickly and comfortably (Miller 1975), but there are several factors concerning the personalities and original settings of migrants which probably have important implications for the development of such disorders. Thus, a proportion of the higher rates might be attributable to particular combinations of genetic and psychological traits which prompt some groups of people to migrate more readily than others; they might be dissatisfied with their home (i.e. family, social, and work) settings, or unable to cope with them.

It could be argued, therefore, that in many cases, the stresses generated in the new environments encountered after migration merely trigger off disorders in these susceptible populations (Sanua 1969). Certainly, some groups of migrants have a pre-migration history of psychiatric illness (Krupinski et al. 1965). Although the majority of migrants move voluntarily, usually motivated primarily by economic and vocational considerations, many have done so unwillingly; studies in Australia, for instance, have shown that wartime and political refugees from Eastern European countries have been particularly vulnerable to many severe forms of psychiatric disorder (Krupinski et al. 1965, 1973).

For many migrants, the stresses generated by actually settling in the new environment of the receiving countries are capable of precipitating psychiatric disorders. Such stresses are clearly greatest for those migrants who differ most markedly from the host populations in terms of such important variables as colour, language, and religion. However, the often traumatic and stressful experience of settling in the new country generally dissipates after a few years, resulting in lower levels of illness (Malzberg & Lee 1956), though for some groups, the problems appear to persist. Thus in Victoria State, Australia, Krupinski (1975) found that high rates had persisted among middle-aged housewives from southern European countries; although they had been resident in Australia for more than 7 years, they were housebound and had not learned English, whereas their husbands and children had become assimilated. A second high-risk group identified by Krupinski comprised well qualified professional immigrants, who had experienced a fall in both social and occupational status because their qualifications had not been recognised by Australian professional bodies.

For many years, interest from this point of view was centred on schizophrenia, and it became almost received wisdom that migrants showed a higher rate of this disorder than the native-born. Though there was not the same degree of agreement on the cause of such a phenomenon, the leading investigator on the subject (Ødegaard 1932) concluded that 'the high incidence of schizophrenia in the Norwegian born of Minnesota is probably not a consequence of factors at work after the arrival of the immigrants to

America . . . (but) that the Norwegians with a schizoid character are more likely to emigrate'. Contrary findings, however, came from a comparison of the emigration rates of schizophrenic samples with control populations in Denmark, which showed that the schizophrenics were in fact less likely to migrate than the controls (Rosenthal et al. 1974). Pope et al. (1983) point out that this is more compatible with intuition, since it seems odd that schizoid or preschizoid individuals would actually be more likely than normals to choose and negotiate the complex process of emigration. On the other hand, a hypomanic individual might well be more likely to migrate than the average, through increased activity and elevated mood; if so, bipolar patients would have a greater tendency to be foreign-born, compared to others in the same setting, whilst a similar excess might be expected in the prevalence of foreign birthplace among the parents of bipolars, in view of the heredity component of manic-depressive psychosis. In fact, their survey of patients admitted to the McLean Hospital, Massachusetts, showed that manic-depressive patients were significantly more likely than either schizophrenics or controls to have been foreign-born, and this excess was even greater in the case of their parents, who represented a wide range of ethnic groups. Therefore, the reported excess of foreign-born schizophrenics in earlier American studies could have been largely due to diagnostic practices at the time, whereas with present-day criteria (such as DSMIII), many of those patients would now be re-diagnosed as manic-depressive. However, in England and Wales in 1971, the hospitalisation rate for schizophrenia in those born in Northern Ireland was 80 per cent higher than that for native-born people, while the rate for immigrants from the Irish Republic was 151 per cent higher than that for the native-born (Cochrane 1977).

In South London, investigation of the characteristics of a large group of hospitalised schizophrenics showed that cases with a positive family history were significantly more likely to have been born in the UK, while those with a negative family history were significantly more likely to have been born in the West Indies. If genetic and environmental factors are inversely related in any individual with respect to the aetiology of schizophrenia, West Indians who were at low genetic risk could have become psychiatrically ill under the stress of immigration. Those findings seem to support the 'environmental stress' theory of an excess of psychosis in immigrants.

INTERNAL MIGRATION AND MENTAL HEALTH

Although international migration continues to form an important component in the population structure of many countries, its influence is essentially selective, episodic, and secondary to that of internal migration. The amount of residential movement by households within western countries is much more important. In European countries between 7 per cent and 12 per cent of households move each year, while in New Zealand, Australia,

Canada, and the US the figure is approximately 20 per cent (Herbert & Thomas 1982).

In the US, this phenomenon has been investigated in considerable detail, together with its implications for mental health, and demographers have been able to discuss a number of important regularities in the spatial patterns and behaviour of different groups of movers. A considerable proportion of the US population migrates over comparatively long distances, i.e. to another county, State, or region of the country. Thus, in 1976, 11.7 per cent of the population aged 14 years and over claimed to have lived in their current State of residence for 5 years or less, and only 55.9 per cent had lived there for their entire lives. In longitudinal terms, it has been estimated that since 1940, the average American will migrate between three and four times in a lifetime (Wilbur 1963).

During the present century, this long-distance migration within the US has been characterised by successive waves, each distinguished by a marked directional bias. Morrill (1965) identified three major streams of migration up to 1960: between 1900 and 1960, nearly 10 million Americans migrated to the western states and 30 million from rural areas to the cities; between 1920 and 1960, 5 million negroes left the rural South for the cities of the North and West US. In the following decade, another million negroes emulated their predecessors (US Bureau of the Census 1981), and by 1970, only 53 per cent of all negroes lived in the South, compared with 86 per cent in 1920. They had also become more urbanised than whites, with 81.3 per cent of them living in urban settlements, compared with 69.5 percent of the whites (US Bureau of the Census 1981). Between 1960 and 1980, a further major shift in the direction of regional migration flows occurred within the USA; during this period, the States of the South and West accounted for 73 per cent of the total population increase in the USA (US Bureau of the Census 1981). The population structure and social fabric of this newly favoured 'Sunshine Belt' (Time 1976) have been radically modified by three fairly new and distinct streams of migrants — older, retired migrants from the metropolitan states of the North East; well educated young professionals, lured mainly from the North East and North Central Regions by the prospects of career advancement in the burgeoning new service and 'hi-tech' manufacturing industries in the region; and hundreds of thousands of footloose young people, who have abandoned conventional social ties and traditional career expectations in favour of alternative, leisure-orientated life styles (Zelinsky 1974). A somewhat similar concentration of new population and employment has occurred in England, in the corridor stretching westwards from London to Bristol, in spite of national policies which have tried to direct this expansion to other regions.

The implications of all these major shifts in population distribution for mental health have yet to be explored systematically; indeed, investigations of such effects of internal migration have a very recent history, in comparison with those of international migration (Kantor 1969). However, the available evidence indicates that the relationship between internal migration and psychiatric disorder is complex, for much the same reasons as those discussed in relation to international migration. Several American investigators have found that admission rates to mental hospitals are higher among inter-State migrants than among nonmigrants. These results were found to hold for white migrants, non-white migrants, and recent migrants, even after corrections had been made to eliminate the effects of age, sex, colour, and recency of migration (e.g. Malzberg & Lee 1956; Malzberg 1967; Locke et al. 1960; Lazarus et al. 1963), though the results reveal substantial variations in the magnitude of the differentials between the population subgroups. These might be attributable to such factors as the selective migration of contrasting groups into different States in the USA, the diverse environments which the migrants experience, or the differential hospital admission policies practised in the receiving States.

Other investigations, however, have yielded divergent findings (e.g. Parker and Kleiner 1969; Sanua 1969; Hunt & Butler 1972), suggesting that when proper statistical controls are introduced, many of the observed relationships between migration and psychiatric illness either disappear, or persist only for very small migrant subgroups. These analyses point to the need to consider the numerous interconnected and mediating factors which are clearly involved in the migration–psychiatric illness relationship, and which include the attributes of the exporting and importing communities, the genetic, psychological, and social characteristics of the migrants, and the particular set of circumstances which actually trigger off any migration. Fischer (1975) suggests that the fact that rural migrants to cities are generally not isolated and disorientated, as might be expected, is due to their movement along social networks, which are used for practical help, for guidance, and in the construction of a personal social world (see Chapter 16).

All of these American studies of internal migration and its mental health repercussions have focussed upon either a single State or a few selected States, but the results of one fairly recent investigation (Smith 1973) raise interesting possibilities for nationwide analyses. This seminal study explored the concept of the 'geography of social well-being' in the USA, on the basis of 47 variables, selected as representing six major criteria of social well-being, for the 48 coterminous mainland States of the USA (i.e. excluding Alaska and Hawaii). Principal components analysis identified six important dimensions in this data matrix, and the structure of the main components is shown in Table 12.2; Smith suggests that Component III can be interpreted as a mental health dimension — it is bipolar in character, with the three high-loading negatively-signed variables interpreted as indicating good mental health (i.e. low patient days in mental hospitals, few residents in mental hospitals, low number of hospital beds). The high positive loading variables indicate high rates of psychiatric illness and related stress-induced pathologies, associated with high rates of expenditure on medical care and low psychiatric hospitalisation. Smith tentatively speculates that this particu-

Table 12.2   Structure of the three leading components of social well-being at the state level

Component I:	General socio-economic well-being (explained variance: 38.56%)	
	Highest loadings:	−.9398 families with income less than $3000
		−.9083 houses dilapidated etc.
		.8951 benefits for retired workers
		.8853 per capita income
		.8651 dentists/10,000 population
		.8556 AFDC payments
		.8086 state unemployment benefit
		.8065 value of owner-occupied houses
		−.7993 households with poor diets
		−.7993 infant deaths
		.7868 public school expenditures
		−.7834 mental test failures
		.7780 eligible voters voting
		.7749 white-collar employees
		.7615 physicians/10,000 population
		.7587 median school years completed
Component II:	Social pathology (explained variance: 13.74%)	
	Highest loadings:	.8384 crimes of violence
		.7236 syphilis cases
		.6719 gonorrhea cases
		.6528 narcotics addicts
		.6422 school segregation
		−.6325 registered voters
		.6043 crimes against property
		.5517 illiteracy
		.5413 tuberculosis deaths
		−.5329 index of home equipment
Component III:	Mental health (explained variance: 11.98%)	
	Highest loadings:	−.8174 patient days in mental hospitals
		.7999 hospital expenses/patient day
		−.7940 residents in mental hospitals etc.
		−.7800 hospital beds/10,000 population
		.6323 divorces
		.5583 suicides
		.4832 mental hospital expenditures/patient days
		.4696 motor vehicle accident deaths
		.4601 crimes against property
		.4568 median school years completed
		.4548 persons attended college

Source: Smith D M (1973) p. 94

lar combination of positively-signed variables might indicate that although good medical care is available, it is expensive, and some of the resulting untreated psychiatric illness is reflected in other forms of social disorganisation. However, he also recognises the possibility that two distinct groups, with differing characteristics, are being revealed within the State populations.

Although the structural 'content' of Component III is rather more ambiguous and complex than that for Components I and II, the mapped scores

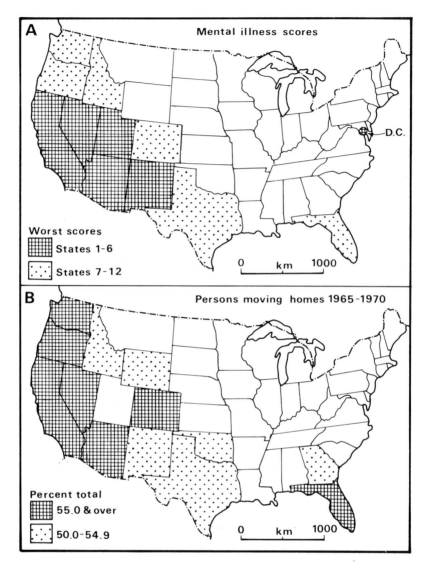

Fig. 12.1

for the dimension are extremely interesting. Fig. 12.1a shows that the high positive scores (denoting 'bad' mental health) are strongly clustered in the core States of the Sunshine Belt. Comparison with Fig. 12.1b suggests that poor mental health here is strongly correlated with a high degree of residential mobility in the population.

Many studies of the impact of national migration upon mental health have attempted to view the two phenomena in the context of the sending and receiving communities. Most commonly, this assessment of the effects of locales on mental health depends primarily upon the comparison of rates obtained from many separate studies of individual rural (i.e. exporting) areas and urban (i.e. importing) settlements. The most recent reviews of the evidence (Dohrenwend & Dohrenwent 1974 a,b; Leighton 1976; Wing 1976) suggest that aggregate levels of treated psychiatric illness are probably higher in urban than in rural areas, though the rates for the psychoses are not significantly different. It is the admission rates for the less incapacitating conditions (especially the neuroses and personality disorders) which are generally consistently higher in urban than in rural populations. Some workers have argued that the disparity between urban and rural rates for these milder disorders may be due to the more stressful social and environmental conditions found in large, rapidly growing cities. Others have argued that the differentials simply reflect the fact that large cities have more comprehensive and accessible psychiatric services than rural areas. A detailed assessment of the literature concerning the relationships between urbanisation and mental health is presented in Chapter 8.

LOCAL RESIDENTIAL MOBILITY AND MENTAL HEALTH

A substantial proportion of the research into the relationships between residential mobility and mental health has focussed upon the comparatively short-distance moves which take place within particular communities or settlements. The range of research strategies which has been employed in these investigations has been extremely varied. However, the relative strengths and weaknesses of these mental health studies can best be assessed by examining them within the context of broader discussions of intra-community residential mobility and socio-spatial patterning; most of this literature has been produced by social scientists, particularly urban sociologists and urban geographers.

Until comparatively recently, social scientists paid relatively little attention to local residential mobility and its impact on community structure (Adams & Gilder 1976). This neglect can be attributed both to the complexities of the phenomenon and to the difficulties of obtaining and analysing migration data at this particular spatial scale. Despite these problems, recent studies have shown that the bulk of all residential movers in western countries cover comparatively short distances, and that the shifts are within, rather than between communities. Furthermore, since the majority of the population in these countries live in urban areas, most of the residential moves are intraurban in character (Adams & Gilder 1976).

During the past few decades, the major cities in western countries have become the foci of the highest levels of residential mobility. In the US, the large metropolitan communities (officially termed Standard Metropolitan Statistical Areas, or SMSAs) have grown faster than any other type of settlement. In 1940, the 168 SMSAs accounted for 52.8 per cent of the US population whereas by 1980, there were 318 SMSAs, housing 74.8 per cent of the nation (US Bureau of the Census 1981).

Despite the comparative novelty of research in this complex field, it has been possible to identify a number of important social and spatial regularities in the migration patterns of local movers within these major urbanised communities. One discovery common to many studies has been that most movers have gone to new homes located either in the same neighbourhood or the same city. Butler (1976) has claimed that movement within SMSAs accounts for at least four out of every five moves that are made. Although longer-distance moves from the central city to the suburban rings of metropolitan communities therefore constitute only a small fraction of the total — 10 per cent of the total moves during 1960–1966 (Butler 1976) — their cumulative effect has been profound. Between 1950 and 1980, the proportion of the total population of SMSAs living in the suburban rings rose from 43 per cent to 60 per cent. Furthermore, the migration has been extremely selective, for most of the movers in the 'suburban flight' have been middle-class whites. In 1980, the suburban rings of metropolitan areas contained 66 per cent of all white residents, compared with only 45 per cent in 1950; they have abandoned the decaying central cities to the blacks and other minority groups (US Bureau of the Census 1981) (see also Chapter 11).

More important than the frequency and distance involved in residential moves, however, appears to be the fact that some 80% of all American movers migrate between census tracts with similar socio-economic attributes (Simmons 1968). Also, most of these movers also tend to remain within the same tenure categories in the intra-urban housing market. In many urban areas, therefore, the frequency and patterning of residential mobility tends to ensure that the social structure of urban meighbourhoods is modified only slowly. In the US, these broad regularities in residential mobility, social structure, and tenure patterns have resulted in a zonal (or annular) differentiation of the city. The core of the city is characterised by rented accommodation, low-income groups (including large numbers of blacks and other poor in-migrants), and very high levels of residential mobility. The second ring is distinguished by mixed housing tenure and relatively low levels of population turnover, while the suburban ring is dominated by owner-occupied housing and high-income groups. Here, high levels of residential mobility are also typical, due to out-migration from the city and to long-distance migration by middle/high-income families from other cities (Moore 1969, 1971). In the UK, both the residential mosaic and the patterns of residential mobility are rather more complex, since the local authority (Council) housing sector constitutes a large element in both the social and housing systems of most cities. Moreover, via letting policies, it exerts marked selective influences on the timing, scale, frequency, location, and character of residential moves among both new and existing tenants (Knox 1982).

The relatively recent and modest body of empirical research concerning the aggregate characteristics of intra-urban residential mobility has been complemented by a second set, which focusses upon the actual precipitants of the mobility; Butler (1976) and Knox (1982) have provided comprehensive reviews of this behavioural literature. Detailed investigations of samples of movers in both the US and the UK suggest that more than half the moves are prompted by changing household needs for dwelling space, triggered by changes in household size. It has also been found that only about 60 per cent of all residential moves are wholly voluntary i.e. that the affected households had an open choice about them, while in some studies, a quarter of all moves could be classed as involuntary, i.e. generated by such influences as urban renewal programmes, demolitions, and evictions. A further 15 per cent of all moves have been categorised as forced, and are most commonly initiated by changes in household circumstances (e.g. marriage, separation, divorce, retirement, ill-health, death) or job changes.

Although the conceptual and methodological frameworks of these behavioural studies are quite diverse, most of the authors emphasise the importance of the role of stress in inducing residential moves, even among voluntary movers. For some social groups, however, the levels of stress are clearly much greater than for others. Thus the residents of older, rented, inner city housing are obviously particularly affected by the precipitants which generate involuntary and forced moves. Several authors in the US have attributed the higher frequency of local, inner city moves among blacks than among whites to the additional constraints induced by living in ghettoes (Butler 1976). These moves have been interpreted as largely vain attempts by black residents to find satisfactory neighbourhoods and housing milieux within the predominantly poor quality rented housing stock found inside the ghetto. The stresses induced by such constraints are particularly marked among those blacks who have high ambitions to improve their educational and socio-economic status. The subject clearly deserves further research, for even those few blacks who have managed to move upwards socially and outwards spatially from the ghetto apparently experience even greater levels of stress (as indexed by mental hospitalisation rates — Levy and Rowitz 1973) than the majority of their brethren, who remain trapped in the ghetto.

Given the scale, variety, and complexity of both the intra-urban residential mobility streams and the underlying social environmental spatial framework within which those movements occur, the assessment of their implications for mental health is clearly a formidable task. Investigators have been obliged to be selective, in terms of their choice of both migrant groups and analytical strategies; many have adopted the ecological method used by Faris & Dunham (1939) in their seminal analysis of the distribution of psychiatric disorders in Chicago, calculating rates of disorder for census tracts, and correlating these with rates of residential mobility and other social and environmental variables. Unfortunately, it is difficult to assess the comparative value of most of this substantial body of ecological research because of several important methodological factors (Giggs 1980; Smith 1980). For instance, it is rare for the same kinds of sub-areas to be used as analytical frameworks, and in the specific case of suicide studies, the sub-areas employed have ranged from Enumeration Districts in Brighton (Bagley et al. 1973) to Metropolitan Boroughs in London (Sainsbury 1955); the fact that these areas differ enormously in size, numbers, and population seriously inhibits accurate comparison of the results.

A second set of problems concerns the attributes of the population cohorts of psychiatric patients selected for analysis. Some authors have deliberately restricted their attention to patients entering psychiatric hospitals for the first time, while other have analysed both first and readmissions. Substantial differences between studies also exist in terms of the duration of the admission period selected for analysis; some workers have been content to analyse data for a single year (e.g. Levy & Rowitz 1973), whereas others have collected data for more than a decade (e.g. Faris & Dunham 1939). However, experience in statistical analysis would suggest a compromise between these two extremes. A short study period may provide too few cases for relatively rare psychiatric disorder, introducing a substantial element of chance into analyses of spatial distributions where the cases are spread over a large number of sub-areas. Thus, in Levy & Rowitz's (1973) study of Chicago, only 131 first-admission senile and arteriosclerotic cases and 197 manic depressives were identified, and were used to calculate age-adjusted rates for 75 Community Areas. In contrast, Faris & Dunham (1939) certainly erred on the side of zeal, because their otherwise very creditable data bases (for 1922–1931 and 1922–1934) mask substantial changes in both the size and spatial distribution of the base populations that were used to calculate rates for the various psychiatric disorders which they analysed.

The review of the social science literature presented earlier would suggest that reasonably accurate psychiatric morbidity rates can only be calculated from data collected for 3 to 5 consecutive years, straddling a given population census. Figure 12.2 emphasises the importance of this issue, demonstrating how marked and spatially variable the impact of residential mobility can be over a relatively short time span, within a large urban area. The example shown is that of the Nottingham Psychiatric Case Register, covering an administratively defined area which had a population of 405 661 in 1971.

A third important limitation of most ecological analyses of the relationship between residential mobility and psychiatric illness patterns stems from the interpretative difficulties inherent in the method itself. The identification of statistically significant relationships between specific measures of psychiatric illness and residential mobility does not necessarily mean that precise cause–effect relationships have been established, primarily because these analyses have been based upon aggregated data (i.e. upon rates for areas) rather than upon information about ill and mobile individuals. Furthermore, all ecological studies have an essentially cross-sectional, or static

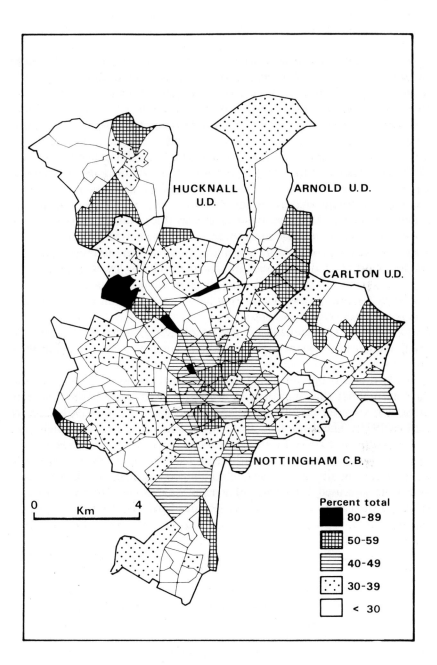

Fig. 12.2

perspective, presenting a picture of the disease–environmental relationship at one point in time, rather than a specifically temporal, cause–effect sequence.

Many of the weaknesses inherent in the ecological method were recognised by Faris & Dunham (1939), and their study raised explanatory issues which remain largely unresolved today. Like most subsequent investigators, they tried to interpret the distinctive spatial patterning found for certain psychiatric disorders in the light of several apparently competing mechanisms, the most common spatial pattern being the gradient or zonal one. Here, the highest rates are found in the inner city neighbourhoods, and then decline progressively outwards to the suburban fringes. Faris & Dunham suggested that this pattern could be ascribed to the inimical social and physical milieux concentrated in the inner city (i.e. the 'breeder' or social causation hypothesis). An alternative explanation (the 'drift' or social selection hypothesis) would be that individuals in the premorbid or early morbid stages of their illnesses drift down the social ladder and inwards from randomly distributed addresses throughout the city to low status inner city neighbourhoods. At this stage, their illnesses would be sufficiently severe for them to require psychiatric hospitalisation, thus inflating inner city admission rates (see also Chapter 14).

Both Faris & Dunham and Levy & Rowitz (1973) attempted to assess the relative importance of these two apparently competing hypotheses in their analyses of Chicago. They did this by mapping separately (and comparing visually) the distributions of first-admission and readmission cases. Figure 12.3 exemplifies this approach, showing the distribution of the high-rate admission areas for all admissions and for schizophrenics in 1961 (Levy & Rowitz 1973). The maps show that in both cases, the tracts with high rates of first admissions are apparently distributed fairly randomly throughout the city. In contrast, the tracts with high readmission rates are massively concentrated in the low-income, black, inner city neighbourhoods. Levy & Rowitz also used Principal Components Analysis — a multivariate statistical method — to analyse the relationships between 17 psychiatric illness variables and 17 social-environmental attributes for the 74 Community Areas in Chicago. Component I (the most important dimension) linked high rates of residential mobility with seven other social–environmental problems and five of the psychiatric illness variables. It was argued that the map and statistical evidence supported the drift hypothesis.

Unfortunately, the use of aggregated statistics for quite large sub-areas does not permit determination of either the relative levels of mobility between normal and psychiatrically ill populations, or the precise directions of the spatial moves which these two groups take within the city. Furthermore, the readmission cases analysed within a specific study period represent the residual element from a preceding period, and no account is taken of either the number or the spatial behaviour of first-admission cases who have apparently recovered or left the study area altogether. These problems

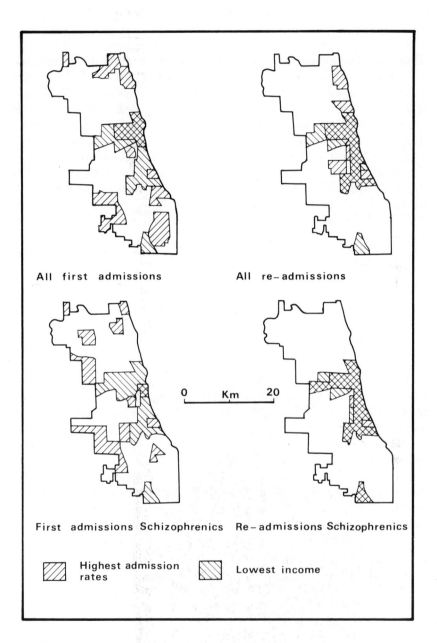

All first admissions

All re-admissions

0   Km   20

First admissions Schizophrenics   Re-admissions Schizophrenics

Highest admission rates   Lowest income

Fig. 12.3

have not been resolved by more recent ecological work, particularly with respect to schizophrenia (Dean & James 1981).

A further problem concerns the effects of using highly aggregated groups. Thus, the distribution of a single diagnostic group such as schizophrenia may conceal dramatic spatial variations in the distributions among population subgroups distinguished by such important variables as ethnicity, age, sex, marital status, and family setting. This issue is briefly discussed by Levy & Rowitz (1973), who found that the total hospitalisation rates (i.e. all admissions, undifferentiated by order of admission or diagnoses) among blacks in Chicago were much higher in community areas where blacks were in a minority, rather than in the inner city areas, where they comprised the majority population. The disaggregation issue has been taken up by a few workers; in a study of the spatial distribution of first-admission schizophrenics in Bristol, Hare (1956) found that cases living with their families did not depart significantly from random. In contrast, the cases who were living out of family setting at the time of admission were markedly concentrated in the central area, but unfortunately, the ecological subdivisions of the city employed in the analysis were very gross and only briefly described. Hare divided the city into only three areas (each comprising five electoral wards) and excluded four wards from the analysis because they were 'notably heterogeneous as regards social characteristics'.

However, more recently, Giggs (1983) has examined the spatial patterning and social–environmental correlates of schizophrenia in Nottingham; the ecological structure of the study area was identified by means of Principal Components Analysis and cluster analysis of 62 census variables for 216 tracts. The spatial distribution for 315 first-admission schizophrenics (admitted during 1969–1973) was then determined, using the total sample and eight sub-groups for the 15 statistically derived ecological areas. The spatial patterning for the total sample was found to be broadly zonal, but the distributions of the different subgroups were extremely variegated. The Poisson probability formula was then used to test the significance of the spatial distributions of the nine schizophrenia variables, and the results for five of the nine groups are shown in Fig. 12.4 and 12.5. The distribution of total cases (Fig. 12.4a) shows the familiar inner city pattern of concentrations, but for the different subgroups of schizophrenics, the patterns are quite varied. Thus, native-born schizophrenics (Fig. 12.4b) and schizophrenics in family settings (Fig. 12.5a) are significantly overrepresented in the inner city. In contrast, the areas with significant excesses of foreign-born cases (Fig. 12.4c) and cases living alone (Fig. 12.5b) are more widely dispersed. The distribution of excess foreign-born cases (i.e. Fig. 12.4c) is particularly interesting, since they are located in areas which had few foreign-born persons in 1971 (Fig. 12.6).

Subsequent analysis of relationships between the distribution of the nine schizophrenic groups and the urban ecological structure suggested that the statistical links between schizophrenia and local residential mobility levels

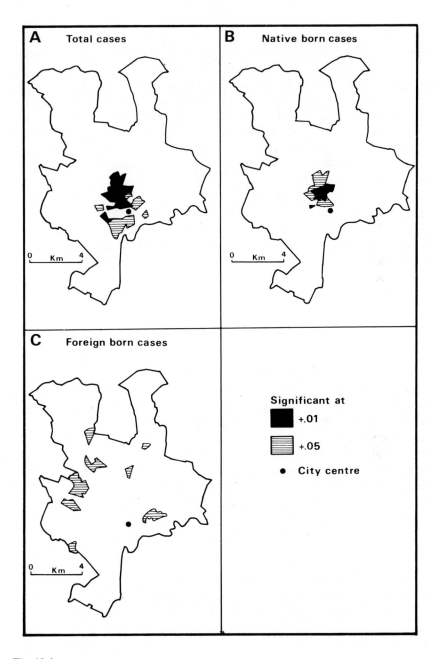

Fig. 12.4

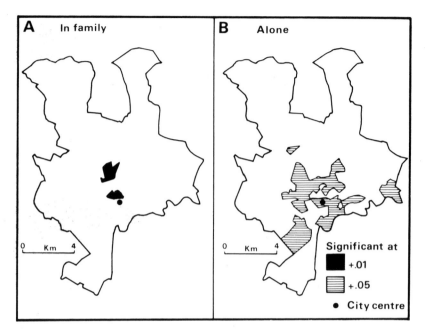

Fig. 12.5

were rather weak. The results of stepwise multiple regression analyses indicated that the strongest predictor of the distribution of seven of the nine groups of schizophrenics was Component I — an axis which measured populations possessing few social or material resources. This axis did, however, include four out of six immigrant population groups.

These findings emphasise the need to deal with disaggregated data in order to identify significant facts about the distributions and social–environmental correlates of important groups within a single diagnostic category. Further supportive evidence for this assertion can be found in a study of ecological variations of three types of suicide in Brighton (Bagley & Jacobson 1976).

Recent contributions to the literature have added further explanatory possibilities for the high concentrations of psychiatric patients in central city neighbourhoods. Some workers have argued that a genetic and social 'pooling' of vulnerable populations may occur in the inner city (Irving 1975). Lei et al. (1974) discovered that the highest rates of mental retardation in Riverside, California, were located in areas having populations which had resided there for protracted periods. It is probably the case, therefore, that high inner city admission rates are the product of a combination of local socially vulnerable and disorganised populations (the breeder hypothesis), the inward movement of similar individuals (the drift hypothesis), and the selective outward movement of those healthy individuals who are both willing and able to do so (the social residue hypothesis).

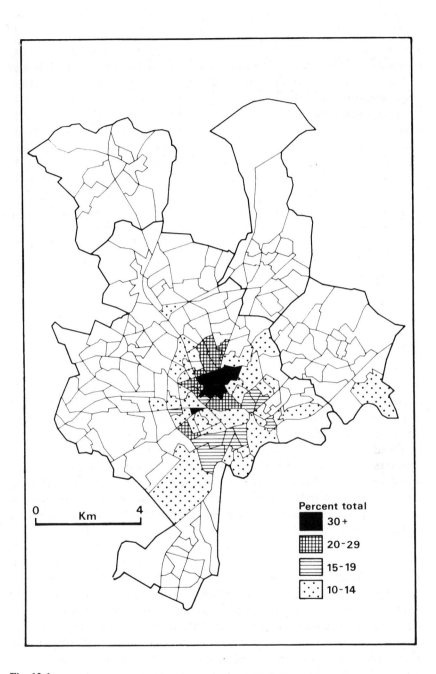

Fig. 12.6

Another important factor which has unquestionably contributed to the high levels of psychiatric disorder in many central city areas has been the implementation of the concept of 'care in the community'. Since the 1950s, the number of long-stay patients in old psychiatric hospitals in the UK and US has declined dramatically, many of these patients having been returned to the community. Since the majority of them have weak or disrupted family ties, they usually end up living in hostels or lodgings, which are primarily located in the older, cheaper, socially disorganised inner city neighbourhoods. Evidence for the effects of this institutionally inspired and (usually) compulsory residential mobility is available from studies in both the UK (Psychiatric Rehabilitation Association 1969, 1970) and the US (Dear & Wittman 1980).

The best evidence of interactions between mental health and residential mobility has come from studies which are essentially bi-level in character. These include consideration of both aggregate area effects (i.e. the ecological scale) and individual behavioural phenomena for samples of both mentally ill and matched control populations. In a thorough review of the literature, Kasl (1977) argues that the mental health of movers should be measured before, during, and after the residential relocation process. Moreover, the findings should be compared at each stage with those for matched controls who have not moved; but unfortunately, few studies have approached this standard.

Many investigators have examined the effects of forced and involuntary moves upon mental health, Hartman (1964) having compared 33 such studies, several of which document the adverse effects of the disruption of established social networks by major urban renewal programmes. Some authors have claimed that strong grief reactions and high levels of intense depression have been identified in affected populations shortly after such compulsory relocation, particularly among the working class, the elderly, and ethnic groups (Fried 1963, 1965; Key 1967; Niebanck 1968). A major study of the rehousing of black families in Baltimore, however, noted a gradual improvement in health after the movers had begun to adapt, and to recover from the initial problems experienced shortly after the move (Wilner et al. 1962).

The findings of studies concerning the mental health effects of voluntary moves are largely inconclusive. In the UK, considerable attention has been given to the populations of Council housing, for this has been the fastest growing sector in the British housing market since 1919. One study found high levels of neurosis on a new council estate in Hertfordshire (Martin et al. 1957), but a comparative study of the mental health status of people living respectively in a deteriorated inner urban neighbourhood and a new council estate in Croydon discovered little difference between the two (Hare & Shaw 1965). Similar conflicting evidence has been obtained from studies of psychological stress among those moving into high-rise council flats in British cities (Bagley 1974; Gittus 1976; Moore 1974).

During the early 1960s, the development of new towns in Britain was the subject of some mental health research. At that time, virtually all the officially designated New Towns were comparatively small communities, located within the rural rings of the major British cities. However, although fairly close to the cities, they were considerably farther out than the typical new suburban council estates. For most of the new residents, therefore, the distance involved in moving to new homes was of a substantially greater magnitude than that incurred by those moving to typical public housing estates. Several studies identified high levels of minor psychiatric illness (e.g. stress-induced dissatisfaction, loneliness, and neurosis) particularly among females (Taylor & Chave 1964; Sainsbury & Collins 1966; Bain & Philip 1975). This subject was comprehensively reviewed by Freeman (1972).

More recently, Hooper & Ineichen have explored the mental health implications of moving house upon young families in Bristol. In a linked series of papers, they have reported the repercussions for mental health of moving to a new home (Hooper et al. 1972), the variations which exist between populations moving to different kinds of new residential areas (Ineichen & Hooper 1973), and the subsequent adjustment to moving among young families in new housing (Hooper & Ineichen 1979). In the last paper, a sample of 262 families was interviewed; these were drawn from seven areas within the city, contrasted by location (e.g. redeveloped inner city, outer suburb) and house type/class (e.g. detached and semidetached owner-occupied houses and high-rise council flats). The results confirmed that there were health and adjustment differences between the population subgroups, which varied according to sex, class and housing type. The follow-up interviews (which took place 18 months later) indicated that few of the sharp differences in mental health identified at first interview had persisted, though several new high-risk groups were appearing (see also Chapter 7).

CONCLUSIONS

This chapter has shown that the literature on the relationship between residential mobility is both long established and substantial. Nevertheless, many important issues still remain unresolved, and several aspects of the relationship have been relatively under-researched. Thus, it has been shown here that accurate comparative assessments of the findings concerning levels of mental ill-health among specific migrant groups are still inhibited by several quite basic psychiatric epidemiological issues. These include variations between studies in the classifications of both levels and kinds of psychiatric disorders, the identification of sick individuals, and the employment of appropriate and accurate population base data in the calculation of rates of disorder among migrant and non-migrant populations. Furthermore, it has been shown that these problems affect all studies to some degree, irrespective of spatial scale or locale. Given the important methodological and data base differences that exist between many studies, it is scarcely surprising that apparently contradictory results have frequently been produced. The elimination of these sources of variation in the epidemiological framework therefore constitutes a necessary and critical step in the development of rigorous, comparative analyses of residential mobility–mental health relationships.

Another limitation of these studies stems from the narrow analytical and explanatory perspectives adopted by most of the researchers. Although the subject has attracted the interest of workers from several disciplines, few have attempted to interpret their findings in terms which go beyond the confines of the perspectives customarily recognised by their individual disciplines. The result of this academic myopia is a series of essentially partial evaluations of the phenomena under review. Relatively few authors have recognised that the residential mobility–psychiatric illness relationship is a complex, evolving equation which includes numerous variables, such as the personality, life experiences, cultural attributes, and reasons for moving characteristic of each migrant prior to the actual residential move. The attributes of the receiving community are also of considerable, though varying importance in relation to the particular assemblage of traits possessed by the movers. The most important influences affecting the mental health of movers on arrival in the receiving area are probably the levels of environmental and cultural congruence with the exporting community, the attitudes of the host population to the migrants, and the opportunities that exist for migrants to fulfil their aspirations and expectations. Numerous studies have shown that most long-distance movers (i.e. international migrants) cluster together in culturally and ethnically homogeneous neighbourhoods, in order to recreate the familiar and reassuring social milieux of their former home environments. Among local (i.e. intra-community) movers, this phenomenon is unusual for, as Simmons (1968) has shown, the majority shift between tracts with similar socio-economic attributes.

The evidence drawn from these diverse studies indicates that there is now considerable potential for interdisciplinary research. There are also sound practical reasons for this, since it is unlikely that any one person now possesses either the breadth of vision or the conceptual and methodological expertise to attempt truly comprehensive research single-handed. Unfortunately, such investigations are unlikely to occur for a long time; but in the shorter term, several aspects of the mobility–mental health equation deserve close attention. For instance, the role of personality factors in relation to migration and mental health has barely been explored, and neither have the mental health implications of contrasting family and social settings in the 'exporting' countries of migrants. The spatial or geographical element in the residential mobility process also merits further research, particularly at the regional and local levels.

For the present, it is difficult to go beyond Miller's view (1975) that the relationship between psychiatric disorder and mobility behaviour is a complex one, and that both the two main hypotheses which have so far been advanced to explain it appear much too simplistic. These two hypotheses, it will be recalled, are respectively of *social causation* (that migration is more stressful than non-migration) and of *social selection* (that those affectedly psychiatric disorder migrate in greater numbers than those not affected).

REFERENCES

Adams J S, Gilder K 1976 Household location and intra-urban migration. In: Herbert D, Johnston R J (eds) Social areas in Cities: spatial processes and form. John Wiley, Chichester

Bagley C 1974 The built environment as an influence on personality and social behaviour: a spatial study. In: Canter D, Lee T (eds) Psychology and the built environment. Architectural Press, Tonbridge

Bagley C, Jacobson S 1976 Ecological variations of three types of suicide. Psychological Medicine 6: 423–427

Bagley C et al 1973 Social structure and the ecological distribution of mental illness, suicide and delinquency. Psychological medicine 3: 177–187

Bain D J G, Philip A E 1975 Going to the Doctor: attendances by members of 100 families in their first year in a new town. Journal of the Royal College of General Practitioners 25: 821–827

Bastide R 1972 The sociology of mental disorder. Routledge & Kegan Paul, London

Binder J, Simoes M 1978 Social psychiatry of migrant workers. Fortschritte de Neurologie, Psychiatrie und ihrer Grenzgebiete 46: 342–359

Boal F W 1976 Ethnic residential segregation. In: Herbert D T, Johnston R J (eds) Social areas in cities: spatial processes and form. Wiley, London

Borrie W D 1975 Population and Australia: a demographic analysis and projection. Australian Government Publishing Service, Canberra

Burvill P W et al 1982 Relation between country of birth and psychiatric admissions in Western Australia. Acta Psychiatrica Scandinavia 66: 322–335

Butler E W 1976 Urban sociology: a systematic approach. Harper & Row, New York

Cassel J C 1974 Psychiatric epidemiology. In: Caplan G (ed) American handbook of Psychiatry, Vol II, 2nd edn. Basic Books, New York

Cochrane R 1977 Mental illness in immigrants to England and Wales: an analysis of mental hospital admissions. Soc Psychiatry 12: 25–35

Dean K G, James H D 1981 Social factors and admission to psychiatric hospital in Plymouth. Institute of British Geographers. New Series 6: 39–52

Dear M J, Wittman I 1980 Conflict over the location of mental health facilities. In: Herbert D T, Johnston R J (eds) Geography and the urban environment: progress in research and applications. Vol 3, John Wiley, Chichester

Dohrenwend B P, Dohrenwend B S 1974 Psychiatric disorders in urban settings. In: Caplan G (ed) American handbook of psychiatry. Vol 2 2nd edition. Basic Books, New York

Dohrenwend B P, Dohrenwend B S 1974 Stressful life events, their nature and effects. John Wiley, New York

Faris R E, Dunham H W 1939 Mental disorders in urban areas. University of Chicago Press, Chicago

Fischer C S 1975 The study of urban community and personality. Annual Review of Sociology 1: 67–89

Freeman H L 1972 Mental health and new communities in Britain. In: Nossiter T J, Hanson A H, Rokker S (eds) Imagination and precision in the social sciences. Faber, London

Fried M 1963 Grieving for a lost home. In: Duhl L J (ed) The urban condition. Basic Books, New York

Fried M 1965 Transitional functions of working class communities: implications for forced relocation. In: Kantor M B (ed) Mobility and mental health. Thomas, Springfield

Friessem D H 1974 Psychiatric and psychosomatic diseases of foreign workers in the Federal Republic of Germany: a contribution to the psychiatry of migration. Psychiatrie, Neurologie und Medinische Psychologie 26: 78–90

Gaw A (ed) 1982 Cross-cultural psychiatry. John Wright, Boston

Giggs J A 1977a The mental health of immigrants in Australia. In: Bowen M (ed) Australia 2000: the ethnic impact. University of New England, Armidale

Giggs J A 1977b Mental disorders and mental subnormality. In: Howe G M (ed) A world geography of human diseases. Academic Press, London

Giggs J A 1980 Mental health and the environment. In: Howe G M, Loraine J A (eds) Environmental Medicine. Second edition. Heinemann Medical Books, London

Giggs J A 1983 Schizophrenia and ecological structure in Nottingham. In: Blunden J, McGlashan N D (eds) Geographical aspects of health. Academic Press, London

Gittus E 1976 Flats, families and under fives. Routledge & Kegan Paul, London

Gordon E D 1965 Mentally ill West Indian immigrants. British Journal of Psychiatry III: 51–56

Hare E H 1956 Family setting and the urban distribution of schizophrenia. Journal of Mental Science 102: 753–760

Hare E H, Shaw G K 1965 Mental health on a new housing estate. Oxford University Press, London

Hartman C 1964 The housing of relocated families. Journal, American Institute of Planners 30: 266–286

Herbert D T, Thomas C J 1982 Urban Geography: a first approach. John Wiley, Chichester

Hooper D, Ineichen B 1979 Adjustment to moving: a follow-up study of the mental health of young families in new housing. Social Science and Medicine 13: 163–168

Hooper D et al 1972 The health of young families in new housing. Journal of Psychosomatic Research 16: 367–374

Hunt G J, Butler E W 1972 Migration, participation and alienation. Sociology and Social Research 56: 440–452

Ineichen B, Hooper D 1973 Wives' mental health in children's behaviour problems in contrasting residential areas. Social Science and Medicine 8: 369–375

Irving H W 1975 A geographer looks at personality. Area 7: 207–212

Jones P N 1978 The distribution and diffusion of the coloured population in England and Wales. The Institute of British Geographers: New Series 3: 515–532

Kantor M B 1969 International migration and mental illness. In: Plog S C, Edgerton R B (eds) Changing perspectives in mental illness. Holt, Rinehart and Winston, New York

Kasl S V 1977 The effects of the residential environment on health and behaviour. In: Hinkle L E, Loring W C (eds) The effects of the man-made environment on health and behaviour. DHEW Publication No 77–8318, Washington DC

Key W H 1967 When people are forced to move. The Meninger Foundation, Topeka

Knox P 1982 Urban social geography: an introduction. Longman, London

Krupinski J 1975 Psychological maladaption in ethnic concentrations in Victoria, Australia. In: Pilowsky I (ed) Cultures in collision. Australian National Association for Mental Health, Adelaide

Krupinski J et al 1965 Factors influencing the incidence of mental disorders among migrants. Medical Journal of Australia 2: 269–277

Krupinski J et al 1973 Psychiatric disorders in Eastern Europe refugees now in Australia. Social Science and Medicine 7: 31–42

Lazarus J et al 1963 Migration differentials in mental disease. Milbank Memorial Fund Quarterly 41: 25–42

Lei T J et al 1974 An ecological analysis of agency labelled retardates. American Journal of Mental Deficiency 79: 22–31

Leighton D C 1976 Behavioural science, mental health and mental illness. In: Kane R L (ed) The behavioural sciences and preventive medicine: opportunities and dilemmas. US Government Printing Office, Washington DC

Levy L, Rowitz L 1973 The ecology of mental disorder. Behavioural Publications, New York

Littlewood R, Lipsedge M 1982 Aliens and alienists: ethnic minorities and psychiatry. Penguin Books, Harmondsworth

Locke B Z et al 1960 Immigration and insanity. Public Health Reports 75: 301–306

Malzberg B 1967 Migration in relation to mental disease. Research Foundation for Mental Hygiene, Albany

Malzberg B 1969 Are immigrants psychologically disturbed? In: Plog S C, Edgerton R B (eds) Changing perspectives in mental illness. Holt, Rinehart and Winston, Inc., New York

Malzberg B, Lee E S 1956 Migration and mental disease. Social Science Research Council, New York

Martin F M et al 1957 Incidence of neurosis on a new housing estate. British Journal of Preventative Social Medicine II: 196–202

Miller W B 1975 Psychological and psychiatric aspects of population problems. In: Hamburg D A, Brodie H K H (eds) American handbook of psychiatry. Vol VI New psychiatric frontiers. Basic Books, New York

Moore E G 1969 The structure of intra-urban movement rates: an ecological model. Urban Studies 6: 17–33

Moore E G 1971 Comments on the use of ecological models in the study of residential mobility in the city. Economic Geography 47: 73–84

Moore N C 1974 Psychiatric illness and living in flats. British Journal of Psychiatry 125: 500–507

Morrill R L 1965 The negro ghetto: problems and alternatives. Geographical Review 55: 339361

Mueller D P 1980 Social networks. Social Science Medicine 14A: 147–161

Niebanck P L 1968 Relocation in urban planning: from obstacle to opportunity. University of Pennsylvania Press, Philadelphia

Ødegaard O 1932 Emigration and insanity: a study of mental disease among the Norwegian-born population of Minnesota. Acta Psychiatric of Neurology (Supplement IV) 1–206

Parker S, Kleiner R J 1969 Mental illness in the urban negro community. Free Press of Glencoe, New York

Peach G C K 1982 The growth and distribution of the black population in Britain 1945–1980. In: Coleman D A (ed) Demography of immigrants and minority groups in the United Kingdom. Academic Press, London

Peach G C K 1983 Ethnicity. In: Pacione M (ed) Progress in urban geography. Croom Helm, Beckenham

Petersen W 1969 Population. MacMillan, London

Pfeiffer J E 1969 The emergence of man. Nelson, London

Plog S C 1969 Urbanisation, psychological disorders, and the heritage of social psychiatry. In: Plog S C, Edgerton R B (eds) Changing perspectives in mental illness. Holt, Rinehart & Winston, New York

Pope H G, Ionescu-Pioggia M, Yurgelun-Todd D 1983 Migration and manic-depressive illness. Compr Psychiatry 24: 158–165

Psychiatric Rehabilitation Association 1969 Mental illness in four London Boroughs. PRA, London

Psychiatric Rehabilitation Association 1970 Mental illness in city and suburb. PRA, London

Ramon S, Shanin T, Strimpel J 1977 The peasant connection: social background and mental health of migrant workers in Western Europe. Mental Health and Society 4: 270–290

Rosenthal D, Goldberg I, Jacobsen B, et al 1974 Migration, heredity and schizophrenia. Psychiatry 37: 321–339

Sainsbury P 1955 Suicide in London. Maudsley Monograph No 1. Chapman and Hall, London

Sainsbury P, Collins J 1966 Some factors relative to mental illness in a new town. Journal Psychosom Research 10: 45–51

Sanua V D 1969 Immigration, migration and mental illness: a review of the literature with special emphasis on schizophrenia. In: Brody E G (ed) Behavious in new environments. Sage Publications, Beverley Hills

Simmons J W 1968 Changing residence in the city: a review of intra-urban mobility. Geographical Review 58: 621–651

Smith C J 1980 Neighbourhood effects on mental health. In: Herbert D T, Johnston R J (eds) Geography and the urban environment: progress in research and applications. Vol 3. John Wiley, Chichester

Smith D M 1973 The geography of social well-being in the United States. McGraw-Hill, New York

Taylor S, Chave S 1964 Mental health and environment. Longmans, London

Time 1976 Americans on the move. Time, New York. March 15, 58–64

U.S. Bureau of the Census 1941 Statistical abstract of the United States 1940 62. Washington DC

U.S. Bureau of the Census 1981 Statistical Abstract of the United States 1981. Washington DC

Wilbur G 1963 Migration on expectancy in the United States. Journal American Statistical Association 58: 444–453

Wilner D M, Walkley R P, Pinkerton T C, Tayback M 1962 The housing environment and family life. John Hopkins University Press, Baltimore

Wing J K 1976 Mental health in urban environments. In: Harrison G A, Gibson J B (eds) Man in urban environments. Oxford University Press, London

WHO 1973 The international pilot study of schizophrenia. World Health Organisation, Geneva

Zelinsky W 1974 Selfward bound? Personal preference patterns and the changing map of American society. Economic Geography 50: 144–179

CASE STUDIES

Stress at Thamesmead

Thamesmead lies within a loop of the Thames, 12 miles downstream from London Bridge. Twenty years ago, much of the site was empty marshland. A large munitions complex, the Woolwich Arsenal, occupied the western half, but soon after the war, the manufacture of explosives there came to an end, and a total of 1690 acres was available for development. This was the largest piece of building land in London and in 1965, the London County Council (LCC) published ambitious plans for a new, largely self-contained community. Thamesmead was not to be just another housing estate: a mixture of private and public housing would ensure a balance of social classes, new industries would enable most of the residents to work near their homes, and higher standards of amenity than before would be set for the public housing. The whole project was seen as the first stage in a cycle of urban renewal in and around London.

The site was a difficult one, at risk of flooding from the river and from rain water off the surrounding hills, so that all buildings would have to be erected on piles, driven down to the deep pebble layer. The final plan proposed a high density of 100 people per acre, and a combination of medium-rise blocks of flats, low-rise maisonettes, terraced houses, and large open spaces. Traffic would be separated from pedestrians, and the whole development linked together by walkways, cycleways, canals, and ornamental water. Housing of high quality concrete panels, terraces and paved spaces, and a special architectural style, would give the new 'town' a distinctive character. In the central area, the main shopping, recreational, and educational facilities would be sited around a yacht marina. Of these early plans, it has been said that, 'the white-walled towers and terraces and yacht harbours promised the kind of *douceur de vivre* that the French were busily building, in a rather more auspicious climate, on the coast of Languedoc' (Esher 1981).

Although planned to be of a similar size to the first postwar new towns, Thamesmead would not be managed, as they were, by a Development Corporation with special powers. The Greater London Council (GLC), which replaced the LCC in 1965, managed the project in collaboration with two London boroughs, Greenwich and Bexley, within whose boundaries

357

Thamesmead lies. The original plans were modified, however, in response to financial and construction difficulties, and in the light of experience, both at Thamesmead and elsewhere; therefore the rate of development has been slower than envisaged, housing densities for the later phases reduced, and the town centre not yet built.

Local industry contracted soon after the first residents arrived, and many jobs were lost; new industry did not begin to move in until late 1970, and even now offers work to only a small proportion of the population. Poor employment prospects, combined with low rates of pay locally and high rents, have ensured that many residents continue to work in Central London, on either side of the river. About 90 per cent (instead of the 65 per cent planned) of the dwellings are publicly owned, and the aim of a balanced community has still to be achieved. However, there are now over 20 000 people in residence (almost half the target population) and despite all the problems, Thamesmead has developed as a lively, articulate community with a character of its own.

Construction began in the south east corner of the site, and this first phase is of striking appearance (Fig. 13.1).

An outer wall of maisonettes, heaped upon each other and disposed in two rows, with internal pedestrian streets at first-floor and third-floor levels, encloses the mass of terraced houses, point-blocks, schools and shops, grouped around a lake and pool. All habitable rooms are above ground level,

Fig. 13.1 Coralline Walk, Thamesmead

in conformity with flood precautions. Garages occupy the ground floor underneath the maisonettes; on the first floor, one-bedroomed dwellings for the elderly are interspersed among the family homes. All the dwellings in this phase were constructed of pre-cast white concrete slabs, produced on the site, with some brick facings. However, the cost proved too high, the factory was closed, and this part of Thamesmead remains distinctive in appearance and in design — 'perhaps the most handsome industrialised project ever achieved in England' (Esher 1981) — in notable contrast both with later phases, and with the conventional housing built for sale.

The first family moved in during June, 1968; by mid-1971, 1000 families were in residence, and their characteristics are described in a GLC report (Skuse 1972). Just under half the families (mainly couples with at most one child) lived in flats, the remainder being equally divided between the maisonettes, usually housing four or five people, and the town houses with families of four or more. The age-structure of the population was — and still is — markedly different from that of the rest of the country, with less than half the normal proportion of people aged over 65 and nearly twice that of children under the age of 15 (Table 13.1). The proportion of professional people and managers was very much lower than in the country as a whole (6 per cent, compared with 22 per cent), the proportion of manual workers being correspondingly greater. About a quarter of families had three or more children living at home, and 6 per cent had five or more.

Table 13.1   Age distribution in Thamesmead compared to Greater London

| Age | Present Study | | | GLC[a] |
| | Males | Females | M & F | M & F |
	No.	No.	%	%
0–4	48	41	15	7
5–9	45	47	15	7
10–14	22	26	8	7
15–19	17	21	6	7
20–34	64	76	24	22
35–64	86	75	27	36
65 or more	13	15	5	14
Total	295	301	100	100

[a] Census population (1971) GLC area

The first two phases were not completed until mid-1975, three years later than planned. Social and community facilities were introduced about a year behind schedule: the first shop in 1970, the residents' club in 1971, and the first youth club in 1973. The first primary school was opened in June, 1969; after two years it had become overcrowded, and a second one in its turn became overfull before long. The first comprehensive school was opened in September, 1972.

Fig. 13.2 Tavy Bridge, Thamesmead

SERVICES

The GLC established an Information Centre in 1968 to deal with enquiries from prospective tenants, and appointed a community development officer to further the growth of community activities. Help in the formation of a residents' association was one of the most important of his many contributions to the life of Thamesmead. The GLC Housing Department converted a dwelling to serve as a local office, but it was mainly to collect rents, and was open for only a few hours a week. The District Office, about 8 miles away and difficult to reach by public transport, continued to be the local centre for housing management.

Access to other public services was also difficult. Bexley's Social Services Department, in the throes of reorganisation, did not establish a local office until August, 1973. The nearest Social Security office lay 3 miles to the south, with no direct bus service from Thamesmead; the Labour Exchange was 4 miles to the east. Their geographical separation and the inadequacies of public transport created hardship for those who had business to do with both services, such as men whose unemployment benefit was insufficient without supplementary benefit. The Churches engaged a social worker in

1969 and on her departure in 1972, an Anglican priest became responsible for community work; he established and edited a monthly newsheet, which did much to further a sense of community, and still flourishes. Anglicans, Methodists, the United Reformed Church, and Catholics had joined together to form the 'Thamesmead Christian Community'; among their aims (both now achieved) were the building of an Oecumenical Centre and the creation of a multi-denominational team to work together in ministering to people's needs.

On the medical side, Thamesmead was seen from the earliest days as an opportunity for a fresh initiative in primary health care planning, with a particular emphasis on the teaching of medical and other health students (Smith et al. 1966). Within the limitations imposed by the slow growth of the development and by financial stringency, many of the aims of the medical programme have been achieved (Higgins 1982ab). I was appointed in 1968 to develop the first group practice, and took up my duties first at the GLC Information Centre and then in a temporary health centre. The first permanent centre, opened in 1972, provides a wide range of services to the 11 000 people living in phases 1 and 2 of the community. The second group practice, serving phase 3, is scheduled to move into a new central health centre. The ten general practitioners (GPs) in these two practices have part-time appointments at Guy's Hospital Medical School; medical students are taught at Thamesmead from their first year, as well as students of other disciplines such as social work and health visiting.

In the early years, the only premises on site and open throughout the working day were the Information Centre and the temporary health centre. As a result, the doctors often found themselves acting as advocates on behalf of their patients, as it became evident that some agencies conduct their battles with each other by using the client as a weapon. Problems such as burst pipes, leaks, or defective heating were aggravated by disagreements between contractors and the Housing Department about who was responsible, and the tenant in difficulties was passed from one to another without finding a remedy. The Housing Department and the Social Security office were unable to agree on a system of support for the rent of those ill or unemployed, and it proved difficult to persuade them even to talk together about the problem. In all these matters, the doctor — the man with the open door and the telephone — was the most readily available source of help.

The temporary health centre served a variety of other purposes. A custom grew up, and still continues, of monthly meetings of all those working in and giving service to the community — clergy, teachers, nurses, health visitors, doctors, dentists, social workers, etc. The centre was also used for other social and business meetings and for the weekly sessions of the Thamesmead and Abbey Wood division of St John's Ambulance Brigade — a useful link between the new community and its longer established neighbour.

PROBLEMS

Many of the problems the residents encountered had been identified from past experience in other housing developments. Incomes are squeezed due to the costs of moving and of setting up new homes, and the cost of travelling to work is often greater; the usual personal support systems are lost (Central Housing Advisory Committee, 1967; Maule 1955). The GLC, however, had presented Thamesmead as something special, and thus set expectations at a level that proved to be unrealistic. People came, read the pamphlets, saw the excellent accommodation, and often decided to move without considering all the consequences. A survey carried out by a group of residents revealed that most people felt they had been given inadequate information about costs and local services and too little time — sometimes, it was claimed, as little as 20 minutes — to make up their minds. The same group of residents, with the help of the clergy, established an office to advise prospective tenants about these matters and to make sure that they had considered all the possible consequences of moving. They also managed in the early years to welcome every incoming family, and to act as a consumer group for the medical service.

Some of the problems were particular to Thamesmead. Those that caused most trouble in the early years were water penetration into houses and financial difficulties. The first, mainly due to defective flat roofing techniques, affected most of the dwellings in the first phase, but the GLC took a surprisingly long time to remedy it. Indeed, action only followed a concerted publicity campaign in 1971, in which almost all tenants participated. The second was the result of changes in policies on rents for public housing at both national and local government level. In 1970, the GLC introduced the concept of a 'fair rent', intended to apply to dwellings on all its estates, and based on the value of comparable accommodation in each locality. Thamesmead dwellings were attractive and well planned, but rents were already generally higher than tenants had been accustomed to paying. The new policy led to an additional sharp increase and as a result, two-thirds of the tenants fell into arrears with their rent. Once in arrears, they were trapped, as the Housing Department's policy was that all debts had to be cleared before a transfer to cheaper accommodation could be arranged. Some tenants, more desperate or less scrupulous than the rest, found a way out by not paying rent at all, so that eviction became inevitable.

Two factors increased the complexity of life for those most likely to be in trouble and least likely to be able to cope with it: the principle of 'selectivity' of benefits (Aberdare 1971) and the lack of a coherent benefit system (Raison 1971). The intended effect of the first was that benefits should go only to those who needed them because their income was below a certain level. The key to benefit was therefore evidence of earnings over a period of time — the pay slips. The effect of the second was that the poorest families, who needed every available benefit had to apply for each to different

Table 13.2   Agencies to whom application had to be made for various benefits

Benefit	Agency
Rent rebate	GLC
Rates rebate	Borough Council
Free milk	GPO or Social Security Office
Free school meals	Education Authority
Unemployment benefit	Employment Exchange
Supplementary benefit	Social Security Office
Free prescriptions	Chemist (leaflet PC11)
Free welfare foods	GPO or Social Security Office (Leaflet W11)
Free dental treatment	Dentist
Free spectacles	Optician

agencies (Table 13.2), most of which required evidence of earnings. If earnings varied, as they did in the case of those on overtime or shift work, frequent applications had to be made as circumstances changed. The greater the applicant's need, the more complicated were the procedures to be followed, and those with least resources had to deal with each agency in turn, relying on each to return the pay slips in time to complete the full cycle of applications before the next round became due. Organisational ability and intelligence of a high order were required to make full use of these benefits, the thresholds for which varied for no apparent reason.

The GLC instituted a rent rebate system that was a particularly severe test of intelligence; it was also overloaded with applications and subject to interminable delays (MacDonald 1972). When political control of the GLC changed again, the new administration set up an enquiry into the level of rents at Thamesmead. This established the validity of most of the grievances, and recommended a reduction of 35 per cent in the rents provisionally fixed under the 'fair rent' scheme; it also drew attention to the 'apparent lack of any real understanding and communication between housing officers and Thamesmead residents' and to 'sour and embittered' feelings amongst many of the tenants.

> At best they take the form of a stoic resignation and expression of total powerlessness to influence the GLC in any way. At worst the resentment about rents boils over into a generalised feeling of anger, directed at most of the authorities which appear to blight their lives . . . The atmosphere is oppressive and potentially very dangerous to the future of Thamesmead (Nevitt 1973).

STRESS AND HEALTH

It is clear that adverse features of the physical and the social environment were responsible for a great deal of stress in the early years, but the effect on the health of individuals cannot easily be judged, since 'stress' and 'health' are vague concepts, impossible to measure directly (see Chapter 2). One definition of stress is a perceived threat, occurring when there are demands on an individual with which he cannot cope (Lazarus 1966). The threat as evaluated by the individual may be difficult to assess, but what happens in response to that threat may be observed and in some instances measured. Emotional arousal may occur, physiological changes result, and various behaviours be adopted; amongst specific behaviours open to people in this position are political action, various forms of protest, or moving. All were made use of at Thamesmead. Moving was not easy, since alternative accommodation was hard to find, but some did manage it even after a relatively short stay. Protest actions and political activities were widely employed, a substantial proportion of the residents participating in them at one time or another.

Another possible specific behaviour is to seek help, and among those to whom people may turn is a doctor. They may consult specifically for social reasons — help in gaining priority for rehousing, for example, or advice about other social agencies and services — or because they feel ill. The illness may be seen by both patient and doctor as a psychological disturbance[1], or may present under the guise of a physical disorder. In some cases, it is the physiological changes accompanying arousal, such as a dry mouth, rapid heart beat, or alterations in breathing that are interpreted by the patient as indicating physical illness; in others, the link between apparently physical symptoms and an underlying psychological disturbance is more obscure. It is reasonable to assume that the act of seeking a doctor's help is an indication that an individual has reached a certain level, or threshold of distress. That threshold is not constant; it varies from person to person and also from time to time for any one individual, as circumstances change. It may vary by the perceived intensity of the threat, by the individual's sense of his ability to cope (which may be affected by past experience or other existing stress), and by the strength of the other supports available to him.

THE GENERAL PRACTITIONER AND PSYCHOLOGICAL DISTURBANCES

The person first consulted in this country by a person seeking medical help is usually the GP, much of whose work is concerned with people whose problems have an important psychological component. General practice offers several advantages for the long-term study of psychological disturbances and of their aetiology. The GP usually stays longer in his community than do members of other health and social services; he accumulates a great deal of information about the people he looks after, and observes all types of emotional and psychiatric disorders, as well as 'normal' reactions to stress. In the decision to seek his help, psycho-social factors are of great

---

(1) The term 'psychological disturbance' is used here to cover all kinds of emotional, psychological or psychiatric disorders or reactions, whether apparently occurring without cause, apparently related to circumstances, or accompanying physical disorders.

importance (Mechanic 1963, 1978; Tuckett, 1963). However, there are difficulties in relying upon GPs' assessments; many psychological disturbances are not detected (Eastwood 1971), even when the GP has had a psychiatric training (Goldberg & Blackwell 1970). An outstanding finding of a major study in London (Shepherd et al. 1966) was a nearly nine-fold variation between the highest and lowest rates of 'formal psychiatric morbidity', reported by the participating GPs. Some of this was believed to represent real variations in prevalence, related to the demographic and social characteristics of the different practice populations, but some undoubtedly reflected the individual doctor's attitude to complex mixtures of psychological disturbance and physical symptoms. Kessel (1960) found that in one London general practice, 90 patients per thousand at risk could be classified as having 'conspicuous psychiatric morbidity'; the rate rose to 380 per thousand if patients presenting physical complaints for no detectable cause were included, and to 520 per thousand with the addition of all cases considered to be psychosomatic.

A high proportion of people present to the GP with psychological disturbance at some time in their lives. In a population comparable to Thamesmead's, 65 per cent of adult patients who consulted their doctor over a period of 5 years were assessed as having a neurotic illness lasting at least a month (Paulett 1956). Most (73 per cent) of those who present to a GP with a psychiatric disorder for the first time recover within 3 years (Kedward 1969), but there is a large group of chronically disturbed people whose recovery rate over 3 years is only 11 per cent (Harvey-Smith & Cooper 1970). Those whose conditions have a prolonged, intractable course are more likely to suffer severe and unremitting social problems (Kedward & Sylph 1974).

SOCIAL FACTORS AND PSYCHOLOGICAL DISTURBANCES

All studies show a greater prevalence of psychological disturbance in women. In the London practices studied by Shepherd et al. (1966), over one year the patient consulting rate, taking both sexes together, was 102 per thousand at risk for 'formal psychiatric illness' and 139 per thousand at risk for 'total psychiatric morbidity'. In most age-groups, the rates for women were double those for men, the highest rates for total psychiatric morbidity being found in women aged 45 to 64 (208 per thousand at risk). For women, the factors associated with higher rates of disturbance include difficult marriage (Bernard 1973), the early stages of child-rearing, the presence at home of three or more children under 15, and the lack of an intimate and confiding relationship with a partner (Brown et al. 1975). For both sexes, the rate is increased in the presence of the following: poorer social status (see Hirschfield & Cross 1982 for a review), loss of a parent during childhood by death, divorce or separation (Hill & Price 1967; Dennehey 1966), and social difficulties (Kedward & Sylph 1974; Jacobsen 1973; Cooper 1972;

Sylph et al. 1969). Some of these factors are interrelated and reinforce each other; working-class wives, for example, are particularly likely to be affected by more than one risk factor (Brown et al. 1975).

Amongst residents in city centres, rates of psychological disturbance are high, though this is in part due to the inward migration of those already in difficulty. In Inner London, admission rates to psychiatric hospitals are higher, as compared with outer London (French 1972), behaviour disorders among children are twice as common as in the Isle of Wight, and psychiatric disorders and delinquency more common in their parents (Rutter 1973).

NEW COMMUNITIES

Freeman (1972), while acknowledging the difficulties, pointed out that new communities are in some ways more accessible to research than are settled ones, and that the efforts made to study their achievements have been puny in relation to the large amount of public investment that has gone into these ventures. Research published to date, however, has not convincingly demonstrated a relationship between stress due to the physical or social environment and psychological disturbance in new communities in this country.

Three major studies have been carried out, all using evidence derived from GPs' diagnoses, utilisation of psychiatric services, and questionnaires; one study also had material obtained by trained lay interviewers. The first (Martin et al. 1957) revealed rates of disturbance that were high, compared with the general population or with the longer established population living nearby. The two subsequent studies — at Harlow (Taylor & Chave 1964) and Croydon (Hare & Shaw 1965) — used for comparison the population of origin in each case, and found no important differences.

Complicating factors mentioned by Freeman are those associated with migration and resettlement. Some evidence suggests that people with psychiatric illness or personality disorder are more likely to move home than are those not so affected (Shepherd et al. 1966; Hall 1964; Tietze et al. 1942). Moving may be followed by a deep sense of loss (Fried 1963; Thorpe 1939), while those who move and are in distress may, without reason, attribute their plight to housing or to other aspects of the new environment (Hall 1966). In addition, any public housing project is likely, as a result of its selection processes, to include a higher proportion of those most at risk. As compared with the general population, more of the residents will be in the poorer social groups and priority may be given to the physically or mentally disabled; those allocated homes may also have spent a long time in housing need and been subject to other stresses, such as the harmful effects of redevelopment programmes or clearance for new roads (Ungerson 1971; Wiggins 1971). Bereavement, divorce, and other changes in life may lead to individuals having to move.

In all these ways, housing selection may favour the more vulnerable, or those passing through a difficult phase in their lives; on the other hand, it may be less likely to favour both the most and the least disturbed: schizophrenics living on their own and single women, who have a lesser risk of depression than others (Porter 1970), both have a smaller chance of being rehoused. Moving has other consequences which may affect the apparent prevalence of psychological disturbance, when assessed by GPs' diagnoses. Factors that influence consultation rates, such as the availability and acceptability of medical services (Brotherston 1958) and the strength of non-medical support systems (Scambler et al. 1981; McKinlay 1973; Friedson 1960), alter with moving; also, doctors who take on work in new communities may be particularly interested in psychological disturbance. As a result of both these factors, rates of recognition of psychological disturbance may be higher than elsewhere.

All the above considerations are important, if the purpose is to compare prevalence rates in a given population with rates in other populations, but less so if it is to identify disturbed individuals within the population cared for by a single medical unit, or to compare the characteristics of those affected and those not affected.

STRESS AND DISTURBANCE AT THAMESMEAD

In the study reported here, information derived from clinical records was used to examine the relationships between environmental stress and psychological disturbance. This was done in four ways: constructing case studies of particular families, measuring rates of psychological disturbance, identifying a group whose disturbance appeared to the doctor to be closely related to environmental stress, and recording utilisation rates of medical services.

An assistant helped me for a year up to July 1970; he was replaced then by my first partner, and the two of us were alone responsible for the general medical care of all the families on our list up to the end of 1972. We agreed a common approach, with emphasis on a full exploration of problems when indicated, and attention to psycho-social factors that might have initiated the consultation or contributed to the 'illness'. Symptoms were noted in detail at all consultations, together with patients' statements about their problems and difficulties.

In the early years, we tended to put fairly precise psychiatric labels on to emotional and psychological problems; but as time went on, and it became clear that relatively few patients could be categorised as having a formal psychiatric disorder, diagnoses became less definite and less medical in nature. The term 'EMI' — emotional and mental illness — came into use to describe all these disturbances, and in the course of our work in those early years, we saw many patients whose disturbances seemed amply justified by the nature and severity of the problems they had to deal with.

Family studies

As might be expected, the larger families seemed most at risk. What follows is a condensed account of voluminous notes and correspondence recording what happened to two such families during their stay in Thamesmead.

Mr and Mrs A moved into one of the terraced houses with their six children, and left in 1976; before coming, the family had been living in a two-bedroomed flat, the two girls having to sleep in the same room as their parents. Mr A had no overt recorded psychological disturbance; Mrs A had been recorded as having symptoms of anxiety due to poor living conditions. These were of course greatly improved by the move, but the cost went up, their rent doubling to £9.14, including £1.60 for a garage which the family did not need, as they had no car. All efforts to gain release from this commitment were of no avail, until Mrs A discovered by chance that another resident had succeeded in this; however, she still had to pay rates for the garage. Mr A obtained employment in the construction firm who were building this part of Thamesmead. His average weekly income before moving was £24.00; in the new job it was £22.00, but fluctuated wildly as a rotating schedule of overtime, short-time, and strikes in turn affected his earning capacity. Over one 21-month period, the family had ten changes of rent, with monthly rebates varying from £11.00 to £19.00 — always, of course, out of phase with actual income at the time.

They soon got into arrears, but managed to pay these off at the rate of £1.30 per week, and were free of debt by January, 1971. Unfortunately, Mr A's income rose temporarily during the following few months, and the rebate was reduced retrospectively. Thus, when the rent book was returned to them, the couple found themselves unexpectedly and without forewarning once more in arrears. A few months later, Mr A had a disagreement with his foreman and was dismissed; in consequence, he was unable to obtain unemployment benefit. Supplementary benefit, first fixed at £15.00 per week, was raised to £21.00 as a result of representations made on his behalf. This sum, however, was expected to cover the whole rent as, in accordance with the procedure then in use, the GLC withdrew the rebate. Arrears steadily increased; the Housing Department issued a notice warning of possible eviction and, without more ado, applied 9 days later to the court for possession of the house. An order for possession was issued, but not enforced. The legal costs incurred by the Housing Department were added to the family's existing debt.

In accordance with the principle of selectivity, whenever Mr A's income rose, benefits were reduced by more or less equal amounts. Mrs A, seeking cheaper accommodation that would allow a greater margin between housing costs and living costs, expressed willingness to move to a three-bedroomed house. She was told that would not be allowed, since such accommodation would result in overcrowding. The family were trapped in every way, unable to do anything to help themselves. Mr and Mrs A both developed anxiety and depressive symptoms; two of the children were also disturbed, one requiring psychiatric treatment. Mrs A consulted a doctor on 139 occasions over the 7 years, the peak consultation rates being during the 3 years from 1971 to 1973, when she attended the health centre a total of 84 times. Some of this was for advice about how to react to the latest blow to the family, but much was for emotional upsets. In addition, she developed a number of apparently physical complaints, some of which required investigation; no serious physical disease was found.

Over that period of 12 months when the Housing Department was fine-tuning the family's rebate to achieve very modest savings to the GLC's budget, members of the family had 126 consultations, 26 prescriptions, ten out-patient consultations, four in-patient days, a number of investigations (including a barium enema, sigmoidoscopy, ECG, chest x-ray, back x-ray and blood tests), 33 social worker contacts, and a case conference involving participants from five different services.

Other families faced similar difficulties. Some found that the mechanisms for coping that they had developed elsewhere were of no use at Thamesmead.

Mr and Mrs B, also with six children, moved in during 1970 but stayed only 2 years. Mr. B's income had always been small, but he had been able to keep out of difficulties by doing odd jobs. He lived in rented accommodation, but it was privately owned and his landlord had been willing to accept work done on the house in lieu of part of his rent. At Thamesmead, these ways of surviving were denied to him; he could not find part-time work and he was of course unable to pay off any of his rent in kind. Soon after moving, he was put on to short-time working and his income fell, but implementation of his rent rebate was delayed, so that all the family's savings were consumed. He too had to pay for a garage to house a car he did not possess and could not afford, while the cost of central heating was included in his rent, restricting his choice of priorities for spending his money. He saw himself as being at the mercy of forces he could not understand. His union made him attend meetings, he said, thus losing earning time; he was not allowed to work more than 5 days in each week ('something to do with the unions I think'); his rent varied unpredictably, and important items of expenditure were outside his control. He contrasted his previous situation where 'my mind was at peace' and he 'always had a few bob in my pocket at the end of the week' with his predicament at Thamesmead — 'a desolate way to live'.

Mr B was also employed by the firm building houses in Thamesmead. The early years were plagued by frequent official and unofficial strikes, the principal causes of which were attempts by the unions, or by a minority of their members, to stop the main contractors using self-employed sub-contructors for some of the work. Whatever the merits of the dispute may have been, the effects of the repeated disruptions were disastrous for men such as Mr A and Mr B, who wanted to work regularly to support their families.

'EMI' in the practice

In the light of these and other cases, there were two important questions: was there a generally high level of disturbance amongst the residents, and was there a group showing good evidence that some factor related to living at Thamesmead was responsible for their disturbance? In assessing the effects of the environment, a past history of psychiatric disturbance was important, since those with such a history or with significant personality problems were unlikely to provide convincing evidence of a direct relationship between emotional illness and stress. Of more significance would be the onset of disturbance in someone hitherto unaffected.

The GLC's list of occupied dwellings was used as a sampling frame, and all 117 households occupied during 1969, as well as one in five (126) of those occupied in 1970 were identified for the purposes of this study — 243 households in all. In 19 of these, no occupant registered with the practice; nothing is known about these people, except that nine households left within 3 years. Sixty-one families (25 per cent of the whole sample) registered, but moved within 3 years; information about many of these families is scanty, some having left after only a few months. We therefore confined our attention to the 163 families in the sample who registered with the practice and remained at Thamesmead for 3 years or longer.

Our working definition of EMI was an illness, involving more than one consultation, in which the doctor assessed the problems as either wholly psycho-social or psychiatric in nature, or as having an important psychological or psychiatric element. A wide range is covered by this definition, from a short-lived emotional upset or worry to quite severe psychiatric conditions. Single consultations (in most of which an emotional disturbance appeared to be a temporary reaction to immediate stress) were not classified as indicating EMI, and are therefore excluded. From the clinical records, a research assistant abstracted onto a family dossier the following information about each member: name, date of birth, sex, occupation, marital status, dates of contact with medical services, physical and emotional illness diagnosed, and referrals to hospital.

Records of individuals identified as possible cases of EMI (because the notes contained either a psychiatric diagnosis or symptoms suggestive of a psychological disturbance, whether presenting as a physical disorder or as an overtly emotional problem) were then reviewed by both investigators, working independently. We accepted or rejected the diagnosis on the basis of the evidence recorded at the time, and assessed its type and severity. Anxiety was diagnosed on patients' statements about worrying, irritability, feeling tense, or inability to relax, which were often associated with fears about the future and feelings of panic. Depression was diagnosed on patients' statements about feeling low, miserable, fed-up or depressed, in the presence of at least one of the following: early morning waking, loss of libido, loss of energy, or loss of ability to cope with daily living; increased irritability or angry feelings, or loss of appetite were also often recorded. If our assessments differed, we reached agreement after discussion; but in no individual case was there a serious difference of opinion.

The nature of the patient's reactions was assessed on a five-point scale, varying from anxiety without any depressive features to depression with little or no recorded evidence of anxiety. Severity was assessed on a five-point scale, from a brief disturbance during the period studied (in which emotional disorder was largely incidental to a social stress or physical illness) up to emotional disorder that was severe, divorced from, or out of proportion to any social or other stress, and prolonged or repeated. It was thus a composite assessment, involving time, the degree of patient-reaction, and a judgement of the appropriateness of the reaction. Statements were recorded at the time about the cause of these disturbances, as perceived by patients, and where these related to some aspect of life at Thamesmead, we assessed the relevance of the statements, in the light of our knowledge of the patient and all the circumstances.

In just over half (85) of the 163 households, at least one member was seen with EMI during the first 3 years of residence. The number of individuals affected was 109 out of 507 (excluding children under five). Table 13.3 gives the proportion of patients with EMI at any time during the first three years of residence. For adults aged 20–64, the average annual prevalence rate, based on the actual number of patients at risk in each year (i.e. taking account of the small number of patients who left or joined the families during the 3 years) was 34 per cent in the case of women and 12 per cent in the case of men. The lowest rate, as might be expected, was that for children. The highest rate was for women aged 20–34, exactly half of whom

Table 13.3 Patients with EMI at any time during 3 years at Thamesmead

		Number at risk	With EMI% All cases	Mod/sev only
Men	All ages	163	18	14
	20–34	64	14	11
	35–64	86	21	15
	65+	13	23	23
Women	All ages	166	42	27
	20–34	76	50	33
	35–64	75	39	23
	65+	15	13	13
Children	5–14	140	6	4
	15–19	38	5	–

were affected at some time within the 3 years, with an average annual prevalence rate of 36 per cent (24 per cent for moderate or severe EMI). Among women, the rate was lower in the older, as compared with the younger age-group, whilst for men, with a much lower general level, the reverse was true. Little can be said about the rates recorded for the over-65s, owing to the small numbers in the sample. Taking the 2 years separately, 35 per cent of the adults in the 1969 sample were affected, compared with 25 per cent of those in the 1970 sample.

Of the women with EMI, the predominant diagnosis was anxiety in 19 per cent of cases and depression in 68 per cent; in the remaining 13 per cent, no clear distinction was possible. The corresponding figures for men were: anxiety 35 per cent, depression 46 per cent, mixed 19 per cent. Anxiety was diagnosed in a higher proportion of those who moved in during 1969, compared with those who came during 1970; 18 per cent of adults at risk in the former group had an anxiety component in their illness, compared with 9 per cent in the latter, the prevalence of depressive illness being the same in each sample. There were also differences in treatment; all but one of the 31 affected women in the 1970 cohort were treated with a psychotropic drug at some time within the 3 years, compared with 27 of the 38 affected women in the 1969 cohort. In 67 of the 99 men and women aged over 19 who had EMI during the 3 years, the condition was assessed as moderate or severe on at least one occasion. During the whole 3 years, only three individuals (two adults, one child) were referred for psychiatric opinion or treatment. Ten children were affected; seven of these came from families who moved in during the first year (1969).

Environmental stress

Thirty-two adults (12 men, 20 women) — nearly a third of those assessed as having EMI — claimed that some factor associated with moving to or living in Thamesmead was a cause of their illness, and in 15 of these cases (six men and nine women in 13 households), we considered that the claim was justified. The main problems were financial (ten individuals in eight households), while difficulties with neighbours were mentioned by seven individuals in six households, all but one of whom lived close together, and near to a large and very disturbed family that was later evicted. Others had a variety of complaints about housing, noise, or other aspects of the environment. Past medical records were also reviewed; of the nine women thought to be affected by environmental stress, only one had been recorded as having a psychological disturbance before moving, as compared with five out of the 11 in whom it was judged that the disturbance was unlikely to have been due to environmental stress. It is of course possible that information in our own notes about past psychological disturbance might have influenced our judgements. We therefore followed-up the women in the original sample, to see if the group identified as likely to have been affected by environmental stress differed from the rest. If the identification was correct, they might be expected to show less disturbance in subsequent years, if stress had been reduced.

In fact, a quarter of the women in the sample left Thamesmead within 9 years. The proportion was the same for three groups: those unaffected by EMI, those affected who did not claim that some aspect of life at Thamesmead had caused the illness, and that sub-group whose claims that their illnesses *were* associated with some aspect of life at Thamesmead we had rejected. Of the disturbed women whose claim was accepted in 1974, a higher proportion — four out of 11 — left during the 9 year period; in those who remained, EMI was diagnosed less often, and was judged as less severe than in the group whose claims were rejected. The two groups also differed in respect of certain risk factors: marital disharmony, acute physical illness, and major illness in the family were recorded more often in those whose illness was judged not to be related to environmental factors.

The numbers are small, but it seems reasonable to conclude that environmental stress was a factor in causing EMI in at least one adult member in 13 (8 per cent) of the 163 households in the sample. The main stress — high rents — was noted as a difficulty at some time during the first 4 years for 21 (13 per cent) of households, though it rarely appears in the records as a problem after 1974. A higher proportion of those with EMI had this noted as a difficulty, but even those not disturbed mentioned it as a problem during the early years. Of the 78 households in which no member was assessed as disturbed, difficulties over rent were recorded in six (8 per cent).

If the information derived from this sample represents the experience of the whole population, then at least 97 out of 747 families who moved in during the first two years had problems with rent, and in 59, at least one individual had an emotional disturbance related to environmental stress. These are likely to be minimum figures, since the information is derived from those who presented to doctors, patients with single consultations for an emotional upset have been excluded, and the sample is restricted to those who overcome their difficulties sufficiently to stay at least 3 years.

Seventy (29 per cent) of the 243 households in the sample moved out within 3 years, and it is reasonable to assume that environmental stress was a problem for a much higher proportion of these. The incomplete records do show that twice as many of those who left had some complaint about life at Thamesmead. In ten of the 22 couples who moved in during 1969 and who left within 3 years, at least one adult with EMI claimed that some aspect of life there was responsible.

Utilisation rates

In the present survey, utilisation has been measured by counting all consultations in normal surgery sessions at the health centre, plus all visits to

Table 13.4 Contacts by year of residence: average number of contacts per year adjusted for number at risk

	Year of residence				
	1st	2nd	3rd	4th	5th
1969 sample	3.9	4.0	4.2	4.3	3.6
1970 sample	3.5	3.4	4.0	4.0	3.8

patients at home by doctors. Contacts for maternity services, family planning, child health, or other clinics are not included. In both groups, rates reached their highest levels in the third and fourth year of residence and fell slightly in the fifth (Table 13.4). Contact rates for the 1969 families were higher than those for the 1970 sample in each year, up to the fifth year of residence.

The contact rate for males assessed as having EMI was three times that for males not so assessed, while for females (in whom a higher proportion of the episodes of EMI were considered mild), it was about double. Having a parent assessed as showing EMI was associated with an increase in the child's contact rates by about a quarter (Fig. 13.3) Contact rates for children were higher in the families who moved in during 1969 than in those who came during 1970.

Fig. 13.3 , Thamesmead

CONCLUSIONS

That the first inhabitants of Thamesmead did experience considerable stress is beyond question, though the effects are difficult to assess, since the findings can be interpreted in different ways.

The basic assumptions of the study were that the two doctors mainly concerned were reasonably consistent with each other, and that neither their approach nor their recording of relevant information varied over the three years. This is unlikely to be wholly true, and although review of the records should have reduced any such lack of consistency, it may not entirely have eliminated it. If the cases assessed as having emotional or mental illness were similar to those included in the category 'total psychiatric morbidity' by Shepherd et al. (1966), then prevalence rates were much higher than average for London at Thamesmead; they were also highest in younger women — the reverse of the pattern found in that study. If only those affected at least moderately are considered, however, the rates are reasonably comparable, and only two adults were identified as needing psychiatric help during the 3 years. There is thus no evidence of a notable excess of serious psychiatric problems.The most that can be said is that relatively more of Thamesmead's residents had an emotional upset during their first 3 years, and that the younger wives were most at risk.

Fig. 13.4 , Thamesmead

Within Thamesmead, the higher proportion of those who moved in during the first year being assessed as anxious, their higher rates of service utilisation, the higher rates of utilisation for their children, and the higher proportion of children assessed as disturbed, all suggest more distress amongst the early settlers than among the families who came during 1970. In prescribing psychotropic drugs less often for them, as compared with the 1970 group, we may either have assessed their disturbance as not severe, or as an understandable response to acute situational stress rather than an illness.

In half the families, at least one member was assessed as having an emotional or mental illness over the three years. A third of those so assessed claimed that some aspect of life at Thamesmead was responsible for their illness, and in half these cases, we accepted this claim. Of the women in this group, only one had a record of a psychiatric disorder in the past; there were differences between them and the women not thought to be environmentally affected in respect of certain risk factors, and of the risk of emotional disturbance, or of moving in subsequent years. The evidence that they constituted a distinct group is therefore reasonably good, and the relationship between stress and the precipitation of emotional disturbance in individuals hitherto unaffected appears clear. This group may, however been more vulnerable than were those not affected. A possible explanation of the high rate of disturbance in younger women in the sample, compared with other studies, is the earlier development of a disturbance which in other circumstances might have been postponed to a later period of their lives. This is referred to by Brown et al. (1975) as 'brought-forward time'.

If the findings in the sample apply to the whole population, and if it can be assumed that those who moved out within 3 years were twice as likely as the rest to have been affected by environmental stress, then of the 747 families who moved in during 1969 and 1970, there were 75 in which at least one adult had an emotional disturbance related to environmental stress. As indicated above, this is likely to be the minimum figure, and includes only those who were distressed enough to seek help from a doctor. The most serious stress appeared to be financial, due to high rents; even those not disturbed are recorded as troubled by this. The physical environment was occasionally held to blame, but in most cases the stress was due not to the problem itself, but to frustration; either the people responsible could not be identified, or they could be identified but not induced to respond.

Thus, the main causes of stress lay in the social environment. In some instances, the adverse social circumstances could not have been prevented. No-one could really be held to account for the effects of a disturbed family on its neighbours. The GLC was not responsible for the system of support for those in need; its component parts had been developed by different authorities, in different circumstances, over the years. The system was — and still is — distinguished by its complexity, its lack of coordination, and by the burdens it puts on those most needing help. There were, however, two elements within the social environment that could not be attributed to the workings of chance. New policies on rent, decided by the GLC and by the Government, bore particularly hard — and, as was demonstrated, unjustly — on the inhabitants of Thamesmead, while the principle of selectivity kept those to whom it was applied within the 'poverty trap'. The situation was made worse by the muddles, delays, and lack of coordination within the Housing Department itself, vividly described by a journalist who happened to be a tenant on another GLC estate at the time (MacDonald 1972).

It seemed as though there was a conflict between the aims of the architects and planners, and those of the Housing Department. The former saw in Thamesmead an opportunity to create a new style of public housing and a new standard of amenity. The latter, on the other hand, appeared to see Thamesmead as just another GLC estate; when challenged about this, the Department's staff replied that difficulties were to be expected — all estates had them — and no prevention or remedy was possible. However, 'psychological tensions were much lightened by the tenants' insistence that they had nothing against Thamesmead itself; they were full of praise for the architects and for their own individual flats' (Nevitt 1973). At Thamesmead, the option of building only to a standard that tenants could afford had been discarded, but the consequence of achieving a higher standard — that rents for most households had to be subsidised — never seemed to be faced. Less thought was given to those aspects of the social environmental most under bureaucratic control than to the physical environment, and it was defects in the former than put at risk the immense investment in the latter.

The problem was that no-one had overall responsibility for this costly and ambitious enterprise, since there was no New Town Development Corporation. Policies on rents, the rate of development, and the balance between private and public housing varied with the 4 yearly cycle of changes in political control. Special provision for Thamesmead could not be made without regard for other GLC estates and their tenants, while the boroughs were anxious to safeguard the interests of their own ratepayers. These major handicaps made proper management difficult, but at the same time more necessary.

However, there were gains as well as losses. The first residents had made a considerable personal investment in their move to Thamesmead; most of them were affected by the early difficulties, and the sense of shared tribulation engendered a strong feeling of common purpose. Those early problems were as great a stimulus to some as they were a burden to others, and much was achieved as a result. In the course of time, housing and rent policies changed and housing management became more responsive. Proposals for a new relationship were developed, culminating in an imaginative scheme for co-management by housing authority and tenants jointly (GLC 1974), but a change in political control prevented its implementation.

Lessons may be drawn from this experience. The effects on such a new

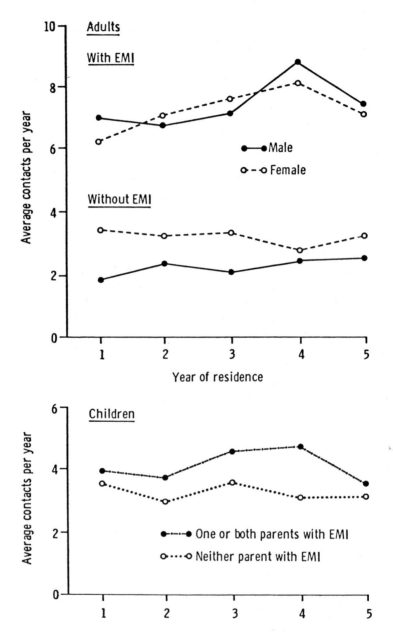

Fig. 13.5 Contact rates by years of residence

community of the social policies followed by the GLC could have been foreseen, and ought to have been avoided. It is too easy for a public service to pass on to others the burden of coping with the effects of its policies. Prevention of social 'disorders' is at least as important as prevention of medical disorders. The present system of welfare benefits is unduly complex, accentuating the paradox that those with the least resources have most to cope with. Perhaps most important, however, is that even with foresight and planning, no new venture can be perfect, and it must be capable of being modified with experience. Just as a new ship has to have a commissioning period, so any new development such as Thamesmead requires to be tested and run-in. This process is dependent on feedback, both from those affected and from those who give service to them. What the local housing manager, social worker, and doctor learn in the course of their daily work should become part of the process of adapting social policies.

The value of the study presented here would be greatly enhanced if it were supplemented by information from the social services and the Housing office serving the population. Each collects a wide range of data, relating to the same people. Although not available in a utilisable form at present, this could provide information, not obtainable in other ways, which is relevant to the effects of both social and physical environments on the wellbeing of people. Combined research of that kind would be of great value in the development of social policy.

Acknowledgements. I am grateful to my colleagues Rodney Turner and Michael Curwen who collaborated with me in this work, and to others who made helpful criticisms. We owe a great deal to the careful work of our research assistant, Eileen Turner. The Greater London Council supplied the illustrations, and we are also indebted to the Endowment Fund of Guy's Hospital Medical School.

REFERENCES

Aberdare Lord 1971 The Times (Parliamentary Report) 8th July
Bernard J 1973 The future of marriage, Bantam. New York.
Brotherston J H F 1958 In: Pemberton J, Willard H (eds) Recent studies in epidemiology. Blackwell, Oxford
Brown G W, Ni Bhrolchain M, Harris T 1975 Social class and psychiatric disturbance among women in an urban population. Sociology 9: 225–254
Central Housing Advisory Committee 1967 The needs of new communities. Ministry of Local Government Circular, HMSO, London
Cooper B 1972 Clinical and social aspects of chronic neurosis. Proceedings of the Royal Society of Medicine 65: 509–512
Dennehy C M 1966 Childhood bereavement and psychiatric illness. British Journal of Psychiatry 112: 1049–1069
Eastwood M R 1971 Screening for psychiatric disorder. Psychological Medicine 1: 197–208
Esher L 1981 A broken wave. Allen Lane, London
Freeman H L 1972 Mental health and new communities in Britain. In: Nossiter T J, Rokken S (eds) Imagination and precision in the social sciences, London, Faber
French E 1972 Admissions to psychiatric hospitals. GLC Intelligence Unit Quarterly Bulletin 19: 25–29

Fried M 1963 Grieving for a lost home. In: Duhl L J (ed) The urban condition: people and policy in the metropolis. Basic Books, New York

Friedson E 1960 Client control and medical practice. American Journal of Sociology 65: 374–382

Goldberg D, Blackwell B 1970 Psychiatric illness in General Practice. British Medical Journal 2: 439–443

Greater London Council 1974 The co-management of homes. Report of a Working Party on the Management and Maintenance of Thamesmead, Greater London Council, London

Hall P 1964 Moving house in the aetiology of psychiatric symptoms. Proceedings of the Royal Society of Medicine 57: 83–86

Hall P 1966 Some clinical aspects of moving house as an apparent precipitant of psychiatric symptoms. Journal of Psychosomatic Research 10: 59–70

Hare E H, Shaw G K 1965 Mental health on a new housing estate. Maudsley Monograph, No 12, Oxford University Press, London

Harvey-Smith E A, Cooper B 1970 Patterns of neurotic illness in the community. Journal of the Royal College of General Practitioners 19: 132–139

Higgins P M 1982a Thamesmead: dream to reality. British Medical Journal 285: 1564–1566

Higgins P M 1982b Thamesmead: lessons learnt. British Medical Journal 285: 1631–1633

Hill O W, Price J S 1967 Childhood bereavement and adult depression. British Journal of Psychiatry 113: 743–751

Hirschfield R M A, Cross S K 1982 Epidemiology of affective disorders. Archives of General Psychiatry 39: 743–46

Jacobsen K 1973 The vulnerable individual: a pilot study. Ungeskr Laeger 135: 2655–2659

Kedward H B 1969 The outcome of neurotic illness in the community. Social Psychiatry 4: 1–4

Kedward H B, Sylph J 1974 Social correlates of chronic neurotic disorders. Social Psychiatry 9: 91–98

Kessel W I N 1960 Psychiatric morbidity in a London general practice. British Journal of Preventive & Social Medicine 14: 16–22

Lazarus R S 1966 Psychological stress and the coping process. McGraw, New York

Macdonald R 1972 The rebate roundabout. Guardian, 20th December

McKinlay J B 1973 Social networks, lay consultation and help-seeking behavior. Social Forces 51: 275–292

Martin F M, Brotherston J H F, Chave S P W 1957 Incidence of neurosis in a new housing estate. British Journal of Preventive & Social Medicine 11: 196–202

Maule H G 1955 Social and psychological aspects of behavior: the family. Advancement of Science 12: 443–448

Mechanic D 1963 Some implication of illness behavior for medical sampling. New England Journal of Medicine 269: 244–247

Mechanic D 1978 Medical sociology. Collier MacMillan, New York

Nevitt D 1973 Thamesmead rents, GLC Report. Greater London Council, London

Paulett J D 1956 Neurotic ill-health: a study in general practice. Lancet ii: 683–685

Porter A M W 1970 Depressive illness in a general practice. A demographic study and a controlled trial of imipramine. British Medical Journal 1: 773–778

Raison T 1971 Making sense of benefits and low incomes. The Times, 14th October

Rutter M 1973 Why are London children disturbed? Proceedings Royal Society of Medicine 66: 1221–1225

Scambler A, Scambler G, Craig D 1981 Kinship and friendship networks and women's demand for primary care. Journal of Royal College of General Practitioners 31: 746–750

Shepherd M, Cooper B, Brown A C, Kalton G W 1966 Psychiatric illness in general practice. Oxford University Press, London

Skuse C M 1972 Thamesmead survey of ingoing tenants. GLC Research and Intelligence Unit, Research Memoranda 321–335

Smith R, Curwen M P, Chamberlain J, Butterfield W J H 1966 The Woolwich and Erith Project: planning a community health service. Lancet i: 650–654

Sylph J, Kedward H B, Eastwood M R 1969 Chronic neurotic patients in general practice. Journal of the Royal College of General Practitioners 17: 162–170

Taylor S J, Chave S 1964 Mental health and environment. Longmans, London

Thorpe F T 1939 Demolition melancholia. British Medical Journal 2: 127

Tietze C, Lemkau P, Cooper M 1942 Personality disorder and spatial mobility. American Journal of Sociology 48: 29–34

Tuckett D 1963 An introduction to medical sociology. Tavistock, London

Ungerson C 1971 Moving home: a study of the redevelopment process in two London boroughs. Occasional Papers in Social Administration, No 44, Bell, London

Wiggins D 1971 The revolt in the cities. The Times, 3rd April

Depression and schizophrenia in an English city

INTRODUCTION

The aim of this chapter is to discuss within a social geographical framework, the distribution of psychiatric illnesses in an English city. The diagnostic sub-groups of depression and schizophrenia have been chosen for a number of reasons. Depression is a concept which covers a number of well recognised syndromes; it also gives scope to investigate illnesses which range from those generally regarded as 'endogenous' to others considered exogenous or stress-related, i.e. 'understandable' results of environmental pressures, (though this differentiation is not accepted by Brown : see Chapter 2). In addition, the literature on the epidemiology of depression is relatively sparse, compared with that on some other psychiatric disorders. Although schizophrenia has been intensively studied, the tendency to group it with indices of social pathology has led in the past to some over-simplified statements about the effects of inner urban environmental stress on mental health.

Social geography is a relatively new discipline, devised from human geography and sociology. Its underlying concepts are the geographical ones of 'space' and 'pattern', and derived from these are 'processes' and practical applications to solving social problems (Jones & Eyles 1977; Herbert & Smith 1979). Urban analysis has been its cornerstone, mainly because of a preoccupation with the effects of the expansion of cities on human life and behaviour in Western society (see also Chapter 11 and Timms 1971). The area studied was Plymouth, Devon, which had a population of 240 652 at the 1981 Census, and is the largest urban area in the South-West of England apart from Bristol, some 120 miles away. The city is well delineated geographically — to the east runs the river Plym, to the west the Tamar; the south is demarcated by Plymouth Sound, and the north by the land barrier of Dartmoor. During the period studied, all psychiatric admissions from it went to a single mental hospital, situated 14 miles from the city centre. There was no catchment area sectorisation within the city, thus removing an important source of possible bias in epidemiological studies. Since the early 1960s, a policy of community-based care, involving two new out-patient departments and a community psychiatric nursing service, had been enthusiastically pursued; this was seen by the professional staff and authorities involved as the most effective way of providing for the needs of patients. Thus, the maintenance of patients in the general community became a service goal, the achievement of which seemed measurable in terms of the frequency of readmissions and time spent in hospital — though it was clearly not the only service goal. Evaluative studies of an out-patient department and of the community psychiatric nursing service used these as primary indicators (Kessel & Hassall 1971; Hunter 1978).

Paradoxically, however, this research into non-residential care suggested that as the amount of observation and support for patients in the community increased, so did the rate of readmissions and even the average length of stay in hospital. It thus confirmed the findings of Brown et al. (1966), in a study of three psychiatric services, that the most community-orientated had the highest rate of readmission for schizophrenia; greater awareness of patients' morbidity by psychiatrists and social workers was seen as the most likely reason for this. Thus, due to the discrepancy between 'system goal' and 'system practice', intervention designed to improve the performance of the system may have an opposite effect, when measured against a declared aim. However, optimum management has to be decided in the light of a patient's social or family setting, the availability of care for him, and the likelihood of harmful effects from him on others. Therefore, the system goal may need to be revised, and our present studies are relevant to this in examining the relationship of social geographical factors to hospitalisation.

THE URBAN DISTRIBUTION OF MENTAL ILLNESS AND ITS EXPLANATION

The non-randomness of the distribution of psychiatric illness in urban areas has long been a subject of debate, the work of the Chicago School of sociologists being perhaps best known. Faris & Dunham (1939) described the distribution of depression and schizophrenia in Chicago, and were able to choose between the Park–Burgess (1925) model of concentric development, which predominantly represents the influence of population structure in an expanding city, and the Hoyt (1939 1964) model, which is sectoral, and correlates more clearly with socio-economic factors. In fact, Faris & Dunham used Park–Burgess zone maps, which comprised concentric circles, arising from the main business district in the middle, and radiating out through transitional, working men's homes, residential, and commuter zones; the populations in the various zones were considered to be produced by the nature of the life within them (see Chapter 6, Footnote 3).

To compare socio-demographic characteristics with mental illness rates, details were compiled of housing types and of social indices, e.g. juvenile delinquency, numbers of restaurants, radio ownership. Their study was the first to examine area differences with respect to the different types of psychoses. When psychiatric first admission rates for the period 1930/31 were studied, a disparity was found in rates for schizophrenia between the higher class residential area, (110 cases per 100 000 population) and the central business district (1757 per 100 000). A study of admissions to state hospitals during the period 1922–1934 showed a similar disparity in rates, but admissions to private hospitals produced a more scattered distribution, as well as an important difference between the proportions of admissions with manic-depressive illness and with schizophrenia, which represented 20 per cent and 23 per cent of the total intake respectively, as opposed to figures of 4 per cent and 30 per cent respectively for the state hospitals. The suggested social difference between schizophrenics and manic-depressives was borne out in analysis of the distribution of each illness. For schizophrenia, average rates still showed an approximately tenfold difference between admissions from the central business district and from the high-class residential area; the high central rates were further emphasised by low rates in the rest of Chicago. Males exceeded females in a ratio of 117:100, although a major component here was the high male rate from 'hobohemia', the central zone characteristically inhabited by impoverished nomadic men, which rarely generated female admissions. First-generation immigrants produced high rates, but only in relation to the fact that they tended to inhabit high-rate areas. Racially, there was a higher rate in negroes, but this was very variable, and again much in accord with the areas inhabited; whites living in predominantly negro areas had high rates, whereas negroes living in these areas had low rates.

With manic-depressive psychosis, the areal distribution was essentially random. Although the absolute rates were similar to those found for schizophrenia, there was no inner urban concentration of cases, no sex or racial differences, and only small differences in numbers between private and state hospitals. Any minor ecological correlates of depression were contrasted with the seemingly absolute randomness of mania. A tendency for manic-depressiveness to come from a higher cultural level was noted; also, in the case of men, the marriage rate was higher for manic-depressives than for schizophrenics, whereas for women, the reverse applied.

In geographical terms, the patterns of distribution of the two psychoses were well defined, and the theoretically possible explanations were as follows:

1. A result of chance, but the degree of statistical significance militates against this.
2. Institutionalisation because of poverty, but neither the rates for manic-depressive illness nor the private hospital statistics support this.
3. A transient phenomenon. This was regarded as possible but unlikely, and in fact, later research showed geographical distributions of the same order.

4. A form of drift because of the schizophrenia itself. This was the first mention of the 'drift hypothesis', but Faris & Dunham discarded it, mainly on the grounds that many of the schizophrenics they studied had spent all their lives in the areas involved, and that there was no preponderance in any particular age-group.
5. Foreign-born patients could have been exhibiting genetic propensities towards development of illness. The overall data do not support this.
6. Social life and conditions were directly aetiological; Faris & Dunham preferred this explanation. They drew analogies with alcoholic psychosis and general paralysis, both of which were prevalent in central areas in propinquity with high numbers of bars and prostitutes respectively, i.e. the causative agent could be defined. Since manic-depressive illness did not show this residential pattern, it was concluded that social factors were not important in its aetiology. Contemporary studies suggested a stronger genetic basis for manic-depressive illness than for schizophrenia, i.e. that they were sensitive to stress in otherwise stable families, as a precipitant to illness, whereas schizophrenics are often isolates, avoiding these stresses. The cause of schizophrenia was thought to be linked to residence in areas of high social mobility and to the resultant 'extended isolation' experienced there; this 'isolation hypothesis' was both a pathogenic and pathoplastic one.

Hare (1956a) studied first admissions to a psychiatric hospital in Bristol for 1949–1953; there were five diagnostic categories, including schizophrenia and manic-depressive psychosis. When patients' home addresses were analysed in terms of Census variables such as single-person households, rateable value, and population density, it was found that schizophrenics tended to come from central areas and showed a correlation with single-person households, while manic-depressives did not, but showed a correlation with rateable value. Neither diagnosis correlated with population density. Hare then divided Bristol into three ecological areas: (a) good central, (b) poor central, and (c) housing estates, finding an excess of schizophrenia in both the good (mostly female) and the poor (mostly male) central areas; an excess of manic-depressive illness in the former was regarded as chance. Hare considered high numbers of persons living alone to be the common explanatory factor for both the good and poor central areas, and put forward five possible explanations for the spatial distribution of schizophrenia:

1. Chance
2. High referral rates from central areas
3. High migration and mobility in the central areas, which would put more single persons at risk
4. Segregation of schizoid personalities in the central area
5. Social stresses acting in a causal fashion

The first explanation was thought unlikely on statistical grounds, as was the second, especially since it would apply only to schizophrenia. The third was also rejected, perhaps a little anecdotally, through the absence of a 'hobohemia', and from a study of 80 patients admitted during 1955, which showed that 53 of them had been living at their current addresses for more than 5 years. The fourth hypothesis (segregation) proposed that solitary, suspicious people move to lodging house areas, which provide anonymity; this implied an active process, whereby morbid individuals break off ties with family life, whereas 'drift' was a passive process in which schizoid individuals become progessively unable to keep better paid employment, and thus move inevitably to the poorer areas. The fifth hypothesis, i.e. that social stresses (social isolation) could be causal, was regarded as an important aetiological factor in one-quarter of the sample, whereas segregation was present in almost half the cases. Hare (1956b) later used 'attraction hypothesis' to describe segregation, and 'breeder hypothesis' for the specifically causal nature of social factors, especially social isolation; he judged that the evidence was much stronger on the side of the former.

These hypotheses had originally been put forward by Gerard & Houston (1953), who generally replicated the Chicago findings in Worcester, Massachusetts. They found that more manic-depressives than schizophrenics continued to reside with their families, but that for schizophrenics still doing so, the spatial distribution was much more random. Many of the schizophrenics living outside families had gravitated to single-person households, and hence to the districts where such accommodation was more available. From analysis of events occurring at the time of removal from the family, three major processes were noted. In about half the cases, personality difficulties were evident, in a third the separation was because of the death of a relative, and in the remaining sixth, the patient left of his own choice. Thus, the premorbid personality difficulties were thought to represent the principal cause, lending support to the 'attraction' hypothesis. Circumstances occurring after drift were considered a secondary cause, encapsulated in the breeder hypothesis.

Amongst other studies, Myerson (1940) suggested that drift could be a process whereby schizophrenics gravitated towards areas where they were protected from competitive social stresses, e.g. where casual unskilled work was available. Dunham (1965, 1977) later concluded that some of his statements about direct causation may have been too hasty, and that there was evidence in Detroit of downward drift or 'social selection'. Levy & Rowitz (1973) in Chicago found that the spatial distribution of first admissions with schizophrenia was random, whereas readmissions were concentrated in the central part. Sundby & Nyhus (1963) found that half of the schizophrenics in two central sections of Oslo (areas of one-room apartments and boarding houses) were migrants to the city, indicating that people without established social and family relationships lived there. Turner & Wagenfeld (1967) concluded that schizophrenics came originally from lower social classes and tended to stay there, failing to achieve expected levels, i.e. a stronger selection than drift effect. Similarly, Harkey et al. (1976) suggested that schizophrenia prevented upward mobility, and that age at entering the labour market was a crucial factor in explaining eventual distribution. Goldberg & Morrison (1963) in Britain found that the socio-economic status of schizophrenics was lower than that of their parents.

The Chicago zonal model can be applied in some instances in Britain; Castle & Gittus (1957) found a central distribution of mental illness and of other 'social defects' in Liverpool, while Bagley et al. (1973) calculated rates of serious psychiatric illness, indictable crime, and child welfare problems in Brighton, down to the enumeration district (ED) level. Close intercorrelations were found between these social and behavioural abnormalities, related strongly to areas of high in-migration, which tended to be rooming house areas near the centre of the city. Some EDs had especially high rates, which again suggested that more than a simple migration factor was operating (see Chapter 6). Similar findings were recorded by Timms (1965) in a study of Luton, but with differentiation between diagnoses, i.e. schizophrenia had a strong positive association with serious crime, and was concentrated in areas of low residential status and high population turnover — the rooming house areas, slums, and older council estates — whereas manic-depressive illness did not show this spatial concentration. Giggs (1973) showed a central concentration of schizophrenia in Nottingham, although some of his conclusions have been questioned (Gudgin 1975; Giggs 1975), especially with respect to clinical data and the acceptance of a direct environmental causation. However, Bain (1973, 1974), working in northeast Scotland, did not obtain findings along the lines of these previous studies, and her research revealed few ecological correlations with the major psychiatric disorders (see also Chapter 2).

Broad conclusions can therefore be drawn from previous work. Schizophrenia tends to be centrally located in cities, and there is evidence that premorbid or morbid processes in affected individuals contribute to this movement. Once drift has occurred, poor social conditions seem to aggravate the illness. Manic-depressive illness, on the other hand, shows very little tendency to be congregated in specific areas. We have studied the distribution of these illnesses in the city of Plymouth in order to re-examine some of the relevant hypotheses.

RESIDENTIAL PATTERNS OF PSYCHIATRIC HOSPITAL ADMISSIONS IN PLYMOUTH

The period studied is 1970–1975 inclusive, and ecological information was obtained from the 1971 Census at both the ward and ED scales. Figures 14.1, 14.2 and 14.3 give an indication respectively of population structure, housing structure and tenure, and of the location of the 22 electoral wards.

Wards with above average (16.5 per cent) rates of retired persons

Wards with above average (17.2 per cent) rates of one person households

Fig. 14.1 Population structure in the city of Plymouth

(a) Inter-ward analysis

Relevant research in Plymouth has been reported elsewhere (Dean 1979; Dean and James 1980, 1981; Dean 1982); generally, it showed quite complex differences between the various diagnostic groups, in terms of their geographical distribution. Also, major differences occurred between males and females, and between first admissions and readmissions. It is likely that social factors have a real effect on the distribution of admissions, even if genetic bases are assumed for some of the illnesses concerned, and also likely that these social influences become more pronounced at subsequent admissions. Other variables are the sources of referral, attitudes of relatives, psychiatric perception of the patient's social background, and degree of development of community care. The last of these, though, has rather a surprising effect, referred to earlier. Other pitfalls in drawing aetiological

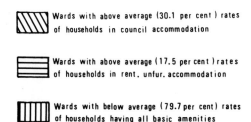

Wards with above average (30.1 per cent) rates
of households in council accommodation

Wards with above average (17.5 per cent) rates
of households in rent. unfur. accommodation

Wards with below average (79.7 per cent) rates
of households having all basic amenities

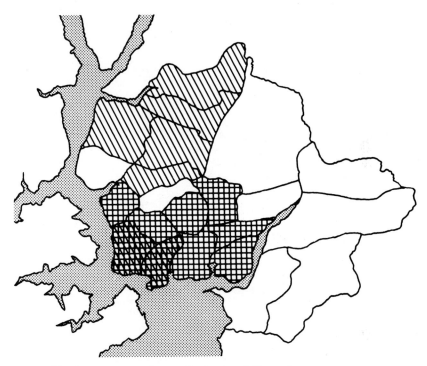

Fig. 14.2 Housing structure and tenure in the city of Plymouth

conclusions concern the 'ecological fallacy' (Robinson 1950): the drawing of conclusions about the effects of social factors on an individual assumes that he is somehow representative of the community under consideration, when in fact this may not be so. This is an important consideration, but one sometimes overstated (Robson, 1969); this issue is also discussed by Bagley in Chapter 6.

Depression

In the case of depressive illnesses, all diagnostic groups covered by the International Classification of Diseases (ICD-8) were examined. Mention will be made here of affective psychoses (296.0–296.9), depressive neurosis

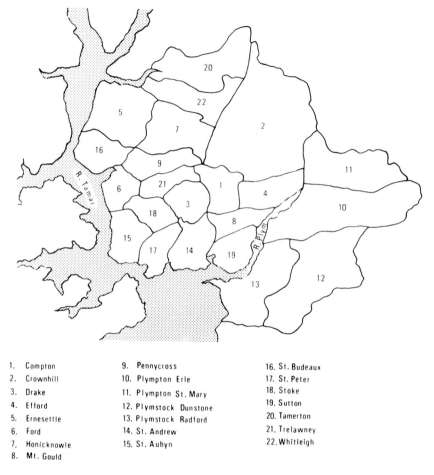

1.	Compton	9.	Pennycross	16.	St. Budeaux
2.	Crownhill	10.	Plympton Erle	17.	St. Peter
3.	Drake	11.	Plympton St. Mary	18.	Stoke
4.	Elford	12.	Plymstock Dunstone	19.	Sutton
5.	Ernesettle	13.	Plymstock Radford	20.	Tamerton
6.	Ford	14.	St. Andrew	21.	Trelawney
7.	Honicknowle	15.	St. Aubyn	22.	Whitleigh
8.	Mt. Gould				

Fig. 14.3 The 22 electoral wards in the city of Plymouth

(300.4), and to a lesser extent 'reactive depressive psychosis' (298.0), which subsume concepts of endogenicity, severity, and reactivity. From the census, variables were extracted covering four categories, representative of the environment. These are: *Housing tenure* (e.g. households per thousand in owner-occupied, council, rented furnished, or rented unfurnished accommodation); *population structure* (e.g. males over 65, females over 60, children 0–14 years, persons of either sex chosen in 5 or 10 year age divisions, migrants in last year, and marital status); *socio-economic status* (e.g. social class I to V, males per thousand seeking work, working wives per thousand married females); and *housing structure* (e.g. proportion of shared dwellings households lacking or sharing a bath, overcrowding, one-person households).

Examination of the relationship between census variables, diagnosis, sex, and first admission/readmission status was made by a regression analysis. In the case of depressive psychosis, the distribution of males was related only to population structure, especially in older stable communities, and this relationship was sustained for readmissions. Females showed no correlation in first admissions, but for readmissions, there was a plethora of associations with rates of unemployment, lower socio-economic groups, shared dwellings and facilities, overcrowding, and rented unfurnished accommodation. Thus, the endogenicity of the psychosis is emphasised for female admissions, but the pattern of readmissions is governed by degrees of social deprivation. However, this analysis — like the others — was limited to the data available; detailed information from personal interviews might give grounds for an alternative view of 'endogenous' depression (see Chapter 2).

In the case of depressive neurosis, which is by far the largest diagnostic category, rather different patterns emerge, with many ecological correlations. Male first admissions continue to have correlations with older populations and also with high concentrations of not-married status. However, there are also correlations with low socio-economic status, unemployment, overcrowding, and persons living alone, as well as a negative association with owner-occupation. These broadly held true with male readmissions, but there is an increasingly strong correlation with poor accommodation, lack of amenities, persons living alone, and renting of unfurnished dwellings. Living in such accommodation implies residence in central locations in the city, and possibly a process of drift towards such an area.

Female depressive neurotics also show important ecological correlations at first admission, which is in marked contrast to female psychotics; also, in contrast with male neurotics, the correlations are with recent migration and with relatively young communities, often the council estates. Readmitted female neurotics show lower correlations with age of population, but an increasingly strong association with low socio-economic status, overcrowding, unemployment, and residence in council estates. This is a strikingly similar pattern to that seen for readmitted female psychotics, and explanations might involve perceptual attributes of the admitting agencies, operating irrespective of diagnostic grouping. Another correlation is with the proportion of wives who work, which is significant for readmitted female psychotics and for both first admission and readmission neurotics, but not at all for males. Employment, or rather the lack of it, has been mentioned by Brown & Harris (1978) as a vulnerability factor leading to depression in women. Presumably, the contrary finding in Plymouth relates to the use of an aggregate areal methodology; at the ward level, the 'working wives' variable appears to reflect stressful circumstances. Another vulnerability factor quoted by Brown & Harris was the number of children in the household; but this does not reach significance for the females studied here, although there is a significant negative relationship with readmitted male neurotics — a population drawn from single-person accommodation.

Reactive depressive psychosis occupies a position intermediate between neurosis and affective psychosis, in terms of spatial distribution and ecological correlation. Female first admissions have small significant correlations with overcrowding, and living in council housing, whereas readmissions have strong correlations with many indices of social deprivation. Males again show an association with migration to single-person households, both on first admission and readmission.

Comparison between the two major diagnostic categories of affective psychosis and depressive neurosis, therefore, reveals important sex and admission/readmission differences. First admissions with psychosis have few ecological correlations: none at all in the case of females, and with age of population only in the case of males, the latter continuing in readmissions. Female readmissions of both types show dramatically similar correlations, suggesting economic and family stress associated with residence in rented council accommodation. Male neurotics show correlations with age (modal age group 40–46, as opposed to females 19–25, $p < 0.001$), low socio-economic status, and an increasing tendency to reside in rented unfurnished accommodation with shared or absent amenities. Figures 14.4 and 14.5

 Wards with above average rates

(> .37 admissions per 1000 p.a.)

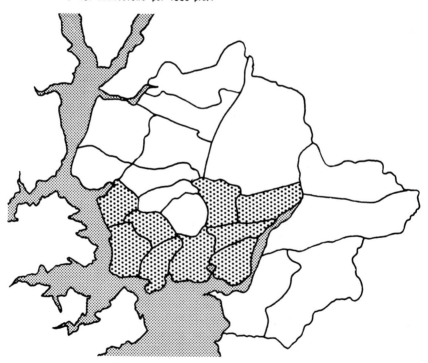

Fig. 14.4 Patterns of residence of male and female admissions with depressive neurosis. Wards with above average rates (> .37 admissions per 1000 p.a.)

Wards with above average rates
(> .49 admissions per 1000 p.a.)

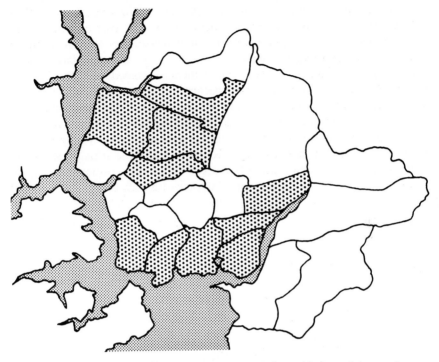

Fig. 14.5 Patterns of residence of male and female admissions with depressive neurosis. Wards with above average rates (> .49 admissions per 1000 p.a.)

show the patterns of residence of male and female readmissions for depressive neurosis.

Explanations for the spatial patterns could be:

1. That the environments producing high rates are inherently stressful. This could explain the similarities between female readmissions for both neurotic and psychotic illness, but does not apply to male readmissions or to first admissions of both sexes for psychosis.

2. Patients living in adverse conditions might be more readily referred and admitted. This would not seem to apply to first admissions for psychosis in females, nor clearly to male psychotics. Male neurotics might be influenced by adverse circumstances, but it is noticeable that they are generally living in these environments prior to first admission, and that there is a progressively higher correlation with very similar stresses on readmission. However, it is not clear why this argument should apply almost exclusively to females, who show major correlations with adverse circumstances on readmission, irrespective of diagnosis.

3. A process of drift could be occurring. Certainly, the movement of males to rooming house areas is very similar to that described for schizophrenia, although a bi-directional movement for females might not fit in with this hypothesis.

4. The effect of population structure could be crucial. Male neurotics, who tend to be older and not-married, would select areas of relative deprivation because of the availability of suitable single accommodation there. However, it would seem that young married women with children are not protected by marriage from becoming depressed, as might be the case with men (Robertson 1974; Briscoe 1982). Recent migration to a council estate would possibly be stressful, even if housing amenities there are good, thus accounting for the preponderance of young married women among readmissions with neurosis from these areas. Probably all these features, which represent stress in vulnerable people, selection for admission, drift, and segregation interact with each other.

Schizophrenia

The distribution of schizophrenia in Plymouth has been investigated in a similar way (Dean and James 1981). Home addresses of patients admitted with a diagnosis of schizophrenia were mapped, and a principal components analysis made against electoral ward census data. Admission status was considered important in assessing processes occurring during the illness; this was broken down into first admissions, second and third, fourth to sixth, and seventh to tenth. The total numbers of admissions studied were 92, 106, 70 and 35 for males, and 107, 173, 169 and 129 for females in these categories respectively, from 1970 to 1975. For each ward, an 'amplification score' was calculated. This represented the ratio of readmissions to first admissions, and together with admission status data, provided ten illness variables to be compared with the census data.

Four components emerged to explain 95 per cent of the variance in a set of 27 census variables. The first ('accommodation') (59 per cent) was associated with loadings on households rented unfurnished, shared, and lacking a bath. The second, explaining 23 per cent, correlated negatively with social class II, positively with class V, and negatively with owner occupation; this is most clearly comprehended as a 'social class' factor. The third component, which correlated most strongly with males (single, widowed, or divorced) and next with similar females emerges as a 'marital status' indicator. The fourth related most strongly to the numbers of single, widowed, or divorced people migrating into the relevant wards — 'single-person migration'.

In the case of males, accommodation and single-person migration were dominant components from the first admission, and were still apparent at the seventh to tenth. It would appear that some form of residential segregation and possibly 'drift' is occurring with male schizophrenics, early in the illness, and that this reappears in those readmitted frequently. With females, accommodation is dominant early on, but by the fourth to sixth admissions and more strongly thereafter, social class becomes a significantly dominant component. This is made more emphatic by there being a positive loading on social class II for early admissions, clearly reversed during later admissions, when there is a negative association with class II and a positive one with class V. The class variable becomes the only significant one on the amplification score for females.

In terms of geographical distribution, the accommodation component relates to the older central wards, analagous in part to Faris and Dunham's zones I and II, since it is predominantly here that poor quality, single-person, unfurnished housing is found. The social class variable is more complicated, since there are two major areas which show a relatively higher loading on class V; these are the central areas, where the accommodation factors operate most strongly, and in the north and north-west, dominated by post-war peripheral council housing. Segregation of housing types could account for this distribution, although drift is often held responsible. Re-admitted patients showed an 11 per cent rate of residential shift, but it operated both in and out of the high-rate areas. This militates against drift being an important explanatory theory; but on the other hand, it has been defined as a premorbid process.

If marital status is compared with admission status, domestic circumstances seem significantly more important to females than to males, but this is probably accounted for by the fact that female schizophrenics were much more likely to be married than male schizophrenics. Robertson (1974) demonstrated a high single:married ratio for male schizophrenics, and in the Plymouth sample, 62 per cent of these had never married, compared with 25 per cent of the females; a similar picture has been reported from Salford (Cheadle et al. 1978). There are two possible explanations for this, which could have an additive effect. Firstly, males tend to be admitted for the first time with schizophrenia at an earlier age; their peak rate for first admission is 20–24 years, whereas for females it is 25–34. Overall incidence rates in females exceed those of males only after the age of 35 (Slater and Cowie 1971). Secondly, males tend to marry later; e.g. for the total population of Plymouth in 1971, in the 20–24 age group, 40 per cent of males were married, compared with 70 per cent of females. The comparable percentages for the 30–34 age group were 86 and 90 (HMSO 1971).

Another factor may be that schizophrenia acts as a bar to marriage in males, but less so in females; whatever the explanation, though, marital status evidently has an important effect on the admission and/or illness process, though the presence of a 'care-giver' is not strictly related to marital status in this sample. Only 25 per cent of males, as opposed to 37 per cent of females were without a 'care-giver' at the time of admission. In the single, widowed, or divorced category, the respective figures were 29 per cent and 58 per cent. This apparent paradox is accounted for by the fact that a high proportion of the never-married schizophrenic males — 62 per cent as opposed to 19 per cent for females — were still residing with one or both parents. This finding is also to be contrasted with Goldberg and Morrison's, discussed earlier, which showed a normal social class distribution for parents of schizophrenics.

The sex differences in the distribution of schizophrenia in Plymouth mirror those for depression, albeit for somewhat different reasons. Males tend to be centrally located, but whether this is because of the accommodation factor, or because of an underlying age-related effect applying to elderly parents, rather than to the index cases, is debatable. Certainly, never-married status prevents the suburbanisation seen in females. They are more likely to be married at admission, and the not-married females are more likely to be widowed or divorced than the males, who are more likely to be never-married. However, suburbanisation is much more likely to have taken place with females, hence their concentration also in the types of accommodation characteristically filled by families; the social class factor would appear to be felt by vulnerable females in conditions of chronic domestic stress. Figures 14.6 and 14.7 show the distribution of first admissions for schizophrenia.

Correlations between illness and census variables, from the inter-ward analysis, allow some explanation of patterns of admission and readmission; as the discussion of schizophrenia has demonstrated, such inferences may be related to individual patient data. However, a finer-grained analysis, involving specific residential settings, is needed to expose the sorts of

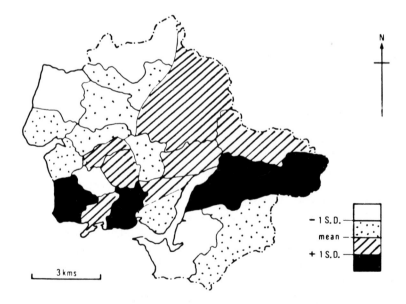

Fig. 14.6 Female first admissions for schizophrenia

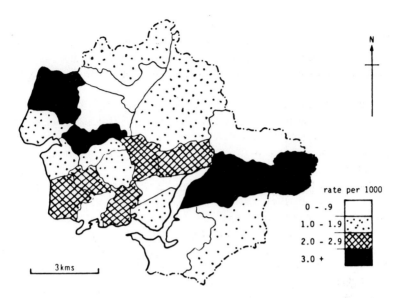

Fig. 14.7 Male first admissions for schizophrenia

environment associated with high rates of admission, and can provide a clearer basis for the examination of case-notes evidence.

(b) Residential environments analysis

The residential environments analysis is designed to confirm and extend the inter-ward one. Rather than the properties of areas alone, individual patients are now considered, to determine whether (after age, marital status, admission number, and diagnosis are controlled) they show a significant tendency to be admitted from particular residential settings.

The residential environments framework

There were (effectively) 492 EDs in Plymouth at the time of the 1971 census; these are classified primarily according to their housing characteristics, but partly by occupational status. Some occupy rather marginal positions, defined by housing tenure and quality, but most can be assigned to groups that represent coherent residential environments. As Table 14.1 shows, 379 EDs, containing 60 834 households, are classified to produce 16 residential environments. The first five (A, B, C, D, and E) have in common high levels of owner-occupation, and three of them (A, B, and E) also have high levels of provision of basic amenities. These desirable environments occur in the suburbs.

In environment C (medium quality owner-occupation), sub-division on the basis of occupational status is possible, but provision of basic amenities is

Table 14.1 Residential environments

	Environment	OWNOC	COUNC	PRENT	ALLAM	EDS	Households
A	High quality owner-occupation I	H	M	L	H	13	1 967
B	High quality owner-occupation II	H	L	M	H	22	3 439
C1	Medium quality owner-occupation I (non-manual)	H	L	M	M	25	7 142
C2	Medium quality owner-occupation II (manual)	H	L	M	M	22	3 561
D	Low quality owner-occupation	H	L	M	L	26	10 696
E	High quality owner-occupation III	H	L	L	H	60	
F1	Local authority flats	L	H	L	H	11	
F2	Local authority neighbourhood estates	L	H	L	H	47	
F3	Recent local authority housing	L	H	L	H	20	15 694
F4	Unclassified local authority housing	L	H	L	H	12	
G	Medium quality privately rented accommodation	M	L	H	M	16	2 692
H1	Low quality privately rented accommodation I (non-manual)	M	L	H	L	15	
H2	Low quality privately rented accommodation II (manual)	M	M	H	L	40	8 536
I	Low quality privately rented accommodation III	L	L	H	L	12	1 621
J	Low quality privately rented accommodation IV	L	L	H	L	29	3 890
K	High quality military accommodation	L	L/M	H	H	9	1 596
All environments		L/M	L/M			379	60 834

appreciably lower than in A, B, and E. As would be expected from this, there is a greater preponderance of EDs in the older, inner suburbs. The lowest level of provision occurs in D — low quality owner-occupation; EDs of this group are confined to the inner suburban areas of Victorian and Edwardian terraces.

EDs with high levels of council housing constitute environment F, which is divisible into three main sub-groups. F1 (local authority flats) consists of inner city flats, built in the 1930s, 1950s and 1960s; but most council EDs fall into F2 — neighbourhood estates, built between 1945 and 1955. F3 (recent local authority housing) is peripheral, built since 1960, while the remaining districts in this group comprise F4 — unclassified local authority housing.

The remaining five environments (G, H, I, J, and K) all display high levels of private renting. G (medium-quality privately rented) consists of EDs with high levels of private renting and moderate levels of amenity provision; they tend to be in the formerly prestigious areas of large Victorian terraces to the north of the city centre. H (low quality privately rented) is similar, but sub-divided by occupational status, and in the older areas.

Environment I (low quality privately rented accommodation III) is characterised by high rates of private renting and low amenity provision, but an appreciable proportion of households (21 per cent) rented from the local authority. This combination of private and council renting is particularly evident in St Peter Ward, where local authority flats have been built as urban renewal schemes in areas previously dominated by private renting. J (low quality privately rented accommodation IV) does not have much council housing; these EDs are concentrated in the older central wards. Finally, the EDs of environment K (high quality military accommodation) are distinctive in having at least half of their households in the armed forces; they are confined to a suburban area, containing a large naval estate.

Admission frequencies in different residential environments

Crude rates of male first admissions for schizophrenia are above average in C1, C2, F1, H1 and J. Overall, the less attractive environments with high levels of renting, represented by F1, H1, H2, I, and J, have significantly more admissions than would be expected from their populations, taking into account age and marital status. The surplus relates essentially to single, widowed or divorced men, and suggests that drift into central areas may be responsible; but the concentration of male schizophrenics in the central areas could be as much the result of their failure to participate in the general suburbanisation of the population. With male readmissions for schizophrenia, a significant surplus occurs in F1, I, and J, within which the highest crude rate of admissions comes from the local authority flats, but this excess again relates to single, widowed, or divorced men.

With female first admissions for schizophrenia, there are no clear associations with housing characteristics, but the significant excess in C1 and H1 indicates a tendency for these females to come from higher status environments. In contrast to the male schizophrenics, this surplus relates to both the married and the single, widowed, or divorced categories. This is also the case with female readmissions for schizophrenia, in which a variety of environments are over-represented, but there is a significant tendency for females not to come from the best quality owner-occupier environments (A, B, and E). Details of rates and frequencies of admission for schizophrenia in the 16 residential environments are given in Table 14.2.

Male first admissions for depressive neurosis are significantly in excess in C2, H2, and F2. This surplus relates mainly to married men, particularly in low quality privately rented accommodation II (manual) and local authority neighbourhood estates; stresses giving rise to depressive neurotic conditions might be more prevalent in such environments. With male readmissions for depressive neurosis, there is an appreciable excess in the local authority neighbourhood estates environment, and also a concentration in those that combine high levels of private renting with low levels of amenity provision. Excesses occur in respect of single, widowed, or divorced, as well as married depressive neurotics.

Female first admissions for depressive neurosis show significant excesses in I and J, (low quality privately rented). Both married and single, widowed, or divorced patients are involved in this, which is also true of the surplus of female readmissions for depressive neurosis. Here, a conspicuous concentration occurs in local authority environments (F1, F2, F3 and F4), but there is also a surplus from environment J — low quality privately rented accommodation IV (See Table 14.3).

(c) Review of possible processes

Residential drift

One of the most likely processes leading to the concentration of admissions in particular environments is residential drift among people already or subsequently defined as mentally ill. For this to result in an areal concentration, it must be out of step with patterns of residential change in the population as a whole, and the classic example is the drift of male schizophrenics into the central areas of cities. Such differential residential movement may occur before or after an initial admission, and can thus explain spatial variations in both first and readmissions.

Environmental causation

The traditional alternative to residential change as a consequence of illness is areal causation, in which the physical or social properties of areas have a direct effect on incidence. The most extreme possibility is 'environmental

Table 14.2 Crude rates, observed frequencies and expected frequencies for schizophrenia admissions

Residential environment	Male first admissions			Female first admissions			Female readmissions			Male readmissions		
	Crude rate	Observ. freq.	Exp. freq.	Crude rate	Observ. freq.	Exp. freq.	Crude rate	Observ. freq.	Exp. freq.	Crude rate	Observ. freq.	Exp. freq.
A	0.00	0	1.99	0.42	1	2.76	2.79	6	5.26	3.35	8	12.70
B	0.89	3	2.51	1.24	5	4.19	0.89	3	6.52	2.73	11	19.15
C1	1.43	5	3.05	2.04	9	4.56	2.85	10	8.72	5.22	23	22.10
C2	1.22	4	2.91	1.04	4	4.16	3.97	13	8.17	8.05	31	19.44
D	0.89	3	3.09	0.50	2	4.09	4.45	15	9.11	5.99	24	19.78
E	0.55	6	7.95	0.73	9	13.28	0.91	10	20.36	1.53	19	60.82
F1	2.37	4	2.38	1.07	2	2.40	10.09	17	6.82	10.73	20	11.17
F2	0.63	6	10.94	1.29	13	11.76	2.53	24	26.82	4.67	47	54.88
F3	0.47	2	3.10	1.28	6	5.57	1.88	8	7.27	6.19	29	23.38
F4	0.83	2	2.84	1.95	5	2.92	2.89	7	7.11	7.40	19	13.48
G	0.80	2	2.29	0.66	2	3.28	0.40	1	6.41	3.65	11	15.58
H1	1.73	10	5.98	0.73	5	7.41	1.91	11	17.89	5.87	40	36.08
H2	0.45	1	2.14	1.98	5	2.66	1.35	3	6.08	13.49	34	12.88
I	0.62	1	2.00	1.18	2	1.83	6.17	10	6.01	4.12	7	8.66
J	2.40	9	4.29	1.19	5	4.58	5.07	19	13.23	8.34	35	22.45
K	0.00	0	0.54	1.14	2	1.55	0.00	0	1.22	0.00	0	5.52
Total	0.94	58	58.00	1.10	77	77.00	2.54	157	157.00	5.10	358	358.00

Table 14.3 Crude rates, observed frequencies and expected frequencies for depressive neurosis admissions

Residential environment	Male first admissions			Female first admissions			Male readmissions			Female readmissions		
	Crude rate	Observ. freq.	Exp. freq.	Crude rate	Observ. freq.	Exp. freq.	Crude rate	Observ. freq.	Exp. freq.	Crude rate	Observ. freq.	Exp. freq.
A	1.40	3	6.62	4.61	11	12.23	0.93	2	4.43	2.09	5	11.84
B	1.18	4	9.75	3.98	16	19.78	0.59	2	6.32	2.98	12	19.45
C1	2.28	8	10.62	4.08	18	20.45	0.57	2	8.08	4.99	22	23.02
C2	4.28	14	9.94	4.67	18	18.70	1.83	6	7.30	1.56	6	19.61
D	3.85	13	10.40	2.74	11	18.50	3.85	13	8.06	5.24	21	20.48
E	2.10	23	32.31	4.19	52	61.78	1.92	21	20.35	2.82	35	60.30
F1	3.56	6	5.86	4.82	9	9.70	2.37	4	4.81	10.19	19	10.26
F2	4.31	41	28.73	5.96	60	50.34	2.84	27	19.12	7.85	79	48.68
F3	2.35	10	12.02	5.34	25	26.43	0.94	4	6.85	4.27	20	21.53
F4	2.06	5	7.36	7.40	19	12.73	2.06	5	4.83	4.67	12	12.44
G	2.81	7	7.37	4.97	15	15.20	1.20	3	5.17	7.29	22	15.33
H1	4.68	27	17.90	4.11	28	33.34	1.91	11	14.06	4.99	34	35.48
H2	2.26	5	6.71	3.17	8	11.91	4.96	11	5.17	4.36	11	13.18
I	2.47	4	5.28	5.89	10	8.10	2.47	4	4.22	5.30	9	8.65
J	3.47	13	12.15	8.58	36	21.20	4.01	15	9.70	8.82	37	21.41
K	2.22	3	2.98	8.00	14	9.61	0.00	0	1.53	2.28	4	6.34
Total	3.01	186	186.00	4.98	350	350.00	2.11	130	130.00	4.95	348	348.00

causation', in which physical properties of an environment, such as noise, overcrowding and general delapidation, directly give rise to illness among residents. Intuitively, such processes may seem unlikely, and research into such pathological effects as excessive population density has so far yielded negative results (Freeman 1978).

Residential sorting

A second example of areal causation involves the concentration of persons who are more likely to cause, experience, or be vulnerable to stressful events and circumstances. Such events may directly promote psychiatric conditions, precipitate episodes in persons with latent conditions, or encourage admission rather than treatment in the community. Access to different types of housing tenure and quality would play an important role in such a process of 'residential sorting', which comes close to residential drift, but there are two important differences. Firstly, it involves the behaviour of other members of the patient's household. Secondly, the accent is not on residential drift as a response to illness, but rather on the spatial sorting of domestic situations which, through their relevance to aetiological and management processes, encourage admission.

Community causation

Community causation represents a third type of areal causation. In this case, the norms of the local community exert an influence on admissions and, since such norms vary from area to area, they are responsible for spatial variations in admission frequencies. Such normative influences may be of the traditional type envisaged by Faris and Dunham, whereby disorganisation or anomie are experienced by individuals. Alternatively, influences may operate in terms of norms concerning what behaviour is tolerable and what is deemed necessary for referral and admission.

Professional practice

The fifth and final process envisages concentrations of admissions created either by the judgements typically made by psychiatrists, GPs, social workers and other professionals, or by the distribution of their deployment, or both. Such effects may be produced in the context of the referral, definition, or treatment and management process respectively. In making judgements about prognosis, for instance, practitioners may take into account not only the non-clinical characteristics of the patient, but also what they perceive to be the nature of his family setting, the general locality, or some combination of these.

Relationships between processes

The operation of one of these five sets of processes does not preclude another, and while there is some merit in discussing them as discrete entities, the boundaries between them are in fact somewhat illusory. Community tolerances may influence doctors' judgements about what is acceptable as a form of treatment or care, while processes of residential sorting will be a determinant of neighbourhood membership and thus, presumably, of local community norms.

(d) Case notes evidence

Access to individual patient histories, as recorded in case notes, may offer a way of appraising the relative importance of these processes. By themselves, case notes are inadequate for such a task, but they do permit valuable insights to be gained into the admission process.

Male admissions for schizophrenia

It was found that schizophrenic males tend not to be first admitted from families; they are more likely to involve referral by the police or courts, and the perceived need to protect other from violent behaviour. In view of this, some process of residential segregation in the direction of less attractive central environments seems highly plausible. Yesavage et al. (1982) studied social class differences between schizophrenic in-patients and their parents, and found that despite the generally higher educational status of the patients, many had dropped significantly in social status (see also Goldberg and Morrison 1963). Moreover, patients who had committed a violent act prior to their admission were almost invariably of lower social status than their parents.

Male readmissions for schizophrenia are much less centrally orientated than first admissions; they are more likely to involve residence with one or both parents, and in such cases, patients are clearly not 'drifters'. Admission occurs because the parents are unable to cope, and request it, or because of an order compelling admission, as a result of the patient's activities in public. The main point, however, is that patients' addresses are determined not by their own performances in the housing market, but by those of their caring parents.

Female admissions for schizophrenia

With female admissions for schizophrenia, the main issue is why re-admissions should be significantly more frequent in poorer quality privately rented accommodation, when first admissions show no such tendency. Part of the explanation may be that female schizophrenics tend to be admitted more frequently from family situations where, as mother responsible for running the household, they occupy vital positions. Thus, the decision to readmit female schizophrenics would be related to the perceived inability of other members of the patient's family to cope.

In a geographical context, it seems most likely that high readmission rates in low social class areas result from families there being less able to manage schizophrenic episodes without the patient being admitted to hospital. Yet even if this is correct, at least three spatial processes are possible. Firstly, through residential sorting, lower class families who are less able to cope might come to be concentrated in certain areas. Secondly, in certain low social class communities, thresholds for tolerating abnormal behaviour may be lower. Thirdly, psychiatrists may more readily perceive situations in lower-class areas as requiring hospital-based treatment, in the interests of other members of the household and additionally or alternatively, may be more successful in imposing judgements concerning the need for admission on lower-class households. To confound matters, these three spatial processes are clearly not mutually exclusive.

Male admissions for depressive neurosis

With this category, the problem is to explain why frequencies tend to be greater in council neighbourhood estates and in environments combining high levels of private renting with low levels of amenity provision. Case note data indicate that admission is frequently in the context of stresses occurring in a family situation. Sexual and other family problems are most frequently mentioned, but financial difficulties are also frequent, relative to other admission categories. Stresses are often associated with suicide attempts or perceived suicide risks.

The areal concentration of male admissions for depressive neurosis may result from greater prevalence of stresses in lower social class and council housing environments, but a number of processes could account for it. Firstly, it may result from the residential sorting of low-income households, which are more likely to generate and experience stresses because of financial difficulties and an inability to manage interpersonal conflicts; such stresses may be intrinsic to families who are less competitive in the housing market. However, stressful behaviour may also be learned from other residents in the locality, i.e. community effects. Thirdly, spatial concentration might be created by the judgements and negotiations which involve psychiatrists and other professional agencies.

Female admissions for depressive neurosis

Female first admissions tend to involve sexual relationship problems, dependent children, and suicide attempts. Such family stresses continue to be important in promoting symptoms, in advance of readmissions, but there is also an emphasis here on patients' inability to cope. This suggests that interpersonal contexts, in which illness is managed (or is perceived to be managed) less effectively, are influential. The combination of greater family stresses and perceived inability of patients to cope is likely to be important in relation to the clear concentration of readmissions in council housing areas. Environmental causation cannot be ruled out here, although three processes seem more likely. Firstly, with residential sorting, that those households less successful in the housing market are also less successful in managing depressive illness without admission. Secondly, a possible community effect on the management of illness. Thirdly, as in previous categories, the practice of psychiatrists and other professionals might show a bias, in terms of housing or occupational status, with a spatial dimension.

INTERPRETATIONS

The earlier analysis has shown that there are possible variations on the older debates surrounding the distributions of psychiatric illnesses. However, on closer examination, the conventional hypotheses tend to break down, while the truly multifactorial aetiology of the admission event emerges more clearly.

Because it does not necessarily relate to behaviour and experience in society, the case note evidence does not constitute an adequate basis for appraising the relative importance of these processes. However, two conclusions are worthy of consideration. Firstly, while other processes cannot be discounted, only that of residential sorting receives support, and this derives from two points. One is that the notes indicate the family or household context to be crucial, in terms both of the stresses that precipitate or cause illness and of its management; it is the relationship of the patient to other family members, rather than to some wider community, that appears to be decisive. Most of the stressful events and circumstances identified as causing depressive illness related to interpersonal relationships within a family or household, which is also the key to understanding the management of illness. Even patients suffering from a primarily endogenous disorder, that involves no significant spatial concentration of first admissions, can be admitted more often from certain areas as a result of their domestic situations. Secondly many of these households appear vulnerable and weak, in the sense that they are unable to manage their internal relationships 'effectively'. Therefore, they may well also lack an ability to control their accommodation and residential location; relatively low incomes are obviously an aspect of this. Such families tend to occupy accommodation rented privately or from the local authority, and within these sectors of the housing market, to live in the least desirable accommodation, such as poor quality private or local authority flats, and some older post-war estates. This combination of family setting and the housing market can account for certain differences in the distribution of illness categories. For example, the lack of spatial pattern in the distribution of male readmissions for schizophrenia may be related to the tendency of such patients to be resident with caring parents; but the performance of these households in the housing market is almost certainly different from that of many of the households from which female schizophrenics tend to be admitted.

Secondly, the case note evidence casts doubt on the appraising of processes such as admission, which are presented as coherent and discrete. At an individual level, these tend to lose their identity, while at an inter-personal level, concepts such as 'professional bias' are undermined by the difficulties inherent in defining objective standards of diagnosis, prognosis, and treatment. There is a profusion of realities experienced, negotiated, and imposed, rather than some single truth. At an individual level, community effects and residential sorting can become interwoven, the latter controlling the community pressures experienced by an individual. In turn, changing residence is one of various responses an individual might make to such pressures. Thus, it is not a simple matter of choosing between discrete processes of residential sorting, community effects, and professional practice.

CONCLUSIONS

This chapter has demonstrated that spatial variations in the rate of psychiatric hospital admissions for different categories of patient and diagnosis often relate significantly to housing, social, and demographic variables. With male first admissions for schizophrenia, it appears likely that some process of residential segregation, probably drift, is responsible for the higher rates, particularly among single, widowed or divorced men, in the central areas. Female first admissions for schizophrenia have little association with census variables and few distinguishing features in the case notes analysis, so that their distribution does not appear to be linked to an ordered set of spatial processes. Male readmissions for schizophrenia also lack a clear spatial order, and it is significant that many of these patients are resident with their parents. This seems to be the main reason for the deviation from a pattern of higher rates in the central areas that is a feature of first admissions. With female readmissions for schizophrenia, family situations can be linked to the spatial concentration of cases in areas of lower social class, private renting and poor quality housing, not so much because these family settings are very stressful but because family members are unable to cope with the illness of a person so central to the running of the household. Partly through their tendency to be divorced, separated, or widowed, and partly because fewer were living with parents, these women were less likely than men to enjoy the protection or support of a care-giver. It seems most plausible that such inabilities to cope are spatially ordered by subtle processes of residential sorting, but the effects of community norms and professional practice cannot be ruled out.

With male first admissions, female first admissions, and male readmissions for depressive neurosis, excesses tend to relate to married persons and to occur in lower social class areas and neighbourhood council estates. Relevant stresses stem primarily from inter-personal relationships within family settings, and the residential sorting of households in which such stresses tend to be generated may well be responsible for spatial concentrations of admissions, but other processes, particularly some form of community causation or spatial bias in professional practice, cannot be ruled out. With female readmissions for depressive neurosis, residential sorting of certain households, from which admission is more likely to occur, seems probable, though the case notes suggest that it is not just the prevalence of stress that characterises such settings, within which patients are often perceived as unable to cope. This complexity of case note evidence is matched at the aggregate level, where there is a separation between excesses of married patients in council areas and of single, widowed or divorced patients in areas of poor quality, privately rented accommodation.

Of the five processes discussed earlier, the greatest support exists for residential sorting. Such an hypothesis seems the most convincing in view of the importance of marital status and family setting in relation to both the precipitation of psychiatric illnesses and their management. Residential drift, as a consequence of illness, seems much less important, except with male first admissions for schizophrenia. Certainly, residential change appears to exercise no appreciable influence over patterns of readmission.

Gottesman and Shields (1982) point out that, in addition to the breeder and drift hypotheses about schizophrenia, there is an auxiliary hypothesis, supported by data, that social selection operates to prevent the upward mobility out of social class V of pre-schizophrenics, whereas their siblings and peers will largely improve their status, compared to the parent generation. This is likely to be relevant to the suburbanisation process in Plymouth during the period after World War 2.

Environmental causation is unsupported by the evidence; poor accommodation, for example, is very rarely regarded in the case notes as having any direct causal significance. Community causation cannot be dismissed, but difficulties of conceptualisation make it a rather unattractive hypothesis. Also, the clinical evidence indicates the importance of intra-family or intra-household relationships, rather than those involving other members of the local community. The role of professional practice remains unclear, largely because it is extremely difficult to test, given the considerable dependence on the definitions and interpretations of individual psychiatrists in the case notes.

In fact, it is doubtful whether the relative importance of any of the five processes under consideration can be assessed in an exact way. The more these processes are scrutinised at an interpersonal level, the more interrelated they appear; an admission to psychiatric hospital becomes an event within a complex process of social interaction in which patients, family members, doctors, social workers and others draw upon both authority structures and informal powers to influence the definition and management of illness. While this chapter has demonstrated the value of case note data in elucidating correlations and patterns established at an aggregate areal level, it has also exposed some of the difficulties in relating individual, subjective realities to positivist explanatory frameworks.

Our studies support the view that greater knowledge of the social geography of psychiatric disorder could have significant applications, e.g. in housing and health service policies, as well as contributing to the scientific understanding of these conditions. It would also throw light on two major themes: the first is the interaction between residential environment and human experience and behaviour, in which different sub-populations of patients may well differ markedly. The second is the importance of subjective and phenomenological perspectives; even if poorer accommodation, larger family size, and greater proximity of neighbours are not immediately stressful for the patient, both relatives and professionals may perceive them as important, thus influencing their judgements and therefore the spatial pattern of care.

REFERENCES

Bagley C, Jacobson S, Palmer C 1973 Social structure and the ecological distribution of mental illness, suicide, and delinquency. Psychological Medicine 3: 177–187

Bain S M 1973 The geographical distribution of psychiatric disorders in the north east region of Scotland. Geographical Medicine 1: 84–108

Bain S M 1974 A geographer's approach in the epidemiology of psychiatric disorder. Journal of Biosocial Science 6: 195–220

Briscoe M 1982 Sex differences in psychological well-being. Psychological Medicine Monograph Supplement 1

Brown G W, Bone M, Dalison B, Wing J K 1966 Schizophrenia and social care. Maudsley Monograph 17. Oxford University Press, London

Brown G W, Harris T 1978 The social origins of depression. Tavistock, London

Castle I M, Gittus E 1957 The distribution of social defects in Liverpool. Sociological Review 55: 43–64

Cheadle A J, Freeman H L, Korer J R 1978 Chronic schizophrenic patients in the community. British Journal of Psychiatry 132: 221–227

Dean K G 1979 The geographical study of psychiatric illness: the case of depressive illness in Plymouth. Area 11(2): 167–171

Dean K G 1982 The psychiatric hospital admission process: a geographical perspective. Unpublished Ph D thesis, University of Hull

Dean K G, James H D 1980 The spatial distribution of depressive illness in Plymouth. British Journal of Psychiatry 136: 167–180

Dean K G, James H D 1981 Social factors and admission to psychiatric hospital: schizophrenia in Plymouth. Transactions of the Institute of British Geographers 6: 39–52

Dunham H W 1965 Community and schizophrenia. Wayne State University Press, Detroit

Dunham H W 1977 Schizophrenia: the impact of sociocultural factors. Hospital Practice 12: 61–68

Faris R E L, Dunham H W 1939 Mental disorders in urban areas. Chicago University Press, Chicago

Freeman H L 1978 Mental health and the environment. British Journal of Psychiatry 132: 113–124

Gerard D, Houston L G 1953 Family setting and the social ecology of schizophrenia. Psychiatric Quarterly 27: 90–101

Giggs J A 1973 The distribution of schizophrenics in Nottingham. Transactions of the Institute of British Geographers 59: 55–76

Giggs J A 1975 The distribution of schizophrenics in Nottingham: a reply. Transactions of the Institute of British Geographers 64: 150–156

Goldberg E M, Morrison S L 1963 Social class and schizophrenia. British Journal of Psychiatry 190: 785–802

Gottesman I I, Shields J 1982 Schizophrenia: the epigenetic puzzle. Cambridge University Press, Cambridge

Gudgin G 1975 The distribution of schizophrenics in Nottingham: a comment. Transactions of the Institute of British Geographers 64: 148–149

Hare E H 1956a Mental illness and social conditions in Bristol. Journal of Mental Science 102: 349–357

Hare E H 1956b Family setting and the urban distribution of schizophrenia. Journal of Mental Science 102: 753–760

Harkey J, Miles D L, Rushing W A 1976 The relation between social class and functional status: a new look at the drift hypothesis. Journal of Health and Social Behaviour 17: 194–204

Herbert D T, Smith D M (eds) 1977 Social problems and the city. Oxford University Press, London

Hoyt H 1939 The structure and growth of residential neighbourhoods in American cities. Federal Housing Administration, Washington DC

Hoyt H 1964 Recent distortions of the classical models of urban structure. Land Economics 40: 199–212

Hunter P 1978 Schizophrenia and community psychiatric nursing. National Schizophrenia Fellowship, London

Jones E, Eyles J 1977 An introduction to social geography. Oxford University Press, Oxford

Kessel N, Hassall C 1971 Evaluation of the functioning of the Plymouth Nuffield Clinic. British Journal of Psychiatry 118: 305–312

Levy L, Rowitz L 1973 The ecology of mental disorder. Behavioural Publications, New York

Myerson A 1940 Review of mental disorder in urban areas. American Journal of Psychiatry 96: 995–997

Office of Population Censuses and Surveys 1971 Census 1971, Devon County Report, Part I. HMSO, London

Park R E, Burgess E W 1925 The city. University of Chicago Press, Chicago

Robertson N C 1974 The relationship between marital status and the risk of psychiatric referral. British Journal of Psychiatry 124: 191–202

Robinson W S 1950 Ecological correlations and the behaviour of individuals. American Sociological Review 15: 351–357

Robson B T 1969 Urban analysis: a study of city structure. Cambridge University Press, London

Slater E, Cowie V 1971 The genetics of mental disorders. Oxford University Press, London

Sundby P, Nyhus P 1963 Major and minor psychiatric disorders in males in Oslo. Acta Psychiatrica Scandinavica 39: 519–547

Timms D W G 1965 The spatial distribution of social deviants in Luton, England. Australia and New Zealand Journal of Sociology 1: 38–52

Timms D W G 1971 The urban mosaic. Cambridge University Press, London

Turner R J, Wagenfeld M O 1967 Occupational mobility and schizophrenia: an assessment of the social selections and social causation hypothesis. American Sociological Review 32: 104–113

Yesavage J A, Werner P D, Becker J M T, Seeman K 1982 Drift and dangerousness: social class differences between acute schizophrenics and their parents in relation to measures of violence. British Journal of Psychiatry 141: 267–270

Mental health and symptom referral in a city

INTRODUCTION

This chapter looks at the health of a city population, on the basis of findings from a survey carried out in Glasgow in the early 1970s; its aims were to find out what symptoms people had in the community and what they did about them. There were three main reasons for asking these particular questions. Firstly, the results of previous research seemed to be contradictory, because while morbidity studies indicated considerable ill-health in the community which did not reach medical attention (Last 1963), surveys of British doctors suggested that GPs felt they were being bothered by trivia (Cartwright 1967). The second reason was that there appeared to be no theoretical explanation of such findings either from a functional (Parsons 1951) or interactionist point of view (Bloom 1963). The third reason was that at the time the research was being undertaken, considerable changes were taking place in the provision of services from the point of first referral in the community. The Social Work (Scotland) Act provided for area social work offices on a geographical basis throughout Glasgow, and at the same time, the traditional lock-up surgeries in the centre of the city were being replaced by purpose-built health centres.

This study was based on the patients registered with doctors practising from one of these new health centres; it housed eight practices, covering over 43 000 patients in all. During the course of a year 1344 home interviews were carried out, representing a 3.1 per cent random sample of the combined average list size. The age-sex distribution of the sample was similar to the population in general, except that young adults tended to be under-represented because of high mobility in an area of urban redevelopment (Hannay and Maddox 1977). Of those interviewed, 964 were adults of 16 years or over and 380 were children aged 15 or less, about whose behavioural symptoms questions were asked of the parent or responsible adult. A considerable amount of information was obtained, including physical and environmental factors. The full results have been published elsewhere (Hannay 1979), but the present chapter will concentrate on those findings relevant to mental health. This includes the prevalence of psychiatric and social symptoms in adults, and behavioural symptoms in children, together with measures of referral behaviour and associated factors. All the questions concerning symptoms referred to the previous 2 weeks only, and therefore the results represent a 2-week period prevalence.

PSYCHIATRIC SYMPTOMS IN ADULTS

The questions on psychiatric symptoms were derived from the Foulds Symptom Sign Inventory (Foulds and Hope 1968). This was designed as a psychiatric screening questionnaire, and each question had been validated against subsequent diagnoses. The most predictive symptoms for each diagnosis were chosen and grouped into eight main questions, except for those on hysteria, which were omitted as relating to the least specific and the most poorly defined diagnosis. No single symptom by itself was highly diagnostic, but taken as a whole, a number of positive responses was likely to indicate psychiatric disturbance.

The results for each symptom question indicated the 2-week period prevalence for individual symptoms. When these were amalgamated into the 8-symptom groups, the results were as follows (expressed as a percentage of all adults interviewed): anxiety, fear or loneliness 20.2 per cent; sleeplessness 20.5 per cent; loss of interest in things 17.6 per cent; worries about other people 8.6 per cent; bothered about periods of excitability 6.4 per cent; bothered by worries about doing things exactly right 12.9 per cent; feeling puzzled 4.8 per cent; and feeling low in spirits 20.3 per cent. Although positive responses tended to cluster together, and indicated general psychiatric morbidity rather than specific diagnoses, it was possible to group the questions into diagnostic categories. Where individual symptoms also occurred in combinations, these were added to the number for the single questions, and the whole expressed as a percentage of the total number of psychiatric symptoms. All the questions fell into one of the original diagnostic categories from the Symptom Sign Inventory, except for the question on loneliness, which was an important subjective response, without itself implying a psychiatric condition. The categories were: anxiety state 26 per cent; psychiatric depression 23 per cent; neurotic depression 20 per cent; obsessional state 11 per cent; paranoid schizophrenia 7 per cent; mania 5 per cent; loneliness 4 per cent; non-paranoid schizophrenia 4 per cent.

About a fifth of the adults who were interviewed exhibited symptoms which suggested an anxiety state and/or depression, with psychotic (or endogenous) depression predominating over neurotic (or reactive) depression. It is not possible to arrive at a precise diagnostic prevalence, because any subject with a positive response was likely to have had other symptoms, which were not specific for particular diagnoses. None of the psychiatric diagnoses were mutually exclusive, and the preponderance of symptoms relating to anxiety or depression may have been due to the fact that these are frequent components of other conditions, such as schizophrenia. Anxiety is also likely to be part of a depressive or obsessional state. Nonetheless, it was striking that 19 per cent of all adults said they felt so low in spirits that they sat for hours on end, 17 per cent had difficulty in getting off to sleep without sleeping pills, and 16 per cent felt anxious at times without knowing the reason why. Of all the adults interviewed, 51 per cent had at least one psychiatric symptom, with a mean of 1.1, and a range of 0 to 7 out of a possible 8.

SOCIAL SYMPTOMS IN ADULTS

The four questions on social symptoms were open-ended, so that details could be filled in, and they covered the broad areas of difficulties with children or teenagers, with other relatives, with money, and with other problems of day-to-day life. These categories were decided on after looking at the commonest reasons for clients presenting for social case work at a family centre in Glasgow (Maddox 1971). Table 15.1 shows the results for each of the four broad categories of social symptoms, but excluding those which were not known to have caused any worry or inconvenience. The results are expressed as a percentage of all adults interviewed; 23 per cent of the adults seen had at least one social symptom, with a mean of 0.3 and a range of 0 to 4. Twenty-one subjects gave positive responses to all four of the main questions.

Table 15.1 Prevalence of social symptoms in Glasgow symptom survey

Social symptom group	Number of adults with social symptoms causing worry or inconvenience	Percentage of all adults (964)
Difficulties with children or teenager	44	(4.6%)
Difficulties with other members of the family or relatives	64	(6.6%)
Financial difficulties	85	(8.8%)
Other difficulties with day-to-day life	90	(9.3%)

In general, the amount of worry or inconvenience caused was more likely to be graded as slight or 'a lot', rather than moderate. Difficulties with other members of the family or relatives produced the highest proportion of those reporting a great deal of worry or inconvenience, and boys seemed to cause more concern than girls. The 6–10 and 16–20 year age-groups gave rise to the most difficulties, and behavioural problems (such as those associated with insomnia, disobedience, and sex) were the most frequent reasons. Although specific illnesses and mental handicap appeared as reasons for difficulties, there was no mention of physical handicap.

It is perhaps surprising that problems with children and teenagers should be the smallest group of social symptoms found, in view of the origins of the Social Work (Scotland) Act in the Kilbrandon Report on children and young persons (Scottish Home and Health Department 1964). Husbands, wives, and grown-up children, followed by parents, were the other relatives to cause most difficulties, especially young adult men and elderly women. Marital relationships, often involving husbands' drinking, caused considerable problems, as did illness and dependent relatives, especially elderly women. Alcoholism was not specifically asked about, and although often alluded to by respondents, it was understated in the results, as much due to the acceptance of social norms of heavy drinking in Glasgow as to possible stigma.

Financial difficulties were the largest group of social symptoms, although the definitions were very subjective, since anyone can claim financial difficulties at some time. Also, the categories for income and expenditure difficulties were not mutually exclusive, nor was the distinction between them always clear. Nevertheless, unemployment (much of it long-term) emerged as the major cause of low income, and the payment of rent and rates as the main difficulty in expense. These were followed by the problem of being ill, and the payment of specific bills. It is interesting that official statistics showed that the rate of financial assistance given by social work departments in Glasgow was over twice that for Scotland as a whole (Social Work Services Group 1974).

The last main group of social symptoms, for other difficulties or problems with day-to-day life, was very broad indeed, as was the explicit remit of the Social Work Department in Scotland (Scottish Education Department and Scottish Home and Health Department 1966). Housing caused by far the most problems, and was at the root of other social symptoms, such as financial difficulties and worries about elderly relatives. Disability or illness, and problems relating to work, were mentioned most frequently after housing in this group.

Although none of these other difficulties or problems with day-to-day life had a duration of more than 10 years, the majority were long-term and a matter of months and years, rather than a few weeks. In his three-factor causal model of depression, Brown (1979) states that the first factor is one of provoking agents, of which one type consists of ongoing major difficulties, such as poor housing, which might or might not have been associated with a severe life event. These difficulties were all markedly unpleasant, had lasted at least 2 years, and did not involve health problems; they were capable of producing depression, but not with the same frequency as severe life events. If Brown's view is accepted, social symptoms would be associated not uncommonly with depression, though in most cases, this would not result in the person seeking medical, still less psychiatric, attention.

BEHAVIOURAL SYMPTOMS IN CHILDREN

The questions on children's behaviour included the most obvious developmental milestones, and covered those kinds of behaviour which the Department of Child Psychiatry in Glasgow had found to be the commonest presenting symptoms for children at their clinic (Stone 1971). The questions were asked of the parent or adult looking after the child about children of 15 years or under. Apart from the first two questions, which were asked about all children, the remaining nine were designed for specific age-groups; 24 per cent of all children had at least one behavioural symptom, with a mean of 0.3 and a range of 0 to 4.

The results for each symptom question indicated the two-week prevalence for each individual symptom, expressed as a percentage of all the 380 children seen. These results were: More difficult to manage than others of the same age 15.8 per cent; difficulty in playing with other children (3–5 years) 0.8 per cent; difficulty with talking or sleeping (3–5 years) 3.7 per cent; difficulty with friends or at school (6–10 years) 4.5 per cent; bed wetting (6–10 years) 4.5 per cent; difficulty with friends or at school (11–15 years) 3.4 per cent; getting into trouble (11–15 years) 1.6 per cent. However, only the first question (in two parts) was asked of all the children, the remainder being for specific age-groups only. A breakdown of the responses by age-groups is therefore shown in Table 15.2.

For both the first two questions, which were asked of all children, and for the specific age-group questions, the 3–5 year-olds appeared to present the most problems, especially difficulty in sleeping. The 6–10 year-olds came next, with school work problems and enuresis, followed by the 11–15 year-olds, whose main difficulties were again related to school work and also to friends. The least troublesome seemed to be babies; not only did they present fewer difficulties of management, but none of them showed marked delay in the early milestones of development.

The acceptability of behaviour to others changes as a child grows, and adapts to new circumstances. Most children can go through temporary 'bad' patches, and quite normal development may be seen as a nuisance or even as 'abnormal' by adults. Figure 15.1 therefore shows the number of positive symptoms for the first two questions, expressed as a percentage of the number of children in each year. These two questions on difficulties in management were asked about all children, and positive responses rose in frequency at the ages of starting and leaving school. One might expect things like crying, temper tantrums, and disobedience to be more common in young children, and these seem to have reached their peak as primary school was started. Positive responses to both questions increased at, or just before the change from primary to secondary school. Finally, there was a marked rise in difficulties of management during adolescence and as school leaving was approached.

Table 15.2   Children's behavioural symptoms

Behavioural symptom group	Number of children with behavioural symptoms (% for each group in brackets)				
	Age group in years				
	0–2	3–5	6–10	11–15	TOTAL
More difficult to manage (cries, temper, disobedience)	1(2%)	12(16%)	15(11%)	5(4%)	33
More difficult to manage (in other ways)	2(4%)	7(9%)	9(7%)	9(8%)	27
Not alert or not smiling	0	–	–	–	0
Difficulty in sitting up, crawling, standing, or walking	0	–	–	–	0
Difficulty in playing with other children	–	3(4%)	–	–	3
Difficulty with talking or sleeping	–	14(18%)	–	–	14
Difficulty with friends or at school	–	–	17(12%)	–	17
Bed wetting	–	–	17(12%)	–	17
Difficulty with friends or at school	–	–	–	13(11%)	13
Getting into trouble	–	–	–	6(5%)	6
Total number of children with behavioural symptoms	3	36	58	33	130
Number of children in each age group	48	77	139	116	380

FACTORS ASSOCIATED WITH SYMPTOM PREVALENCE

The age–sex distributions for psychiatric and social symptoms in adults showed that women were more likely to have such symptoms than men, although the difference was only significant for psychiatric symptoms. The 30–44 year-olds were also the most affected, apart from psychiatric symptoms in men, which were most prevalent between the ages of 45 and 64.

Unemployment (especially due to illness), lack of an active religious allegiance, and living in high-rise flats compared to other types of housing, were all associated with significantly more psychiatric symptoms. The same was true of high neuroticism and low extroversion scores (Eysenck 1958). It was interesting that those who had difficulty in contacting their doctor, or who had criticism of the health centre or of the interview, or whose previous

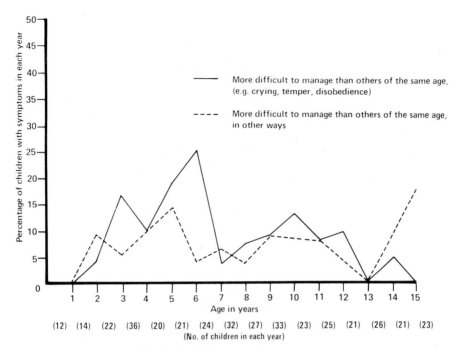

Fig. 15.1 Management difficulties in children according to age

experience of doctors and hospitals was ranked as bad, all had significantly higher frequencies for psychiatric symptoms.

The association between symptoms and living in the upper floors of high-rise flats remained significant, even when allowing for the effects of age and sex (Hannay 1981) and is discussed below. On multivariate analysis for possible predictors of psychiatric symptom frequency, ten variables had significant regression coefficients in the following order of importance: neuroticism score, number of short hospital stays, sex (female), age of housing (older), unemployment (not due to illness), age, intelligence score (low), religion (no active allegiance), social class (lower), and high-rise flats.

Factors which indicated a lack of personal stability, like unemployment, morbidity, separation or divorce, neuroticism, absence of religious allegiance, or contact with relatives, all correlated significantly with the frequency of social symptoms. Measures of the physical environment, such as living at high densities and lack of basic amenities, were also associated with significantly more social symptoms, as were estimates of poor health and increased use of health and social services. On multivariate analysis, the following eight variables had significant regression coefficients as possible predictors of social symptom frequency: neuroticism score, unemployment (not due to illness), age, separation or divorce, number of short hospital stays, high-rise flats (not living in), religion (passive allegiance), years in present residence (few).

It seemed, therefore, that it was the more intelligent adults in less favourable circumstances such as old tenement buildings, who externalised their problems as social symptoms, whereas it was the less perceptive in better physical surroundings, like modern high-rise flats, who internalised their problems as psychiatric symptoms.

For children, there were more behavioural problems amongst boys and amongst those who were not being looked after by their parents. Behavioural symptoms also increased significantly with measures of illness and disability. On multivariate analysis, three factors emerged with significant correlation coefficients as being possible predictors of behavioural symptoms in children, in the following order of importance: number of long hospital stays, relationship of respondent (not a parent), neuroticism score of respondent. These are all factors which would tend to lessen the security of children and indicate some degree of maternal deprivation (Bowlby 1965).

MENTAL HEALTH AND HIGH FLATS

In view of the significant correlation between those living in high flats and an increased prevalence of psychiatric symptoms, this association was analysed further, allowing for age and sex (Hannay 1981). As can be seen from Table 15.3, there were considerable differences in the average number of psychiatric symptoms per person, according to the type of housing. The difference between these means was tested by a one-way analysis of variance, and was significant at the 5 per cent level. In particular, those on the fifth floor or above of high-rise flats had twice the prevalence of psychiatric symptoms as those living in houses, or on the lower four floors of tower blocks. The majority of subjects lived in traditional low-rise tenement flats and had an intermediate prevalence of psychiatric symptoms, similar to the mean for the whole sample.

Table 15.3   Effect of type of housing on prevalence of psychiatric symptoms

Type of housing	Mean number of mental symptoms per person	Number of subjects
Detached or semi-detached	0.8	66
Terraced house	0.8	78
Low rise — up to 4 floors	1.2	702
High rise — lower 4 floors	0.7	36
High rise — 5th floor or above	1.6	67
Other	1.4	15
Total sample	1.1	964

$p < 0.05$ for significance of difference between means, tested by oen-way analysis of variance.

The significant correlation between psychiatric symptoms and housing, particularly high-rise flats, may have been due to the intervening variables of age and sex — for instance, if more middle-age women tended to live on the upper floors of tower blocks. A partial correlation was therefore carried out, using SPSS computer programmes. The zero order partial correlations were not significant at the 5 per cent level between living in high-rise flats and either age or sex, but there was a significant correlation at the 0.1 per cent level between female sex and the prevalence of psychiatric symptoms. When controlling for the effects of age and sex, the partial correlation coefficient between the mean prevalence of psychiatric symptoms per person and those living on the fifth floor or above of high-rise flats was 0.082. This was calculated for 959 adults with five missing values, and was significant at the 0.5 per cent level.

Although only 7 per cent of those interviewed lived in the upper floors of high-rise flats, even this number accounted for a small but significant change in the variance of psychiatric symptom prevalence for the total sample studied. The effect could well have been greater if there had been a larger proportion in the high-risk group. This is not unimportant when overall, only 25 per cent of the variances in psychiatric symptom frequency was accounted for by the many variables studied. The data came from a study which was not specifically designed to test an hypothesis relating to mental health to high flats, but rather to describe the prevalence of symptoms in the community with associated factors. The results do not prove a causal relationship between mental health and high flats, but strongly point the way to this for further research, involving controls with stratified samples giving equivalent numbers in the postulated high-risk group, as well as an extended period of time. The traditional height of Glasgow tenements is four storeys, which is the reason for making a distinction between those living in the lower four floors of high-rise flats and those living on the fifth or above. Glasgow started building such flats in the 1950s, and by the end of the 1960s, there were 15 000 people in tower blocks, over three-quarters of which were between 11 and 31 storeys high. There has been increasing concern about the possible effects of life in them such as isolation and loneliness, and the above findings support this concern.

THE REFERRAL OF SYMPTOMS

The action taken for each positive symptom was asked, and this was graded into a ranking scale of: 1 for no referral, 2 for an informal or lay referral, and 3 for a formal or professional referral. A lay referral was an informal referral to a relative, friend or acquaintance, which did not primarily involve a professional role, as opposed to a formal professional referral. Because any one person might refer different symptoms in different ways, these types of

Table 15.4　Referral of symptoms by percentage in each group

Referral	Physical (all subjects)	Mental (adults)	Behavioural (Children)	Social (adults)
None	55.6%	71.5%	60.2%	40.7%
Lay or informal	10.2%	11.5%	20.4%	9.3%
Professional or formal	34.2%	17.0%	19.4%	50.0%
Total	100% (5631)	100% (1060)	100% (103)	100% (248)

referral are compared by individual symptoms rather than by subjects in Table 15.4

Subjects were most likely to do nothing about psychiatric symptoms, followed by children's behavioural symptoms, whereas action was most often taken over social symptoms, which were also those most likely to be formally referred. The most frequent formal referral of social symptoms was to the social security office or employment exchange, followed by referrals to a doctor or hospital.

Apart from social symptoms, the majority resulted in no action at all and with the exception of children's behavioural symptoms, there was little evidence that lay referral was important. Only about a third of all physical symptoms were referred for formal advice, and the proportion of psychiatric symptoms formally referred was half this at about one-sixth. Whereas adults tended to do nothing about the majority of psychiatric symptoms, it is striking that half the social symptoms were formally referred-a much higher proportion than any other group. However, only 3 per cent of adults who were known to have formally referred social symptoms did so to a social worker. In general, adults who tended not to seek medical advice had more mental symptoms, which were a major component of the 'Symptom Iceberg' (Hannay 1979).

DISCUSSION

One of the starting points of this study was the concept of the sick role (Parsons 1951), and the importance of the social as well as the medical response to illness (Gordon 1966). Variations in sick role behaviour have been associated with cultural differences (Twaddle 1969), illness frequency (Petroni 1969), and family size (Petroni 1971). Some have viewed illness as a way of coping with failure (Shuval 1973), and others have distinguished between disease as a biologically altered state and illness that is behavioural (Fabrega 1973). It has been suggested that the medical definition of disease tends to limit the perception of people's troubles (Zola 1972), and therefore illness behaviour should be converted to problem behaviour as the main object of primary care (Lamberts 1974).

Theoretical approaches to the utilisation of services also imply some perspective on the services themselves (Mechanic 1966). Differences between the need and demand for services can reflect different public and professional expectations (Office of Health Economics 1971). These varying perspectives of patients and doctors might require new approaches from professional training, as part of an adaptive process (Kennedy 1973). There is nothing immutable about the caring professions or the way in which they practise. It has been pointed out that there is something anomalous in the splitting off of social work from medicine at a time when the problems of industrial living require an ecological perspective from services that have to locate themselves within the process of social change (Mead 1972). This involves establishing priorities for primary medical care (Office of Health Economics 1974) and for the social services, within what has been called social development planning (Cullingworth 1970). Such plans should not be stationary, but continuous processes, for which feedback from patients and consumers is essential (Vermost 1974). Without this the system cannot adapt, with resulting imbalances between the availability of services and need, which may become inversely proportional, as described by the inverse care law (Hart 1971).

Goldberg and Huxley (1980) propose that psychiatric disorder in the population can be seen in terms of a model which has five levels; level one represents the community, and level two represents morbidity among patients attending primary care doctors. Between the two is a 'filter', and the factors which determine whether or not an individual passes through it are often referred to as 'illness behaviour' — a term devised by Mechanic. In Britain, females are relatively less likely to pass through than males, which may be related to the presence of small children at home in some cases.

Illness behaviour can also be viewed as a form of adaptation. Such a perspective seems more appropriate than considering illness as a form of deviance (Twaddle 1973), which has been criticised on the grounds that illness is, in fact, the norm rather than deviant (Pflanz and Rohde 1970). The findings of the present study suggest a complex interaction between different types of symptoms, personal characteristics, and the physical and social environment, in which factors causing instability were important. These included things like mobility, housing, unemployment, and marital breakdown, as well as specific behaviour such as cigarette smoking. Symptoms can therefore best be looked at in terms of people's adaptation to their environment, which implies a broader view of aetiology than is usually defined within the traditional research interests of the medical and social sciences. Perhaps the boundaries between these disciplines should be less important than they are. From the point of view of prevention, the practical measures required lie largely outside the conventional remit of medical and even social services, which function more by picking up the pieces than by preventing the breakages, possibly related to factors like housing and unemployment. These require political initiatives, as was perceived in the last century by the pathologist Rudolph Virchow, who wrote that 'politics is medicine writ large'.

The idea that health is a form of biological and social adaptation is not new (Dubos 1959). It is an ecological concept, relating health and illness to the physical and social environment. Moreover, adaptation embraces not only disease but illness behaviour; it also involves a time dimension, and implies that health and illness are not just static but continuous processes (Robinson 1971). The stage at which health becomes illness depends not only on perspectives and criteria, but also on the level of analysis, which might be biological and pathological, or behavioural. The behavioural aspects of health and illness are the adjustments that are an essential part of adaptation, mediated through self-awareness and through the perception of norms and sources of assistance.

If symptoms can be viewed as an expression of maladaptation to the environment, then their referral may also show failure of adaptation, on the part of both individuals and society. Personal problems may not be perceived as being appropriate for professional advice. These perceptions may have been acquired in the past and failed to adjust to changing circumstances, or the services may simply not be available. Just as the adaptation of an individual depends on self-awareness, so the adaptation of society depends on social awareness. It is this social awareness, expressed through public conern, that enables society to adjust. Such adjustments tend to be slow and imperfect, partly because of the nature of political processes, and partly because of attitudes to change. Change means uncertainty, and in general people prefer the security of what they know, so that attitudes become out of step with reality as history changes behind our backs.

The results of regression analysis in this survey suggest that the perception of symptoms was more important than the perception of services in determining referral behaviour. However, the appropriateness of a particular symptom for referral was also relevant, especially for the non-referral of psychiatric symptoms. Theoretically, the concept of a functional 'sick role' as some kind of consensus behaviour is an inadequate framework for the observed facts. One way of representing the marked variation in the extent to which different types of symptoms are referred for formal advice is shown in Figure 15.2. The amount of referral is proportional to the distance from self; psychiatric symptoms are closer to a person's integrity than the physical symptoms of the body, and both are more obviously part of an individual than social symptoms due to external circumstances in society. The extent to which people internalise or externalise their perceptions of reality is similar to the dichotomy between personal responsibility and the social determinants of behaviour, between nature and nurture, and even between right- and left-wing views of society. In this model, the place of contemporary medicine lies somewhere in the middle.

Acknowledgements. The research upon which this chapter is based was made possible by a grant from the Social Science Research Council. The full

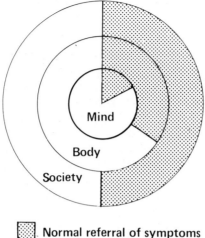

▓ Normal referral of symptoms

Fig. 15.2 Extent to which different types of symptoms are referred for formal advice (stippled area: formal referral of symptoms)

findings have been published in a book entitled 'The Symptom Iceberg, a Study of Community Health' (Hannay 1979) by Routledge and Kegan Paul, by whose kind permission some of the results have been reproduced.

REFERENCES

Bloom S 1963 The doctor and his patient. Russell Sage Foundation, New York
Bowlby J 1965 Child care and the growth of love. Penguin, London
Brown G W 1979 A three-factor causal model of depression. In: Barrett J E (ed) Stress and Mental disorder. Raven Press, New York
Cartwright A 1967 Patients and their doctors: a study in general practice. Routledge and Kegan Paul, London
Cullingworth J B 1970 Social planning in Britain. Gerontologist 10: 211–13
Dubos R 1959 The mirage of health. Allen & Unwin, London
Eysenck H J 1958 A short questionnaire for the measurement of two dimensions of personality. Journal of Applied Psychology 42: 14–17
Fabrega F 1973 Towards a model of illness behaviour. Medical Care 11: 470–84
Foulds G A, Hope K 1968 Manual of the symptom sign inventory. University of London Press, London
Goldberg D, Huxley P 1980 Mental illness in the community. Tavistock, London
Gordon G 1966 Role theory and illness. College and University Press, New Haven, Connecticut
Hannay D R, 1979 The symptom iceberg: a study of community health. Routledge and Kegan Paul, London
Hannay D R 1981 Mental health and high flats. Journal of Chronic Diseases 34: 431–432
Hannay D R, Maddox E K 1977 Missing patients on a health centre file. Community Health 8: 210–216
Hart J T 1971 Inverse care law. Lancet 1: 405–12
Kennedy D A 1973 Perceptions of illness and healing. Social Science and Medicine 7: 787–805
Lamberts H 1974 Illness and problem behaviour. Huitsarts Wetensch 17: 56–62
Last J M 1963 The illness iceberg. Lancet II: 28–31

Maddox E J 1971 Analysis of some data from the Drumchapel family centre. Unpublished paper

Mead A 1972 The future of general practice in the United Kingdom. A sociological diagnosis. Paper at 3rd International Conference on Social Science and Medicine, Elsinore

Mechanic D 1966 The sociology of medicine: viewpoints and perspectives. Journal of Health and Human Behaviour 7: 237–48

Office of Health Economics 1971 Prospects in health. London

Office of Health Economics 1974 The work of primary medical care. London

Parsons T 1951 The social system. Routledge and Kegan Paul, London

Petroni F A 1969 The influence of age, sex and chronicity in perceived legitimacy to the sick role. Sociology and Social Research 53: 180–93

Petroni F A 1971 Preferred right to the sick role and illness behaviour. Social Science and Medicine 5: 645–53

Pflanz M, Rohde J J 1970 Illness: deviant behaviour or conformity? Social Science and Medicine 4: 645–53

Robinson D 1971 The process of becoming ill. Routledge and Kegan Paul, London

Scottish Education Department and Scottish Home and Health Department 1966 Social work and the community. HMSO, Edinburgh

Scottish Home and Health Department 1964 Children and young persons in Scotland. HMSO, Edinburgh

Shuval J T 1973 Illness — a mechanism for coping with failure. Social Science and Medicine 7: 259–65

Social Work Services Group 1974 Scottish social work statistics 1972. Scottish Education Department, HMSO, Edinburgh

Stone F H 1971 Personal communication

Twaddle A C 1969 Health decisions and sick role variations. Journal of Health and Social Behaviour 10: 105–14

Twaddle A C 1973 Illness and deviance. Social Science and Medicine 7: 751–62

Vermost L 1974 Counteracting medical power: the sociologist's task. Paper at 4th International Conference on Social Science and Medicine, Elsinore

Zola I K 1972 Concept of trouble and source of medical assistance. Social Science and Medicine 6: 673–9

Mental health and the environment in developing countries

INTRODUCTION

During the century now drawing to a close, developing countries have been undergoing extraordinary changes, which bring with them a questioning of formerly unquestioned beliefs. However, whether rapid cultural change inevitably produces stress, and if so, whether this stress affects everyone in the population concerned, or only those with vulnerable personalities, are questions that have still to be answered (Carstairs & Kapur 1976). The theory of change-induced stress is not one which can be universally generalised, but should always be considered in the light of specific conditions; for instance, is migration viewed by population as admirable in those prepared to face hard work, or as a desertion or betrayal of the home community (Murphy 1977)? Thus it should not be regarded as a unitary concept in social psychiatry, but examined in terms of its components, such as whether or not close-knit social nuclei are established which newcomers can join — the successful tradition of doing this by overseas Chinese seems to have resulted in relatively little psychiatric disorder occurring in them through migration. However, Murphy found that in Singapore, where the Chinese population was sub-divided by marked language differences, there was a strong inverse correlation between the size of the language group and the incidence of functional psychoses in females and of suicide and arteriosclerotic psychoses in males. This would be predicted by the 'social fit' hypothesis (see Chapter 2).

One of the most important of the socio-cultural processes now affecting developing countries is rapid urbanisation, and Lin (1969) has suggested that this may become 'over-urbanisation', i.e. growth of cities to an extent which is disproportionate to the economic development of the rest of the country. In these circumstances, their westernised pattern of life shows an enormous discrepancy of culture with the rest of the country's population, which is mostly rural, so that the city may appear — in cultural terms — as an alien implant. Furthermore, the rate of penetration of foreign influences can mean that even old-established city residents may be troubled by cultural conflicts. It is quite possible that the emotional tensions, feelings of insecurity, disharmony of beliefs, and disruption of familiar habits which are likely to occur in this situation of social disintegration will lead to mental health problems, which could be either psychiatric illnesses, psychosomatic disorders, addictions, or forms of deviant behaviour. However, because medical and social services in such cities are so poor, most of these disorders will remain unrecorded, and untreated in any appropriate way.

From the anthropological point of view, Gutmann (1980) states that 'cities are in large part founded and settled by young people, refugees from village gerontocracy . . . they go to the city as a kind of revolution against patriarchy, and against the omnipresent extended family'. But as a result, the relative homogeneity of rural societies is lost, other people can no longer be understood through self-reference, and 'remain unfamiliar and unpredictable, despite years of physical proximity'. Related to this concept, Wittkower & Prince (1974), surveying evidence mainly from developing countries, concluded that social change is especially likely to be harmful to mental health when associated with such stress factors as anomie, role deprivation, or value polymorphism (i.e. the coexistence of antagonistic values in one community). On the other hand , the original village situation can be regarded as one of social rigidity (see Chapter 2).

In South America, migrants from distant rural areas generally settle on the outskirts of large cities and remain in a state of 'marginality', mostly in shantytowns which are without any services such as sewage or water (Bernstein 1976). Heads of families are usually the first to migrate, and may then be vulnerable to the development of alcoholism, or such adverse emotional states as brutalisation, apathy, or depression. If the man is unable to find work, or suffers some misfortune, or if communication with his relatives breaks down for some reason, permanent disruption of the family may occur. Such migrants often experience a sense of grief, originating from the decay of the home community, and followed by an idealisation of what they have left behind; to reaffirm their identity, they are likely to remain within the migrant group, which provides social support but makes integration into the wider society more difficult. The main city, with its unfamiliar norms and culture, tends to be feared; but in the shantytown, some features of the home environment can be reproduced. Studies in Buenos Aires, comparing areas of differing social status, showed that the migrant inhabitants of shantytowns had the highest rates of alcoholism, violence, mental retardation, epilepsy, and learning difficulties in children.

Migration has occurred throughout human history, but the main difference between the urbanisation of the older industrialised countries in the nineteenth century and that of developing countries today relates to birth and death rates (Gulbinat & Emberg 1978). Whereas growth of cities required an enormous rural influx, because of lower urban fertility and higher mortality rates, these differences have been eliminated or reversed in developing countries, so that the city population itself is multiplying as never before. At the same time, migration continues from the country, because population growth there threatens to overcrowd the land, and though the proportion of rural residents moving to the cities is about the same as in the past, the absolute numbers of people involved are vastly greater. Thus in Asia, Africa, and South America, cities which for many years had remained in the range of 250 000 to 500 000 now have between five and ten million inhabitants, with every sign of their growth continuing inexorably.

The background to this vast migration is that in 1980, 1.34 billion people were estimated to be living in the rural areas of 68 developing countries — just over half of them in absolute poverty. Worldwide recession, growing protectionism, and erratic prices for agricultural commodities were among the factors hindering development programmes in these rural areas (FAO 1983). Lin (1983) defines absolute poverty as 'an extreme condition of human deprivation which endangers survival, health, and physical and intellectual growth.' He adds that:

> The Third World with its absolute poverty, political instability, social upheaval from wars and migration, rapid population growth, and unequal distribution of wealth does not provide the conditions favorable to healthy human growth and development. Only ten to fifteen per cent of its people have access to basic health services. High infant mortality, epidemic and endemic disease, and malnutrition sap the vitality of adults and impair the physical and mental development of their children'.

Forms of treatment

In many traditional societies, both the causes of serious illnesses and their relief are attributed to malign or beneficent supernatural powers. When a healer is consulted, the group of anxious relatives who usually accompany the patient are especially concerned about two things: can this healer be trusted absolutely? And even if he is a trustworthy person, is his healing spirit strong enough to overcome the evil power which made the patient ill in the first place? A consultation reflects the need for help which is felt not just by the patient, but by the whole family. For many centuries, healing has been seen in these societies as a contest between good and evil spirits: if the sick person survives, the healer's guiding spirit has prevailed, but if the victim dies, then the gods or healing spirits have not intervened in time. Since expectation by the patient is an important element in therapy, it would be reasonable to anticipate that both emotional stress and psychiatric illness of non-organic origin would often be alleviated by healers whose treatments have been seen to be successful in his community in the past (Foster 1977).

Very little is known by barely literate villagers about Western medicine, though year by year, more and more of them are being urged to make use of cosmopolitan medical products, either in the local dispensary or in the 'medicine shops' which in India, are to be found in every town and in some large villages. These are often used together with whatever traditional healing may have to offer. However, the progress of modern medicine there has been slow, not least because the shop proprietors have only a limited knowledge of the drugs they sell,and although their shelves are crowded with medications — some of which are both potent and expensive — all too often the wrong one is used in any particular case.

Under these circumstances one can only hope — on behalf of both psychiatric and other patients — that the government-backed primary health centres (PHCs) and smaller sub-centres will gradually build up an awareness on the part of both staff and patients of which preparations should be employed in which conditions. Since rural Indians, like villagers in most cultures, share misgivings about the new drugs, it is also to be hoped that the centres will continue to practise their role as medical educators, as well as dispensers of medicines. In that case, the villagers will slowly learn that new treatments will only be effective in their proper contexts. This applies particularly to patients with psychiatric illness or epilepsy, because it is only in relatively recent decades that potent drugs have been discovered for these conditions.

RESEARCH AND THE ROLE OF WHO

In the years immediately after the Second World War, the citizens of advanced countries were calling for a number of reforms, including social welfare, freely accessible health services, and the emancipation of mental health care. The third of these was given added impetus because it coincided with the discovery of a number of psychotropic drugs which at least relieved the conditions of a majority of the mentally ill. The post-war years were also a period in which many of the former colonial countries attained their independent statehood. Among the pressing needs for educational, social, and economic advancement there, health care had a rather low priority, and mental health an even lower one.

The World Health Organisation (WHO) can be forgiven for considering that the pharmacological treatment of psychiatric disorders could not be rapidly introduced in developing countries, since the psychotropic drugs began to be used globally only from the late 1950s, and it took a considerable time before practising doctors everywhere became familiar with them. However, in recent years, advisors on mental health have been appointed to the staff of each of WHO's Regions, while a Division of Mental Health was established at its Headquarters.

Even during earlier years, though, a number of outstanding pioneers achieved advances in psychiatric care in their respective developing countries: Sansingkeo in Thailand, who improved the standard of teaching and patient care through the respect he had acquired among public health planners in his country's Ministry of Health; Yap of Hong Kong, who clarified the nature of forms of mental illness found only in the developing world (Yap 1951); and El Mahi, the first Sudanese psychiatrist, who established a constructive collaboration between his few staff and the many Mollahs, or Moslem clergy, to whom relatives bring cases of mental illnes for treatment. His outstanding pupil, Baasher, has done a great deal to inspire the Arab countries to improve the quality of their psychiatric care. Yet another pioneer has been Leon of Cali, Colombia, who emulated Pinel by striking the chains from patients in the local mental hospital.

Tsung-yi Lin, was the first Taiwanese psychiatrist and the first medical student from the island to receive a postgraduate fellowship at the Imperial University in Tokyo, where he studied psychiatric epidemiology. There was a far-sighted reason for this: he believed that only rigorous surveys of such morbidity, carried out in his own country, would convince those in other medical disciplines that psychiatric illness also presents a serious threat to the health of the general population. Once this had been convincingly demonstrated, it would be easier to persuade his medical school colleagues that psychiatry required a larger place in the teaching programme.

In addition to psychiatric teaching, Lin spent parts of 1946, 1947 and 1948 carrying out studies on defined populations. These were: Baksa, a rural village with an adult population of nearly 6000; Simpo, a country town of 6800 inhabitants; and Ampeng (19 000), a crowded peripheral suburb of the island's capital, Taipeh. He gave an opinion on diagnosis, when the field workers were in doubt about this, and his criteria were based on those first used in northern Europe, and then by Japanese epidemiologists (Lin 1953). The pooled results showed a lifetime prevalence rate of 10.8 per thousand for all psychiatric disorders, and of 3.8 per thousand for psychoses. In general, the levels of serious illnesses were not unlike those found in the West, except that disabling neurotic illnesses were recorded in only 1.2 per cent of the total sample surveyed. This low rate for neurosis suggested either that such illnesses were rare among these Chinese respondents, or that the criteria for identifying neurotic disability were set at a very high level.

An unprecedented morbidity survey was next carried out among the aboriginal tribes in the Eastern mountain region; this village-by-village study yielded a prevalence rate of psychosis of 3.9 per 1000 — very close to the 3.8 per 1000 of his previous survey. However, it was noted that in many subjects, the psychotic illness appeared to have remitted in a relatively short time. To verify this finding ,a series of follow-up visits were made to monitor the recovery rate for psychotic patients. It was found that of the whole group, 48 per cent had recovered within 3 months ,52 per cent within 6 months, 65 per cent within a year, and 84.6 per cent within 2 years (Rin & Lin 1962). Other favourable reports of the prognosis for schizophrenia in developing countries are referred to below.

The same survey was repeated in each of the three target populations, in 1961, 1962, and 1963 (i.e. 15 years later, in each area). Among the findings were a significantly high rate of population growth in Ampeng, the city suburb, as compared with Baksa and Simpo; there was also a significantly higher rate of psychiatric morbidity there, shown especially in excess prevalence of neurotic and psychosomatic disorders, but with a less marked increase in psychotic illnesses. The growth in population in Ampeng was primarily attributed to internal migration of followers of Chiang Kai Chek, who found themselves marooned on an unfamiliar island , from which they were unlikely ever to be able to return to their ancestral homes in mainland China (Lin et al. 1969). Lin would be the first to recognise the methodological limitations of his pioneer morbidity surveys, yet his criteria were abreast with those employed by leading Western research workers of the time. This work also had the desired effect of convincing relevant authorities that psychiatric illness presented a major challenge to health care in developing countries.

During and after the 1950s, psychiatric research workers in more advanced countries became impatient with the inadequacy of their scientific methods. Clinicians looked in vain in the published works for criteria which would convince others that they were discussing the same clinical entities. This was equally the case with follow-up studies of particular psychiatric illnesses — were they quite the same ones? Reports of the incidence or prevalence of schizophrenia or any other supposedly specific form of psychiatric illness often raised questions as to whether or not the cases had been unambiguously identified. A few years earlier, senior teachers were not troubled by these uncertainties: they stated their (sometimes idiosyncratic) criteria for diagnosis, and expected no further discussion. However, it came to be realised that unless commonly agreed criteria for diagnosing schizophrenia, depression, or other types of illness were stated, the advancement of knowledge about these entities would remain slow.

A consequence was the study of Leighton et al. (1963), in which African investigators worked together with Americans to see whether the experience of social stress and social decline would be associated in rural and small-town Africa (as they had been to some extent in Maritime Canada) with an increase in neurotic and psychosomatic symptoms. In a series of community surveys in Stirling County, coupled with prevalence studies of minor as well as more marked forms of psychiatric disorder, social disintegration had been investigated in relation to the frequency of neurotic illness. Most previous field surveys had ignored such minor forms of malfunctioning, but Leighton showed that certain communities were in a state of general decline and that minor psychiatric morbidity was more common among their inhabitants (see Chapter 2). It was, however, an undertaking of a different order to determine whether indices of social decline and check-lists of neurotic symptoms (developed by Macmillan) would prove as reliable after translation into Yoruba as they had been in North America. It seemed likely, though, that the disintegration of traditional cultural norms and systems of social support in Africa would be having adverse mental health consequences.

Leighton had the courage to preservere, in spite of knowing that such translations tend to be inescapably imprecise renderings of the original; some languages do not even have separate words to describe the different moods of depression, irritability, and anxiety (Leff 1977) and in any case, such concepts do not carry medical implications in most African cultures. However, these translations were close enough in meaning to be used as measures of the presence of symptoms ,or as indicators of social decline, and significant correlations were indeed found among the respondents in Nigeria, as had been shown to occur in Canada. This finding was the more interesting because it conflicted with those of many previous population studies of the prevalence of neurotic complaints, which were reported at a higher rate in women than in men. In this Nigerian study, though, men reported such complaints significantly more often than women.

It may be significant in this connection that many of the men had left traditional agriculture, in which they had worked side by side with their village kinsfolk, and sought unfamiliar labouring tasks in small towns. Their new employment was lacking in both status and community support. The women , on the other hand, brought with them their accustomed cultivation of small plots of land, which helped to feed their families and provided a surplus to be sold in the local market, these activities being as familiar in their new homes as they had been in the old. Shepherd (1980) comments on these findings that:

> Whereas the Yoruba acknowledged the concept of major mental disorder and recognised its various symptoms, their views on causation differed radically from those of Western observers. By contrast, the phenomena of what in Western culture would be regarded as minor mental disorders were widely recognised but were not necessarily classified as illness. Further, the decisions concerning their status as morbid phenomena were made by native healers.

Thus, depressive symptoms were recorded at much the same rates in men and women in Nigeria, as was also found in Uganda (Orley & Wing 1979). Depression was four times more common in the Nigerian sample than in Stirling County, and was twice as common in Ugandan women as in those of an inner London suburb. This contradicted earlier suggestions that depression is unusual in African populations, which probably resulted from the fact that patients there generally do not complain directly of depressive symptoms, but one reason for the greater morbidity might be that depressive illnesses in rural Africa remain untreated. Orley & Wing also suggest that other untreated endemic disorders, such as parasite infestation, might be relevant as contributory, causes. However, the social model of depression (see Chapter 2) was developed in Western settings, and until recently, few studies had been reported of demographic or environmental factors which might be relevant to depression in an African context. It was remarkable, though, that Vadher & Ndetei (1981) found that 68 per cent of a sample of depressed Kenyan patients had experienced at least one independent severe life-event in the 12 months preceding the onset of their depression, while the figure for depressed women in London had been 67 per cent (Brown & Harris 1978).

In a further study of depressed patients in an urban area of Kenya (Ndetei & Vadher 1982), lack of regular income or employment and being first-born were found to operate as vulnerability factors; the first of these was also found to be significant in London. However, having an intimate confidant and active religious affiliation did not seem to protect against depression in a Kenyan setting; thus, the same degree of intimacy may well have different meanings for different cultural groups. Being first-born was the most significant factor associated with the depressed group, and this was related to the fact that in Kenyan culture, the first-born traditionally has a special position in the family, which approaches and may even supersede that of a parental role in relation to brothers, sisters, and other members of the extended kinship group. This entails responsibilities for others, including finance, major decision-making, and deep moral and practical concern for each person in the family group, all of which could clearly result in stress and adverse life-events. Unlike the situation in London, the number of children aged under 14 who were at home had no significant association with depression; but in Kenya, baby minders are readily available within the extended family, so that the mother need not be tied down by this responsibility to the same extent.

Psychiatric morbidity was found in 29 per cent of general hospital outpatients in both a rural and a semi-urban area of Kenya (Dhadphale et al. 1983); since there were no significant demographic differences between the psychiatric patients from these two areas, or between psychiatric and non-psychiatric patients with respect to literacy, socio-economic class, education, or tribal origin, psychiatric problems are clearly not confined to an educated, urbanised minority in developing countries. As in the African studies of depression and unlike European findings, there was a notable absence of differences in psychiatric morbidity between the two sexes; the most likely explanation for this is the social role of African women, which provides both constant social support and a wide range of activities; but the effects of westernisation may be likely to include a greater liability to psychiatric disorder.

There have now been a number of joint studies in which scholars from other countries have brought with them techniques and instruments for morbidity surveys, as was done by Giel & Van Luijk (1969) from Holland, who helped to establish psychiatric teaching and research in a new medical school in Addis Ababa with a series of field studies in Ethiopia. It should be appreciated, though, that the reported prevalence rates for neuroses, psychosomatic disorders, personality disorders, alcohol abuse, and other socially defined conditions can differ very widely from one country to another, or even between different surveys carried out on samples of the same population. This is partly for methodological reasons, since some investigators have chosen narrow criteria for case identification, while others have used much wider measures. But even when allowance is made for these factors, at least some psychiatric morbidity rates appear to vary with differences in social and environmental conditions.

Giel was one of those who, like Leighton, recognised that it is difficult to separate persons whose behaviour is socially embarrassing, or disapproved of from others who are considered to be mentally disturbed, rather than only anti-social. In his own surveys with Van Luijk, psychiatric morbidity was identified in 8.6 per cent of persons living in a small Ethopian town, and in 9.1 per cent of those in a village. These figures contrasted with the findings of the Leighton & Lambo team in Nigeria, among whose respondents no less than 40–45 per cent were judged ill, but only 15–19 per cent 'significantly impaired', whereas in the Ethopian studies, only 5 per cent in the town sample and 6 per cent in the village sample were judged to be significantly impaired. Giel & Van Luijk also carried out a study in the out-patient service of the teaching hospital in Addis Ababa. Here, it was found that no less than 18 per cent of this unselected sample of general out-patients attended with primarily psychiatric disorders — a proportion surprisingly close to a similar screening of out-patients in a rural clinic in northern India (Dube 1970) and to results from a study of out-patients in a suburban area of Nairobi (Ndetei & Muhengi 1979).

A particularly interesting paper by Giel & Workneh (1975) describes the behaviour of a group of patients in an Ethiopian clinic ,who have their counterparts in many developing countries, and also in Europe. These are essentially dependent personalities, who seek comfort and support from repeated attendance at the hospital or primary health centre. In many cases, it comes to be recognised that what they are seeking above all is reassurance. Kapur has pointed out (personal communication) that for Moslem women, hidden from social contacts through purdah, attendance at a psychiatric out-patient clinic provides a welcome occasion to go out and visit the hospital. Indeed, their return attendances tend to become numerous, but this pattern of behaviour has not yet manifested itself among women patients in the rural clinics.

Social disintegration has been reported particularly in respect of island territories in the South Pacific, with dissolution of tribal societies in which members would spend most of their time engaged in communal activities, and replacement of their hierarchical structuring by a cash economy. Alcoholism has become a significant problem in these circumstances, in and around towns, and particularly in association with the depopulation of outlying islands into the capitals. Little epidemiological study has been made of psychiatric disorder in this region so far, but it seems reasonable to assume that mental health might be promoted by bringing some of the advantages of urban living, such as education and medical care, to the smaller island communities, as an alternative to the migration of their people into what are often no more than urban slums. Modern communication systems would make this possible in many cases (Schmidt 1974).

Another aspect of the same disintegration process has been reported from Nigeria by Arth (1968). Young Ibo men who have acquired independent wealth from wage work no longer rely on their fathers for a bride price. As a result, the father's prestige declines, and 'psychosenility' is said to be prevalent among elderly male Ibos, who have been affected by this aspect of modernisation and the consequent dissolution of traditional society. So far as attempted suicide is concerned, under-reporting of cases is very likely to occur in developing countries, but published rates have been as low as 11 per 100 000 in Papua New Guinea and 7 per 100 000 in Benin, Nigeria, compared with up to 600 per 100 000 in industrialised countries. The Nigerian study (Eferakeya 1984) found that more attempts were made by males than by females — the opposite of the situation in developed countries — and that the peak age-group was younger (i.e. in late adolescence). Most attempts were by taking drugs, whereas an earlier Nigerian series (Asuni 1967) found that over 60 per cent were by physical self-injury.

During the 1960s and 1970s, WHO contributed to improving the reliability of diagnosis through the study on Psychiatric Diagnosis in New York and London (Cooper et al. 1972) and the International Pilot Study of Schizophrenia, which included centres of research in Colombia, Denmark, India, Nigeria, Taiwan, Czechoslovakia, UK, USA, and USSR. Two of the major findings of this latter study were: firstly, that cases were reliably identified and judged to be schizophrenic, both by local psychiatrists and by most from the other participating countries, although those in Washington, DC and in Moscow each had some idiosyncratic concepts of the symptoms describing this condition; and secondly, that after a 2-year follow-up, schizophrenic patients in the developing countries appeared to have had a significantly better level of recovery than was the case with those in the advanced countries.

This was confirmed by a number of other findings, notably those of Murphy & Raman (1971) who showed that a better rate of remission occurred among schizophrenics of Chinese and Indian races in Mauritius than among similar patients in Britain. The rates of severely disabling and chronic schizophrenia in the two countries were very similar, supporting the concept of a 'process' form of the illness, largely immune from social influences. However, if the disease is relatively mild, circumstances in Mauritius seem to encourage the disappearance of symptoms, whereas some European conditions at least promote their persistence. In fact, Shepherd (1977) suggests that 'The elaborate and mostly unrealized recommendations of community care and rehabilitation programmes have long been anticipated by the social structure of some supposedly unsophisticated societies'.

Comparison with other international data suggested that neither climate nor race could explain this difference (though diet was another possible factor, not entirely eliminated). The same authors (Raman & Murphy 1972) proposed that the degree of social recovery which a schizophrenic patient can achieve is largely determined by the social assistance he receives and by the social demands that meet him as he emerges from the initial phase of the illness. If so, environmental factors, including culture, would be more important in determining prognosis than had previously been thought, and in fact, the generally accepted European prognostic indicators for schizophrenia were found not to apply to any great extent in these Mauritian patients. There are various possible explanations for the view that the Mauritian social environment is relatively more favourable in this respect — for instance, the nature of the family structure, its expectations and emotional interactions, or differences from developed countries in the social networks of villages and extended families.

Waxler (1979) followed up 66 schizophrenics in Sri Lanka, 5 years after their first admission, and found that the overall social adjustment and clinical state of the sample were significantly better that those reported from industrialised countries. This good outcome was not thought to be explicable in terms of sampling or diagnostic methods, type of treatment, or the family's willingness to tolerate deviance. An alternative explanation would be at the cultural level, and the similarity of these results to others from India suggested that comparable family structure, native treatment systems, beliefs about madness, and values may all play a part. Whereas expectations of mental illness and the operation of the treatment system might tend to alienate schizophrenics from normal roles and to prolong illness in developed countries, Sinhalese families usually see the cause of mental illness as external to the patient, regard it as quickly curable, and always provide positive social support to the sick person.

However, Westermeyer (1984) criticises this view on the grounds that samples derived from psychiatric clinical facilities might be expected to produce more acute cases (probably with a better outcome) than one based on a community survey. His own survey was in pre-communist Laos — a predominantly peasant society, in a country which then contained no mental health facilities or practising psychiatrists. The Mauritian work suggested that chronic mental disorder in a developing country may lead to little or no loss of productivity and little loss incident upon treatment, family crisis, property destruction, or assault. But in fact, the average Laotian subject with long-term psychosis represented a considerable drain on the financial resources of the family, extended kin, and in some cases neighbours or community; the expense was mostly for traditional healers, and could easily equal a person's lifetime savings. These sums were particularly significant because the line between economic survival and disaster tends to be a thin one in such societies. Nor was there evidence that the mentally disordered person there is productive, or even partially self-sustaining in general, though there were a few in the sample who contributed more than would have been likely in a competitive industrialised society. Other losses caused by the mentally ill included damage to their homes or contents, destruction of food through paranoid delusions, and fines or recompense for the consequences of their disturbed behaviour affecting others.

Investigation of the social function of this Laotian group (Westermeyer 1980) showed that psychosis tends to be associated with severe dysfunction, even in a subsistence peasant society; most subjects were dependent on others for food and shelter, ceased recreational, sexual, and communal activities, and often became alienated from family or friends. Sociological critics have claimed that 'labelling' by psychiatrists and their institutions is a major cause of the social disability associated with major mental disorder, but in this sample, the label of madness was attributed only by kin or fellow villagers. Similarly, institutionalisation has been blamed for much of the disability of the chronic mentally ill; but none of these subjects had ever entered an institution, yet they showed the same social disability as is associated with psychosis elsewhere.

Their social networks were found to be reduced in size (Westermeyer & Pattison 1981), as has been reported from industrialised countries, in spite of the fact that the Laotian subjects had mostly lived in the same village all their lives, and had had daily face-to-face contact with a limited number of people. Without the ability to exchange goods or labour with friends, neighbours, or co-workers, they became dependent on a few family members or self-appointed sponsors to care for them. However, a few subjects still had extensive networks, even after years of mental illness, apparently due to a 'social capital', built up through having given to others more than they received before their disability came on, which was then drawn on for assistance when reciprocity was no longer possible.

In Kiribati (formerly the Gilbert Islands), with a population of about 60 000, the primary determinant of psychiatric contact is the degree to which symptoms cause social upheaval, rather than distress to the patient himself; as a result, there is a strong male excess among identified patients, since females are more easily managed by families and are perceived as being less threatening (Daniels et al, 1982). Outside the main island, there is a subsistence economy, except for some copra production, but in this 'island paradise', free from some of the pressures of industrialised societies, a community survey of 4000 people revealed nine cases of alcoholic psychosis. Petrol fume inhalation is also common among the young, especially boys, and is a group activity with much social pressure to participate. Schizophrenics admitted to the central hospital in 1982–3 were found to be more likely than controls to have a history of such inhalation, to a highly significant extent.

In Micronesia, a prevalence study of schizophrenia (Dale 1981) showed that in island populations which were separated both by long sea distances and by race and culture, there were substantial differences in the rate of the disorder. It was not identified in some islands at all, was a rare occurrence in others, and in yet others was at a high rate — eight or nine cases per thousand adults; in general, the rate became progressively higher, moving from east to west. Various hypotheses can be proposed to explain this, including genetic differences, and diet — i.e. the marked increase in use of grains with partial westernisation; chronic schizophrenics are reported to be rare in tribal populations, eating mostly root crops, whereas neuroactive peptides from grain glutens may be pathogenic in those with the genotype(s) for schizophrenia (Dohan et al. 1983). Another report from the same area (Wilson 1981) states that a prominent problem for many of its communities is that of the disturbed, wandering schizophrenic, who may be placed in jail periodically, having been eventually rejected and abandoned by his family.

Years of scientific work have resulted in the revision of the American Psychiatric Association's Diagnostic and Statistical Manual (DSM III) and the decennial revision of the psychiatric section of WHO's International Classification of Diseases. Differences of opinion still underlie some of the assumptions on which these two instruments are based, but considerable progress has now been made towards creating a common diagnostic language between different schools. WHO and the US Alcohol, Drug Abuse, and Mental Health Administration have also recruited scientific working groups, to assist in reaching a clearer understanding of the different forms in which psychiatric disorders and drug abuse are found to occur world-wide. Thus, diagnostic precision and epidemiological method make their special contributions towards advancing mental health care.

For instance, whether or not the clinical features of schizophrenia are constant in societies at different stages of development can only be determined on the basis of very stringent diagnosis. Though low prevalence rates of Schneiderian First Rank Symptoms had been found in several developing countries, as well as in West Indian and West African immigrants to the UK, Ndetei & Singh (1983) found that when Kenyan schizophrenic patients were carefully matched with those in English hospitals, the rates were the same. After they disgarded symptoms which might relate to a social-cultural context, the rest were very similar to those of English patients, and were highly discriminant of schizophrenic illness.

During the past two decades, research workers in developing countries have in fact played a very positive role, both in epidemiological fieldwork and in exploring new paradigms of patient care in rural areas, where mental health has tended to be neglected. One example is a survey of suicide and attempted suicide in Fiji (Haynes 1984), where those of Indian race form 50 per cent of the population, but account for 90 per cent of suicides; in the decade 1972–1982, suicides increased in number by 80 per cent, compared with a population increase of 19 per cent, and Hindus were over-represented, compared with Moslems. In one province, which mostly consists of sugar cane farms, worked by Indians, suicides in 1979–1982 were by hanging in 74 per cent of cases, and the rest by poisoning, mostly using paraquat. (Similarly in Western Samoa, which had an average of only six suicides per annum up to 1971, when paraquat was introduced, the number rose to 42 in 1981, mostly by paraquat poisoning). In this province of Fiji, 80 per cent of female suicides were aged under 30, but above that age, the male rate exceeded the female, and there was a dramatic peak in males aged over 60, all of whom had a long history of chronic ill-health.

Haynes reports that those committing suicide nearly all lived in rural areas, and particularly on sugar cane farms, which are sometimes very isolated, usually based on extended family units, and tend to develop a claustrophobic life, in which stresses become greatly magnified. These farms,many of which also grow rice, are under severe pressure of work throughout the year, with constant anxiety about financial survival. Many suicides of young Indian men followed trivial arguments with the parents; those who do not do well academically have to return to the family farm, and to an authoritarian father, resulting in great frustration, after the expectation of a different life has been aroused. For their part, young women tend to be devalued, and often live a life fraught with difficulty, both before and after marriage; they represent a powerless group, for whom it is not socially permissible to display anger or frustration. Many suffer from chronic anaemia and, faced with multiple domestic chores, frequent pregnancies, and relative poverty, may become too exhausted (both mentally and physically) to cope any longer. In contrast, the Fijians still pursue a traditionally communal way of life — especially in these northern provinces — and receive much support both from relatives and from other social groups; however, increasing urbanisation is likely to diminish these traditional ties, with the passage of time.

An isolated community

An unique epidemiological survey of an isolated community is that by Rawnsley & Loudon (1964) of the inhabitants of Tristan da Cunha, which is situated 1700 miles from the nearest large settlement. The 264 islanders were evacuated to England following a volcanic eruption in 1961, but were almost unanimously eager to return to the island at the earliest possible moment. The community was 'closed', in the sense that for half a century, there had been no in- or out-migration, but was not truly 'isolated' because of improved communications and the turnover of resident officials. However, in relation to psychiatric disorder, the important social factor was the high degree to which major life experiences are shared exclusively by members of the community; this is promoted by the small population, nearness of the houses, universal inter-relatedness, and necessary cooperation in the economy. A notable homogeneity of values and attitudes prevailed, together with a very low tolerance of departures from the generally accepted standards of behaviour.

During the previous hundred years, there was documentary evidence that four islanders had had severe psychotic illnesses, including one man who became violent in his early twenties and was chained up alone in a house for several years, until his death. The 1962 survey revealed four current cases of psychosis (three organic dementia and one depression) representing a point-prevalence of 2.1 per cent; there were also six adults with marked mental retardation. Epidemiologically, the main features of interest were two minor disorders — epidemic hysteria (principally in 1937–1938, affecting over 10 per cent of the population) and headaches associated with anxiety, which seemed to have become much more common in the few years before the survey. Disability from the headache was mainly trifling, but psychogenic factors were clearly evident in many cases, and it had become an endemic syndrome in the community.

It seemed likely that the isolated, monotonous life, regulated by many unwritten laws, might predispose to hysteria, which satisfied a hunger for events. About the time of the 1937 epidemic, a few young couples wanted to get married, but were under pressure not to do so because relationships between their families had been strained for some years. Thus in a situation where strong needs were counterbalanced by strong controls, the abnormal behaviour might provide the means for openly acting out the satisfaction of an impulse, without fear or guilt. This exemplary work by Rawnsley & Loudon provides a valuable framework for the study of mental health in many isolated communities of developing countries.

PROMOTION OF MENTAL HEALTH CARE

The epidemiological studies mentioned above helped to demonstrate the size of the problem of psychiatric disorder, and a growing number of research workers in the developing countries became interested in showing how mental health could be allied with new forms of health care delivery. At a WHO workshop on methods of improving rural mental health care in 1973, several reports were made of the successful employment of field medical aides, in situations where both psychiatrists and qualified nurses were very few. Quite simply trained workers could be taught to recognise schizophrenia, manic-depressive psychosis, and uncontrolled epilepsy among villagers under their care; they also learnt how to administer first aid until the patient could be shown to a doctor, and his future treatment prescribed.

A meeting of WHO's Expert Committee on Mental Health in 1974 ,which considered the high rates of psychiatric disability revealed by prevalence studies in several developing countries, concluded that this morbidity was too widespread to remain the responsibility of specialists in mental health alone. Instead, experiments were needed to establish whether modestly trained health assistants (both male and female) could be employed on a large scale to recognise common forms of psychiatric illness in such societies, and to supervise their care. Following publication of the Committee's report (WHO 1975), action research groups were recruited in India, Colombia, Sudan, Senegal, the Philippines, Brazil, and Egypt.

The writer was working in India from 1978–1981, and spent much of his time attached to Chandigarh's Post-Graduate Institute for Medical Education and Research, enabling him to learn at first hand about this project (Wig & Murthy 1981). At the start, like other teams, they recognised that mental ill-health was neglected by the local population, and considered an unimportant element in sickness. Where such illnesses occurred, they were attributed to supernatural causes, and until recent years, there were few examples of successful treatment for these patients, if they should be brought to any village-based PHC. This was also the case at the PHC situated in the village of Raipur Rani, about 40 kilometres from Chandigarh, which became the base for these studies on rural mental health care.

As a first step, a health census was carried out in a village (Manka) with a population of 1000, where almost 20 patients were found to be suffering from epilepsy, schizophrenia, or depression. Two-thirds of these cases were considered to be significantly disabled, but half of them had not been taken to any medical centre, because they were popularly believed to be incurable. However, when treatment was offered close to their homes, they accepted it without hesitation, especially when improvement was seen to have been achieved in others.

The project was given the task of testing whether basic mental health care could be provided by the personnel (medical and auxiliary) of the general health services, which also raised a number of questions:

1. Can mental health care be integrated into general health services?
2. What are the priorities to be included at the primary health care level?
3. Are there training tools and manuals suitable for the training of the peripheral health personnel?
4. Can intervention and treatment at the village level bring benefits to the individual, the family, and the larger community?
5. How can the villagers themselves be involved in the task of caring for the mentally ill in their community?

The first four of these questions were answered in the affirmative during 5 years of village work. The fifth has provided a model upon which a simple level of family care can be taught to the patient's family, while he is receiving medication.

The defined population served by Raipur Rani's PHC amounted to 60 000; the centre has three doctors, while a multi-purpose worker and a health supervisor monitor the activities of less highly trained staff at the village sub-centres. In addition to the health care activities supervised by the PHC, there are also a number of Ayurvedic dispensaries, where practitioners of this school of medicine continue to practise their ancient teachings, with government support and widespread public acceptance.

At an early stage of the project, members of the village health staff were interviewed. They had had very little training in the recognition and management of psychiatric disorders, and the only psychotropic drug with which they were familiar was diazepam. They had not had experience of using either chlorpromazine or imipramine, but were eager to learn more about these hitherto little known drugs. Members of the research teams in Cali and in Chandigarh then agreed on a 24-item Self-Reporting Questionnaire, to be used to identify 'probable cases'.All these cases were next to be given an abbreviated version of the Present State Examination (PSE), which was also administered to a random sample of people who had been rated as normal in the preliminary screening.

After practicing the administration of the screening instruments until they had attained a high degree of inter-observer reliability, four teams (Cali, Chandigarh, Khartoum, and Manila) carried out a systematic screening for mental health in a random sample of adult patients attending their rural clinics. At the same time, the clinic's nursing and medical personnel were asked to indicate whether or not their patients were currently suffering any form of psychiatric illness.

Not surprisingly, the rates of such illness were reported at somewhat different levels from the four centres, varying from 10.6 per cent to 17.7 per cent. The disorders most frequently observed were neuroses and psychosomatic disturbances, which together represented 90 per cent of all the positive psychiatric cases. Psychoses were detected relatively rarely in the general medical clinic; to ascertain their true prevalence, it would have been necessary to look for them in people's homes, because of the likely degree of disability of many cases.

Of the relatively small number of patients judged to be psychiatrically disturbed (as shown by the research workers' two-stage screening tests), only one-third were observed to be mentally ill by the regular staff of the clinic. Cases which were missed were mildly disturbed, while severe illness was seen in nine out of ten cases. This is a finding which has been reported in numerous studies of the prevalence of psychiatric disorders in general practice clinics in developing countries. Clearly, it has proved far from easy to distinguish symptoms of neurotic illness from physical symptoms on the one hand, and from behaviour within the range of human eccentricity on the other.

Previous epidemiological studies in India were hampered by many difficulties, including the relatively high rate of illiteracy and lack of resources for investigation. Dube (1970) in a mixed rural and urban population, found a period prevalence rate of 18 per thousand for 'severe'psychiatric cases. In two rural communities, Elnaggar et al. (1971) obtained a prevalence rate of 27 per thousand for psychiatric morbidity, whereas Sethi et al. (1972a) found 39 per thousand; psychiatric disorders were found to be commoner in migrant than in settled families (Sethi et al. 1972b). In an urban society, the same investigators (1974) found a two-year period prevalence rate of 67 per thousand; this included mental retardation, but not psychophysiological reactions or personality disorders. Psychiatric disorders were significantly more common in those aged over 30, in illiterates, and in persons belonging to small families; anxiety and depression occurred at high rates (14.7 and 13.6 per thousand respectively), whereas these conditions were uncommon in the rural samples. Although this overall prevalence rate appears high, it is lower than those for Stirling County and Midtown Manhattan (see Chapter 2).

Earlier Indian studies had not explored the relationship between psychiatric morbidity and socio-economic status, but this was done by Nandi et al. (1980) in a survey of a cluster of villages in West Bengal. The population consisted of three different groups: firstly, tribal people, with a simple, non-specialised society, marked by strong ethnocentric feeling and kinship bonds; secondly, scheduled castes, who were economically weak and painfully aware of their low hereditary social position; and thirdly Brahmins, who constituted a distinct and isolated cultural group, but were losing their traditional prestige. Depression was commoner in females in all these groups, but there were differences in relation to other disorders, anxiety and obsessional states being absent among the tribes, but most common among Brahmin women, where it fitted well with their cult of purity and ritual-ridden life. On the other hand, hysterical disorders were most prevalent in scheduled caste women, whose low status was least likely to be disrupted by attention-seeking behaviour.

In all three population groups, there was a significantly higher rate of morbidity amongst members of higher socio-economic classes, as there was in Hagnell's study of rural Sweden (1966). It may be that as tribal people gain in prosperity, they lose some of the stability and security of a traditional unstratified society, causing a higher rate of morbidity (especially psychosis) in those economically better off. It may also be relevant that in the period following independence, those who had previously accepted the *status quo* found that the conditions of life could now be changed for the better by human efforts; the stress resulting from this knowledge particularly affected the upper classes, and their recorded higher psychiatric morbidity may reflect this change in their way of life. The drift hypothesis (see Chapter 2) is not relevant in a rural, traditionally agricultural society such as this, where there is little occupational specialisation or competitiveness, and little scope for occupational mobility. By contrast, Nondi et al. state that these communities have been characterised by a close-knit family system, from which each member — well or ill — derives emotional support.

Having taken note of the high prevalence of minor forms of nervous illness in the general medical clinic, the WHO teams reviewed their decision to treat only sufferers from psychosis or epilepsy, as being rated highest in their priorities. It was impressive in 1978, when the writer first visited a number of villages within a few miles of Raipur Rani, to be introduced to chronic schizophrenics and controlled epileptics who were already so much better that they were able to resume work in the fields. The aim of this collaborative study on strategies for extending mental health care was to test the feasibility of introducing a few high-priority psychiatric illnesses into the conditions already regarded as within the competence of village health workers. This represented a new initiative in rural health care.

In Botswana (Ben-Tovim 1983), a psychiatric service has been provided to the more remote areas of the country by regular visits from a psychiatrist or psychiatric nurse from the capital to as many as possible of the primary care facilities. These remote communities lie more than 300 kilometres west of the narrow easterly strip, which contains 80 per cent of the total population of 930 000, the whole country being approximately the same size as France. During the visits, patients are seen who have previously been identified by the primary care staff, and continuing care is offered to those with functional psychoses and convulsive disorders. Though the regions concerned were racially and tribally heterogeneous, this did not seem to result in marked clinical differences between patients from the various populations.

A total of 119 patients who were seen in three of the remote Botswana regions contained: 48 schizophrenics, 35 epileptics, 13 alcoholics, 12 neurotics (particularly complaining of functional headaches), seven organic cases (including some with mental retardation), and two cases of affective psychosis. The low rate of the last category was thought to be due to the persistent failure of health workers, presumably for cultural reasons, to identify depressive psychoses as disorders requiring treatment, though reference has been made earlier to the fact that African patients generally do not complain directly of depressive symptoms. Estimates of prevalence in one region were 3 per thousand for schizophrenia and 2.3 per thousand for epilepsy, which are of the same order of magnitude as those reported from other developing countries.

In spite of the enormous distances involved, Botswana has been fortunate in having a well developed system of primary health care, an administration which has been interested in mental health, and the resources to provide transport for psychiatric personnel. But as far as developing countries in general are concerned, Lin (1983) warns that 'We still await documented results attained through systematic and objective evaluation research in order to assess the feasibility and applicability of the community-based model for treatment and care'

INDIAN RURAL LIFE

India's post-independence history has some features in common with other rapidly developing countries. Since 1947, its population has been increasing at a disquieting rate, and the 1981 decennial census reported that the proportion of the national population who were living below the basic minimum for nutrition had increased to 42 per cent. Yet this forbidding statistic is found in a sub-continent whose output of cereals has multiplied since the 'green revolution' began in earnest in 1966–1967; new seed grains, short-stemmed crops, and greater use of fertilisers and irrigation had successfully increased the crop yields by the mid-seventies. Since then, India has been able to keep stores of food-grains in reserve against failures of the monsoon rains, and also to export some to neighbouring countries. Now, at least for a time, the threat of total starvation has been lifted, although among the poor, malnutrition continues to take its toll of infants and the elderly. At the same time, India's manufacturing capacity grows slowly but steadily, producing more and more factory products for the nation's needs.

The writer has had the opportunnity of visiting Sujarupa, a remote village of farmers, in Rajasthan, North India, twelve times between 1950 and 1981. The older members of this community could recall severe droughts in 1900–1901, and in 1919–1920, and lesser ones up to 1973–1974. Even in the 80s, if villagers of Sujarupa were asked to define 'happiness', they commonly replied, 'To eat two meals a day'. Like most Indian villages, it has seen a transformation in communications with the nearest market town, a little over 50 miles distant; the roads have improved, and buses increased greatly in number. Here also, the crop yields have increased, but in some important respects these farmers have not moved with the times; for instance, all of their women and more than half of their men remain illiterate, although free schooling is available within walking distance. Boys, but rarely girls, are sent to school for 1 or 2 years before being set to work on the farm. Until quite recent years, the boys were pleased to escape early from school; but nowadays, a minority of clever youngsters have become aware of what they have been missing — and a still smaller fraction of the parents have begun to realise that education can improve the prospects of some at least of their sons. Several of the older men have spent a few years either in the army or as semi-skilled workmen in the cotton mills of Ahmedabad, more than 200 miles away; these were the first to be taught to read and write.

Among the present younger generation of Sujarupa is Laxman Singh, aged about 25 in 1981. He was the first to complete 10 years of study, and chose to enlist in India's navy, on the sensible grounds that it gives opportunities to train as a medical assistant, a cook, an engineer, or a radio and electronics technician. When he returns home on leave, at least once a year, he treats his elders with due respect; but in private conversation, he told me that he now found village life too constrained and cramping. He is (perhaps through having completed his medical assistant's course) the only villager of my acquaintance who finds the lack of hygiene and the swarms of flies and other insects distasteful. In March, 1981, he took me to see his newborn first child. To my surprise, I found that he had brought a mosquito-net with him from Bombay, and had erected it over his wife's string bed, so that she and the baby would be shielded at least from the flies.

Laxman Singh enjoys his service, as did the older men who had served in the army. They like to talk about their travels and adventures, but especially the recollection of making friends with fellow-soldiers drawn from India's far-spread states. Both military service and life in city slums had provided a delayed educational experience. From either of these experiences, men from Sujarupa returned home with a much fuller knowledge of Hindu legends, prayers, and hymns, and had often learned to play a musical instrument. The last thing that a European would expect of illiterate villagers' time in the services or in the slums would be that they had generally undergone a conversion experience: but this was precisely what had happened to most returned villagers. It was they who led their fellow villagers in frequent late evening sessions of *bhakti*, songs of worship to Lord Krishna.

This was not, however, what happened to every villager who explored the world outside: some took to drink, and some to frequenting brothels, but they were a small minority. Their custom of living in close association with kinsmen and acquaintances from their own locality ensured that they enjoyed (in Emile Durkheim's terminology) the 'solidarity' of inhabiting a compact, inter-related community, whose members helped each other in time of need. Few became alienated from their families, or lost their adherence to the values of the village. However, as pointed out earlier with reference to South America, there is a consequent absence of integration into the larger community of the city.

Since it has been taken for granted by most scholars, from Thomas Jefferson to the present day, that the displacement of villagers, long familiar with agricultural work, to become city dwellers and factory workers is usually detrimental to their mental health, it is timely to refer to a study (Inkeles and Smith 1970) which seriously challenges this contention. This covered a large sample of Indian men aged 18–32, who were either agricultural workers, newly arrived migrants to the city, urban workers in small-scale enterprises, or employees in industry. Its schedule of enquiry aimed to measure the respondent's adjustment, and to elicit any psychosomatic symptoms, but the results failed to support the expectation that urban life is more frequently stressful and detrimental to mental health than that in the village. The authors conclude that:

> If security, calculability, support, trust, respectful treatment and the like are assumed to make for psychic adjustment . . . in developing countries, such salubrious experiences are no less enjoyed by those who have moved to the city and have taken up industrial employment than by those who continue to pursue the bucolic life of cultivators in the bosom of their traditional villages.

It is gratifying that there are twentieth century sociologists who have drawn attention to the fact that city life is not invariably unrewarding.

In India, as in most developing countries, social values are often transmitted by oral tradition. Even illiterate villagers often memorise lengthy sections of song from their great epics. These are sung far into the night, to the music of small brass cymbals, seven-stringed guitars, and hand-drums (tabla). Sometimes, a particular village may consider itself to have received a supernatural instruction that they are to perform episodes from the *Ramayana*, an epic poem, for the benefit of neighbouring villages. Their performances are fervent, if much less finished than those of itinerant singers and dancers.

The Indian film industry, although a late-comer, has grown to become the second largest in the world, and seems likely soon to be the largest. Much of its output is crudely melodramatic, punctuated with popular songs and dances; but even these naive entertainments reiterate moral teachings, such as the wrong behaviour and ultimate punishment of villains, and the hardships but ultimate reward of the good. Many of their most popular films have been re-enactments of heroic episodes in India's two great verse dramas, the *Ramayana* and the *Mahabharata*. These tales are full of heroic deeds, of examples of right and wrong behaviour, and of each earning his (or her) inescapable reward. As they watch these heroics, even the most simply educated cinemagoers are imbued with the teachings of an ancient tradition, and with the unending confrontations of Good and Evil.

STRATEGIES FOR BETTER CARE

Modernists among the citizens of many recently independent countries argue that their first task is to improve the economic, health, and educational status of their fellow-countrymen. They believe that only by learning the technology of the world-embracing material culture will their people be able to emerge from present poverty. Others (including the Ayatollah Khomeini) insist that their peoples' loyalty to a stern, unrelenting religious code is their most compelling value; but the rest of the world observes his holy extremism with apprehension. Nearer to our medical interests and capability is our desire to make a contribution towards attaining WHO's target of Health for All by the Year 2000. Though there are formidable obstacles, which make it seem unlikely that this will be accomplished quite so soon, it is perhaps realistic to consider WHO's more modest aim of Strategies for Increasing Mental Health Care as our psychiatric contribution towards the wider undertaking.

Some forms of psychiatric illness can be recognised by either physical, behavioural, or biochemical changes, and have been referred to as *organic* or *functional* disorders. The former of these terms presents little difficulty: physical or chemical changes exist, and reveal themselves to scientific observation. Functional disorders are harder to pin down; there are even people, including some psychiatrists and many more social scientists, who argue that these conditions are only the legacy of stressful life experiences. Others adopt an intermediary position, believing that life events upset the body's functioning so profoundly that it is justifiable to presume that bodily processes have become deranged, and that even though we are not yet capable of demonstrating the nature of the resulting biochemical disturbance, this will soon be achieved.

The history of psychiatry, though, has been punctuated by premature assertions that its secrets have been revealed. A more realistic approach, however, is to recognise that many curative or life-saving medications have been discovered during and since the Second World War, and that some of them are as simple and inexpensive as rehydration fluid for children suffering from dysentery. Others, including phenothiazines and antidepressants, have more limited efficacy, but can improve the quality of patients' lives. In developing countries, there is a growing impatience over the slow pace at which Health for All is being approached. In 1978, India had the same number of psychiatrists as Denmark, whose population was then less than 1 per cent of India's (Wig et al. 1980). In most developing countries there are less than one psychiatrist and two psychiatric nurses per 100 000 population, and in many less than one of each per million population; in some countries, there are none (Lin 1983). International research teams have shown that village health workers can bring mental health care to the villages; but there are nearly 600 000 villages in India alone. Can events be speeded up?

One reason for the delay that has been experienced was put forward by the late D M Mackay (1981) in an article entitled 'Primary health care is needed, but is it wanted?' The implication is not that the villagers have simply rejected our medicines, but rather that we have not exerted ourselves strenuously enough to demonstrate to them how their seriously ill relatives can in many cases be helped back to life or health.

A different argument has been put forward by an Indian Professor of Social Medicine, who is both a doctor and a graduate in anthropology. Banerji (1976) believes that Indian health care has not yet recovered from its long indoctrination by British teachers. 'Western medicine was used as a political weapon by the colonialists to strengthen the oppressing classes and to weaken the oppressed . . . This western and privileged-class orientation of the health services has been actively perpetuated and promoted by the post-colonial leadership of India' (Banerji 1979). There are, it must be admitted, some public hospitals in India where the poor and the uneducated are given less attention than the wealthy and well-educated (to whose society most doctors aspire to belong); but it is also true that there are many doctors in district hospitals who give disinterested medical treatment to rich and poor patients alike. In many such hospitals, a patient's relatives are encouraged to stay near him and provide his nursing care, and at the same time to learn how to treat him when he comes home.

The concept of primary care being made accessible to villagers within a few kilometres from home was advocated as early as 1938 in a report on Basic Health Care drawn up by members of the Indian National Congress, and then lost from sight for nearly 40 years (Cassen 1978). Its ideas are now commanding attention among the health planners, who include not only doctors but also those concerned with education and village development. Perhaps stimulated by the accounts of China's barefoot doctors, many developing countries are experimenting with different variations on the employment of basic health workers at the village level.

Banerji has also reproached the teachers of Western medicine for virtually ignoring the content of Ayurvedic medicine and Moslem Unani, both of which have been practised in India for hundreds of years. Research on the pharmacology of ancient remedies has in fact been carried out in Calcutta since the First World War, and in numerous other centres since Independence — but the resulting contribution of new, valuable remedies has unfortunately been slight. On the other hand, teachers of these indigenous systems of medicine have included instruction on Western physiology, pathology, surgery, medicine, and therapeutics as part of their teaching, while practising Vaids and Hakims do not hesitate to use Western medicine as part of their own prescriptions.

It has to be admitted, however, that one of the finest Medical Libraries in India (that in the Post-Graduate Institute for Medical Education and Research, Chandigarh) contains not a single book on Traditional Medicine. Does this matter? It is very likely, in fact that this total indifference towards India's legacy of ancient medical lore is damaging to the modern doctor's rapport with his patients. At least some knowledge of the vocabulary and teachings of Ayurvedic and Unani medicine would be helpful, even though he may make it clear that his own practice is of another kind.

Villagers are well aware that a doctor will best be able to help an ailing patient if the patient understands and trusts what he is doing; and even where the doctor's explanation is not fully understood, the patient will feel encouraged, provided that the trust is there. The British were misguided in regarding their allopathic medicine as though it were the sole repository of medical science, but Banerji was surely also mistaken in attributing all the shortcomings of medical care in his own and other developing countries to the hubris of the Colonial Power.

Medical care seems on the verge of making a further major breakthrough, particularly in the developing countries. We have been confronted by the enormous logistical problem of manufacturing (at a reasonable cost) the medicines which can be safely issued at successive levels of the chain of expertise, from the village sub-centre via the PHC to its back-up district hospital. The step-by-step training of village health workers needs to be reinforced by their support from more highly trained staff, who move between the front line of the remoter villages and the point of convergence at the PHC.

Awareness of the high prevalence of handicapping depression, anxiety, and psychosomatic disorders was widespread in the eighteenth century in Europe. It lapsed during the nineteenth century because such sweeping advances were being made in the fields of infection and pathology that doctors believed every illness — including every psychiatric illness — would soon reveal its aetiology. During the present century, functional psychiatric illnesses have again attracted widespread attention, at first in the developed, but now also in developing countries. Anthropologists have confirmed that some persons in every society know what it is like to experience periods of anxiety, depression, and fear as well as the bodily distress to which these give rise.

By recognising these conditions and prescribing shared acts of reparation to relieve them, traditional healers have played a useful role in their communities for many centuries. However, it is not only in developing countries, but in every society that people turn to a wide variety of healers who inspire confidence. They achieve this for two reasons: because they have insight into areas of stress in their culture, and because they possess a certain charisma which inspires confidence in their clientele. They have never completely ceased to practise even in developed countries, nor are they likely to do so, either there or in the developing world, for years to come.

THE WORLD ENVIRONMENT

The human environment includes not only physical surroundings and the abundance or scarcity of food, but above all the amount of aggressiveness of one community against another, or their ability to live and work in mutual cooperation. The human race likes to think of itself as a social species, but in fact we are frequently reminded how little we have progressed towards achieving cooperation in place of strife. The UN itself is all too well aware that the superpowers have each armed themselves with thousands of nuclear missiles, capable of annihilating many millions of each others' populations in the first fusillades; millions more would die painfully from their injuries because nuclear warfare destroys habitations, transport, communications, doctors, nurses — the catalogue of destruction seems to have no end. In comparison with the holocaust which is already a potential reality, the death and destruction happening daily in local theatres of war may seem to be on a small scale, but it does not seem so to the families of the killed and wounded.

Blacker (1946) observed that during the years of the blitz in Britain, admissions of cases of psychosis to London's psychiatric hospitals were largely unchanged, whereas attendances of patients with neurotic complaints remained significantly less than had been the case in the waiting period of the 'phoney war'. He drew the conclusion that to share danger and physical hardship with one's fellow-citizens was a stimulus towards recovering — or simply sustaining — one's mental health. Civilian morale was at its highest when British citizens were being intensively bombed, and when in every street, groups of fire-watchers no longer went into bomb shelters or underground railway stations, but busied themselves with the prevention or control of fires.

During recent years, a similar display of a people's cohesion under stress has been shown to the world by Poles in the creation (and eventual suppression) of their own independent trade union, Solidarity. Even under martial law, the Poles have continued to show support for their own free but now proscribed union, and it is remarkable that in 1981, the rate of attempted suicide is reported to have fallen by 30 per cent, compared with the previous year, indicating the positive effect of a common purpose. They are not alone, though. In many countries, violence, suppression, and all too often death are the fate of political dissidents, who may even be pronounced insane, and submitted to involuntary treatment.

The prospect for mankind has never been so bleak, since our forefathers never knew weapons of such unprecedented destructive power; entire local populations could be annihilated, and many more die a lingering death among the ruins of whole cities and their devastated surroundings. If even relatively few nuclear missiles are fired into their targetted cities, the survivors, when they approach the epicentres, will see evidence of many thousands dead or dying, and for several miles' radius, the destruction of houses, schools, hospitals, of telephone, television, and radio communications, broken water-mains and sewage outlets. In 1945, in Hiroshima and Nagasaki, many survivors became temporarily deranged by the horror of the scene which confronted them: the enormously more destructive weapons of the mid-80s will present an even more horrific spectacle.

Human cleverness has brought us into the possession of bombs powerful enough to kill a large proportion of our fellow-men, together with the destruction of cities, factories, and roads. Human cleverness would be more wisely employed in drawing up agreements to stop the further increase in nuclear weapons, and then to move suspiciously, step by step, towards a prospective dismantling of the death-dealing salvoes of bombs which are already poised to start.

Unless the Great Powers understand how near we are to mutual destruction, and act accordingly, the future of mankind could easily turn out to lie with the developing countries, because a madness of self-annihilation has spread over the 'advanced' countries of the world. Enough nuclear weapons have been made, held in readiness, and targetted for the major cities of the USSR — just as they have missiles targetted on cities in Europe and the US — to ensure a nuclear holocaust. We can only hope that enough mental health will prevail among the peoples on both sides to persuade them to dismantle these deadly weapons, before they cause our shared destruction, and so surrender their future — and ours — to the developing countries.

REFERENCES

Arth M 1968 Ideals and behavior. A comment on Ibo respect patterns. Gerontologist 8: 242–4
Asuni T 1967 Attempted suicide in Western Nigeria. Central African Journal of Medicine 13: 289–292
Banerji D 1976 Formulating an alternative rural health care system for India. Jawaharlal Nehru University, New Delhi
Banerji D 1979 The place of the indigenous and the western systems of medicine in the health services of India. International Journal of Health Services 9: 511–519
Ben-Tovim D 1983 A psychiatric service to the remote areas of Botswana. British Journal of Psychiatry 142: 199–203
Bernstein M 1976 Causes and effects of marginality. International Journal of Mental Health 5: 80–95
Blacker C P 1946 Neurosis and the mental health service. Oxford University Press, London
Brown G W, Harris T 1978 Social origins of depression. Tavistock, London
Carstairs G M, Kapur R L 1976 The great universe of Kota. Hogarth Press, London

Cassen R H 1978 India: population, economy, society. Macmillan, London

Cooper J E, Kendell R E, Gurland B J, Sharpe L, Copeland J R M, Simon R 1972 Psychiatric diagnosis in New York and London. Oxford University Press, London

Dale P W 1981 Prevalence of schizophrenia in the Pacific island populations of Micronesia. Journal of Psychiatric Research 16: 103–111

Dhadphale M, Ellison R H, Griffin L 1983 The frequency of psychiatric disorders among patients attending semi-urban and rural general out-patient clinics in Kenya. British Journal of Psychiatry 142: 379–383

Dohan F C, Harper E H, Clark M H, Rodrigue R, Zigars V 1983 Where is schizophrenia rare? Lancet ii: 101

Dube K C 1970 A study of prevalence and biosocial variables in mental illness in a rural and an urban community in Uttar Pradesh. Acta Psychiatrica Scandinavica 46: 327–359

Eferakeya A E 1984 Drugs and suicide attempts in Benin City, Nigeria. British Journal of Psychiatry (In press)

Elnaggar M N, Maitre P, Rao M N 1971 Mental health in an Indian rural community. British Journal of Psychiatry 118: 499–503

FAO 1983 Report to the biennial conference. Food & Agriculture Organisation, Rome

Foster G M 1977 Medical anthropology and international health planning. Social Science & Medicine 11: 527–534

Giel R, Van Luijk J N 1969 Psychiatric morbidity in a small Ethiopian town. British Journal of Psychiatry 115: 149–162

Goldberg D, Blackwell R 1970 Psychiatric illness in general practice. British Medical Journal ii: 439–443

Gulbinat W, Emberg G 1978 Demographic considerations and trends. International Journal of Mental Health 7: 18–33

Gutmann D 1980 Observations on culture and mental health in later life. In: Birren J E, Sloane R B (eds) Handbook of mental health and aging. Prentice Hall, Englewood Cliffs, NJ

Hagnell O 1966 A prospective study of the incidence of mental disorder. Svenska Bokforlaget Norstedts-Bonniers, Stockholm

Harding T W, De Arango M V, Baltazar J, Clement C E, Ibrahim M H A, Ladrigo-Ignacio L, Murthy R S, Wig N N 1980 Mental disorders in primary health care. Psychological Medicine 10: 231–241

Haynes R H 1984 A preliminary survey of suicide in a province of Fiji. British Journal of Psychiatry (In press)

Inkeles A, Smith D M 1970 The fate of personal adjustment in the process of modernisation. International Journal of Comparative Sociology 11: 81–114

Leighton A M, Lambo T A, Hughes C C, Leighton D C, Murphy J M, Macklin D B 1963 Psychiatric disorder among the Yoruba. Cornell University Press, New York

Leff J P 1977 The cross-cultural study of emotions. Culture Medicine & Psychiatry 1: 317–350

Lin T Y 1953 A study of the incidence of mental disorder in Chinese and other cultures. Psychiatry 16: 313–316

Lin T Y, Rin H, Yeh E, Hsu C, Chu H 1969 Mental disorders in Taiwan fifteen years later. In: Caudill W, Lin T Y (eds) Mental health research in Asia and the Pacific. East-West Center Press, Hawaii

Lin T Y 1969 Effects of urbanization on mental health. 24–33

Lin T Y 1983 Mental health in the third world. Journal of Nervous & Mental Disease 171: 71–78

Mackay D M 1981 Primary care may be needed, but is it wanted? Journal of Tropical Medicine and Hygiene 88: 93–97 (also published in World Health Forum, 1982)

Murphy H B M 1937 Migration, culture and mental health. Psychological Medicine 7: 677–684

Murphy H B M, Raman A C 1971 The chronicity of schizophrenia in indigenous tropical peoples. British Journal of Psychiatry 118: 489–497

Ndetei D M, Muhengi J 1979 The prevalence and clinical presentation of psychiatric illness in a rural setting in Kenya. British Journal of Psychiatry 135: 269–272

Ndetei D M, Vadher A 1982 A study of some psychological factors in depressed and non-depressed subjects in a Kenyan setting. British Journal of Medical Psychology 55: 235–239

Ndetei D M, Singh A 1983 Schneider's first rank symptoms of schizophrenia in Kenyan patients. Acta Psychiatrica Scandinavica 67: 148–153

Orley J, Wing J K 1979 Psychiatric disorders in two African villages. Archives of General Psychiatry 36: 513–520

Raman A C, Murphy H B M 1972 Failure of traditional prognostic indicators in Afro-Asian psychotics: results of a long-term follow-up survey. Journal of Nervous and Mental Diseases 154: 238–247

Rin H, Lin T Y 1962 Mental illness among Formosan aborigines as compared with the Chinese in Taiwan. Journal of Mental Science 108: 134–146

Schmidt K E 1974 Report on mental health services in the South Pacific. WHO, Manila

Sethi B B, Gupta S C, Kumar R, Kumari P 1972a A psychiatric survey of 500 rural families. Indian Journal of Psychiatry 14: 183–187

Sethi B B, Gupta S C, Mahendru R K, Kumari P 1972b Migration and mental health. Indian Journal of Psychiatry 14: 115–121

Sethi B B, Gupta S C, Mahendru R K, Kumari P 1974 Mental health and urban life: a study of 850 families. British Journal of Psychiatry 124: 243–246

Shepherd M 1971 A critical appraisal of contemporary psychiatry. Comprehensive Psychiatry 12: 302–320

Shepherd M 1980 Mental health and primary care in the seventeenth century. Acta Psychiatrica Scandinavica, Supplement 285, 62: 121–130

Vadher A, Ndetei D M 1981 Life events and depression in a Kenyan setting. British Journal of Psychiatry 139: 134–137

Waxler N E 1979 Is outcome for schizophrenia better in nonindustrial societies? Journal of Nervous & Mental Disease 167: 144–158

Westermeyer J 1980 Psychosis in a peasant society: social outcomes. American Journal of Psychiatry 137: 1390–1394

Westermeyer J 1984 Economic losses associated with chronic mental disorder in a developing country. British Journal of Psychiatry (in the press)

Westermeyer J, Pattison E M 1981 Social networks and mental illness in a peasant society. Schizophrenia Bulletin 7: 125–134

WHO 1973 The International Pilot Study of Schizophrenia. WHO, Geneva

WHO 1975 Organization of mental health services in developing countries: The 16th report of the Expert Committee on Mental Health. WHO, Geneva

Wig N N, Murthy R S, Mani M, Arpan D 1980 Psychiatric services through peripheral health centres. Indian Journal of Psychiatry 22: 311–316

Wig N N, Murthy R S 1981 A model for rural psychiatric services — Raipur Rani experience, 1975–1980. Department of Psychiatry, Post-Graduate Institute of Medical Education and Research, Chandigarh, India

Wilson L G 1981 Utilizings dispersed mental health para-professionals for scattered Pacific islands: a Micronesian experience. Community Mental Health Journal 17: 161–170

Wittkower E D, Prince R 1974 A review of transcultural psychiatry. In: Caplan G (ed)
. American Handbook of Psychiatry, 2nd edn., Vol 2. Basic Books, New York

Workneh F, Giel R 1975 Medical dilemma. Tropical & Geographical Medicine 27: 431–439

Yap P M 1951 Mental illness peculiar to certain cultures. Journal of Mental Science 97: 313–327

EPILOGUE

Continuity and sense of place: the importance of the symbolic image

The continuity of our lives is preserved by being surrounded by the solidified substance of time which has lasted for a given period. Take, for example, a small drawer, which the carpenter has made for the convenience of some household. With the passage of time, the actual form of this drawer is surpassed by time itself and, after the decades and centuries have elapsed, it is as though time had become solidified and has assumed that form. A given small space, which was at first occupied by the object, is now occupied by solidified time. It has, in fact, become the incarnation of a certain kind of spirit. (Mishima 1959)

The action of time makes man's works into natural objects . . . In making them natural objects also, time gives to man's lifeless productions the brief quality of everything belonging to nature — life. (Lee 1902)

In this fictionalised account of a true story, Mishima gave the story of a mad monk who burned down the 500 year-old Golden Temple because it represented the beauty he himself lacked. In his story, Mishima identified one of the most important, yet intangible attributes of an historic object — time.

In 1967, I had the opportunity to see and photograph the machine shop of the Crown and Eagle Mills in North Uxbridge, Massachusetts. This cotton mill, built in 1825–1850, had survived for almost half a century empty and unused, having been closed well before the Great Depression. It had been carefully preserved on the estate of its wealthy owner until his widow died in about 1969. It was one of the oldest factory buildings in the US, and also one of the most beautiful ever built. It stood like a Loire Valley chateau, spanning the Mumford River on a graceful arch with two parallel canals on either side — a majestic and breathtaking combination of architecture and landscaping (Fig. 17.1). Yet until about 1970, this seminal historic building was almost completely unknown outside its region.

On entering the machine shop, behind the main mill, I was confronted by a scene which veritably took my breath away. In front of me was a room filled with tools and machines, left as if nothing had been changed since the workmen had departed 50 years before (Fig. 17.2). To see this was an awesome experience, enhanced particularly by the fact that the building was not 'preserved' as a museum, but was simply existing, having survived the ravages of time to deliver its historical visual message to me. That room, without question, had a kind of spirit. The profound meaning of the Industrial Revolution, the early history of the rise of American capitalism, and

Fig. 17.1 Crown and Eagle Mills, North Uxbridge, Mass, USA, 1967

Fig. 17.2 Machine shop, Crown and Eagle Mills, 1967, before the machinery was purchased and removed by the Old Sturbridge Village Museum

the origins of modern technology and labour seemed to converge and focus upon that one place at that moment. The scene was so charged with feeling, information, and emotion from the past that to touch each item in the room was to touch an icon. One could almost feel the workmen rise from the faded photographs to be present in that space.

The experience of discovering an historic man-made environmental artifact like that called to mind a comment that Samuel Johnson is reported to have made: 'Depend upon it, Sir. When a man knows he is to be hanged in a fortnight, it concentrates his mind wonderfully' (Johnson 1776). Sadly, this beautiful building proved to be a fragile image. First the machine shop was stripped of its machinery by Old Sturbridge Village Museum, ironically destroying the real thing in order to create a museum exhibit commemorating it. Then, in 1975, vandals entered the mill and, when the fire that they had started was out, this remarkable building had been reduced to a broken shell (Fig. 17.3). To find such a building and room, caught as this was between the historic past and an uncertain future, heightened my sense of communication with the past, and embedded the image on my memory, just as it did on the film in my camera.

It is clear that for almost every person, the man-made environment is important in some way, and that the historic environment is significant for a large section of the population. Hearst Castle, in San Simeon, California,

Fig. 17.3 Crown and Eagle Mills, 1977, after the fire started by vandals

for example, a remarkable palace created from the fragments of European monuments, attracts over 940 000 visitors a year, bringing a $1.3 million annual profit to the State of California which owns it. It is difficult, however, to isolate exactly what the ingredients are which give certain old buildings their value. Is it their history, their adherence to certain aesthetic principles, their particular place in certain peoples' lives, or changing styles and taste? One thing is evident: certain buildings, when threatened, can be the subject of an enormous outpouring of emotional energy by those who feel in some way attached to them.

Throughout my work as a documentary photographer and preservation advocate, I have found myself constantly confronted with the issue of how to assess objectively the value of a building or group of buildings when so many intangible qualities such as taste, aesthetics, history, and time are involved. It is often possible to assess rationally the historical or architectural significance of something, but what is more elusive, and ultimately more significant to people, is an historic building's ability to become the focus of human emotion — to become the incarnation or symbol of something much larger and closer to our own lives. It is at this level that the forlorn and ramshackle former slave cottage can seem as potentially more moving, and in many ways more important, than a carefully restored palace. We must never lose sight of the need to understand the elusive quality of spirit in the objects which make up the man-made environment. If we do, then even when we are successful in preserving something, we may find that we end up only preserving the hollow shells of what once existed.

This observation goes beyond the issue of simple preservation of an artifact to an assessment of how it is to be preserved. It may be clear what the history of a building is, and also its architectural value, but what is its emotional content? What ingredient gives it the power to move people — to make them think about the mysteries of the place's history and to engender love for it? Preservation can at times be superficially successful. A building or district may be 'preserved', but made over into something so new that all the visual time depth has been excised.

An example of this is The Faneuil Hall Markets in Boston. Until the wholesale produce market was moved out, this complex was Boston's Covent Garden. It was then restored as an elegant shopping area, and has even been the model for the similar restoration of Covent Garden in London. As a shopping centre, it has been fabulously successful, and is reported to attract more people than Disneyworld. However, like Disneyworld, it is history reduced to a storybook. Only the stone facades and timber floors of the old buildings were preserved; all effects of age were removed, and all of the residue of its former uses sanitised or cleared away. The complex no longer seems like an historic part of the city, but is a carnival precinct, separate from the real city around it. Despite this limitation, the commercial success of the project is such that in Baltimore, where no old buildings existed, a new Marketplace was constructed for a similar development, showing that the old buildings, which started as a genesis of the urban renewal idea, end up being so extraneous that they are not even a necessary ingredient of the next project. Has preservation been achieved then? Superficially, it has. The Boston project is a financial success, the shells of the historic buildings are still there. But as one walks through the complex, one has a feeling that the buildings have been in a sense 'lobotomised' — their genuine history excised. Time has been flattened, and the effects of age have not been left for people to see. We are still left with the challenge of how to preserve an historic area and make it vital, without destroying the intangible quality which gives it the power to move people — the power to engender attachment and love.

Human attachment to the man-made environment is not a simple concept, and its nature and importance to people varies according to individual needs. Preservation advocates often speak of the need to preserve something for the public good, and ironically, most of the public may be totally unaware of this effort unless, should it be unsuccessful, they notice the ensuing demolition. The geographer Tuan (1974) calls the concept of environmental attachment 'topophilia' which:

> can be defined broadly to include all of the human being's affective ties with the material environment. These differ greatly in intensity, subtlety, and mode of expression. The response to environment may be primarily aesthetic . . . (or be) tactile, a delight in the feel of air, water, and earth. More permanent and less easy to express are feelings that one has towards a place because it is home, the locus of memories, and the means of gaining a livelihood.

He goes on to say that topophilia is not the strongest of human emotions, though when it is compelling, we can be sure that the place or environment has become the carrier of emotionally charged events, or is perceived as a symbol. This observation is important because it is exactly these ingredients which can help define an historical environment as important enough to people to be preserved. Tuan also suggests that for people to be conscious of the importance of an historic environment, whether a building or a whole city district, they must be aware of a connection to important historical events, or informed enough to be able to make the connection between the environment and the symbol: 'the appreciation of the landscape is more personal and longer lasting when it is mixed with the memory of human incidents . . . Homely and even drab scenes can reveal aspects of themselves that went unnoticed before, and this new insight into the real is sometimes experienced as beauty.'

In my work, I have focussed upon the early industrial areas of both England and New England, documenting landscapes and buildings which to many are the epitome of the 'homely and drab'. However, I was inspired by what I found to be a certain kind of beauty in these scenes, and my experience has given me insight into how the historic environment becomes meaningful to people. For me, there were two stages to this experience: firstly, the personal transformation that came from discovering specific historic buildings and environments, which in my view had profound value; secondly, witnessing the public respond when confronted with the photographic images of these places, giving me the chance to become aware of the kind of attachments which people have to even the harshest of landscapes.

In his discussion of 'Rootedness versus Sense of Place', Tuan makes the point that sense of place is built upon knowledge of history, and can apply to anyone, newcomers and oldtimers alike. Rootedness, however, depends less on thinking and knowing about history than upon living it as it has been lived for generations. Preserving something is to become conscious of it in a new way, and thus to lift it out of the daily context of life and transform it in peoples' minds into something of special importance. Thus, in discovering historic sites and bringing them before the public as a preservation issue, I was both experiencing, and focussing people's attention on, 'sense of place'. Furthermore, in the act of photographing these sites and then confronting the public with the images, I was participating in an historic transformation of their perception; this documentation and display was helping to convert rootedness to sense of place, which is the essential basis for active preservation. Rootedness relates to passive preservation, which results from continued use through custom and lack of need for change, but active preservation movements have occurred when people have found their environment changing too rapidly. It is at this point that an awareness of the environment as something distinctive and unique can emerge — an awareness which is the sense of place.

In studying and documenting the industrial landscapes of Lancashire and West Yorkshire, I was confronted by exactly this kind of transformation of attitude. For generations, the landscape was complete — a seemingly limitless world of factories, chimneys, rows of terraced houses, canals, railways, and coal pits. It was not a landscape which anyone considered attractive, nor, with its dirt, darkness and smoke, was it even particularly healthy. So with zeal, urban planners and politicians worked for change, and during recent decades, this has been sweeping (Figs. 17.4, 17.5). The air became much cleaner with the effects of the Clean Air Act, but as the pall receded, it revealed a rapidly changing and eroding built environment. The rows of terraced housing have been the hardest hit. What had once seemed ubiquitous has been wiped out so quickly that it is now difficult to find any but fragmentary clusters of workers' terraces. Mills and their chimneys have also disappeared at a rapid rate, helped by government subsidies whose goal, until recently, was the almost total removal of them and their associated housing. At first, these efforts were applauded, and it would have been unreasonable to expect that this vast environment could or should remain unchanged. But what occurred is massive change almost everywhere at once, so that the historic industrial environment, which was once universal in these regions, is now rarely found intact anywhere.

One may say, 'What does it matter? This was not an important or beau-

Fig. 17.4 Stockport Mills and Viaduct, 1969

Fig. 17.5 Stockport Mills, 1978

tiful environment.' But an interesting phenomenon indicates that the human connection to this historic scene is deeper and more positive than many will admit. L. S. Lowry, a now well known English painter who had lived his life in almost complete obscurity until his late 60s — all the while painting a unique series of images of this industrial landscape — suddenly found himself catapulted to extraordinary fame. He had captured the image of this landscape and interpreted it in his work for the preceding half century, but is was not until the real landscape had noticeably disappeared that he became popular. Now, the extent of his popularity provides a strong evidence of the collective sense of loss which people finally felt when a once familiar world had all but disappeared.

This example is not unique. When the organisation Save Britain's Heritage produced an exhibition of photographs which I had taken of the mills and industrial landscapes of Lancashire and West Yorkshire at the Royal Institute of British Architects in 1979, one visitor kept returning day after day. He visited it during his lunch hour, and for a period of over a month, did not miss a single day. I met him on the final day of the exhibition, and he said he had grown up outside Manchester, but had moved to London and become a magazine writer. When he saw the exhibition, he was profoundly moved; for years, he had been aware of his roots in this industrial area, but the photographs served to provide that sense of attachment with a visual image, and it is significant that he chose to come repeatedly to see the photographs, rather than simply return to look at the area. They served to isolate and focus the view, making the landscape itself into a kind of icon. Until this exhibition, most of what he had seen and heard about the industrial North criticised and condemned it as an environmental disaster, but the exhibition gave it legitimacy as an historic landscape, and in so doing, helped to convert his rootedness into an awareness of his own sense of place.

Other examples of this process occurred during the exhibition; there were visitors who wrote letters or poems, and some long-time residents of the areas concerned sent their own works of art, which portrayed the mills. One woman's long letter almost poetically described the social context of this historic environment:

> 'I thought I was the only person in the world who loved old mills. We would see twenty five or so factory chimneys from the school window. One mill was particularly beautiful . . . equal (in my opinion) to the Chateaux of the Loire, complete with tower and wrought-iron ornamentation . . . I used to pass the weaving shed of the Stack Mills on the way to school. The flagstones were hot and vibrating. Children would take their mothers chips, black peas, steak and kidney puddings in at dinner time. There was a creche at Aston Bros. a long time ago to cater for women who worked the machinery . . . my mother-in-law started work in the paper mill at 11 years old — 6 o'clock start, bread and dripping for breakfast at 8, soup at 12, bread at 4, finish at 6. And no talking allowed'.

The number of people who came to the exhibition was far greater than had been expected, even though it took place far away from the industrial areas portrayed.

Fig. 17.6 Amoskeag Millyard, Manchester, NH, USA, 1968

This exhibition followed a similar one which I produced in Manchester, New Hampshire, in 1975, focussed upon a single corporation, the Amoskeag Manufacturing Company, which had established and planned the city, beginning in 1838. The pictures emphasised the architectural and urban design quality and legacy of the huge Amoskeag plant, which at the turn of the century, was acclaimed as the world's largest textile mill (Figs 17.6, 17.7). In preparing it, I had no reason to expect that it would be seen by many people beyond the usual attendance of the museum — members of the design professions, those interested and informed about the arts, etc. However, the exhibition deliberately incorporated social history material, including photographs and taped oral history of former workers in the mills (Fig. 17.8). After it opened, the museum reported gradually increasing

Fig. 17.7 Amoskeag Millyard, during demolition, 1969

attendance, until the gallery was crowded on almost every day; when it closed, it had set a museum record. On the final Sunday, over 1000 people came through in less than 4 hours, but what was most remarkable was that they were mostly those who had worked or were presently working in the mill. Whole busloads came from old people's homes, and many people returned repeatedly, bringing their friends. On one occasion, I witnessed the reunion of two men who had worked together in the mill, but had not seen each other for 30 years.

It may be asked whether this response to the exhibition showed any attachment to the millyard itself, or whether it was simply a reunion with the past, without any expression of concern for the physical remains. Also, do these former workers agree with or appreciate the aesthetics of the architecture and planning of the mill, or care whether it survives? Many of the former workers clearly responded mostly in personal ways; one was surprised and delighted to find the front door to her former house displayed, and another remarked, when she looked at a photograph of the loomfixers, 'I never thought I would ever live to see a photograph of my husband in a museum.' More revealing is the comment that: 'When I walk through the millyard, I feel like a young man again.' Few of the former workers verbalised any directly aesthetic response, but a certain number did express regret to see the ensuing demolition of many of the mill buildings. Aesthetics in everyday life is rarely isolated from other issues, and expressions of attachment to place can rarely exclude an implied feeling that a certain beauty exists as well; the very fact that so many former workers embraced the exhibition in such a positive way seems to show that they accepted the

Fig. 17.8 Anore Deselets, Loomfixer, Manchester, NH, USA, at the Currier Gallery Exhibition, 1975, standing next to the photograph of himself taken at the mill in 1975

notion that the millyard had aesthetic quality. For them, the conscious recognition that it was important to the outside world because of its architecture was probably a revelation, but the knowledge that it was, served to reinforce and expand their own sense of place, just as happened during the exhibition in England.

It was during this first exhibition that I became aware, not only of the former workers' emotional ties to their environment, but also of a disagreement between their own point of view and that expressed as being their point of view by the planners, city officials, and leaders of the business community. Countless times I had been told that 'it might be nice to save the mills, but people see them as symbols of their own exploitation, and wish to see them destroyed.' The response to the exhibition and the subsequent oral history project has proved this to be generally untrue, raising the question of why these civic leaders had a distorted impression of the situation. While documenting the mill districts of England, I found a similar conflict in points of view. Again, civic leaders often claimed that working people hated the old industrial environment, but the workers themselves more frequently spoke with affection towards it, as shown in the letter quoted on page 462.

The reason for these apparently conflicting attitudes is that the local leaders attributed such views to the workers in order to support their own strongly held beliefs that the old mills and houses should be cleared to make way for a new civic image. Some of these elite people had come into the communities from outside, and saw the old and deteriorating mills as symbols of economic stagnation. For them, salvation lay not only in renewing the physical fabric, but also in changing the image; and ironically, these people often do understand the historic meaning of the buildings they wish to destroy. The problem is that they are motivated to destroy them precisely because it is the cultural and historical messages inherent in these buildings which they wish to erase.

In Huddersfield, ICI, a major multinational company which has grown out of the historic dyestuffs industry, is one of several modern industries attracting new people to the area, and for many of these new people, change and modernity is the symbol of their own success. As one long-time resident said in 1977:

> The people that have come into Huddersfield, and have tried to reshape it in the last 20 or 30 years, they're the people that worry me because all they want to do is to march with the tide of 'progress' that's flooding over the country . . . They seem to want to knock Huddersfield down and replace it with major ring roads and faceless buildings that are 'armoured' with concrete, and black panels, and things like that . . . I don't think they've got any root depths in Huddersfield. To them it's merely a removal of certain so-called 'eyesores', that are eyesores to them.
>
> Taped interview with Trevor Burgin, May 1977

This difference in attitude has had a very important impact on the historic landscape in both England and America. In this respect, there are two categories of people. The first is a largely inarticulate, long-time local population, who are attached to the physical environment in a variety of different, but largely personal ways. Their expression of attachment derives from the experiences of their own lives, and may or may not include a conscious desire for preservation of the surroundings. It usually takes major demolition and change for them to become conscious and aware that the physical fabric is something historically important to themselves. Witness, for example, the prints of Lowry paintings now commonly hanging in pubs and private homes throughout the region. In the second group, we have people for whom personal identity and feelings of success are intertwined with the remaking of the local image from that of a decaying mill town into a community with modern buildings. As the preservation movement has expanded, increasing numbers of these people have embraced the notion that older structures can be remodelled into this new image; but until recently, most believed that major physical change was necessary in order to achieve 'progress'.

In addition to these two categories of attitudes and experiences, there are always individuals from either group who are conscious of the historic fabric, and wish to see it preserved; but an interesting diversity of view can also be found among them. My own experience has been that of an outsider, discovering the aesthetic and historical value of each area by relating it to a wider knowledge of other places in the world; but for some, the awareness has grown out of a personal connection with the area. L. S. Lowry was able to achieve the necessary distance between himself and his own world to develop the specific images into an all-encompassing visual symbol. One former local resident was so strongly affected by the rapid disappearance of the mill chimneys, which had been the strongest visual elements of the area, that he has moved about the region buying the chimneys from the mill owners. His approach is unique in that he has taken title to just the chimney, usually for very little money, becoming responsible for the maintenance, which he does at weekends. The mill owners would otherwise have demolished the chimneys, since few are still in use. In another example, a mill engine machinist became an amateur photographer, and proceeded to achieve recognition for his photographs of the other workers taken in the mill where he worked. This was done, as it turned out, just before the mill was closed and demolished.

Another local historian of working-class background made a comment which revealed something about the difference which can exist, even among the conservation orientated, between those whose roots are in the area, and those who, coming from the outside, recognise the place for its historical and aesthetic qualities. He said, 'I would almost prefer that they knock down the mills than let the trendies get them.' By this, he meant those who convert the mills into elegant shops or other uses, which wipe out the everyday, local, hard, industrial character. For him, it was an issue of a way of life, and he therefore felt a loss in what most people from the outside might perceive as a gain. His sense of place included the way people lived; the buildings were important to him, but the kind of change that occurred at Faneuil Hall Markets in Boston would be tantamount to destruction. When remodelled like that, the buildings lose their spirit, which is the product of the human life which went on in them.

Apart from confirming my belief that the preservation of parts of those environments is important, my experience with these exhibitions made me aware of a particular aspect in the process of human growth and awareness. What had attracted people's attention was not just the historic environment itself, but the particular image of it which I and others had isolated from the rest of the scene by the use of the camera or paint brush. It was these specific images which became the symbols for the place, bringing people to awareness of the issue of preservation, as their attention was focussed by the images on the 'classic views'. Such images can then become so pervasive in the public consciousness that they continue to turn up. Shortly after the SAVE exhibition, for example, a cigarette advertisement used a photograph of an industrial canal in Manchester (England) taken from precisely the same vantage point as one of my published photographs.

Tuan stated that topophilia is most compelling when the environment has come to be perceived as a symbol, and when I first witnessed the Lancashire and West Yorkshire industrial landscape, I was aware of a certain excitement, which comes from discovering the visual incarnation of an historical symbolic scene. I felt that I was already familiar with it; it was a part of my culture, rising from the pages of Dickens, the Brontes, and many other writers. The views of this landscape coalesced into an image which constituted a universal type, transcending the individuality of each to become a veritable visual symbol of the Industrial Revolution. 'For all its faults, it is Europe's most romantic industrial landscape. A landscape so true, so honest, that a well known film director taken to a hill above Halifax said simply, "It's too much." In other words, so perfectly "West Riding" that the uninitiated would have had difficulty in accepting the scene as anything but a grossly heightened version of reality.' (Willis 1975).

When such a view becomes a symbol, conveying a deeper human meaning about the place, it becomes enhanced in people's minds, whether or not it is generally regarded as beautiful. That filmmaker was responding to the drama of seeing the scene for the first time and finding it familiar. It is this enhanced image which people are often trying to preserve when an effort is made to save a building, a group of buildings, or a whole landscape. Significantly, even a nationally known natural wonder such as Yosemite Valley contains scenic views which are similar to many found elsewhere in the Sierras, but the shape of the valley and the number of similar waterfalls all combine to provide a visual image of much greater formal intensity than anywhere else. Early on, the place became a focus for the natural landscape preservation movement. It provided an image which the public readily identified as a symbol; it was complete — the apotheosis of the Western mountain landscape of the United States. More recently, Ansel Adams has continued to reinforce its symbolic importance with his photographs. People now acknowledge and reinforce the importance of these artistic images by buying prints and postcards of his photographs from a gallery in the valley itself.

Buildings gain meaning through their association with history, but beyond this, it is out of a focus on the symbolic image of a place that active preservation efforts often emerge. More importantly, this transformation of the perception of a place beyond the everyday reality to this more abstract connection with human history and life is how a conscious sense of place is created and reinforced in a community. Continuity in the evolution of the environment is achieved by man's conscious actions to encourage this awareness, be it through literature, art, or social and political efforts.

The challenge to contemporary planners is to help people gain an awareness of the larger meaning of time and human association inherent in the
historic environment, and thus renew the image of a place, while preserving
rather than replacing the historic fabric. In this way, people will achieve
continuity in the human environment without erasing the best that man has
created.

REFERENCES

Johnson S 1776 In: Boswell's *Life of Johnson*
Lee V 1902 In praise of old houses London
Mishima Y 1959 The temple of the golden pavilion (translated by Morris I). New York
Tuan Y F 1974 Topophilia. A study of environmental perception, attitudes, and values.
    Prentice-Hall, Englewood, Cliffs, NJ
Willis R 1975 Yorkshire's historic buildings. Robert Hale, London

Photographs by Randolph Longenbach

Index